NASEBY

The Decisive Campaign

THREE
LETTERS,

From the Right Honourable
SiR THOMAS FAIRFAX,
Lieut. Gen. *CRVMWELL*
and the Committee refiding in the Army.

Wherein
All the Particulars of the Great Uictory obtained by our Forces againſt His Majeſties, is
fully related, fought the 14 of *Iune*, 1645.

With a Liſt of the Names of ſuch Colonels, Captaines,
Lieutenants, Enſignes, and other Officers, both of
Horſe and Foot there taken priſoners. And the
Reſolution of both Houſes upon the ſame.

Die Lunæ, 16 Iune, 1645.

ORdered by the Lords and Commons *Aſſembled in Parli-*
ament, that theſe Letters, with the Liſt of the Priſoners,
be forthwith printed and publiſhed, with the Order of both
Houſes concerning the ſame.

Io. Brown. Cler. Parliament.

LONDON,
Printed for *Iohn Wright* at the ſigne of the Kings-head
in the Old-baily. 1645.

NASEBY
The Decisive Campaign

Glenn Foard

Pen & Sword
MILITARY

First published in Great Britain in 1995 by Pryor Publications
This edition published by
PEN & SWORD MILITARY
an imprint of
Pen & Sword Books Limited
47 Church Street
Barnsley
South Yorkshire
S70 2AS

ISBN 1 84415 132 8

A CIP catalogue record for this book
is available from the British Library.

Printed and bound in Great Britain by
CPI UK

Pen & Sword Books Ltd incorporates the imprints of
Pen & Sword Aviation, Pen & Sword Maritime, Pen & Sword Military,
Wharncliffe Local History, Pen & Sword Select,
Pen & Sword Military Classics and Leo Cooper.

For a complete list of Pen & Sword titles please contact:
PEN & SWORD BOOKS LIMITED
47 Church Street, Barnsley, South Yorkshire, S70 2AS, England.
E-mail: enquiries@pen-and-sword.co.uk
Website: www.pen-and-sword.co.uk

CONTENTS

To

Mike Westaway

LIST OF ILLUSTRATIONS

Frontispiece : pamphlet containing letters of 15th June 1645 from the army

ACKNOWLEDGEMENTS

My greatest debt is to Mike Westaway, a native of Naseby, who has followed in the footsteps of Mastin, Fitzgerald and Hamson in the detailed study of the battlefield. It has held a fascination for Mike ever since he was a young boy, back in the 1930s, when his father first told him about the battle. He has probably devoted more time and energy than any other person before him in studying, walking and surveying the area, recovering numerous finds from the fields between Naseby and East Farndon. I have spent many enjoyable and very valuable hours with Mike exploring almost every hill and valley across three miles of battlefield and talking over the issues. His friends Peter Burton and Tim Bevin have also played a crucial role in this re-interpretation of the battle, sharing their information on and ideas about the battlefield. Peter in particular has spent innumerable hours in recent years scouring the landscape for evidence of the fighting and has made the single most important discovery, finding the first evidence of the Royalist retreat and then leading the pursuit of that evidence across into Clipston. He has also lent me finds from the field and on various occasions offered us hospitality on evenings spent studying maps and discussing the significance of the discoveries until the early hours. Without the three of them this book could never have been written, but the interpretations of their evidence presented here are my own because, inevitably, there have been issues on which we each have different ideas.

Eric Westaway has also played an important role over the years by maintaining a public interest in the battle, through his Naseby Farm and Battle Museum, and has at times aided me in my research with information, providing contacts in the village and has also loaned the negative for figure 67. I have also been helped by Stuart Kendal who has taken me on a tour of the landscape between Sibbertoft and Farndon and has reported a few additional finds. In each case I am also indebted to the landowners who, through these individuals, have allowed me access to their land.

I must thank the staff of the Northamptonshire Record Office, Public Record Office, British Library, Leicestershire Record Office, Northamptonshire Reference Library and all the other record offices and collections consulted in researching this book. Also the Northamptonshire Record Society who have given permission for a number of illustrations in their library to be reproduced. Help has also been given by Mark Curteis of Northampton Museum, Steph Mastoris of Market Harborough Museum, and by Yolanda Courtney, with information and illustrations relating to the siege of Leicester, and by Fred Hartley of Leicestershire Museums Service. Owners of several country houses have also assisted in my research, whether with information about or by providing access to their private collections of artefacts. Only the collection at Wistow Hall was not made accessible to me.

Various other friends and acquaintances have provided advice and help. David Hall, Tony Brown and Peter Taylor have very kindly given me access to unpublished work on the open field system and enclosure of several parishes. I have however also drawn upon many original sources in preparing the reconstruction and hence I must take full responsibility for any inaccuracies therein. I must also acknowledge my debt to an earlier county historian of Northamptonshire, George Baker, who made extensive extracts and an index of Civil War material for the county that he found within the Thomason Tracts. I have drawn heavily on this material because in many cases I have not had the time to go back to the original sources. Thanks also to Brian Giggins who has assisted with the identification of several illustrations and has provided figures 17 & 68, and to Mick Nicholson for figure 27. All the other illustrations, unless otherwise stated, are from the author's own collection.

I am particularly indebted to Keith Roberts for detailed advice on practical military operations in the 17th century with regard to Chapter 8, including the correction of a number of errors of interpretation made in earlier drafts. Thanks also to Nigel Jackson and Alastair Bantock for reading and commenting on parts of the text. Various other individuals too numerous to mention have provided me with advice and information, either in response to letters or during my site visits. It has been remarkable how kind and friendly almost everyone has been.

Last, but not least, I must thank my wife Anne. She has not only drawn most of the maps and plans but has also put up with my almost continual work on the book over the last year, which has meant that she has hardly seen me for weeks on end and has had to deal with frayed tempers as the deadline for completion drew ever closer!

PREFACE

Sitting on the steps of the battlefield monument looking out across Broadmoor on a warm and sunny July evening the air is almost still. The noise of the new road can just be heard faintly in the distance, but it hardly disturbs the peace of the battlefield. Now a light aircraft towing a glider passes overhead, as often happens here, intruding far more into the consciousness. You cannot escape the 20th century! But there again, it seems rather odd to be worrying about peace and quiet on Naseby field - the incident about which we come to muse was quite the opposite. On such a pleasant evening there is little to connect one with the tumultuous events of the 14th June 1645 - the noise and smoke of battle, the death and destruction.

Almost every time I visit Naseby there are other visitors and the same is true today. He is a tourist, like many perhaps, who just happened to be driving through Northamptonshire. He saw the finger-post to Naseby and thought, 'Ah! Let's make a brief detour'. Such is the wide knowledge of the significance of the place - though to admit the truth, his wife had said: 'Naseby; what's so special about that, what happened there?' Well it is that question this book sets out to answer. In the short time that has elapsed since that chance encounter the research for this book, allied with that by my metal detecting friends, has resulted in a story very different, more complex and far more interesting than that which anyone could have recounted on that July evening.

Glenn Foard
Earls Barton
9th April 1995

PREFACE TO PAPERBACK EDITION

It is now nine years since the original publication appeared. None of the data newly recovered since 1995 would seem to warrant a major reassessment of the battle, and thus it has been decided to reprint the original volume exactly as it was first published.

In the interim, one new book has been published on the subject (M. Marix Evans, P. Burton and M. Westaway, 2002, *Naseby: English Civil War – June 1645*). It provides substantial new insight in just one aspect, deriving from its presentation of further metal detecting evidence collected by Peter Burton. This has enabled them to suggest a location for the destruction of Rupert's Bluecoats that is very different to the tentative conclusions made in 1995. But this data also raises questions over the initial deployment and action of Okey's dragoons. The new shot distribution on the royalist side of Broadmoor begins to link the main action to the shot pattern adjacent to Sulby hedges. This could be taken as support for the alternative interpretation that the scatter on the north western edge of the field represents fighting later in the battle, as part of the royalist infantry retreated into the cover of the enclosures. But the question must remain unresolved because we lack the systematic, fully recorded archaeological survey here and on the other English battlefields, comparable to those regularly conducted on sites in the USA. Until we have such a survey, we will not know the degree to which concentrations and, equally important, the gaps in the plotted distribution, represent the actual distribution of the action, as opposed reflecting the many biases that can influence the recovery of finds.

Also since the first publication, we have identified two significant documentary sources, one for the battle and the other for the historic terrain. The first, rediscovered in the Bodleian Library, is the original plan by de Gomme, in Dutch, which like his plans of other battles shows only the royalist deployment. This is further confirmation of the argument made in 1995 that the well known de Gomme plan, in the British Library, was a secondary work which drew its evidence of the parliamentarian deployment from Streeter's plan. The other, is the sheet from the 2 inch Ordnance Surveyors' Drawings of circa 1815, in the British Library, showing the extent of ancient enclosures and the road network through the open fields of Naseby prior to enclosure. It elaborates the evidence presented in 1995, which was derived from the much faded 17th century plan of Naseby. Sadly, neither source assists in the resolution of the important question as to the exact position and extent in 1645 of the closes in Sibbertoft township, at the boundary with Naseby and Sulby, which are critical to the interpretation of the action in that part of the field.

Glenn Foard
Creaton
13th May 2004

INTRODUCTION

After Hastings and the Battle of Britain, which respectively began and ended our millennium, Naseby was undoubtedly the most important and decisive battle ever fought in England. Where those other battles were the result of challenges to the very basis of the English State by foreign foes, Naseby was the culmination of a bloody Civil War and the stepping stone for a political revolution.

The primary objective of this book is a simple narrative of military events.[1] Where it strays, as it inevitably must, into wider issues it does not claim to be in any way an exhaustive analysis and its perspective often remains at best regional in scale. If useful insights into wider issues do result then this is an unexpected bonus. It is to be hoped that the failure to address such matters in more detail has not devalued this work or led to inadvertent misinterpretation, for as a landscape archaeologist rather than a military historian the potential for such errors is always in ones mind when writing on a military theme. Though there is a brief consideration of the political and social background to the battle, there are others far better qualified to review such matters and Maurice Ashley's recent book has already set Naseby within this wider context. The present book does aim to place the military action in its 17th century landscape setting, a landscape very different from that which we see today, and to view the events within the wider context of the Civil War within the region. Finally it tackles the historiography of Naseby fight and considers the potential for future conservation, investigation and interpretation of the battlefield. This seemed an appropriate way to end, for the study of the battle and the political, religious and tourist interest in the battlefield over the last 350 years is another fascinating story in its own right, while the conservation and interpretation of battlefields has recently been recognised in England as an important issue in heritage management.

It might be asked why another book on Naseby is justified when two have already been published within the last ten years. The answer is two fold. First there is completely new information, both documentary and archaeological, which enables a fundamental revision of the battle and battlefield. Second there are the limitations in the previous publications. Naseby is probably the best documented of the major Civil War battles and yet it has not been the best understood. It is very surprising, for such an important battle, that there has never been a comprehensive study which draws upon all the major sources of evidence. Peter Young's book, published in 1985, is a mine of valuable information but it is not of the same standard as his other excellent studies of Civil War battles, suffering not only from a lack of plans but also from an inadequate synthesis of the evidence presented. On the other hand Maurice Ashley's book, published in 1992, was concerned far more with the wider historical context of the campaign, rather than the detail of the battle itself. Various other useful books and booklets have considered Naseby fight but the most effective and accessible analysis of the military action has remained the brief account by Woolrych. However, it is inevitable with a book which covers all the major battles of the Civil War, that he could not be expected to devote sufficient time to any one battle to provide a comprehensive review. In recent years the study of the battle has been bedeviled by the controversy of the 'Second Battle of Naseby', over the construction of the new A14 road, and in this the eccentric analysis by Colonel Rogers has caused untold confusion. His analysis has been followed, to a greater or lesser degree, by a number of other studies of the battle and it is to be hoped that with the present work that particular ghost will finally be laid to rest. The most recent assessment of Naseby was that produced by David Smurthwaite as part of the documentation for the English Heritage 'Battlefields Register', however even that valuable analysis has been completely overtaken by the new evidence. The objective of the present book is a complete reinterpretation of the battle using all the evidence that is now available, but it cannot claim to be a definitive study, for one lesson of the research has been the amount of new information that can still be brought to bear on an already well known event.[2]

Unlike most previous books written about the battle of Naseby, which have generally been prepared from a national perspective, the present work is based on detailed local study. Behind it lies an intimate knowledge, built up over many years, of both the county of Northamptonshire and, thanks to the assistance of others, of the battlefield itself. In this the present author has followed in the footsteps of a number of well and not so well known local historians, from this and previous centuries, who have found people at Naseby with a detailed understanding of the battlefield who were keen to share their knowledge. It is my experience that any history which involves events taking place in the landscape, whether over decades or even centuries, can only be properly understood if, first of all, the character of that landscape is understood. This is a lesson which, as an historical geographer or landscape archaeologist, one learns early on from the pioneering work of people like Hoskins and Beresford.[3] Through careful reconstruction of the historical geography, supported where appropriate with archaeological evidence, historical events can sometimes be dramatically revised and it was the realisation that this applied equally well to battlefields, where those historical events took place over just a few hours, which led to my involvement with Naseby.

NOTES

1. The origins of the present book lie in an article, Foard, 1992, which was to have been published in the *Journal for Post Medieval Archaeology*, however, due to delays in publication, it has been overtaken by events.
2. Young, 1985; Ashley, 1992; Woolrych, 1961; Rogers, 1968; Young & Holmes, 1974, p.236-250; Denton, 1988; English Heritage, 1994.
3. For example, Hoskins, 1955; Beresford, 1971.

CHAPTER 1

THE EVIDENCE
AND THE LANDSCAPE

Reviewing the numerous secondary accounts of the battle and campaign one thing that becomes clear is the ease with which errors and distortions can be carried though and elaborated. The article by Stead is a classic example.[1] It has un-referenced comments that others then take up and refers to traditions which are then distorted and further altered by subsequent writers until it is almost impossible to see where they originated. Therefore here, when dealing with the events of the 14th June 1645 and the days that immediately preceded it, all the original sources have as far as possible been re-examined and their accuracy and value assessed. Inevitably there will be documents that should have been consulted but were not found, although hopefully no major source has been missed. That is of course with the exception of the material in the Public Record Office, particularly in the Commonwealth Exchequer papers. Undoubtedly important documents still lie there whose significance is as yet unrecognised by anyone, just as the list of seriously wounded New Model Army soldiers had lain unused and apparently unrecognised until I accidentally discovered it while conducting research for a paper on the Civil War defences of Northampton.

Accounts of a battle, even though written by people who were with the armies, can often be at variance with one another even if there is no element of propaganda distortion. This is inevitable in a battle situation, for no two people will have seen exactly the same things. Some may, from their perspective, have accurately presented particular events of the battle because they saw them at close quarters, others may only have had a glimpse of those events, have been told about them by someone else, not have been aware or even may not have thought it worth recounting. Therefore in piecing together the battle it is essential to try to balance the accounts, one with another, and where possible support the assessment using topographical or archaeological evidence.

For the rest of the Naseby campaign secondary sources have been more extensively used as the information was less crucial to an understanding of the battle and with the limited time available it was the area that could most safely be left. In studying this secondary material particular effort has however been made to scour the local historical sources for Northamptonshire and Leicestershire, to identify the more obscure references to events and people, including the many local traditions about the battle.

The documents that were produced at a local level at the time of the Civil War provide the most important body of written information which has not previously been used in the study of the Naseby campaign. Neither have they been used to any significant degree in the study of the Civil War generally in Northamptonshire, for the history of that county during the war has yet to be written. The materials for such a study are however extensive and have the potential to add to the understanding not only of the context of the Naseby campaign, but also directly to the battle itself. Of particular importance are the parish accounts, submitted by each constable after the war in order to claim repayment for the exactions that had been placed upon the parish by Parliament's forces. Few such documents seem to survive for Leicestershire, but Buckinghamshire and Warwickshire have a similar if not better survival than Northamptonshire. For the purposes of the present study this enormous body of information has only been systematically searched for Northamptonshire, while for Warwickshire it has been possible to draw upon the evidence from this source quoted by Tennant.[2] Undoubtedly further detailed study of the Warwickshire and Buckinghamshire accounts would add yet more minor detail to the campaign. Accounts do not appear to survive for every parish in Northamptonshire, unless a substantial number are scattered in other boxes un-indexed to the county, which is a distinct possibility given the inadequacy of the organisation of the Exchequer papers. Where they do exist there is enormous variability between different parishes, some giving great detail while others provide little more than a summary cost. This means that if a parish account does not refer to the Naseby events it does not mean that there was no impact on that parish, although it seems likely that if there were large scale losses to the Parliamentarian army then some reference would have been made. With regard to the Royalist impact the evidence is very sparse, simply because the accounts were claims for money from Parliament. As there was no money to be claimed for losses suffered at the hands of the Royalist army so such losses are only rarely reported and then with little detail. Very occasionally there are constables' and churchwardens' accounts surviving in the local parish records that may far more accurately show the overall demands and may give more accurate dates for these events. These however exist for only a handful of Northamptonshire and Leicestershire parishes for the Civil War period. The incompleteness of local records is best exemplified by Naseby itself, for it is not simply a case of whether records survive but also what the local officials chose to record. Mastin, the vicar of Naseby whose name was inextricably linked with the study of the battle in the late 18th century, censured his 17th century predecessor in Naseby for his failure to make even a passing reference to the battle in the parish registers, 'an utterly inexcusable omission in a resident clergyman'.[3]

The other major collection of material that has yet to be comprehensively studied are the army accounts, warrants and pay records for the New Model Army and the various other armies and local forces. As with the parish accounts, there is a great body of evidence among which there is undoubtedly important information, particularly concerning the exact size and composition of the Parliamentarian army that fought at Naseby. A limited search of these sources has been conducted for this book in an attempt to clarify specific questions, such as the identification of Bartlet's regiment which provided the rearguard at Naseby. However this work has only scraped the surface and important new insights will probably result from comprehensive analysis of this material in the future.

The most important sources for the battle itself, which surprisingly have not all been fully exploited by previous authors, are the various independent accounts of the battle written either on the 14th June or in the following few days. Most are Parliamentarian letters and reports published in the newspapers and pamphlets in the week following the battle, although there are several contemporary Royalist perspectives, particularly the diaries of Slingsby and Symonds. It is to these contemporary sources that the greatest weight has been given in our analysis of the battle. In addition there are other accounts, such as Belasyse's *Life*, written later but by or for individuals who were present and based upon their own or colleagues' experiences of the battle. Finally there are the accounts written years after the battle that were essentially historical works based mainly upon other published and unpublished sources and not upon the experiences of the authors, even if some were present at the battle. In this category are the histories by Sprigge and by Clarendon, though in both these examples it must be accepted that the authors had access to first hand accounts from various of the key protagonists. This is confirmed in the case of Clarendon's *History* by the fact that several documents, such as the so-called *Prince Rupert's Diary*, were actually drawn up for Clarendon's use by people directly involved in the events. Rushworth and Whitelocke also appear occasionally to have had access to first hand accounts of certain events. For the wider campaign there are also the letters of various of the protagonists, including the correspondence to and from Sir Samuel Luke, governor of Newport Pagnell, and the records of the proceedings of the Commons and Lords. A list of the main sources for the battle itself, with a brief comment on their value, is given in appendix 2.[4]

Naseby is exceptional in having two graphic representations of the battle.[5] That by Sir Bernard de Gomme is one of a series for the major Civil War battles. It is stylised and draws its information for the topography and the Parliamentarian deployment from the earlier depiction of the battle by Streeter. The latter, drawn for and published in Sprigge's *Anglia Rediviva*, a history of the New Model Army, is a unique document in England. It has been copied several times, once for inclusion in Rushworth's *Historical Collections* and again in the late 18th century to illustrate Mastin's history of the parish of Naseby.[6] Streeter's engraving, although of great value, has also caused difficulties in the understanding of the battle. Our detailed study of Naseby has shown it to be a remarkably accurate representation of the landscape to the north west of Naseby village in 1645, but the realism of the depiction has deceived many into believing that it very accurately locates the initial battle formations. This is seen in its most extreme in Rowley's booklet on Naseby, in which he attempts to use the engraving as though it was an accurate map.[7] In reality the deployment is as stylised as that on de Gomme's plan. Whereas Streeter did visit Naseby to draw the prospect and, the excellent artist that he was, made a very good job of representing the landscape as it was a year or so after the battle, his representation of the armies can only have been an interpretation. It must have been dependent upon information drawn from the memories of various people, together perhaps with a copy of Skippon's original 'form of battle', drawn up on the 11th June 1645. A comment by Rushworth might also show that he had access to the equivalent Royalist document, for Rushworth says that he had before him the plan of battle from the papers of the Royalist Major General, Sir Jacob Astley. He also says that the depiction of the Parliamentarian deployment had been approved by the senior commanders. However one has to consider what there is in the depiction that is stylised or the result of artistic licence. For example, did the Royalists in fact form up on Dust Hill, where they would have had the advantage of the ground, instead of in Broadmoor? It would have been impossible for Streeter to have given an accurate representation of the army if he had placed it on the hill because it would have been too distant and distorted. Hence the evidence from both Streeter and de Gomme on the exact positioning of the two armies must be treated with care.

There are three other types of evidence that have not previously been adequately explored in connection with Naseby. Many of our Civil War battlefields are surrounded by traditions but, as Evans wrote of Edgehill in the early 20th century:

> 'many local traditions of the fight have doubtless been irretrievably lost, and in these days when village boys and girls quit their homes as soon as they can for the excitement of town life..., any that remain are less likely than ever to survive; but they are always worth listening to when they can be arrived at.'[8]

That local traditions were passed down about the events of 1645 is beyond doubt. One knows from ones own grandparents' stories the sort of things that are passed on by word of mouth. They include the special personal views of major national events which happened locally. From earlier this century the stories in my own family relate to the great period of unemployment, with the memories of the Raunds March passing through Rushden, or to the R101 passing over on its fateful maiden flight. As Beesley recorded in about 1833, the traditional story of the battle of Edgehill was a reasonably good account and the same seems to be true at Naseby but, although such stories have a limited role in enhancing our understanding of the campaign, they must be handled with great care. So, where traditions are recorded particularly early, especially in the 18th century, or if they support other independent sources of evidence, then they may well add a small piece to the jigsaw of reconstruction. Most of all they are of interest in their own right as an indication of the enduring local interest in the battle over the last three hundred and fifty years.

Of far greater importance than tradition are the physical remains of the battle. However, because the techniques of landscape archaeology have never been systematically applied to the study of battlefields in England, it is essential that the methodology be explored here so that not only the potentials but also the limitations of the evidence are recognised. Naseby may have been the first battlefield where the distribution of artefacts and burials from the battle was used as evidence to interpret the distribution and nature of the fighting. This pioneering work was conducted by Edward Fitzgerald in the mid 19th century but sadly it was not used by Thomas Carlyle, the famous historian of the Civil War, for whom the fieldwork was carried out. As a result, no attempt was made to build upon Fitzgerald's excellent work and so today we still do not have a well developed methodology for battlefield archaeology. The techniques for systematic recovery of artefacts such as pottery and flints from the ploughsoil were established for the study of archaeological sites in the 1970s, but the systematic recovery of metal artefacts has been far more slowly established as an archaeological technique.[9] This was an approach pioneered by the late Tony Gregory from about 1976, but still not completely integrated into archaeological fieldwork even today. As a result, although there are many archaeological reports on the physical remains of defensive structures from the Civil War, the study of artefacts from battlefields and siege sites has been left almost completely to metal detectorists. The lack of archaeological work on battlefields can be seen from the fact that a recent book on the archaeology of the Civil War devoted only two out of its sixty-four pages to battlefields and no space at all to the study of artefact scatters in connection with siege sites.[10] The one apparent exception has been the fieldwork on the Marston Moor battlefield, conducted by Newman and Cammidge. However, the detail of this work has never been published and so the potentials and limitations it may have revealed have not been available to guide the development of battlefield studies.[11]

The metal detector is a very valuable archaeological tool, but like many tools it can be used in a constructive or a destructive manner, dependent upon the intentions and the knowledge of the user. At Naseby it has been used by three keen detectorists in a very effective way. Indeed, such has been the purpose and focus of their work that, like some other detectorists, they should be better described as amateur archaeologists. They developed an interest in the battle and have collected artefacts and made records of their discoveries in such a way that the information can be used to cast dramatic new light upon the nature of the battle and the location of the fighting. My only involvement has been to find myself in the fortunate position of being given access to their information, to combine their three sets of records and then to integrate it into an overall study of the battle. All that I have been able to bring to the analysis of the finds distribution is experience from working with metal detectorists on various archaeological projects since the late 1970s. Knowing what we now know about the nature of the evidence, the three fieldworkers, Mike Westaway, Peter Burton and Tim Bevin, are the first to admit that a new survey would need to be pursued very differently, using a systematic technique. This cannot however be levelled as a criticism of their survey, for this was pioneering work. The limitations in the Naseby data must be recognised but this must not be allowed to detract from the very great achievement of the survey.

The objects recovered are almost all musket balls, approximately one thousand in all. In contrast, just a couple of dozen pistol balls have been found. In part this is because they are smaller and more difficult to locate, but it is also probably because far fewer pistol balls were actually fired during the battle. As a result the archaeological evidence shows us much about the action of musketeers and dragoons but hardly anything of the action of cavalry, which seems to be represented by the gaps in the distributions. There are other important factors, particularly of geology and land use, which influence the patterns of recovery, not just the distribution of infantry and dragoon action. For example, where permanent pasture exists, recognised by the survival of ridge and furrow, then almost no musket balls are found. This does not mean that there are no artefacts, for if the topsoil is removed there may be many musket balls lying close to the subsoil.[12] Similarly the detectorists report 'heavily mineralised soils', encountered for example on Sulby Hill, causing problems in the locating of musket balls. Another potential for bias in the distribution is of course the unsystematic survey method. The effects of such an approach are well known from archaeological fieldwalking surveys - by concentrating, however unintentional it may be, in the areas where larger numbers of finds are being made there is a tendency to reinforce positive patterns and to under-represent the lesser scatters. Although it is impossible to turn a low into a high density distribution, it is possible that spurious concentrations within the lower density scatters may be created by more intensive survey. Account must also be taken of previous removal of artefacts. At Naseby there has been a long history of collection of objects from the battlefield, including the recovery of musket balls in large numbers for sale to antiquaries and tourists in the 19th century. All these factors need to be taken into account and any interpretation must be tempered by the careful combination of the archaeological with documentary information. The survey team at Naseby and Sibbertoft are continuing to collect new evidence and in places will inevitably prove that my interpretations are wrong, which is all to the good for it will mean that the study of the battle is continuing to bear fruit, as I hope it does for a long time to come.

Finally there is the evidence for the reconstruction of the contemporary landscape, both of the battlefield and of the wider countryside, for which information has been drawn from several types of source. There are the national maps such as Ogilby's *Britannia* of 1675, which provides the major roads of England in the mid 17th century. There are also several county and area maps that have been drawn upon, but the main sources have been the local estate maps, surveys and other documents which enable the detailed reconstruction of the landscape at a parish level. The survival of these documents is very variable and hence some areas are easily understood whereas others are almost impossible to accurately reconstruct. When fitting the events of the campaign and especially the battle within this landscape, we must also not forget Gardiner's concerns that the distances given by the contemporary sources appear to be too short. In part this may be explained by the continuing use in 1645 of the old English mile of 2427 yards, though this is probably not the whole story because, in the absence of accurate maps, there were undoubtedly some simple errors in the contemporary judgement of distances.[13]

THE LANDSCAPE IN 1645

The events of the Naseby campaign took place in a landscape very different from that which exists in the south and east Midlands today, yet that context is very important to the understanding of the battle and of the campaign as a whole. A comprehensive 17th century historical geography of the region has yet to be compiled and so we must make do with a simplified study which focuses on Northamptonshire, and especially on the Naseby area, where the main action of our story took place. Northamptonshire lies in the centre of England and at the heart of that very distinctive landscape of open fields and nucleated villages that stretched across England from Wessex to Northumbria. The majority of battles of the Civil War were fought in this largely unenclosed countryside, most notably Edgehill, Marston Moor and of course Naseby itself. The reason was that such a landscape generally lacked hedgerows or stone walls and was therefore ideal for 17th century warfare with its set piece battles which required great open spaces, especially for cavalry action. At the beginning of the Civil War the Royalists had the choice as to where they drew the Parliamentarian army to battle. It could have been in the mainly enclosed landscape of the Severn valley around Worcester, where the Earl of Essex had taken control of the city in late September 1642, but instead they chose to place their forces between the Parliamentarian army and London. This forced Essex to engage them in an open field landscape of the Midlands where a decisive full scale battle could be fought. There the King could make the best use of his superiority in cavalry which provided the chance of decisively defeating Essex and ending the war almost before it had started. Whereas in an enclosed landscape musketeers could dramatically affect the outcome of a battle from the cover of hedgerows, the opportunity for this where the countryside was dominated by open fields was very limited. However where small areas of enclosures did exist, as Okey's action at Naseby demonstrates,

View of Buckton church now in Ruins with a View of the Town.   Sept 1721

Fig. 1. Boughton Green, near Northampton, where the Northampton horse clashed with detachments of Royalist cavalry several days before the battle of Naseby. Drawn in 1721, this view is typical of the Northamptonshire and Leicestershire landscape in 1645, when most of the countryside lay in great open fields lacking any hedgerows or even trees. Apart from the isolated church, only around Boughton village is there a cluster of small enclosures, hedges and trees, though in the far distance are the hedged closes of one of the relatively few enclosed parishes. (By permission of The British Library, Add. 32467, f.79)

the influence of hedgerows on a battle could be significant. The open field landscape also provided the opportunity for a defeated army to be wholly destroyed as can be seen from the two truly decisive battles of the English Civil War. Both Naseby and Marston Moor were fought in an open field context where infantry, once detached from their cavalry and without the cover provided by the small hedged fields and lanes of an enclosed landscape, were very vulnerable.

While some regions of England never had open fields and in others they had long since disappeared, in the heart of England they survived over a greater part of the countryside. In Northamptonshire and Leicestershire in particular the open field system survived reasonably intact well into the 18th century in the vast majority of parishes. So it was that in 1712 John Morton, in his *Natural History of Northamptonshire*, could still write that 'Enclosures lie dispersedly up and down in the County..... And yet for the greatest Part of the County is still open....'. However, we cannot simply assume that all the action of the Naseby campaign in Northamptonshire and Leicestershire took place in an unenclosed landscape, for significantly Morton adds, 'One of the largest... knot of Pastures, begins in that Angle where the three Counties of Leicester, Warwick and Northampton meet....'[14] By the mid 17th century a few parishes there had been completely enclosed for sheep farming, a process which had begun after the Black Death, while in some others there had been partial enclosure, although even in this part of the county the vast majority of land still remained open at the time of the Civil War. Because of the fragmentary nature of such enclosure in Northamptonshire, it will be necessary, in order to understand the events of the 14th June, to reconstruct the landscape of the Naseby area in some detail to determine which land was enclosed and which was open in 1645.

The other open landscape of Northamptonshire was its heathland, but this was mainly restricted to four areas of the county which were not very extensive. The largest lay to the north west of Peterborough, another in the south west of the county near Brackley and extending mainly into Oxfordshire. Of the two smaller areas of heath, one lay immediately north of Northampton, the other near Guilsborough. Just across the county boundary lay Dunsmore Heath where Rupert, mainly as a propaganda ploy, had challenged the Earl of Essex to a major set piece battle in 1642 to decide the war at the outset. Though this event did not take place, and though these heaths do not play a major role in our story, many other places in the county had small fragments of heathland and several of these do figure briefly and significantly in the Naseby story. As Morton wrote in 1712, the heathland had 'heath or Ling upon it (....from whence a tract of it has frequently here the Name of Lings, Linches, or Links) but also Furze, and Broom in some Places, and Fern or Brakes....'.[15] Today one is hard pressed to find even a tiny fragment of heath in Northamptonshire. It was almost completely swept away during the Agricultural Revolution, mainly as a result of the Parliamentary Enclosure Acts of the 18th and 19th century. However, the natural vegetation of these areas has not been wholly suppressed. In the former heathland zones of the county, if one ventures beyond the beaten track, there are traces of furze, bracken and broom still to be found encroaching where agricultural control is relaxed. So, for example, if one visits Borough Hill, where much of the Royalist army was encamped while at Daventry in June 1645, one can see furze encroaching on the ramparts of the Iron Age hillfort. This is exactly what had happened by the 17th century at Naseby, Sibbertoft and Clipston in small areas of less intensively used land and this was a factor determining exactly where the battle was fought.

Woodland was another major element of the Northamptonshire landscape but this figures hardly at all in our story, for it lay mainly in the southern and north eastern extremities of the county. These were the ancient Royal forests of Whittlewood, Salcey and Rockingham, by now shrunken to a tiny part of the area they had covered in the early medieval period. The final type of landscape which must be taken into account is the fenland, which extended from the eastern corner of Northamptonshire, as it was then, across to The Wash. In 1645 this was still an undrained land, largely impassable except along the few causeways and was significant during the Civil War because it represented an important barrier to movement into East Anglia from the east Midlands. In late May 1645 this was the frontier zone which Cromwell was sent to defend as the Royalist army marched towards East Anglia.

An understanding of the road system of the region is also important to understanding the events of 1645, for it helps to explain why armies followed particular routes and why garrisons had been established in particular places. The Enclosure Acts of the 18th and 19th centuries led not only to the enclosure of the Northamptonshire and Leicestershire landscape, they also resulted in a major redrawing of the local road pattern. Even more significant, the Turnpike Acts of the 18th century caused radical changes to the network of major roads. Because Northamptonshire's enclosure was generally so late, Parliamentary Enclosure Acts only beginning in 1728, while most Turnpike Acts date from the mid to late 18th century, we have a county map which precedes most of these major changes.[16] Though not published until 1778, the Thomas Eayre map was mainly surveyed around 1720 and almost completed in the 1730s.[17] It therefore shows the Northamptonshire landscape, and especially its road pattern, very much as it was in 1645. To complement this we can correct and supplement Eayre's information with the county map by Robert Morden, published in the late 17th century, which shows major roads, and by John Ogilby's road map of England and Wales published in 1675 which shows the nationally important routes in great detail. That the roads recorded by Ogilby and Morden reflected the pattern in use earlier in the century is confirmed by various sources. For example, one finds that the route from London via Stony Stratford and Daventry then on to Coventry was chosen by John Taylor in his 'pennyless pilgrimage' just before the Civil War. In our reconstruction of the wider landscape the main towns have been identified using John Speed's atlas of Britain published in 1616, and the extent of the fenland and the main roads crossing the fen from Blaeu's map of 1648.[18] Whereas the major routes were typically very wide, often sixty or seventy feet, which would have been important for the movement of Civil War armies, the condition of the roads was generally poor. The inability of the unimproved road system of the 1640s to cope with the transport of heavy goods is well recorded and so the hundreds of carriages and the thousands of horses with a major army must have found them almost impassable when the weather was wet. The description of the Northampton to Welford road in the 1720s, before it was turnpiked, must have been fairly typical of roads in 1645: 'The highways.... have been chiefly spoiled by the Great Number of Carriages and Waggons which are continually passing through the same with heavy Burthens and tearing up the roads.' Transport was difficult because 'most part of the soil where the Said Roads lie, consists of clay, and is of such a swampy nature, that it doth suck up all the stones cast into them.' Such roads are seen in 18th century illustrations of the county, rutted, unfenced and wandering across the open fields.[19]

It is not just the configuration of the landscape which is important in understanding the events of 1645, it is also the perception that contemporaries had of that topography. Today we have a better overview of England as it was in 1645 than anyone could possibly have had at the time. In considering the marches of the two armies as they approached each other in the days and weeks before the 14th June, one has to remember the inadequacy of 17th century cartography. The best maps available at the time were the atlases by Christopher Saxton, published in 1579, and by John Speed in 1612.[20] They accurately depict the location of all the towns and villages, the main rivers and, in a very stylised form, the major hills and woodlands. However, they do not record a single road and it would not be until thirty years after the war that the first 'route maps' were published. So, even if the military commanders had access to the relevant county maps or to a complete atlas by Speed or Saxton, they would still not have been able to plan their campaigns or predict the action of their adversaries using maps alone. As Cruso wrote in 1632, 'guides can better direct them then the usuall maps, which (if not false) are too generall'.[21] Commanders in the Civil War would therefore have been extremely dependent, far more than in later wars, upon the scouts of their nearest garrisons or upon local guides in determining where to march and where to fight.

NOTES

1. Stead, 1891.
2. Tennant, 1992.
3. Mastin, 1792, p.117.
4. Belasyse; Clarendon, 1702; Sprigge, 1647. Firth, 1898. Rushworth, 1722; Whitelocke. Tibbutt, 1963; *CSPD*; Lords Journals; Commons Journals.
5. BL Add.16370. There was also apparently an original copy in Dutch. Warburton, 1849, vol.3, p.104. Sprigge, 1647.
6. Rushworth, 1722, contains the '*I.Sturt sculp:*' copy of the Streeter engraving. The copy in Mastin, 1792, is the only one on which the church is shown. Occasionally this has led to confusion, as for example in Carlton, 1994, plate 5. A modified copy was produced for the reprint of *Anglia Rediviva* in 1854. Other views of the battlefield are derived from Streeter, for example that in Lockinge, 1830, and Young, 1985.
7. Rowley, 1989.
8. Evans, 1938, p.121.
9. For example Foard, 1978.
10. Harrington, 1992. There are a number of excellent archaeological studies of defensive sites and of sieges explored through excavation evidence combined with documentary study. The most significant early study was RCHM, 1964; of recent studies the most notable include Atkin and Laughlin, 1992, and Courtney & Courtney, 1992.
11. Other metal detectorists have worked on the battlefield, maintaining detailed maps of their discoveries, but these also have not been published. Pers.comm. Greg Sparham.
12. The Midland Archaeological Research Society conducted a detecting survey on the site of a proposed barn at Prince Rupert's Farm. The absence of musket balls in the initial survey was completely overturned when the land was resurveyed after the topsoil had been stripped, with 14 musket balls being recovered: Pers.comm. Bob Kings.
13. Gardiner, 1893. Denton, 1988. The old English mile of 2427 yards (1500 double paces) was still in use although the modern mile of 1760 yards had been legally defined in the Tudor period. Adams, 1976, p.8.
14. Morton, 1712, p.15.
15. Morton, 1712, p.9-10.

16. The first two Turnpike Acts were the Stony Stratford - Dunchurch road in 1706 and the Northampton - Welford road in 1721. Steane, 1974, p.250-2.

17. Brown & Foard, 1994, p.177.

18. Eayre map. Ogilby, 1675. Speed maps. J.Blaeu, 1648, *Regiones Inundatae*, a map of the Fens (reprinted 1992 by Cambridgeshire Libraries). John Taylor's poem, *The Pennyless Pilgrimage*, quoted by Burke, 1942.

19. Steane, 1974, p.247-253 and plates 8 & 24.

20. Ravenhill, 1992. Speed maps.

21. Cruso, 1632, p.68.

CHAPTER 2

A REGIONAL PERSPECTIVE

'the people can bear the war no longer,
and will enforce you to a dishonourable peace.'
Oliver Cromwell

The battle of Naseby must be viewed in two contexts, one national and the other regional. Whereas the former has been explored by various authors, not least because it relates to the creation of the New Model Army, the latter has not been adequately considered. The focus here is more to the regional context in order to redress the balance, for through an understanding of local conditions it may become clearer why nationally important events unfolded where and in the way they did. The campaign in the early summer of 1645 evolved quite differently than anyone had expected, for it was not focused in south west England, where the last Parliamentarian garrisons were in danger of being finally removed, neither was it focused in the north of England. There the Royalists might have recruited amongst the former soldiers of the Earl of Newcastle, whose army had been destroyed at Marston Moor, then they might have challenged the advancing Scottish army and, in coordinated action with Montrose in Scotland, have attempted to recover the North for the King. Instead, against all expectation and against the sound advice of Prince Rupert and his other military commanders, the King turned the campaign in a way which the Parliamentarians interpreted as a threat to the heartland of their power. This led to the most important battle of the war being fought where the Royalists were further and the Parliamentarians closer to the areas where they could concentrate their greatest military power.

THE MILITARY BACKGROUND

It had been said in 1642 that the King chose Leicestershire, Northamptonshire and Warwickshire to be 'the seat of our war.'[1] It was here that the first great battle was fought, at Edgehill, and more than two and a half years later it was here that the decisive campaign would be played out, but unfortunately there has never been a detailed study of the war in the south east Midlands. This was the important frontier zone between on the one side the Parliamentarian heartland of East Anglia, typically referred to as the Association, and London, and on the other the King's capital at Oxford together with the important Royalist enclaves of Ashby de la Zouch and Newark. Sherwood's study of the Midlands does provide some information, but the region is peripheral to his main area of interest.[2] Although there are several countywide studies, most notably for Warwickshire, the Civil War in Northamptonshire has not been reviewed since Page's compilation of contemporary sources in the late 19th century. Buckinghamshire also has only a few articles, mostly from the early 20th century, while in Leicestershire the best overview remains the single chapter in Nichols' early 19th century county history.[3]

Fig.2. Gloucester was of great strategic importance, maintaining Parliamentarian influence in a region which was mainly under Royalist control. Communications with the city were maintained only with great difficulty and Northampton was a key link in the supply route, with convoys regularly waiting at the town for a favourable chance to proceed to Warwick and thence into the West, because all along this route the convoys were within striking distance of Oxford and Banbury. This was only one of several key communication routes which passed through Northamptonshire.[4]

For Parliament this region not only had a value in its own right, it served two other very important roles. The Parliamentarian garrisons, particularly Newport Pagnell, Northampton, Coventry, Warwick and Leicester kept communications open between London and Gloucester, the west Midlands and the North West. Of equal importance, Northamptonshire and Buckinghamshire, together with the adjacent areas of Leicestershire, Lincolnshire and the fenland were a vital frontier zone. The garrisons of Newport Pagnell and Aylesbury were considered the 'bulwark of the Association', while Northampton, Rockingham and Crowland closed the north western border of East Anglia. These garrisons protected the Association and London throughout the war from almost all military action. East Anglia was therefore in a unique position in the country, for the region largely escaped the destructive local fighting and the incursions of major armies which ravaged almost every other part of England and Wales. This was particularly

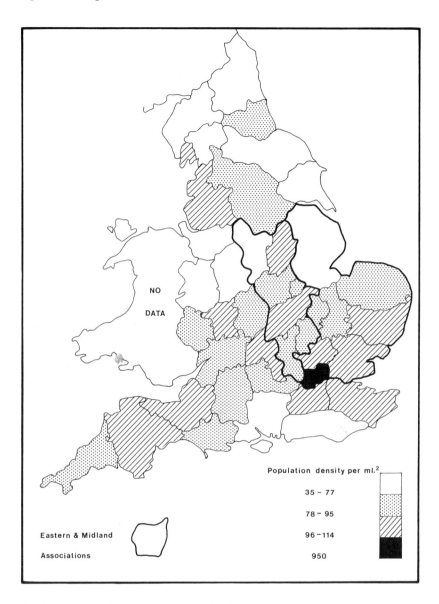

Fig.3. The density of population in England circa 1600[5]

important because it was also the wealthiest and most populous region in the country. Behind these defences, apart from brief disturbances such as the siege of Kings Lynn in August 1643 and the pillaging of Huntingdon in August 1645, the eastern counties were a haven of peace and security where economic activity could continue comparatively unscathed. The counties of East Anglia therefore had a strong common interest in maintaining their frontier by collective action and this provided a unique political context where a single military organisation could be made to work. Behind the frontier this collective approach, within a relatively secure and wealthy region, enabled the creation in 1643-4 of the most effective Parliamentarian army that the war had yet seen. In contrast the Royalists lacked such a base, although they had held much of the North until July 1644. Its loss after the battle of Marston Moor was a great blow but, with the exception of Lancashire, it could not compare to East Anglia in wealth or population and was never wholly secure. Wales, most of which was in Royalist hands, was again not a very wealthy or populous region. Only south west England could begin to compare with the Parliamentarian heartland, especially once the Royalists held Bristol, at that time England's second city.

The focus of our story, the south east Midlands, had been a well populated and fairly prosperous region earlier in the century but, because it was a disputed area throughout the war, much of it fared very badly. Buckinghamshire, for example, suffered almost constant incursions from Royalist forces based in Oxfordshire and proved incapable of maintaining major garrisons in its own right. The garrisons at Newport Pagnell and Aylesbury had to be partly manned and funded by the Eastern Association. At the beginning of the war, in the summer of 1642, the majority of the region had been secured for Parliament, with all the county towns apart from Oxford coming into Parliamentarian hands either immediately or by early 1643. Northampton was fortified in August 1642 and became one of the most important garrisons in the region, being chosen as the assembly point for the first Parliamentarian army in the weeks before Edgehill. Sir John Gell secured Derby and John Hutchinson achieved the same in Nottingham, Lord Brooke garrisoned his castle at Warwick, while the nearby town of Coventry also declared for Parliament. In Buckinghamshire the county town of Aylesbury was successfully held in the face of a Royalist attack soon after Edgehill and, despite other later and less serious threats, it remained in Parliamentarian hands throughout the war.[6] Under the leadership of Lord Grey of Groby a Parliamentarian garrison had also been established at Leicester by the beginning of 1643, but there were several major towns which surprisingly were never fortified by either side. The best example is Stamford. It was said in 1646 that the town was 'scituated... in such a place, that the most skillfull engineers, which, in these civill warrs have surveyed the same on both sides .... could never find a way to make it a towne tenable either for defence or offence.'[7] In most counties there was however a proliferation of subsidiary garrisons. Many of these were established in close proximity to substantial market towns which would otherwise in themselves be indefensible, at least with the limited forces and resources that were available. Hence the garrison of Astley was near Nuneaton, Bagworth near Market Bosworth, Kirby Bellars near Melton Mowbray and so forth.

The predominance of Parliamentarian control in the south east Midlands should not be taken as an indication that the whole region was Parliamentarian in sympathy. It has been said of Stamford, for example, that although the town was more inclined to support Parliament than the King it was probably the action of a vocal and influential minority which determined the position of the community.[8] Parliamentarian or Royalist control of a territory did not necessarily even reflect the dominant sympathy of the local people. Banbury was a case in point, for Joshua Sprigge's home town was strongly puritan yet it fell under Royalist control soon after the battle of Edgehill and remained so throughout the war.

In December 1642 the counties of Leicestershire, Derbyshire, Nottinghamshire, Northamptonshire, Rutland, Bedfordshire, Buckinghamshire and Huntingdonshire were brought together under a single committee as an Association. Lord Grey was given command, as Major General, of all the military forces of this Midland Association.[9] It was however ineffective and the war effort in the region continued to be run by individual County Committees. It is true that there is evidence of troops from one county taking quarter in another, when involved in action in that county, as with the Warwickshire troops in Leicestershire.[10] Only occasionally however did they cooperate effectively, as in 1644 when Lord Grey's Leicestershire forces combined with Gell's troops in Derbyshire to destroy the newly established Royalist garrison at Wilney Ferry. But this was a case where the common interests of both counties were deeply concerned, because Wilney Ferry controlled the main road between Leicester and Derby where it crossed the Trent, interfering with all communication and trade between the two.[11]

Royalist interests in the region were not firmly established until after the battle of Edgehill, when Oxford became the Royalist capital. The city was heavily fortified and its control of the county was reinforced by the establishment of a number of lesser garrisons. Of these the most important was Banbury castle, which had been taken by the Royalists immediately after Edgehill and from where they controlled much of south west Northamptonshire as well as north Oxfordshire and south Warwickshire. Other minor garrisons secured the road north from Oxford to Banbury and also much of the rest of the shire. This was very necessary given the presence of large Parliamentarian garrisons which encircled Oxfordshire on the north, east and south. The value of such lesser garrisons can be seen from the case of Boarstall House. The Parliamentarians at Aylesbury 'had experienced much inconvenience from the excursions of their neighbours' at Boarstall but in the spring of 1644 it was abandoned, only to be taken over by the Parliamentarians. Oxford found the new Boarstall garrison greatly disrupted their control of the region and so it had to be retaken. When they had recaptured it they refortified the house and demolished the church to provide a clear field of fire around its defences, improvements that were obviously effective for it was to withstand two later attempts to storm it. Boarstall served its purpose well for it 'nearly supported itself.... by depredations in Buckinghamshire, particularly in the neighbourhood of Aylesbury.'[12] It was undoubtedly the action of such garrisons which played an important role in the

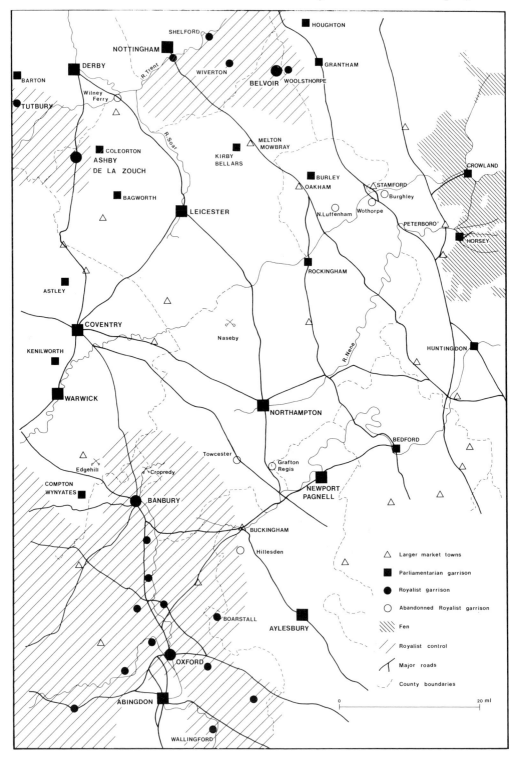

Fig.4. Garrisons and areas of influence in the south east Midlands early in 1645.

disruption of the economy of Buckinghamshire to a state where in 1645 the county was unable or unwilling to support even its own Parliamentarian garrisons.[13]

Elsewhere in the region it was in early 1643, as the various County Committees began to suppress the last pockets of Royalist resistance, that two key Royalist bases were established, one at Newark and the other at Ashby de la Zouch. When the Hastings family had failed to secure Leicestershire for the King in the summer of 1642 they had withdrawn from the county but now Henry Hastings returned to garrison his father's castle at Ashby, on the north west edge of Leicestershire. Although the town itself was Parliamentarian in sympathy, under the shadow of Ashby castle it was to remain a Royalist stronghold throughout the war.[14] In response to the establishment of the Parliamentarian Midland Association under Lord Grey, the King appointed Hastings as Colonel General of Leicestershire, Rutland, Derbyshire, Nottinghamshire and Lincolnshire. From Ashby he not only dominated north west Leicestershire, providing a continual threat to Leicester, but also, together with the garrisons in Staffordshire, he 'disquieted' the Parliamentarians in Derbyshire, Warwickshire and Staffordshire.[15] Hastings' control of the Ashby enclave was strengthened later in 1643 with the capture of Lichfield.

Fig. 5. Newark was established as a Royalist garrison early in 1642. During the war the defences of the medieval castle were enhanced by the addition of massive defences of earth and timber which encompassed the whole town, making it one of the strongest of Royalist garrisons.

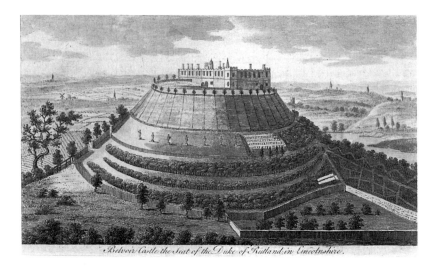

Belvoir Castle the Seat of the Duke of Rutland in Lincolnshire.

Fig.6. Belvoir castle was garrisoned for the King in January 1643 and controlled adjacent parts of Leicestershire, Nottinghamshire and Lincolnshire. As the Parliamentarian threat increased in 1645 the whole village at Belvoir was cleared away for strategic reasons. The castle may have been 'one of the strongest and fairest buildings in the Kingdome', but it eventually surrendered to its besiegers in February 1646. Command of the garrison was then given to Markham, who had been wounded at Naseby after which Cromwell had supposedly promised to 'show him favour'. The Civil War defences were levelled in 1647, when the constable of nearby Branston records men being sent from the village to Belvoir to throw down the bulwarks, although the castle itself was not demolished until 1649. This view shows Belvoir in 1735, after a rebuilding in the 1650s and 1660s following the plan and incorporating remaining parts of the earlier castle.[16]

Newark, on the eastern side of Nottinghamshire, was heavily fortified as the key Royalist garrison in the east Midlands, but more significant for our region was the subsidiary garrison at Belvoir Castle, which was established in January 1643.[17] The castle was:

'by reason of the situation on a hill of difficult accesse, and being built upon the confines of Lincolne and Leicestershires, with a very fair prospect also into that of Nottingham, is thought to bee of speciall consequence and importance for his majesties service, as having a strong power and influence on all those three counties.'[18]

Belvoir was to Newark what Banbury was to Oxford. From Belvoir, under the overall command of Henry Hastings, now Lord Loughborough, the Royalists dominated north east Leicestershire and the adjacent areas of Nottinghamshire and Lincolnshire. At various times throughout the war the Belvoir and Newark forces also made incursions into Rutland and Lincolnshire, where Stamford suffered frequently, to Peterborough and into the fenland. These two relatively small Royalist enclaves based on Ashby and Newark remained under Royalist control throughout the war. Though always isolated, they were crucial staging posts for Royalist communications between Oxford and the North. The Royalist garrisons in the region, from Oxford to Newark, also ensured that the natural wealth of the south and east Midlands could not be employed unchecked to support the Parliamentarian war effort - if it had then Parliamentarian power nationally would have been overwhelming. For these reasons Ashby, Newark, Belvoir and Banbury were heavily fortified and a very high priority was given to their retention.

1643 was the high point of Royalist fortunes in the south east Midlands. In October they made a major attempt to expand their control eastward from Oxford and Banbury. This was a pattern which would be repeated in the winter of 1644-5 here and elsewhere. When the Royalist army was in winter quarters its power in the region was greatly enhanced, making military expansion a possibility, indeed a real necessity if its troops were not to over tax the resources of their own territory. In the summer, when the forces were withdrawn to reconstitute the field army, the garrisons and their territories were far more vulnerable. So it was that in 1643 a large detachment of the main Royalist army marched to Northampton and faced the town, having a plan to take it by treachery. When this failed, on the 15th October they marched on into north Buckinghamshire and Bedfordshire.[19] Shock waves spread right through the Eastern Association, for the approach of Prince Rupert's forces raised the hopes of all Royalists in the region and even in Cambridge, the headquarters of the Association, there were moves to raise forces for the King. The Parliamentarian response reveals a fear that would arise again in May 1645:

'Since the Cavaliers have come into Bedfordshire, Which county they have woefully plundered, they have seized upon the town of Newport Pannell in the upper part of Buckinghamshire .... and have forced the inhabitants thereabouts to come in and strengthen and fortifie it, their drift being to intercept all cattell and other provisions that shall come out of all the adjacent counties to London, hoping thereby to cut off all victuals from this city, and so to starve it, if they be not timely prevented and unnestled out of that place. Besides infinite danger may befall the eastern Associated Counties if the Cavaliers be suffered to proceed in this enterprise, because they will have opportunity to draw all the malevolents out of those Counties to their side .... and thereby bring all the quietest parts of the kingdom into combustion and distraction.'[20]

The Parliamentarians responded in force. Major General Philip Skippon, leading the London Trained Bands, marched north and at this news, due to a disastrous misunderstanding, the Royalists abandoned Newport Pagnell. The Earl of Essex was at St.Albans at this time and decided to stay there with his army 'untill Newport Pannell be strongly fortified and well manned for the defence of those parts to keep the Cavaliers from thence another time.'[21]

Buckinghamshire already had to support the garrison at Aylesbury and did not have the resources, especially in the light of continual Royalist incursions, to maintain another major garrison. Because of its strategic importance, the Newport garrison was therefore to be maintained by the Eastern Association counties of Hertfordshire, Huntingdonshire, Cambridgeshire, Suffolk, Essex and Norfolk, as well as Northamptonshire, Bedfordshire, and the three Hundreds of Newport Pagnell.[22] The Royalists fell back on a new garrison at Towcester, and established outposts at Grafton Regis and Hillesden, thus maintaining their control of the key routes from London to Northampton, Coventry and beyond. Skippon, supported by local garrison forces, took Grafton by storm on Christmas Eve, which also led the Royalists to abandon Towcester early in the new year, pulling back to Banbury and Oxford. By this time Rupert had shifted the focus of Royalist preparations for the 1644 campaign to Wales and the Welsh Marches. The Royalists still tried to retain control of north west Buckinghamshire through their Hillesden garrison but this was finally cleared in March by Eastern Association forces, again supported by troops from Northampton and Newport Pagnell.[23] The Association army was now powerful enough to take a major responsibility for defence of the region and so Skippon was able to withdraw the London Trained Bands.

Further north 1643 was also a high point for Royalist fortunes, where the 'flying armies' from Ashby and Newark were the scourge of the Parliamentarians. In response to these incursions, in March 1643 the Northamptonshire County Committee established a garrison in Rockingham castle to secure the north east of the county and the adjacent parts of Leicestershire and Rutland. However, after their victory at Ancaster Heath on 11th April the Newark and Belvoir forces extended their influence to Grantham, Stamford and Peterborough. They were pushed back from Peterborough by Cromwell, who then drove them from the Stamford area, storming their newly established garrison at Burghley House on the 27th July. This established a continuing pattern in which the Eastern Association appear to have taken direct responsibility for the maintenance of military control in the far north east of Northamptonshire. The other minor Royalist garrisons in Leicestershire, such as North Luffenham, were also cleared and later in the year the Eastern Association forces recovered most of Lincolnshire.[24] In response to the threat from Belvoir, a garrison was also established at Burley in Rutland, set on a hill top in a superb defensive position just two miles north east of the county town of Oakham.[25] The garrison there, under Colonel Waite and then in 1644 under Major Layfield, played an important role in controlling the incursions of the Belvoir Royalists, but was ultimately responsible to Lord Grey and its troops operated at various times in conjunction with the Leicestershire forces.[26] Although Burley was drawing provisions and taxes from the villages in the immediate environs, and presumably from the whole of Rutland, these villages were also required by

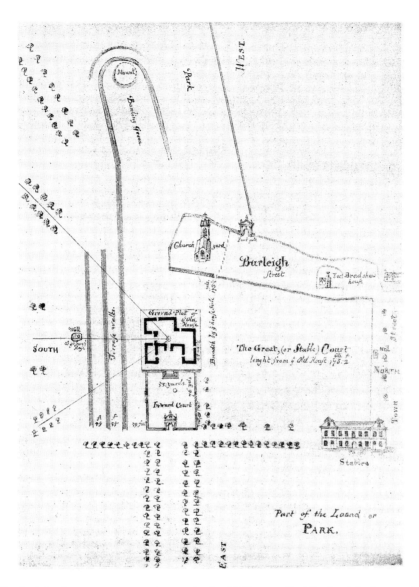

Fig. 7. A Parliamentarian garrison at Burley Hall controlled Rutland during much of the Civil War. The Duke of Buckingham's house, which lay on the site of the present house, had been built on a grand scale in the 1620s. Its impressive hill top position gave commanding views to the north, south and west, where it overlooked Oakham, the county town. It was recorded in the survey of 1651 that 'The Mansion house usually called the Hall standing within the Wall of the Park was in these late Wars utterly consumed by fire soe that att present there remains nothing but certain ruinous parts and pieces of the Walls being built of freestone....' The stables have survived, but landscaping for the gardens and park of new Hall has swept away all trace of the Civil War defences.[27]

warrants under Lord Grey to support the much stronger garrison across the county boundary at Rockingham.[28]

Following a successful campaign in 1643, by early 1644 Parliament held almost the whole of Lincolnshire with some 5000 foot and about twenty troops of horse. This expanding Eastern Association army was more than a match for the local Royalist forces and soon Belvoir was the only significant garrison holding out beyond Newark.[29] However, while the Association forces were concentrating their effort in north Buckinghamshire, at Hillesden, the Royalists pushed back into Lincolnshire and retook the major garrisons, wiping out almost all the Parliamentarian gains. The fall of Lincolnshire was, at least in part, the result of the inability of the Parliamentarian commanders in the various adjacent counties to work together. The flying armies of Ashby and Newark, so named because they could move very quickly as they were not encumbered by a large train of artillery and baggage, ranged widely over the north of the region. They waged an effective campaign of destruction in the Parliamentarian areas but never had sufficient power to tip the balance and deliver any of the major enemy garrisons to the King. Then, in the early summer of 1644, the newly strengthened Eastern Association army moved into Lincolnshire once more, drove the Royalists back onto the defensive and Lincoln together with most of the county fell to Parliament. The appearance of a major field army had completely tipped the balance of power. Such an army could place local garrison forces in an untenable position so long as it was not countered by an opposing field army. This was a lesson that the Parliamentarians would also learn to their cost in May 1645. Only massively defended garrisons like Newark could hope to withstand a concerted assault by such an overwhelming force. However, once the Association army marched on into the North to the siege of York, the local Royalist garrisons which had survived, in Belvoir and Newark, could once more move onto the offensive. With 500 troops they attempted to garrison Wothorpe, in a strategic location overlooking Stamford and commanding the important Ermine Street route. This time, for once, the local forces did cooperate, Lord Grey bringing together Leicestershire and Northamptonshire troops to expel the Royalists.[30]

While the bulk of the Eastern Association army were involved in the siege of York, in June 1644 the King led an army through the Midlands. He was shadowed by two armies, those of Essex and Waller, but then in a typically disastrous move Essex divided the Parliamentarian forces. As the King marched into the south east Midlands, only Waller was left to shadow him. In a scenario very similar to that which would arise in 1645, again through incompetence involving the Earl of Essex, as the King advanced into Buckinghamshire the Association and the local County Committees had to look to their own defence as Parliament desperately tried to raise other forces, under Major General Browne, from the home counties, London and East Anglia, to meet the threat. Although some troops were assembled they proved ineffective, due to the fragmentary, county based organisation of most of the

Parliamentarian forces, and Browne never joined with Waller or played any significant part in the campaign. Waller finally had little choice but to challenge the King at Cropredy Bridge, just to the north of Banbury, on 29th June. He was defeated and, if the King had pursued his advantage, the Parliamentarian army might have been completely destroyed in the field. Instead Waller was allowed to fall back to Northampton where his army took up quarters around the town.[31]

Despite having the upper hand, Charles took no territory, not even a single major garrison fell to him. Even before he received news of Rupert's crushing defeat at Marston Moor the King had retreated to Evesham, fearing that Waller would join with Browne's forces. In reality Waller's army was a wholly inadequate force comprising mainly trained bands and local levies. From his own and Browne's experiences Waller drew the inevitable conclusion that:

> 'an army compounded of these men will never go through with your service, and till you have an army merely your own, that you may command, it is in a manner impossible to do anything of importance.'

Parliament had been given the first clear statement of what was needed to bring the war to a successful and speedy conclusion.[32] Twelve months later that army would exist, though not under Waller's command, and it would march into the region to fight the decisive battle of the Civil War.

Despite the setback that Waller had suffered, the total defeat of the two Royalist armies at Marston Moor near York on the 2nd June 1644 had more than redressed the balance, for it was not only the garrisons of Yorkshire which fell to Parliament as a result. As the Eastern Association army returned southward other strongholds began to tumble. The whole Royalist cause was under threat and the Newark and Ashby enclaves must have seemed particularly vulnerable, indeed senior commanders in the Association army were only stopped from besieging Newark by the unwillingness of their Lord General, the Earl of Manchester, to complete the destruction of the King's forces. Though the opportunities were not fully exploited, Marston Moor had dramatically changed the military position in our region, for with the fall of the north of England the two Royalist enclaves of Ashby and Newark became completely isolated. Though they could still prove a great annoyance to the local Parliamentarians, as in the autumn of 1644 when they were able to attack the fenland once more while the Association army was at Newbury, the Royalists were forced back on the defensive for most of the rest of the war. It was in this climate of overwhelming Parliamentarian success that the local forces from Northamptonshire, Warwickshire and Buckinghamshire combined, under the command of Colonel John Fiennes, to lay siege to Banbury castle. With part of its forces having been withdrawn into the Royalist field army the garrison was at its most vulnerable. Fiennes encircled Banbury and had soon entered the town, which lacked any substantial defences, but the garrison in the castle, under Sir William Compton, held out bravely. Extensive siege-works were constructed and following a very destructive artillery bombardment the Parliamentarians twice attempted to storm the castle. In September they were joined by Eastern Association troops, while Cromwell's cavalry deterred any Royalist attempt to relieve the castle. The fate of the siege of Banbury mirrored the apparent decline in Parliamentarian fortunes nationally in the autumn of 1644, represented by the failures at Lostwithiel and Newbury. By mid October, as the garrison was nearing the point when it would have to surrender simply because of the lack of supplies, a relieving force was dispatched under the Earl of Northampton. There were claims of gross mismanagement of the whole affair when on the 26th October, without the Association cavalry to support them, the besieging force had to raise the siege and flee. In a fighting retreat many were said to have been killed, although the majority of the troops with some of their artillery and supplies were safely drawn away.[33]

It is true that the attempt to reduce Banbury in the summer of 1644 had ended in failure and that Newark had not even been invested by the Eastern Association army, however, despite these lost opportunities, the winter of 1644-5 still saw the Parliamentarian forces in the region in the ascendancy. Compton Wynyates, which had been taken on the 8th June as part of the offensive against Banbury, continued to be held for the rest of the war, despite a fierce Royalist attack in January 1645. So the Warwickshire Committee retained an improved hold over south Warwickshire, restricting the influence of the Banbury garrison.[34] In the summer of 1644 there had also been other significant Parliamentarian advances around Oxford, when Major General Browne had been given command of a force for the reducing of Oxford, Wallingford, Greenland House and Banbury, as well as command of the forces of the counties of Oxfordshire, Berkshire and Buckinghamshire.[35] Greenland House, near Henley, capitulated and although Browne failed in his siege of Boarstall House, far outweighing any failures of the summer was the seizure and fortification of Abingdon, which had been abandoned by the Royalists in May 1644.[36] Like Aylesbury and Newport Pagnell, Abingdon's garrison was supported by Eastern Association forces during the winter of 1644-5. Just six miles from Oxford, Abingdon was a major threat to the Royalist capital and so during the winter they attempted to regain the initiative. First they garrisoned Besselsleigh House, on the Faringdon road, but were driven out and then Rupert attempted to storm Abingdon itself on the 11th January. Though the town was poorly supplied and had incomplete fortifications, Browne repulsed the Royalist attack, a defence in which the presence of Eastern Association troops must have been crucial. Rupert made one final attempt to restrict Browne's freedom of action by attempting to destroy Culham Bridge and to create a fort there to stop Parliamentarian incursions across the Thames into south east Oxfordshire, but again the Royalists failed.[37] Rupert suffered considerable losses in these attacks, even the garrison commander of Oxford, Sir Henry Gage, was killed. So the advantages they had given up in the spring when the King's field army marched away had not been recovered in the winter when the forces returned.

The Royalists, though everywhere on the defensive, could still launch destructive and worrying forays. In the north of the region they showed this when the Newark and Belvoir troops captured the key frontier garrison at Crowland. The greatest fear of the Parliamentarians, that the Association would be attacked, was renewed yet again. Association troops were rushed forward to besiege the fort but it was well protected and so the most realistic response was a protracted siege to starve out the small Royalist garrison. By October 1644 we find Sir Thomas Fairfax's cavalry from Yorkshire joining with Gell, in the Vale of Belvoir, to defeat the Royalist relief force as it headed for Crowland. They fell upon the enemy 'with singular good speed and good success, and bravely surprised the greatest part of them.' Thus they 'prevented that most desperate and dangerous design (as it might unquestionably have proved) of breaking in, like a furious overflowing flood, into the associated counties.'[38] In May 1645 we will find Fairfax, though with a far more important command, once more rushing to protect the Association from a far greater Royalist threat. Even after Crowland was retaken the Belvoir Royalists continued to make occasional expeditions to plunder Rutland and the adjacent areas, as for example in January 1645 when they captured two sequestrators and 12 troopers from Burley House. However the Royalist association of the East Midlands was finished as a major fighting force and as the King's fortunes declined there were growing disputes within the Royalist camp, which led at this time to the replacement of Lucas as governor of Belvoir.[39] They were now confined to the grim task of retaining their strongholds in the face of growing Parliamentarian power and encircled by a string of small enemy garrisons. Around Ashby for example there were four: in Warwickshire Astley Castle had been held for Parliament since 1642; since at least March 1644 at Bagworth in Leicestershire, in the house of Lady Manners, there had been a quarter for horses to scout abroad in that part of the county; a garrison had been established by Gell at Barton in Derbyshire in autumn 1644 and then in November the Royalist outpost in Sir John Beaumont's house at Coleorton, just two miles from Ashby, had also fallen to the Parliamentarians. Temple, the new governor of Coleorton refortified the house and it is said that from the garrison his artillery could actually fire upon Ashby castle.[40] These were of course only tiny garrisons, Coleorton and Bagworth each comprising no more than about 50 men, but they were important because they restricted the ability of the Royalists to plunder the region and to collect taxes and supplies in the territory they had previously controlled.[41] Though the County Committees of Leicester, Warwick and Rutland had established various small strongholds facing the Royalist bases, it is notable that in Northamptonshire and Buckinghamshire there was no proliferation of such sites. Parliamentarian power in those counties depended almost completely upon well defended major garrisons. As Sprigge explains, 'It hath been held great wisdom by ancient and well experienced Souldiers, to have but few Garisons, and those very strong, which may hold out long without relief...'[42] The importance of such an approach would become only too apparent to the defenders of Leicester in May 1645, when they found they had desperate need of the artillery and several hundred troops that had been temporarily deployed in the lesser garrisons of the county. The Northampton Committee was also instructed by Parliament to prepare a garrison close to Banbury with the intention that, like Ashby and Belvoir, it should be placed under pressure. Perhaps half heartedly, the Committee garrisoned Fawsley Hall near Daventry in January but it was abandoned after a few weeks at the news of approaching Royalist troops. This failure is not perhaps surprising since substantial Royalist forces were in winter quarters around Banbury. Despite further instructions in March, it would not be until early 1646 that Parliament's wish would be achieved, when Thorpe Mandeville manor house was garrisoned as a base for the final siege of Banbury.[43]

The Parliamentarian ascendancy in the region during the winter of 1644-5 is best seen from the fortification of Erasmus de la Fontaine's house at Kirby Bellars, just two miles west of the market town of Melton Mowbray in Leicestershire. This was again a tiny garrison of about 50 troops, but of sufficient scale to disrupt Belvoir's collection of supplies.[44] The intention was that Kirby would 'preserve that side of the country, and recover the lost hundred, which lay towards Newark, Belvoir, and Wiverton...'[45] Parliamentarian influence was now so strong that they were able to draw labour for the construction of Kirby's defences from villages within a couple of miles of Belvoir. Hence there is at this time reference to Kirby Bellars in the accounts of the constable of Branston, who recorded between the 17th and 25th February 1645 'charges when wee went to Kirby 2/6d' and then 'spent at Melton when wee work about... ye bulwarkes at Kirby 2/0d.'[46] The Royalists did not accept such action lightly and attempted to expel Captain Hacker, but on the 4th February the troops from Newark and Belvoir 'were repulsed very gallantly with little losse, and the fortification goes on notwithstanding.' Then on the 25th the Royalists again attacked Kirby but this time the garrison fled back to Leicester after firing the house, though the Parliamentarians claimed the destruction was accidental.[47] Despite this setback the County Committee soon re-established the garrison, while at this same time there are also reports of failed attempts by the Ashby garrison to re-take Coleorton; indeed such was the success of the Parliamentarian forces during the winter that they were able to fortify Grantham and at one point had actually blocked up Belvoir Castle.[48] However the attempts to reduce the main Royalist garrisons came to nothing, for even where the local forces did combine to mount a long siege they did not have the resources to maintain it against relieving forces from outside the region. So Newark for example was relieved in February 1645 by Langdale's Northern horse during their expedition to relieve Pontefract.[49] In the case of Ashby it was simply that 'the enemy are very strong, and their works good..... There are also many Irish there; who have lately made a new fort, a very strong work...'[50] Despite these various difficulties, and even after the reverse suffered at Melton Mowbray in March at the hands of Langdale, the Parliamentarian pressure on the local Royalist enclaves was maintained. By the end of April the Newark Royalists even had to release their stranglehold on Nottingham, abandoning their fort on the edge of Nottingham and destroying the southern suburbs of the town as they retreated.[51] Royalist strength in the region was gradually but inexorably being worn down.

Though in the ascendancy the Parliamentarians did not have everything their own way, as can be seen from the experience of the tiny garrison at Burley.[52] Their control of Rutland was still being affected by the Royalist troops at Belvoir as late as May 1645, when the following requirement was issued by the County Committee:

'To the Constables occupiers or Tenants of Gunthorpe. By virtue of an ordinance of ye Lords and Comons assembled in Parliament for maintayneing of forces for ye defence of ye kingdome and for yt we desire ye ease of ye country, of billeting and free quarter of souldiers and for ye satisfieng for oates and provision formerly brought into this garrison and in regard we find ye Country very forward to leavy collect and carry in greate summs of money to the enemie, att Belvoir and Wyverton these are therefore strightly to charge and comand you forthwith upon the sight hereof to assesse and collect within your constabulary the summe of fower poundes and eighteen shillinges imposed upon your sayd towne for one monthes tax for ye purposes aforesayd and yt you bring in and pay the same att this garrison to Jo.Cole gent, treasurer of ye County att or before the six and twentieth day of this instant May... faile not att your utmost perills given undeer our hands att Burleigh the 19th May 1645. Jo.Osborne Jo.Hatcher.'[53]

In those areas where the Parliamentarian cause appeared strong there could still be fundamental weakness. During the winter the condition and morale of the Newport Pagnell and especially the Aylesbury garrison had deteriorated dramatically. Lack of pay brought the troops near to starvation, forcing them to pawn their clothes for bread and driving many to desertion. It was not simply the result of the usual arrears in the payment of taxes from Bedfordshire and the Eastern Association counties like Essex. The quartering of Eastern Association troops in Aylesbury and the towns and villages nearby, and around Manchester's headquarters at Newport Pagnell, must have placed a great strain on the resources of the county. At the same time substantial forces from the Royalist army were also quartered in north west Buckinghamshire and in the adjacent parts of north Oxfordshire and south west Northamptonshire.[54] The Royalist army wished, as far as possible, to exploit Parliamentarian territory during the winter because this would relieve the pressure on the limited resources of its own now much shrunken area of control. If not, then Oxford and its subsidiary garrisons would be badly placed to withstand the new campaigning season. So we find reports in Buckinghamshire that the 'king's forces there plunder and play such reaks that the poor country is like to be utterly undone by them.'[55] The situation was exacerbated by the friction between Newport and Aylesbury garrisons, and between the garrison commander at Newport and the Buckinghamshire County Committee. Things were so bad that it was said that Aylesbury was in danger of being lost and the Royalists did actually face the town during the winter, though they did not attack.[56] The peace negotiations of the Treaty of Uxbridge between King and Parliament brought a temporary but very welcome lull in the conflict during January and February 1645, but this did not remove the drain on the resources of the county.[57] As we shall see, Buckinghamshire was not the only Parliamentarian county ill prepared to withstand a sustained Royalist offensive in 1645.

So at the opening of the Naseby campaign Parliamentarian fortunes in the south east Midlands were in the ascendancy. Although there were underlying problems on the Parliamentarian side it was simply that the Royalist forces were in an even weaker condition. The local Parliamentarian forces had sufficient resources to keep the local Royalists on the defensive and in the long term they could probably wear down the Royalist garrisons, but what they did not have was sufficient resources to take them quickly. In the short term at least it was a stalemate, but one which meant that the region was unlikely to be decisive in determining the outcome of the war. However, the local garrison forces were no match for the battle hardened troops of the major armies and it is no coincidence, for example, that when the Northampton horse met the cavalry of the Royalist field army they were more often than not defeated, as at Middleton Cheney in 1643 and at Weedon in early 1645.[58] If a major army was to enter the region the local forces would not only be outnumbered, they would also be outclassed. In May 1645, quite unexpectedly, this is exactly what would happen, completely transforming the military situation and resulting in the decisive battle of the Civil War being fought in the south east Midlands.

THE IMPACT ON THE PEOPLE

After two and a half years of war this region, like many others, was suffering badly and could not continue to sustain this level of exploitation and destruction. Studies, like that by Tennant on Warwickshire, have shown very clearly that the local community was far from isolated from the events of the war and that there were no rural backwaters where national events passed by largely unnoticed.[59] Every parish was intimately drawn into the war effort and saw and felt, in one way or another, the impact of the destruction. Even if a parish was not visited by hostile forces, the villagers would see the effect the war was having on others. It was quite common to find refugees passing through ordinary villages, often from considerable distances, as at Lowick in Northamptonshire where in 1644-5 the churchwarden gave 'to 3 poore people with a letter of request which came out of Ireland 1/-' and later 'to a Minister which came out of Ireland and going to the parlyment driven out by the Rebbells 1/-'. In late March or April the churchwarden also gave 'to 3 men and 2 women with a letter of request which came out of Yorkseare undone by the kings army 1/-', then 'to a poore man which came out of Darby sheare undone by the kings army 1/-' and finally 'to a poore man of Yorkesheare 28 July undon by ye kings armye 1/-'. Depending on where one was there might also be a major impact on religious practices. In those parts of the county controlled by the Northampton and Rockingham garrisons the people were required to accept the Solemn League and Covenant (a religious vow which united the English and Scottish people for the preservation of themselves and their religion) and to make various changes in their religious practices. So the churchwarden at Lowick recorded after April 1644 that they spent four shillings 'when wee wente to Northampton about the Covenant'. Later he paid three shillings and ten pence 'for taking downe ye Roode lofte and for filling the holes and for whiteing of it' and later in July twelve shillings and six pence 'for glasing the windowes when the Crusifixis and scandolus pictures was taken downe'. Finally in 1645-6 a further nine shillings and six pence were 'payd to Workmen for levilling and taking away ye alter'. With such fundamental changes taking place at the heart of their community in an ordinary village nobody could be unaffected by the dramatic events of the war.[60] The greatest impact for most parishes was of course financial. Everyone from the richest lord to the very poorest villager was taxed by someone. If they were unlucky they might be regularly taxed by both sides. By 1646 the parishes in Northamptonshire under Parliamentarian control were paying, in addition to the costs of maintaining their own garrisons, regular assessments for the Scottish army, the New Model Army and to support 'the five Garrisons'.[61] For Great Houghton, near Northampton, the costs of the war dramatically increased the sums the constable had to raise from the parish. In 1642-3 the total was just £3/8/3d, by 1643-4 this had increased to £15/8/0d, in 1644-5 the expenses were £23/4/9d and then in 1645-6 it reached a peak of £33/17/5d. In the following year, as the war ended, we see a dramatic fall to £10/8/10d.[62]

Already before the war there was a comprehensive administrative system in place, and this was exploited by both sides in the 1640s. In Parliamentarian areas the County Committee, which had been created out of the pre-war Commission of the Peace, ran local government.[63] They issued the requirements for taxation and other payments, often on printed proforma sheets, to the constable of each parish. The Northamptonshire Committee acted through the High Collectors for the east and west divisions of the

county, who took the ordinance and allocated the amounts to be met by each
of the parishes in his division. The assessments varied between parishes
according to their ability to pay. This can be seen from the record for 1645
for the Eastern Division of the county, which lists all parishes in each
hundred, the constables and churchwardens, and the payments due under the
Parliamentary ordinance.[64] The requirements were passed down via the High
Constables of each Hundred, who would oversee the activities of the parish
constables. Over and above the weekly taxes and excise duties, there were
other requirements imposed on the parishes. For example in November 1644
assessments were issued to the eastern division of the county requiring extra
payments towards 'maintaining of a troop of horse, for security of the East
Division of the County of Northampton, and service of Rockingham Castle;
as the Committee for the said County shall direct.'[65] Other levies in 1645
included that for the Scottish Army and for the New Model Army. The
constable's accounts also of course record the standard payments, dating from
the late 16th century, for the relief of maimed or sick soldiers and for the
upkeep of the county gaol. In addition, the county treasurer could grant a pass
to wounded soldiers to enable them to get to their homes by obtaining relief
from each parish en route and similar payments were made to civilians in
need. The constable was also responsible for the maintenance of several
soldiers of the militia and, even in peacetime, for the village arms and
armour.[66] It was he who actually collected taxes, as well as dealing with the
serving of warrants and various other legal and administrative services. He
allocated taxes and assessments against the individual households of the village
according to their ability to pay, as for example when the constable of
Harringworth made a levy in September 1645 for 'the last six moneth taxes
and a peney a cowe for the house of correction', in which the charges on
individual householders varied from 7/- down to 2d. The constable then
delivered the parish's payment to the High Collector of his division of the
county or his representative, or in some cases they were collected directly by
an officer of the relevant garrison. Hence in October 1645 the constable of
Harringworth was required to pay the parish's excise duty 'at Lewis
Whitwell's at Rockingham', whereas payments for the maintenance of a troop
of horse in the east division was to be paid to the High Collector for that
division, then again in January and February 1645 we find monthly receipts
for payment of the weekly tax signed by 'Richard Grimesditch Ensign to
Captain Dickenson'.[67]

This was an efficient administrative system, far better as a result of the
overall control exercised by the County Committees than that employed in
Royalist areas. However, whether equitably distributed or not, such financial
demands placed a major burden on the people. The experience of local
communities would of course vary considerably according to their location
and also, at least for the wealthier families, according to their allegiance. For
parishes which were in a disputed area the impact must have been far greater

than for villages close to a major garrison. There would be the losses resulting from the military conflict itself and from the plundering outside any formal taxation system and they might even be subjected to taxation by both sides. The situation of a parish could change quite dramatically depending how the military situation developed. This can be seen in the case of Branston in Leicestershire, which lay within three miles of the Royalist garrison of Belvoir, because the Branston constable's accounts give a view right through the Civil War. Until early 1645 the demands on the parish came almost solely from Belvoir. In 1644 for example they were sending men to work on defences of the castle, supplying provisions and quartering small numbers of Royalist troops, but with the establishment of the Parliamentarian garrison at Kirby Bellars in early 1645 Branston found its situation transformed. From then on one finds almost equal demands coming to the village from both sides. Hence in April the constable 'payd in pte to Kirby for 2 monthes tax £7/15/0d', but then a few days later he 'sent to Belvoir a veale 7/6d'. Indeed for the whole of 1645, unlike previous years, he records equal receipts of tax of £10 each for Kirby and for Belvoir.[68] This must have represented a dramatic and very damaging increase in demands for the people of Branston. A similar story is told in the accounts of the parish constable of the village of Stathern, also just three miles from Belvoir. Again one sees how the village provided Belvoir with supplies, taxes and with labour for the construction of the bulwarks of the defences, but when Royalist control waned the Parliamentarians began collecting taxes from them as well.[69] It was this Parliamentarian stranglehold on the territory supporting garrisons like Belvoir which was progressively destroying the Royalist ability to wage war.

The demands on villages could also be greatly increased by specific large scale military actions. Hence the parish of Burton Latimer in central Northamptonshire, though 19 miles from Grafton Regis and 34 miles from Banbury, was required to provide supplies at Christmas 1643 to support the siege of Grafton and then in the summer of 1644 to support the siege of Banbury. Other villages closer to Banbury were also required to send in men to dig the siege-works or men and horses to carry supplies.[70] Many parishes became used to the occasional quartering of a handful of troops at any time, whether local garrison forces or detachments from more distant parts passing through, particularly those on the main roads. For example, the parish of West Haddon reported the innumerable times that troops from Coventry, Warwick and Northampton had been quartered on the village as they moved between the garrisons.[71] Sir John Isham of Lamport also complained of 'frequent quartering of Parliamentary troops, my house standing on two great rodes', though as a recognised Royalist sympathiser he may have fared worse than others and certainly suffered troops at least once breaking into his house.[72] Such relatively small numbers of troops, though a burden, were nothing compared to the impact of an army quartered on a group of adjacent parishes. The effect could be as devastating as the plundering of the village by a hostile force. The worst excesses would occur when an army was quartered on an area for a long period of time, as in early 1644 when the people of Hertfordshire had petitioned Parliament against 'the intollerable burden of free quarter' when Essex's army spent 17 weeks there without pay.[73] The villages around Northampton suffered similar impositions, though not for as long, when Waller's army was quartered about the town after his defeat at Cropredy Bridge.[74] In Northamptonshire in the mid 17th century most villages had a population of between 100 and 500.[75] An army of five or ten thousand men descending on a settlement of this size would be dramatic in its impact, even if it only stopped for a single night. Whether the taking of provisions, stock, goods or money was treated as an unwelcome tax or as plundering might depend upon the way in which the soldiers treated the inhabitants and also, to a degree, upon the allegiance of the people in question. There was wanton destruction by both sides, but if it was an opposing army to that which controlled the territory within which the parish lay then the impact of quartering on the village could be disastrous.

For the individual or the community the effects of the war might be enormous. For example, in 1644 the churchwarden of Great Houghton paid eight pence 'to a poreman of Ecton being pillaged of his goods when prince Robert came by that way.'[76] When Langdale returned from Pontefract through Leicestershire, intending to rejoin Rupert who was then at Ludlow, he:

> 'lost more reputation than he got by his former actions; for such inhumanities and insolencies and outrages wer committed by his souldiers at Harborough and other places in that county as will render him and them not only odious to the present age but infamous to all posterity.'[77]

Sympathiser and 'malignant' alike amongst the local population would frequently be treated equally badly by a force entering the territory controlled by the opposition, but it was not just as a result of the major campaigns that villages were hard hit. In disputed areas there were places which reported major losses at other times, such as the puritan village of Kilsby near Daventry which records 'Losses sustained by Banbury forces January 10th 1644. Sir William Compton with a party of about four hundred horse tooke by imprisonment of men and plundered by violence the sume of £1000 and upwards.' Then again, in September 1645, Sir William with a party of horse quartered in the village for one night and plundered by violence the sum of £200 or more.[78] Though in such cases there may have been considerable exaggeration, the general scale of the impact cannot be doubted. Throughout the kingdom the progressive impact of such taxation, quartering, pillaging and destruction had by the winter of 1644-5 reduced many areas to a very sorry state. It was increasingly recognised by both sides that the country could not and would not accept such demands for much longer.

By the winter of 1644-5, as a result of two and a half years of fighting, the whole country was weary of war. In some areas the common people were so exasperated by the continual and oppressive nature of the exactions that they even began taking up arms against their oppressors. Though such extreme action was restricted to Royalist areas in the South and the West, even if the people did not rise up in arms they could pose almost as great a threat if they became disaffected. They might refuse or perhaps simply reach the stage of being incapable of paying their taxes and providing supplies. The Parliamentarians began to worry that the population in many areas they controlled were so disillusioned that they might easily betray their garrisons to the enemy. It was in part a result of the realisation that the country could not sustain continued warfare that 1645 came to be viewed by both sides as the decisive year. It encouraged both to take more determined action to win the war before they were forced to concede an unwelcome peace through the inability or unwillingness of the general population to maintain the war effort.

NOTES

1. Tennant, 1992, p.30.
2. Sherwood, 1974.
3. Tennant, 1992. Page, 1893. Firth, 1890. Nichols, vol.3, appendix 4.
4. Whetham & Whetham, 1907, p.58.
5. After Darby, 1976, p.252.
6. Gibbs, 1885, p.154-173. RCHM, 1913, vol.2, p.26-32.
7. Butcher, 1646, p.46, quoted by Davies, 1992, p.30.
8. Davies, 1992, p.28 & 53.
9. Nichols, vol.3, appendix 4, p.31.
10. Record of quarter taken in Leicestershire by troops from the Warwickshire garrisons of Astley, Coventry, Warwick and Edgbaston, PRO SP28/161, unfol..
11. Nichols, vol.3, p.676 and appendix 4, p.33. Ogilby, 1675, plate 40.
12. *Gentlemans Magazine Library*, p.278-280.
13. RCHM, 1913, vol.2, p.26-32. *CSPD*, p.557. Clarendon, 1702, bk.9, par.34-36 .
14. Nichols, vol.3, p.737.
15. Nichols, vol.3, p.611.
16. Vicars, 1646, part 4, p.361. Constable's accounts, Branston, LRO DE 720-30. Pevsner, 1984, p.96.
17. Nichols, vol.2, p.50-57.
18. *Mercurius Aulicus*, p.58.
19. *The True Informer*, 21st-28th October 1643.
20. Quoted by Bull, 1900, p.155.
21. Bull, 1900, p.157, quoting *Certaine Informations*, no.19.
22. Ordinance of 18th December 1643, quoted by Bull, 1900, p.160.
23. Foard, 1994, p.20-25.
24. Nichols vol.3, p.251. Mee, 1967, p.67 & 216. Pevsner, 1984, p.491.
25. Not to be confused with Burghley House immediately south of Stamford whose spelling Burley sometimes shares in 17th century sources.
26. Vicars, 1646, p.110. Warrant from 'the Committe att Bourligh', 14th December 1644, LRO DE 730/3, f.42. Finch, 1901, p.7.
27. Survey of manor of Burley, 1651, LRO DG7/1/70. Pevsner, 1984, p.459. Finch, 1901.

28. Mr Barker of Hambleton supplied horses & oats under warrant to the Rockingham garrison, some taken by Lieutenant Barry for Colonel Horsman, others by Captains Wollaston and Butler's troops. Similarly supplies to the Burley garrison. LRO DE 730/3, f.50.

29. Kingston, 1897, p.151.

30. *CSPD*, 1644, p.138.

31. Eg: Floore Account, SP28/173 unfol..

32. Gardiner, 1893, vol.1, p.351-363; vol. 2, p.4-5. Smurthwaite, 1984, p.154.

33. Tennant, 1992, p.197. Beesley, 1841, p.366-385.

34. Tennant, 1992, p.161-4 & 205-6.

35. 27th June 1644. Civil War Tracts in the Bodleian calendared in *Bibliotheca Buckinghamiensis*, p.55-68 & 88, Aylesbury Reference Library local studies collection.

36. RCHM, 1913, vol.2, p.26-32.

37. Firth, 1890, p.287.

38. Vicars, 1646. Kingston, 1897, p.177-181.

39. Vicars, 1646, p.103.

40. Astley was held by Colonel Bosevile's regiment and then later in 1644 by Colonel Purefoy, PRO SP28/219 unfol.. In addition to the main garrisons at Coventry and Warwick, the garrison at Kenilworth also appears to have been retained at this time. Muster for May 1645 at Kenilworth, PRO SP28/122, f.338. *Narration of the siege*. Nichols, appendix 4, p.33 & 39.

41. Symonds, p.178. Bennett, 1980. Pevsner, 1984, p.136-7. Nichols, vol.3, p.737 & appendix 4, p.40. The 17th century Hall was demolished and replaced in the early 19th century. The Hall and church are detached at some distance today from the straggling village, lying on a hill side in parkland. There are no standing remains of the garrison, and even amongst the archaeological earthworks no trace of the Civil War defences have yet been recognised.Pers.comm. F.Hartley, Leicestershire Museum Service.

42. Sprigge, 1647, p.14.

43. Foard, 1994a. Whetham & Whetham, 1907, p.93.

44. Nichols, vol 2, p.232. Symonds, p.178. Bennet, 1980, says that Belvoir was constrained by a garrison at Stonesby.

45. *Narration of the siege*.

46. Constable's accounts, Branston, LRO DE 720-30.

47. *Perfect Diurnal*, 4th February 1645. NRO, ML 1423. *Mercurius Aulicus*, p.1402. Nichols, vol.3, appendix 4. The mansion house was repaired or rebuilt after the war and a stable block added. All except the latter was demolished in 1756. The stable block, now a farm, stands in a large area of parkland, which once surrounded the mansion, on the north side of the A607 on the east side of Kirby village. Though there are earthworks on the site of the mansion, to the west of the stable block, there is no evidence of any Civil War defences. Pers.comm. F.Hartley, Leicestershire Museums Service, and Mr A.Fox of Kirby Bellars. Pevsner, 1984, p.192.

48. Nichols, vol.2, p.232. Letter of February 1645 quoted in the 1824 edition of the *History of Ashby Castle*. NRO, ML 1423.

49. Nichols, vol.3, appendix 4, p.41.

50. *Perfect Diurnal*.

51. Tibbutt, 1963, p.263.

52. Supplies taken by Burley between December 1644 and 22nd May 1645, LRO DE 730/3, ff.42-54.

53. LRO DE 730/3, f.53.

54. In January 1645 Parliamentarian forces quartered at Aylesbury, Hartwell, Eythrope, Newport Pagnell, Wing, Bierton, Waddesdon, Leighton, Stoke Mandeville, Wendover, Ellesborough, Missenden, Amersham, Chesham, St.Leonards, Lee and other nearby villages. The Royalist quarters included Buckingham, Somerton, Winslow, Bicester, Thame, Islip, Chippingworth, Audley, Brackley, Brill, Haddenham, and adjacent villages. Gibbs, 1885, p.169. RCHM, 1913, vol.2, p.3 & 26-32. Tennant, 1992, p.242-3.

55. *Perfect Occurrences*, 27th December 1644.

56. Johnson, undated, p.174-236. Shehan, 1862, p.50.

57. Firth, 1890.

58. *Mercurius Aulicus*, 6th May 1643.

59. Tennant, 1992.

60. Lowick, churchwarden's accounts, 1645-6, NRO 199P/77/29.

61. Marston Trussell account, 1646, PRO SP28/173 unfol..

62. Great Houghton parish records, NRO 175P/38. This cost of course does not represent the whole cost of the war to the village, which was a much higher figure.

63. For a summary of pre-war local administration see the introduction to Goring & Wake, 1975.

64. Estreat Rolls for the 10 Hundreds of the Eastern Division of Northants, August 1645, NRO Montague 18/1945/6.

65. Constable's accounts, Harringworth parish records, NRO 156P/104/120.

66. Dare, 1926.

67. Constable's accounts, Harringworth parish records, NRO 156P/104/1-122.

68. Constable's accounts, Branston, LRO DE 720 - 30.

69. Constable's accounts, Stathern, 1630-1687, LRO DE 1605/56.

70. PRO SP28/171, f.14.

71. PRO SP28/173, unfol..

72. Isham, 1955, p.xl.

73. Kingston, 1897, p.153.

74. Eg: Burton Latimer account, September 1646, PRO SP28/171. Flore account, PRO SP28/173 unfol..

75. Compton Census, 1676.

76. Great Houghton churchwarden's accounts, 1644, NRO 175P/28.

77. *The Kingdomes Weekly Intelligencer*, 11th-18th March 1645.

78. Kilsby account, 1647, PRO SP28/172 unfol..

CHAPTER 3

BUILDING TWO ARMIES

'till you have an army merely your own, that you may command,
it is in a manner impossible to do anything of importance.'
William Waller

The battle of Marston Moor on the 2nd July 1644 had been the most dramatic victory of the war so far. It was the result of the entry of the Scottish army into the conflict and their linking up with Parliament's Northern forces and new Eastern Association army. Success on the battlefield had enabled Parliament to take control of northern England and seemed to provide an opportunity to rapidly win the war, yet within several months the Parliamentarian cause had been thrown from elation into despair. The Earl of Manchester proved unwilling to capitalise upon the success as his army returned south, there was the disintegration of Sir William Waller's army in the weeks following his defeat at Cropredy Bridge and then the Earl of Essex's total humiliation at Lostwithiel, a campaign in which his military incompetence was revealed for all to see. Finally there was the debacle of the second battle of Newbury on the 27th October, which showed any who were still not convinced how incapable the senior commanders were of working together and how weak and demoralised the Parliamentarian armies had become. A restructuring of Parliament's forces was essential if they were not to disintegrate completely. The events leading to the victory at Naseby must therefore be traced back to the autumn and winter on 1644-45 and can only be understood in the context of the close working relationship which developed between Oliver Cromwell and Sir Henry Vane the younger.[1] They represented the Independents, a radical political and religious grouping that believed in religious toleration and rejected state controlled worship in favour of autonomous congregations. The Independents had come to the view that the King was an untrustworthy dissembler who could not be believed in any negotiation and that the only course of action was the complete destruction of the Royalist army on the battlefield. That is what Vane and Cromwell set out to accomplish and that is what they achieved on Naseby field. Parliament had always controlled the necessary resources to win the war, what it lacked was the will and the organisation to do it. The great political success of the Independents was that they achieved the creation of an army capable of and committed to the defeat of the King. So, the decisive campaign of the English Civil War was won as much on the floor of the House of Commons as it was in the open fields of Northamptonshire.

John Pym above all others had guided Parliament into the war and following Pym's death, in December 1643, the mantle had been taken on by Vane. Working in close cooperation with Cromwell and other Members of

Parliament like Oliver St.John, Zouch Tate and John Lisle, he guided Parliament and their Scottish allies along a far more radical path than that which they would otherwise have followed. But the Independents were a minority in Parliament and so to achieve their goal they exploited the feelings of war weariness in the country and the concern that this engendered among many in Parliament, and then played upon the fear that the Parliamentarian forces would not be ready in time to face the King's army in the new campaigning season. Their argument that 'the enemy draws his greatest advantages as well from our divisions as treacheries' was not lost on the majority of Members.[2] Through skilful political action they created a situation where their objectives were being forwarded in Parliament by a much larger 'war party' which, though it included Presbyterians like Zouch Tate, was led by the Independents. They were opposed by a 'peace party' dominated by the more numerous Presbyterians and led by Essex and Manchester, who were soon joined by the Scots. The Independents also used the committee system in Parliament to very good effect. Vane had played an important role in the creation of the Committee of Both Kingdoms, a small executive body which included Scottish commissioners, that directed the war effort on behalf of Parliament. Although Essex and Manchester were both members, it was this committee that had begun to wrest control of the war effort from the Earl of Essex. The Committee of Both Kingdoms had an even representation of the two factions but this was significantly different to the natural balance within the Commons and so in the committee the Independents were able to take a leading role. In the important Committee for the Army the Independents had similar influence especially as they had the support of the chairman, Zouch Tate.

Within their own spheres of action Vane and Cromwell pursued their objectives in a series of calculated steps and with a skill which at first took in their natural opponents in Parliament, the army and even the Scots, and then, when the deception was clear to all, they simply out-manoeuvred them. For example, in 1644 Vane had championed the Scottish cause in Parliament and was influential in bringing them into the war. The agreement with the Scots had been achieved by making them believe that they had a common purpose with the Independents and it was only towards the end of the year that the truth became apparent. The Independents suffered minor setbacks and in some situations had to propose less than they really wanted but, because they always took a pragmatic approach, they were still able to ensure that their overall goals were achieved. For example they had wanted to see Cromwell as commander of Parliament's army in 1645, but they realised that both Houses could not be persuaded to agree to this and so instead they proposed the appointment of Sir Thomas Fairfax, an excellent young military commander from Yorkshire, whose views and approach were compatible with their own. Once they had created the army that they wanted, they needed to ensure that authority to run the military campaign was delegated by the Committee of

Both Kingdoms to the field commanders. To achieve this they waited until the time was right to win the argument, using the fear engendered by the Royalist threat to the Eastern Association in early June 1645. Similarly they intended that Cromwell be appointed as second in command of the army and so they kept open the post of Lieutenant General of Horse until the very last moment. Again they chose the crucial time to act, after the fall of Leicester and as the decisive battle approached, when through fear the Commons were most likely to give their assent. That this was the way in which Vane and Cromwell worked was clear to contemporaries like Baillie, whom they had outmanoeuvred. There seems little reason to doubt the truth of his assessment that there was 'a high and mighty plot of the Independents to have gotten an army for themselves under Cromwell'.[3] The Independents were the most resolute and confident men on the Parliamentarian side, with a clear, long term agenda which they skilfully pursued, making best use of the opportunities that presented themselves.[4]

It was the conflict in the Eastern Association army between Cromwell, as Lieutenant General, and the Earl of Manchester, the Commander in Chief, which was the catalyst for these fundamental changes. This dispute was already under way by March 1644 when Cromwell had defended Lieutenant Colonel Packer against the complaints of Major General Crawford, Manchester's closest ally.[5] As the military situation deteriorated in the late summer and autumn of 1664 the conflict in the army became increasingly intense between those, led by Cromwell, who wished to see the war pressed home to achieve the ultimate defeat of the King and those, led by Manchester and Essex, who wanted a negotiated peace and could never contemplate the King's total destruction. By the end of November Essex, Manchester and Denzil Holles, a leading ally in the Commons, were conspiring with the Scots to remove Cromwell and to secure the ascendancy of the Presbyterian cause.[6]

At first Cromwell intended to purge the Eastern Association army to create a fully committed force but rapidly this was transformed into a scheme for the total remodelling of all of Parliament's armies, using the same arguments which had first been put forward by others of less radical view such as Waller. The Independents exploited the disasters of 1644 to get approval for this New Model Army. The failure of the Parliamentarian forces:

'was generally attributed to the ill Conduct of certain eminent Commanders ... of whome some were thought too fond of a Peace, and others over-desirous to spin out the War, and others engaged in such particular Feuds, that there was little vigorous Action to be expected from such disagreeing Instruments.'[7]

Lady Hutchinson, writing after the Restoration summarised the situation very clearly:

'It was too apparent how much the whole Parliament cause had been often hazarded, how many opportunities of finishing the war had been overslipped by the Earl of Essex's army; and it was believed that he himself, with his commanders, rather endeavoured to become arbiters of war and peace, than conquerors for the Parliament; for it was known that he had given out such expressions.[18]

Cromwell was seen quite differently by many:

'on a great plain called Marston Moor, [they] had a bloody encounter, and the Scots and Lord Fairfax had been wholly routed, and the battle lost, but that Cromwell, with five thousand men which he commanded, routed Prince Rupert, restored the other routed Parliamentarians, and gained the most complete victory that had been obtained in the whole war.'[19]

There have been many who have challenged Cromwell's right to such approbation but, whatever the truth, this was certainly the popular perception at the time. Cromwell and Sir Thomas Fairfax, who had also achieved important military successes in the North, had come to be seen as dynamic, effective, even charismatic commanders while Essex and Manchester had demonstrated their incompetence as generals.

The political battle over the organisation of the army during the winter of 1644-5 was not however simply a matter of the interests of a small group of military and political leaders, it also reflected a long standing tension in English society between the county and the state. Militia forces had always been maintained at a county level and England had never had a nationally funded standing army. National military power had in the past been created by cooperation between the individual counties and so, from 1642, the Parliamentarian war effort had been based primarily on the establishment of military forces in each shire. Counties saw the removal of their forces to support an army in distant places as weakening their local defence and it did indeed leave them open to destruction, whether through pillaging by the enemy or the capture of their garrisons. Not surprisingly therefore the County Committees often secured their own interests at the expense of the overall Parliamentarian cause. The attempt in 1642-3 to weld these county forces together in Associations, with the aim of creating larger and more efficient armies, was also almost bound to fail because regional government was not something that England was used to. There was just one exception, the counties of the Eastern Association. Local interests were not absent from the eastern counties, it was simply that they could see that to keep the war at a distance from their homes they had to work together to maintain a common frontier. Yet when it came to the creation of a national army the Eastern Association sided with the other counties. It was only after three seasons of warfare in which these divisive local interests had caused armies to fragment at crucial times, bringing the Parliamentarian cause near to defeat, that there was a chance of persuading a majority of Members of Parliament to place national above local interests. It was therefore a remarkable achievement that the New Model Army was created at all, for although recruits were still raised locally it was funded by national taxation administered through the Treasurers of War in London. It was truly a national army, the first such army that had ever existed in England. So in a sense, as Everitt has said, the success at Naseby was 'the triumph of the State over the county community as much as of Parliament over the King.'[10]

The two key pieces of legislation were considered in November and December 1644, the Self Denying Ordinance, proposed by Zouch Tate and Henry Vane, and the New Model Ordinance. The former was aimed at removing military command from all those who sat in Parliament and replacing them with professional soldiers. The latter was intended to create one new army out of the remnants of the three broken armies of Essex, Manchester and Waller. These were the central planks of the war party's programme, but they could not both be pushed through Parliament at that time. First of all it was necessary to demonstrate that a negotiated peace with the King was impossible and therefore the Independents cooperated in the peace negotiations of the Treaty of Uxbridge in February. Slingsby observed of this treaty that it was 'great in expectation, tho' in conclusion it brought forth nothing yt gave any hopes of peace, but rather gave either side warning to prepare ye sooner for battle...'[11] After the failure of the negotiations the Independents were able to persuade Parliament that it should support their two key pieces of legislation. As Vane said at this time:

> 'There can no argument I know be more prevalent with you than the shortening of the war; the Houses of Parliament have been willing to end it either way, by treaty or war; but they think all treaties will be useless till they be in a posture to show themselves able to repel that opposition that can be made against them.'[12]

The central issue was clearly articulated by Cromwell: 'if the army be not put into another method, and the war more vigorously prosecuted, the people can bear the war no longer, and will enforce you to a dishonourable peace.' After intense political debate and many delays, mainly imposed by opposition in the Lords, the remodelling of the army and the withdrawal of the members of Parliament from military commands were both agreed.

The political battle did not of course end there, for once the principles had been established the argument continued over the exact composition of the army. Sir Thomas Fairfax was proposed as commander in chief because Cromwell simply would not have been acceptable to Parliament. The two men had built up a good working relationship as a result of their joint action in Lincolnshire in the autumn of 1643 and during the Marston Moor campaign in 1644. They respected each others military abilities and, equally important, they appeared at this stage to have compatible religious and political views. The Independents also gained agreement that Fairfax propose the composition of the new army, although they had to concede that Parliament should have the right to approve the list of senior officers. This was to prove another long, drawn out and very bitter wrangle, but during March they achieved agreement to the whole list as it had been submitted by Fairfax. Though one cannot dispute Gentles' statement that 'it is unlikely that we shall ever know precisely who advised Fairfax on his selection for higher officers,' it seems almost inconceivable that Cromwell did not have a leading role in drawing up the list.[13] This does not mean that one must agree with Holles who, in his *Memoirs,* insinuates that Cromwell was the real mover in the new army and that Fairfax was simply appointed as his tool. Holles was after all a very hostile witness.[14] It is however clear from Fairfax's own memoirs that he was completely surprised by his appointment and had very little idea at the outset as to what exactly he was about.[15] He had been thrust from a peripheral northern arena into the heart of the war effort, was a complete outsider and at the beginning must have been almost wholly dependent upon the advice that he was given by his allies. Cromwell had after all worked with the majority of the officers concerned for more than a year, had been planning for the creation of a new army for a good deal of that time and had been active in the Committee of Both Kingdoms in February making plans for the new army establishment. The officers chosen gave the New Model a committed and competent officer corps and included most if not all of Cromwell's closest supporters. With this important political battle won, the implementation of the remodelling could be left in the capable hands of Fairfax and his Major General, Philip Skippon.

The new army was to comprise 12 regiments of foot, each with a nominal strength of 1200 men, 11 regiments of horse, each of 600 men, and 10 companies of dragoons, each of 100 men, giving a full complement of 22000. Of these, three regiments of horse and four of foot came from Essex's army, two regiments of foot from Waller's army, and the remaining nine regiments of horse and four of foot from the Eastern Association army. To partially make up the numbers in the regiments of foot, given their very low strength, other regiments were reduced into them and new recruits were also to be conscripted. Money was raised to fund the New Model Army well before its composition was agreed, a large loan being obtained in London to fund the initial preparations before the first county assessments were paid. The first approvals to the list of senior officers came on the 5th March and so preparations could begin, but it was not until the 18th that the full list was agreed.

The purchasing of equipment for the army had also been put in hand and during April it began arriving in large quantities. This was not simply a case of restructuring existing forces, for although the troops from the old armies will have brought their equipment with them, the contracts reveal a major re-equipping of the New Model.[16] The following discussion is primarily based upon the orders made before June 1645 because the majority of this equipment is likely to have been ready for the army when it marched, particularly that which is detailed in the 1st April summary of contracts already let. These contracts are summarised in Appendix 4. There were three main groups of purchases, for the train, the infantry and the cavalry. The train had been placed under the command of Lieutenant General Thomas Hammond and although no new artillery pieces were ordered, apart from a new brass mortar, there were purchases of munitions and equipment for the existing guns. There was equipment for sakers and demi-culverin, the field pieces of the day, and for culverin and cannon, which were normally reserved for siege work. There were also 600 round shot for demi-culverin and 2000 for the sakers, 300 shells for the mortars or 'grenados', barrels of powder and 8 tons of match, as well as 1000 hand grenades for the infantry. Streeter's engraving of the battle of Naseby suggests that the artillery with the train comprised fourteen field pieces and three siege pieces. The guns assigned to the New Model in April included two brass demi-culverin and eight brass sakers while in addition a saker and three drakes, shorter and lighter versions of the standard artillery pieces, were sent up to Windsor for the army.[17] So the artillery train is likely to have comprised at least three demi-culverin and a mortar together with at least nine sakers and three drakes. The train was also to be supplied with eleven new open waggons and twenty two new enclosed waggons, six of the latter for Sir Thomas Fairfax's and two for Major General Skippon's own use. The order for 100 horse harnesses specifies every fifth one to be for a 'thiller', the horse ridden by the carter at the front of the team, which shows that teams of five horses were the norm. A further 300 harnesses were also ordered, presumably some for the remaining waggons and others perhaps for the artillery. In all the train had been voted 1038 horses in early March and so with something of the order of 200 horses required to pull the artillery this would have left enough for about 175 waggons.[18] There were then the basic supplies and equipment for the train, including 400 pick axes and 800 shovels and spades for the pioneers and 200 tents as well as various equipment for the maintenance of the waggons themselves. The artillery also required a substantial number of waggons for its supplies. When the ten pieces had been sent up to Windsor from London on 29th April they had been accompanied by 12 waggons and carriages comprising 5 loads of match, 2 loads of bullets and 6 carriages for the ordnance.[19]

At full strength the army would have included about 9600 musketeers. 5600 matchlock muskets and 6000 bandoleers were ordered, showing that the vast majority of the soldiers, mainly the new recruits, were to be newly equipped. Dragoons also carried muskets and it seems likely that the 1050 snaphance muskets[20] were purchased for them. According to Vernon:

'the Dragoones arming is only offensive, having a good fire lock musket something awider bore than ordinary hanging in a belt by a sweble at his side, with a good sword and ordinary horse, it being only to expediate his march, for he must perform his service on foot....'[21]

Fig.8. Pikemen originally wore armour such as this, though by 1645 most were probably no longer equipped in this way. They were armed with a steel tipped pike about 16ft long and a short broadsword. Organised in blocks of several hundred the pike provided effective protection for the foot against cavalry attack. Musketeers comprised approximately two thirds of the infantry by the time of Naseby. On the battlefield the musketeers from each regiment or brigade were typically formed up in two blocks six ranks deep, flanking a single body of pike. They carried matchlock muskets, smooth bore muzzle loading firearms, in which a slow burning cord or 'match' set off the charge of gunpowder. For safety reasons, those guarding the train of artillery were provided with 'firelocks', muskets in which the charge was ignited by a spark produced as a flint struck a metal plate. In hand to hand fighting they might resort to the use of the sword but were noted for more often using the butts of their muskets as clubs. (reproduced by permission of Northamptonshire County Council)

Five tons of musket bullets were also purchased. The complement of pikemen would have been about 4800 and for them 2400 pikes, mainly 16 footers, were to be supplied. The proportion of pikes to matchlock muskets ordered was at a ratio of just over 1:2, confirming the balance of pikemen to musketeers in the army. There were however no purchases of armour for the infantry, the back plates, breast plates and helmets being restricted to orders which comprise equipment for the cavalry. This supports the argument that armour was no longer issued to pikemen by this time in the war, although some soldiers may have brought such equipment from the old armies. It is not surprising therefore that amongst the equipment recorded as having been found at Naseby in the centuries since the battle there is not apparently a single piece of pikeman's armour, not even a helmet. The musketeer of the New Model Army cost about £2/7/5d to equip, the pikeman just £1/10/11d. At about £1 per suit, the cost of equipping a pikeman with armour would have increased the cost to £2/10/11d and presumably the near doubling of cost could not be justified, especially in view of the rate at which the foot were known to desert. Armour would also of course restrict the ability of the infantry to move quickly. The most expensive single item for the infantryman were his coat and breeches, at 16/-, while shoes cost 2/3d, a shirt 2/10d, stockings 1/-, a sword and belt 4/8d, and a pike 4/2d, then for the musketeer his bandoleer cost 1/2d and his musket 11/6d. The 9000 swords and belts purchased were presumably for both infantry and dragoons, for it matches almost exactly the total of muskets and pikes purchased. Sufficient shirts (4000), stockings (3500), coats (4000), breeches (4000) and shoes (5000 pairs) were purchased to equip about 4000 men. It was not until later that the orders specifically describe the coats as being red with blue linings but undoubtedly they were so from the very beginning. Not only had red coats been the norm for the Eastern Association army in 1644, but in the New Model purchases of April 1645 the coats were said to be distinguished by coloured tapes, in six different colours, something that would only make sense if the coats were otherwise of a standard colour.[22] There were also 60 new drums purchased, sufficient for six regiments of foot.

The New Model orders included 2000 saddles, presumably all for the cavalry as 600 dragoons saddles had been separately purchased, 1100 suits of armour comprising back, breast and headpiece and 2250 pair of pistols with holsters. There were also 400 horse harnesses and 200 cavalry swords. Thus the New Model cavalry were equipped rather as Vernon's harquebusier, that is 'his defensive Arms [being] only an open Caske or Head-peece, a back and brest with a buffe coat under his armes.' For offence Vernon recommends 'a Carbine hanging on his right side .... and to good fire-lock pistols in houlsters. At his saddle a good stiffe sword sharp pointed, and a good poll-axe in his hand...', although it seems from the purchases that the New Model cavalry were only supplied with the pistols and sword. The cost of equipping a cavalryman far exceeded that for either the infantryman or even the dragoon, a reflection of the great value of the cavalry on the Civil War battlefield, but the supply records also clearly show that far less cavalry equipment had to be purchased compared to that for infantry and dragoons. Undoubtedly this was because the vast majority of the cavalry were simply transferred from the regiments in the other three armies, bringing with them most of the equipment they required. In contrast some 7000 new infantrymen had to be recruited and fully equipped if the army was to be brought up to full strength.

Fig. 9. For protection cavalry troopers usually wore back and breast plates of metal, over a leather buff coat, as well as a helmet. They were armed with a pair of pistols and a sword. Some cavalry may also have carried a short flintlock musket or 'carbine' though this was not common during the Civil War. This cavalry armour, which comprises a back plate and two lobster tail helmet, is typical of that used by the cavalry on both sides. All these artefacts, including the two iron cannon balls, are said to be from Naseby. Most of these items were previously in the collection of Naseby relics which William Hanbury built up at Kelmarsh Hall, were then at Lamport but are now preserved in Northampton Museum.

There were several other cavalry units present at the battle on the Parliament side which were not part of the New Model Army and it will be seen later that some of these units included dragoons as well as cavalry. These dragoons presumably fought as though they were cavalry, although their regiments were placed in the reserve not in the front line. It is not clear how

Fig. 10. A cavalry trooper with 'harquebusier' equipment. Probably like some of the poorly equipped Royalists at Naseby he lacks body armour but is wearing a buff coat. He has two pistols in holsters and a flintlock carbine over his shoulder. During the Civil War few cavalry troopers appear to have carried carbines. In contrast, dragoons were mounted infantry, just using their horses to ride to the action but fighting on foot. They were equipped like musketeers, though with a flintlock musket, again carried on a belt over the shoulder. They could move rapidly into action yet their muskets provided more effective fire power than pistols or carbines. [23]

they were equipped but presumably both they and the New Model dragoons lacked the body armour which had been issued to most if not all of the New Model cavalry. The value of the dragoon was his greater mobility compared to the infantry, together with the greater firepower provided by his musket compared to the pistols with which the cavalry were equipped. Both cavalry and dragoon clothes, including items such as buff coats, appear to have been the responsibility of the men themselves because no central purchases are seen. The senior officers will also have purchased their own arms and equipment as well, so one must look to the evidence of the engravings of the senior commanders to gain an impression of character and quality of their arms and armour, although several items have been collected from the battlefield at Naseby, including the pieces of body armour previously in Ravensthorpe church and two swords, all now in Northampton Museum.

Fairfax travelled to Windsor on 3rd April 1645 where he called a general rendezvous of the army and there he remained until the end of the month 'busie in Modelling his Army'. He had to deal with the discontent of common soldiers, whose regiments were being disbanded and who were being transferred into other regiments, and he had to contend with officers whose services were no longer required, who had to be discharged or found alternative service elsewhere. There were also new recruits to be integrated and trained and the artillery train to be prepared. This was a major task in which Major General Skippon had a key role. He travelled to Reading on the 6th April where five regiments and five companies from the Earl of Essex's army were quartered and there he had the difficult task of reducing these troops, some of whom were near to mutiny, into three regiments.[24] He was the ideal man for the task because he had the respect of his men, for it was he as their Major General who had stood by them during the surrender at Lostwithiel when their commander in chief had fled. Though there were some limited disturbances and a significant number of men did eventually desert, Skippon and Fairfax achieved the task of remodelling far more

Fig. 11. An officer's sword from Naseby.

effectively than many had imagined possible.

There have been various views as to the character and significance of the New Model Army. On the one side was the idea, most strongly developed in the 19th century, that it was a dramatically new force which from the outset had a radical character and religious zeal with at its heart Cromwell's 'honest godly men'. At the other extreme lies Kishlansky's picture of the New Model as just another 17th century army, very little different to its predecessors, suffering arrears of pay and with the same problems of pressed infantry who readily deserted. He has even suggested that the Independents only took control after the war, but his analysis has been challenged more recently by Gentles in his detailed review of the New Model Army.[25] A Captain from Sir Samuel Luke's regiment, who was with Cromwell's force in early May, had certainly reported: 'We are here in an army where as yet I never saw a black coat minister and cannot hear of above one belonging to the army.'[26] It is true that the force which Cromwell commanded in May was only a part of the New Model and might be viewed as an army within an army, but the New Model certainly contained from the outset a number of Independent chaplains, the most famous being Hugh Peters, while the strength of Independency in the army horrified the Presbyterian Richard Baxter who visited the New Model two days after Naseby. Although undoubtedly a wide range of political and religious views were still represented, Baxter found Cromwell's 'hot headed Sectaries' had already seized the highest places in the army.[27]

One unique characteristic of the new army was its freedom from county or Association committees. It was both separately funded, via a committee of Parliament, and was of sufficient size not to need large scale support from locally managed troops. Fairfax did call in local forces as the major battle approached, but they only ever comprised a small percentage of the army and many did not arrive in time to fight because of the disruptive effects of local interests and bureaucratic delay. The New Model was thus able to act without continual worry about the local interests of particular regiments and commanders. The burden of funding had been spread across the main areas of Parliamentarian control but, although the County Committees were to collect the money, they had to render it to Parliament which gave the responsibility for the maintenance of the New Model to the Committee for the Army. The tax was apparently allocated according to the ability of the counties to pay, which can be estimated crudely by relating the assessments to the approximate area of each county. The heaviest burden was placed on London, Kent and East Anglia, the wealthiest counties which had been almost completely shielded from the military action. Adjacent areas, which had also escaped most of the fighting and the destruction, including Bedfordshire and Huntingdonshire, were slightly lower rated. Then came the counties which continued to suffer directly from military action. By now Lincolnshire was relatively well secured and was expected to pay slightly more than neighbouring counties. Warwickshire and Leicestershire paid even less than

Shillings per ml.²

0

1 - 30

31 - 60

61 - 130

350

Eastern

Association

Fig. 12. Taxation to fund the New Model Army in 1645.[28]

Derbyshire and Northamptonshire, but Buckinghamshire and Nottinghamshire were not rated at all. The latter were the counties which had suffered the worst from Royalist action in the past. The burden on the war torn counties was not simply from direct Royalist action, they had a wide range of other demands to meet, greater perhaps than the more secure counties, as can be seen by examining just one Northamptonshire parish in 1645. Burton Latimer paid a weekly contribution to the New Model of 7/6d from the 1st February to the 1st December 1645, £16/2/8d in all. In contrast the village had to pay a weekly tax of £2/1/6d to maintain the garrison at Northampton, 8/- per week for the Rockingham garrison, for Newport Pagnell 13/8d per week, and for the Scottish army in England approximately 10/- per week.[29] There were also, on top of this, the various demands for the provision of supplies, of labour for the construction of defences and so forth. In the north and the west of England there was no assessment at all for the New Model, because not only had those areas been badly affected by the war but they also continued to maintain their own regional armies.

The foundations of the New Model had been laid in the army of the Eastern Association. Shielded by the fenland and by the Midland Parliamenta' ian garrisons, East Anglia had been able to mobilise its enormous resources to establish a large and efficiently organised army. Cromwell in particular had used the opportunity provided by the Eastern Association to great effect. Rising to second in command under Manchester, he had a fundamental role in moulding the whole Eastern Association army. According to Baillie, 'Manchester himself, a sweet, meek man, permitted Lieutenant-General Cromwell to guide all the army at his pleasure.'[30] Cromwell was certainly the prime mover, although some contemporaries gave the credit elsewhere:

> 'that they might be all of one mind in religion as of resolution in the field, with a severe eye he (the Earl of Manchester) hath looked into the manneers of those who are his officers, and cashiered those whom he found to be in any way irregular in their lives or disaffected to the cause...'[31]

Cromwell built the whole structure soundly from the bottom up, first of all with the creation of his own regiment of horse. Known as the Ironsides it grew to a total of 14 troops and was without doubt the best trained, most committed and most effective cavalry unit to fight on a Civil War battlefield. The principles which underlay the success of the Ironsides were also applied to the other regiments of horse of the Association army, which formed the core of the New Model cavalry. He had also been instrumental in the creation of a series of infantry regiments with a highly committed officer corps. As with every other army of the Civil War, and most which followed in later centuries, the majority of the infantry were pressed men, men who might desert their colours as soon as an opportunity arose. In an infantry regiment it was therefore above all the quality of the officers which was crucial. Cromwell had brought into senior command in the army younger men who shared his vision and belief, men like Colonels Montague and Pickering. It is also generally agreed that the Eastern Association army was better disciplined and more committed than most other forces.

As a result of Cromwell's experience in the building of the Eastern Association army, and of the close political alliance between Vane and Cromwell, the Independents' political agenda had been implemented with a deep understanding of the military requirements. The result was arguably the best organised, best officered and most efficient military machine that existed in England before the 20th century. In a later century, unlike Fairfax, even Wellington was to be saddled with incompetent officers appointed by his political masters. This effectiveness was not something that simply evolved during 1645-6, it was a direct reflection of the original composition and organisation of the army as it was established in the spring of 1645. The New Model Army was the product of three years of war, brought together from three armies and, as a result of the political victory achieved by Vane and his allies, its composition was determined wholly by the military commanders who were to lead it. The ability of these senior officers was therefore crucial to the success of the army. Whereas on the Royalist side a renowned military commander, Prince Rupert, had joined the Royalist cause at the outset, Parliament had lacked a dynamic, charismatic leader. It was only as the war progressed that several men began to stand out as effective commanders. It was they who in 1645 supplanted the incompetent or poorly committed old guard, but the remodelling was an even more dramatic transformation. For the first time in English history the overall command of the military machine had been taken from the nobility and placed in the hands of the gentry. The three senior officers were Sir Thomas Fairfax as Lord General, Philip Skippon as Major General and eventually Oliver Cromwell as Lieutenant General of Horse. Unlike the Parliamentarian armies which had preceded it, the New Model was a single army with a team of senior officers with a common purpose, and in many respects compatible views on religious as well as military matters. They also each had a military record which would place them in good standing with their men. Cromwell and Fairfax had fought side by side in Lincolnshire in 1643 and during the Marston Moor campaign, and clearly respected each other. Cromwell had fought alongside Skippon at the second battle of Newbury and he, or at least some of his senior officers in the Eastern Association, had worked with him in the south Midlands in the winter of 1643-4. They also both shared a distaste for the incompetence of the Earl of Essex, as Sir Samuel Luke's comment makes clear: 'To expect any good from the Maj. Gen. I cannot, for he that dealt so unworthily with his Excellency in Cornwall, I cannot expect he can deal better with me.'[32]

Sir Thomas Fairfax was just 33 years old when he took command of the New Model. He had gained his first brief military experience in 1630 in Holland and his first command was as a Colonel of foot in 1639 in the war against the Scots. From the beginning of the Civil War he had fought as a commander of horse alongside his father, who was commander in chief of Parliament's northern forces, and it was there in his native Yorkshire that Fairfax served his apprenticeship, in skirmishes and lesser battles. His charisma was already becoming apparent in the first winter of the war as he led his men from the front with great courage, though like Rupert his impetuosity could lead him into unnecessary danger, but he learnt by his mistakes and defeats as well as from his victories. He showed an ability to act quickly and decisively, perhaps even recklessly at times, but this was an attribute that he shared with all the most effective senior commanders of the war, for at this time the dynamic leader was always to be seen at the front, in the thick of the action. He had already come to the notice of Parliament in the autumn of 1643 in Lincolnshire where, with Fairfax seconding Cromwell's charge at Winceby, there began the most effective military collaboration of the whole war. Fairfax came to wider notice after his success at Nantwich that winter. At Marston Moor he commanded the right wing of horse, later on joining Cromwell, after his own wing was routed, as Cromwell's left wing of horse carried all the field before it. His concern for both his men and, by his control of plundering and wanton destruction, his attention to the fair treatment of the civilians upon which the armies depended for their support, would bode well for the New Model Army. So too would his discipline and sense of honour, for he would stamp his authority on the army without delay. Neither would there be special treatment for any troops under his command. For example, on the return march from the South West in May 1645 the General's regiment claimed exemption from the duties of the rearguard. In response Fairfax is said simply to have dismounted and led them on foot himself at the rear of the army. Thus he soon gained the trust and respect of the men under his command in the New Model just as he had with his troops in Yorkshire.[33]

Fig. 13. Sir Thomas Fairfax, Commander in Chief of the New Model Army.

Fairfax was simply a military commander and was respected and liked by almost all who came into contact with him. In contrast Cromwell, who was 45 years old, was a country squire from the Isle of Ely who had been a Member of Parliament at the beginning of the war but had lacked any kind of military experience. He had however a genuine religious zeal which was his

Fig. 14. Oliver Cromwell was a leading figure in the remodelling of Parliament's forces over the winter and spring of 1644-5, the only one closely involved in the process who combined a high level of both military and political expertise and authority. He had a great influence on the character and composition of the New Model Army and just a few days before the battle was appointed as Fairfax's Lieutenant General of Horse. (National Portrait Gallery)

central driving force and through the war he grew to become a highly respected military commander but he made many enemies in his rise to prominence. He had fought in a number of the major battles of the war. Starting as a Captain of horse at Edgehill he had become Lieutenant General of the Eastern Association army by the time of Marston Moor and his political influence had grown alongside his military success. From the outset he had a clear view of the true nature of the conflict and understood what was required to win. He steadily built up his power base within the Eastern Association army, his military reputation and his political influence to a point where he could put those ideas into practice, playing a decisive role in the creation and then the use of the New Model Army. As Firth has said, 'as a soldier he not only won great victories, but created the instrument with which he won them .... The New Model [was] but his regiment of Ironsides on a larger scale.'[34]

Whereas the great generals of the English Civil War were all first and foremost courageous cavalry commanders, the armies also required the solid professional control of the older, experienced men to exploit the strengths of the infantry. The choice of Philip Skippon, at the age of about 45, as Major General of the army was therefore no surprise. He had learned his military skills through years of continental warfare, serving in Holland and Germany. At the beginning of the war he had been given the important task of preparing the London Trained Bands for action and as a result he missed Edgehill but was ready with those forces a few weeks later when Prince Rupert advanced on London. Skippon had served as Major General under Essex and was Parliament's most experienced and respected infantry commander. After suffering under the disastrous leadership of the Earl of Essex during the Lostwithiel campaign he must have broadly shared Cromwell's assessment of what was needed for military victory. His religious inclination was also not incompatible with the Independents for his was one of the 'preaching and praying' regiments so criticised by Presbyterians like Luke and Baillie.

Fig.15. Philip Skippon, Major General of the New Model Army, who commanded the infantry at Naseby.

At the outset of the Naseby campaign the most senior cavalry commander in the New Model was Colonel Vermuyden but he resigned his commission at the time that Cromwell was appointed Lieutenant General of Horse. A Commissary General of Horse had to be found and not surprisingly Cromwell chose his close ally and friend the 34 year old Henry Ireton. He had commanded a troop of Nottinghamshire horse at Edgehill, but had fought alongside Cromwell since July 1643. He had seen action at Marston Moor and was Cromwell's second in command in the Isle of Ely. In Ramsey's view:

'His military genius does not rate on a level with his literary and debating abilities; he is not a master of strategy and there are some evidences of weakness and imprudence in judgement, but his enemies vouch for his courage, his application was undoubted and he cared for his men.'[35]

Fig.16. Henry Ireton, promoted to Commissary General of Horse in the New Model Army on the 14th June 1645. Ireton commanded the left wing of cavalry at Naseby.

It is impossible to overestimate the importance of an effective Council of War in which a decisive leader was willing to listen to the arguments, to be able make up his own mind and then to have the support of all his senior officers in the implementation of those decisions. This was a very different team to that which had attempted to run the Eastern Association army in 1644, when Cromwell and his followers, men like Pickering and Montague, seem to have been in almost continual conflict with Manchester and his Major General. The New Model's Council of War, once it was allowed to make its own decisions free from the shackles of the Committee of Both Kingdoms, had the will and the ability to act decisively in a way that no earlier Parliamentarian army had. Certainly it was able to function far more effectively than the Royalist Council of War which was now more divided than it had ever been and led by a King who was more indecisive and ineffective than even Essex or Manchester.

The composition of the officer corps of the New Model was also in some respects different from previous armies and that difference was not lost on their enemies, Royalist and Presbyterian alike. According to Holles:

'All of them, from the general (except what he may have in expectation after his father's death) to the meanest sentinel, are not able to make a thousand pounds a year lands; most of the colonels are tradesmen, brewers, tailors, goldsmiths, shoemakers, and the like. These to rebel against their masters!'[36]

Though this is exaggeration by a hostile observer, it reflects a genuine change that all could see. These were 'ordinary' people rising above their station, so far as the elite were concerned, for they saw military authority moving from the nobility to the gentry and below. According to Sir Samuel Luke 'the officers you will hardly distinguish from common soldiers', while Clarendon summed up the Royalist view when he described the officers in the New Model Army as all 'dirty people of no name'.[37] Almost the whole existing team of officers in some regiments were transferred directly into the New Model. If this applied across the whole army then it was the choice of the regiment and its commander not of the individual men themselves that led to the particular balance of officers in the new army. Cromwell had not tried to make the army a wholly Independent force, but had ensured that many of the Independent regiments were included. Though the remodelling was not a genuine purge of the army, in the end that is how it would begin to look as many Presbyterian officers simply refused to serve in the New Model once they had lost the argument over its composition. The result must have been a body of senior officers who were wholly committed to the support of Fairfax, Cromwell and Skippon. If Pickering's and Montague's regiments are any guide then the colonels will have had compatible views with those of the senior command and can have expected a similar level of support and commitment from their own commissioned officers, with whom they had presumably built up a good working relationship over the preceding year or more.[38] In this at least Rushworth had some confidence, for he wrote after the battle:

'this new moulded Army, so much contemned by many and left as sheepe to the slaughter by others, but from the beginning I was confident, a blessing from heaven did attend this Army, there were in it so many pious men, men of

integrity, hating vice, fighting not out of ambitiousnesse or by ends, but ayming
at Gods glory and the preservations of Religion and Liberty, and the destruction
of the Enemy.'[39]

The composition of the officer corps was of particular importance with regard
to the infantry because, unlike the cavalry troopers, the common soldiers were
composed mainly of pressed men and had a rapid turnover. The character and
commitment of the New Model was therefore determined by the whole of the
cavalry but only by the officers and a small core of infantry, the majority of
the foot being very brief and unwilling members of the army.[40]

Perhaps of even greater importance in the summer of 1645 was another
fundamental difference between the New Model Army and those which it
replaced, and indeed with the Royalist army. This was the dramatic reduction
in the number of officers in relation to common soldiers, especially in the
infantry. For example, Pickering's was one of the weakest of all the Eastern
Association infantry regiments, having never reached anything like its full
complement during 1644.[41] The maximum number of soldiers was 738 in May
1644. As a result of the hard and almost continual fighting between May and
October, the sickness and the high level of desertion which resulted from the
bad conditions and the lack of consistent pay, by January 1645 the regiment
was down to just 243 men. Despite this the number of officers did not vary
greatly, for in May 1644 there had been 135 officers while in January 1645
there were still 124. The cost of maintaining such an imbalance of officers to
men must have been dramatic for the finances of the army and so the New
Model was intended to have a far more appropriate balance. When Ayloffe's
regiment was reduced into Pickering's the number of officers was not
increased, instead all of Ayloffe's officers were discharged.[42] If Pickering's
were in any way representative then immediately the army must have almost
halved its bill for officers' pay. Moreover, Pickering's regiment were being
recruited at the same time with pressed men yet further improving the ratio
of officers to men. As a result, by the time of Naseby the New Model was a
far more balanced army than that which was fielded by the Royalists, although
all the infantry regiments still remained well below strength and undoubtedly
the balance will have deteriorated again as the year progressed, just as it had
in the Eastern Association army during 1644.

It cannot be assumed that from the outset the New Model was, throughout
its ranks, a committed and professional force, because there were fundamental
tensions within the army at this time. The mere process of welding together
troops from three separate armies, with many of the officers being discharged,
was a recipe for conflict. Add to this the open hostility between Independent
and Presbyterian and almost inevitably the problems developed to the stage of
mutiny in the regiments of the Independent Colonels Montague and Pickering.
In the latter, the disorder was almost certainly amongst the men from the
regiment of the Presbyterian Colonel Ayloffe which had been reduced into
Pickering's. The tension continued into early June, when many of Pickering's

men deserted at Newport Pagnell, and may well have contributed to the failure of both Pickering's and Montague's regiments to hold their ground at Naseby. Amongst the cavalry there had also been problems with some regiments that did not want to transfer. However the Eastern Association horse, which formed the core of the New Model cavalry, were already in 1644 more than a match for the Royalists, who had until then held a decisive advantage in cavalry actions. Neither were the cavalry troubled by desertion and the imbalance of officers to men that is seen in the infantry. During 1645 more than 7000 men needed to be conscripted into the infantry, half the total complement. In contrast the cavalry was almost completed from the existing troops in the three armies and hence they were well organised and trained already. This was particularly important for an army which would fight its most important battle within two and a half months of being formed, because the training of a cavalryman was far more involved and time consuming than that of an infantryman.

Another concern with the New Model was to ensure that the troops were well paid and disciplined, in order that they did not alienate the local population in the areas through which they marched. The provisioning of the army and the degree of impact it had on the countryside is explored later, but what is clear is that in the first few months the troops were adequately paid and hence able to pay for their needs.[43] Even Luke, who was hostile to the New Model, had to admit when Fairfax's army marched through Newport Pagnell a few days before Naseby that it was 'the bravest that ever I saw for bodies of men, both in number, arms or other accoutrements, and pay for the officers', while the 'ordinary men are the likeliest that ever I saw...', and to the Earl of Essex he wrote it was 'the gallantest that I have yet seen in England for stout soldiers and willing men to fight, and if God will do his work by multitudes I am confident it will be done now...'. Not surprisingly however he also added elsewhere that 'I think these New Modellers knead all their dough with ale, for I never saw so many drunk in my life in so short a time,' a comment in accord with the general assessment that the new recruits for the infantry were the dregs of society. In this last aspect the new army was no different to those that had preceded it, yet, how different in this regard was it from many later professional armies?

If the New Model was not respected by the Royalists, who disparagingly called it the New Noddle, it was held in equally low esteem by many Parliamentarians. James Chaloner wrote to Lord Fairfax on 24th February 1645 about his son's appointment to command the New Model and his arrival in London that 'it is as little pleasing to some here as to them at Oxford.'[44] According to Fairfax himself:

'had it not been in the simplicity of my heart, I could not have supported myself under the frowns and displeasures of those who were disgusted with these alterations, in which many of them were much concerned; and therefore they sought by all means to obstruct my procedings in this new charge. Though they could not prevent what the necessity of affairs prest most to do, which was to march speedily out with the army, yet were we by them made so inconsiderable, for want of fit and necessary accomodations, as it rather seemed that we were sent to be destroyed, than to do any service to the Kingdom.'[45]

It would seem that knowledge of the intrigue against Fairfax had even reached the Royalists, for Edward Nicholas wrote to Rupert on the 16th May that Cromwell 'is now the principal counsellor of the rebels, who are much dissatisfied with Thomas Fairfax; and if Cromwell should miscarry, neither Scots would advance, nor the rebels be able to raise any considerable army.'[46] Yet both the Royalists and the Presbyterians, through their elitist views and their experience with earlier armies, were deceiving themselves. By late April, when the New Model was reportedly between 19000 and 20000 strong, it had been transformed into a committed, well organised, well equipped and effective fighting force. This was a very different army to that which had been brought to its very knees by the Newbury campaign just seven months before.[47]

THE ROYALIST ARMY

In July 1644 the Marston Moor campaign had seen the destruction of the Royalist army of the North, both on the field and then through the reduction of its garrisons, as well as the army which Rupert had built up with such great effort in Wales and the Marches in the winter of 1643-4. Northern England was effectively lost to the King, with just a few hard pressed garrisons like Pontefract, Scarborough and Chester holding out. To a degree Charles himself had redressed the military balance with his victories at Cropredy bridge, Lostwithiel and even in the Newbury campaign, for although the latter was not a victory it had enabled him to relieve the garrisons of Hampshire and Berkshire. After Newbury the King dispersed his forces in quarters around Oxford for the winter but the city was under greater pressure than ever before, with Reading and Abingdon in Parliamentarian hands, and the difficulties of provisioning his troops led many of them to desert. The national military situation had been stabilised but the King had not recovered the losses of Marston Moor. In the winter and spring of 1644-5 a new force had to be built out of the ruins of three Royalist armies but from a far smaller territory than they had controlled the previous winter.[48] Indeed such was the parlous state of the Royalist cause by early 1645 that it was suggested that if the New Model was established and the King's army drawn out of Oxford then 'they will not be able to subsist, without foreign help, six months after.'[49] The Royalists simply did not control sufficient territory to build and maintain an army which could defeat all the forces which Parliament was able to mobilise. Even Rupert had apparently concluded that outright military victory was no longer achievable, but Charles would not countenance a negotiated settlement.

Fig. 17. Prince Rupert, nephew of Charles I, was Lieutenant General of the Royalist army in 1645 but commanded the right wing of cavalry at Naseby.

Prince Rupert was now appointed Lieutenant General of the Royalist army, in place of the elderly Lord Forth. A younger son of the Elector of the Palatinate, Rupert had trained for a military career from early childhood in Germany. He had seen his first military action in Holland in 1633 when just 14 years old and served his apprenticeship as a trooper and later as a colonel of horse. When he arrived in England at the beginning of the war he already had a great military reputation as a courageous and skilful leader. Charles I had appointed his nephew as his cavalry commander in August 1642 and so Rupert led the right wing of horse at Edgehill. Clarendon's hostile picture of a swashbuckling troublemaker had distorted history's view of Rupert until more recent studies redressed the balance. In fact his dynamic leadership and courage gave him the devotion of his men and the respect of his enemies, once they had met him. In Parliamentarian propaganda however he was a cruel devil, 'Prince Robber', for he had brought to England the far more harsh continental military attitudes of the Thirty Years War. Rupert had built up around him a group of trusted soldiers, his closest ally in arms being his brother Prince Maurice, and once appointed Lieutenant General he brought his friends and allies into positions of power within the army. For example, Bernard de Gomme was appointed as Quartermaster General and William Legge became governor of Oxford. In the spring of 1645 Rupert also attempted to coordinate the surviving Royalist forces to create an effective military machine but what was not undertaken, or what he was not allowed to conduct, was a fundamental reorganisation of the Royalist forces comparable to that which Parliament would soon authorise. This might have proven an impossible task for Rupert, even without the continual undermining of his position by the King, but it was not even attempted.[50]

Fig.18. King Charles I, as Captain General of the Royalist army, had overall command at Naseby.

Charles I, who retained overall command of the army as Captain General, was a weak man unsuited for kingship or for military command, being unsure of himself and unable to take decisive action. He was also very impressionable and so could not be trusted to keep to a course of action, even when it had been fully agreed, often changing his decisions according to the last person who spoke to him. Most dangerous of all, Charles was devious in his dealings with both his enemies and his supporters, sowing dissention and division within his own military command as effectively as he had done in the political sphere in creating the Civil War in the first place. This is most clearly seen in 1645 in his granting to Lord Goring of an independent command in the South West, responsible only to Charles himself. Goring, who had fought well as a commander of horse in important battles such as Marston Moor, could be a very effective commander but his deficiencies more than outweighed his strengths, for he was not only a drunkard and a womaniser but was also unreliable and untrustworthy. The King fuelled Goring's personal ambition by allowing him to act independently at the very time when a united military command was crucial to the severely weakened Royalist war machine. This decision was to rebound badly during the forthcoming campaign.

Fig. 19. Lord Digby, a courtier responsible for some of the King's most disastrous decisions.

Even more damaging for the Royalist cause was the King's lack of judgement in taking Lord Digby as one of his closest advisers. This courtier and amateur soldier, who had been appointed as one of the Secretaries of State in the winter of 1643-4, was an untrustworthy intriguer who used his position to undermine Rupert. It was Digby above all others who would be responsible for the disastrous string of decisions made by the King in late May and early June 1645 which led to the crushing defeat at Naseby. It was also Digby who encouraged the King in his unrealistic confidence that victory was still possible, especially if his enemies continued to fall out and if troops could be brought over from Ireland. In reality it was the Royalist cause which was in the greatest danger from internal dissension, for while the discord within the Parliamentarian camp was being fuelled by a struggle to fundamentally reorganise their military forces, that within the Royalist camp was purely destructive. As defeat came ever closer so the intrigues, encouraged by weak leadership, became ever more damaging.

Fig.20. Lord Astley, Major General of the Royalist army.

A commander upon whom Rupert could depend was Lord Astley. At 66 Sir Jacob Astley was perhaps rather too old for the stresses of the battlefield, but he was by far the most experienced and capable of Royalist infantry commanders. He had seen long and distinguished service on the continent, having fought first in the Low Countries, then under the King of Denmark and later under Gustavus Adolphus, under whom he had risen to become Major General. While on the continent he had also served for a time as Rupert's military tutor. Astley had been Charles's Major General at Edgehill, a command he had retained throughout the war. The other main Royalist commander at Naseby was to be Sir Marmaduke Langdale. This austere and autocratic Yorkshire catholic, who was about 47 years old, had faced Fairfax in the North on several occasions. Rupert had given him the task of bringing together the scattered remnants of cavalry of the Royalist Northern army after the defeat at Marston Moor and he retained command of the Northern horse in 1645. The Royalist army also had a far greater number of experienced officers than the New Model, some of the more senior having served on the continent as well as in three years of Civil War in Britain.

Fig. 21. Sir Marmaduke Langdale, who commanded the left wing of cavalry at Naseby.

Preparations for the forthcoming campaign were under way by January 1645, with work on the artillery train beginning by the time Rupert visited Oxford at the end of the month.[51] There Rupert had discussions with various people including William Legge, a good friend of the Prince who was not only governor of Oxford but also master of the Armoury. It was intended that transport, tools and other supplies for the train be drawn from Bristol and other Royalist garrisons in the South West to supplement those already available in Oxford. Warrants were to be sent out for teams of draught horses and carts, while several garrisons were required to make covered waggons which were to be ready by the 22nd March.[52] Forty were required, of which ten were to come from Oxford, ten from Worcester, fifteen from Bristol and five from Bridgwater. They were to be supplied with all their gear and with carters to handle them, together with proportional numbers of spades, pickaxes and shovels. The ironworks in the West Midlands were to supply round shot for the artillery, orders being sent out for 200 twelve pound, 1200 six pound and 200 three pound shot, 260 'granado' shells for mortars and 1400 hand grenades. 8000 pike heads were to be supplied via Worcester and 1900 from a supplier in Stourbridge while others were to produce the staves for the pikes. Shrewsbury was to provide 12 large leather boats, which were to have their own four wheeled carriages and all the necessary equipment together with horses and carters. These were intended for the construction of pontoon bridges to transport the artillery across rivers. There were also to be 30 scaling ladders of twenty and fifteen foot in length. Smiths, carpenters, wheelwrights and collarmakers in and around Oxford were all set to work to produce various of the equipment while supplies of planks, boards and spokes were to be drawn from Witney and Faringdon, and pike-staves from Blewbury. The necessary organisation was put in place immediately to insure that 'no tyme or meanes for the expediting, or advancing of any the Provisons or services concerning this yeares Proportion for the Traine may bee neglected or omitted.' However the supply of equipment for the train, as for the rest of the army, was to be affected by the deteriorating fortunes of the Royalist cause in the Welsh Marches. With the fall of Shrewsbury in February the boats in particular would in the end have to be built at Oxford, where they would be tested out by taking two of the largest guns across the river.[53]

The previous artillery train of forty pieces had not been fully used in 1644 and so it was to be reduced in number this season to just twenty out of the thirty or so which were available in the Oxford artillery park. There were to be two demi-cannon, two whole culverin, two demi culverin, four twelve-pounders and ten six-pounders. The six largest guns were intended for siege-work while the remaining fourteen were field guns which might fire case shot as well as ball. The responsibility for the train rested with the Waggon Master General and to transport all the equipment, supplies and artillery pieces he would need a large number of draught horses, carriages and carters. These were ordered to be ready by the 20th March, but again the military situation would lead to a change in plans before the army drew out of Oxford in early May. To pull the guns there would need to be at least 200 horses, the manuals of the period indicating for example that a culverin required at least seventeen horses while a six pounder needed six horses. There would also need to be at least as many again to pull the ammunition and supply waggons, for each of which the normal complement was five horses.[54] Oxen could be used, but with their far greater pulling power horses were always to be preferred, especially for the artillery which required great traction. If at all, the oxen were most likely to be used for pulling waggons containing provisions.[55] Though we do not have a complete record of the supplies actually taken in May 1645, we can gain an idea of what was involved from the train of sixteen brass pieces planned in June 1644 for the Cropredy campaign. It had required round shot and case shot in three 'tumbrels', two wheeled heavy carts, a waggon with ten barrels of powder and a hundredweight of match and three carts each to move the munition tents, barrels, harness and other equipment. Another cart carried nails, horseshoes and other supplies, a further cart for shovels, spades and the like, then finally for the infantry two waggons with forty barrels of powder, two with match and two with musket shot. In all this made 15 waggons or carts, each of which required a team of five horses giving 75 horses in all. There was then a carter for each waggon, 2 coopers, 1 collarmaker, 3 smiths, 2 wheelwrights, 3 carpenters, 19 pioneers, 40 matrosses, 25 gunners, 11 conductors, a surgeon, quartermaster, clerk and various controllers and gentlemen of the ordnance, in all some 130 men.[56] Though the train in 1645 would have less pieces they included heavier siege artillery and so the supporting munitions and supplies will have been even more substantial, hence the provision of a total of forty waggons. The train will also of course have been supplemented by the impressment of 'county teams', that is waggons with their horses and carters from individual parishes.[57] These waggons would have been needed to transport not just the supplies for the artillery, some of which may have been moved in the open waggons, but also to move the provisions, for which there would have been enclosed waggons. There was also the baggage of the various senior officers to be carried while some of the waggons would of course be used later to transport the sick and, after a military engagement, the wounded.[58]

During the Spring of 1645 Oxford was building up its resources ready for the coming campaign. On the 9th April it was reported that:

'His Majesty is still at Oxon, where his stay will be very requisite, until that garrison be in a condition to defend itself .... as soon as the train is ready to move, Prince Rupert will draw unto the King, and then Northward; if in the West they can subsist without their army.'[59]

This points up the dangers inherent in the way in which the Royalists had to strip troops from front line garrisons to put together their main field army. It was a fundamental weakness under which they had suffered in previous years, placing important garrisons like Banbury under threat and why places like Oswestry and Sudeley had fallen to Parliament in 1644. As in the previous year, it was expected that the withdrawal would be followed by a concerted attempt to reduce key Royalist garrisons and so every effort had to be made to put them in a state in which they could survive the onslaught. For example, on the 9th April Trevor reported:

'my Lord Northampton defeated a convoy passing from Gloucester towards London with cloaths and plate to a very great value: which added to a former brush of that kind, will make the enemy look about him, and put Banbury castle in a good condition to entertain the young illuminated warrior Mr Fiennes this next summer, if he think good to come and fetch his guns he left there the last.'[60]

London and East Anglia, which remained secure behind a frontier, could supply most of the troops for the Parliamentarian field army but, to a lesser degree, the Parliamentarians faced a similar problem as the Royalists. They too had to remove troops to make up the field army but they were better placed to meet the challenge. The remodelling of the Parliamentarian field army was extended to some of the local forces, in particular those of Major General Browne, who had been given command of Buckinghamshire, Berkshire and Oxfordshire. His own regiment for example was strengthened by the transfer of troops from other regiments, as well as by the recruitment of new soldiers. This was essential because Browne was about to lose the Eastern Association regiments which had been garrisoned in the region over winter and some, like Ayloffe's, for most of the previous year.[61] His position was also strengthened by transferring forces between garrisons, bringing troops in from stronger garrisons to support the weaker ones and troops from counties away from the fighting into the front line garrisons.

The Royalists did not have this kind of luxury. Indeed, in Wales and the Welsh Marches the whole process of rebuilding the Royalist army was under threat in the winter of 1644-5. First there were the Parliamentarian attacks which attempted to further destabilise the Royalist resource base by expansion into Wales. From Cheshire in the north and from the far south west of Wales small forces captured significant territory, while in the south Massey also posed a threat to Herefordshire. The greatest Parliamentarian success was the capture of Shrewsbury in February. This threatened the Royalists' whole programme of recruitment in north and central Wales, for Shrewsbury was the base where many of the new recruits were brought together and prepared for action. The situation was compounded by a fundamental threat to the 'nursery of the King's infantry', not by Parliamentarian forces but by the very populations on whom the Royalists depended. Already in August Rupert had experienced difficulty in recruiting men for his devastated army in the Chester area, but the situation across much of Wales and the Marches had deteriorated rapidly by the beginning of 1645. The Royalists had experienced a degree of indifference and open hostility from local populations throughout the war, but in the winter of 1644-5 in this region it became particularly strong and threatening. To create the army which had fought at Marston Moor Rupert had drained Wales and the Marches of seasoned troops, new levies and money. Now large remnants of the Royalist armies had returned and were quartered there. The continual pressure of free quarter, compounded by the mismanagement of local administration, led to increasing problems. There was open hostility to the quartering of Rupert's defeated troops in Shropshire, while the Northern horse were forced to move from area to area and faced actual physical attack in Monmouthshire. There was a general rising up of the local people against the demands placed upon them to support not just the local but also the national forces. A war weary people began to demand peace.

This can be compared to the Parliamentarian weakness in some areas. We have already seen the inability of Buckinghamshire to support even its own garrisons while the Midland region in general could only be allocated a very limited contribution towards the support of the New Model Army. The impact of continual conflict had been exacerbated by the King's policy of quartering his field army in Parliamentarian areas over winter and the quartering of Eastern Association and other Parliamentarian army forces in the county at the same time. The effect would be clearly seen in early June by Fairfax as his army tried to requisition supplies as they marched through the county. In December the King had moved the quarters of many of his field army from around Oxford across to the Cotswolds, the area upon which Massey's Parliamentarian forces from Gloucester depended for their support. Here again the impact was devastating. Massey's men began to desert and mutiny, placing his whole command in danger and requiring troops to be brought in from the south east Midland garrisons to reinforce his depleted ranks. However, unlike the Royalists, Parliament did not have to depend on such territories for its main field army as it had the secure areas of East Anglia and London to support the New Model. The territories which were still fully under Royalist control were not only much smaller but also in comparison far less wealthy or populous and so Rupert will have had to press those territories far harder. This may have been why in Wales and the Marches the situation deteriorated much further than in the south east Midlands. There was great tension between the unpaid soldiers and the local population in several Royalist areas and this pressure had been compounded by the impact of the war on the local economy and hence their ability to pay. In some parts of the region the very basis of the economy, the cattle trade to London and the Midlands, had been cut completely by the war. They also had to suffer free quarter, the high handed approach of some local commanders and, perhaps worst of all, the lack of discipline amongst the regular soldiers. The result was an anti-military not an anti-royalist movement. The local Associations encouraged by Charles as a way of rasing local forces to expel the Parliamentarians increasingly appeared as a threat to the Royalists as well.

Most significant was the rise of militant neutralism - the so called clubmen - and across much of the region in February and March local people took up arms to defend themselves from all military threats and exactions. There were clubmen in Shropshire, Worcestershire and Monmouthshire, but the rising in Herefordshire was the most aggressive. The resource base essential for the creation of the Royalist army for the 1645 campaign was in danger of being destroyed by both external and internal forces. Rupert wrote in March that 'I fear all Wales will be in rebellion'.

Prince Maurice, who had been given command in the region, succeeded in reversing the deteriorating situation. Already by the late summer of 1644 the administrative system in Worcestershire had been reorganised and the small broken regiments remodelled into a new, more effective force. Similar action was now extended to Monmouthshire, with the ending of free quarter and the extra taxes. The action mirrored the administrative and military reorganisation which Rupert had undertaken in 1643-4, attempting to conciliate and build cooperation by moderating and regularising the demands and actions of the Royalists. Then, in March, a combined force under Maurice and Rupert implemented the military element of the solution. Chester and Beeston were relieved and the Royalist forces recruited there, after which they moved south. They harshly suppressed the Herefordshire clubmen and quartered the army on the county as though it was a captured territory, while elsewhere the rule of law was carefully followed. Herefordshire was held down by force and the other counties cowed into submission at the example. The situation had been dramatically reversed in a very short time and Rupert could now concentrate on the recruiting and supply of the new army.

To keep a check on these developments Massey's forces at Gloucester, which as we have seen had become severely weakened, were reinforced with small bodies of horse from the south east Midlands. He was joined by 250 cavalry from Northampton and Warwick and a little later by two troops of horse from Newport Pagnell. 'The auxiliaryes were in all three hundrd and forty; his owne so few, weake, and ill armed, that he coud scarce muster a hundred fighting horse....' By this time Rupert had some 6000 horse and foot in Hereford and Worcester. Massey followed the enemy's movements and advanced to Lidbury, which had risen up against the Royalists in late March, and there with just 400 horse and 500 foot he skirmished with Rupert.[62] The engagement was inconclusive and Rupert returned to Worcester and Herefordshire where he 'vigorously endeavour'd to supply his Army with large Recruits out of those Parts.'[63] On the 9th April 1645 it was reported:

'P.Rupert came hither [Bristol] late yesternight, but stays not long. His army is quartered in the parts about Hereford, where the late insurrection was, and shall continue there, until they give him 800 men armed for their contempt. His army is in a very good condition, and he is hopeful to increase it much; for he hath presses for 1400 men out at this time.'[64]

In south west Wales Gerard ruthlessly quartered in Montgomeryshire, which had become an enemy territory, and after refreshing his army there he struck in late April in Pembrokeshire pushing the Parliamentarians back into just two garrisons. Across Wales the situation had now been reversed and it was an increasingly secure base from which they could maintain their war effort. Gerard recruited his army and now had 700 horse and 2000 foot, a force which could be of great value to the main Royalist field army if it could be brought up to join them. The presses to raise infantry for Rupert's army were also effective and by late April these new recruits had joined existing regiments to bring up their strength. The army was now reasonably well supplied and by early May they were ready to march with Rupert and Maurice to join the King at the opening of the campaigning season. For the second year running Wales and the Marches had produced and supported the assembly of the greater part of the Royalist field army.

In south west England the situation had remained in a far better state, but there was still the need for improvement. In early March the King had sent the Prince of Wales with a team of privy councillors, including Hyde and Culpepper, to Bristol to coordinate the war effort in the region.[65] As a result of their efforts the local administrative system appears to have improved somewhat in its ability to support the war and the military situation was also dramatically improved. Parliamentarian advances were halted and they were thrown back once more into several strongly defended garrisons, with Taunton in particular being placed under great pressure. Despite their successes however there was a problem within the Royalist camp which would play a significant role in the forthcoming campaign. Goring had been given command of the western forces with responsibility direct to the King and independent of Rupert. Instead of decisive leadership from an effective single military command Charles was promoting tension and division - the seeds of defeat had been sown. Rupert wrote on 24th March 'I expect nothing but ill from the West; let them hear that Rupert says so...'[66] Goring would not follow his orders in the weeks before Naseby, with disastrous effect, while in the South West Goring's high handed actions would encourage clubman risings ultimately more damaging than those in Wales. The final element of the Royalist strategy for the new campaign was the attempt to negotiate a peace treaty with the Catholic rebels in Ireland to release more troops to fight in England. Charles was willing to achieve this at almost any cost:

'if taking away of the penal laws against papists by a law will do it, I shall not think it a hard bargain, so that freely and vigorously they engage themselves in my assistance against my rebels of England and Scotland, for which no conditions can be too hard....'[67]

To Charles the chances of a major influx of seasoned troops from Ireland still seemed good, but one can imagine that Rupert was under no such illusions. So, at the opening of the campaigning season the Royalist cause looked better

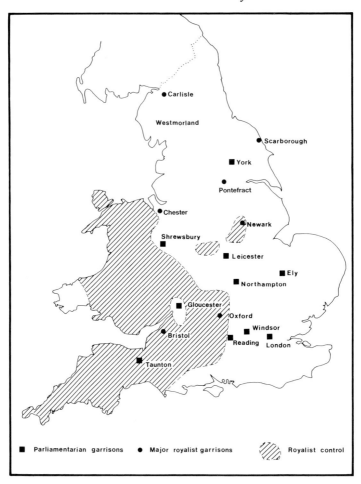

Fig.22. The territory controlled by each side in early 1645.[68]

than could ever have been expected a few months earlier. Rupert had rebuilt an army in Wales and the Marches and a substantial force had been raised in south Wales under Gerrard. Goring had some 5000 foot and 5000 horse in the South West and was recruiting well and even in Scotland there were the Royalist victories of Montrose to divert the attention of the Scottish army. Though now under severe pressure, there were also areas in the Midlands under the control of well fortified Royalist garrisons and in the north key garrisons still held out, representing important bases around which the North might perhaps be rallied once more to the King. Whereas Parliamentarian spirits were low, the Royalists had good reason to be hopeful for 1645. However, despite their improved fortunes, Rupert was in little doubt that the war was already unwinnable. In early April he supported Lord Hertford in arguing that the Royalist forces which had been raised with such difficulty should be used to gain the best possible peace. As so often, the King ignored advice that was unpalatable, preferring to hear Digby's unrealistic optimism.

NOTES

1. The following discussion draws heavily on Gentles, 1992, and Adamson & Folland, 1973.
2. Bell, 1849, vol.1, p.155.
3. Laing, 1841, vol.2, p.246.
4. Laing, 1841, vol.1.
5. Kingston, 1897, p.152-3.
6. Rushworth, 1722, vol.6, p.2.
7. Rushworth, 1722, vol.6, p.1.
8. Hutchinson, 1908, p.183-4.
9. Hutchinson, 1908, p.182.
10. Everitt, 1969, p.9.
11. Slingsby, p.140.
12. Vane quoted by Adamson and Folland, 1973, p.231-2.
13. Gentles, 1992, p.23.
14. Holles, 1699, p.34.
15. *Short Memorials*, p.375.
16. Mungeam, 1968.
17. Firth, 1962, p.158.
18. *Commons Journals*, vol.4, p.71. Hexham, 1639, part 3, p.4-7, specifies 13 horses for a field piece or quarter cannon.
19. Firth, 1962, p.158.
20. Again a muzzle loading, smooth bore firearm, but whereas in matchlock muskets the charge was set off by a slow burning cord or 'match', in the snaphance it was set off by a spark created by a flint striking a metal plate.
21. Vernon, 1644, p.42.
22. Foard, 1994, p.27-8, although the comments attributed to Cromwell there are in error. Gentles, 1992, p.44.
23. Cruso, 1632, p.30-31. Vernon, 1644, p.42. Haythornthwaite, 1983. Firth & Davies, 1940, p.17-18.
24. Rushworth, vol.6, p.16. Sprigge, 1647, p.9. Bell, 1849, vol.1, p.173.
25. Kishlansky, 1979, Gentles, 1992. While Gentles has used the army records preserved in the Public Records Office and is aware of the evidence the Exchequer papers include, his analysis of this material, though detailed, does not attempt to be definitive. These records will enable a far more detailed understanding than is presently available of the composition, character and strength of each regiment in the army, their casualty rates, losses to sickness and desertion, and the detail of their equipment and supply. Similar study of the armies from which the New Model was drawn will also be possible, assisting in the understanding of the forces which were brought together in 1645 to form the new army. Only when this has been done, building a story from these many thousands of small pieces of information, will an accurate overall picture be compiled that does full justice to the potential which exists.
26. Tibbutt, 1963, p.537.
27. Stearns, 1954, p.247-9.
28. The New Model monthly assessment (with county areas in square miles, as in 1960, in brackets) was Northamptonshire £450 ($910ml^2$) = 10/- per ml^2, Leicestershire £250 ($830ml^2$) = 6/- per ml^2, Bedfordshire £1000 ($400ml^2$) = 48/- per ml^2, Warwickshire £300 ($980ml^2$) = 6/- per ml^2, Rutland £180 ($150ml^2$) = 24/- per ml^2, Sussex £3927.15.6d, 3 farthings ($1460ml^2$) = 54/- per ml^2; Derbyshire £516 ($1000ml^2$) = 10/- per ml^2, Surrey & Southwark £2000 ($720ml^2$) = 56/- per ml^2, Kent £7070 ($1520ml^2$) = 93/- per ml^2, Huntingdonshire £1020 ($450ml^2$) = 45/- per ml^2, Cambridgeshire £2171.6.8d ($870ml^2$) & Ely £728.13.4d (with Cambs) = 67/- per ml^2,

Hertfordshire £2432.10.0d (630ml^2)=77/- per ml^2, Lincolnshire £2070 (450ml^2)=15/- per ml^2, Norwich £366 (see Norfolk) & Norfolk £7070 (2050ml^2)=72/- per ml^2, Suffolk £7070 (1090ml^2)=130/- per ml^2, Essex £6750 (1530ml^2)=88/- per ml^2, London and Middlesex £8059.15.0d.(453ml^2)=355/- per ml^2. Rushworth, vol.6, p.9.

29. PRO SP28/171, f.10-11.

30. Baillie to Dickson, quoted by Ramsey, 1949, p.21.

31. *Weekly Account*, 1644, quoted by Kingston, 1897, p.153-4.

32. Tibbutt, 1963, p.324.

33. Markham, 1870. Wilson, 1985.

34. Firth, 1947, p.467.

35. Ramsey, 1949, p.204.

36. Holles, 1699, p.149.

37. Tibbutt, 1963, p.304, 309-10 & 319. Clarendon, 1702, bk 4, p.261.

38. Foard, 1994.

39. Rushworth letter.

40. Gentles, 1992, p.40-1.

41. Holmes, 1974. Foard, 1994.

42. List of officers of Ayloffe's regiment mustered 2nd May 1645 prior to discharge, PRO SP28/122, f.171.

43. Tibbutt, 1963, p.537.

44. Bell, 1849, vol.1, p.162.

45. Scott, 1811, vol.5, p.391.

46. Nicholas to Rupert, 16th May, Warburton, vol.3, p.91.

47. Gentles, 1992, p.35.

48. The following discussion draws heavily upon Hutton, 1982.

49. 24th February 1645, Chaloner to Lord Fairfax, Bell, 1849, vol.1, p.164.

50. Morrah, 1976. Kitson, 1994.

51. Discussion of the train is based mainly on Roy, 1964.

52. Souldern and Fritwell, between Banbury and Bicester, were amongst the Oxfordshire villages which supplied carts in mid March. Tennant, 1992, p.246.

53. Slingsby, p.142.

54. Roy, 1964, p.353-5, 399 & 521-2. Hexham, 1639, p.4-7.

55. Toynbee, 1961, p.37.

56. Roy, 1964, p.21 & 353-4.

57. Toynbee, 1962, p.15-16.

58. Toynbee, 1962, p.17.

59. Carte, 1759, vol.1, p.80.

60. Trevor to Ormond 9th April 1645, Carte, 1759, vol.1, p.80 & 83.

61. Foard, 1994, p.96-7.

62. *A true and impartial History of the Military Government of the Citie of Gloucester*, 1647, reprinted in Scott, 1811, vol.5, p.370-1. Sherwood, 1974, p.176.

63. Rushworth, vol.6, p.23.

64. Trevor to Ormond, 9th April 1645, Carte, 1759, vol.1, p.83.

65. Ludlow, 1698, vol.1, p. 151-3, repeating Slingsby, p.143.

66. Warburton, vol.3, p.68-9.

67. Charles to Ormond, 27th February 1645, Petrie, 1968, p.152.

68. After Young & Holmes, 1974, p.226 with amendments.

CHAPTER 4

THE CAMPAIGN OPENS

'This day is yours, great Charles; and in this war
Your fate and ours alike victorious are.'
Robert Herrick

The urgency of the task was continually in mind as the remodelling of the Parliamentarian forces was being planned and implemented. The wrangling in Parliament had so delayed the creation of the new army that there were worries it would not be ready before the King took the field. On 11th March Thomas Widdrington wrote with some concern saying Rupert had gone northwards to join Maurice and Langdale to form a large army but that 'the new model is not yet grown into an army.'[1] Parliamentarian fears must have been reinforced when Maurice sent out instructions on the 3rd April for Worcestershire to prepare for the arrival of the Royalist army and although the Warwick Committee sought to countermand the instructions their words probably had little impact.[2] Rupert was well aware of the delays in the remodelling process and, encouraged by Langdale's relief of Pontefract, the Royalists had thrown themselves into the task of preparing their forces as quickly as possible. They could see the potential to wreak havoc before Parliament had a field army which could challenge them.[3] While the New Model waited for the completion of its train of artillery, Fairfax was ordered to send Cromwell with 1500 horse and a few dragoons to disrupt the Royalist preparations. He was to intercept the 2000 horse being sent from Worcester to Oxford because the King was in desperate need of cavalry support if he was to take the field with his infantry and train of artillery, which was approaching readiness in and around Oxford.[4] So, when Cromwell arrived at Windsor to resign his commission, under the requirements of the Self Denying Ordinance, he found himself instead being given command of several of Fairfax's regiments. Cromwell's military successes over the last three years had made him an indispensable commander at such a difficult time.

From Windsor he advanced along the main Worcester road, reaching Watlington on the 23rd April. The road, which passed north of Oxford, was controlled at Islip Bridge by a brigade of cavalry under the command of the Earl of Northampton comprising his own, the Queen's, Wilmot's and Palmer's regiments of horse. On the 24th Cromwell defeated them in what was the first action of the New Model Army. It was claimed that at least 39 Royalists were killed in the encounter, with 500 horses and 200 prisoners taken, while about 50 Royalist horse fled from Islip to Blechingdon, which was the next obstacle to Cromwell's advance. In the meantime a troop of Oxford horse were sent out to defend Gosford Bridge, which controlled the main road back to the city, and later that night they were supported by some

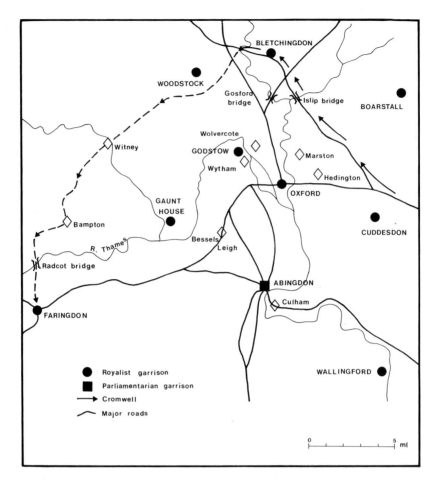

Fig. 23. Cromwell's actions around Oxford in April 1645.

commanded musketeers from Oxford and Colonel Palmer's regiment of horse, who had already been beaten at Islip.[5]

Bletchingdon was one of the largest houses in Oxfordshire, for in 1665 it is recorded as having 30 hearths, but the building one sees today is a Palladian villa, remodelled in the early 18th century. Colonel Widebanke's garrison, which comprised 200 foot, had no works to defend the house and provisions for only two or three days. Cromwell commanded their surrender, deceiving the defenders into thinking he had infantry who were ready to fall on when in reality he had only cavalry. In the early hours of the morning of Friday the 25th, Widebanke surrendered without a shot having been fired. In the garrison Cromwell took 200-300 muskets, 70 horses and other supplies which were all sent to Aylesbury. For a garrison defending the environs of Oxford to surrender without a fight, and to just a body of horse, was not something that the Royalist high command could countenance. As an example to the other garrisons in the area, Widebanke was sentenced to death and his senior officers debarred from bearing arms again. Although initially reprieved, he was shot a week later.[6]

On the morning of Saturday 26th units of cavalry from Faringdon and a troop of horse from Wallingford as well as the Oxford horse were all drawn out, but by then the Parliamentarians had gone.[7] That morning, as Cromwell marched on towards Witney, Colonel Fiennes' regiment was sent out to skirmish with the Royalists, an action in which he supposedly took 150 horse, 3 colonels and 40 foot.[8] Later in the day, at Bampton Bush, Cromwell dealt with a body of some 350 foot under Colonel Vaughan, who had been sent to hold Radcot Bridge which controlled the road from Witney to Faringdon. At seven that evening the Queen's troop of the lifeguard were also beaten up, with 6 men and 60 horse taken, all the day's prisoners being dispatched to Abingdon, the nearest Parliamentarian garrison.[9] Then on Sunday Colonel Lisle's regiment of foot, under Lieutenant Colonel Littleton, were pursued and 200 of his 350 men were said to have been taken or killed.[10] Later in the day yet more horse and foot were drawn out of Oxford to meet the continuing threat.

Though the losses were undoubtedly exaggerated the actions were disrupting Royalist preparations. But now Cromwell took on a more difficult challenge, Faringdon castle, which controlled the road from Oxford to Bristol. At this time the garrison was still under the command of Colonel Lisle although in May he would leave with his regiment to join the Royalist army and be replaced by Colonel Rawdon.[11] No other garrison was likely to fall as easily as Bletchingdon, to just a party of horse, and so Cromwell called up infantry support from Abingdon which was just 13 miles away. In all some 500-600 men, which included regiments formerly in the Eastern Association but now part of the New Model, marched up to support the attack on Faringdon. At about three in the morning of the 30th April they assaulted the defences but 'were repuls'd with the loss of fourteen Men kill'd, and Capt.Canon (who rear'd the first Scaling-Ladder and ascended himself) taken Prisoner, with an Ensign, and eight common Soldiers and divers Wounded.'[12] Twice they assaulted the castle and twice they were repulsed 'with great losse'.[13] They remained there for the next few days but on the 3rd May, having news that Goring was coming to relieve the garrison, Cromwell raised the siege.[14] Goring seized Radcot Bridge and a party of horse which Cromwell had sent out under Major Bethel to establish the enemy positions was caught in a skirmish and came off with some loss.[15] Though they were forced to retire, Luke could still write with some confidence in early May that 'Cromwell has almost frightened them out of their wits at Oxford by killing and taking multitudes.'[16] He had also cleared the area of heavy draught horses, which had not yet been brought into Oxford because there were insufficient resources within the defences to maintain them.[17] This was an important blow because the King desperately needed them to transport his artillery and baggage train. However on the 4th May Prince Rupert and Prince Maurice arrived at Oxford, followed the next day by Goring.[18] The King now had a sufficiently large body of cavalry to allow his army to take the field. For almost a fortnight Cromwell had disrupted their preparations, buying time while the New Model was being completed, but he could now no longer delay their departure.

The mistakes in the management of previous campaigns now began to be repeated in 1645, removing any advantage that had been gained by the delays to the Royalist departure. This is not surprising because Fairfax was receiving detailed instructions from the Committee of Both Kingdoms in London throughout May and early June.[19] It placed him in an almost impossible situation because the war was being run by a committee which was at times over a hundred miles from the real action, and on which the discredited former commanders Essex and Manchester were prominent members. Ironically therefore, despite the dramatic political victories of the preceding winter, the same men were in charge of the new campaign as had been in command in previous years. Despite having created a single new army capable of winning the war, the Committee of Both Kingdoms were intent upon fighting on all fronts by fragmenting that army. What Fairfax and Cromwell wanted was to unite all their forces and confront the enemy in one great battle which would decide the war, but in the Committee of Both Kingdoms the debate on the 28th April centred around whether Oxford or Taunton should be the first objective. Fairfax was ordered, against his better judgement, to march to the relief of Taunton, which was in desperate straights and expected to fall within a few days.[20] He travelled from Windsor to Reading on the 30th and then, leaving some troops under Cromwell and Browne to secure Oxford, Fairfax marched with 9000 men into the South West.[21] Yet, by the 8th May, when Fairfax had reached Blandford, the Committee decided that he should return north now that the Royalist army had taken the field. He was to send just 3000 foot and 1500 horse to the relief of Taunton. This brigade was commanded by Colonel Weldon and comprised infantry from his own, Fortescue's, Floyd's and Ingoldsby's regiments, accompanied by the horse from Graves's regiment, and supported by troops from the local garrisons. In a typical move, Fairfax set out towards Dorchester with the whole army only then turning away with the main body to return to Oxford. The Royalists, thinking the whole army was advancing to Taunton, raised the siege.[22] Though the objective had been achieved, this great new army had been fragmented into three separate bodies. Had the Royalists struck with force at any one of these they might have severely weakened the whole Parliamentarian war effort. Fairfax's force as it marched northward once more was particularly vulnerable because he had so few cavalry. Moreover, when Fairfax finally arrived at Oxford on the 22nd, the 190 mile round trip would have taken a great toll on the army through desertion and simple exhaustion. While the resources of the New Model were thus diverted and divided, there was no force of sufficient size anywhere in the Midlands capable of challenging the Royalist army.

The King's objective for the opening of the campaign was for the troops from Oxford to link up with those of Rupert and Prince Maurice from Hereford and Worcester and then to march north to relieve Chester and Pontefract. The continuing success of Montrose in Scotland, with his victory on the 9th May at Auldearn, would further raise the Royalist spirits as they marched, for the Scottish army might now have to withdraw from England completely.[23] The King also had great hopes that a peace treaty could be reached in Ireland which would release large numbers of troops to reinforce his army in England, just as they had during the winter of 1643-4. Not surprisingly perhaps, the court astrologer also predicted a Royalist victory.[24] The intelligence which Luke received from Oxford in the days before the Royalists marched suggested that 'though they intend to plunder the country yet till they had routed our army they would not venture upon any place.'[25] This may have been their intention, but within three weeks their strategy would have changed dramatically.

In the Welsh Marches Rupert's forces were nearing completion. The Parliamentarians saw that 'The princes army is the maine rest of the Kings affaires, which they strengthen daily, by impressing the countrey, taking lesser brigades, and draining the garrisons.'[26] Part of Goring's army had crossed the Severn to join them at Hereford and after a short while they were ready to march. In Oxford munitions were issued from the Magazine in New College while from the artillery park, in the close behind Magdalen College, the King drew out just 14 instead of the intended 20 guns. The twelve-pounders and two six-pounders had to be left behind and only eight of the intended fourteen boats could be taken because there were simply not enough horses to pull them. The Royalist artillery train in 1645 therefore comprised 8 six-pounders and 2 demi-culverin (firing a 9-10 lb ball), which were the field pieces, and 2 whole culverin (15-16 lb) and 2 demi-cannon (27-30 lb), the siege pieces. Though smaller than in 1644 the train was at least somewhat more mobile and it was certainly well supplied. Although there had been delays in the arrival of supplies from Worcester, it was mainly thanks to Cromwell's action over the previous fortnight that the Royalist army began the campaign not just later but also weaker than had been intended. In early June the King would try to arrange for the other guns to be brought up to the army, but they would not arrive by the 14th June. However, the weakness of the train of artillery did not ultimately contribute to the Royalist defeat in the forthcoming battle.[27]

When Fairfax marched into the South West he had left Cromwell around Oxford with his horse and dragoons together with four regiments of foot under Major General Browne.[28] Although he did not have a commission in the New Model, Cromwell had under his command a large proportion of the new army, mainly the Eastern Association troops which he had been instrumental in raising and training over the last two years. In many ways this was already Cromwell's army, for in both its politics and its religion this was the nucleus of the radical force that would dominate the next fifteen years of British history. In addition to the New Model infantry he also appears to have had some soldiers from local garrisons, including at least one company from Newport Pagnell.[29] His instructions were to follow the progress of the King's army and so when the King set out for Woodstock on the 7th May with only the lifeguard of horse, the Oxford infantry and the train, Cromwell began to follow.[30] At Woodstock the King was joined by Goring with a large body of cavalry to keep Cromwell's horse from attacking the rear of the army. On the 8th there was an alarm at one o'clock and later that morning, near Burford, the Parliamentarians took one Royalist colour but in response Goring captured forty of Cromwell's horse including, they claimed, two colonels. The news reached the King at daybreak as he marched out of Woodstock Park, now with the support of further cavalry under the Earl of Northampton whose regiment had been quartered over winter around Banbury.[31] The force comprised fourteen pieces of artillery, eight boats on carriages and the ammunition, part of the Lifeguard in the vanguard and then Sir Thomas Dalyson's and Northampton's regiments at the rear.[32] As the Royalists marched north, Colonel Purefoy's small garrison at Compton Wynyates also took up the challenge, engaging them in several minor cavalry skirmishes. On the 7th near Stow he took various prisoners including Rupert's gunsmith and four of his lifeguard, as well as Prince Maurice's surgeon, head cook and farrier. Then on the 9th Purefoy attacked the rear of the Royalist army at Chipping Camden, killing 14 and wounding some others.[33]

On the 8th May on Bradford Down there was a rendezvous where the King was joined by the two Princes and by Langdale with the Northern horse, making in all 3000 foot and 4000 horse.[34] That evening, a few miles to the west at Stow on the Wold, the Council of War considered the strategy for the new campaign. Rupert argued for a march to relieve Chester and Pontefract and then presumably to clear the North and avenge the defeat at Marston Moor. Until he had a secure northern base he did not want to challenge the New Model. In contrast, Digby and Goring argued for a rapid engagement with Fairfax's army. In typical fashion the King tried to follow both courses at once by splitting his army, sending Goring into the South West to deal with Fairfax while the rest of his troops were to march north to relieve Chester.[35] Given his disagreements with Goring, who was becoming increasingly unreliable with phases of inactivity reinforced by bouts of drunkenness, Rupert probably acquiesced simply to be rid of him and the potential for conflict within the Royalist army. This is of course if Rupert really had any say in the matter, or in any other key decisions of the campaign, because it has been argued that the King's devious personality meant he could not cope with debate in a large, semi-formal forum and that he therefore excluded the whole area of strategy from the debate of his Councils of War. Whether there was genuine debate or not, in this case the King had made a disastrous decision for Goring's horse would be sorely missed at Naseby.[36]

While Rupert had marched with his cavalry and a few foot to help bring off the King's forces from Oxford, Sir Jacob Astley had marched from Hereford and lay between Worcester and Bewdley with the rest of the infantry.[37] At Evesham on the 9th the King was joined by Astley with 3300 foot and by Colonel Bard, governor of Chipping Camden, with his 300 foot.[38] Chipping Camden house, which had been Bard's garrison and which Symonds thought 'so faire', was wantonly burned. According to Slingsby:

> 'Least ye enemy should make use of yt for a garison, when we had left it, being so near Evesham, ye prince likewise command'd it to be burnt; wch I set on a light fire before we march'd off. A house as my Ld Cambden says yt had £30,000 in building and furniture.'[39]

It is surprising, given his antipathy towards Rupert, that Clarendon did not make anything of the fact that it was Rupert who ordered the destruction. This was however just one of many houses which the King's forces destroyed between Oxford and Bristol for fear that they might be garrisoned by Parliament while the field army was away in the North.[40] The damaging effect of Parliament's seizure of Abingdon in the previous summer meant that Rupert would take no chances this year. At Evesham the army was also joined by reinforcements from Worcester comprising the regiment of foot which had been under the command of the late Sir Gilbert Gerard and 150 horse under Sandys.[41] This would have made an army of some 11000 troops, but by now of course Goring had left with his 3000 horse and dragoons.[42]

On the 10th the army continued northward taking many of the Evesham troops with them, a weakening of the garrison that they would later regret.[43] The King quartered at Inkborough Magna that night and then on the 11th there was a rendezvous of the whole army as they marched to Droitwich.[44] In addition to stripping troops from the area as they marched north they were also able to take in the supplies they needed, because provisioning had apparently been planned in advance with the sort of military precision one would expect from Rupert. The warrants issued to High Constables in Worcestershire in early April had presumably enabled large quantities of supplies to be laid in or made ready for transport to the army by carts, teams and carters requisitioned for the purpose.[45] On the 14th the King went to Cofton Hall while Rupert laid siege to Hawksley House, a Parliamentarian garrison of just 100 men. Astley's tertia of foot made the approaches and:

> 'in a short time they carry their Line close by ye Moat Side (for it was moat'd about) and by trenches draws away ye Water; which ye beseig'd perceiving after we had made a shot or two, they call for a parley; and at last were sain to yeild ye house, their arms, and ymselves prisoners, wth out any loss great either of men, or time...'[46]

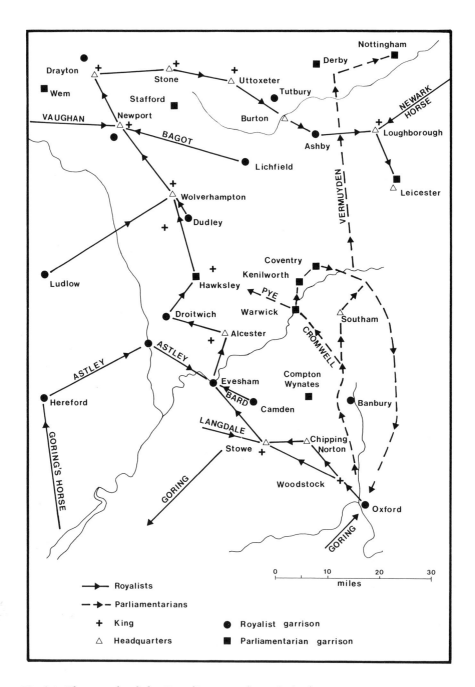

Fig.24. The march of the Royalist army from Oxford to Leicester in May 1645, followed first of all by Cromwell's large detachment from the New Model and then shadowed by a smaller brigade under Vermuyden. As the Royalist army marched north it was strengthened with cavalry and infantry from various garrisons in the region.

After its capture the house was pillaged then fired, as was nearby Frankley Hall the next day.[47] There were apparently other minor actions as they marched north, as for example when the Parliamentarian Shrewsbury horse were caught in a skirmish near Wenlock.[48] Whether such actions had a strategic purpose or were primarily intended simply to give the troops experience of real action is unclear.

After the skirmish with Goring's cavalry, Cromwell and Browne had left the Woodstock area on the 11th May, marching north with some 7000 horse, flanking the King's army but at least 15 or 20 miles to the east. The Royalist intelligence was that Cromwell intended to draw out troops from the garrisons in the region and pursue the King to Chester, but his instructions from the Committee of Both Kingdoms were to follow in order to protect the Association and then to join with the Scottish and Northern forces. He was not to engage the King beforehand unless he had a significant advantage.[49] Skirting Banbury on the 13th May they marched north along the Warwick road, drawing provisions from the villages north of Banbury, including Avon Dassett, Fenny Compton and Warmington. As they marched Cromwell will have sent out scouts to cover the advance and when he quartered his troops small parties of horse, each of about a dozen men, seem to have been sent forward to various other villages to provide warning in case the Royalists made an approach. For example, while at Warmington it would appear that a 'court of guard' was established two miles to the west at Ratley and another three miles to the north at Northend. Later, when they reached Southam, a court of guard was similarly established at Ufton, about two miles to the west on the Warwick road. Other detachments at Kineton and Chadshunt seem to have maintained a guard on the Stratford road at Combrooke.[50] This was good military practice, as defined in the manuals, and was undoubtedly followed by the other commanders during the campaign, though the evidence which could show this is generally lacking.

On the 14th, the day Hawksley House was taken, Cromwell's army had reached Warwick, from where Colonel Pye was dispatched with a party of 1500 horse towards the enemy, to gain intelligence and, if appropriate, to harry them as they marched. Cromwell remained at Warwick on the 15th, where other troops from Northampton, Newport and Aylesbury had also begun to assemble. Browne had already established the army headquarters further east in the small town of Southam and on the 16th the rest of the army moved there.[51] The cavalry were dispersed in surrounding villages, such as Marton and Long Itchington, mainly perhaps because of the need for large quantities of grass for their horses, particularly as the troops were to remain in the area for the next four or five days. The infantry were at or near the headquarters and so the villages in the adjacent Hundreds, including Priors Hardwick and Wolfhampcote, were required to send in supplies to Southam on the 14th and 15th May.[52]

Browne argued that it was time to retreat until Fairfax brought up the rest of the New Model because, following the rendezvous at Stow and Evesham, the King's army was now so strong that it would be unwise to engage them. According to Luke there were only 8000 Parliamentarian troops facing a Royalist force said to number some 12000, besides those that Goring or Gerard might bring up to them. Even if Cromwell could draw out yet more men from the local garrisons he could not afford a full blown battle. However, newspaper reports and even correspondence between Major Bridges at Warwick and Sir Samuel Luke make clear that a major battle was exactly what was expected. Even Cromwell believed that Fairfax would soon join him and that they would then be able to pursue and engage the King.[53] Sir William Brereton, who was still besieging Chester and therefore very vulnerable as the King's army approached, suggested that the Royalists were playing into Parliament's hands and that if Cromwell was to quickly join with the Northern army and the Scots then they could defeat the King before his army was grown too large. It was not to be. The Committee of Both Kingdoms had debated whether Fairfax should besiege Oxford or follow the King and the former had been resolved upon. It was felt that Parliament already had a great Scottish army in its pay in the North which, together with the forces in Cheshire, Derbyshire, Nottinghamshire and the other northern counties, could on their own deal with the Royalist threat.[54] Cromwell was instructed that if the Royalist army marched any further north then he was to return southward to garrison Bletchingdon and join Fairfax in besieging the Royalist capital.[55] Cromwell wrote to Brereton that 'no man is more troubled (that I cannot advance to the assistance of friends) than myself. I must obey commands...', though whether he really wished to engage the King without the rest of the New Model, even with other support, is unclear.[56] Because the Scottish army was weak in cavalry, Cromwell was however instructed to dispatch Vermuyden with 2000 horse and 400 dragoons, who were quartered near Rugby, to join the Scots in Derbyshire.[57] The old commanders in the Committee of Both Kingdoms in London were matching the King in their inability to take decisive action, continuing to divide their forces and pursuing several different objectives at once, in the North, the South West and now at Oxford. The great new army which had been created to rapidly end the war had now been split into four separate divisions! So, Vermuyden set out with his own, Rich's, Pye's and Fiennes' regiments of horse and Okey's dragoons to rendezvous with the Scots, although if the King altered his course and marched into Yorkshire then Vermuyden had the authority to follow.[58] The prospect of the great battle that so many had expected now receded from view, at least for the moment.

While at Cofton Hall the King was joined by yet more troops, from the Hereford, Ludlow and Dudley garrisons.[59] On the 15th, after burning the Hall, he moved on to the old moated manor house of Himley Hall and the next day to Bushbury, while Rupert had his headquarters at Wolverhampton. On the 17th they reached Newport, where they were joined by Vaughan's 400 horse from Shrawardine, a garrison near Shrewsbury, and by Colonel Bagot who had brought 300 foot and 200 horse from Lichfield.[60] The local Parliamentarian garrisons were still harrying the army as it marched, but with little effect because Charles wrote from Chetwyne that night, 'we are (God be thanked) all well and in hart, the Rebelles having twyce offered to beate up some of our quarters, but wth losse to themselves.'[61] On the 20th they continued north to Market Drayton, where the army rested for a day. Intending to make the most of their opportunities, that night Langdale set out with a party of horse and foot to surprise Wem, a nearby Parliamentarian garrison of just 150 men, but he arrived too late to achieve his objective. It was while they were at Market Drayton that Lord Byron, governor of Chester, came to the army with a party of horse bringing news that the siege of his garrison had been raised.[62] Brereton had had no alternative but to withdraw because the Scottish army had not advanced to challenge the King. Instead, due to the growing threat posed by Montrose's victories in the Highlands and probably also because they did not want to face the Royalist army alone, the Scots had withdrawn to Westmorland. Brereton had intelligence of the King's approach with some 14000 - 15000 men and he knew that without the support of the Scots he could not afford to be caught between Chester and such a formidable force.[63]

On hearing of the relief of Chester the Royalist army turned eastward. The King had not yet made up his mind where he would march after Chester, but Pontefract and Scarborough were both hard pressed by besieging Parliamentarian forces.[64] To reach the area he could march to the south of the Parliamentarian controlled areas of Derby and Nottingham, via the Royalist enclave around Ashby and Lichfield and then across to the garrison at Newark, where he could detach the Newark horse to strengthen his cavalry. At this time Baillie, who was with the Scottish army, recorded in his journal: 'The King is turning his head southward, to my great joy; for I was much afraid, that the north of England should have joined with him, and fallen first on our army, and then on Scotland.'[65] Even so, the Scots were not going to take any chances, for the King could still turn north once more and march into Yorkshire, so they moved south very slowly. They would wait and see what happened to the New Model Army first.[66]

But where was the New Model while these events were unfolding, and why did Fairfax not act to counter the Royalist threat? On his return from the South West, Fairfax had received instructions from the Committee of Both Kingdoms to lay close siege to the Royalist capital at Oxford. It seems that they had received some very dubious intelligence that Oxford could be taken by treachery and, as the Lords were informed on the 17th May, the Commons 'out of a desire to put an end to this miserable war, do think it fit that siege be laid to the City of Oxford, for the taking it, it being the centre of our troubles.'[67] William Legge had continued recruiting and strengthening the fortifications of the Royalist capital throughout May. It was inevitable that he

would continue to prepare for the siege and so, in order to restrict his freedom
of action, on the 17th May the Committee had instructed Fairfax and
Cromwell to rapidly send up some horse to Oxford to 'hinder the carrying in
of Provision to Oxford, and the Burning and Spoiling of the Country.'[68]
Cromwell acted immediately, ordering a night-time march of troops from
beyond Coventry towards Daventry and, following a rendezvous on Dunsmore
Heath, moving south to Brackley on the 21st, reaching Marston near Oxford
on the 22nd.[69] Both commanders obeyed their orders but they had little doubt
as to the futility of the action. As Fairfax wrote in early June, just before the
siege was raised:

> 'I am very sorry we should spend our time unprofitably before a town, whilst
> the King hath time to strengthen himself, and by terror to force obedience of all
> places where he comes; ..... It is the earnest desire of this army to follow the
> King, but the endeavours of others to prevent it hath so much prevailed.'[70]

The return to Oxford had at least brought a substantial part of the New Model
back together but the city was well garrisoned and, having spent more than
£30000 on its defences, was very heavily fortified. With a major Royalist
army in the field unopposed, the idea of a long drawn out siege was quite
inappropriate.[71] The Scots, though they might not themselves wish to
challenge the Royalist army, could also see the absurdity of the situation and
conveyed their views to London, the Earl of Calander writing on the 18th
May to the Scotch Commissioners in the capital:

> 'when a puissant enemy is raging through the kingdom acquiring strength and
> subduing whole counties, that it is not reasonable to employ armies for the
> reducing of towns and lieing down before strengths, but that it were much better
> for the security of the kingdoms and putting an end to our troubles to pursue the
> enemy in the field.'[72]

Fairfax knew only too well how the campaigning season would rapidly take
its toll on the New Model, just as it had on the Eastern Association army the
previous summer. The greatest threat would be sickness and desertion,
problems which would increase as difficulties inevitably arose over pay and
provisions and especially once the weather began to deteriorate later in the
year, indeed Fairfax had already seen large scale desertion begin as a result
of the abortive march into the South West.[73] He knew that the wisest course
of action was to concentrate all his forces and challenge the King in battle at
the very earliest opportunity, before the strain began to tell on his own army.
The sooner the battle came then the longer he would have to exploit the
success before the campaigning season was over. However, for the moment
Fairfax was held back by the detailed instructions he was being given by the
Committee of Both Kingdoms in London.

As Fairfax approached Oxford from the south, Captain Gardiner was sent

Fig. 25. The Siege of Oxford as depicted by Jan de Wyck. (Et Archive)

out from the city with a party of horse and foot to skirmish with the
Parliamentarian cavalry but was repulsed with the loss of 200 foot, who were
taken as prisoners to Abingdon [74] On the 22nd Fairfax reached Marston,
which was to be his headquarters during the siege.[75] Over the following days
they built a breastwork on the east side of the river Cherwell and a bridge
over the river near Marston to enable communications between the besieging
forces on the east and west sides of the city. Cromwell and Browne took
quarters on the west side of the river, at Wytham and Wolvercote, while four
regiments and thirteen carriages were stationed at the new bridge.[76] The city
was now beleaguered on all sides. In response the Royalists flooded the
meadows to hinder the Parliamentarian approach to the town and fired houses
in the suburbs to give a clear field of fire from the defences.[77] Rupert had
given the governor of Oxford authority over all the surrounding lesser
garrisons, except Banbury, with instructions that they were to aid him in
whatever was required for the protection of the city.[78] So, on the 23rd, in
order to reinforce the defence of the city itself, he ordered the garrison at
Godstow House to retreat to Oxford. They fired the house but they were not
quick enough, for a party from Sheffield's regiment arrived in time to put out
the fire and recover the powder and ammunition that had been left there, even
capturing the governor and some of his men as they fled.[79] The other Royalist
garrisons remained in place and so, because it was essential for the besieging
force to be secure from attack from the rear, on the 24th May Fairfax went
to view Boarstall House and left a party there to face the garrison.[80]

*Fig.26. The ruins of Godstow, a minor Royalist garrison two miles north of Oxford,
taken by the New Model in May 1645.*

The Committee in London may have ordered the siege of Oxford, but they had failed to put the necessary preparations in hand and it was not until the 23rd that Parliament ordered the necessary equipment and supplies. There were two whole culverin and one demi-cannon ready at Northampton, which appears to have served as a Parliamentarian supply depot for the region, and one of each at Windsor, while the 'pocket pistol' at Cambridge was also to be requisitioned. The other supplies they ordered included 1500 spades and shovels, 500 pickaxes, 200 scaling ladders, 500 barrels of powder, 40 tons of match, 30 tons of bullet, 600 grenado shells, 1000 hand grenades, 50 tons of round shot and 20 carriages for provisions. The overall cost was more than £6000.[81] There was even a shortage of military engineers to oversee the construction of the siegeworks and so recruitment enquiries had to be made in Holland.[82] It was to take more than a fortnight before the artillery and other essential equipment arrived, by which time the New Model had already been instructed to abandon the siege. As a result Fairfax spent his time quite unprofitably, unable to achieve anything apart from blocking up the city and stopping them taking in any provisions.[83]

Fig. 27. An exceptionally large siege piece called Queen Elizabeth's Pocket Pistol, seen here on a 19th century carriage. Such pieces could be very effective at breaching garrison defences. This gun is said to have been captured by the Royalists at Lostwithiel but a siege piece called the Pocket Pistol was called up from Cambridge for the siege of Oxford, a gun previously known as the Queen's Pocket Pistol when captured in the North by the Association army in 1644.[84]

Many could see the futility of the whole enterprise. Luke wrote, 'Sir Thomas Fairfax is before Oxford with such a strength as is not so considerable as I could wish for such a work, the enemy in the out-garrisons being very bold and no whit daunted.'[85] To maintain the siege it was necessary to call in troops from various places in the region and thus weakening local garrisons, some of which were already known to be in a poor state and all of which were about to find themselves in the front line. At least 700 men were drawn in from the main garrisons in the region, including part of Colonel

Martin's regiment from Aylesbury which was at the siege from 24th May to 14th June 1645, about 300 more from Newport Pagnell and 400 from Northampton, while as late as the 31st May Parliament was still ordering the assembly of troops for the siege from Kent, Suffolk, Middlesex and Bedfordshire.[86] The Committee of Both Kingdoms had deployed the New Model around Oxford and left the centre of England exposed without an army to face the King, intending that the Scots and the northern forces tackle that threat. This was a mistake that had been made in previous years, trying to command forces to work together in a coordinated strategy when those forces lacked the will to cooperate. Entering the south east Midlands the Royalist field army completely tipped the balance of power, as they had in late 1643. The local forces were powerless to halt the Royalist advance and had to retreat behind their defences. The response of the Committee of Both Kingdoms was once more too little and too late. As the King entered Staffordshire Parliament was concerned for the safety of the county town and ordered that the troops there should not be called away to any other service.[87] By the 24th it was still uncertain where the King was marching and so Vermuyden was told to wait near Nottingham and to unite his horse and dragoons with those of Lord Fairfax, Sir John Gell, Colonel Rossiter and Colonel Hutchinson. Although they could in theory muster about 4000 horse and dragoons, this was no match for the whole Royalist army and they could do little more than watch as the King marched through the Midlands unopposed. Indeed, as Hutchinson made clear, the local forces were actually in no state to assist because by the 24th the Derby and Lincoln horse had not yet arrived while those from Nottingham were 'in such ill case to march for want of pay, that they will rather mutiny than obey commands.'[88]

Right up to the 31st May the Committee in London continued to issue instructions for the troops in Lancashire, Cheshire, Derbyshire, Nottinghamshire, Lincolnshire, Staffordshire and Yorkshire to rendezvous with the Scottish army and to interpose themselves between York and the King in case he should march north.[89] In fact Parliament's strategy of leaving the Scots to deal with the Royalist army had collapsed and the results would be disastrous, with events which at the time seemed to have tipped the whole balance of the war. By the 29th Vermuyden was at Grantham, keeping at a safe distance from the Royalist army but protecting the Association and ready to take whatever advantages he could against the King.[90] Meanwhile, by the 25th the Royalist army had reached the area controlled by Lord Loughborough. The rendezvous was on Eggington Heath after which the King stayed that and the following night at the Tutbury garrison while the headquarters were nearby at Burton on Trent. Now Brereton's intelligence was indicating 10000-12000 Royalist troops and by the 29th this would be revised down again to 8000 although it was expected that 1500 horse would join the army from Newark.[91] While at Burton on Trent, Rupert marched to Barton and reviewed the Parliamentarian garrison there but he 'misliked their complexion' and decided not to attack, probably because there were more important objectives in mind.[92] However, whereas the Parliamentarian infantry could not venture beyond their defences, where they remained in expectation of a Royalist attack, the horse could at least take the field to gain intelligence and harry the Royalists in their quarters. So for example, while the army was at Burton, some of the Derby horse gave Colonel Cary's quarters an alarm and the Barton horse also skirmished with the Royalists. The action seems to have had the desired effect because it was reported from Derby that 'we are every day forth with our regiment and force them to keep close.'[93]

Charles was at Tutbury when the news arrived of the threat to Oxford. It was expected and in some senses perhaps even wished for: 'Oxford was known to be in so good a condition that the loss of it could not be in any degree apprehended, and nothing could more reasonably have been wished than that Fayrefax should be thoroughly engaged before it.'[94] A Council of War was held at Burton, where it was discussed whether to march on the north or the south side of the Trent.[95] As Slingsby reported:

'being once come into ye Northside of Trent, our Northern horse chiefly were made glad wth hope yt we should still have march'd Northward, yet they were not much inquisitive, and hitherto shew'd a mind indifferent wt way they went so they follow'd their General...'[96]

Rupert also still wished to march north to relieve the beleaguered garrisons and in order to recruit in Yorkshire amongst the men who had fought in the Earl of Newcastle's army in 1644. According to intelligence receieved by Brereton, the Yorkshire gentry had promised that 8000 men would join the King's army if it marched northward.[97] Once strengthened they could then meet the Scottish threat, while the New Model were busy around Oxford. On the other side it was argued that Oxford might need to be relieved and so the army should not march into the North. Rupert proposed that, if this was to be the objective, then rather than relieve Oxford directly it was better simply to ensure that Fairfax drew away from the city and this could be achieved if the King was 'to fall upon some place posessed by Parliament'.[98] The decision was yet another compromise. The next day Digby advised Nicholas, the other Secretary of State who had remained in Oxford, that it was considered best if they did not have to relieve the city for some weeks and he requested that Nicholas did not call them back to Oxford unless it was absolutely essential. In the meantime they would march towards Leicester, 'the best way we can take in case we are to march immediately unto you.'[99] The King's decision may have been influenced by the letters written by Culpepper to Digby on the 24th, 25th and 26th May. When Charles had left Oxford he had promised to return to the city to relieve it as soon as Nicholas and the governor informed him that they could hold out no longer.[100] Culpepper now urged a speedy relief because the loss of the city would be as destructive to the Royalist cause as the loss of a battle. However, he did not expect Oxford to fall through lack of provisions, nor did he fear that the New Model had the ability to storm the city. It was because of 'the temper of those within the town, the disaffection of the townsmen, the neccessities of the soldiers, and the vast importance of the place and persons within the town....'. This seems to mirror the view in Parliament that there was the possibility of Oxford being yielded to Fairfax by treachery.[101]

The King had expected that when they reached Ashby they would be joined by Gerard and by the Newark horse, while on the 19th Rupert sent orders to Goring for him to march out of the South West with at least 3500 horse and all of Goring's own and Grenvile's foot, without waiting for the new levies.[102] Once joined by these troops the King would be outnumbered only in ordnance, and even this could be remedied because it was ordered that the rest of the artillery train be made ready at Oxford for Goring, who was instructed to bring it up to the army as he marched north. Given the antipathy between Goring and Rupert, the letter was accompanied by one from Lord Digby confirming that the instructions to:

> 'march presently with all strength you can make to Market Harborough in Leicestershire are sent you by the unanimous advice of all here as a thing most absolutely necessary to our preservation, the Rebels setting their whole rest upon encountering and distressing this army, where the King's person is, as will appear to you by their particular forces drawn this way whereof I have given an account..... If their aims had been at the West all things had been laid aside to succour you and now vice versa you must do the like. For God's sake use diligence and come as strong as you can. In my conscience it will be the last blow in the business. Bring with you what powder and match you can possibly, as it is neccessary that your design be kept very secret, and that it may be understood that it is for Surrey and Sussex.'[103]

With such reinforcements they could feel confident about meeting the New Model in battle but without them Rupert knew their situation would be impossible. Culpepper, with the support of Goring, wrote that to fight 'in my opinion (if his Majesty have joined with him Goring and Gerard), is not to be declined; a battle we must have, and I know not how it can be struck upon better terms...' and if Fairfax were to retreat then the whole of the East would be open to the King.[104] It was Digby's view that 'ere one month be over we shall have a battle of all for all. ..... If we can be so happy as that [Goring] comes in time, we shall infallibly crush them between us.' Therefore Rupert, according to Clarendon, 'despising the New Noddle, as it was called, because most of the old Officers were either omitted by the Parliament, or had quitted their Commands in the Army, judging himself Master of the Field, marched towards Leicester...'[105]

The garrisons which had been faced or taken by the Royalist army in its advance towards Chester were minor places of no great strategic significance but their next target was a very different matter. The decision to march on Leicester was not taken at random. The King had been there in July 1642 but it was Rupert who in September had been rebuffed by the town in his high handed threats to extort money at the beginning of the war, action which had been disowned by the King.[106] It has been suggested by Everitt that the attack on Leicester may have been prompted by a wish to avenge this affront, but this cannot have been a serious consideration. At Burton they will have been fully briefed by Lord Loughborough as to the condition of the Parliamentarian forces in the region. As Luke commented at the time, 'It is thought his Majesty would not have marched so far out of his way but that he had good assurance that he should make no long work of it.'[107] Indeed Skipwith, at whose house Charles stopped just before the siege, later claimed that the King had approached Leicester because of 'the certain intelligence that he had of the weakness of that Committee, and their want of experience in military affairs.'[108] Lord Loughborough had advised Rupert in 1643 as to the inadequacy of the town's defences and the situation had still not significantly altered by 1645. A few weeks earlier Lord Loughborough had already organised an abortive plot to take the town by deception but now the King would be able to exploit Leicester's weakness to good effect because of the absence of a Parliamentarian army nearby.[109] The town was in an important strategic location and its capture would link the Royalist enclaves of Newark and Ashby to create a powerful counterbalance to the growing Parliamentarian power in the region. With the massive forces at his disposal the King could complete in a few days what Lord Loughborough had been trying to achieve throughout the war, but the decision was however guided primarily by short term needs. The capture of Leicester would encourage the New Model to raise their siege of Oxford and would provide control of a Parliamentarian area which could be stripped of supplies to relieve the city.[110]

Even at this late date the Parliamentarians still considered it more likely that the Royalist army would advance into Yorkshire, but as they marched unopposed through the Midlands the Committee of Both Kingdoms finally began to take steps to counter what now appeared to be a threat against the heartland of their power, the Eastern Association. As Brereton wrote on the 29th May, 'I fear Prince Rupert may rather aim at some counties in the Association that may lie convenient, being able to make little opposition and to yield great benefit to the soldiers.'[111] On the 26th May the Committee ordered Cromwell to leave the siege of Oxford with just three troops of horse and march immediately to the Isle of Ely, where he was to be joined by the Cambridge forces, and at the same time Vermuyden was also called back towards the Association.[112] Instructions immediately went out to draw forces into the Midland garrisons, including troops from Gloucester which were to move up to Evesham and others from Stafford to march down to Coventry. Hertfordshire forces were also to come up to Aylesbury to cover for garrison troops sent forward from there towards Oxford. For Leicester however the

Committee of Both Kingdoms had little constructive support and whatever they might order now was already too late.[113]

The Royalist army marched south eastward on the 27th into Leicestershire to Lord Loughborough's headquarters at Ashby and then the next day through Coleorton, where the Hall was held by a small Parliamentarian force.[114] The 350 soldiers in the garrison must have remained behind their defences in great fear as this massive army marched by, but they denied Lord Loughborough's demand for their surrender and sallied forth to attack the rear of the Royalist army as it marched on.[115] The King had far greater concerns. Such small garrisons could be dealt with after the fall of Leicester and so the army marched on to the town of Loughborough while the King himself went to nearby Cotes.[116] He stopped the night at the house of Henry Skipwith, a strong Royalist supporter who had been High Sheriff of the county in 1636 and later a Commissioner of Array. Skipwith entertained the King nobly, for which support he would later be fined to the value of £1114 by the Parliamentary sequestrators, but for the moment the King's supporters in and around Leicester must have felt very confident.[117] About this time the Royalist army was estimated at 8000 horse and foot, but they had also been joined by some of Lord Loughborough's troops and, while at Cotes, they were reinforced by 1200 horse under Sir Richard Willis, governor of Newark.[118] To support the army, demands for money were already being made of the gentry in Leicestershire, with loans of £40 being required from several of the more wealthy residents in Loughborough.[119] In less civilised fashion the plundering of the county was also begun, a process which would continue unabated until the destruction of the King's army on the 14th June.[120]

Preparations were now begun for the siege of Leicester. On the 28th Langdale had been sent with the Northern horse, whose strength was estimated at about 1400, to lie between Coventry and Leicester 'to hinder provisions, or any of ye Country people, for coming into Leister.' They marched to within four miles of the town and, while feeding their horses in a meadow, their scouts reported enemy horse half a mile away. The Leicester cavalry, probably supported by now with some of the Scottish horse, drew up in three bodies. However, as Langdale formed up his men to charge them the Parliamentarians withdrew to the town, one body facing the Royalists to cover the retreat.[121] Langdale then took command of a hill overlooking the town in preparation for the whole army, which would arrive the next day.

Whereas differences of interest between the counties had led to the failure of the Midland Association, feuds had not generally affected the ability of counties to secure their own defence. In Northampton for example the County Committee was relatively united, included various nationally influential figures and had maintained effective control over most of the shire from the very beginning of the war. In contrast, in Leicestershire the tensions which in peacetime had divided the ruling classes had continued and were undermining effective local government. Problems had already become apparent in 1643 but by 1644 the problems between Lord Grey, governor of Leicester, and his County Committee had come to a head.[122] The bulk of the Committee were local merchants and traders with just a few nobility and gentry led by Lord Grey. Grey was not willing to see his social inferiors rise above their station and, as in some other counties, the governor took strong measures to curb his Committee. This was not simply a personal conflict with Grey, for in May 1644 there were more general differences reported between the Committee and the soldiers at Leicester.[123] In an attempt to resolve the increasing difficulties and so provide for the more effective defence of the town, Parliament had reformed the County Committee. But this had simply led to more friction and the problems appear to have caused Lord Grey to leave Leicester for London. A petition had been presented to the Commons by the inhabitants of Leicester in September 1644 and another in November which requested that Lord Grey 'be sent back to them to unify his officers and that the gentlemen of quality who should serve on the County Committee be enjoined so to do and not thus leave it to those of the "mean middling sort".'[124] Grey did not return.

The defences of the major Parliamentarian garrisons in the region had not previously been seriously tested, but they were certainly not of the same standard as Oxford or Newark, and Leicester's defences were considered particularly inadequate.[125] Leicester castle, of which the medieval walls still survived, had been re-fortified during the Civil War as the core of the garrison. Immediately outside and accessible from the castle lay the Newark, a suburb of the town which was also encompassed by a medieval wall and gates, but which could not be entered directly from the town. Luke describes this whole complex of castle and suburb as the 'Newark Fort which is in the manner of a citadel.'[126] The rest of the town had already lost its medieval walls by the beginning of the 17th century, except for the town gates, but during the war the whole of Leicester had been encompassed by new earth and timber defences.[127] In the absence of a contemporary plan such as that which exists for Newport Pagnell, documentary evidence like that for Northampton or archaeological evidence comparable to that from Gloucester, it is currently impossible to accurately reconstruct the defences of the town as they were in 1645.[128] It is however clear that a substantial part of the suburbs were not encompassed by the fortifications. When George Booth, Lord Grey's brother in law, visited the town on 12th April 1645 he wrote to the governor saying:

'I shall make bold to present your lordship with the weak condition it is in, most obvious to the unobserving eye. By all men's account, there are not above 200 soldiers in the town, and those as peremptory against discipline, as their governors are ignorant of it... 500 resolute well-managed soldiers at any time might one day make themselves masters of this town...'.[129]

In response Grey ordered repairs to be undertaken on the defences and these works were begun by the Committee:

'for the necessary defense and safety of the towne and to prevent the enemyes
approaches to the ffortifications thereof and the danger thereof It is ordered that
the Grange howses and all buildings walls thereto belonging or adjoyninge
lyinge neare the publicke works on the South side of the towne shal be taken
downe and removed and the ground there levelled before Wednesday next. And
the owners and inhabitants of the said Granges and premisses are ordered and
required to take downe and dispose the same according to this Order.'[130]

By late May they had implemented some of the re-fortification, reducing the
length of their defences, but the works were still not adequate, it being argued
for example that there were too few bulwarks to provide covering fire along
the curtain and that those which did exist had been placed too far apart.[131]
Moreover, as Innes later claimed, they had failed to demolish the suburbs of
the town and had left major houses standing within pistol shot of the
fortifications.[132] Had they carried out similar works to those later required by
Fairfax, after he had retaken the town, then Leicester might have held out far
longer against the Royalist siege. However, the whole blame cannot be placed
with the Committee. They had reported in May that their greatest need was
artillery, yet the order in Parliament of the 15th May to provide more artillery
to Leicester had still not been implemented by the 27th.[133] As a result the
defenders had just nine pieces of ordnance in the town when it was attacked,
a wholly inadequate number given the length of the defensive circuit. Also
significant was Lord Grey's failure to return to the town before it was
attacked.[134] So, although Leicester had not been caught wholly unprepared, it
was still in a very weak state.[135]

The ability of the county to defend itself will also have been reduced by the
continual impact of the Ashby and Belvoir garrisons. As a Parliamentarian
newspaper reported in February 1644, Lord Loughborough 'hath made the
country poor by robbing and pillaging them...' and it was said in July that:

'the county of Leicester is in very great danger, by the frequent incursions of
the enemy's forces and garrisons in and near it; by reason whereof, neither the
persons nor the goods of the inhabitants, and well affected to the Parliament, are
secure in any part of the county.'[136]

Indeed, the Royalist commander from Ashby had gained himself the name
'Rob-carier' from his continual action against trade in and passing through the
county. As a result, convoys were necessary to protect goods as they were
transported to Nottingham or Derby.[137] Although the Parliamentarians had
been able to restrict the incursions by the winter of 1644-5, with the
establishment of garrisons such as Kirby Bellars, the impact of Royalist action
over the previous two years in weakening the county can be clearly seen from
its very low assessment for the financing of the New Model Army.

The Committee at Leicester had corresponded first with Cromwell and
then, after he retreated to Oxford, with Vermuyden when he was shadowing

the Royalist army. They had also written to the adjacent counties for support. The appeals had brought some assistance because by the time the Royalist army arrived the town had been reinforced by several hundred cavalry from the Scottish army, but most effective was the action taken within the town itself. About 900 townsmen were listed under the captains of the garrison to assist the regular soldiers, while arms and ammunition were dispersed at various locations around the town for its better defence. In all the garrison comprised some 600 foot and 420 horse, but the Leicestershire forces had been overstretched by the offensive against Ashby and Belvoir. Some troops had been stationed at Bagworth, Kirby Bellars and Coleorton and it was the failure to bring back most or all of these men to Leicester that was perhaps the Committee's most significant failure in the days leading up to the 31st May. Despite having several days notice of the close approach of the King's army, the 350 troops with their artillery were not pulled back from Coleorton and only 100 of their horse had been drawn out from Kirby Bellars leaving a further 160 horse and foot. In all this gave the Leicester garrison only 480 foot and 240 horse, whereas they could have had over 1200 regular troops.[138] In addition there were of course the 900 townsmen but the support from the rest of the shire was very poor, no more than 150 men coming in from the county in response to the warrants issued by the Committee. Both Colonel Pye and Major Innes, who assisted in the defence of the town, considered the numbers of troops wholly inadequate to man nearly 3 miles of defences, especially as estimates of the strength of the Royalist army at this time were of the order of 10000 or 12000.[139] Luke considered he needed at least 1200 men to defend Newport Pagnell where the defences were less than two miles long and so, even with the active support of the townsfolk, Leicester had a daunting task to defend the whole circuit of defences against such a large force which would be thrown against them at six or seven places at once. By the time the attack came, because of the shortage of men, the defenders were exhausted through having to maintain their position at the defences for three nights on end.[140] There was also a lack of the necessary equipment to repair the fortifications, such as spades and shovels, and of gabions to protect the gunners and musketeers from incoming musket fire. There were not even enough draught horses to move the cannon from place to place around the town as the need arose. The Committee of Both Kingdoms had made an important miscalculation in not urgently reinforcing the town, whose garrison would be quite simply outnumbered and outgunned. One of the few advantages the defenders did have was that two experienced officers happened to be in the county when the Royalists approached. Colonel Pye, a cavalry commander with the New Model, was passing through the town to rejoin Vermuyden and so he was immediately appointed to assist the garrison commander, the inexperienced Colonel Grey.[141] They also had the assistance of Major Innes and his 200 horse from the Newport Pagnell garrison, who had hastened into Leicester just as the Royalist army arrived.[142] While Colonel

Grey took the north and east side of the town Pye was given command of the Newark side and, together with Innes, he proved to be 'a great meanes of resisting the Prince'.[143]

On the night of the 29th the Royalist foot marched to Leicester and invested the town, burning down several windmills and one water mill, which lay to the west on the river Soar. The next day at about eight o'clock they pitched their tents and the foot came up to the south side of the town.[144] Both horse and foot quartered in the field while the town was besieged, as did Rupert who 'laye in the workes before Leycester', while Charles stayed close by in the vicarage at Aylestone.[145] Though the house today from the outside looks mainly 19th century, having been restored in 1850, illustrations of circa 1600 show it as a timber framed building on a stone plinth. Behind the later facade most of the building, except the north wing, remains today much as it was in 1645.[146] While the King lay at the vicarage his troops, under constant cannon and musket fire from the defenders, raised a battery of six great pieces against the town on a 'deep, large, and strong dry ditch' known as the Raw Dykes.[147] In response Major Innes sallied from the north gate of the town to drive the Royalists out of the northern suburb at St.Sunday Bridge, firing the houses there so they could not be used again to cover an approach.[148]

Fig.28. This fanciful early 19th century engraving shows Prince Rupert with one of the gun batteries set up on the Raw Dykes to bombard the town. The artillerymen are protected from incoming fire by gabions, large wicker baskets filled with earth. Remnants of the Raw Dykes, which was probably an embankment for a Roman aqueduct, still remain today on the south side of the town close to the A50. At the time of the siege they were far more substantial, but in the late 18th century Nichols reported 'the ramparts are daily diminishing, for every purpose of levelling.'[149]

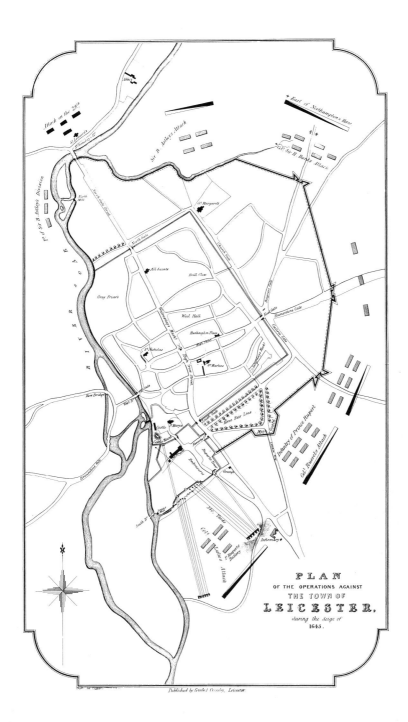

Fig.29. Conjectural plan of the Civil War defences of Leicester in May 1645, by Hollings, showing the positions from which the main assaults were made by the Royalists during the siege.[150]

Later that day Rupert fired two great shot at the town and then sent a trumpeter to request the surrender. The garrison detained the envoy while they discussed their situation, but Rupert was impatient at the lack of response and so about three in the afternoon he began the barrage. The battery had been set up facing the stone wall of the Newark which, because it had not been lined with earth, would not survive for long. The defenders responded with cannon and musket fire 'as fast as they could charge and discharge, and so continued all day, and all night'. They could claim some success having put one Royalist piece out of action with a direct hit.[151] However, by six that evening a large breach had been made in the Newark wall and the firing continued as the defenders, including women from the town, laboured in great danger to repair the damage.[152] Within a short space of time they had succeeded in erecting a retrenchment with three flankers within four or five yards of the wall to protect the breach.[153]

Fig.30. A 19th century view of the main breach in the Newark wall created by the bombardment on the 30th May 1645. Cannon balls have actually been found embedded in the north wall of the Newark, opposite the breach, and must represent overshots. On the east side of the Newark the gate into the suburb from the town also survives, though now sadly encompassed by major modern roads. It was used at the time of the Civil War as the garrison magazine. Though the buildings have gone, one can still climb to the top of the castle mound and look out over the Newark. Before the modern buildings were constructed one would have been able to see the Raw Dykes where the Royalist battery exchanged fire with the artillery set upon the castle mound. Within the Newark most of the buildings which stood in 1645 have also been demolished, except for the medieval chapel of the Trinity Hospital and the Newark Houses museum.

That evening the Royalists prepared to storm the town in six or seven places and at midnight, upon the firing of six big guns, the attack began. The main and most fierce assault was mounted by Lisle's tertia against the breach in the Newark, but the defenders brought up one of their best cannon and loaded it with case shot, which 'did wonderful execution' upon the attacking forces. With great courage the Royalist commanders led their men in the assault and Colonel St.George, seconding Sir Thomas Appleyard's attack, 'in a bravery, came up to the cannon, and was by it shattered into small pieces, and with him many more...'[154] Appleyard was more fortunate and was the first to enter the town, an achievement that was later rewarded when he was granted the governorship of Leicester in recognition of his bravery. So they came to 'push of pike' and entered the breach but Major Innes' dragoons, supported by a charge of horse, drove them out. In the next assault Lisle's troops were seconded by the King's lifeguard of foot, who lost at least two colours to the defenders. Three times the Royalists came on and three times they were repulsed, leaving many dead in the breach. This was the main attack on the defences and yet it failed, for the Newark was defended by a competent professional soldier, Major Innes, with a very committed force.

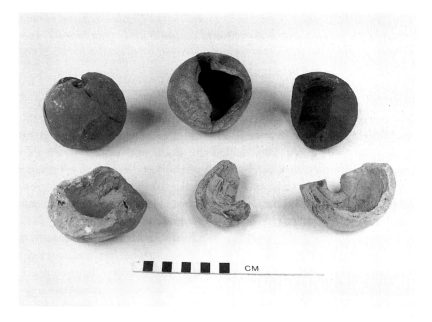

Fig.31. These broken but unused ceramic grenades from the Civil War period discovered in Leicester may be similar to those used to such good effect by the Royalists in their attack on the 30th May 1645 (Leicestershire Museums Service)

Elsewhere about the town the Royalists fared much better as their approach was made easier and safer because there were houses still standing in the suburbs within pistol shot of the defences.[155] Astley's tertia fell on at the north side of the town by the river and at the drawbridge next to the Abbey. Bard

Fig.32. The embrasures for musketeers to fire through the southern wall of the Newark, from behind which the garrison successfully defended this part of the town from the fiercest Royalist attack. A section of the north wall of the Newark, between the museum and the church, still survives and has a series of similar but more crudely cut holes.

probably attacked near the Belgrave Gate and Page at the Galtrey Gate, seconded by a body of Newark cavalry who attacked on foot with pistol and sword, while others assaulted the hornwork in front of the drawbridge on the east side of the town. As they scaled the earth and timber defences with ladders they were met with the butt end of muskets and were repulsed with some loss, but in the next assault the first wave of troops threw hand grenades which burnt many of the defenders and drove them back from the ramparts. The defenders lacked any reserves to second them and so the Royalist musketeers, numbering two or three hundred at each place of assault, were able to scale the defences and get into the town. Once they had entered they broke down the drawbridge and levelled the works in two or three places so that the horse could enter. So far the storming had taken about two hours.[156]

Once inside, the Earl of Northampton's horse began to scour the defences, but this was not the end of the fighting for they were soon met with a counter attack by Colonel Pye leading a body of cavalry.[157] The defenders, soldiers and townsmen alike, would not surrender but instead they fought street by street, house by house, retreating into the market place and to St.Martin's churchyard where they made a brave stand, only surrendering when faced by a charge of horse. Throughout the rest of the town fighting continued and, according to Walker, it was this resistance which drove the Royalists to such excesses against soldiers and civilians, men and women. Walker claimed that 'they fired upon our men out of their windows, from the tops of the houses, and threw tiles upon their heads .... and finding one house better manned than ordinary, and many shots fired at us out of the windows, I caused my men to attack it, and resolved to make them an example for the rest; which they did; and breaking open the doors, they killed all they found there without distinction...'[158]

In contrast to the rest of the town, the Newark and the castle, the most heavily defended part of the garrison, held out under Major Innes and only surrendered upon conditions.[159] Given more troops it seems likely that the rest of the town could also have withstood the siege for much longer and have inflicted even greater losses on the Royalists, who had certainly suffered heavily in the attack on the Newark, the place they had considered to be the weakest part of the defences.

Though the immediate Parliamentarian accounts of the storming exaggerated the scale of the destruction, the sack of the town was without doubt a bloody revenge for its tenacious defence. It was claimed that 'they gave no quarter, but hanged some of the Committee, and cut others in pieces. Some Letters said that 'the kennels ran down with bloud.'[160] It was reported that many of the garrison were killed, that the Committee and the Scots in particular were refused quarter and that the slaughter was only halted when Rupert himself intervened, though he did not protect the Scots.[161] The town was 'miserably plundered' and by daybreak scarcely a cottage remained which had escaped the looting.[162] Later reports from Leicester, received in London on the 7th June, corrected the earlier more wild stories and showed that the Committee and the Scots there were not killed in cold blood but that 'the King's Forces killed divers who prayed for Quarter; and put divers women to the Sword, and other women and children they turned naked into the streets, and many they ravisht.'[163] It was even claimed by the Parliamentarian press that Colonel Bard, following his reputation for harsh action, had actually encouraged the rape and pillage. The Parliamentarian and Royalist accounts also differ as to whether the King sought to stop or simply allowed such destruction. At Charles' trial a witness claimed that on the day of the storming the King had ridden through the town in his bright armour and had said of the atrocities in the Newark: 'I do not care if they cut them 3 times more, for they are mine Enemies...', but in later years a tradition developed, undoubtedly a Restoration attempt to excuse the King from any blame, in which Charles himself was seen riding through the streets shouting 'Cry mercy, good subjects!'[164] Not surprisingly perhaps, some commentators later saw this extreme action against the people of Leicester as the reason why God's wrath was brought down upon the heads of the Royalists with their defeat at Naseby.[165] Though the killing stopped that night, the plundering continued for several days to the extent that on Sunday 1st June, when the King attended a service in the town, 'ye Mayor of ye town had a foul disaster happen'd him;

for when he should have given his attendance upon ye King to ye Church, his mace was plunder'd from him.[166] Even by the standards of the day, at least in England, the sack of Leicester was considered extreme. It may be that the Royalist troops' lack of pay contributed to the scale of their plundering, but it was not just random action by individual soldiers, the organised plundering was probably even more damaging. It is claimed that a few days later some 140 cartloads of the best goods of the town shops were sent away to Newark with a convoy of 2000 horse while other spoils were taken to the garrison at Belvoir.[167] Such had been the losses in the town that, once it had been retaken by Fairfax, there was a voluntary collection made in London towards the relief of the citizens of Leicester.[168]

Despite their success, the Royalists had suffered considerable losses, with even more bodies lying just within the line of the defences than there were outside or in the ditch. At the Newark there were 30 or more in the breach and as many outside, while other bodies were scattered in almost every street in the town. Some Parliamentarian sources claimed that 709 Royalist soldiers were buried in Leicester, besides those that later died of their wounds, compared to only about 100 defenders. On the other hand Symonds estimated less than 200 Royalists were killed, while a generally reliable Parliamentarian newspaper reported 300 Parliamentarian and 400 Royalist dead, although according to Walker the Royalists 'lost three for one in the assault'. Amongst the officers alone there were nearly 30 killed including Colonel St.George, Major Bunnington and a major of Rupert's firelocks.[169] There were more than 300 Parliamentarians taken prisoner including Colonel Gray and Captain Hacker, both of whom were wounded, Colonel Pye and Major Innes.[170] Hardly any of the garrison had escaped from the town, perhaps just the ten or so that had discovered the Royalists' word for the night who, at about daybreak, were able to get out by the riverside.[171] At first light the King returned to his quarters and going by the defences he was shown the members of the Committee who had been taken prisoner and the bodies of the dead, whose exploits were recounted to him.[172] That morning the Parliamentarian cavalry of Vermuyden and Rossiter had gone to a rendezvous at Melton Mowbray with the intention of trying to draw off the enemy from Leicester, but not surprisingly the Nottingham and Derby horse did not appear as they had been instructed, while later in the day Parliament was still considering the deployment of forces to relieve the town. The speed with which Leicester had fallen had taken everyone by surprise.[173]

Robert Herrick, from Houghton, celebrated the victory in a poem:

> 'This day is yours, great Charles; and in this war
> Your fate and ours alike victorious are.
> In her white stole now Victory does rest
> Enspher'd with palm on your triumphant crest.
> Fortune is now your captive; other Kings
> Hold but her hands; you hold both hands and wings.'[174]

The success at Leicester had a dramatic effect on the Royalist confidence, as letters intercepted at this time reveal. They began to make exaggerated claims that the King had 16000 troops, while Gerard had substantial forces coming up to him. Moreover Goring had 11000 in the South West, was recruiting rapidly and was expected to come up to join the King to make such an army that they had little doubt they would make an end of the business this summer.[175] The victory had also placed the local Royalist garrisons in a position where they could once more consider taking the offensive. Not surprisingly Parliamentarian reactions were of great fear and concern. To many it seemed the most shocking setback during the whole war, not simply because of the viciousness of the destruction but also because of the closeness of the garrison to the Association. According to the petition of the citizens of London there was the danger of 'iminent ruine which is comming upon both, through the releiving of Chester, the unexpressible losse of Leicester, the barbarous cruelty executed there, the danger of the rest of our Garrisons...'[176]

The Royalist army was thought to number at least 11000 and in order to keep the Parliamentarians guessing the King made moves in various directions. On the 1st June a party of 2000 horse faced Derby and on the 2nd June 140 carriages were reported ready to set forth in that direction. Gell's claim that he did not fear them because he had 3000 men in the town to defend it was undoubtedly a case of bravado because, although it would be a much tougher challenge than Leicester, no commander in the region could have been other than very concerned that their garrison might be the next target.[177] Other reports claimed that Rupert was going to unite with Goring, Gerard and Grenvile to relieve Oxford, while at the same time there were some 2000 Royalists in Rutland, at Oakham and at Burley, and Luke had intelligence that a large party of Rupert's horse were going to be sent out towards Coventry. With the fall of Leicester the Royalist territories of Newark/Belvoir and Ashby/Lichfield were linked. Even if the King's army moved on, the balance of power in the region had been dramatically altered and the Royalist garrisons could now go onto the offensive. There were fears that a party of horse would join with the Newark forces to fall on Grantham 'which it is probable they may carry very easily by storm', and a week or so later, on the 10th June, Rossiter was indeed forced to draw out 300 foot from Grantham to tackle an assault mounted by the Newark and Belvoir troops on his subsidiary garrison at Hougham.[178] Lady Hutchinson, wife of the governor of Nottingham, wrote that the fall of Leicester 'was a great affliction and terror to all the neighbouring garrisons and counties....' and it was even feared that disaffected people were now offering to betray important garrisons like Cambridge and Derby.[179] The requests from Lord Fairfax in Yorkshire became even more urgent that the Scots march south to Nottingham to meet the Royalist threat. As he said, by the exploit of taking Leicester the King has:

'much increased his repute is now able to attempt either Nottingham, Derby, Grantham, or any other garrison of the Parliament in those parts, or to march into this country and possess himself thereof, and acquire a great addition of forces by aid of the Papists and malignants here....'[180]

The impact of the fall of Leicester cannot be over estimated. Booth had warned in April that if Leicester were lost it 'will take away all commerce from all the north-west of England...'[181] This was far more dramatic and effective than the action in 1644, when the Royalists took Wilney Ferry to control the crossing of the Trent, or even perhaps than in 1643 when Rupert had fortified Newport Pagnell and then Towcester.

On the Parliamentarian side the recriminations soon began.[182] William Lilly wrote of the Leicester Committee:

'Unworthy men have wearied my pen, disheartened the gentry to our inevitable loss, and impoverishment of those towns committed to their charge. Let the town of Leicester be hereof an unlucky precedent, which hath been these three years fortifying, and now on a sudden transmitted to his Majesty's forces. What became of the vast sums of money there raised? why the valiant gentlemen displaced, and men of inferior rank exalted? Who gives any reason, unless it was purposely done to betray the town to our enemies, or, by loss of this, to prolong the wars another year? You shall see if his Majesty's providence fortify not that town in less months than we in years? It must be discovered who or whom have played the plain knaves with us; or else we shall never be at quiet. Many complain the taxes of that county have exceeded the income of rent.'[183]

Though Lilly's criticisms were not wholly unfounded they cannot be taken simply at face value because of the fundamental conflict within the Parliamentarian cause in Leicestershire. There were however other stinging criticisms from Major Innes, one of the two Parliamentarian commanders who had played a key role in the defence of the town, charging the Committee at Leicester with incompetence.[184] Some of the blame also undoubtedly rested at the door of the Scots, for they were in the pay of Parliament and had been instructed to march south to follow the motions of the King's army, but instead they had withdrawn into Westmorland. Had they marched south and joined with Vermuyden and the local forces they should have been more than a match for the Royalist army, the combined force numbering perhaps 21000.[185] Others believed that the greatest blame lay with the Committee of Both Kingdoms, as a petition submitted by the citizens of London made quite clear. If the petition had not actually been engineered by the Independents they certainly capitalised upon it because, although the sack of Leicester was a devastating loss which none could have wished for, it gave the Independents the opportunity to complete the work of remodelling the army.   The Committee of Both Kingdoms had been created to control Essex and his allies but was now being used by those very people to control the New Model and this had to be stopped.

While such matters were discussed in London the Royalists began to exploit their success. On the 1st June Charles levied a charge of £2000 on Leicester for the support of the army, by which time the administration of the town had already been replaced because the letter was addressed to the 'late' mayor and corporation of the town.[186] Having taken Leicester, administrative and military control of the county also naturally fell into their hands and so command of the shire was given to Lord Loughborough, with Lisle as his Lieutenant General and Colonel Appleyard as governor of Leicester.[187] According to the New Model's scoutmaster, the King now had as great an opportunity as he ever had to gain recruits. Charles summoned into Leicester the whole county to list themselves under Lord Loughborough and between 400 and 1000 countrymen came in to join the army.[188] When Parliament once again had control of Leicester we find local Royalists, from wealthy gentlemen to ordinary tradesmen, being very heavily fined for their support of the King at this time.[189] So for example Clement Tookie of Galby, gentleman, was fined £50 on 16th June 1645 for 'appearing in Leicester whilst the King's forces held it', while at the other extreme lay Richard How of Woodhouse, butcher, who was fined £5.[190] At best the recruiting probably did no more than make up for the losses that had been suffered in the storming of Leicester, and perhaps of almost equal value to the army were the 2000 horses taken in the town, which people had brought into Leicester for security before the siege.[191] The King also sent out warrants for men to come into the town to assist in the demolition of large parts of the suburbs to make the town more easily defensible.[192] Over the next two weeks work progressed rapidly on re-fortification, especially of the Newark, the Parliamentarian newspapers reporting that Lord Loughborough 'fortifies it so earnestly as if he meant to command the whole country'.[193]

The lesser garrisons in the area had been established at a time when Parliamentarian fortunes in the region were in the ascendancy, in order to straighten the garrisons of Ashby, Belvoir and Tutbury and to protect the region from Royalist plundering and taxation. These small garrisons were now untenable and so on the same day as Leicester fell, Bagworth, Kirby Bellars and Coleorton in Leicestershire, Burley in Rutland and Barton in Derbyshire were all abandoned.[194] Indeed, the sack of Leicester put such fear into these garrisons that some of them fled leaving behind their artillery, ammunition and supplies.[195] It is unclear where the troops from Coleorton and Bagworth went, though they probably fell back on Derby, but on the 1st June the garrisons from Kirby Bellars and Burley, together with those Leicester troops that had been posted to Kirby to support the offensive against Belvoir, fell back on the nearest Parliamentarian garrison at Rockingham in Northamptonshire.[196] Others may have fallen back on Northampton or beyond, for around this time the constable of Great Houghton 'payd for quartering of two shogers one nyght apon 1/2d givn to two shogurs that cam from lester'.[197] The troops that came to Rockingham 'to recrute' were quartered, for at least a night or two, in the town and the surrounding villages.[198] The governor of the castle immediately sent Major Butler with 25 or 30 of his horse back with the Burley forces to recover their ordnance, arms and ammunition before the enemy could take them. Finding a party of the Royalists already in the town Butler fired Burley Hall to stop the King from establishing a garrison there.[199]

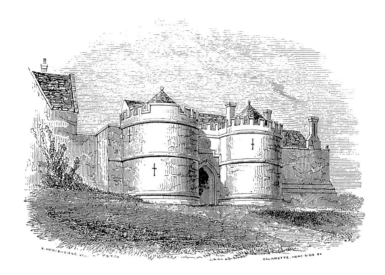

Fig. 33. The gatehouse of Rockingham castle. A garrison was established in 1643 in the medieval castle at Rockingham, which lies in a commanding position overlooking the Welland valley. Part of the outer wall and several towers had been demolished before the war but the keep and gate remained and the whole site had been strengthened by the addition of earth and timber defences in 1643. In 1645 the governor was Sir John Norwich, who had raised a regiment of dragoons at the outset of the war to secure Northampton and the county for Parliament. The small market town of Rockingham used to extend right up to the castle gate but the church and a large part of the settlement was demolished, probably at the time of the fall of Leicester, to provide a clear field of fire from the castle defences.

For a brief moment Rockingham became Parliament's front line garrison. There was little else between the King and the Eastern Association than the five hundred cavalry based behind the medieval walls and new earthen defences of the castle at Rockingham. Though small, it seems to have been far stronger than the other small garrisons which had been abandoned. It had been held for Parliament since March 1643 and stood in a commanding position dominating the Welland valley with steep scarps on all but the south side. The castle, which still retained its massive medieval stone gatehouse and its keep, had been extensively refortified in earth and timber under its first governor, Colonel Horseman, and the keep, set on top of a large motte, provided an ideal gun platform and by 1644 it had ordnance planted on its roof. At some time, possibly in the days immediately following the fall of Leicester, the

church and half of the small town of Rockingham was demolished to provide
a clear field of fire from the defences.[200] The horse which had fallen back on
Rockingham from Kirby and Burley were now placed under the command of
Rockingham's governor, Sir John Norwich, who dispersed them in
Uppingham and the surrounding district while others returned to Burley, even
though the House had been fired. In all Norwich now had under his command
some 500 horse ready for immediate action, in addition to whatever infantry
he had to hold the castle itself.[201]

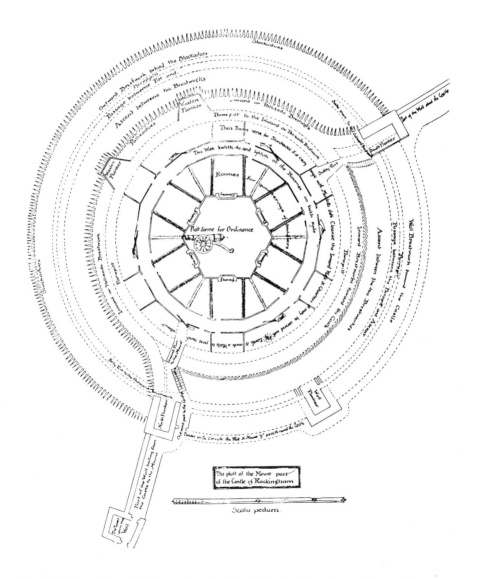

*Fig. 34. Plan of circa 1644 showing the Civil War fortifications of the castle motte at
Rockingham, with palisadoes and stockadoes outside the medieval walls and artillery
placed on the roof of the keep.*

The Royalists were now in a position of overwhelming dominance. Norwich reported that 'they straggle up and down the country, plundering, imprisoning and laying great impositions on the country.' This did however make the Royalist troops vulnerable and the best response for a front line garrison, even if it was small, was to take the offensive in as bold a way as it could. So Norwich sent out all of his own, the Kirby Bellars and the Burley horse who:

> 'divided themselves into parties severally and had very good sport, brought in as many prisoners as our little garrison can well contain, some taken within 4 miles of Leicester, some nearer hand, some officers, the Queen's trumpeter, some of the Queen's Life Guard, others killed outright and but one of all our party wounded. We have so fallen on them with our party, though but small, that I hope it will make them keep nearer home.'

The intelligence they gained from these prisoners was to prove inaccurate for, according to them, the King's next move would be to march into the North to relieve Pontefract.[202]

The approaching storm put all the Parliamentarian garrisons to the south of Leicester in great fear. After Rockingham the nearest was Northampton, a far more formidable challenge than Leicester, which appears to have had a united and determined Committee, an effective military command and a substantial garrison which had wide support both within the town and in the county. As Everitt has said, whereas Leicester had been one of the least committed county towns in the region at the outset of the war and was, at least in 1645, the weakest and most vulnerable of the garrisons, Northampton was perhaps the strongest.[203] The town had been developing its fortifications almost continuously since August 1642 and over a period of nearly three years had added an earth and timber reinforcement in front of its medieval walls around most of the circuit of the town, replacing the wall in some places to reduce the length of the circuit. Mounts had also been constructed on the north side, to provide covering artillery fire where there was slightly rising ground outside the defences, and the castle had been refortified as the core of the garrison. There were limitations in the works, particularly on the east side of the town where the medieval wall had not yet been reinforced with an earthen curtain, but there were artillery positions around the whole circuit to provide covering fire. With the impending siege, Northampton had hurriedly taken on a new engineer and had begun constructing further defences. Had the feared assault come, as it most surely would if the battle at Naseby had ended differently, then the defences of Northampton would have been found wanting. The artillery on its 'scare crow Mounts', as its new engineer described them, would soon have been dismounted by the Royalist artillery and the unlined medieval walls on the north east side of the town would rapidly have come tumbling down into the ditch. So worried were the Committee that they continued with their major scheme of refortification even after the battle of

Naseby, completing the earthen defences around the whole eastern circuit of the town in the winter of 1645-6.[204] The sack of Leicester had had a dramatic effect on the town, for Luke wrote from Newport Pagnell on the 31st May that it:

> 'has struck such a terror into Northampton people that our inns and houses are full with them and I believe that if this success should alter his Majesty's resolution from going northward and come and ask Northampton, he may have it on easier terms than he had Leicester.'[205]

Such a reaction is not perhaps surprising given the lurid stories which came out of Leicester with the refugees and even Fairfax's Scoutmaster, Major Leonard Watson, had likened it to the sack of Magdeburg.[206]

The weakness of Leicester was not unique amongst the garrisons in the region and Parliament was made aware in no uncertain terms that the garrison of Aylesbury was also in danger of being lost if the enemy should appear before it. It was in need of urgent financial support, the country not being able to maintain their supply of provisions or money, while there was great laxity in the watches of the garrison which meant that they might easily be surprised.[207] Bedford, which had never been heavily fortified, was short of ammunition and powder and the Committee even considered slighting 'the Mount' and sending their 100 or so troops to Cromwell in Ely to avoid a Royalist attack. The advice they got from Luke was that 'to demolish it at this present will be rather a means to invite them thither than to drive them away.'[208] At Newport Pagnell Luke had accepted the need to supply troops to the siege at Oxford, but at that time the Royalist army had not been an immediate threat. The governor had however made it clear that he had less than 1100 troops in the town and that to secure its defences, which were almost two miles long, he would need far more troops, requesting the support of a regiment or two as well as adequate supplies if a siege was feared.[209] Whereas the New Model was being relatively well resourced, local garrisons such as Newport seem to have been starved of resources. This was not necessarily intentional, but rather perhaps because the extra taxation to support the New Model and the Scottish armies made the Association counties even further behind with their payments for the garrisons. In the case of Newport and Aylesbury the problems were also due to the impact of both Royalist and Parliamentarian armies quartering in the county over the winter of 1644-5 which, as we have seen, had severely strained the resources of the county. As a result, at Newport it had already been reported in May that 'our men steal away apace' through want of pay. The garrison was said to be very poorly supplied, while the local population could not even be persuaded to come in to work on the fortifications of the town, difficulties that were not helped by the fact that Luke was in dispute with his County Committee. As far as possible he intended to control his Committee, not like Northampton where he claimed the Committee governed the governor. There are shades here of the problems at Leicester, indeed the whole garrison at Newport appears to have been rent by conflict, with competition between officers for command and even claims of embezzlement of money by officers in the garrison.[210] According to Luke, as a result of desertion and the removal of troops to the siege of Oxford and to support Massey, he now had no more than 500 troops to defend the town and felt that his garrison was another weak target which might attract Royalist attention, encouraging the King to bypass Northampton. He wrote to Fairfax on the 5th June with reports that the King intended to advance on his garrison, saying that Newport was ill prepared for an attack and requesting the return of his infantry, which had been sent to the seige of Oxford:

> 'how ill we are provided you cannot but know; our Horse and Men being commanded away, and we not Six hundred Foot left in the Town, I desire you as you tender either your own or our Good, to haste hither what Men you can, for we had need of Two thousand Men to Man these Works, they are so large, and at this time so Indefensible.'[211]

Given the difficulties of the Aylesbury and Newport garrisons, the commanders there had every reason to fear that the King might advance on them. He had carefully chosen Leicester as a weak garrison and his intelligence about the condition of these other places is likely to have been just as good. Later, as the direction of the Royalist march became apparent, it was also feared that Evesham might be one of their targets.[212] In the winter of 1643-4 there had been a similar push by the Royalists into the south east Midlands, severing the same communication routes, with the establishment of garrisons at Newport Pagnell, Towcester and Grafton Regis. This had met with a rapid and substantial response from London, but in 1645 the situation was very different. It was the beginning of the campaigning season, the main Royalist field army would soon be encamped within a few miles of the next major Parliamentarian garrison, Northampton, and it clearly worried many that the whole region was in danger of falling to the King. Shocked into action by these events, Parliament finally began to take notice of the needs of the garrisons in the region, for on the 1st June they required arrears of tax to be speedily paid and authorised the garrison commanders to bring in provisions and forces from adjacent counties to Newport Pagnell and Aylesbury.[213] For most of the garrisons however the best that could be done was simply to offer reassurance.

Though Parliament was concerned about the region, ordering deployments to secure Evesham and other garrisons, they were far more worried about the threat to the Association, which was the heart of their military and economic power.[214] Whereas the Northamptonshire troops were used to fighting against some of the most effective of Royalist forces and had adequately fortified their garrisons to fend off all but the most sustained attack by a major army, the garrisons of the Association had so far had an easy war and were wholly unprepared. The troops of the region needed organising ready to defend it against any Royalist advance, while some important towns were hardly fortified at all. Huntingdon for example, when attacked by the Royalists in August 1645, was said to have only very light defences. When Parliament gave the control of forces in particular areas to individual commanders Rossiter had been given Lincolnshire but the most important charge, the Isle of Ely, had been retained by Cromwell.[215] Already on the 26th May, before the fall of Leicester, Cromwell had been ordered to march to the Isle of Ely to put the defences in order.[216] This northern half of Cambridgeshire was in effect the gateway to the Association, for it was mostly undrained fenland with only a few causeways crossing it, and was described by the Lords as 'a place of so high consequence in a time of so great danger'.[217] A handful of strategically placed garrisons could control access to the whole region, unless the Royalists were to march much farther south through Northamptonshire and Bedfordshire, and so Cromwell was specifically instructed to guard the passes out of Lincolnshire into the Isle of Ely.[218] They were heavily fortified and although some at least of the fortifications existed before May 1645 they were certainly strengthened by Cromwell in the weeks before Naseby. On the 29th May Parliament authorised the provision of powder, match and bullet for the Isle of Ely and then, on the 1st June, further powder and gunners.[219] Cromwell was also given the use of the trained bands of Cambridgeshire and artillery from Cambridge and was told 'As you need workmen for the fortifications you are hereby authorized to send for them out of any of the neighbouring counties of the Association or from Northampton.'[220] He had found the whole area ill prepared and over the next few days was continually on the march, backwards and forwards across the region, arranging its defence.[221] By the 1st June he was near Grantham and then on subsequent days at Stamford, Peterborough and Huntingdon and later at the headquarters of the Association in Cambridge.[222] Briefly he seems to have taken command over Vermuyden, who was quartered first at Stamford and then at Deeping Gate on the south side of the Welland where the bridge controlled the main and most easterly road from Sleaford and Bourne to Peterborough.[223]

Most important however were the forts of Crowland, Horsey and Earith, which were strategically placed at river crossings on the only significant causeways through the fen into the Isle of Ely. As one travels today downstream across the fen towards Crowland from Market Deeping, the main road follows close to the course of the only causeway which existed in 1645 and there, dominating the skyline is Crowland Abbey. Set on a small fen island Crowland was the lowest bridge over the Welland while all around it is the open fen landscape. Though now all drained it would in 1645 have been impassable except for the causeway. The Crowland fort was apparently constructed around the Abbey itself, for the antiquary Stukeley recorded in 1744 that 'Oliver's fortification ditch runs across the choir, exactly where St.Guthlac's shrine stood.'[224] To the south of Crowland the next approach to the Association was via Peterborough. Though it was then part of Northamptonshire, the Soke of Peterborough appears to have been controlled in military terms by the Eastern Association rather than by the County Committee of Northampton. From Peterborough a causeway led out of the Soke across onto Whittlesey Island. This access was commanded by Horsey fort, which is one of the best preserved of all Civil War sites. Further south at Earith another fort, also well preserved today, controlled the next causeway to Ely itself. When well manned and provided with sufficient artillery these garrisons will have proved an effective frontier defence. However, despite what Parliament might order and whatever local commanders on the ground might do, until a major field army met the Royalist challenge no territory and no garrison was completely safe.

Fig. 35. Horsey Hill was one of the key defensive sites which protected the Isle of Ely, and hence the frontier of the Association, as the Royalist army marched eastward in late May and early June 1645.[225] The fort lay on a small island controlling the fen causeway from Peterborough to Whittlesey island and must have been almost unassailable. It is one of the best preserved of Civil War sites, a classic sconce where the bastions and curtain are clearly visible. Today the busy A605 from Peterborough to Whittlesey runs right by the fort yet, because of the trees, the passer-by would not even notice the site as they negotiate the bend as the road turns on the corner of the defences.[226] (Cambridge University Collection : copyright reserved)

While the disastrous events unfolded at Leicester the New Model Army had remained around Oxford. On the 31st May Sir Thomas Fairfax had viewed Gaunt House, a small garrison controlling the crossing of the Isis at Newbridge, and had then sent Rainsborough, together with three troops of Sheffield's horse, to summon the garrison. This was a large moated manor house near Standlake and although the house still stands today only a fragment dates from the time of the war.[227] Rainsborough bombarded the house all day but, because of the moat, he could not easily storm it and so the governor refused the first summons. The next day however the garrison was once again summoned and this time the governor did surrender. Rainsborough took 60 prisoners and all the arms, ammunition and provisions. A new garrison was then put in the house, under the command of Major General Browne, and it was to remain in Parliamentarian hands for the rest of the war, one of the few positive results of the time the New Model spent around the city in 1645.[228]

The Royalist defenders of Oxford were however in no way daunted by the losses, for they made a number of sallies from behind their defences. At one o'clock on the morning of the 3rd June they attacked the Parliamentarian guard near Heddington Hill, seizing part of the outworks, killing 11 and taking 84 prisoners.[229] In response, the following morning the Parliamentarians took 12 of the garrison and brought away 50 cows from under the walls.[230] But these were all minor engagements and the city was never in real danger, indeed when the New Model was leaving Oxford the Royalists sallied out yet again and took another 100 prisoners who were then exchanged for the Royalists that had been taken at the beginning of the siege.[231] By the 2nd June orders had at last arrived from London telling Fairfax to prepare the New Model to march towards the Association and immediately he began to make arrangements. The 700 foot which had joined the siege from Northampton, Newport and Aylesbury were placed in garrison at Abingdon, together with 200 of Fairfax's horse, although the next day the Northampton troops were finally allowed to return home for the better defence of their garrison, which was thought to be the next Royalist target.[232]

On the 4th June, the day the King departed from Leicester to march south, instructions arrived for Fairfax to raise the siege and march eastward towards the Association.[233] Fairfax was not to 'amuse' himself about garrisons such as Boarstall House but rather to march immediately to join with Vermuyden and with Cromwell's Eastern Association forces.[234] Moreover, the Committee of Both Kingdoms at last gave him some of the freedom of action he needed: 'We desire you to attend the King's motions in such way as, being at the place, you may judge to be best.'[235] The bridge over the Cherwell was pulled up, the New Model troops on the other side of the river Ray ordered to march to Islip Bridge to join the rest and the siege placed in the hands of Major General Browne, who had been given command of all forces in Oxfordshire, Berkshire and Buckinghamshire.[236] So, on the 5th June, after nearly a fortnight wasted in a pointless and ineffective siege while the Midlands were left exposed to the full force of the Royalist army, the New Model finally marched north eastward along the main road towards Buckingham. In a final gesture, Fairfax ordered one last attempt on the garrison at Boarstall House, where the siege had continued since the 23rd May. Fairfax himself visited Boarstall, bringing 1200 foot from Marston with ladders and various other equipment. They summoned the house but were denied and hence 'that night Skippon caused the House to be stormed, but the Moat being much deeper than they expected, the Assailants were beat off with Loss, and so the next day raised that Siege also....'[237] Although the New Model would return in March 1646 it would take them over two months to force the garrison to finally surrender.[238] Inevitably the Royalists made the most of the New Model's failure at the siege, with accounts that the forces storming Boarstall were beaten off with the loss of at least 400 men and that the enemy had been given a blow on the rear by the Boarstall, Wallingford and Oxford troops together with some of Goring's Horse. The Royalist propaganda even included reports that Fairfax and Browne had fallen out at the siege 'and cudgelld one another'.[239]

Fig.36. Boarstall Tower is the only surviving part of the garrison which Skippon attempted to storm on the 5th June 1645. It is now in an idyllic setting, the water filled moat encompassing the medieval gatehouse and its gardens on three sides. I visited the site close to the 349th anniversary of the siege and with my chance companions I followed Dr Hall who took us on a tour of the house. Painfully slowly we followed the old gentleman up the spiral stair to the great chamber on the first floor. From this room a door led into one of the corner turrets - his bedroom, overlooking the moat. The old gentleman produced a tiny cardboard box from a shelf. In it were musket balls collected from the gardens, several of them heavily distorted as though they had impacted upon the fortified walls. He had also in the past discovered at least one cannon ball in the grounds, but that unfortunately was now lost.[240]

NOTES

1. Bell, 1849, vol.1, p.182.

2. Sherwood, 1974, p.183-4.

3. Slingsby, p.142.

4. Rushworth, vol.6, p.23. Ludlow, 1698, vol.1, p.150-1.

5. Symonds, p.163. Ludlow, 1698, vol.1, p.150-1. Sprigge, p.11.

6. VCH, 1959, vol.6, p.56. Sprigge, p.11. Rushworth, vol.6, p.23. Symonds, p.163-4.

7. Symonds, p.163.

8. Ludlow, 1698, vol.1,p.150-1. Rushworth, vol.6, p.23. Sprigge, 1647, p.12.

9. Rushworth, vol.6, p.23. Sprigge, 1647, p.12.

10. Symonds, p.163-4. Ludlow, 1698, vol.1, p.150-1. Firth, 1890, p.287-8. Sprigge, 1647, p.12.

11. Symonds, p.165.

12. Ludlow, 1698, vol.1, p.150-1. Foard, 1994, p.81. Rushworth, vol.6, p.26. Digby to Rupert, 30th April 1645, Warburton, vol.3, p.81.

13. Symonds, p.164. Sprigge, 1647, p.13.

14. Symonds, p.164.

15. Rushworth, vol.6, p.26. Sprigge, 1647, p.16.

16. Tibbutt, 1963, p.266.

17. Roy, 1964, p.22.

18. Gardiner, 1893, vol.2, p.204-5. Digby to Rupert, 30th April, Warburton, vol.3, p.80-1.

19. There are a series of letters, reproduced by Rushworth, from the Committee of Both Kingdoms to Fairfax instructing him as to the exact actions he should take.

20. Rushworth, vol.6, p.23. Trevor to Ormond, 8th May 1645, Carte, 1759, vol.1, p.84-5.

21. Tibbutt, 1963, p.266. Rushworth, vol.6, p.26.

22. Sprigge, 1647, p.17. Warrants re pay for 'that part of Col Ingoldsbyes regiment which marched lately in Col Barcleyes regiment', under the command of Lieutenant Colonel Pride according to a muster of 16 June, July 1645, PRO SP28/31, f.25. Rushworth, vol.6, p.28.

23. Rushworth, vol.6, p.29.

24. Wharton, 1645.

25. Tibbutt, 1963, p.268.

26. Scott, 1811, vol.5, p.371.

27. Records of the Train of Artillery, 29th January to 6th February 1645, Roy, 1964, p.57, 146 & 427-9. Slingsby, p.142.

28. Sprigge, 1647, p.15.

29. Tibbutt, 1963, p.537.

30. The itinerary of the Royalist army's march is mainly drawn from *Iter Carolinum* and Firth, 1898.

31. Slingsby, p.143. Tennant, 1992, p.245. Sherwood, p.188.

32. Symonds, p.165.

33. Tennant, 1992, p.216.

34. Slingsby, p.143. Trevor to Ormond, 8th May 1645, Carte, 1759, vol.1, p.84-5.

35. Scott, 1811, vol.5, p.371.

36. Morrah, 1976, p.177. Roy, 1962.

37. Scott, 1811, vol.5, p.371.

38. Slingsby, p.143. Symonds, p.165.

39. Slingsby, p.144.

40. Tennant, 1992, p.215.

41. Hutton, 1992, p.174n.

42. Slingsby, p.143. Rushworth, vol.6, p.29. Warburton, vol.3, p.85. Symonds, p.166.

43. Walker, 1705, p.126.

44. Symonds, p.166-7.

45. Sherwood, p.183. Tennant, 1992, p.54 & 247.

46. Slingsby, p.144-5.

47. Tennant, 1992, p.217. Symonds, p.167.

48. *Mercurius Aulicus*, 25th May to 8th June.

49. Browne was at the Heyfords and Cromwell between Woodstock and Banbury. Tibbutt, 1963, p.276. Nicholas to Rupert, 16th May, Warburton, vol.3, p.91. Sherwood, 1974, p.188.

50. Tennant, 1992, p.251-4. The association of courts of guard with quarters is a suggestion by the present author, based on proximity but without reviewing the original sources.

51. Tibbutt, 1963, p.536.

52. Tennant, 1992, p.250-6.

53. Tibbutt, 1963, p.281.

54. Rushworth, vol.6, p.29-30.

55. Rushworth, vol.6, p.32. Tibbutt, 1963, p.283. Nicholas to Rupert, Warburton, vol.3, p.97.

56. Rushworth, vol.6, p.29-30. Tibbutt, 1963, p.537. Cromwell to Brereton, 18th & 19th May, Dore, 1984.

57. Major Bridges, Tibbutt, 1963, p.540.

58. Rushworth, vol.6, p.32. *CSPD*, p.515. Rich's regiment was at this time still known as Sidney's. Gresley reports 3000 horse and dragoons under Vermuyden under the four colonels. Gresley at Derby to Brereton, 26th May, Dore, 1984, p.496-7.

59. Tennant, 1993, p.217.

60. Rushworth, vol.6, p.29. Symonds, p.172.

61. Charles to Nicholas, 18 May 1645, Bray, 1827, vol.5, p.128.

62. Rushworth, vol.6, p.29.

63. Tibbutt, 1963, p.281-4.

64. Charles to Nicholas, 16th May 1645, Bray, 1827, vol.5, p.127.

65. 17th June 1645, Baillie, 1775, vol.2, p.116-7.

66. Whitelocke, p.144.

67. Bray, 1827, vol.5, p.127n.

68. Charles to Nicholas, 18th May 1645, Bray, 1827, vol.5, p.128. Rushworth, vol.6, p.32-3.

69. Tennant, 1992, p.256.

70. Sir Thomas Fairfax to Lord Fairfax, 4th June 1645, Bell, 1849, vol.1, p.228.

71. Varley, 1932, p.113-4.

72. Earl of Calander to Scotch Commissioners in London, 18th May 1645, HMC, 1891, p.224.

73. Kingston, 1897, p.171. Foard, 1994, p.68-9.

74. Rushworth, vol.6, p.32-3. Sprigge, 1647, p.21.

75. Rushworth, vol.6, p.32-3.

76. Rushworth, vol.6, p.34.

77. Varley, 1932, p.128.

78. Rupert to Legge, 7th May, Warburton, vol.3, p.83.

79. Sprigge, 1647, p.22. Rushworth, vol.6, p.34.

80. Rushworth, vol.6, p.34. Sprigge, 1647, p.22.

81. *CSPD*, p.515-6. Orders by the Committee of Both Kingdoms for the restocking of the store at Northampton with arms and ammunition so that various places in the region could be supplied, implies Northampton was a depot and hence why the cannon were held there. Report of Committee of Both Kingdoms, 10th June 1645, HMC, 1891, p.227.

82. *CSPD*, p.516.

83. Rushworth, vol.6, p.34. Wharton to the Committee of Norwich, 21st May 1645, Bell, 1649, vol.1, p.227. Firth, 1890, vol.5, p.280-292.

84. Blackmore, 1990. *A Journal and a True and Exact Relation*, BL TT E.4/9.

85. Tibbutt, 1963, p.295.

86. Sergeant Harris's account in Col. Martin's Regiment, 44 days when the regiment marched to Henley and back to Aylesbury, 18th January to March 1644-5; John Lewis under Martyn, 24th May 1645 to 8th Sept 1645, 'being out with the party at Abington'; Thos Smith's Account, sergeant of foot in Col. Martin's regiment, including 24th May 1645 to 14 June 1645 'at Oxford'. PRO SP28/219, unfol.. Tibbutt, 1963, p.261-2.

87. *CSPD*, p.515.

88. Hutchinson to Lord Fairfax, 24th May 1645, Bell, 1849, vol.1, p.222.

89. *CSPD*, p.548-9.

90. *CSPD*, p.549 & 518-9.

91. Nichols, vol.3, appendix 4, p.35. Rushworth, vol.6, p.29. Intelligence on Royalist troop numbers from a Royalist deserter. Gresley to Brereton, 22nd May, Dore, 1984, p.482, 494 & 507. The rendezvous was on Foson Heath according to letter from Brereton to Leven, 27th May, Dore, 1984, p.500 & 499.

92. Captain Barton to Brereton, 27th May, Dore, 1984, p.498.

93. Symonds, p.178. Barton to Brereton and Swettenham to Brereton, 27th May, Dore, 1984, p.498-9.

94. Clarendon, 1702, bk 4, p.38.

95. Slingsby, p.145.

96. Slingsby, p.146.

97. Dore, 1984, p.480.

98. Young & Holmes, 1974, p.237.

99. *CSPD*, p.522.

100. *CSPD*, p.522.

101. *CSPD*, p.520.

102. Clarendon, 1702, bk 4, p.38.

103. Lord Digby to Lord Goring, 19th May, HMC, 1891.

104. *CSPD*, p.520.

105. Ludlow, 1698, vol.1, p. 151-3.

106. Nichols, vol.3, appendix 4, p.28 & 31.

107. Tibbutt, 1963, p.294.

108. *Narration of the siege*.

109. Nichols, vol.3, appendix 4, p.41.

110. Clarendon, 1702, bk 4, p.38.

111. *CSPD*, p.532-3. Brereton to Committee of Borth Kingdoms, 29th May, Dore, 1984, p.507.

112. Sprigge, 1647, p.27. Rushworth, vol.6, p.34 says four troops of horse.

113. *CSPD*, p.533-6.

114. Rushworth, vol.6, p.29. Nichols, vol.3, p.737.

115. *Narration of the siege*.

116. Rushworth, vol.6, p.29.

117. Nichols, vol.3, p.367. Lloyd, *Worthies*, p.649.

118. *CSPD*, p.532. Symonds, p.179.

119. *CSPD*, p.531.

120. *CSPD*, p.544.

121. Slingsby, p.146.

122. Fleming, 1981-2, p.33. Nichols, vol.3, appendix 4, p.33 et seq.

123. Nichols, vol.3, appendix 4, p.35.

124. Richards, 1988, p.688.

125. *A Glorious Victory*. A detailed discussion of the defences and siege is presented in the article by Courtney & Courtney, 1992.

126. Tibbutt, 1963, p.297.

127. Speed maps.

128. Foard, 1994a. Atkin & Laughlin, 1992.

129. Nichols, vol.3, appendix 4, p.41-2.

130. Stock, 1923, p.336.

131. *A more perfect and exact relation*

132. *Narration of the siege.*

133. Nichols, vol.3, appendix 4, p.42.

134. *CSPD*, p.529.

135. *CSPD*, p.589.

136. *Mercurius Britannicus*, 6th February 1643-4. *Commons Journals*, vol.3, p.557.

137. Nichols, vol.3, appendix 4, p.37-8.

138. Symonds estimated that in all there were six hundred foot and three troops of horse within the town.

139. *Narration of the siege*. Sir John Norwich, should have had the best intelligence, for his was the closest Parliamentarian garrison and sent out scouts towards Leicester. Norwich reported that there were before Leicester 6000 horse and 4000 foot, 8 field pieces and 3 great pieces, 60 carriages, thirty of which laden with ammunition and provisions while the rest were for baggage. Norwich then reported on the 1st June 7000 horse and 4000 foot. Tibbutt, 1963, p.548 & 552.

140. *A more perfect and exact relation.*

141. Not to be confused with Lord Grey the overall commander of the Leicestershire troops, who was not present.

142. *Narration of the siege.*

143. Symonds, p.180.

144. Tibbutt, 1963, p.294.

145. Firth, 1898, p.739. Nichols, vol.3, appendix 4, p.42,n.4, quoting Stukeley.

146. Pevsner, 1984, p.266.

147. Nichols, vol.4 ,p.25.

148. *Narration of the siege*. Sir John Norwich, Tibbutt, 1963, p.548.

149. Nichols, vol.4, p.25.

150. From Hollings, 1840.

151. Sprigge, 1647, p.23. *Narration of the siege.*

152. Symonds, p.180.

153. Symonds, p.180. Whitelocke, p.143

154. Sprigge, 1647, p.23. Cox, 1738, p.1360.

155. *Narration of the siege.*

156. Clarendon, 1702, bk.9, p.33. *A more perfect and exact relation*. Later it was falsely claimed that some of the defenders had betrayed the town and let down the gates. Whitelocke, p.143.

157. *Narration of the siege. A more perfect and exact relation.*

158. Walker, 1705. Newspapers, quoted by Nichols, vol.3, appendix 4, p.46 et seq.

159. Tibbutt, 1963, p.292 & 323.

160. Cox, 1738, p.1360. A kennel is a roadside gutter.

161. Tibbutt, 1963, p.298. Whitelocke, p.143.

162. Symonds, p.180. Whitelocke, p.143.

163. Whitelocke, p.144.

164. Sherwood, p.191. Rushworth, 1722, vol.7, p.1411. Firth, 1926, p.6.

165. 17th June 1645, Baillie, 1775, vol.2, p.116-7.

166. Slingsby, p.148.

167. *A more perfect and exact relation*. Tibbutt, 1963, p.298-9.

168. Nichols, vol.3, appendix 4, p.65.

169. Symonds. Slingsby, p.147-8. Whitelocke, p.144. Rushworth, vol.6, p.35. Sherwood, 1974, p.191-2. Walker, reprinted in Nichols vol.3, appendix 4. Sprigge, 1647, p.23.

170. Whitelocke, p.143. Walker, reprinted in Nichols, vol.3, appendix 4.

171. Slingsby, p.147-8.

172. Slingsby, p.147-8.

173. Tibbutt, 1963, p.552. *CSPD*, p.550.

174. Herrick, 1648, quoted by Nichols, vol.2, p.632-3.

175. Tibbutt, 1963, p.294.

176. Vicars, 1646, p.155.

177. Tibbutt, 1963, p.555.

178. Tibbutt, 1963, p.553-5. Tibbutt, 1963, p.319.

179. Hutchinson, 1908, p.224. *CSPD*, p.564.

180. *CSPD*, p.551.

181. Nichols, vol.3, appendix 4, p.41.

182. *Narration of the siege*.

183. William Lilly, quoted by Nichols, vol.3, p.750 n.3.

184. Nichols, vol.3, appendix 4, p.50.

185. Sprigge, 1647, p.25-6. Tibbutt, 1963, p.296.

186. Digby to the late Mayor and Corporation of Leicester, 1st June 1645, in Stocks, 1923, p.337.

187. Symonds, p.184.

188. Tibbutt, 1963, p.551. Symonds, p.184.

189. *Exchange Intelligencer*, 13th June 1645.

190. Similarly William Inge of Belgrave was fined £550; George Ashby of Quenby £450; Edward Blunt, parson of Walton, £140; Captain Cave of Brokesby £100; John Cave, rector of Pickwell, £40; William Leader of Wimiswould, gentleman, £20; John Wayland, parson of Skeffington £20; Thomas Bren of Tugby £10 and Richard How of Woodhouse, butcher, £5. Nichols, vol.2, p.569 & 773; vol.3, p.1135.

191. Tibbutt, 1963, p.297.

192. *Exchange Intelligencer*, 13th June 1645.

193. Tibbutt, 1963, p.297 & 552. *A Glorious Victory. Mercurius Britannicus*, no.86, quoted by Hensman, 1911, p.222.

194. Warburton, vol.3, p.90. Symonds, p.183-4. Ryves, 1685. Mercurius Aulicus, 25th May to 8th June claims that the Parliamentarians also abandoned Melton Mowbray and Akington.

195. Tibbutt, 1963, p.298.

196. Tibbutt, 1963, p.552.

197. Great Houghton parish records , NRO 175P/38.

198. Rockingham accounts. Thomas Russell: 'Item five roodes of meddow destroyed in a place called the followe meddowe by kerby bellowes troopers a bout Nasebey fight £1-5-0'. Lewes Whitwell: '4 acres meadow by kerby bellowes and Leicester forces'. Thomas Harrison: 'Medow ground yt was destroyed by Kerkby Bellors Men when Leicester was taken £2. Item for Leicester Souldiers yt came to ye Garrison to recrute when Leicester was taken £1-6-8.' PRO SP28/171, f.385-6 & 391. Several other nearby parishes record in their accounts the quartering of Kirby Bellars troops for one or two nights and, although they do not specify when, it is almost certainly at this same time.

199. Tibbutt, 1963, p.298 & 556. *Mercurius Civicus*, 29th May to 5th June 1645.

200. Klingelhofer, 1983-4. Account Book of the Committee for Rutland, PRO SP28/173 unfol.. Particular of Lord Rockingham's Account, PRO SP28/171, unfol.. The buildings were demolished by Sir John Norwich, the second governor, so this may have been carried out in response to the threat from the Royalist army in late May and early June 1645.

201. Norwich to Luke, 12th June 1645, Tibbutt, 1963, p.570. The Rutland Committee had at least a company of foot and a troop of harquebusiers in 1645. Committee of Rutland, November 1645, Col.Waite's troop; Col. Waite's foot company November 1645; July 1644 Waite's troop of harquibusiers; PRO SP28/219 unfol.. *The Scottish Dove*, 30th May to 6th June. The Lords determined to enquire into the dispute about the abandonment and burning of Burley garrison, *Lords Journals*, 14th June 1645. The detailed documents relating to Rockingham and its garrison in the Exchequer papers have yet to be studied in detail.
202. Sir John Norwich, Tibbutt, 1963, p.548.
203. Everitt, 1969. Whetham & Whetham, 1907.
204. Foard, 1994a.
205. Tibbutt, 1963, p.292.
206. Tibbutt, 1963, p.555.
207. *CSPD*, p.597.
208. *CSPD*, p.564. Tibbutt, 1963, p.292 & 549.
209. Tibbutt, 1963, p.262-3.
210. Tibbutt, 1963, p.268, 278 & 282.
211. Rushworth,vol.6, p.38.
212. *CSPD*, p.577.
213. *CSPD*, p.564.
214. *CSPD*, p.541.
215. *CSPD*, p.542.
216. *CSPD*, p.523.
217. Ramsey, 1949, p.39.
218. *CSPD*, p.560.
219. *CSPD*, p.564.
220. *CSPD*, p.540.
221. Rushworth, vol.6, p.37.
222. Tibbutt, 1963, p.551, 553, 555 & 556.
223. Rushworth, vol.6, p.37.
224. It had required the construction of forts on the three roads to Crowland, at Brother House, Dowesdale Bank and Barrow Bank, to block up and reduce the garrison when it had been captured by Royalists in December 1644. Kingston, 1897, p.178-181. *Stukeley's Diaries and Letters*, vol.2, 1883, Surtees Society, entry for 29th August 1744. The plan of 1856 purporting to show the earthwork remains of the fort is of dubious accuracy. Gresley, 1856.
225. Grid reference TL224960. RCHM, 1926, p.248. O'Neil, 1960. Harrington, 1992, p.44.
226. RCHM, 1926, p.247-8.
227. Sherwood & Pevsner, 1974, p.778.
228. Rushworth, vol.6, p.36. Whitelocke p.143. Sprigge, p.22.Tibbutt, 1963, p.552.
229. Tibbutt, 1963, p.300 & 555. Rushworth, vol.6, p.36. Symonds, p.188.
230. 3rd June, Whitelocke, p.143.
231. Sprigge, 1647, p.21.
232. *CSPD*, p.561 & 556-7.
233. Whitelocke, p.143. Rushworth, vol.6, p.36.
234. *CSPD*, p.566-7 & 676.
235. *CSPD*, p.565.
236. Rushworth, vol.6, p.36. *CSPD*, p.562.
237. Rushworth, vol.6, p.36.
238. Smyth, 1864, p.233-252.
239. According to *Mercurius Aulicus*, 25th May to 8th June, all three senior commanders brawled, while Cromwell 'fled' to Ely.
240. Hall, 1989. Pevsner, 1973, p.69.

CHAPTER 5

THE ARMIES APPROACH

'They straggle up and down the country, plundering,
imprisoning and laying great impositions on the country.'
Sir John Norwich

There was great uncertainty as to what the Royalists' next move would be, because they sent troops in various directions, to Burton on Trent and into Derbyshire, Staffordshire and Northamptonshire.[1] Intelligence came in from refugees leaving Leicester and while some reports indicated the King would march north other news suggested that Northampton was their next objective. Some even said they might bypass that town and attack Newport Pagnell instead.[2] However, while the King's army was at Leicester news had arrived of the fall of Evesham, which had only been left with a garrison of 550 troops when the King had marched out less than two weeks before.[3] They had already lost control of the key garrison at Shrewsbury, which commanded the iron-works of Coalbrookdale and communications into north Wales. Transportation of supplies had become increasingly difficult by 1645 and the iron products of the west Midlands could only get through to Oxford via Worcester and then only with strong convoys. The fall of Evesham effectively closed this crucial route.[4] The Royalist capital was therefore not only under siege, it was also becoming increasingly isolated from its areas of supply for cannon, shot, grenades and other materiel.[5]

At Leicester a Council of War was called to decide the army's next move and naturally the plight of Oxford was a central issue. There were several options. They could march south to the relief of Oxford; go towards Worcester to join up with Gerard's 3000 troops and so, having strengthened the army, restore the losses in the west or engage the New Model; or they could continue north, as Rupert had long been arguing, and might even attempt to come to terms with the Scots, in view of their great disgust for the Independents who were now in the ascendancy. The courtiers on the Council lent eager support to the idea of marching to Oxford. It has been argued that Oxford was now of little practical value to either side, but the city did have more than just simply symbolic value.[6] Not only would its fall have been a major propaganda victory for the Parliament, it would also have been a significant blow to the Royalist war effort. Oxford was still the centre of the King's administrative system and the refuge of many of the most important Royalist supporters. It had also become a major production and supply centre for ordnance, small-arms and other military supplies and was probably the most important production centre for gunpowder. It also contained the craftsmen to maintain and repair the train of artillery and had a major magazine and armoury.[7] The question was not over the value of the capital,

Fig. 37. Evesham, which controlled a crossing of the river Avon, was an important staging post on the Royalist communication route between Worcester and Oxford. Its fall in late May 1645 was a severe blow to the Royalist cause.

but rather over its ability to hold out against a close siege. Hyde had written to Rupert on 27th May that 'We receive strange alarms every day from Oxford; but if such a town cannot endure the face of an army for some time, I would dwell hereafter in the fields and villages, and think no more of fortifying towns...'[8] Rupert was in correspondence with his close friend William Legge, governor of the city, and had there been a real threat then Legge would surely have advised Rupert, who would have responded positively. However, Slingsby does say that at this time there came from Oxford 'some intimation .... yt ye town was not so well provid'd for a seige; wch stopt ye King in his march & turn'd his thoughts how to relieve it'.[9] The other important factor was the wish amongst some on the Council to see an early meeting with the New Model. Nicholas, the King's Secretary of State who had remained in Oxford, had written to Rupert on the 22nd May saying:

> 'If Fairfax and Cromwell should receive some considerable blow, it would not only check... [the] Scots and Northern rebels, in advancing hither, but add so much to the present distractions at London, as would prepare an easy way for a happy removing of the present miseries of this Kingdom...'[10]

This view was very much encouraged by the common feeling amongst the Royalists that Fairfax's army was inferior to the King's, especially as Cromwell was away in the Association. Even though the New Model might outnumber them at present, this would not be the case when Gerard's and Goring's forces reached the King. Rupert and the other soldiers on the

Council apparently argued strongly that the army should march north while the courtiers, particularly Digby and Ashburnham, encouraged by the success at Leicester, argued for a march towards Oxford and an early battle with Fairfax.[11]

Fig. 38. When the Royalist army marched out of Leicester on the 4th June 1645 they fired Leicester Abbey, the Countess of Devonshire's house, where the King had been staying for the previous two nights. The ruins of this Palladian mansion, built by the Earl of Huntingdon, remain to this day at the north west corner of Abbey Park. Enclosed behind a long stretch of medieval park wall they stand as a tribute to the wanton destruction of the Civil War.[12]

As usual Charles tried to get the best of both worlds and ended with the worst. The army was to march south to relieve Oxford but then, rather than face the New Model, it would march north again to pursue the other objectives. The King wrote to Nicholas on the 4th June that his army was so weak he was unwilling to hazard it in the relief of Oxford before Goring or Gerard joined with him, and so he urged Nicholas to send all the unnecessary people out of Oxford so that the provisions could last longer. He requested that Nicholas did not require him to relieve the city unless it was absolutely necessary, saying that he was intending to stay at Harborough for a time to 'gather up straglers and to make provision to supply you for this service...'[13] Had he immediately engaged the New Model while Cromwell, Vermuyden and Rossiter were away from the army then the outcome might have been somewhat different. Had he marched northward he would have had time to recruit in Yorkshire and then face either the Scots or the New Model on ground of his own choosing with a far stronger army. Instead, as at other important moments during the Civil War, the King's lack of leadership qualities, his inability to take bold decisions or even to recognise his own limitations and let his senior commander take the military decisions, placed his army in the worst possible situation.

So it was that on the 4th June the Royalist army began the march towards Oxford, leaving a small garrison in Leicester to hold the town and to continue with the re-fortification.[14] While the foot marched out of the town, the horse assembled from the various adjacent villages and hamlets where they had been quartered because of the need for extensive pastures to feed so many horse. They all marched to a rendezvous in the open fields of Newton Harcourt, some five miles south of Leicester on the main Northampton road. From here Colonel Willis, governor of Newark, returned to his garrison with some 400 horse. This was a planned redeployment, but of far greater concern was the decision by the Northern horse, after days of uncertainty, that they would also march to Newark in what was in effect a mutiny.[15] They had been very unhappy in Oxford over winter and had only been placated by being allowed to march north in February in that remarkable dash to relieve Pontefract. They had become discontented once more with the recent decision to march to Leicester and when they discovered that they were to march south once more they:

> 'began to hang backward, and discover their discontent. At ye next Randevous ye King talk'd wth ym, but still they shew'd an unwillingness. Sr Marmaduke was sent to use his power and perswasions among ym but yet nothing could move ym.'

After a night of uncertainty and following further persuasion, based on the King's earlier promise that the army would march into Yorkshire within 15 days once Oxford was relieved, the Northern horse did rejoin the army the next day.[16]

Already by the 4th June the vanguard of the army had reached Market Harborough, where they let it be known that Northampton was their next objective, and some of the Royalist horse must already have begun making forays into Northamptonshire because there is a report that some stragglers going to plunder a fair in the county were captured by the Northampton horse.[17] Sir John Norwich, governor of Rockingham which was the nearest Parliamentarian garrison to Harborough, was preparing himself for what he felt was the inevitable assault:

> 'I expect them before me ere morning. We shall not be wanting to entertain them according to the utmost of our abilities, being recruited by the addition of some horse and foot from Kirby and Burleigh not doubting a place of such importance as this will be looked on with a vigilant eye, and considerant of our disadvantages which I shall not particularise lest I should discover too much if intercepted.'[18]

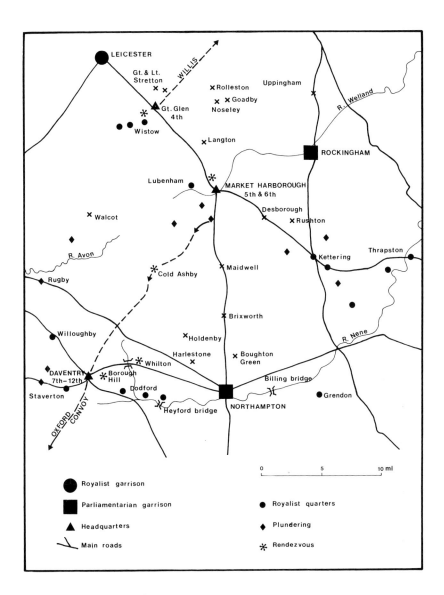

Fig. 39. The Royalist march from Leicester to Daventry.

Norwich maintained a positive approach throughout and by the 11th he was even making serious proposals that, if just 1500 dragoons were sent to join with the forces at Rockingham, he might easily retake Leicester. He reported that very few Royalist troops had been left to defend the town and that:

> 'The country much distrust their last base carriage unto them, sparing almost none, that they would join therein, and of those that are in leaguer many are countrymen - how courageous they will be (many of them being forced) I make question.'[19]

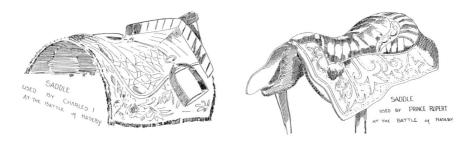

Fig. 40. The Wistow saddles, probably left as a present by Charles I and Prince Rupert when the King stayed at Wistow Hall on the 4th June 1645.

On the night of the 4th the Royalist headquarters were in the village of Great Glen which straddled the main Northampton road. It must have been at this time that a house in the village gained the name *Rupert's Rest*, for in the late 18th century this 'ancient residence' still contained a large chamber known as Prince Rupert's room. The tradition was however already distorted by this time, for it had become the place where Rupert slept on the night before the battle of Naseby.[20] The King himself lay that night at nearby Wistow Hall, in the parish of Kilby, while his horse guards were quartered in the adjacent villages of Kilby and Foston.[21] When on campaign Charles seems to have been careful in the choice of his quarters, usually picking out the houses of Royalist supporters, as indeed he had from the beginning of the war.[22] Wistow was the home of Sir Richard Halford, an ardent Royalist who had been one of the King's Commissioners of Array for Leicestershire in June 1642 and had raised troops and provided large sums of money for the Royalist cause.[23] It is said that after Naseby, in the succeeding weeks and months, Halford was under constant danger and his house plundered repeatedly under the pretence of seeking for the King, while in August 1645 he was fined £2000 for his delinquency.[24] The Hall, though modernised in later centuries, retains much of its early 17th century core and upstairs there are three rooms with 17th century panelling, the one at the south west front being known as King Charles' room. In the late 18th century even the bed in which the King had supposedly slept was still shown to visitors. They were also shown the two embroidered velvet saddles with bronze stirrups, which are still at Wistow Hall, said to have been used by Charles I and Prince Rupert at the battle of Naseby, together with a sword which was also said to have been left by Charles. The saddles are certainly of the right date and of sufficiently high quality workmanship to have been given to Halford as a present by the King, but probably on the 4th June and not, as the tradition suggests, when he escaped from the battlefield. Though the story that Charles returned to Wistow to change his horse during the flight from Naseby is almost certainly wrong, in a most bizarre way Charles did in a sense return. Sir Henry Halford, who was physician to George IV, was present at the opening of Charles I's coffin, on 1st April 1813. It was then that he acquired one of Charles' cervical vertebrae cleft by the executioner's axe. This single bone Sir Henry Halford 'used to display at his dinner table at Wistow, where there are several portraits and relics of Charles I, and he was much criticised for his want of nice feeling.'[25]

On the 5th June the army continued south to a rendezvous at Market Harborough, a small market town in the upper reaches of the Welland valley, on the border between Leicestershire and Northamptonshire.[26] Harborough had been an important staging post throughout the war for Royalists travelling between Oxford, Newark and the north.[27] The headquarters for the nights of the 5th and 6th were established in the town but the King stayed at the nearby village of Lubenham, at Mr Collins' house.[28] At the time a Parliamentarian newspaper suggested that the Royalist army was marching into Northamptonshire in case Cromwell with other forces fell upon them before they were ready.[29] This was of course pure propaganda, because Cromwell's troops were at this stage in no condition to fight with anyone. The only significant forces between the King and the Association were the garrison at Rockingham and the cavalry under Vermuyden, who had now begun to move southward flanking the King's march but at a safe distance.[30]

One may well ask why the King followed such a circuitous route towards Oxford. It may simply be because this was the major road, always a consideration when an army was encumbered by a large baggage train, but it was more likely to have been with the intention of deceiving the local garrisons as to his exact objective. Interestingly, already in late May it was to Market Harborough that Goring had been instructed to march in order to rendezvous with the army, implying that the decision to move to Harborough had been taken before the fall of Leicester. The Parliamentarian newspapers were however quite clear as to where they marched and why: 'In their countie course they leave none of the fattest soyles, for they come by Walcot, Langhton, Harborough, Rugby, and so dispersing themselves in Northamptonshire....'[31] As they marched the army:

'made an utter desolation in most of the Towns between Deintry and Leicester, driving away not only many thousands of sheep and other cattle, but even the Countrymen themselves ..... inforcing them to purchase their liberty...'[32]

There are various records of the army plundering villages around Rugby which almost certainly relate to this time. The village of Shawell, in the south west corner of Leicestershire, estimated its losses at £235 when Rupert burnt the place, while at Rugby on about the 5th June a certain John Jones was:

'plundered by prince Rupert his forces by my Lord of Northampton's Regement and imprisoned by them, being but newly Relesed from imprisonment at Naseby fight, being in the hands of the cavaliers nine or tene dayes, which did prededuce me £20.'[33]

Sprigge also claims that some of the local people had 'their children taken from them, and sold before their faces to the Irish of that Army, whom the parents were enforced to redeem with the price of money.'[34]

As the King advanced through Leicestershire and Northamptonshire the main body of the army will have marched together, but some at least of the horse were dispatched on wide ranging forays. We are fortunate in having the diary of Richard Symonds, who was in a troop of the King's lifeguard, as he gives a hint of such action. Symonds was a keen antiquary and made records of the various churches he was able to visit on his marches and, as a result, we can see not just where he was quartered but some of the other places he visited during the day. So, on the 4th June, he visited Great and Little Stretton, Rolleston and Goadby before returning to Great Glen, which was the headquarters that night. His troop may have been dispatched to face the nearby Rockingham garrison, to ensure there was no unexpected attack on the army as it marched, but equally they may have been collecting stock and other supplies from the surrounding territory. The quartering and supply of the Royalist army had been improved considerably from the situation early in the war where troops were 'sent out without any manner of forecast or design, or care to preserve or quarter them when they are abroad.'[35] Again on the 5th June, while the army was at Harborough, Symonds was some seven miles forward at Desborough and Rushton and it was probably at this time that the villages in central and eastern Northamptonshire were plundered by Royalist troops.[36] For example we find that at Burton Latimer 'The King's souldiers tooke away from [Thomas Lee] a few dayes before Naseby fight in money £8' and from other villagers four horses worth £22. At Weekley 'When the King's soildiers came to plunder the Towne they layd a tax on it to the value of £20' and some of the inhabitants were 'plundered by them to the value of £13/10/0d'. At Thorpe Malsor 'Henry Giniley had his papers taken from him by the Cavaliers in June 1645' while 'Wee of east Farndon have had our houses plundered and pillaged by the Kinges army....' and at nearby Great Oxendon the villagers estimated that their losses of 'household goods and cattell about Nasbey fight and a weeke before were above £400.'[37] A little further west, the village of Sibbertoft also reported:

> 'the losse which was sustained in the towne of Sibbertoft att (Navesbye fight) and in the weeke before by the Kings forces in monie horses beast and sheepe, with linnons wolons Corne and other provisions to the undoing of the greatest part of the inhabytance was att the least to the value of £300.'[38]

With the exception of the places where the New Model Army was actually quartered, the scale of these losses to the Royalists far outweighs anything recorded by the villages supplying the Parliament army a few days later.

While the headquarters were at Harborough the cavalry were certainly deployed well into Northamptonshire, with detachments already quartered within seven miles of Northampton by the 5th. Other reports suggest they had advanced right across the county along the main road from Harborough to Huntingdon, 'lying all the country over' in the small towns of Kettering and Thrapston and in adjacent villages. From this particular approach, as far as Thrapston, the local forces could not 'but conceive that his sole intentions are for the Association' and letters from Huntingdon reported daily that they expected the King that way.[39] On the afternoon of the 5th June two hundred Royalist cavalry also faced Northampton, but the garrison was not yet overawed because they sallied forth and claimed to have captured a captain and a good part of his troop. Most of the following day the Royalists continued to face the town, in full view from the defences, but again the Northampton horse responded, skirmishing with the enemy at Boughton Green where they claimed to have had the better of them and to have taken several prisoners.[40] This time however Colonel Whetham's men lost two of their colleagues in the engagement and only managed to withdraw with great difficulty, even with the support of dragoons sent out from the town. Rupert had once before been driven off from Northampton, in October 1643, and although this time he had a far greater force at his disposal, the Northampton garrison were not going to give in without a bloody fight. On the night of the 6th June Royalist forces also faced Rockingham castle but made no attempt upon it. Throughout this period, as one correspondent from Northampton reported, their horse continued to skirmish with the Royalists, while the Rockingham governor 'hath sent out his troope daily, who have taken many prisoners, he sent hither 30 at one time to be kept here.' Not surprisingly perhaps, all the prisoners were found to be 'full of money and good cloathes' that they had plundered from the two counties.[41]

While this military action continued so too did the plundering. On the 6th the King had already sent out warrants for the western half of Northamptonshire to send in provisions to Daventry, in preparation for his march there, and on the 6th and 7th substantial detachments of cavalry continued taxing the county.[42] They:

'sent out their warrants all over the North East parts of this County, and taxed every Town some at 100 pound some 200 pound, and some lesse some more, upon penalty of being plundered of their goods and their houses fired, and by this meanes they have gathered great sums of mony: and some of the Townes having payd the sum first set, another company comes and chargeth them again...'

On the 6th a large body of Royalist horse were said to have advanced through Maidwell and by the afternoon were as far as Brixworth and adjacent villages, within six miles of Northampton.[43] One villager perhaps did not pay as he should, for at about this time the churchwarden of Great Houghton paid 'to

a poore man of Spratton that had his house burned £2/0/8d. [144] Some reports
say the royalists even crossed the Nene and quartered as far south as Grendon,
their scouts being seen within four miles of Newport Pagnell. By now
however troops were beginning to arrive to support the local Parliamentarian
garrisons which were also collecting supplies in case of a siege. Newport, like
Leicester before it, had been offered limited support by the Scots, for on the
6th June two troops of Scottish horse under Captain Middleton were deployed
to the north of Olney to counter the Royalist threat. By the night of the 6th
Vermuyden had followed the Scots in towards Newport Pagnell, marching to
rejoin Fairfax. Vermuyden's men were quartered in the town of Olney, which
controlled the bridge on the main road south to Newport Pagnell, and in the
adjacent villages of Lavendon and Weston Underwood. With Vermuyden's
arrival, the next day the Scots withdrew into Newport itself, to bolster the
garrison's defence. [45]

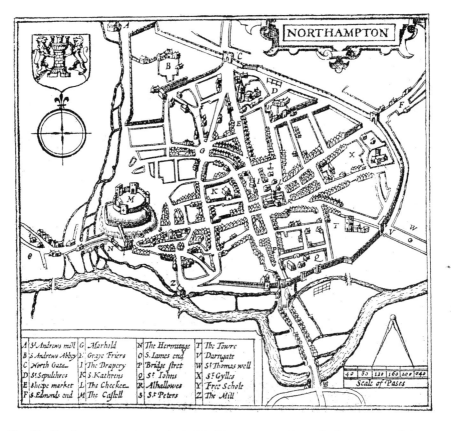

A	St Andrews mill	G	Marhold	N	The Hermitage	T	The Towre
B	S Andrews Abbey	H	Gray: Friers	O	S. Iames end	V	Darrigate
C	North Gate	I	The Drapery	P	Bridge stret	W	St Thomas well
D	St Sepulchres	K	S. Kathrens	Q	St Iohns	X	St Gylles
E	sheepe market	L	The Checker	R	Alhallowes	Y	Free Schole
F	s Edmonds end	M	The Castell	S	St Peters	Z	The Mill

*Fig.41. Northampton as it was in 1610. The town was from the beginning of the war
one of the most important Parliamentarian garrisons in the region. Its medieval
defences and those of its castle were refurbished and enhanced with earth and timber
fortification during the war. In early June, after the fall of Leicester, it was feared
that Northampton would be the King's next target.*

On the morning of the 7th there were Royalist horse still quartered around Northampton, as they had been for two days, but now the whole body of the King's army began to move south. Still observed by the Rockingham scouts, they marched out of Harborough towards Kelmarsh on the Northampton road, crossing the Welland by the small stone bridge, but then they turned across country on minor roads towards Daventry because the rendezvous that day was at Cold Ashby.[46] There were various Parliamentarian reports on the 7th that the King was at Holdenby House, within six miles of Northampton, while other reports also put him there on the 10th June. This was a place Charles would come to know very well in 1647, when he was imprisoned there, but he did not stop at Holdenby in 1645 unless it was very briefly during the day. All other accounts are clear that the King was with the army on the night of the 7th in the small market town of Daventry, 11 miles west of Northampton.[47] That night the foot lay in the field and the cavalry were quartered in surrounding villages, but while the army was at Daventry the King himself stayed in the town at the Wheatsheaf Inn.[48] Though now an old peoples home, the Wheatsheaf still survives at the south end of Sheaf Street and just over fifty years ago the landlord would still show interested visitors the suite of rooms supposedly occupied by the King in the days before the battle of Naseby.[49] It had originally been intended by some of the King's advisors that Charles should continue on to Oxford but when the army reached Daventry news arrived that the siege of Oxford had been raised and that the New Model had marched east towards Bedfordshire.[50] Rupert's letter of the 8th June contains a most revealing comment about the struggle that was going on between the military commanders and the courtiers for control of the campaign:

> 'There was a plot to send the King to Oxford, but it is undone. The Chief of the Council was the fear some men [viz., Digby and Ashburnham] had that the soldiers should take from them the influence which now they possess with the King...'[51]

This was a struggle in which the courtiers would continue to have the upper hand, resulting in the destruction of the King's army at Naseby.

There has been much written about the mistakes made by the King in the fortnight after the fall of Leicester, but once the decision had been taken to relieve Oxford the actions that followed made good military sense. Rupert it would seem was making the best of a bad situation, for as Lieutenant General he was at least in control of the detail of how the King's decisions were to be implemented. Marching south he took control of the most commanding position in western Northamptonshire, the great Iron Age hillfort of Borough Hill, immediately to the east of Daventry. Rupert must have known Daventry from the time he had assembled his forces there in 1643, when preparing to escort the Queen in her passage from York to Oxford, and the defensive possibilities of Borough Hill must also have been known to other commanders

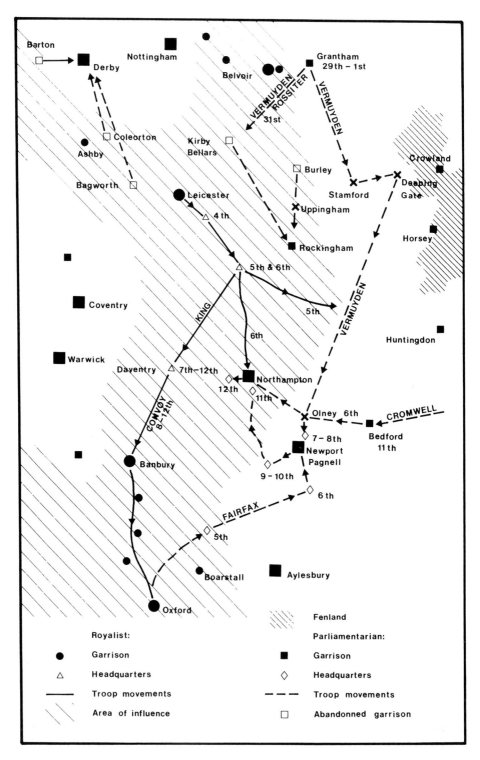

Fig.42. The south east Midlands after the fall of Leicester.

from the region, such as the Earl of Northampton, because convoys from Oxford to Ashby and Newark frequently passed through the town.[52] In establishing the army at Daventry, Rupert not only placed himself in an ideal position to relieve Oxford, he also severed the last road link from London to the Midlands, the North West and to Gloucester. The strategic significance was not lost on the Parliamentarians in London, for the newspapers recorded that the Royalists 'diverted their course; and as if they intended to draw a line from Newark to Oxford (and stop our Commerce with diverse Counties) they return into Northamptonshire...'[53] For those few days in June the King had command of a broad swathe of central England from the Thames to the Trent.

For millennia Borough Hill had dominated western Northamptonshire. As far back as the Iron Age the massive hillfort had controlled the most important lines of communications from south eastern England through the Watford gap to the Midlands and the North West. Now the King's army sat down behind the surviving earthen rampart of the hillfort, just as a Danish army had probably done nearly eight hundred years before, making use of the ancient defences to control the region. The Royalists appear to have thrown up new works at this time for there are Parliamentarian reports 'That he indeavours to intrench himself about Daventry hills, to prevent our falling on before the coming up of their Foot, and to that end have summoned the County to bring in shovels and Pike-Axes...'[54] At this time Borough Hill was an area of common pasture and, although the southern slopes were heavily wooded, on every other side there were wide open views over many miles. The hill commanded the road to Northampton, which passed immediately to the north of the fort, and the main London to Coventry road, just half a mile to the south, while two miles to the east ran Watling Street. This was a commanding position on one of the main communication routes in England.[55] The fort had changed little by the time Walpoole visited the hill in the late 18th century when he described it as:

'lofty and insulated : the area is of oblong, or oval form, about a measured mile in length, and near two in circumference; the whole is surrounded by two, three, or four deep trenches, and the same number of great ramparts or banks; according as the strength or weakness of the ground required....'[56]

A modern visitor will however find it difficult to trace the ramparts and ditches because they were levelled by ploughing, which began following enclosure in 1803. Today only at the very southern end of the fort does a well preserved length of rampart and ditch survive, marking the southern extent of the hillfort, while at the northern end, though now much altered by the golf course, there are the smoothed over ramparts of the smaller but more heavily defended later Iron Age fort.[57] Of the brief Royalist stay on Borough Hill nothing has yet been revealed on the site itself, except perhaps the single cannon ball reported in 1923 as having been 'discovered many years ago....on the outskirts of Borough Hill'.[58]

Fig.43. Borough hill as it was in the early 18th century, overshadowing the small market town of Daventry. It was here that part of the Royalist army was encamped while the King waited for the relief convoy to return from Oxford and where the whole army stood in battalia all night on the 12th June 1645.

The Royalists needed just one more major garrison to secure their control of central England - the town of Northampton. On 4th June the Committee at Northampton wrote to Fairfax that the Royalist army 'is within twelve miles of us; their design is thought to be for this Place: we doubt not but you will take us into your thoughts for a speedy Relief, and in the mean time we shall provide for them to the best of our strength.'[59] Having heard the graphic stories of the sack of Leicester, probably at first hand from the refugees, the people of Northampton must have been terrified at the thought of a Royalist attack on their town. The only comfort they received was the return of the 400 foot that had been detached from the garrison to assist in the siege of Oxford, who had now been ordered home 'for the better defence of the place'.[60] But Northampton was not the immediate objective of the Royalists and presumably their show of strength before the town was simply to deter an attack on their army as it marched from Harborough to Daventry. Though far outnumbered, the garrison was for the moment safe behind its defences and could immediately sally forth onto the offensive whenever the Royalists were at a disadvantage. As the Royalist cavalry drew away from the town to Daventry a party of the Northampton horse followed, skirmished with them and took twenty horse and various prisoners without loss.[61] Though willing to take the initiative when it could, Northampton waited nervously for the arrival of the New Model Army to meet a challenge which was well beyond its own modest resources.

While at Daventry much of the Royalist cavalry were dispersed in the surrounding villages. On the 7th June the King's lifeguard were at Staverton, controlling the main road towards the Parliamentarian garrison at Warwick, and then on the 10th they were at Willoughby, controlling the north western approach to Daventry along the main road to Coventry.[62] Others troops were quartered as close as three or four miles from Northampton and yet more to the north of the town. From Daventry they took effective control of a wide area of Northamptonshire and Warwickshire, though they could still not act with impunity, for Colonel Whetham and Sir John Norwich both continued to harry the Royalists wherever they could. Because there were so many cavalry they had to be quartered on a wide range of villages and this made them vulnerable to surprise attack. The local force, making the best use of their intimate knowledge of the area, could move in rapidly to strike, beat up the quarters of the enemy cavalry and then withdraw just as quickly to the safety of their garrison. They also ventured out from behind their defences to attack small detachments of Royalist troops pillaging or 'taxing' the villages nearby. So we find the newspapers continuing to report 'many skirmishes have been betwixt Northampton forces and Parteis of the Kings, and prisoners taken on both sides.'[63] Not only did such attacks limit the Royalists' opportunity to ravage the surrounding countryside, it also gave Whetham the opportunity to gain valuable intelligence. For example, on the 9th June he took some prisoners who informed him that it was the King's intention to join up with Goring's troops and then to engage the New Model and if this engagement was successful the King would then march northward.[64]

On the 8th the King's cavalry made a rendezvous at Whilton and from there dispatched a force comprising five from each troop of horse in a convoy to deliver the stock and other plunder to Oxford, the rest returning to their old quarters within three or four miles of Northampton.[65] Though one must recognise the exaggerations that propaganda reports in the newspapers can contain, the claim that the Royalists took 30000 sheep and 8000 cattle to Oxford does give an impression of the scale of the plundering.[66] With knowledge of the approach of the convoy, cavalry were dispatched from Oxford and the surrounding garrisons to guard it as it came in.[67] The opportunity also seems to have been taken, while sending provisions to Oxford, to resupply the army with munitions, presumably to replace those expended at the storming of Leicester, because when the convoy returned to the army at Daventry it appears to have brought back with it at least one waggon of 'fire works' from the King's firemaster in Oxford.[68]

Even when the convoy to Oxford had departed there was still no respite for the people of Northamptonshire and Warwickshire. On the following days the 'marauding Teames' of Royalists continued collecting provisions, extending as far afield as Brackley. Flecknoe, less than four miles west of Daventry, is one of the few villages to have defined in detail the losses to the King's army at this time. So, for example, we see that a wealthy merchant in the village not only had to provide free quarter but also lost 21 yards of woollen cloth, pairs of sheets, jewels, linen, clothes and money, all 'taken away by violence'. Other villages at least as far west as Upper Shuckburgh seem to have suffered equally at the hands of the Royalists.[69] On the 9th they came within half a mile of Northampton and drove away a herd of beasts and at the further end of Harlestone heath, within three miles of the town, 'they made a great fyer about 12 of the Clock.'[70] The governor of Northampton reported that 'Ye enemy has been very barbarous in beating and torturing weemen to make them tell where there money is', but for some villages such treatment was not new. Since August 1642, when Royalist troopers attacked the village of Kilsby, the people within the Rugby-Banbury-Buckingham triangle had become accustomed to being taxed by both sides and in some cases ruthlessly plundered by the Royalists.[71] However for other villages, in the areas under more secure control of the Northampton and Rockingham garrisons, such incursions were unusual. It was only when major detachments of Royalist troops passed through the area that they had been affected, as for example in 1644 when the churchwardens of Gt.Houghton paid 8d 'to a poreman of Ecton being pillaged of his goods when prince Robert came by that way'.[72] The fears expressed in London about the impact of the Royalist depredations on the provisioning of the capital reflect the economic value of Northamptonshire and Leicestershire to the Parliamentarian cause, particularly for the supply of cattle. Despite the efforts of the Northampton troops, the Royalists continued to 'spoil and destroy both Corn and Hay, saying they will make our Garrison seek further off for their provision, and boast how many fat Cattle they have made stop of for comming to London.'[73] On the 11th the Royalists still had several parties which 'straggle up and down the county about Northampton, which drive away cattle and sheep in abundance and took away great store of bacon, butter, salt and all other provisions, which they spend but little of but preserve it in wagons.....'[74]

Clarendon, in a very disparaging manner, criticised the King for staying at Daventry 'where, for want of knowing where the Enemy was, or what he intended to do, the King remained in a quiet posture the space of five days.'[75] In fact Clarendon was quite wrong, because while the army was at Daventry there were forces sent out towards Nottingham and Derby as well as being active around Northampton. Intelligence from prisoners taken by the Northampton garrison also makes it clear that the King was waiting in expectation that he would be joined by Goring's force. But whatever he might want to do, from the 8th until the 12th June the King had little alternative but to wait at Daventry for the return of the 1200 cavalry which had escorted the convoy to Oxford, only then could he march north to the relief of Pontefract and Scarborough.[76] The army was entrenched in a strong position at Daventry and they were well aware that the New Model had advanced to Newport Pagnell, for on the 10th June a trumpeter had arrived from Fairfax to discuss the exchange of prisoners.[77] However, whereas the New Model was on the move, the Royalist army was stationary and so Fairfax could prepare for the coming action by discerning the Royalist deployment but the King could not do the same. If we are to believe Walker's account, which was followed by Clarendon, from the 10th June the Royalists suffered from a breakdown in their intelligence gathering system and thereafter would be on the defensive and thus, in some respects, at a disadvantage.

The logical course of action for the King to take now was laid out in a letter from someone, possibly Hopton, in the Bridgwater garrison on the 10th June:

> 'I shall trouble you no farther but with this humble suit, that Oxford being now relieved you would well consider before you engage your person southwards, where you will meet with far greater forces to oppose you than the rebels are able to bring thither, and that, your affairs being now prosperous, you would not expose your person and cause to the hazard of a day before you shall be joined with Gerard and assisted by your northern forces, which, I fear, will hardly be persuaded to go far from their own country, and before all those western forces may be in the rear of the enemy's; to the speedy effecting whereof we shall apply all our counsels. The rich country of [?] will feed your whole army, and the advantage of the Trent will give liberty to [?Gerard] to come up to you before it can be compelled to fight; in the meantime the influence of your Majesty's armies and victories, with the assistance of parties, will not only relieve all your besieged garrisons in the north, but likewise give such encouragement to your well-affected subjects of those parts, that all this Kingdom beyond Trent will probably return to their loyalty, which will so add to the fears and distractions of the rebels that the disorders amongst themselves will be instead of a third army in the southern and eastern counties.'[78]

This letter may have been intercepted and so never reached the King, but the arguments expressed can have been little different to those propounded by Rupert in the Councils of War which decided the actions of the next few days.

Though we know that the decision to march north had already been taken by the 4th June, there is a traditional explanation as to why the King supposedly had a change of heart. It is said that on the night of the 7th June:

> 'about two hours after the King had retired to rest, some of his attendants, hearing an uncommon noise in his chamber went into it, where they found his Majestie sitting up in his bed, and much agitated; but nothing which could have produced the noise they fancied they heard. The King, in a trembling, enquired after the cause of their alarm, and told them how he had been agitated in a dream, by thinking he saw the apparition of Lord Strafford; who after upbraiding him with unkindness told him that he was come to return him good for evil; and that he advised him by no means to fight the Parliament armie that was at that time at Northampton, for it was one which the King should never conquer by arms ..... Prince Rupert, in whom courage was the predominant qualitie, rated the King out of his approbation the next day, and a resolution was taken to meet the enemie...The next night however the apparition appeared to him a second time, but with looks of anger assured him that would be the last advice he should be permitted to give him; but that if he kept his resolution of fighting, he was undone.'

Afterwards it is reported 'he was often heard to say that he wished he had taken the warning and not fought at Naseby; the meaning of which nobody knew but those to whom he told his appearance at Daintree; and they were all of them afterwards charged to conceal it.'[79] If this story had any basis in fact then it is not perhaps surprising that it should have been thoughts of Strafford that came into Charles's mind at this difficult time, for his desertion of the Earl weighed heavily upon his conscience and it is said that even on the scaffold he referred to Strafford's fate. However if Charles' correspondence at this time is a genuine representation of his mood then he cannot have been too worried about the prospects, for on the 9th June he wrote to Edward Nicholas: 'if we Peripatetiques get no more mischances than you Oxfordians ar lyke to have this somer, we may all expect probably a merry Winter.'[80] Indeed Charles was even persuaded to take time out to relax by hunting in the nearby Fawsley Park.

The events following the fall of Leicester had finally prompted Parliament to instruct Fairfax to leave the siege of Oxford and deploy his forces to secure the Association.[81] He was now receiving intelligence from Luke which suggested that the Royalist army was marching towards Huntingdon and as long as Fairfax believed the King might be advancing against the Association he moved rapidly, using the best and most direct route. On the night of the 5th June the troops were quartered between Brill and Bicester, with the headquarters at Marsh Gibbon. Their intention was to march the next day to Buckingham, following the main Oxford to Cambridge road, but the plans were changed when it was discovered that the King's horse were already facing Northampton.[82] It was not considered safe to venture so close to the Royalist army for, although we know that the Royalists had decided against such a strategy, Luke's scouts reported that the King would try to force the New Model to fight near Brackley. This must have weighed heavily in Fairfax's deliberations, especially as a large body of the New Model horse had still not returned from the north. Because of the foolish decisions of the Committee of Both Kingdoms to divide its forces, the New Model was now at its most vulnerable and if compelled to fight they would be heavily outnumbered in cavalry.[83] To avoid such dangers Fairfax marched on a more southerly course to Great Brickhill, which he reached on the 6th June.

Before they marched towards Buckinghamshire instructions had gone out to the County Committee to send in provisions to the army but, just as Luke reported in connection with his garrison so with the New Model, their endeavours proved fruitless and no provisions came in. According to Luke:

> 'the hearts of the people in these parts being so stricken by the loss of Leicester, together with the late alterations in Parliament affairs, that though I have summoned in this county and Beds. to my assistance, yet cannot get one man, and but very little provisions. Neither can I get but very few to come into the works without forcing them.'

The county had probably not yet recovered from the enormous burdens which had been placed upon it during the previous winter. On the 7th, when he arrived at Newport Pagnell, because of 'this great strait the soldiers are in', Fairfax had to request that Luke provide the New Model with what supplies he could out of the stores of the garrison. The problems in gaining supplies in Buckinghamshire incidentally enables us to see exactly how the New Model was attempting to minimise its impact on the territories through which it marched, because Fairfax wrote that the failure of supplies to arrive 'much discontents the soldiers and necessitates them to straggle abroad, which may prejudice the inhabitants in the county.'[84] Taken together with the evidence for supply of the army when it reached Northamptonshire it will be seen that control was achieved by keeping the army, particularly the infantry which contained the most unruly elements, tightly together in a few well controlled quarters each night and not allowing them to roam widely across the countryside.

By the time he reached Newport Pagnell, on the 7th June, Fairfax will have been aware that the Royalist army had moved south westward to Daventry.[85] Now there was no need for haste as there was no immediate threat to the Association and so, over the next five days, he made a more gradual advance towards the enemy, biding his time as he strengthened his army for the coming battle. The headquarters for the nights of the 7th and 8th June were established on the south east bank of the Ouse at Sherington, just two miles north east of Newport Pagnell, with troops quartered in various adjacent villages.[86] With the garrison commanding the crossings on the west and with cavalry deployed three miles to the north at the small town of Olney, which controlled the other main bridge, the army was in a well protected location.[87] Fairfax had secured his first base for the advance on the Royalists and had placed the New Model between the King's army and the Association.

Newport Pagnell was one of the garrisons which had felt most under threat from the Royalist advance and so, despite the demand for supplies, the garrison and population must have been very pleased to see the New Model Army arrive. Luke wrote on the 7th, 'we want men exceedingly, and the want of victuals, ordnance and arms are as great, yet I fear them not this time, Sir T.Fairfax being so near....'[88] Despite the relief at the arrival of the New Model, the governor did not however entertain Fairfax and his commanders, making the excuse that there was a lack of accommodation. He restricted his hospitality to showing them around the defences, saluting them with a 'peale of ordnance' and providing wine.[89] One cannot help thinking that this muted welcome was a reflection of Luke's distrust of the New Model Army and it certainly seems to have been taken as an insult. The garrison was demoralised and mutinous, largely due to a lack of pay and supplies, and so it is not surprising to see that there was tension between the garrison and the New Model forces, something which cannot have been helped by the realisation that, under the Self Denying Ordinance, the governor would soon be replaced. There had also been dissatisfaction amongst Parliamentarian forces that had not been incorporated into the New Model because they saw the latter given all the resources while they were left with little support, but perhaps most significant was the inevitable conflict over religion, the New Model being viewed by Presbyterians such as Luke as an army of Independents whom they despised as much if not more than they did the Royalists. What is perhaps remarkable is the degree to which this animosity boiled over into actual physical conflict. Already in mid May 1645 Luke had written:

> 'There is such an antipathy here between my men and the New Model that you will every day hear of new encounters. My party which encountered Col. Pickering is returned with the loss of one man only, whom I intend to relieve so soon as I know where he is.'[90]

When one of Fairfax's officers preached in Newport on the Sunday following the battle they were actually imprisoned by the governor![91]

One of the most distinct images one has from the previous accounts of the Naseby campaign is of a Royalist army poorly served by its scouts and wrong

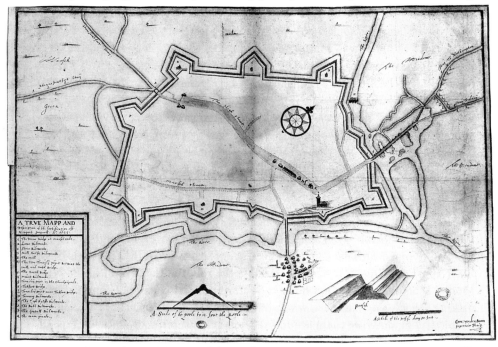

Fig. 44. The Civil War defences of the Parliamentarian garrison at Newport Pagnell, described as being one of the strongest places in the Kingdom, yet repeatedly in the weeks leading up to the battle of Naseby the governor reported the lack of sufficient troops and supplies to hold the town against the expected siege.[92] It lies at the junction of the Ouse and the Lovat, controlling the crossings of both rivers. The defensive ditch and rampart of the Civil War curtain are still visible as a slight earthwork, much confused in places by later quarrying, in the Bury Fields, common land on the north west side of Newport Pagnell. (By courtesy of the Bodleian Library)

footed on several crucial occasions because it did not know exactly where the New Model Army was. In contrast Fairfax seems always to have had detailed knowledge of the whereabouts and strength of the Royalist army. If this apparent failure is not, in part at least, a distortion of the facts by the faction at court that were critical of Rupert, then we must establish why it occurred. The reason the Royalist intelligence system failed them so disastrously may be partly explained if one considers the way in which information was collected during the Civil War. The local garrisons will often have been the most effective sources of intelligence because they knew their own territory so well. Apart from the Banbury garrison, which was very familiar with the south western part of Northamptonshire, there were no Royalist bases in the combat zone and so they were immediately at a disadvantage. In contrast the Rockingham, Northampton, Newport, Coventry and Warwick garrisons were all working on home territory and encompassed the Royalist army on both sides. Moreover, Sir Samuel Luke had been Scoutmaster General to the Earl of Essex from January 1643 until January 1645 and on the 6th June instructions were issued for Luke's intelligence system to be funded directly by Parliament and his information provided to the New Model while it was in the area.[93] Luke had a network of contacts in the region and one can see from his letter books how rapid and frequent was the exchange of intelligence between the local garrisons. These garrisons were continually sending out scouts or small parties of troops who would view enemy positions and capture enemy soldiers, who could be made to talk 'by faire promises of Reward or threatenings of great punishment...'[94]

There was also the information gained from the interception of correspondence and, at least in the case of Luke, information coming from spies within the Royalist garrisons, including Oxford itself. Rockingham had provided the most important intelligence while the Royalist army was in Leicestershire, but now that they were in western Northamptonshire it was the Northampton garrison which was the most significant source of information. Northampton already had a scouting service by 1643 and since at least the summer of that year it had maintained a posting service which was run in 1645 by Nathaniel Sharpe, postmaster to the garrison.[95] These messengers of the Committee at Northampton were required to take letters and news of alarums and other events to the commanders throughout the region and beyond.[96] Sharpe and his assistants were involved in numerous journeys to London, Coventry and other garrisons in the region and this is how the intelligence was so rapidly transmitted from one place to another.[97] The post riders and other men from Northampton would also at times act as guides for forces coming into the region, and undoubtedly this occurred in June 1645.[98] In the fortnight immediately following the battle of Naseby, Sharpe would be involved in journeys to London, Newport Pagnell and Leicester and this must have been one of the main ways that the news of the successes at Naseby and Leicester reached London and the other garrisons. The intelligence from

Northampton in the days leading up to the battle, at least initially, seems to have reached Fairfax via Sir Samuel Luke. For example, there is the letter from Whetham to Luke on the 9th June and then, on the following day, a letter from Luke to Fairfax passing on the information. Such rapid communication meant the garrisons were well aware of the developing regional and national situation and for Fairfax it meant he was aware of enemy deployments and intentions soon enough to enable him to react while the intelligence was still relevant. Indeed Fairfax made full use of the resources at Northampton as he neared the town, even its senior commanders, for on the 12th Luke reports 'there is a party as I hear going out of the army and Col.Lydcot attends them because of his experience in the country.'[99]

So it is not surprising that as soon as he moved into the area Fairfax was better served with intelligence than the King's army. The Royalist troops, spread far and wide across Northamptonshire collecting provisions, were very vulnerable to attacks from the local garrisons. Fairfax on the other hand manoeuvred as close as possible to the Parliamentarian garrisons, kept his army as close together as possible and only advanced into the combat zone a few days before the two armies met. There was therefore very little opportunity for the Royalists to gain intelligence as to his movements or the real strength of his army. This is not to suggest that the Royalists were wholly without information or knowledge of the area because they surely had with them scouts from their Banbury garrison, but the scouts were dependent, to a degree, upon local support and this was a territory which was generally well disposed towards Parliament, while the scale and apparently indiscriminate nature of Royalist plundering must have discouraged many of those who were sympathetic from providing assistance.

Both armies also, of course, collected intelligence by their own means, for each had its own scouts. In the New Model they were under the command of Major Leonard Watson, Scoutmaster General to the Army, who had during the Naseby campaign a complement of 20 mounted scouts who will have been supplied with the best and ablest horses in the army.[100] The Royalist scouts, presumably with similar numbers, were under the command of their Scoutmaster General, Sir Francis Ruce. The armies would also use larger bodies of cavalry to discover enemy dispositions and so, for example, on the 8th Fairfax dispatched several parties of horse under Colonel Butler as far as Towcester to determine where the King's forces were deployed. From there Butler then sent a dozen horse right forward to within a mile of the enemy's main cavalry quarters. Not only did they view the situation, they also captured some stragglers from Langdale's Brigade and these prisoners confirmed that the Royalist army was still at Daventry.[101] Fairfax also sent a trumpeter to the Royalist headquarters, who arrived at Daventry on the 10th June, to discuss terms for the exchange of prisoners.[102] As Cruso says, a trumpeter must:

'be discreet and judicious; not onely to be fit to deliver embassies and messages
as they ought, but (at his return) to report what he hath observed concerning the

enemies works and guards, and what he hath further gathered and spied.'[103]

Fairfax was making careful preparation for the forthcoming battle by gaining intelligence as to the strength and disposition of the King's forces. Although most of the advantages lay with Fairfax, the intelligence gathering process was not completely one sided. The Royalists also sent out parties to approach close to the New Model and they may even have had spies out, for on the 10th Fairfax sent Edward Woodhall to Luke saying he had been 'taken under very strong suspicion of being a spy or some way employed by the enemy, but pretending to be servant to Sir Rowland Egerton and sent by him to London.' Luke was to keep him in custody for a week until his intelligence was no longer valuable and then release him.[104]

As the battle approached the final build up of the army began and the very last steps in the whole process of remodelling the army were now initiated. Fairfax had been continually frustrated in the early weeks of the campaign because the Committee of Both Kingdoms were directing the war by remote control from London. Finally, on the 9th June, the Committee relinquished their control, giving him a free hand to find and engage the King's army.[105] It had taken the disaster of Leicester, the ravaging of Leicestershire and Northamptonshire and, most of all, the fear that the same fate might be in store for the Association, to force their hand or perhaps to give the Independents on the Committee the opportunity to get the policy changed. Now that effective control had been given to Fairfax the potential of the New Model Army could at last be realised. How desperately must Rupert have wished for similar authority to manage the Royalist campaign! Immediately Fairfax wrote to Parliament saying that he was about to advance towards the enemy and was resolved to engage them if they would stand and fight, for he realised how important it was for the New Model to beat the enemy before Goring's cavalry joined them.[106] But first there was one other objective to be fulfilled. The Independents had prepared their ground and bided their time, looking for the best moment. As the decisive battle was just a few days away, Parliament was manoeuvred into a situation where, despite the Self Denying Ordinance which had disposed of Essex, Manchester and Waller, it could not refuse to give Cromwell a commission in the army, as Lieutenant General of Horse. There was no time for anyone to oppose the appointment and once the battle had been won it would be impossible for his enemies to refuse to continue his commission. Fairfax was clearly party to the whole scheme, for not only had he left the post of Lieutenant General open for several months but it was Fairfax himself who made the proposal to the Council of War at Sherington. Not surprisingly the officers concurred and Hammond was sent with a letter to Parliament from the chief officers of horse desiring Cromwell be given this command. After a debate on the 10th June the Commons empowered Fairfax to make the appointment, without waiting for approval from the Lords.[107] The final piece in the jigsaw was now in place. This was, it would seem, the last straw for a number of officers who had accepted the move into the New Model. Now that Cromwell was to be second in command several officers 'petitioned the General that they may have their liberty to leave the army, they being not able to live with that ungodly crew.'[108] Of these Vermuyden was by far the most significant although his leaving, as Luke intimates, was surely because he knew that under Cromwell he would not be made up to Commissary General as his experience might have justified. There was clearly no doubt amongst his opponents that this was now in reality Cromwell's army, even though it would be several years before he finally gained the senior command.

At Newport Pagnell Fairfax had been joined by Vermuyden's brigade of 2500 horse and dragoons, although they were said to have been wearied by their long marches and needed to be recruited.[109] There were also some Scottish horse who had recently arrived at the garrison, but whether they remained with Luke or accompanied the army to Naseby is unclear.[110] Reports now put the New Model strength at about 12500, but Cromwell was also urgently raising forces in the Association and the greater the time available to him the more troops he would be able to assemble to swell the ranks of the army for the coming battle.[111] Letters were sent out to the various counties by the Committee of the Association in Cambridge, such as that to the Suffolk Committee, signed among others by Cromwell, which said 'because we conceive that the exigence may require Horse and Dragoons, we desire that all your Horse and Dragoons may hasten to Newmarket; where they will receive orders for further advance...'[112] However, although large numbers of troops were brought together in East Anglia, the Suffolk horse would be the only ones to arrive in time to fight in the battle. On the 6th June instructions had already gone out for the troops Cromwell was assembling to march to join Fairfax and within a few days 500 horse accompanying the Lieutenant General were already nearing the army but the other troops, comprising at least 3000 foot and 1000 horse, were left far behind.[113] On the 11th June it was said that the Hertfordshire horse and dragoons were also ready and were ordered to join with Cromwell that night, but in contrast the Essex horse had still not moved from Cambridge.[114] Other Parliamentarian cavalry in the north were instructed to unite with Gell, who was to be under Fairfax's command, and assist at the rear of the Royalist army.[115]

'The Grand Armye', as Luke describes the New Model, would need all the additional support it could get because not only had various regiments been sent to Taunton, the regiments that Fairfax still had with him were still nowhere near their full strength even though they had continued to receive recruits throughout May. The Commons had issued reminders in late May to the City of London and several counties to hasten up their recruits and money, while the counties of the Association had been reminded of the need for their recruits to be ready to be sent up to the army by the 8th June.[116] As late as 4th June 400 recruits were ordered to be raised by the counties of Sussex and

Surrey and a further 400 by the Committee of the Militia for Sir Hardress Waller's regiment, which implies it was still seriously under strength.[117] A common problem at this time was the desertion of these new recruits even before they reached the army, as was the case with those coming up to Montague's regiment via Newport Pagnell in late May who had to be rounded up by the governor and sent on to the regiment. Although in this case it would seem it was mainly due to the drunkenness of their 'conductors', Parliament did point out that part of the problem was that Fairfax's officers sometimes failed to attend the places of rendezvous and so many of the new recruits simply ran away.[118] The problem was so bad that Parliament had found it necessary to issue another Ordinance to empower Fairfax, for a further month, to press men within the counties through which he marched, while on the 31st, in an attempt to stem the loss of existing troops, they had also authorised the severest punishment of those soldiers that deserted.[119] Despite this, problems continued when the army marched away from Newport Pagnell, because Fairfax found that many of his soldiers had gone into the garrison and enlisted there, especially the men from Pickering's regiment who had formerly been stationed at Newport Pagnell. Fairfax's instructions to Luke were clear:

'Cause proclamation to be made on pain of death to return them to their colours. You know how needful it is to have our regiments as complete as may be. Therefore I desire all means possible may be used for clearing your garrison of the said soldiers.'[120]

To try to make up for some of the shortfall in numbers, Fairfax began to strip the local garrisons of their troops to bolster his army, for Luke reported on the 10th June that 'they past all throughe this towne yesterday and have allmost gott all my soldiers from mee...'[121] The Newport garrison was left with at most 600 foot and one troop of horse.[122] It was of course a common practice to detach troops from garrisons in this way, with cavalry sometimes being sent to quite distant parts of the country, as for example with the troops of horse of Captain Sticke and Captain Clarke from the Northampton garrison who had been dispatched in May to bolster the severely weakened forces of Colonel Massey at Gloucester and were still with him in late June.[123] However, the calling up of troops in this way could have disastrous effects on the garrisons concerned and so we find that Rossiter complained that the instructions to send his forces out would place Grantham under threat from the Royalists at Newark.[124] In response he was instructed, on the 9th June, only to march to join the New Model if the Newark horse and dragoons were also drawn out to assist the King.[125]

After their brief rest, the army marched westwards through Newport Pagnell on the 9th June, following the main road on the south side of the Ouse. They travelled just seven miles and established their headquarters in the small town of Stony Stratford, with other troops quartered in the surrounding

villages.[126] Stony Stratford lay astride Watling Street, the major road running
north to King's headquarters at Daventry, nineteen miles to the north west.
The town lay on the south side of the river and so, as at Sherington, it was an
easily defensible location with just two bridges controlling access across the
Ouse. Fairfax was making a very careful approach, taking full advantage of
the available defensive locations to protect his advance and he was wise to do
so for the Royalists did not rest quietly at Daventry. They had scouts and
small parties out. On the 10th for example there was a party of firelocks out
in Whittlewood forest, just to the north of Stony Stratford, who captured some
stragglers from the New Model. This was an ideal area in which small bodies
of infantry could scout and ambush the enemy, for there was an extensive
tract of woodland stretching in patches from close by Towcester almost to the
Ouse at Stony Stratford.[127] It was also reported that a party of some 700
Royalist horse and foot advanced as far as Towcester on the same day,
plundering the villages thereabouts and 'committing some cruelties in [Greens]
Norton'.[128] Rupert was clearly continuing to gain intelligence as to the New
Model's position and intentions and so, despite the disadvantages that Rupert's
scouts were working under, it is still difficult to understand how over the next
three days his scouts could have failed him so completely. Fairfax himself had
new intelligence on the 10th suggesting that the Royalist army might be
preparing to march, for carriages were apparently drawn out of their quarters,
but it was not yet known where they were heading, some saying Harborough
and others Banbury. They had also made some adjustments to their quarters,
withdrawing their guard from Heyford Bridge but leaving a strong guard of
300 horse at Whilton Bridge, implying perhaps that they were pulling their
troops back from the Northampton area and concentrating them around
Daventry. The Royalists were certainly very fearful that the New Model
might interpose themselves between Daventry and Oxford and so stop their
convoy of cavalry from returning, which would have put the army at a great
disadvantage. Luke had indeed sent a hundred cavalry to watch this road in
case reinforcements were sent up to the King, but one wonders whether
Rupert might also have suspected that Fairfax was about to advance to
Northampton and that this Royalist withdrawal back towards Daventry on the
10th was a direct response.[129]

It was four o'clock on the morning of the 11th June when the first
detachments of New Model cavalry, comprising 800 men under Colonel
Whalley, reached Northampton.[130] They had intended to beat up the Royalist
quarters but were too late as it would soon be light. Their arrival gave the
town some comfort for Colonel Whetham remarked, 'they will bee a good
security of the Quarters neere us', while the news that Cromwell himself was
already at Bedford was heard with even greater relief: 'we are not a little
ioyful to heere of Col.Cromwell advance, for wee know not how soone wee
may stand in neede of his assistance...'[131] It was a stormy day as the rest of
the army marched from Stony Stratford to Northampton. They probably

followed the main London to Derby road, passing through the village of Grafton Regis, which will have been very familiar to Skippon because eighteen months earlier he had commanded the siege of the Royalist garrison which had been established there to cut this important communication route. Luke however says they advanced through Hanslope which, although on a minor road and further out of their way, was on the east side of the river Tove and away from Whittlewood forest and so would have made the army less vulnerable to attack while in line of march. This would have required the New Model to have first marched back towards Newport Pagnell, but this might have been part of Fairfax's strategy to deceive the Royalists as to his real intentions, because on the 12th the Royalists still believed that the New Model had marched eastward towards Bedford and the Association. Whatever their exact route, the army had a hard march on the 11th due to the continual rain, causing Fairfax to write in evening that 'The ill Weather hath been some disadvantage to us, but I hope a fair day may recover what a foul day loses.'[132] The roads had no doubt deteriorated badly in the wet, with the passage of such a large body of troops and a large train, but the army completed the 11 mile march and lay that night in the villages astride the road, immediately to the south of Northampton.[133] The quartermasters of the regiments, each accompanied by several troopers, must have ridden forward to seek out suitable quarters, sending back the troopers to direct their regiments to their billets for the night.[134]

Again Fairfax was placing his army in relative security close to a major garrison, establishing his headquarters at Wootton, although because there was inadequate accommodation in the village the senior officers were entertained in Northampton by the mayor and magistrates of the town.[135] This was a very different reception to that which they had found at Newport Pagnell, though not surprising given the radical nature of some within the town and county, with Committee members such as Gilbert Pickering and Sir John Dryden. This was after all the county which had produced Robert Browne, who had been buried in St.Giles church in Northampton, whose Brownist sect has been considered the origin of the Independents. There was insufficient space for all the infantry at Wootton and so four regiments of foot were quartered in the adjacent village of Collingtree and, as usual, the regiments of horse were dispersed in slightly more distant villages, with Butler's for example at Hackleton.[136] Though dispersed to some degree, the army was not scattered across a wide area in the way that the evidence from Warwickshire would suggest was normal for a Civil War army.[137] They were also of course close to the enemy, another reason to keep the troops tightly concentrated in a few villages, and undoubtedly causing Fairfax to be equally careful to ensure adequate sentinels and courts of guard were posted. Such sentinels would usually have been placed in pairs at some distance from the quarters, often at the meeting of ways, to warn of an enemy approach and though during the daytime they will have been placed on the hills, from which they could gain a wide view, at night they will have been in the valley.[138]

On the 11th Fairfax wrote that he intended to move closer to the enemy the next day in order to discover their resolution and 'If they appear forward to engage, I shall take the best advice I can upon the place, but as yet I see no great reason to decline.' However, if they were to march westward or stay until further supplies came up to them from the west, then he would wait. His most revealing comment is that he needed additional horse from Lincolnshire, Nottinghamshire and Derby because he was concerned that if Goring's cavalry joined the King 'we shall be much inferior in Horse'.[139] This will have been based on the intelligence available to him on the 11th from Watson, his scoutmaster, that the Royalists had '6000 effective foot, their horse more' and other reports from 'those that have seen both armies [who] say they differ not much in numbers, the Kings horse seeming more, but not so good nor so well armed, and his foot nothing so well provided as ours.'[140] As the great fight approached Fairfax's first priority was therefore to bring in as many additional troops as possible to reinforce his army and so from Wootton on the 11th dispatches had been sent out to the garrisons at Coventry, Warwick, Nottingham and Northampton, to Sir John Gell in Derby and to Colonel Rossiter in Lincolnshire to 'come up' to the army with all the strength they could muster.[141] Fairfax had also received intelligence that it was the intention of the Royalist army to march on Friday 13th and so he wrote urgently to Cromwell requesting his speedy return to the army. Fairfax instructed him to bring back the cavalry that he had taken with him to Ely, and any others that could be spared from the support of the foot that were preparing to march up to the army from the Association.[142] As a newspaper later reported, 'our party waited on the coming of other forces before attempting the enemy.'[143]

Some of the reinforcements were already on their way, including the Suffolk Horse who accompanied Cromwell, and when the army marched from Kislingbury on the 13th it would be joined from the Northampton garrison by 2 troops of horse and 200 foot as well as two whole culverin to reinforce the train of artillery.[144] It may be that these Northampton soldiers were from the companies of Major Johnson and Captain Melvile, for on the 26th and 30th June respectively their soldiers were said to be 'lately returned from state service'.[145] Some troops would not reach the army until the very last moment, most notably Rossiter from Lincolnshire with his Eastern Association cavalry and dragoons, while others who had been summoned, such as Gell's Derbyshire forces, would miss the action though they would encounter shattered remnants of the Royalist army in the days after the battle.[146] Most of the rest of the Eastern Association forces which had been instructed to join the army simply never arrived and instructions were still being repeated on the 14th June for Hertfordshire to send 500 horse. The latter would in fact reach the army on the 14th in time to assist in the pursuit after the battle, but the 500 Norfolk horse which were still at Bedford, the 500 Norfolk horse at Thetford and the 600 Essex horse never arrived.[147] Such ineffectiveness in assembling supporting troops demonstrates very clearly how much still remained to be done in reorganising the other Parliamentarian forces which were not part of the New Model, and it would be a considerable time before all the military forces in England were placed under one effective command structure as a single army. So, it was not just the King who had difficulty in bringing together his forces.

On the 12th June the New Model marched through Northampton, just as more than two and a half years earlier, before Edgehill, Parliament's first field army marched from the town in pursuit of the King. This was however a very different force to that which Essex had assembled at Northampton in September 1642, which had been an ill disciplined rabble, poorly equipped, poorly supplied and lacking in pay. The New Model moved just five miles, marching 'in very good order' because they were in such close proximity to the enemy, and taking up a position on the west side of Northampton. The headquarters were established at Kislingbury facing the King's quarters which were eight miles further west.[148] This village lay on the south side of the Nene, which separated the quarters from the main Northampton to Daventry road and so there was just a single bridge to be defended against attack. While they had been to the rear of the main garrisons or at a distance from the enemy the army had been somewhat dispersed in quarters in a number of villages, but now a new stage of the campaign was about to open. The army was far more exposed and so the troops were not dispersed for, as the constable of Kislingbury later recorded, 'Sr Thomas Fairfax quartered with us one night with great pt of his horse, and all his foot'[149] That night there were some 2000 horses in the meadows of Harpole, which lay just across the bridge from Kislingbury, and presumably at least as many in Kislingbury parish, while Colonel Fiennes' regiment of horse were at Rothersthorpe.[150] At Flore, three miles closer towards the enemy, there is a record of the quartering troops from Whalley's and Fleetwood's regiments which must be from about this time, and if it was on the 12th then these presumably represented the vanguard of the army, deployed forward to protect the New Model from surprise attack, but if so then there were Royalist cavalry to be dislodged first.[151]

Fairfax had made a deliberate, unhurried approach and preparations were now well advanced. On the 11th Skippon had been directed to draw up a 'form of battle' and the army 'was divided into several Brigades of Horse and Foot, in order to their being better disposed for an Engagement.'[152] However, Fairfax was not quite ready to force the King to a battle, not at least until Cromwell had reached the army. Nor did he want to engage the Royalists in their present position because they had 'the advantage of ground, with intrenchments which his Majesties Army had at Daventry...' within which they had planted their ordnance.[153] Baillie estimated that Fairfax had gathered together some 11000-12000 troops as he approached the enemy but, although the King was known to be much weaker in foot, yet he reported that 'we were exceedingly afraid for the Parliament's forces: albeit lusty, well-armed, and well-paid men; yet without officers of experience.'[154] The New Model was greatly despised by friend and foe alike and so it is not surprising to find Rushworth commenting on the 10th that 'I hope the Lord will be with this poor condemned army'.[155] Baillie perhaps typified the view of many Presbyterians when he wrote: 'This new-modelled army consists, for the most part, of new inexperienced soldiers; few of the officers are thought capable of their places.' Other Parliamentarian supporters were at least more confident of victory and one of these was William Lilly, the famous astrologer and an acquaintance of Bulstrode Whitelocke. It was reported that, on the news of the two Armies being near one another, Lilly told one of his friends in London, 'If they did not engage before the 11.day of this month, the Parliament would have the greatest Victory that they ever yet had.'[156] Coincidentally, Lilly's Starry Messenger, with its predictions of the fate of the Royalist cause, was actually published on 14th June 1645.[157]

As Fairfax prepared for the coming battle his troops still had to be provided with supplies and now that they had entered Northamptonshire this had proved a much easier task. The Royalist army, because it was in a hostile area, had gathered its provisions in a way which was almost universally viewed as plundering but the New Model was supposed to approach the matter of supply in a more organised and sympathetic fashion. On the 16th May instructions had been issued to the Parliamentary commissioners sent to reside with the army to prevent false musters, plunder and the like:

> 'For the Ease of the Country, the said Commissioners are to endeavour that no Officer, or Soldier be Quarter'd in any Place but by the Quarter-Master, first shewing his Commission ...... and giving a Ticket of the names of every person which he shall quarter, expressing of what Regiment, Troop or Company the same Person so Quarter'd is....'

No provisions or quarter was to be taken without payment of ready money unless through lack of pay, in which case the provisions and quarter taken were to be detailed by the Captain or Quartermaster. Where the army was on the march and not stopping more than one night then payments were 4d a night for hay, 3d for grass, 4d for oats, 6d per peck of beans and pease, 7d per peck of barley and malt, 8d per day for diet of every horseman, 7d every dragoon, and 6d every soldier. Under no account was anyone to be forced to provide more than he had in his own house.[158] It was intended in this way to ensure that the army did not alienate Parliamentarian supporters, as previous armies had.

Gentles has argued that during the first months of its existence the New Model Army was in fact no different in its impact to any other Civil War army and he bases this conclusion upon the Northamptonshire evidence.[159] However, when one analyses the information in detail on a countywide basis a different conclusion may perhaps be drawn. This is not of course to dispute that the impact of the army could still be seen as oppressive, the needs of any large army were bound to place pressure on the resources of an area, however carefully the provisioning was controlled. For example the village of Boughton, which did not apparently see the quartering of troops, reported 'we find yt at Navesby fight we weere continually oppressed with foote and horse that did belong to the Parliament untill we had neither horse meate nor mans meate lefte us to our expence of £30'.[160] The evidence does however indicate that the soldiers did usually pay for their quartering. Luke, who had no reason to be charitable to the New Model, reported on the 12th June that 'the foot officers pay well and drink well.'[161] At Collingtree on the 11th 'some men payd slenderly for their quarters' while a fortnight later near Warwick, as the triumphant army marched south once more, we find the village constable at Milverton specifically stating that Pickering's soldiers 'generally paid for their quarters. But some of the horsemen and Officers did not pay.'[162] There may still have been some problems, given this comment about the officers and the cavalry, and it was not perhaps an isolated case, for the villagers of Marston Trussell reported that Rossiter's cavalry also took free quarter in their village on the 14th June. Though his was not a New Model regiment, the complaint is echoed by Luke who said that 'the great officers so far as I can hear pay no quarters, nor the horse.'[163] There was certainly no excuse for such failures because there was no lack of pay in the New Model through much if not all of June.[164] There was also a further £10000 ready at Windsor on the 27th May for the army, and this or yet more money was instructed to be sent by convoy via St.Albans and Newport Pagnell on the 13th and by the 15th June Cromwell would instruct Luke to provide a convoy to bring this 'treasure' up from Newport Pagnell to Northampton where it would be collected.[165] Not only were the troops adequately paid, Fairfax also seems to have made every effort to ensure that the rules were adhered to. It can be seen from numerous events during his commands that Fairfax cared about the condition of his soldiers but that he would stand no indiscipline, which he punished severely. Already he had executed two soldiers for disorder and desertion on the march into the South West and on the return journey another had been executed, making it clear 'that it should be death for any man to plunder.'[166]

To ensure that the New Model was efficiently provisioned with the minimum of impact on the local population, before they marched from Oxford instructions had been sent out to the County Committees of Northamptonshire, Bedfordshire and Buckinghamshire to bring supplies to the army. When they had marched into Buckinghamshire, as we have seen, Fairfax made every effort to supply the army through the local administrative system and to control his forces to stop them ranging widely to take provisions. That he was unsuccessful was a reflection as much on the state of the county as the discipline of the army. Supplies had however been sent to the army all the way from the Eastern Association and, unlike the soldiers who should have joined Fairfax from East Anglia, most of these supplies did arrive.[167] When

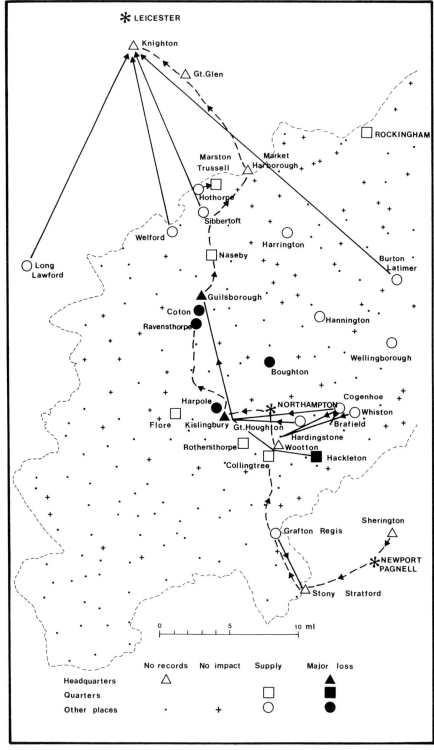

Fig.45. The impact of the New Model on Northamptonshire parishes in June 1645.

the New Model moved into Northamptonshire the local administrative system was brought into action with far greater success. As a result the army could be concentrated in a few villages close together, with the infantry at the headquarters and, where necessary, in one or two adjacent villages, while the cavalry were in the immediately surrounding villages. Hence on the 11th the infantry were at the headquarters, Wootton, and the adjacent village of Collingtree, while regiments of cavalry were each apparently in a separate village, with Butler's for example at Hackleton. This dispersal of the cavalry was almost inevitable due to the need for grass for the horses. A similar situation would be seen on the 14th, when the headquarters were at Market Harborough but Rossiter's regiment was at Marston Trussell. It would have been impossible to have put all the horse together at the headquarters because there were already more than a thousand horses in that quarter every night from the train as well as the horses of the officers. Indeed, when the headquarters were at Wootton they found it necessary to place at least 200-300 of the horses from the train and the officers in the adjacent village of Collingtree. The presence of 2000 horse in the meadows of Harpole on the night of the 12th must surely have been an exception, the cavalry usually being concentrated due to the proximity of the enemy, as indeed were all the infantry, the train and some of the rest of the horse which were concentrated in Kislingbury, while Colonel Fiennes' regiment of horse were at Rothersthorpe.

In Northamptonshire the Commissary General of the army and the County Committee, presumably working through the High Constable of each Hundred, required the constables in individual parishes to provide money or supplies. The mobilising of this support can be seen spreading forward of the army as it approached. So we find the parish of Grafton Regis, in Cleyley Hundred, providing provisions to Stony Stratford on the 10th June to the value of £2/7/8d for three troops of horse and the next day they sent further provisions, to the value of £3/6/4d, to the same town for the troops of Captain Nevell, an officer in Rich's regiment of Horse.[168] As the army arrived outside Northampton the surrounding Hundreds were similarly brought into the supply chain and so, for example, in Hamfordshoe Hundred it is recorded in the Wellingborough 'Town Book': 'Paid towards the charge laid on the Hundred of twenty fat sheep and three heyfers, for Gen.Thomas Fairfax's army.....£1'[169] A number of the villages in Wymersley Hundred also record supplies sent to the army. The village of Whiston carried 10 dozen loaves of bread and 20lb of bacon with a total value of 16/- to Hardingstone, adjacent to the headquarters at Wootton. They also had to provide a load of wood to Northampton, again for the use of the army, while another villager had one of his horses purchased.[170] The adjacent village of Cogenhoe delivered 10 dozen loaves and 40 pounds of cheese, again to Hardingstone, as well as more wood for their use. They also provided 3.5 bushels of malt to Brafield for the use of the army, though it is unclear whether it was for troops quartered there or for trans-shipment.[171] This is certainly very different to Tennant's interpretation of the provisioning of Waller's army in Warwickshire in the days leading up to the battle at Cropredy in 1644, which he claims was a chaotic process with 'supplies filtering in apparently at random from far and wide.'[172]

The exact process involved in collecting and transporting these supplies is revealed as a result of the exceptional survival of the constable's accounts for 1645 for Great Houghton, another village in Wymersley Hundred. On the 11th or 12th June a small detachment of cavalry arrived at Houghton to oversee the delivery of provision to the army. William Denton, constable of the village, had to pay 'for 8 shogers quarteryng when they com for provyson for the Army to Kislingburie and 8 horses 6/-'. It would appear that the soldiers organising this provisioning were from the baggage train, for Cogenhoe had to give free quarter for 16 horses and 5 men of Sir Thomas Fairfax's train at the time when the supplies were being organised.[173] This is as might be expected, for the supply of the army was the responsibility of the Commissary General, who was specifically named by the constable of Welford as having provided the valuation of the supplies provided by that village on the 16th June.[174] Not only did the constable of Houghton have to quarter the soldiers and organise the victuals, he was also required to provide the parish team and waggon to deliver them. We know this because Denton records in his account: 'givn to Georg Brown and Carvill when our Teame was lost at Navsbie fight 7/-; givn to Turton at samn time 6d.' The reasons for these payments are unclear, unless they were the carter and his assistant who went with the team. By the time the cart arrived at Kislingbury one must assume the army was ready to march and they were ordered to accompany the baggage train. The reference to the loss of the team might be interpreted as their destruction when the Parliamentarian baggage train was attacked by Rupert, but alternatively they may perhaps simply have been requisitioned by the New Model and never returned. The constable later reimbursed himself and a certain Tomson 'for goyng to lester for to sue for Teame and Cart (4/-)' and then a further payment to himself and Robert Carvell for a further 'two days seaking for our teame and cart 3/6d.' They were unsuccessful for later Denton records: 'A ssesment made the 14 of June for the raysing of mony for to pay for Our Team and Cart that was lost at Navsby fight after two months tax'. The village was clearly finding it difficult to make good the loss because Denton records 'Another ssessment made the 20 of october for the eaysing of mony after on monthe tax and a half to pay for the arears for the horses and cart which was lost when the Generall went by and provigyon sent for to Kislingburie'.[175] This could be taken as evidence that the New Model was, as Gentles argues, acting very little different to previous armies. It is however interesting to note that although this was a very substantial sum that had to be found to replace the cart and team, no reference is made to the loss in the accounts submitted by the village in 1647 seeking reimbursement for losses during the war.[176] Indeed, although there are a large number of parish accounts surviving for Northamptonshire only a small proportion of them claim any reimbursement for the costs of supplying the New Model Army during the Naseby campaign, even though we know their Hundred was required to provide supplies. It would seem that the majority of the supplies requisitioned must have been paid for either immediately or reimbursed at a later date on the submission of the tickets that had been issued.

The use of parish teams to transport supplies seems the normal practice, because the village of Cogenhoe similarly had to supply 'a teame and men 7 dayes for carrying carriages after the army', at a cost of £3/10/0d. This would mean that they also were present with the baggage train at Naseby, but they were not so unlucky as to lose their team.[177] As the army marched north other Hundreds and parishes were drawn into the supply chain, such as Hannington which supplied 'one quarter of oats and one strike of beanes to a captaine under Sr Thomas Fairfax about May 1645 12/4d.'[178] It was not just that the army was on the move that led to teams being sent long distances with supplies. When the army had passed by, the parishes still had to send provisions, as with Burton Latimer which had to deliver them to the army when it was nearly 30 miles away at Leicester.[179] Sibbertoft, which had lost goods to the value of £300 to the Royalists also had to deliver provisions for the New Model Army while it was at the siege of Leicester, so this was not a case of supplies being brought into Leicester because the area had been badly pillaged and could not support the army.[180]

Most villages do not record anything about the supply of the army in their accounts, but those that do seem to show how well organised the process was compared to the Royalist plundering which had preceded it. However, if one could compare this to the way in which the King's army had been provisioned in Worcestershire in early May would it be significantly different? Where an army was marching through its own territory it may, by this time of the war at least, have been supplied efficiently and to have spread the burden relatively equitably. It was however a very different matter for the very few villages on which the New Model Army was actually quartered and occasionally on immediately adjacent parishes. When they reached Northampton the troops were quartered first in the villages on the south and then, on the 12th, to the west of the town. One can trace the progress of the army from the impact on the villages in which it stayed. So at Collingtree:

> 'Sr Thomas Fairfax quartered here 3000 foot at the least and 200 or 300 horse and men, which belonged to the officers and carriages. Some men payd slenderly for their quarters, yet ye towne was indamagd at the least by Coll:Pickering Coll:Mountegu & 2 more'[181]

While the New Model infantry regiments were quartered at Collingtree we find an example of what must have happened to villagers in most of the parishes on which the army descended, with the churchwardens of Collingtree recording in 1645, 'payd to Stormer for his beere drank out by souldiers 6/8d'. Though undated within the year, this is presumably the impact of the New Model for 6/8d would buy at least six gallons of beer.[182] At the nearby village of Hackleton:

> 'there came 600 Troopers having with them Captaine Garner and Captaine Ferrie father wth maine other commanders under the command of Sr Thomas Fairfaxe whoe weare marching towards Naseby fight and stayed wth us one day and night to the charge of £60'.

At the same time apparently:

> 'There came some officers and soldiers in ye night tieme and came into mens houses and took away provisions to be carried away to Sr Thomas Fairfax's armie lying in the feeldes thay took away great store of meale and cused it to be baked in bread and besides toock bread butteer sheepe bacon beere and what provision they could fiend giving noe sattisfaction at all for it and causing this provission to be caried away in a cart to kislingbery and from thence to Gilsbouroe being ye day before Nasebe fight to the value of £8.'

They also took from the village fields 10 lambs and 7 sheep the same night without giving any satisfaction at all for the sheep.[183]

The impact of the army as a whole is best seen on the nights of the 12th and 13th June. On the 12th all the foot and a substantial part of the horse were quartered in Kislingbury, a fairly average Northamptonshire village of some 80 households, where the impact of the army was dramatic.[184] With over 7000 infantry and at least 2000 cavalry, the majority of the army must have lain in the field that night. The constable of Kislingbury estimated that the army 'did eate and spoile in the towne and feild to the value of £100', with individual householders suffering in various ways: Mr Harris lost 18 sheep and lambs and 3 strike of malt, Mr Cox lost 9 sheep and Mr Asbie one fat calf, while a Mr Holloway suffered the 'whole traine of Artillery lying and eating up my inclosure and cutting down my trees etc £8.'[185] The depredations also extended just across the river into the adjacent parish of Harpole where:

> 'Besides the great Charge of his Excellencyes Sr Thomas Fairfaxe armye when he quartered at Kislingbury before Nasebye fight we had at least 2000 horse feeding on our grasee and Corne and divers sheepe and lambs taken away from us and all most all our provisions in our houses was eaten up and carryed away.'

Again there were also small quantities of stock stolen: 3 sheep, one wether and five or six lambs.[186] With so many soldiers descending on a village it must have been simply impossible to enforce full discipline. Moreover, unlike garrison troops who had to depend on the same people for several years, the army on campaign had no local ties to reinforce respect for the villagers on whom they were quartered. On the following night, when the army moved on to Guilsborough, a somewhat smaller village, it would appear to have been similarly concentrated.[187] The depredations spilled over once more into several immediately adjacent villages and hamlets, in Coton, Ravensthorpe and Teeton, which were probably the villages through which the army marched that evening. The villagers of Ravensthorpe and Teeton, though they do not appear to have suffered direct quartering of troops, lost 50 sheep, 26 lambs and provisions worth £1/17/0d, at an overall cost of about £25.[188] At Guilsborough, where most if not all of the army were quartered that night, the impact was far greater. One villager recorded the:

'Losse Sustained by the foote souldiers of Sr Thomas Fairfax his army the night before Navesby fight quartering at my house as followeth, Loss in Lynnens and apparell in one Chest and ells where to the value of £10, grase eaton by their horses and wood burnt the same tyme to the value of £2/10/0d, Lost more in Cheese and butter the same tyme £1/0/0d.'

Other villagers recorded loss of sheep and lambs, household goods and food, as well as coal, wood, hedges, turves and gates burnt, and straw, grass and oats taken for the horses. The numbers of soldiers quartered on a single household could be as many as 50.[189] The use of large quantities of wood and other fuel is a typical loss to the armies and Tennant suggests for a similar case, at Kineton at the time of Edgehill, that it was for camp fires. They were frosty autumn nights whereas this was mid June, but the nights may still have been cold and they were certainly wet, at least on the 11th and 12th. However, it seems likely that a good deal of the fuel was simply required for cooking purposes, because there were after all perhaps as many as 10000 soldiers at the headquarters on the nights leading up to the battle.

Such losses in the villages in which the army actually quartered far outweigh any other losses to the New Model in parishes which provided supplies on a large or small scale. For the rest of the county the impact was in fact very small compared to the overall costs incurred in funding the war effort. As Fairfax intimated in his comments about Buckinghamshire, it seems the way in which he was restricting the impact on the local population was first and foremost to keep the troops concentrated in just one or two villages. To enable him to do this he was using the local administrative system in an efficient way to deliver the necessary supplies, with a charge being placed on each Hundred thus ensuring, as far as possible, an equitable spread of the demands. So, although the impact on a village like Guilsborough may have been little different to that of Essex's army on a village like Butlers Marston just before Edgehill, in 1642 that impact was apparently widespread across south east Warwickshire whereas in June 1645 in Northamptonshire it was restricted to just a handful of parishes.[190]

NOTES

1. *A Glorious Victory. The Scottish Dove*, 30th May to 6th June.

2. Tibbutt, 1963, p.300. *The Scottish Dove*, 30th May to 6th June.

3. Evesham taken with 12 royalists killed and 545 taken prisoner. Col.Massie to Wm.Lenthall, 27th May, HMC, 1891, p.225.

4. Roy, 1964, p.47.

5. Roy, 1964, p.35-6.

6. Kenyon, 1988, p.141.

7. Roy, 1964, p.26-7, 34 & 53.

8. Clarendon to Rupert, 27th May, Warburton, vol.3, p.91.

9. Slingsby, p.144-5.

10. Warburton, vol.3, p.97.

11. Nicholas to Rupert, 22nd May 1645, Warburton, vol.3, p.97-8. Ludlow, 1698, vol.1, p. 151-3.

12. Pevsner, 1984, p.249.

13. Charles to Nicholas, 4th June 1645, Bray, vol.5, p.130-1.

14. Whitelocke, p.143.

15. Firth, 1898.

16. Slingsby, p.149. Symonds, p.186. Whitelocke, p.144.

17. *The Weekly Account*, 4th June.

18. Tibbutt, 1963, p.556.

19. Tibbutt, 1963, p.570.

20. Throsby, 1791, vol.2, p.321. Although in 1875 it was reported that the house had been demolished, it seems that at least part of the original survives at the back of the present building, for in 1961 the house on the west side of Main Street called Rupert's Rest still had 'great oak cross beams that are ages old'. Hill, 1875. Village history article in Leicester Advertiser, 3rd March 1961, LRO DE 2148/114-115. Particulars of Rupert's Rest, Great Glen 1979, LRO L333.

21. Symonds, p.185. *Iter Carolinum*.

22. Tennant, 1992, p.43.

23. Nichols, vol 2, p.870.

24. Nichols, vol.2, p.870. Though Sir Richard did not himself take up arms, his tomb in Wistow church shows this keen Royalist supporter in full armour.

25. The Wistow sword was presented in the 19th century to George IV. Pevsner, 1964, p.426. 'The arrangements of the floor boards in the King Charles' room and the smaller panelled room which now adjoins it, indicate that the former room was originally longer than it is now.' The changes were probably part of the extensive mid 18th century alterations to the house. Information from Lord Cottesloe of Wistow in c.1935 reported in *The Wistow Hall Tradition*, c.1935, typescript by Frank P. Strongman. LRO DE 2102, 2. *NN&Q*, 1890, vol.3, item 522. *Northampton Herald*, 9th December 1893. Halford, 1813. Mee, 1967, p.184. Firth, 1926, p.212. Throsby, 1791. Jones, *1829*, vol.1, p.113.

26. Symonds, p.186.

27. For example, Langdale passed through Harborough en route to the relief of Pontefract. *The Kingdomes Weekly Intelligencer*, no.91, 11th-18th March 1645.

28. *Iter Carolinum*. Davies, 1964.

29. *A Glorious Victory*.

30. Lomax to Lord Fairfax, 6th June 1645, Bell, 1849, vol.1, p.292.

31. *A Glorious Victory*.

32. Tennant, 1992, p.258.

33. Tennant, 1992, p.257 & 262 in which the Rugby event seems to have been incorrectly related to a period after the battle. If Jones was released on the 14th June then he must have been taken prisoner on or about the 5th June.

34. Sprigge, 1647, p.32.

35. Wilmot to Rupert, 1st December 1642, quoted by Tennant, 1992, p.55.

36. Symonds, p.185-187.

37. Burton Latimer account, September 1646, PRO SP28/171, f.15 & 21; Weekley account, f.187; Account of East Farndon, f.750. Thorpe Malsor account and Great Oxendon account, PRO SP28/172 unfol.. The loss of papers has parallels at Upper Shuckburgh in Warwickshire a few days later and so may not simply be an excuse. Tennant, 1992, p.261.

38. PRO SP28/171, f.124.

39. The Royalists were quartered in Barton Seagrave, Finedon, Woodford, Thrapston and villages thereabouts. Tibbutt, p.302-3 & 305. On the 6th there was a regiment of Horse quartered in Kettering, *The Kingdomes Weekly Intelligencer*, 3rd-10th June 1645. *Mercurius Civicus*, 29th May to 5th June 1645.

40. Tibbutt, 1963, p.559. *The Kingdomes Weekly Intelligencer*, 3rd-10th June. *The Kingdomes Weekly Intelligencer*, 3rd-10th June. *The Weekly Account*, 4th-11th June.

41. *A Perfect Relation*.

42. Tibbutt, 1963, p.305-6. *A Perfect Relation*.

43. *A Perfect Relation*.

44. Gt.Houghton churchwarden's accounts, NRO 175P/28.

45. Rushworth, vol.6, p.39, gives Oundle, as does Vermuyden in his letter, but it must mean Olney as that is adjacent to Lavendon and Weston. Tibbutt, 1963, p.558. Tibbutt, 1963, p.302-307.

46. Tibbutt, 1963, p.558. *The Kingdomes Weekly Intelligencer*, 3rd-10th June.

47. *The Kingdomes Weekly Intelligencer*, 3rd-10th June. *Iter Carolinum*. *Mercurius Britanicus*, 9th-16th June. Whitelocke. *Mercurius Civicus*, 5th-12th June. Tibbutt, 1963, p.559.

48. Symonds, p.188. *Iter Carolinum*.

49. Edgar, 1923, p.13. Brown, 1991, p.21, 25 & 36. Harrison, 1948, p.163.

50. Symonds, p.188.

51. Rupert to Legge, 8th June, Warburton, vol.3, p.100.

52. Tennant, 1992, p.109.

53. *A Glorious Victory*.

54. Letters from the army, 9th June, *Mercurius Britanicus*, 9th-16th June. *The Moderate Intelligencer*, 12th-19th June.

55. Brown, 1991.

56. Walpoole, 1784.

57. Baker, 1822-1830, vol.1, p.342.

58. Edgar, 1923, p.68.

59. Rushworth, vol.6, p.37.

60. *A Perfect Relation*. Whetham & Whetham, 1907, p.94-6.

61. *A Glorious Victory*.

62. Holme, 1891, p.40. Symonds, p.191.

63. *A Glorious Victory*.

64. Whetham to Luke, 9th June, Tibbutt, 1963, p.563-4.

65. Whetham to Luke, 9th June 1645, Tibbutt, 1963, p.563. Letters from the army, 9th June, *Mercurius Britanicus,* 9th-16th June.

66. *A Glorious Victory*. *Mercurius Verdicus*, 12th June.

67. Tibbutt, 1963, p.318.

68. Roy, 1964, p.149 & n.160.

69. Tennant, 1992, p.257.

70. Tibbutt, 1963, p.309 & 563.

71. Whetham to Luke, 11th June, Tibbutt, 1963, p.567-8. *The Moderate Intelligencer*, 5th-12th June.

72. Gt Houghton churchwarden's accounts, NRO 175P/28.

73. *A Glorious Victory*.

74. Norwich to Luke, Tibbutt, 1963, p.570.

75. Clarendon, 1702, p.506.

76. Tibbutt, 1963, p.310 & 564. Letters from the army, 9th June, *Mercurius Britanicus*, 9th-16th June. Rushworth, vol.6, p.40.

77. Symonds, p.190.

78. *CSPD*, p.581-2.

79. Quoted by Edgar, 1923, p.61-65 and Mastin, 1792, p.187-9, from Rastall, 1787. Harrod, 1808, p.81. Nichols, vol.3, p.531. Savage, 1671.

80. Quoted by Baker, 1822.

81. Whitelocke, p.143.

82. Tibbutt, 1963, p.303.

83. Sprigge, 1647, p.27-8.

84. Fairfax to Luke, 8th June, Tibbutt, 1963, p.560.

85. *Mercurius Britanicus*, 7th-16th June. Inexplicably other correspondence suggests Fairfax was at Brackley on the Wednesday night. Lomax to Lord Fairfax, 6th June, Bell, 1849, vol.1, p.292.

86. For example, Pickering's regiment were apparently quartered at North Crawley, just to the north east of Newport, Tibbutt, 1963, p.313. There is a local tradition that the Parliament army encamped in the field before the Rectory House at Sherington. Shehan, 1862, p.464. Staines, 1842, p.90n.

87. *A more exact and perfect Relation*

88. Tibbutt, 1963, p.306.

89. Bull, 1900, p.167.

90. 19th May, Tibbutt, 1963, p.279.

91. Hobson's discourses which so enraged Luke were published in Hobson, 1647.

92. *CSPD*, Dec 1644. Johnson, undated.

93. *CSPD*, p.573.

94. Vernon, 1644, p.37.

95. Provender for scout horses, PRO SP28/238 f.183; scout horses and scouts to ride them were ordered to be provided in June 1643 to preserve the town from sudden dangers and surprises, Cox, 1898, vol. 2, p.440. Warrant to pay Nathaniel Sharpe, 18 July 1645, PRO SP28/239 unfol..

96. The duties are clear from Michael Betts' bills of 1643, PRO SP28/238, f.184, 196 & 209.

97. PRO SP28/35, f.443, 445, 446, 458, 466, 474 & 479, all for 1645; SP28/238, f.58, 73, 76, 79, 82, 83, 84, 120, 114, 117, 124, 125, 127 & 222, from March to December 1643.

98. PRO SP28/238, f.101.

99. Tibbutt, 1963, p.318.

100. Warrant to pay Major Leon Watson Scoutmaster £98 for 14 days pay for himself and for 20 men and horses, 19th July 1645. PRO SP28/31, f.37.

101. Rushworth, vol.6, p.39. Sprigge, 1647, p.28. *A Glorious Victory*. This information must however be treated with care, for the same account quite incorrectly says Fairfax later removed his quarters to Towcester. Letters from the quarters of the army 'certifie his advance from Stony-Stratford to Sir Hatton Farmers house near Towcester, with intention to fight the King; that this day Cromwell was expected.' *The Moderate Intelligencer*, 5th-12th June.

102. Symonds, p.190.

103. Cruso, 1632, p.14.

104. Tibbutt, 1963, p.564-5.

105. *CSPD*, p.578.
106. Whitelocke, p.144.
107. Rushworth, vol.6, p.39. Whitelocke, p.144.
108. Luke, 12th June, Tibbutt, 1963, p.317.
109. *CSPD*, p.563.
110. Tibbutt, 1963, p.304.
111. Whitelocke, p.144.
112. Kingston, 1897, p.200.
113. Whitelocke, p.144.
114. *CSPD*, p.586.
115. *CSPD*, p.569.
116. *CSPD*, p.524 & 564. Wharton to the Committee of Norwich, 21st May 1645, Bell, 1849, vol.1, p.227.
117. *CSPD*, p.563.
118. About the 26th May, Tibbutt, 1963, p.289. *CSPD*, p.548.
119. Whitelocke, p.144.
120. Tibbutt, 1963, p.561.
121. Luke to Whetham, 10th June, Tibbutt, 1963, p.313.
122. Tibbutt, 1963, p.321.
123. 21st May 1645, PRO SP28/239 unfol.. 23 June 1645, PRO SP28/35 f.64. One of Captain Clarke's men is said to have been imprisoned in the West and taken when the Northampton forces were there in July. PRO SP28/238 f.241. Later, in October 1645, one similarly finds four troops of Northampton horse sent out to serve under General Poyntz. 21st October 1645, PRO SP28/239, unfol..
124. *CSPD*, p.579.
125. *CSPD*, p.579.
126. *A more exact and perfect Relation*.
127. Pettit, 1968, map 2.
128. Tibbutt, 1963, p.315.
129. Tibbutt, 1963, p.316.
130. Whalley may perhaps have had under his command some of the other regiment of Ironsides as a result of Cromwell's absence in Ely.
131. Whetham to Luke, 11th June, Tibbutt, 1963, p.567.
132. Rushworth to Luke, 11th June, Tibbutt, 1963, p.567. Fairfax's letter, Rushworth, vol.6, p.40. Tibbutt, 1963, p.317.
133. *A more exact and perfect Relation*.
134. Vernon, 1644, p.40.
135. Sprigge, 1647, p.30.
136. Collingtree account, PRO SP28/171 f.401. Hackleton account, PRO SP28/172 unfol..
137. Tennant, 1992, p.117 & 176-7.
138. Cruso, 1632, p.72-75.
139. Rushworth, vol.6, p.40.
140. Tibbutt, 1963, p.568. *A Perfect Relation*.
141. Rushworth, vol.6, p.40.
142. Rushworth, vol.6, p.39.
143. *Moderate Intelligencer*, 13th June.
144. Whetham to Luke, 13th June 1645, Tibbutt, 1963, p.574.
145. PRO SP28/239 unfol..
146. Vicars, 1646, p.157.
147. *CSPD*, p.591-3.
148. Tibbutt, 1963, p.571. Sprigge, 1647, p.30.

149. PRO SP28/173 unfol..

150. 'For quartering Colonell Fines Regiment one day and a night one day afore Naisby fight', Rothersthorpe account, PRO SP28/173 unfol..

151. 19 villagers had cavalry quartered in their houses. This account of cavalry quartering is not dated but is almost certainly from 12th June 1645, because there is no obvious alternative context for these particular troops being here in such numbers, and because Major Bethel is referred to and he was killed in September 1645 at the siege of Bristol. PRO SP28/173 unfol.. There is however conflict with Sprigge who states Flore was a royalist quarter that night. Sprigge, 1647, p.31.

152. Bell, 1849, vol.1, p.231. Rushworth, vol.6, p.40. Sprigge, 1647, p.29.

153. *A True Relation of a Victory*. Tibbutt, 1963, p.565.

154. 17th June 1645, Baillie, 1775, vol.2, p.116-7.

155. Tibbutt, 1963, p.566 & 571.

156. Whitelocke, p.144.

157. Nichols, vol.3, p.737. Lilly, 1715.

158. Rushworth, vol.6, p.32-3.

159. Gentles, 1992, p.45.

160. Boughton account, PRO SP28/171, f.330.

161. Tibbutt, 1963, p.317.

162. Collingtree account, PRO SP28/171, f.401. Tennant, 1992, p.264.

163. Tibbutt, 1963, p.317. Marston Trussell account, PRO SP28/173 unfol..

164. *CSPD*, p.523.

165. *CSPD*, p.590. Whetham & Whetham, 1907, p.102.

166. Sprigge, 1647, p.15 & 19.

167. *CSPD*, p.589.

168. PRO SP28/171, f.31.

169. Palmer & Palmer, 1972, p.74.

170. PRO SP28/171, f. 581.

171. PRO SP28/171, f.610-1.

172. Tennant, 1992, p.177.

173. PRO SP28/171, f.612.

174. Account of Welford, PRO SP28/173 unfol..

175. Great Houghton parish records, NRO 175P/38.

176. PRO SP28/172, unfol..

177. PRO SP28/171, f.612.

178. PRO SP28/173 unfol..

179. For Provision sent to Sr Thomas Fairfax Armie at Leicester presently after the fight at Naseby: more then wee did received £3, PRO SP28/171, f.10.

180. PRO SP28/171, f.120.

181. PRO SP28/171, f.401.

182. Churchwarden's accounts, Collingtree parish records, NRO 74P/31. Young, 1972, p.xii.

183. PRO SP28/173 unfol. This must be captains Gardner and Perry with Colonel Butler's regiment of horse, Sprigge, 1647.

184. 86 households in Hearth Tax, 1674; 89 households in 1720, Bridges, 1791.

185. PRO SP28/173 unfol..

186. Harpole account, PRO SP28/171, f.720-3.

187. 55 households, Hearth Tax, 1674. 43 households in 1720, Bridges, 1791.

188. Ravensthorpe & Teeton account, PRO SP28/172, unfol..

189. PRO SP28/173 unfol..

190. Tennant, 1992, p.56-57.

CHAPTER 6

FROM FLORE TO NASEBY

'they all drew on Burrow hill neere Daventry,
and in all haste indeavoured to get away; the news being brought
that Ironsides was coming to join with the Parliaments Army.'
A Gentleman in Northampton

The Royalists were aware of Fairfax's arrival at Newport Pagnell because an exchange of prisoners was discussed on the 10th June. However, despite having scouts and small parties of horse deployed as far south as Whittlewood forest, some of which approached close to the New Model at Stony Stratford on the 10th, the speed of Fairfax's approach to Northampton caught Rupert by surprise, Fairfax coming to Kislingbury 'so privately, that the Royal Army had little intelligence of him.'[1] Perhaps his precautions of sending a strong body of horse to Towcester, to cover the advance, and of approaching via Northampton rather than directly along Watling Street to Daventry, had deceived the Royalists. Later events would also suggest that the Royalist army was somewhat lax in deploying guards, scouts and sentinels, a surprising thing for Rupert to have allowed at such a crucial time.

On the evening of the 12th June the King was persuaded to relax with a hunting trip in the deer park at Fawsley, just three miles south of Daventry. Fawsley might seem an unlikely choice for it was the seat of the Knightley family, puritans who had been active opponents of the King long before the war began and represented on the Parliamentarian County Committee. However at this time the estate was let to the Palmer family, old Royal servants who will have given Charles a warm welcome, perhaps in the hunting lodge, which still survives today as a ruin called the Dower House.[2] It was at about seven that evening, while the King and his retinue were pursuing deer, that the alarm was raised.[3]

Colonel Whalley had led the vanguard of the army into Northampton on the 11th, with the intention of beating up the Royalist quarters, and it was perhaps Whalley who was deployed on the night of the 12th to complete the task.[4] There were two roads leading from Northampton to Daventry, both crossing the Nene at Whilton Bridge, where a substantial Royalist guard had been placed on the 10th, apparently as part of a withdrawal from around Northampton back towards Daventry. At Heyford, although the guard on the bridge had been removed two days earlier, by the 12th Colonel Cary with his regiment of horse was quartered in the village and a little further west at Flore, presumably to cover approaches from both the south and the east.[5] The scouts first located Cary's quarters and then the 'forlorn hope' caught them completely unaware, with their horses at grass 'having no thoughts of the so near Advance of the Parliamentarians...'[6] This seems an amazing failure on

Cary's part because his was the most forward Royalist position, just six miles away from the main Parliamentarian garrison in the region and it was also known that the New Model was at most 15 miles away. There should have been sentinels and guards out on the Northampton road and the lesser approaches to the quarters because, after all, the Northampton troops had been active on previous nights and this attack could just as easily have been by a party sent out by Colonel Whetham. Indeed the King assured his troops that that is exactly what it was, for the Royalists are said to have believed that the New Model had marched eastward to secure the Association.[7] However another account, apparently relating to the same action, claims it was simply an encounter between scouts with two men captured on both sides.[8] If that was true then Cary had deployed a guard forward of his position, perhaps in Heyford, while the regiment was several miles to the west at Flore. Even so, his troopers were clearly taken completely by surprise. Whatever the exact details, this failure of the Royalist scouts and sentinels would continue the next day and then, with even more disastrous results, on the morning of the 14th. This was in complete contrast to the efforts of the Parliamentarian scoutmaster whose 'continued diligence in getting timely intelligence of the Enemies motion, then, and alwayes, redounded not a little to the enablement of the Army.'[9]

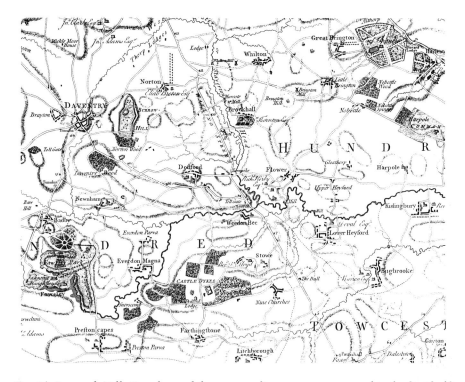

Fig. 46. Borough Hill, Fawsley and the surrounding area, as surveyed in the first half of the 18th century by Thomas Eayre, when the landscape and road pattern had changed little from 1645. (Northamptonshire Record Office)

The alarm threw the Royalists into great confusion, especially as it appeared that the New Model was far stronger than had been expected. In fear of a Parliamentarian attack Rupert drew together all his forces in a general rendezvous on Borough Hill at midnight.[10] There, as Slingsby says, 'yet one may see ye intrenchments of an army, and so high as it overlooks a good part of ye Country between it and Northampton; and there upon yt Hill ye whole army of horse and foot stood in arms yt same night.'[11] Much of the New Model must also have lay in the field all night, but resting at Kislingbury because Fairfax had no intention of attacking the Royalists while they were in such an advantageous position on Borough Hill. That night the horse sentinels of the two armies were within pistol shot of each other, never alighting from their horses, always ready to ride at a moment's notice with warning of enemy movements. It is possible that they faced each other at Whilton Bridge, where the two main roads from Northampton crossed the Nene, though here it was little more than a small stream. Others undoubtedly guarded the lesser roads which crossed the river from Brockhall and Flore.[12] In contrast to his enemies, Fairfax seems to have followed the guidance of the military manuals to the letter. Not only did he ensure that adequate guards were placed forward of the army, he himself was 'abroad almost all night within 2 miles of the enemy who neither attempts to beat up quarters nor give alarms.'[13] As Cruso says:

'the guards, being disposed in their places, must be every night visited by the Commissarie Generall (which often the Lieutenant Generall, and sometime the Generall himself ought to do) to keep the souldiers in the greater awe.'[14]

Fairfax only returned to Kislingbury at four that morning and it was as he rode back to the headquarters that a sentinel is said to have made the Lord General stand in the rain because he had forgotten the password, not being allowed to pass until the Captain of the Guard was summoned. The soldier is said to have been rewarded for his diligence.[15]

The Royalists had no intention of taking the offensive although their cavalry remained on horseback for much of the night and there was much running about amongst the foot as they prepared the carriages. They had always intended to march as soon as their convoy returned from Oxford, as it had done that night, so all the alarm did was to increase the urgency of that march. It was clear to Fairfax that the Royalists intended to march away, because as he was inspecting the guards he had himself seen fires on Borough Hill as the Royalists burnt the makeshift huts that soldiers often built when they were required to lay in the field for more than a night or so.[16]

It was about five in the morning that the Royalists began marching through Daventry and they were clear of the town by nine, the whole army when in line of march being perhaps up to about six miles long. The Parliamentarian scouts reported that the enemy had drawn off at least some of their train towards Southam on the Warwick road, while to cover the retreat the

Royalists sent out about 3000 of their best horse which were placed 'on each side of the Rivolet' to face the New Model.[17] The Nene by Watling Street seems the most likely location, but there are several other small streams to the east of Daventry where these cavalry could have deployed. As both main roads led through the town they were well placed to cover the retreat, whichever road was taken. A convoy was also said to have been sent out towards Oxford, while another body of horse had left Daventry on the Leicester road whom the Parliamentarians at first suspected had simply been sent 'to amuse us', though they did wonder if the Royalists were dividing their forces.[18] In fact, as when he relieved York in 1644, Rupert was attempting to deceive his enemy as to his real intentions, but this time he was dealing with a very different commander. Fairfax was himself skilled in such deception and he also had a very efficient scoutmaster. It was soon recognised that the forces which had marched out on the Southam road were just a feint, because they 'left the way to Warwick, which was Woodland, ...and wheeled to Harborough, which we having full knowledge of, advanced after...'[19] Their march seems to have taken them as far as Shuckburgh, the first point from which a road led north east to rejoin the Leicester road, at Kilsby.[20]

It is very unlikely from this evidence that the Royalist line of march was the same as they had used in advancing to Daventry, through Cold Ashby and Naseby, the route which it is usually assumed they took on the 13th.[21] The Cold Ashby road would after all have required them to march towards not away from the New Model, something they were clearly trying to avoid. Rupert did not want Fairfax to fall on the army when it was so vulnerable, in line of march, and made every effort to deceive the enemy as to his real intentions. The cavalry that had marched out on the Leicester road were closer to the New Model than the rest of the Royalist army and at that time the Leicester road from Daventry ran immediately north from the town, through Kilsby and on to Lutterworth.[22] Moreover, the weather had been very wet for the last two days and, as we have seen, the roads across the claylands of Northamptonshire became exceptionally difficult in wet weather, particularly when one had several hundred carriages, waggons and artillery pieces to transport. The difficulties in moving a train of artillery in bad conditions is clear from Hexham's manual: 'a halfe Canon mounted upon its carriage, drawn with seven coupple of horse and a Thiller, and this to be understood in a good way: but if the way be foule, morish, and durty, then ....for a halfe cannon eleven couple and a thiller...'[23] If the army wished to move quickly this was another good reason for them to stay, as far as possible, on the main roads in the valleys and away from the clayland.

Their objective was not however the town of Leicester, they were marching for Melton Mowbray and then to Newark, intending to strengthen their foot with troops from that and other garrisons, and then to march to Pontefract.[24] Hence, as one report relates, in the afternoon the King wheeled about to Harborough, which must have meant the army turning as it reached the Avon

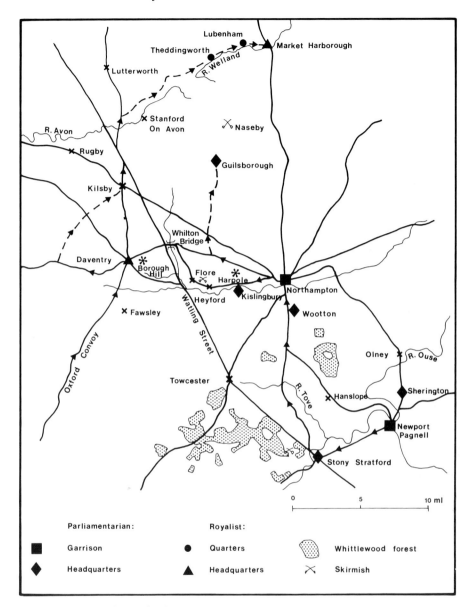

Fig. 47. The marches of both armies up to the night of the 13th June.

valley and marching eastward, up the valley.[25] Though this was a long march
for one day, some 23 miles compared to 19 for the more direct route, it was
not impossible because when the New Model marched into the South West
after Naseby they made 20 miles a day on some legs of the march. Those
from the Royalist army that travelled first along the Warwick road to
Shuckburgh will however have travelled almost 30 miles, a much more
demanding distance, especially as artillery pieces seem also to have been
involved. The Royalist army had every reason to march as rapidly as possible

on the 13th and, to complete this long distance to Harborough, they may even have begun to send away their carriages on Thursday night.[26] The Parliamentarian scouts also reported that when the King's army marched that morning 'seven horse Collors were sett upon Baggage Waggons and marcht as a Regiment of horse, besides a 1000 weemen and 500 Boyes at least.' The Royalists were trying every ruse they could to deceive Fairfax as to their strength as well as their intentions, but none of these deceptions were effective. Nor did the Royalists manage to get away wholly unscathed, because the Northampton horse were once again active and brought in twelve prisoners that morning.[27]

There are many quite wild traditions regarding the movements of several of the key commanders on the day before the battle, one for example places the King in Rugby and another puts him in Lutterworth. Of these traditions one in particular seem to ring true. There is a small ruined bridge, next to the modern road, that crosses the river into the small hamlet of Stanford on Avon and which is known to this day as King Charles' Bridge. It is said that it was over this bridge that Charles came into and later went out of Stanford on the 13th when he took his midday meal at the Hall.[28] Stanford was the home of Sir Thomas Cave, who had been one of the deputy lieutenants of Northamptonshire and had shown himself a strong supporter of the Royalist cause, having supplied arms and ammunition earlier in the war.[29] What is not generally realised is that in 1645 the Hall was on the south side of the river, next to the church, and was only moved to its present site, on the north side of the river, at the end of the 17th century.[30] Had the army been marching on the route we have suggested then the King would indeed have had to cross the bridge to reach the Hall. It will have made good military sense for the army to have marched north to the Avon and then turned eastward to cross into the Welland valley. The main road lay on the north side of the valley and so they will have been able to keep the rivers between their army and the Parliamentarian forces. Though both rivers are here just small streams, they still had some defensive value. Certainly later, after the battle, it was at the fords across the Welland that various of the Royalist troops were caught and killed, implying the difficulty of rapidly crossing the streams with substantial bodies of horse.

As the Royalists had begun marching through Daventry, Fairfax was preparing to follow while his scouts maintained their surveillance, bringing news back to the headquarters. In Kislingbury at about six that morning Fairfax called a Council of War to decide exactly what to do next. While the Council met, a great shout of joy went up from the cavalry. Cromwell had just ridden into the village and, as the newspapers reported, as much as the Royalists feared him, his own men loved him.[31] When the orders had arrived for Cromwell to join the army with all speed he had been collecting his forces at Bedford and so on the 12th he had advanced to cross the Ouse at Olney, marching on to Northampton where he is said to have arrived that night.

There is a tradition that Cromwell stayed at Hazelrigg House, just to the east of St.Peter's church in Northampton, before the battle of Naseby. Hazelrigg, known in the early 20th century as Cromwell House, and one of the few properties surviving in the town today which existed at the time of the Civil War, was a grand house which lay close to the castle, an obvious place for a senior commander to have been quartered. If Cromwell did stay there on the night of the 12th June this will explain how he was able to reach Kislingbury so early the next morning.[32] Other reports, less plausibly, place him at Lady Throckmorton's house in Weston Underwood near Olney but it is more likely that it was the Suffolk horse who stayed there, because the cavalry who accompanied Cromwell are said only to have arrived in Northampton at eleven or twelve on the morning of the 13th, marching on straight away to join the army.[33] The Essex horse, comprising some 1100 cavalry and 600 dragoons, were also expected to be following but they never arrived.[34] As Luke reported, Cromwell would have 'brought 3 or 4000 more had not the Earl of Warwick commanded back 2000 coming from Essex, which makes those at Cambridge which were ready to march, stay behind.'[35] Despite the creation of the New Model Army, the war effort was still being jeopardised by the lack of an effective overall command structure for the rest of the Parliamentarian forces. Colonel Rossiter should also have reached the army on the 13th but he too failed to arrive when expected. As the Council of War met, Fairfax must still have been concerned that he might not have sufficient cavalry to match the enemy, particularly if the King received reinforcements.[36]

The Royalists were still marching through Daventry that morning as the Parliamentarian drums called the infantry to arms and the trumpeters summoned the cavalry. Soon the troops were marching out over the narrow ironstone bridge from Kislingbury village, that one can still cross today, to a rendezvous just across the river in Harpole fields, the nearest area of open land in the direction they would be marching.[37] The rendezvous was probably held in the fallow field, or perhaps on the large common to the north east of the parish, rather than unnecessarily damaging crops, because the Harpole account makes no reference to any such damage, only to the grass and corn eaten by the horse the previous night. From here Major Harrison of Fleetwood's regiment was sent forward with a 'great body of our horse' towards Daventry, presumably along the road to Whilton Bridge, to determine the King's movements and intentions by both observation and by taking prisoners.[38] Meanwhile the army assembled and, under the experienced eye of Major General Skippon, the officers busied themselves organising their troops in line of march. If they were deployed as they had been a few weeks earlier then the carriages and the main body of the train will have been in the centre of the army, flanked on all sides by troops of horse, with two pieces of artillery between each of the regiments of foot.[39] Just as Rupert's lifeguard were in the vanguard of the Royalist army, as was usual when near the enemy, now that Cromwell had arrived he led the vanguard of the New Model.[40]

Fairfax must have waited for intelligence from the scouts or from Major Harrison before he ordered the army to move off. News soon came in that the march by the Royalist cavalry on the Leicester road was the true course of the army, for Whetham reported later that day that the whole of the King's army 'is marched towards Leicester'. In addition to the work of Watson's scouts, because they were in such close proximity to the enemy Cromwell will undoubtedly have sent out parties of horse, each under a corporal, 'to scout, and scoure the high wayes before the body', both the roads on which the army marched and the byways.[41] He would not have wanted his forces to be caught by a surprise attack. The main body marched to flank the enemy, not approaching too close for, according to Slingsby's report, Fairfax 'follow'd with his army upon ye side of us 6 miles distant.' Writing from Guilsborough that night, Rushworth confirmed that the New Model was not following the Royalist army but that 'our army flanks him'.[42] To flank the Royalists, Fairfax probably first marched north westward on the Daventry road turning north at Little Brington, or possibly on the main Coventry road, past Althorp and Great Brington, then north through East Haddon, Ravensthorpe and Coton to Guilsborough. This will have kept them about six miles east of the Leicester road, where the Royalist cavalry had certainly marched that morning. That the New Model did indeed use this road is supported by the evidence of pilfering from the villagers of Ravensthorpe and of Coton 'before Navesby fight'.[43] There is no evidence that troops quartered in the two settlements but they may have been nearby in the open fields or perhaps they even stole the provisions as they marched through.

Sprigge claims there was in 'the Countrey much rejoycing at our comming, having been miserably plundered by the Enemy.' Though it is true that the area had been badly affected over the previous week or more by the Royalist army, it seems unlikely that William Jenaway, William Giles, Robert Trassler and the other villagers of Ravensthorpe, Coton and Guilsborough who lost stock and goods to the New Model will have shared the sentiments![44] That night the army quartered 'in, and about Guilsborough' while local tradition records that Cromwell slept that night at Thornby Grange, which is just over a mile to the north of Guilsborough.[45] It is a very plausible story, for Cromwell was commanding the vanguard and may be expected to have been in advance of the main body and, as at other times when the army was on the march, it is likely that some of the horse were quartered in adjacent villages rather than the headquarters. Thornby Grange as it now stands is an early 20th century building though fittingly, and perhaps not unintentionally, it has been rebuilt in 'neo-Stuart' style.[46] Later that evening Okey's dragoons, who had the vanguard on this as on previous nights, would be quartered at Naseby, but for the moment that village was in Royalist hands.[47] Most if not all the foot and many of the horse were however at the headquarters in Guilsborough, judging by the losses claimed by the villagers. On 'the night before Naseby fight' there were households in the village that had to suffer the quartering of up to 50 soldiers each.[48]

Rupert established his headquarters in Market Harborough, ten miles from Guilsborough, but while the Royalist infantry will have been kept together in the town itself some of the cavalry were deployed in surrounding villages, such as East Farndon.[49] The King's troop were certainly at Theddingworth, while the King himself was at Mr Collins' house at Lubenham, where he had stayed during the previous week when the army was marching south.[50] Whereas most traditions surrounding the whereabouts of the main combatants on the night before the battle are wrong, as with the claims that Rupert was at Great Glen or that Cromwell was at Hazelrigg House, those which surround King Charles and Lubenham are quite different.[51] The Old Hall still remains to the south of the A427 on the eastern edge of Lubenham, along Old Hall Lane, although only a single wing remains today of the large H shaped manor house, the rest having been pulled down in 1774.[52] In the 19th century visitors to the Hall were still shown the 'little room', called the King's room, where Charles was said to have slept during his stays at Lubenham.[53] It is claimed that it was here, for a second time, that Strafford appeared to Charles in a dream and warned him not to fight.[54] Today all there is for the visitor to see is 'Charles I's chair' which now stands in the church, as it has for at least two centuries, but which originally came from the Old Hall. According to Nichols 'Tradition says it was occupied by that unfortunate monarch, King Charles I a few days previous to the fatal battle of Naseby.'[55]

The letter written to Sir Edward Nicholas by the King that Friday night, when he was going to supper, shows that Charles had no idea of the forthcoming battle and that it was still his intention to march on to Melton Mowbray and Belvoir.[56] As on previous nights, the Royalist army was completely unaware of the proximity of the New Model, believing that their diversionary tactics had been successful. Their illusions were soon shattered, as they had been on Thursday evening, by a Parliamentarian attack on one of their outlying positions. Ever since he had left Newport Pagnell, Fairfax had managed to retain the upper hand. The Royalists were on the defensive and always uncertain where he was, how strong he was and where he would strike next. This time it was Ireton who had been given command of a detachment of cavalry with instructions to fall on the flank of the enemy if the opportunity arose.[57] That Friday evening Rushworth wrote, 'Our army flanks him 5 miles short of Market Harborough, the headquarters at Guilsborough. I expect every hour to hear of the party sent to fall on the rear.'[58]

Naseby must have been the southern-most of the Royalist positions, over six miles from Harborough, and therefore presumably it was a 'Court of Guard', the main cavalry quarters probably being much closer to the headquarters. At Naseby a small party of cavalry would have been in an ideal position to warn of a Parliamentarian approach and, although most of the guards were apparently captured, some appear to have escaped to raise the alarm. However, in view of the previous performance of the Royalist guards, it is perhaps not unreasonable to accept the claim of one Parliamentarian newspaper that 'wee tooke divers of Prince Ruperts Life Guard playing at Quoits for handfulls of money at Naseby, these were about twentie men.'[59] According to other sources the troopers were from both Rupert's lifeguard and Langdale's brigade, while there is a local tradition that claims some of them were dining in Shuckburgh House, opposite the church at Naseby, when they were surprised.[60] This was not the only skirmish on Friday night. Slingsby reports that the enemy gave the Royalists an alarm, which may have been the encounter at Naseby:

> 'but presently were encountr'd wth a perty of our horse, and chas'd untill they came to see where they had made their fire, in an open feild. Upon ye charge Liet.Coll.Sair, receiving a Shott near ye shouldier, was brought off to Harborrow, to Sr Marmaduke Langdales Quarter.'[61]

The news did not reach the King until at least eleven in the evening, some accounts say midnight or two in the morning, but within a short time he and

Fig.48. The small market town of Market Harborough is seen here with coaches and waggons in the market place in the early 19th century, when it still lay on a major communication route. The church and school look very much as they did in 1645. It is no coincidence that it was through Harborough that both armies would march in June 1645, for Harborough had frequently seen forces from both sides passing by throughout the war. It lay on an important route from London, through Northampton to Leicester, Derby and the north, while for the Royalists it was on an important east-west route because, with Leicester and Northampton in Parliamentarian hands, their convoys passed though Harborough when travelling between Oxford and Newark.

his retinue were riding eastward the two miles to the headquarters at Market Harborough.[62] According to tradition it was in the building now known as the King's Head Inn that he found Rupert resting in a chair in a low room. The inn, which had formerly been a manor house and is now much altered, still lies at the corner of Church Street and King's Road.[63]

By two in the morning the Council of War was in session. Within a few days it would be said by Rupert's enemies amongst the Royalists that it was he who decided at Market Harborough that the army should turn to fight and these lies, spread by Digby, were repeated by various later historians. For example, Whitelocke says 'There it was resolved (and chiefly by P.Rupert's eagerness, old Commanders being much against it) to give Battel...'[64] In fact the Council saw Rupert, supported by Astley and the other soldiers, arguing that the army should continue to march north but, as had happened on other crucial occasions earlier in the campaign, the courtiers lined up against Rupert, 'it being our unhappiness, that the Faction of the Court, whereof the most powerful were the Lord Digby and Mr John Ashburnham, and that of the Army were ever opposed and were jealous of others.'[65] The degree to which the Royalist cause was riven by often very personal jealousies can be seen from the re-surfacing of the dispute within the family of the Earl of Northampton which, while the army was at Daventry, had begun to draw in leading Royalist figures like Rupert and even led to accusations of treachery.[66]

In early June Charles had been very clear, when writing to Nicholas, that his army would be too weak to fight the New Model until it had been reinforced by Goring or Gerard. Neither had yet arrived, indeed Goring had ignored his instructions and was still in the South West, while on the 12th the King had discovered that the New Model was far stronger than he had suspected. This was why the Royalist army had marched away from Daventry, to avoid a battle, trying to deceive Fairfax as to their real intentions and to trick him into thinking that their army was stronger in cavalry than it really was. Why then was the decision taken at Market Harborough to turn and fight? The explanation perhaps exists in the twisted lies of Digby who says 'it was then the unanimous opinion of all that if Fairfaxe should follow us neere wee ought to turne upon him and fight with him before he could ioyne with the Scots....'[67] Fairfax clearly intended to force an engagement and in these circumstances, it was argued, if they continued to march north then the rear would be attacked so endangering the whole army. It is certainly true that, as a Parliamentarian newspaper claimed, with the great size of the Royalist train, some 200 or 300 carriages, they would have had difficulty in marching away fast enough.[68] Digby, supported by Ashburnham, the Treasurer of the army, also claimed that retiring from an enemy which had already been discomforted at Oxford would only provoke danger and demoralise their own soldiers. There was a general feeling amongst the Royalists at this time that the New Model was an inexperienced army and in particular that its officers were men of low birth with little military experience. Several weeks earlier Digby had claimed that the combined Royalist forces were 'equal to any the rebels have at this time', while Charles himself had written to his wife that 'I believe they [the New Model] are weaker than they are thought to be, whether by their distractions, which are very great ... or wasting their men, I cannot say.'[69] News had also recently arrived of Montrose's success at Auldearn against a much larger force and the King must have considered the New Model Army could be as easily dispatched as his enemies in Scotland.[70] The Royalist soldiers were certainly told, while at Harborough, that the New Model was weary and weak and that they would beat Fairfax and be in Northampton by Sunday.[71] It is not too surprising to find the Royalists holding the New Model in low esteem as many Parliamentarians considered it in the same light, Rushworth describing it on the 14th June as 'our poore despised and contemptible army'.[72] But Rupert clearly did not share the view of the New Model held by Charles and his courtiers, not least because he had already faced many of the same troops at Marston Moor, led by Cromwell and Fairfax, and had been soundly defeated. Rupert did not underestimate the threat and was still hoping that, if they delayed the engagement, they would be joined by Goring and Gerard and knowing that he could also draw reinforcements from Belvoir and Newark as the army marched north.[73] However, Rupert's position as Lieutenant General of the army counted for nothing in such matters, the final decision on strategy always resting with the King, as Captain General. At Market Harborough Charles took the advice of his courtiers against that of his experienced military commanders and this was to prove the King's most disastrous decision of the whole war. He had ignored Prince Rupert's advice before, in the autumn of 1644, when he took on the three Parliamentarian armies in the second battle of Newbury. Then he had survived the encounter, but only because of the inability of the Parliamentarian commanders to work together and the poor condition of their combined forces. At Naseby Charles would not be allowed to escape the consequences of his actions, for if the King was willing to engage in battle then Fairfax was certainly 'very glad of the proffer having long expected it.'[74]

Though he had been overruled, Prince Rupert undoubtedly threw himself into the preparations for the next day's action, for he had now recovered much of the energy and enthusiasm that he had lost as a result of his defeat at Marston Moor. One can imagine that for the rest of the night he was busy making plans and preparations with his senior commanders, for there was a strategy to agree upon and ground to be chosen for the deployment of the army. First light may have seen him riding out of Harborough with his local guides to view the ground on which the army would probably have to fight.

That night, as the Royalist Council of War had debated and the King made his fateful decision to turn and fight, the rearguard and the vanguard of the respective armies lay within three miles of each other. Colonel Okey's dragoons were at Naseby and the Royalists were probably at East Farndon and adjacent villages. Scouts had been sent out by each army in case the enemy made a move. There was however no more action that night and so the riders watched each other 'untill day light appeared, where the Scouts on both sides saluted one another....[75] After three years of war the decisive moment had arrived.

NOTES

1. Slingsby, p.149. *Moderate Intelligencer*, 14th June.

2. Isham, 1962.

3. Rushworth to Luke, Tibbutt, 1963, p.574-5. *A more exact and perfect Relation*. Symonds, p.192. *The Moderate Intelligencer*, 12-19th June.

4. That it was perhaps Whalley, with the other troops attached to his regiment, that provided this 'forlorn hope' is supported by the fact that Whalley's and Fleetwood's regiments appear to have quartered at Flore on the night of the 12th June. However this seems to be in conflict with Sprigge who says that Flore was a royalist quarter unless he is confusing this with the situation earlier that evening. Sprigge, 1647, p.31.

5. Probably Upper Heyford, which lay on the Northampton road, rather than Nether Heyford.

6. *The Moderate Intelligencer*, 12-19th June 1645. Rushworth to Luke, Tibbutt, 1963, p.575. Rushworth, vol.6, p.40.

7. Tibbutt, 1963, p.575. Sprigge, 1647, p.30. Fairfax may have intentionally encouraged this belief if on the 11th he had indeed marched east from Stony Stratford and approached Northampton via Hanslope.

8. *A more exact and perfect Relation*.

9. Sprigge, 1647, p.31.

10. Clarendon, 1702, bk.9, p.37. Rushworth to Luke, Tibbutt, 1963, p.574-5. *A more exact and perfect relation*. Symonds, p.192. *The Moderate Intelligencer*, 12th-19th June.

11. Slingsby, p.149-150.

12. Tibbutt, 1963, p.318. However, Sprigge says that when Fairfax inspected the guards he was 1.5 miles from Flore which was a royalist quarter. Sprigge, 1647, p.31.

13. Rushworth to Luke, Tibbutt, 1963, p.575.

14. Cruso, 1632, p.70.

15. Rushworth, vol.6, p.40.

16. Symonds, p.193. Sprigge, 1647, p.31.

17. *A more exact and perfect Relation*. Another report rather dubiously claims they also sent a convoy towards Oxford. In working out the space likely to have been occupied by the baggage train, and in calculating the likely length of the train in line of march, I have taken the following estimates for the size of a waggon (using measurements of a surviving wain) and team of five estimated very roughly with Eric Westaway: waggon width 7ft, length 15ft, team of horses in two pairs with a thiller 35ft, giving a total length of roughly 50ft per waggon and team. No attempt has been made to accurately check these figures as they have simply been used to determine an approximate order of scale. In line of march the baggage, with about 200 carriages must have covered something like 2.5 miles. For the rest of the army, the cavalry if marching four wide with a strength of about 5000 must have added up to 2.5 miles, while the infantry at 8 wide with 6ft between ranks with 4500 men would add another mile, giving in all about 6 miles.

18. Rushworth to Luke, 13th June, Tibbutt, 1963, p.575.

19. *A True Relation of a Victory*.

20. Tennant, 1992, p.260.

21. For example, Warburton, vol.3, p.102 n.3, claims the army marched over 'a wide and very open country, in the centre of which stands Naseby...'. He is followed by Ashley, 1992, p.65.
22. Ogilby, plate 22 & 61. Brown, 1991, p.42.
23. Hexham, 1639, p.4-7.
24. *Brief Memorials* . Sprigge, 1647, p.31.
25. *The Moderate Intelligencer*, 12th-19th June.
26. *A Glorious Victory*.
27. Whetham to Luke, in Whetham & Whetham, 1907, p.101, summarised in Tibbutt, 1963, p.574.
28. Dyson, 1913, p.57. Markham, 1870, p.213.
29. Nichols, vol.4, p.352.
30. Sandon, 1883.
31. *A more exact and perfect Relation. A True Relation of a Victory*.
32. Kingston, 1897, p.205. *The Northampton Reporter*, 1st May 1899, article by J.T.Page.
33. The sources give numbers ranging from 600 to 800. Rushworth, vol.6, p.40. Sprigge, 1647, p.32. Cromwell is said to have passed through Wellingborough on his way to the battle. A letter referred to by Cole was exhibited in Wellingborough in about 1890 by Mr Dolben of Finedon Hall. G.M. Dulley, 1892-3, 'The Hind Hotel', *NN&Q*, vol.5, p.177. Cole reported that the Hind Hotel 'is stated to have been in building when Cromwell's army marched through Wellingborough, immediately previous to the battle of Naseby; a letter in the hand-writing of the Protector, was formerly in the posession of a neighbouring family, in which he desired forage might be prepared here for his troops at that juncture.' Cole, 1815, p.244.
34. Tibbutt, 1963, p.319. Col.Thomas Long to Luke, 13th June, Tibbutt, 1963, p.574. It is not stated where Long was but only Northampton makes sense in the context of the other information in the letter.
35. Tibbutt, 1963, p.319.
36. *The Moderate Intelligencer*, 14th June.
37. Whetham to Luke, Tibbutt, 1963, p.574.
38. *A more exact and perfect Relation*.
39. Gentles, 1992, p.44.
40. Warburton, vol.3,p. 102. Whetham to Luke, 13th June, Whetham & Whetham, 1907, p.101.
41. Vernon, 1644, p.40.
42. Slingsby p.150. *The Moderate Intelligencer*, 12th-19th June. *The Parliament Post*, 10th - 17th June. Rushworth to Luke, 13th June, Tibbutt, 1963, p.574-5. *A more exact and perfect Relation*. Sprigge, 1647, p.32.
43. Ravensthorpe and Teeton account, PRO SP28/172 unfol..
44. Sprigge, 1647, p.32. Guilsborough account and Ravensthorpe account, PRO SP28/172 unfol..
45. *A True Relation of a Victory* . Sprigge incorrectly names the place as Gilling, though Guilsborough is clearly named in his *'Journall of the Armies Martches'* in Sprigge, 1647, p.332. Despite this, attempts have been made to locate 'Gilling'. Mastin in the late 18th century identified it with the site called Calendar, a medieval monastic grange which had probably been deserted centuries before.Mastin, 1792, p.127. 'The Haselrig Mansion', *Northampton Mercury*, 6th November 1896, article by J.T.Page. Mee, 1945, p.325, attributes the tradition to the 'Elizabethan Hall' at Thornby.
46. Pevsner, 1973a, p.427.
47. *A More Particular and Exact Relation*. Wogan, reprinted in Young, 1985, p.367.
48. Roger Garner of Coton had household goods and provisions taken on the night before Naseby fight. Account of Guilsborough, PRO SP28/172 unfol..

49. Bridges, writing in 1720, says they were quartered in East Farndon and other adjacent villages; Bridges notes. It seems likely that Royalist troops may have been quartered in Marston Trussell village, which lay between Theddingworth and Lubenham. However, there is no record of this. The account submitted to Parliament in 1647 as usual makes no reference to Royalist exactions, while the constable's account for the parish, which has been annotated in a much later hand as 1645, is in fact from the late 17th century on the evidence of the constables named. Its references to 'two soldgers 6d' and 'charges for the King careges 15/1d', again highlighted by a later hand, have nothing at all to do with the Civil War. Marston Trussell Constablecs accounts, 1616-1704, NRO 206P/102 unfol..

50. Symonds, p.193. Davies, 1964, incorrectly places the train at Theddingworth. *Iter Carolinum*.

51. A tradition records that Prince Rupert stayed in Great Glen on the night preceding the battle. This, like the tradition about Cromwell being at Hazelrigg House in Northampton and Charles being at Wistow is quite wrong. It seems likely that what was said in the past was that they were there before Naseby fight, meaning some days if not a week or more but this was corrupted to the night before. For example, Firth, 1926, p.212. The misreading of these traditions has led some authors to suggest that Prince Rupert quartered on the night of the 13th at Great Glen, while Langdale had pushed north almost to Leicester. Hollings, 1840, p.65. A detachment of Royalists are also said to have been in Lutterworth on the night of the 13th June. Anon, 1881, p.133.

52. Nichols, vol.2, p.699. By the mid 19th century the house lay in ruins. Hill, 1875, p.139. Mursell, 1861, p.31. Harrod, 1808. This contains a plan of Lubenham Manor with moats.There were in the 19th century, according to Nichols, earthworks on the site of the Hall. He identified them as a Roman camp, but in fact they were merely the moat of 3 acres while the large enclosure was no more than a medieval headland. Although now much altered and with modern extensions, in the west gable a stone mullioned window is still visible from the road and the Hall is still surrounded today on two sides by the earthworks of its medieval moated enclosure.

53. Manuscript notes for a history of the parish of Lubenham extracted from various sources by Rev. Edwards, 1896, LRO DE 1369/73. J.T.Page, 'The Night before Naseby', *Northampton Herald*, 25th November 1893.

54. Rastall, 1787, quoted by Warburton, vol.3, p.101.

55. Archdeacon's Visitation, 2nd August 1882, quoted in LRO DE 1369/73 Archdeacon Bonney's Visitation, 18th September 1838. Visitation, 20th August 1842. Nichols, vol.3, addendum p.705. Inspection of the chair indicates Nichols is wrong in saying that the back part of it formed part of the wainscoting against the south wall of the Nave and one piece with the pew.

56. Charles to Nicholas, 13th June, Bray, 1827, vol.5, p.134.

57. Sprigge, 1647, p.32.

58. Rushworth to Luke, 13th June, Tibbutt, 1963, p.575.

59. *The True Informer*, 21st June.

60. Sprigge, 1647, p.32. Page, 1893a.

61. Slingsby, p.150.

62. *Iter Carolinum*. Whitelocke p.145.

63. Hill, 1875, p.1. Davies & Brown, 1984, p.47-9. Articles and papers by Strongman, LRO DE 2101/131/6, p.2.

64. Whitelocke, p.145.

65. *Brief Memorials*.

66. Tennant, 1992, p.260.

67. Digby to Legge, quoted by Morrah, 1976, p.188.

68. *A more exact and perfect Relation*.

69. Wedgwood, 1974, p.442. Charles to Henrietta Maria, 8th June, *The King's Cabinet Opened*.

70. Warburton, vol.3,p. 102.
71. *The True Informer*, 21st June.
72. *A True Relation of a Victory.*
73. Warburton, vol.3, p.102.
74. *A Relation of the Victory.*
75. *A more exact and perfect Relation.*

CHAPTER 7

THE ARMIES AND THE BATTLEFIELD

'Never hardly did an army go forth to war
who had less of the confidence of their own friends,
or were more the objects of the contempt of their enemies'
A Breviary of the History of the Parliament

Before we can examine the events of the battle itself we must consider two issues, firstly the strength and composition of the two armies and secondly the landscape over which the events took place. Almost everyone, from those present on the day to the most recent modern commentators, agrees that the New Model was larger than the King's army. What is a matter of great dispute is the degree to which the King was outnumbered and so, because of the influence that numbers will have had upon the events of the battle, it is necessary to review this issue in detail. The question of the equipping and nature of the troops has already been dealt with in Chapter 3 while the composition of the two armies, in terms of the regiments and officers that fought at Naseby, has already been analyzed in detail by Young and so will not be duplicated here.[1]

The estimates of the numbers of troops involved at Naseby which were made in the days and weeks before and immediately following the battle vary considerably, as do the calculations made by historians whether writing a few years or centuries later. Belasyse, an influential Royalist who was a volunteer with the King's reserves during the battle, estimated the New Model Army had about 15000 and the Royalist army no more than 12000 men. De Gomme and Clarendon on the other hand claimed the Royalist army was no more than 7500 strong, while Walker, from whom most of Clarendon's evidence on Naseby was drawn, gives incomplete estimates which are compatible with Clarendon's. In contrast Rushworth, who was writing on the day, says that the two armies differed by no more than 500 men while Rupert probably had a greater number of cavalry than Fairfax, and his account was followed by Sprigge and by Whitelocke. Various assessments over the last century or so, beginning with that by Ross, lie about half way between these two extremes, whereas Ashley concludes that Belasyse's figures were reasonably accurate. Gentles however, in his recent study of the New Model Army, has suggested a more extreme variation between the two armies arguing that Fairfax probably had at his disposal nearer 17000 men at Naseby while the Royalists had less than 9000. If the New Model really did outnumber the King's forces by almost two to one then we must agree with Hutton when he says that the Royalist army simply committed suicide at Naseby.[2] In this case the main consideration must be the greater ability of the Parliamentarians to deliver the resources which won the battle. On the other hand, if the assessments of numbers made by those on both sides who actually saw the armies that fought at Naseby were closer to the truth then, in assessing the battle, we can justifiably concentrate our attention more upon questions such as relative experience and tactics.

Most assessments of the strength of the two forces have depended upon the broad contemporary estimates of the numbers of infantry and cavalry in each army. The one major exception to this has been Young's detailed examination of each regiment in the Royalist army but unfortunately, because of the paucity of detailed documentary evidence for these regiments, his analysis is unable to advance us far beyond the calculations made from the standard sources. Indeed, we can never expect a definitive study of the strengths of the Royalist regiments because the necessary documents do not appear to exist. With the New Model Army the jury is still out, and will remain so until a comprehensive study is made of the vast body of warrants, accounts and other documents in the Exchequer papers. All previous calculations of Parliamentarian numbers have been based almost solely upon the estimates given in the newspapers and the contemporary histories, but there is a very good chance that in the Exchequer papers sufficient evidence exists to enable almost exact calculation of New Model army numbers, regiment by regiment. The most important source will be the pay records related to the army musters, but these can be supplemented by documents such as the parish accounts, which occasionally specify the number of troops quartering in a village. For example, there is a warrant of 1st July 1645 for the pay for 53 soldiers in Major Wilde's troop in Vermuyden's regiment, according to the muster taken on the 23rd April 1645. For Colonel Pye's regiment another record specifies £108 as 11 days' pay for the men & officers in the Colonel's own troop together with the staff officers of the regiment, according to the muster of 25th April, while another specifies £201/5/8d for 13 days' pay according to the muster of 20th May.[3] Although some evidence from these sources is used here, there has been no attempt to carry out the vast undertaking of scouring the hundreds of boxes of Exchequer papers that will be required for the definitive study of the Parliamentarian army strength in May and June 1645. What has been done is to temper the evidence of the general sources with a small selection of data from these more detailed records.

There are wide discrepancies between many of the general sources. Some of the writers were obviously poorly informed but others can be shown, on the basis of the Exchequer papers, to be fairly accurate. For example, there are the newspaper accounts which refer to Colonel Rossiter as having 500 men when he joined Cromwell at Naseby. That evening, when they were at Marston Trussell, the regimental strength was accurately recorded by the constable of the village when he set down the cost to the parish of quartering Rossiter's men and horses. The record has survived and shows that Rossiter had 493 troopers on the evening of the 14th June. As he had lost only one man seriously wounded in the battle, the newspaper estimate is seen to be remarkably accurate.[4] Some other newspaper accounts are however far less reliable, such as that which on the 7th June put Fairfax's forces at 11000 and the Royalist army at 13000.[5] Baillie also estimated between 11000 and 12000 Parliamentarian troops, but he was not present and Gentles has argued that he had reason to underestimate numbers as he wished to establish the mistake in excluding the Scots from the war effort.[6] Other Parliamentarian newspapers put the army at over 13000, which accords reasonably well with Sir Samuel Luke's estimate of 8000 foot and 5-6000 horse, made after he saw the whole army march through Newport Pagnell on the 9th June. By the time the other regiments under Rossiter and Gell joined the army Luke estimated it would be nearer 7000 foot and 8000 horse, making a total of about 15000, although his second estimate for the foot was reduced by 1000 showing the limitations in his evidence, while we know that Gell did not reach the army before the battle.[7] Lord Belasyse, who was in the field with the King on the 14th June, also estimated the Parliamentarian force at 15000.[8]

How close do these figures accord with the more detailed evidence for the New Model Army? It would appear that in late April some at least of the regiments of horse were not up to full strength, because we have seen for example that Major Wilde's troop of Vermuyden's regiment had only 53 troopers instead of 100. By June the numbers had increased, though it seems unlikely that all the regiments had reached their full complement of 600. If all nine New Model regiments that were at Naseby had been at full strength then they would have numbered 5400, but at the 5th June muster there were apparently only 3014 horse.[9] The difference can in part be accounted for by Vermuyden's brigade, which had not yet rejoined the army. His brigade, comprising his own, Rich's, Pye's and Fiennes' regiments of horse and Okey's dragoons, numbered between 2000 and 2500 troopers, one source specifying about 2000 horse and 500 dragoons.[10] Each regiment would appear to have been nearer 500 than their full complement of 600, while Okey's dragoons must have been well below strength, unless only part of his regiment were with Vermuyden. The source giving the details of the 5th June muster claims that with Vermuyden's brigade (and presumably the troops taken by Cromwell) the horse would total 5969. Amongst Vermuyden's 2500 troopers about 1800 must have been from the New Model. Also missing from the 5th June muster were the three troops of horse, no more than 300 men, which Cromwell had taken to Ely. This would give a total of about 5100 rather than the full complement of 5400 for the nine New Model regiments of horse. In other words, the horse appear to have been close to but not completely up to full strength by the time of Naseby. Moreover, when Vermuyden's brigade returned to Newport Pagnell in early June they were said to need 'recruiting' as a result of their heavy service over the preceding weeks. That most of the regiments were close to full strength is supported by the fact that Colonel Butler's Regiment, when it quartered at Hackleton on the 11th June, is said to have numbered 600, though of course this was probably only an estimate.[11]

In addition to the New Model forces there were a limited number of other cavalry which Fairfax had called up to the army in the days and weeks preceding the battle, which were needed to redress what Fairfax feared would be a deficiency in cavalry if Goring was to rejoin the King. Colonel John Fiennes, who was Member of Parliament for Oxfordshire, commanded a regiment of horse that had originated in North Oxfordshire and which had been with Cromwell and then with Vermuyden since at least late April. The regiment had been severely under strength while in quarters at Abingdon during the previous winter but, as we have seen, the regiment may have numbered about 500 by June when it accompanied Vermuyden.[12] Rossiter's regiment of horse, which was not strictly part of the New Model but rather based in Lincolnshire, had remained actively engaged in that county until a couple of days before the battle.[13] Their arrival at the very last moment added another 494 horse and dragoons. The only other major unit of cavalry to arrive in time to fight at Naseby were the Suffolk horse and dragoons under the command of Colonel Brampton Gourdon, Member of Parliament for Sudbury.[14] They were among the 600 horse that joined the army with Cromwell on the 13th, but only about 300 of those were probably the Suffolk horse because Cromwell was also returning with the three troops of horse he had taken to Ely from the siege of Oxford. That there were only 300-400 Suffolk horse is confirmed by the fact that when they were divided into two divisions at Naseby, one to each wing, there were only 200 allocated to Ireton left wing. No reference is made in any account of the battle as to the participation of forces from the local garrisons, other than the Northampton horse that joined in the pursuit. However, two companies of horse had been sent out from Northampton on the 13th to join the army. Perhaps the reference to the Northampton horse as only joining in the pursuit was a reference to the other horse from Northampton and Rockingham who may have arrived later in the day. If the two Northampton companies did fight then, on the basis of the advice in the manuals, one must assume that they were placed in the reserves, probably with the Association cavalry. Together they will have made at most 500-600 horse and probably considerably less.

Sprigge's claim that Fairfax had nearly 6000 horse on the field at Naseby might therefore represent a slight underestimate.[15] If one takes Luke's estimate of 5-6000 horse and adds to this those which joined from the Association and Northampton then one has a total of 6300-7400. We have seen that if one adds Vermuyden's brigade to the 3014 mustered on the 5th June and those joining from the Association and Northampton one has a total of between 6308-6908. This is significantly below the 7200 which would have prevailed had all the regiments been at full strength. Each of these independent estimates are relatively close and would tend to support the presence of up to about 6600 horse under Fairfax's command at Naseby.

The New Model infantry, like that of the Eastern Association army in 1644, never reached anything like their full strength. At the 5th June muster there had been only 7031 foot.[16] It must be assumed that the two companies of firelocks under Captain Lieutenant Desborough who guarded the train, which probably numbered at most 130 men, were also included in this figure.[17] No other infantry joined the army thereafter, except for some local garrison troops which probably numbered no more than about 400. We cannot be certain however that there were no significant losses through desertion or any additions by the arrival of new recruits over the nine days leading up to the battle. Some troops certainly deserted at Newport Pagnell on the 10th and they may not have been returned to the army before the 14th. With this caveat the Parliamentarian infantry at Naseby can be estimated at less than 7500, which is half way between Luke's two estimates of the infantry strength.

This gives an average of about 860 for each New Model regiment with a further body of some 550, comprising mainly the firelocks and the local troops, to defend the train. Pickering's, Montague's and two other regiments of foot quartered in Collingtree on the 11th June numbered over 3000 men, tending to confirm regimental strengths averaging over 750 men but well below the full complement of 1200.[18] This is supported by the evidence after the battle for two of these regiments. When marching through Warwickshire the following week, Pickering's regiment was between 700 and 800 strong, while one company of Montague's numbered 80 men, again suggesting a regimental strength of the order of 800.[19] These numbers are bound to be lower than on the 14th June as both regiments lost up to 50 killed and wounded and are likely to have lost at least a few other troops, if the stories of desertion with pillage after the battle are correct. It is of course possible that some regiments were considerably weaker and others significantly stronger than the average of about 860. For example, Sir Hardress Waller's Regiment was awaiting 800 recruits at the time of the battle and so may have had no more than perhaps 400 men at Naseby. Indeed it would appear that Sir Hardress Waller himself and some of his officers were not present at Naseby, for he was instructed on the 14th June to return to the army and leave some of his officers to bring up his recruits.[20] If this is correct then he was not the only commander absent from his regiment, because Colonel Pye had been captured at the storming of Leicester, had only been released on parole a few days before Naseby and so he too was unable to fight.[21] If Hardress Waller's regiment was severely under strength then it would help to explain the relatively low casualty figures for the regiment which are discussed below.

In contrast, the regiment commanded by Lieutenant Colonel Pride at Naseby seems to have had other troops attached to it at this time. This was Colonel Sir Edward Harley's regiment, which had been originally intended for Colonel Henry Barkley or Barclay, from whose old regiment several companies had been drawn. Some of the records for June and July 1645 describe the regiment as 'formerly Barclay's', in several cases corrupted to 'Bartlett's'. Harley did not serve during 1645 because he had been wounded and so that is why the regiment was commanded at Naseby by Pride.[22] Attached to it at this time were two companies of Colonel Ingoldsby's regiment, the rest having been included in Weldon's brigade when it was sent to the relief of Taunton.[23] 200 infantry had also been dispatched from the Northampton garrison to join the New Model on the 12th, while others had been detached a few days earlier from the Newport Pagnell garrison, perhaps also no more than 200 as Luke only had about 600 infantry at this time. One might expect local infantry units to have been with the reserves or rearguard, which would explain how Pride's was strong enough to provide two separate units in the battle, though they may instead have defended the train.

To these maximum estimates of 6600 horse and 7500 foot must be added Okey's dragoons, which may have had as few as 500 men although its full complement was 1000. Finally there were the 20 scouts under the command of the scoutmaster, Major Watson.[24] If Okey's dragoons were at full strength then Fairfax's army could have comprised at most about 15000 men, the number estimated by Belasyse and at the top of the range estimated by Luke.

In determining the actual strength of the two armies it is also essential to take account of the likely number of officers, for all commentators agree that the Royalists had a far larger proportion of officers than the New Model. The degree to which this might distort the size of an army can be seen from the example of Pickering's regiment. When it was in the Eastern Association in 1644-5 it was at its greatest strength immediately after its establishment in April 1644. At that time it had 110 officers out of a full complement of 165 but only 805 common soldiers out of a complement of 1200, giving a ratio of 1 to 8. This very high ratio of officers to men is a result of the fact that in the armies of the Civil War it was normal for the officer list to include not just the commissioned officers but also the sergeants, corporals, drummers, gentlemen at arms, clerks and gentlemen of the company. In our figures we have also added the five or so support staff for the regiment as a whole who would be accounted for with the Colonel's company, including the waggoner, quartermaster, provost marshall, surgeon and surgeon's mate. By 8th May 1644, after the regiment had suffered at the storming of Lincoln, it had 140 officers but only 523 men, a ratio of 1 to 4. By February 1645, when in winter quarters at Abingdon and at the low point of its fortunes, it had 126 officers but only 243 men, a ratio of 1 to 2.[25]

Fairfax commanded a new army which represented a total restructuring of three previous armies, a process which involved a large number of officers being discharged or transferred elsewhere. As a result we can be fairly certain that the total number of officers in the New Model was very close to the full complement for each regiment. As in the Eastern Association army, the infantry regiments would have had 16 officers for each of the ten companies plus about 5 support staff for the regiment, giving a total of 165 per regiment. At full strength this gives a ratio of 1 to 7 and so for the eight regiments present at Naseby this gives a total of approximately 1320 officers. It is important to know whether or not the figures quoted by the various sources for the armies take account of the numbers of officers, for if they do not then it will be neccessary to add those numbers to the totals already arrived at. When the full complement of a regiment is specified in the documents of the period it appears only to relate to the number of common soldiers and this is apparently true for the numbers quoted for musters.[26] If this is correct then to calculate the total strength of the New Model infantry it is probably necessary to add 1320 to the estimated 7400 men, giving 8720. For the horse one may judge from Cromwell's Ironsides in February 1644-5, just before incorporation into the New Model, where the number of officers for a troop was maintained fairly close to the full complement.[27] Eleven companies of Cromwell's regiment had 88 officers and 914 troopers, giving a ratio of 1 to 10. There were nine New Model regiments of horse, three other regiments and two companies of Northampton horse. This gives a total of nearly 600 officers, which produces an overall total for the horse of about 7200. In addition there were Okey's dragoons. If the muster records reported in the newspapers are indeed just for the common soldiers then in all the army may have numbered up to 17000 including officers compared to a maximum of 15000 if the numbers quoted from the musters did include the officers.

There are various Parliamentarian estimates of the strength of the Royalist army as a result of the work of the scouts while the King marched north. One report which reached Sir Samuel Luke suggested that the King's army numbered about 12000, but he dismissed the wilder estimates such as the 14000 claimed by Sir Robert Pye, who was involved in one sortie against the Royalists. Another improbable estimate is the 15000 reported to Brereton by a captured Royalist quartermaster, who said the King had 8000 horse and 7000 foot.[28] With such large numbers being reported it is not perhaps surprising that Fairfax was concerned that the Royalists might prove stronger in horse than the New Model, especially if joined by Goring. Immediately after the battle the letter from the army by the two Parliamentary Commissioners, Leighton and Herbert, specifies 12000 Royalists and this is repeated by several newspapers, while another account from the army suggested that the Royalists were 14000 strong.[29] One might dismiss the figures quoted by these Parliamentarian sources as over-estimates of the Royalist strength intended to emphasise the success of the New Model, but the same cannot be said of Belasyse's estimate. He was a senior Royalist who was present at the battle, and within the circle of the King's advisors, and he says the King's army did not exceed 12000.[30] At the other extreme we have the figures from Clarendon, Walker and de Gomme of approximately 3500 horse and 4000 foot.[31] Whereas for the New Model most authors in modern times have tended to increase the numbers, for the King's army some have accepted these relatively low figures without question.

By far the most significant source for the strength of the Royalist army is Symonds' diary. He gives what appears to be direct and accurate information from two musters, one near Stow on the 8th May and the other at the siege of Leicester, although the evidence is more detailed for the horse than for the foot. The Royalist army had been assembled gradually as they marched first north and then east. At the first muster, near Stow, the King had 6300 horse according to Symonds. Of these the King then sent 3000 back with Goring into the South West, leaving himself 3300 horse, which may explain Slingsby's figure of 4000.[32] By drawing out troops from other garrisons in the Midlands the King rebuilt his cavalry to number 5620 when the muster was held at Leicester at the end of May. Of the 1200 Newark horse that had joined the army just before the siege of Leicester 400 returned with Willis to Newark on the 4th June, leaving the King with some 5220 horse for Naseby. Why then did the King write on the 4th June to Nicholas saying that he had scarcely 3500 horse?[33] The explanation may be straightforward. It seems likely that this letter was written on the evening of the 4th, after both Willis with his 400 Newark horse and the whole of the Northern horse had departed. However, the 1600 or so Northern horse returned the next day and therefore both the King's and Symonds' figures are actually in reasonable accord at about 5200. By the time of Naseby there may have been some additional volunteers because, according to Clarendon, on the 14th there were 500 in the King's reserve of horse compared to 130 at the previous muster.

Symonds provides a summary of the Royalist infantry that were present at the muster at Stow on the Wold.[34] These comprised 3300 under Lord Astley and 500 under Colonel Lisle, together with Rupert's foot which consisted of 500 in Rupert's own regiment and some 500 Shrewsbury foot, the remnants of the Irish regiments which had come over to England in the winter of 1643-1644. In addition there were 200 men in the King's lifeguard and 300 with Colonel Bard, giving a total of 5300 foot. After the muster there were only 300 more that joined the army, with Colonel Bagot, while just a handful of men were lost at the siege of Hawksley House. There should therefore have been a total of 5600 foot in the army at the end of May, but this cannot be checked as Symonds does not provide a record of the numbers of infantry at the Leicester muster. These totals are somewhat larger than the figures of 4000 Royalist infantry and 6000 horse reported at the siege of Leicester by Pye and Innes. Theirs was however only an estimate and they may have had reason to underestimate the numbers as their statements were within very critical reports, blaming the Committee at Leicester for the loss of the town.[35]

From these totals a number of deductions have to be made. By far the greatest impact will have been the losses sustained in the storming of Leicester. A Parliamentarian newspaper claims that 709 Royalists were killed but, although accepted by Sprigge and later by Ross, this figure may be an exaggeration. Symonds, who had nothing to gain by distorting the truth, perhaps gives a more accurate estimate when he claims that less than 200 Royalists died at Leicester. To this must be added the number wounded that would not have recuperated by the time the battle was fought. Judging from the casualty rates compared to deaths in the battle itself, a maximum figure for wounded may be 800 compared to 200 killed.

Ever since Clarendon's *History*, there seems to have been an over-estimate of the impact of garrisoning Leicester upon the Royalist army. Sir John Norwich, governor of Rockingham, who had good intelligence from Leicester after the King marched south, was certain that there were no more than about 500 infantry and two troops of horse left in the town by the 11th June.[36] These cavalry may have numbered no more than 100, judging by the small size of many of the Royalist troops of horse, and Young has suggested that they were probably men from Lord Loughborough's regiment, which had been at the siege but did not apparently fight at Naseby.[37] It seems quite likely that some of the 500 foot came from Appleyard's regiment, as he had been made governor, but some of his officers were listed amongst the Naseby prisoners and so at least part of his regiment was present at Naseby. A significant proportion of the 500 soldiers left at Leicester were in fact local people, according to Norwich. There were certainly enough recruited, for Slingsby claims he saw nearly 1000 men joining the army, although no more than 40 of the former garrison troops agreed to join Lord Loughborough's regiment of foot, with some of those who did join deserting to Coventry soon after.[38]

A final drain on Royalist numbers was the desertion of troops with their plunder after the sack of Leicester, for which we have no figures although Ross suggested as many as 1000. Considerable desertion was also suffered by the New Model at this time, for which again we have no details and so to a degree the losses on either side may cancel each other out. Moreover, the King wrote that while he waited at Daventry he was gathering up stragglers from his army and so some of the men he had lost following the storming of Leicester may have returned.[39] In all perhaps no more than 1100 were lost from the Royalist army as a result of storming and garrisoning Leicester but, given the recruiting which occurred while at the town, the total net loss may in fact have been no more than 500.

On the 4th June, as the army marched south, the King had written that he had no more than 4000 foot, a figure that is repeated by de Gomme, while Walker gives just 3300.[40] If one deducts the estimated 1100 lost or left at Leicester from the total of 5600 given by Symonds then we have about 4500 foot. The estimated total of infantry and horse together is, consequently, about 9500. As a rough check against this we can compare the evidence for those taken prisoner, wounded and killed, the figures for which are discussed in detail in chapter 9. There were 4508 common soldiers taken in the battle and marched into Northampton on the 15th June, while almost 4000 Royalist horse are said to have escaped from the field.[41] To this must be added at least 500 seriously wounded who were not apparently listed amongst the prisoners on the 15th, many having been quartered in Naseby and surrounding villages for some days after the battle. Finally there were between 700 to 900 killed. This again gives a total of just over 9500, to which one will need to add the number of officers captured, at least some of whom were dealt with separately.

It is known that most Royalist regiments were seriously under strength and that as a result, relative to the New Model, the army had a very high proportion of officers compared to common soldiers, because the Royalist army had not undergone a significant reorganisation. Sprigge states that the enemy had amongst its officers at least 1500 who were old soldiers, but the total number of officers will have been considerably more than this, because the ideal complement of officers for this number of troops was about 1350. It seems likely that the Royalists will have had double that figure, significantly narrowing the difference between the two forces if the muster totals only refer to common soldiers. We have seen the degree to which imbalances could build up in a Parliamentarian regiment but the Reading garrison of April 1644 may provide a more reasonable guide to the ratios for Royalist regiments. The full complement for Reading's twelve Royalist regiments would have been 9000 common soldiers, but in fact it comprised just 2231 soldiers and yet still retained 923 out of its full complement of 1002 officers.[42] This gives a ratio of less than 1 to 2.5, not very different to the worst ratio in Pickering's regiment in the winter of 1644-5, while the most complete of the regiments at Reading could still only manage a ratio of 1 to 3. The strongest single Royalist regiment at Naseby appears to have been Rupert's bluecoats, which comprised 10 companies and contained in all 500 men in May-June 1645. If it had a near full complement of officers, as one might expect, then it would have had a ratio of 1 to 3. Vaughan's regiment was probably the strongest of the Royalist regiments of horse at Naseby with 400 men in 7 companies, giving a ratio up to 1 to 4. Taking an average ratio of 1 to 3 would give 12000-12500 officers and men in the Royalist army if officers are not included in Symonds' figures, still far less than the 17000 which is the absolute maximum estimate for Fairfax's army. Whatever calculations are made there remains a very significant difference between the two armies. Only if the Royalist army were as far below strength but as well provided with officers as Pickering's had been in the winter of 1644-5 would the gap narrow, a ratio of 1 to 2 giving closer to 14000 Royalists, but this seems impossible.

How do these estimates compare to those made by contemporaries? The least plausible claims are from the Parliamentarian accounts, such as that by Rushworth, repeated in various newspapers and by Sprigge, which suggests that the difference between the two armies was no more than 500 and that in cavalry the Royalists were actually stronger. Sprigge wrote that the Royalists took themselves for 'a more considerable force then we, especially in Horse, on which they chiefly depended; being also as confident, they might relye upon their Infantry for valiant resolute men...'.[43] Okey, writing immediately after the battle, also considered that, at least on the Royalist right wing, the enemy horse outnumbered those of Parliament.[44] In part such claims may have resulted from the ruses that the Royalists employed in the day before the battle to give the impression of greater strength. It may also, in part, be due to the Parliamentarian exaggeration of numbers to make the victory appear more dramatic and the failure of the left wing more acceptable. However, Belasyse gives less than 12000 Royalist and 15000 Parliamentarian troops, a difference of only about 3000 men. This is supported on very good evidence by Digby who wrote a few weeks after Naseby that there were 3000 more Parliamentarians in reserve than the Royalist army had, which Sir William Vaughan 'who charged quite through those bodies which were in our eye, positively affirms.'[45] Neither Belasyse or Digby had obvious reason to distort the figures by increasing the Royalist numbers, indeed if anything the opposite is true because Digby's letter was critical of Rupert for not identifying the disparity earlier. Our calculations of likely strengths has given 9000-9500 Royalist and 15200 Parliamentarian soldiers and perhaps 12500 Royalists and nearly 17000 Parliamentarians if the officers do need to be separately added. The discrepancy here is somewhat greater than the Royalist eye witnesses suggest. There seems little chance of further clarification of the Royalist figures but the same is not true for the New Model. Given the problems which will be seen later when we attempt to apply the numbers to the calculation of frontages for the Parliamentarian army at Naseby one begins to wonder whether, when the Exchequer papers have been fully studied, it may be neccessary to significantly scale down the Parliamentarian strength, though probably not as far as Rushworth would have us believe.

Not only in numbers but also in composition the two armies seem to reflect the state of the respective causes. The balance between horse and foot at Edgehill had been approximately 1 to 2.5, which was already well below the ideal of 1 to 5 required by some of the military manuals. As the war progressed there had been a general deterioration on both sides as it became increasingly difficult to raise and keep infantry.[46] By the time of Naseby the balance in the two armies was still remarkably close, with approximately 1 to 1 in the New Model and about 1.15 to 1 in the Royalist army. However in other ways the armies differed enormously. The New Model represented a complete rebuilding of the Parliament's forces based to a high degree upon Cromwell's experience with the Eastern Association. It comprised regiments of horse which were almost up to full strength, well trained and most of them highly committed, and just eight regiments of foot which, although well below full strength, were not overloaded with officers. Despite the views of many Royalists and Parliamentarians, most of the officers in the New Model had proved themselves in several years of Civil War, indeed it is too easy to overlook the degree to which the New Model was in reality an old army reborn and expanded. The Eastern Association regiments, both horse and foot, formed the core of the army that fought at Naseby, especially as all the troops that had been detached to relieve Taunton were regiments which had not come from the Association. The officers were often men of fairly ordinary background but, despite the views of many of their 'betters', this did not affect their ability. Amongst the common foot soldiers there were, however, large numbers of new recruits who had been conscripted to make up the great shortfall in numbers and who undoubtedly lacked both the training and the commitment seen amongst the cavalry and the officers. To compensate for the large body of troops which had been detached to relieve Taunton, there was also a relatively small supplement of local troops drawn in by Fairfax, comprising some 400 foot and about 1200 horse and dragoons, which would all be used in the reserves or rearguard, in addition to the New Model's own regiment of dragoons. Rossiter's certainly contained some dragoons, as did the Association horse. Whereas the New Model had its own regiment of dragoons, the local cavalry units, because they normally fought in small engagements, may have included dragoons to make them more flexible fighting units. We have seen the importance of dragoon support for cavalry, as for example when they had to move through a wooded district, and we have also seen that it was cheaper to equip a dragoon than a cavalry trooper, another important consideration for County Committees. The same considerations presumably affected the Royalist army, because there was one guidon[47] reported amongst the captured Royalist colours at Naseby. In addition to their greater numbers, the New Model was also very well equipped, well paid and relatively well provisioned.

In contrast, the Royalist army comprised the shattered remnants of many regiments from various armies and garrisons and, according to Pye and Innes, many of them were poorly armed, especially amongst the horse.[48] Some of the more experienced horse had been sent into the South West with Goring and would be sorely missed. The infantry however were well seasoned troops with large numbers of experienced officers, many having seen service throughout the war, while some had also been professional soldiers before the war, in Ireland or on the continent. For this reason they were looked upon by the Royalists as the 'old infantry', having been in arms for such a long time. Although a substantial number of men were conscripted into the Royalist infantry in Wales and the Welsh Marches in the Spring of 1645, the army probably did not have anything like the same proportion of new recruits as the New Model. The army had been pulled together from garrisons across the Midlands and Wales, reflecting the great difficulty the Royalists had in supporting a large field army on a much reduced territory. As a result of this, and the lack of dynamic and effective overall leadership, the Royalist forces had not been reorganised into efficient, large fighting units and still retained large numbers of officers, out of all proportion to the number of common soldiers. The army was therefore far more costly to maintain and supply than the New Model, but on the battlefield, particularly amongst the infantry, it must surely have made for a stronger, more experienced force. As Sprigge says:

'they had on their side not so few as fifteen hundred Officers, that were old soldiers, of great experience through long experience in forraign parts; when on the other hand, we had not ten Officers that could pretend to any such thing, as the experience of a souldier, save what this war had given them...'[49]

Though it is a propaganda caricature of reality, the contemporary descriptions of each army suggests that the Civil War was, in the last analysis, decided between an army of ordinary godly men and an army of gentlemen. Though the Royalists despised the men of the New Model as their social inferiors, which was undoubtedly a significant influence encouraging the King to fight on the 14th June, they would soon learn that in battle these men were their equals.

Naseby was therefore far from being the largest battle of the Civil War, for at Edgehill there had been about 30000 and at Marston Moor some 40000 men. Already at Marston Moor Parliament was able to muster a far larger force than Rupert and at Naseby the balance was again apparently in Parliament's favour. A major factor in any military campaign is the ability of a commander to ensure that adequate resources are available in the right place at the right time, which includes not only numbers of men but also their quality and motivation and the adequacy of their supplies and equipment. That Fairfax and Cromwell achieved this advantage at Naseby should not be used as an argument to devalue their victory, for it is also the case that a commander needs skill to exploit his advantage in such a way that his enemy is forced to come to battle and then to ensure that the enemy force is destroyed.

THE BATTLEFIELD IN 1645

The troops themselves were obviously the most significant resource available to the commanders, but the landscape was another important factor which provided opportunities to exploit and problems to overcome. Few authors who have written about the battle of Naseby have made sufficient effort to understand the topography and to place the events within the contemporary landscape. The best attempt was by Woolrych, but he mistakenly imagined this area to be an 'ill drained, furze dotted heath, varied here and there by the great open fields....', while Warburton, writing in the 19th century, says the parishes were divided from each other by hedges even in 1645.[50] Before we can continue the narrative we must therefore digress once more to review the landscape within which the battle took place. Only then can we begin to put ourselves in the position of the commanders and consider the options they must have reviewed, so assisting us in determining the initial deployments, in understanding why the battle was fought exactly where it was and in resolving the dispute of recent years as to the exact extent of the battlefield.

Visiting Naseby today one sees a landscape which was transformed between 1650 and 1820 as a result of a series of Parliamentary Enclosure Acts which led to the laying out of rectangular hedged fields and straight roads. What did the area look like at the time of the battle, when the contemporary accounts talk about this being 'champion' land?[51] In 1645, apart from the small area of hedged paddocks around the villages, such as Naseby and Sibbertoft, only the parish of Sulby on the west, a part of the land of the former hamlet of Nobold in Clipston on the east, and a small area of Sibbertoft fields had been enclosed with hedged fields or 'closes'.[52] There were a few other old enclosures in Clipston field and further north the whole of the townships of Little Oxendon and Thorpe Lubenham had been enclosed, but all the rest was open field. Even today a few fields around the battlefield remain in ridge and furrow, the earthwork remains of the strip cultivation which was still being practised in all these open field parishes in 1645. Each ridge generally represents a single ownership, the land of each farmer comprising a number of such strips scattered throughout the field system. Groups of parallel strips were known as 'furlongs' and these in turn were grouped into 'great fields'. Only rarely were these great fields enclosed by a hedgerow even by the mid 17th century. However, where hedgerows did exist they will have been well managed, stock proof barriers which will have provided effective cover and a significant barrier to the movement of men and horses, particularly if lined by dragoons or musketeers.

The reconstruction of the mid 17th century landscape between Naseby and the Welland has proved a difficult task and the picture presented here cannot be considered definitive. In some parishes definition of the extent of the old enclosed land proved very problematic, particularly in Sibbertoft, yet in others like Naseby it has been very easy because of the late date of enclosure. Of all the man made elements of the landscape, the road pattern would appear to have remained the most stable between 1645 and the first Ordnance Survey maps in the early 19th century, particularly in Sibbertoft where there was hardly any change in the road pattern as a result of enclosure, while even in Naseby the roads did not generally alter very much.[53]

In Naseby and Sibbertoft, as in the majority of Northamptonshire parishes during the 17th century, there were three great fields in which crops were annually rotated with one field each year being left as fallow.[54] It was a remarkably open landscape in which, according to Mastin who was writing in 1792, there was 'not a hedge, or a tree for more than a mile together, a few scattered thorns only and patches of gorse or furze'.[55] In many parishes, since the population decline of the late medieval period, limited areas within the open fields had been allowed to revert to heathland and there were also small areas of poorly drained land in the valley bottoms, but in general this was a relatively well managed and heavily exploited agricultural landscape in 1645. Naseby itself was the last parish in this part of the county to be enclosed, in 1828, and so it is to that place that we must look for the best evidence for the character of the open field landscape. One cannot accept the romantic vision of Naseby before enclosure painted by James in 1860, who imagined it as 'a wild, half-cultivated field, without any well defined road, and which few ventured to cross after nightfall'.[56] It is necessary to go back to accounts which predate enclosure to get a good idea of its true character in 1645. William Pitt, the surveyor of the state of agriculture in England in the early 19th century, described Naseby following a visit in 1806, just fourteen years before enclosure:

> 'The open field is extensive, and in as backward a state as it could be in Charles the First's time, when the fatal battle was fought. The lower parts a moist rough pasture, with furze, rushes and fern abounding; the rest of the field a strong brown deep loam, in the usual bean and wheat culture. Pasture enclosures near the village, and a good many cows kept. The parish is as much in a state of nature as any thing I have seen in the county. The avenues across the field are zig-zag, as chance has directed, with the hollows and sloughs unfilled, except with mire.'[57]

The way in which the open fields of Naseby were run can be seen from the description made by a former resident of the parish in the early 19th century. Naseby Field was:

> 'divided into four parts - one for wheat, one for barley and beans, the fallow field, and the sward for the cattle. All round the outskirts of the field were the pastures, where the sheep and cows were sent in herds to graze, and an enclosure called "The Wolleys" was kept for the purpose of bringing up calves and yearlings. There were two herdsmen for the cows who went round every morning during the summer and took them to pasture, bringing them home to the different farmhouses in the village in the evening to be milked and put up for the night....The 1st of May was the day on which the pasturing commenced..... Much the same arrangements were carried out with respect to the sheep..... There were two shepherds to manage the flocks, and after their day's work was done they "folded" them on the fallow ground for the night to manure it. These folds were removed to different positions at intervals over the whole of the fallow ground, and the next year it was sowed wheat......Round the village of Naseby there were little homesteads where the cattle which were ill were put to graze...The part of the field which was sowed wheat was divided into furlongs, most of the farmers having a land in each... On the end of each land, on the knoll where the horses were "flit", were the land marks in the shape of letters of the alphabet cut or painted on small posts...The same arrangements prevailed in the barley, bean and fallow fields.'[58]

The only significant change since 1645 appears to have been the laying down to pasture of the land at the extremities of the parish, which took place in 1733, part of a process during the 17th and 18th centuries in which increasing amounts of land were being put down to permanent pasture within the open fields of Northamptonshire.[59] Mapping the distribution of these leys, unenclosed furlongs turned over to permanent grass, is not an easy task and

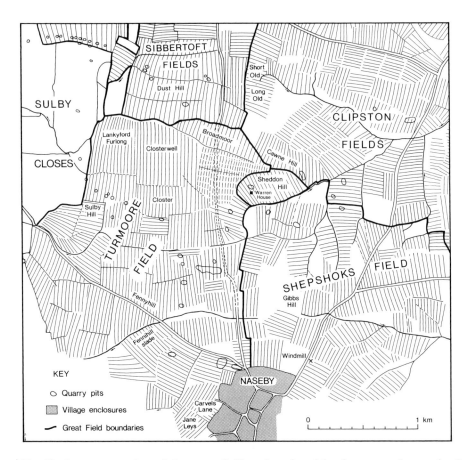

Fig. 49. A reconstruction of the open field and enclosed landscape to the north of Naseby as it was at the time of the battle.

yet the distribution of ley grass may have had a limited influence upon deployments during the battle, perhaps for example in the choice of sites for the baggage trains as it will surely have been much easier to move hundreds of waggons on permanent grass than on ploughland. In Naseby a good deal of land had already been converted to grass when the map of the parish was surveyed in 1630, most of it lying around the village itself.[60] Various other key topographical features represented on Streeter's engraving of the battle can be located from the 1630 map and later documents. Leane Leys Hill, the location of the Parliamentarian baggage train, can for example be identified as the hill immediately north west of the 19th century 'Jane Leys'.[61] Fenny Hill, Rutpit and the windmill, also all shown by Streeter, can similarly be located using the 1630 map.[62]

The great field on the north west side of Naseby was called Turmore Field in 1630 and comprised an open, arable area of about 1000 acres. It was encompassed by a single hedge running along the parish boundary on the west side, where this abutted the anciently enclosed pasture fields of Sulby, which is often described as Sulby Hedges. Lantford hedge, referred to on Streeter's engraving of the battle, was probably just that part of Sulby Hedges where it lay adjacent to Lankyford furlong.[63] Running across Turmore field were at least two roads, one leading north west to Welford, the other north to Sibbertoft. The latter, though laid out in its present form during the enclosure of the parish, runs close to the same line as in the 17th century.[64] Within the open fields of Naseby, Sibbertoft and Clipston there were small areas of heathland, depicted on Streeter's engraving and mentioned in the accounts of the battle. In 1891, despite the effects of agricultural improvement, there were 'furze bushes, whose descendants still give a golden livery to the slope over which Langdale's troopers were driven...' but today all trace of them has now gone.[65] In 1712 Morton wrote of the Northamptonshire heaths, 'These also are the Places for Warrens; as consisting of such a lax and dry Earth as Rabbets delight to burrow, and affording an Herbage peculiarly fit for them... and accordingly... we have Warrens well stored.'[66] A warren was a very specific area of land set aside for the breeding of rabbits, not simply a piece of open ground where rabbits happened to burrow. Naseby warren lay on the east side of the Naseby to Sibbertoft road, butting on to Turmore field and to Clipston parish. Warrens were often enclosed by a wall to stop the rabbits from straying and in the case of Naseby there was a warrener's lodge, the 'Warrn House' depicted amongst a clump of trees on Sheddon Hill on the 1630 map of Naseby. Mastin states that 'Upon a dry hill north of the village, called lodge hill, was formerly a rabbit warren, upon which was a house...'[67] It is still enclosed today by a hedge on the line of the warren boundary, which can be reconstructed from the great field boundaries on the 1630 and later maps. The majority of furze appears from Streeter to have lain in the area of Long Old and Cawne Hill in Clipston and on what may have been common land at the south east corner of Sibbertoft field. It may have extended south into Broadmoor for Symonds describes marching 'through a bottome full of furze bushes' during the Royalist advance, while Bridges refers to the problems caused to the Royalists by the bushes in both Clipston and Naseby fields, but if so it is surprising that Streeter does not show any such furze in Naseby.[68] Unfortunately the surviving documentary evidence does not enable the reconstruction of the full extent of heathland in the open fields in 1645.

Careful analysis of Streeter's engraving shows that the open land depicted is not just in Naseby but also in Sibbertoft and a small area of Clipston. On the right hand side of the engraving the land is not constrained by a hedge but rather by the slope of a hill. This is Dust Hill, encompassing the whole of the southern extremity of Sibbertoft and extending into Clipston, where its eastern end was known as Cawne Hill in 1633. Broadmoor was, as it is now, the valley between Sheddon and Dust Hill through which the parish boundary runs, but then there was not even a hedgerow dividing Naseby from Sibbertoft because the boundaries of unenclosed parishes were not normally hedged.[69] Northward from the shallow valley of Broadmoor one climbs a short distance

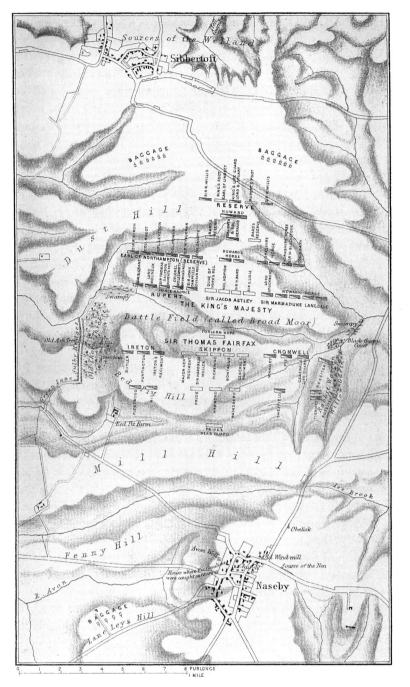

Fig.50. The importance of understanding the landscape in order to better understand
the events of the battle has long been recognised. Although one must disagree with his
exact placing of the armies, Markham's plan of 1870 shows very well the physical
form of the landscape between Naseby and the northern edge of the Sibbertoft plateau.

to the top of Dust Hill on to a small clayland plateau that stretches for more than a mile to just beyond Sibbertoft village. Strangely it was claimed by some in the 17th and 18th centuries that this area around Naseby, with its extensive views, was the highest ground in England. To the north and north east of Sibbertoft the land falls dramatically into the Welland valley and there are a number of narrow valleys, known as coombs, which cut deeply back into the plateau with slopes which plunge in places as much as 50 foot down almost vertical scarps. The unique morphology of this tiny corner of Northamptonshire was to have a minor but significant impact on the events of the battle. The character of the landscape here can be best appreciated from the Sibbertoft to Clipston road. As one travels east from Sibbertoft just beyond Lowe Farm the ground begins to fall away as the road passes through the old enclosed land of the deserted hamlet of Nobold, where hedged fields lay on either side of the road in 1645. Clipston has one of the last remaining extensive areas of open field landscape, fossilised as ridge and furrow earthworks within the later hedged fields. Sadly, however, even here the majority of the land has been ploughed in recent times and the ancient field pattern is in danger of being lost completely, threatening to remove our last major link with the landscape in which the battle was fought. As you leave the Sibbertoft to Clipston road, turning north towards Marston Trussell, on either side are fields of pasture covered with ridge and furrow. It is across this land that the Royalist army marched in battle formation on the morning of the 14th June, and it was back across these open fields that many of the troopers returned, fleeing in total defeat a few hours later. From the hill top a wide view opens out across the Welland valley and then a little further on one passes through an area of ridge and furrow with no hedgerows on either side of the road. Once through the gate the ground suddenly falls steeply away as one drops down into the valley, the road running on towards Marston Trussell and the infant river Welland. In this journey from Lodge Hill to Marston Trussell one can broadly follow in the footsteps of Royalist troops as they first retreated and then, at the end of the battle, as they fled with Cromwell's cavalry in hot pursuit.

NOTES

1. Ross, 1888, is the most comprehensive analysis but there is various information now available of which he was not aware. A discussion is also in Warburton, 1849, vol.3, p.103-105. Young, 1985.

2. Hutton, 1987, p.17. Ashley, 1992, p.154-6, gives a summary of 19th and 20th century estimates of the strength of both armies.

3. Major Wilde's company, PRO SP28/31, f.4. Col.Pye's troop, PRO SP28/31, f.6. If the evidence is restricted for most companies to the many records for the amounts of pay issued to each company then it may still be possible to provide relatively accurate estimates of numbers. It is reasonable, given the nature of the remodelling process, to assume that every New Model regiment in June 1645 had a full complement of officers. It may therefore be possible to

estimate the numbers of soldiers having first taken account of the proportion of the money to be allocated for officers. Comparison may be possible between the late May and 16th June musters. For example there is a warrant of 1st July to pay to Capt Hopkins in Ireton's regiment £66/6/0d as 9 days' pay for men and officers for his men mustered 24th May 1645 commencing 7th June last, and £59/2/0d as 9 days' pay according to the muster of the 16th June last commencing 16th June, PRO SP28/31, f.5.

4. Marston Trussell account, PRO SP28/173 unfol.. The exact number has been calculated from the costs listed as two entries do not give the number of men only the cost, but that does appear to be standard for each man and horse.

5. *Kingdomes Weekly Intelligencer*, 3rd-10th June.

6. Baillie, 1775, vol.2, p.116-7. Gentles, 1992, p.36 n.63.

7. *Mercurius Civicus*, 12th-18th June. *The Kingdomes Weekly Intelligencer*, 10th-17th June. Tibbutt, 1963, p.310 & 319. *The Exchange Intelligencer*, 4th-11th June, claims 17000 Parliamentarian troops, but this can be corrected by the fact that this includes the 3000 cavalry and 1000 horse which Cromwell was assembling in the Eastern Association but which never reached the army.

8. Belasyse.

9. *Scottish Dove*, 6th-13th June.

10. Rushworth, 15th May. Tibbutt, 1963, p.323. Gresley claims Vermuyden had about 3000 horse and dragoons. Dore, 1984, p.496-7.

11. Hackleton account, PRO SP28/172 unfol..

12. Young, 1985, p.151.

13. Firth & Davies, 1940, p.163. Tibbutt, 1963, p.320.

14. 'Recd.16 days pay as Collonnell to Nasbe at 39s'. Entry in Gurdon Papers at Repton Hall, quoted by Kingston, 1897, p.201. Gurdon must surely be the Colonel Gorden reported in *The Exchange Intelligencer*, 18th-24th June. Named as Gourdon by Carlyle, 1858, vol.2, p.383.

15. Sprigge, 1647, p.35.

16. *Scottish Dove*, 6th-13th June.

17. Asquith, 1981, p.9.

18. Collingtree account, PRO SP28/171, f.401.

19. Pickering's regiment at Milverton. The date given by the original source and quoted by Tennant seems unlikely and probably relates to 21st June when the army headquarters were in the adjacent village. Montague's were at Leamington on the 21st June. Tennant, 1992, p.264.

20. *CSPD*, p.592.

21. *CSPD*, p.602.

22. Harley was the colonel under whom Lieutenant Colonel Pride commanded the regiment. Firth & Davies, 1940, vol.1, p.359. Barlitts is the name in *Accompt of the Maior and Mr Rushworth of Northampton*, PRO SP28/173 unfol.. A Colonel Bartlet had been at Newport Pagnell in 1643, *Camden Miscellany*, xii, 69-119, but he was no longer there in 1645, Tibbutt, 1963, p.709, and so this reference is unlikely to refer to the Newport troops. Temple, 1986, n.71.

23. Pay for that part of Col Ingoldsby's regiment which marched lately in Col Barcleyes regiment according to a muster of 16th June, warrant of July 1645, PRO SP28/31, f.21 & 25.

24. Warrant to pay Major Leonard Watson, Scoutmaster, £98 for 14 days pay for himself and for 20 men and horses, 19th July 1645. PRO SP28/31, f.37.

25. Foard, 1994.

26. For example in Pickering's regiment in April 1644. Foard, 1994, appendix 2.

27. Firth & Davies, 1940, vol.1, p.16.

28. Tibbutt, 1963, p.281.

29. *The Kingdomes Weekly Intelligencer*, 10th-17th June. *Mercurius Civicus*, 12th-18th June. *The Weekly Account*, 11th-18th June.

30. It should however be noted that Belasyse comments that the battle was very ill contested by the Royalists and so it is just possible that he did inflate the Royalist numbers to assist in this argument.

31. Clarendon, vol.2, p.505.

32. Slingsby, p.143.

33. Charles to Nicholas, 4 June 1645, Bray, 1827, vol.5, p.129. This letter may well have been the source of the numbers of horse quoted by de Gomme, Walker and Clarendon. De Gomme's numbers for Marston Moor have also been shown to be in error. Newman, 1981.

34. Symonds, p.166. Slingsby, p.143, claimed just 3000.

35. *A Perfect Relation. A More Exact Relation.*

36. Tibbutt, 1963, p.570. Ross estimated 1400 but was not aware of Norwich's letter.

37. Young, 1985, p.234.

38. *A Perfect Relation.*

39. Charles to Nicholas, 4th June 1645, Bray, vol.5, p.129. Ashley makes an un-referenced statement that Charles collected additional troopers from various garrisons, notably during the stay at Daventry, but I have found no evidence to support this.

40. Charles to Nicholas, 4th June 1645, Bray, vol.5, p.129. Walker, 1705.

41. *A More Exact and Perfect Relation.*

42. Symonds, quoted by Young, 1985, p.22. Roberts, 1989, p.16.

43. *Scottish Dove*, 13th-20th June. Sprigge, 1647, p.33.

44. *A More Particular and Exact Relation.*

45. Belasyse. Digby to Legge, undated, Warburton, 1849, vol.3, p.127.

46. Carlton, 1994, p.98.

47. The 'colour' or company flag carried by the dragoon cornet was called a 'guidon'.

48. *A More Exact Relation.*

49. Sprigge, 1647, p.41.

50. Woolrych, 1961, p.121. Warburton, vol.3, p.102 n.3 & p.106.

51. *A True Relation of a Victory. A More Particular and exact Relation.*

52. A 'close' was a small field which was usually enclosed by a hedge. Denton, 1988, and Young, 1985, have apparently misinterpreted the solid bounded plots on the 1630 map of Naseby as closes. They in fact represent unenclosed tenurial units within the open field.

53. In reconstructing the landscape of 1645 I have drawn upon the work of David Hall and of Tony Brown. Hall has given me access to his unpublished map of the furlongs cf Sibbertoft and Brown has provided access to information from his documentary work on Sulby, Sibbertoft and Clipston, though the majority of the reconstruction of old enclosures and road patterns has resulted from my own documentary research. The main sources were: Map of Naseby, 1630, Suffolk Record Office HB56. All the following in NRO: Field Name maps, 1932, for Naseby, Sibbertoft, Marston Trussell, Sulby and East Farndon; Sibbertoft Enclosure Award, 1650, YO934; reconstruction maps of Sibbertoft in 1650 and of East Farndon in 1781, by P.Taylor; Map 556; FS36/1-18; Maunsel(Sulby)689; Map 1646; Map 4798; YZ4346; Clayton 164; L(C)1599; Map 701; Map 562; Naseby Inclosure Map and Award; Clipston Inclosure Award; Marston Trussell Inclosure Map. Hall, 1977. Hall & Harding, 1979. The Eayre map has been used, where other information is absent, to define the likely road pattern for the area between Naseby and the Welland. Only Sibbertoft (1650) and possibly Kelmarsh were enclosed between 1645 and the Eayre survey. The other dates of enclosure are: Great Oxendon 1768; Clipston 1777; Little Bowden 1779; E.Farndon 1780; Marston Trussell 1825. The enclosures before 1645 were Thorpe Lubenham before the mid 16th-century; Haselbech 1599 and Lt.Oxendon probably 16th-century.

54. The system of rotation by great field was still in use at Naseby in the 19th century. NRO YZ7403. For a detailed description of the open field systems of Northamptonshire in the 17th century and before see D.Hall, 1995, *The Open Fields of Northamptonshire*, Northamptonshire Record Society, vol.37.

55. Mastin, 1792, p.48.

56. James, 1864, p.28.

57. Pitt, 1809, p.304.

58. Page, 1889.

59. Mastin, 1792. This can be seen for example from a comparison of terriers of Clipston in 1633 and 1686, NRO Clipston Glebe Terriers.

60. This is identified on the 1630 map of the parish with individual leys named while the large area of consolidated demesne, also around the village, is described as 'part in grass'.

61. The exact location & extent of Leane Leys is defined by Fitzgerald's sketch of 1842, Terhune & Terhune, 1980, vol.1, p.343. Fitzgerald took detailed advice from villagers who knew the parish before enclosure and his information on this is therefore likely to be more accurate than Hall, 1977, because the historical evidence now surviving for such matters for Naseby is not wholly adequate.

62. Stainwright, 1991, p.88-90, incorrectly refers to Charles I witnessing the defeat of his army from the windmill on Mill Hill, Naseby. He also wrongly identifies the windmill depicted by Streeter as the one on Mill Hill.

63. The name on the 1630 map is 'Lankyford', rather than 'Lanford' as quoted by Hall. The identification with Streeter's 'Lantford' is however not in doubt.

64. The existence of this road is crucial to the interpretation of Streeter's engraving and so must be discussed in detail. The Naseby Inclosure Award records the laying out of the road 'to the end of a road in the parish of Sibbertoft', showing it crossed the parish boundary in the same position as it had before enclosure. Typically with such early 'enclosures by agreement' as that at Sibbertoft (1650) the roads remained exactly on their previous course and so, in the absence of a pre-enclosure map or other evidence, the alignment of the enclosure road has been taken as almost certainly the exact pre enclosure line. The map of Northamptonshire by Thomas Eayre, published in 1775, some 40 years before Naseby's enclosure, shows the Naseby-Sibbertoft road crossing Broadmoor almost as it does today. Careful examination of the 1630 map of Naseby confirms the existence of the road in the mid 17th century although unfortunately the northern section of the road has faded and disappeared from the map, as have various other roads and other features. This explains the apparent omission of some roads but others may be missing due to the very selective presentation of information on the map. The Sibbertoft road is absent from Hall's analysis and from the transcription of the 1630 map by Greenhall but its southern half is clearly visible on the original. Hall, 1977, and Greenhall, 1974, p.23. Both this and the Clipston road, also not visible on the 1630 map as Woolrych pointed out, are depicted on the pre-enclosure Eayre map. The 1630 map was first used in an analysis of the battle by Fitzgerald (see below). Woolrych, 1961, used the map again but incompletely and incorrectly, as with his identification of roads and the plotting of the open field boundaries, closes etc. For example, he calls the Sibbertoft road 'only the most vestigial of tracks'.

65. Stead, 1891, p.73.

66. Morton, 1712, p.9-10.

67. Mastin, 1792, p.20. The extent of the warren can be defined from the great field boundaries on the 1630 and the Naseby Inclosure Map, NRO. None of the 17th century sources specifically refer to a wall or pale so it is possible that none existed. The hill was still known as Lodge Hill earlier this century, but in 1630 it was called Sheddon Hill. Hamson, 1906.

68. Symonds, p.193. The 'burts and water' described in Slingsby's diary may perhaps be an incorrect transcription of furze and water. Bridges notes.

69. Carlyle, 1858, p.174, incorrectly records Broadmoor as the wide table of upland north of Mill Hill. Occasionally hedges did exist on parish boundaries, as with a short section of the Clipston / Marston boundary where the 'meare hedge' is specifically named because it was so exceptional. Hall & Harding, 1979.

CHAPTER 8

THE BATTLE

'After a doubtfull battaile a most glorious victory,
greater than that of Yorke.'
Rushworth

The Royalist army was drawn out of its quarters early on the morning of the 14th June and Symonds, who was with the King's lifeguard, was already on the move at two o'clock. By six the Royalists began to march out of Market Harborough to a rendezvous of the whole army on the hills immediately south of the town.[1] Probably the last of all to leave were the waggons and carriages of the train because, as Vernon says, when the enemy is to your fore the waggons must march at the rear, guarded by a squadron of horse.[2] The cavalry, most of which had been dispersed in the villages surrounding Harborough, will have approached the rendezvous along various roads, from Lubenham, Theddingworth and probably from Great Oxendon, Little Bowden, East Farndon and other places. At about seven o'clock, apparently on the high ground at East Farndon, the troops halted for prayers and it was here that Astley began to draw up the army in battalia. In the early 19th century John Nichols, Leicestershire's county historian, recorded the local tradition that it was on the hill south of the town, between Farndon and Oxendon, that the Royalist army formed up that morning.[3] Should we believe this local story? According to Slingsby, who was with the Northern horse, they 'had not march'd a Mile out of Town, having taken a Hill whereon a Chappell stood...'[4] This chapel might be the small, isolated church of Great Oxendon, a very distinct landmark which lies to the north of the village, but it is more likely to have been East Farndon church, which stands near the top of the hill while the village itself is out of sight on the slopes to the north.[5]

Although the open fields of East Farndon, Great Oxendon and Clipston were not enclosed until the 18th century, there were several areas of hedged fields, both large and small, which Rupert will have seen when deciding the best place to embattle the army. Half way between Farndon and Oxendon lay the deserted medieval village of Little Oxendon, whose fields had been enclosed in the 16th century.[6] There was therefore a swathe of hedged fields right across the centre of the Farndon/Oxendon ridge in 1645. The battle line is not likely to have been drawn through these hedgerows if open land was available, for they would severely restrict the movement of the troops, especially the cavalry, which were Rupert's greatest strength. Further east lay the crofts and closes in and around the village of Great Oxendon, which occupied most of the hill top, and so there could be no deployment this far along the ridge. In contrast, at Farndon there was only a tight grouping of closes around the village on the northern slope of the hill. Further southward

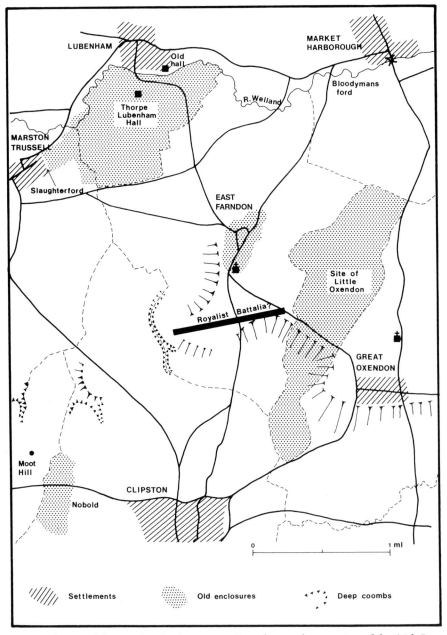

Fig.51. The possible Royalist deployment at Farndon on the morning of the 14th June 1645 set within a contemporary landscape (only selected slopes are shown).

on either side of the road leading to Naseby, the land was completely open and so here on the hill top an army could be deployed, facing south towards the Parliamentarian quarters. The Royalists would have had the advantage of the ground, for the land falls away southward as a modest but still significant slope. To the north west there is the steep slope where the land drops down into the Welland valley, but most important on that side is the small but dramatic coomb, in places perhaps thirty or forty feet deep and with near vertical sides. Infantry, let alone cavalry, would find it impossible to negotiate the steep slopes and so there was no chance here of Fairfax making an outflanking move. On the east lay the pasture closes of Little Oxendon, where Rupert could deploy musketeers in the hedged enclosures to secure the army's left flank, just as Fairfax was to use the Sulby hedges to such great effect later in the day.[7] The ground was almost a mile wide from the coomb, which would have guarded the right flank, to Little Oxendon closes, protecting the left flank, almost the same distance that would be occupied by the Royalist battalia later that day at Naseby. Farndon Hill must surely be the 'rising Ground of very great Advantage' upon which the Royalist army stood, waiting for the despised 'New Noddle' to appear.[8]

According to Slingsby, as soon as they had arrived on the hill 'we could discerne ye enemy's horse upon another Hill about a Mile or two before us, wch was ye same on wch Naseby stood.' Was he perhaps late in reaching the rendezvous, for his statement is in conflict with Walker who claims the army waited in battalia but that there was no sign of the New Model?[9] Walker says that by eight o'clock they began to fear their intelligence was wrong and so Francis Ruce, the scoutmaster, was sent out to establish the Parliamentarian position. In a short time he 'returned with a Lye in his Mouth, that he had been two or three Miles forward, and could neither discover or hear of the Rebels.' Was it perhaps that the Parliamentarian forces had not yet deployed at Naseby? An advance of two to three miles would have placed Ruce in the far south of Clipston field, below the scarp where New House Farm now stands and, unless they had already deployed on the ridge, here he would indeed have been unaware of the Parliamentarian army. However, in such a situation any competent scout would surely have ascended the scarp to take a view from the commanding ground because, as Cruso makes very clear, the scouts played a vital role in the army: 'They must see that with their own eyes which they inform, the least errour of theirs misleading the whole bodie'. To compound the failure, it would appear that another report then came in that the New Model had retreated. We have already seen how the inadequacies of their scouts had twice placed the Royalist army at a disadvantage, when they had failed to discover Fairfax's approach to Northampton on the 11th and then on the 13th when they had failed to realise that the Parliamentarian army had followed their march so closely. Cruso goes on to say that the scouts should 'be led by an able officer, it being a task so difficult, that many have lost that reputation by it which they had been long in gaining of.' There can be little doubt that Ruce lost that day any reputation he may have had left!

The next question is one that was later posed by Digby. Though he was responsible for spreading many lies about Rupert's actions during the campaign, we cannot simply dismiss his comment that 'wee should rather have tryed to bring them to our Post then to have assaulted them instantly in theirs....', unless of course the disinformation runs even deeper than has been previously considered.[10] Given we know that some crucial facts about the days and hours leading up to the battle were intentionally distorted by Digby to place the blame on Rupert and others, we must ask whether Walker's narrative should be trusted where it places doubt on Rupert's actions. Did his 'official' account create the idea of uncertainty where none really existed, placing blame on Ruce simply to support the case against Rupert? Did Walker, as Digby was to do so blatantly, twist the facts to make it appear that Rupert made a number of disastrous mistakes and miscalculations when in fact he was following a well thought out strategy? In the following description the account by Walker has been taken at its face value, but the question must still remain in mind.

It is unlikely that we will ever know for certain why Rupert quit the ground on which he stood. It may have been, as Walker says, simply his impatience, alternatively it might be seen as a sensible response to the report of the New Model's retreat, but it could equally have been that Rupert wanted to gain the initiative. Whatever his reasons, the Prince drew out a party of cavalry supported with musketeers and marched forward to discover and engage the enemy, while the rest of the army remained in battalia on Farndon hill. By the time he had advanced about a mile Rupert saw the vanguard of the New Model Army. The road from Farndon to Naseby dips into low ground whereby the Naseby hills are obscured, but as soon as one passes through Clipston village, about a mile and a half from where the Royalist army was probably deployed, the Naseby ridge comes into view. Today, unfortunately, the visitor will find the ridge is dominated not by an army but by a radio mast, New House Farm and the traffic of the new A14.[11]

Fairfax had marched out of his headquarters at Guilsborough by first light that morning, knowing from his scouts exactly where the Royalist army had quartered the previous night.[12] His main concern was that the King might have continued his march north, for he had been informed that in the night the Royalists had drawn some carriages through Harborough towards Leicester. This was after all their most sensible course of action and exactly what Rupert and his senior officers had wanted to do. Fairfax's first intention was to deploy his horse as rapidly as possible, to harry the rear of the Royalist army and so to retard their march.[13] It will have taken about an hour for the infantry to cover the two and a half miles from Guilsborough to the rendezvous in Naseby field.[14] All the roads in the parish lead through the village and so it seems likely that almost the whole army will have passed through Naseby that morning. As they marched along the highway and through the village the cavalry will have been deployed four wide to take up the full width of the road. A Naseby tradition, recorded in 1865 from an old labourer who supposedly had heard it from his grandfather and he from the person to whom the incident had happened, recounts how:

'a child of about four years old, was standing at his cottage door on the morning of the battle, when Cromwell's troopers came riding through the village. The cottage was on the south side of the churchyard in a narrow part of the village, a high wall at that time separating the churchyard from the road. The little boy seeing the horses ran across the road in front of them, as children will, and the foremost trooper, fearing that the child would certainly be killed, stooped from his saddle, caught the boy by the nape of his neck, and flung him over the wall on his right. The child fell happily on soft ground in the churchyard, with no injury done to him, and he lived to tell the story....[115]

Whether the tradition is genuine or not, one can well imagine that, as the great bodies of cavalry passed through Naseby, the villagers came out of the houses to stand and stare. Streeter depicts them later that morning close by the windmill on the Clipston road viewing the battle from a safe distance. From this position the villagers would certainly have been able to see the fight raging on the hill top to the north west, especially as there were none of the trees which today obscure part of the view. Did they really stand there to view the dramatic events - the greatest thing not just in their lives but in the whole history of the village of Naseby - or was it just artistic licence on Streeter's part? We shall never know, though local tradition does tell of women coming out of the village to watch the battle and suffering as a result.[16]

Fig. 52. Local villagers, depicted by Streeter, viewing the battle from close by the Naseby windmill, where the obelisk monument now stands.

The road towards Harborough, where the Royalists were known to be, still runs north east from the village on almost the same course as in 1645. The Parliamentarian rendezvous was probably along this road, somewhere near where the obelisk monument now stands, because another tradition, recorded in the mid 19th century, speaks of 'a place in a field, a good deal to the north east of Naseby, a little out of the Clipstone road, where it is said the Parliament Army heard prayers and a sermon on the morning of the 14th.'[17] This rendezvous may have been held on the ley grass which apparently covered a large area north of Naseby village extending as far as the windmill. As the army stood there around seven or eight that morning any doubts as to the enemy's intentions were soon dispelled, because great bodies of Royalist horse were seen about three miles away on the hills to the south of Harborough. The King was obviously drawing up his army in battalia. In response Fairfax ordered his troops to be deployed so that they were ready to receive a Royalist attack or, if the Royalists maintained their ground, then to advance in battle formation towards them.[18]

The New Model was probably drawn up in battalia along the hill top on both sides of the road, though on the west the slope is not quite as steep or as long as on the east. As soon as Rupert had passed through Clipston village he would have seen the Parliamentarian army deployed at the top of the scarp, but as he advanced he found that the New Model was in a very commanding position, for he was 'hindred of any nearer approach, by reason ye place between us and ym, was full of burts [?furze] and Water...'[19] It would have been folly to attack across this ground and up the steep slope. On the west side of the road many small streams issue from the bottom of the scarp and the land is dissected by numerous small valleys cutting back into the plateau. The ground below the spring line is clayland and can be very wet even today and, despite the drains and the deep ditching of the streams, water still runs over the land in places during the winter. In the 17th century this must have been very boggy, especially after the heavy rain which had fallen during several previous days. In contrast, the higher land is a very well drained ironstone soil but on the steep slopes, even as late as the 1950s, there were several fragments of furze still surviving. One of the last areas to be cleared and 'improved' was the Lynch Banks, in what is now the second field to the west of the Clipston Road. Here, on the steep valley side, there was a dense growth of gorse with many rabbit burrows and with bluebells on the hedge banks. This was an idyllic place, a last contact with the landscape of 17th century Naseby. Sadly, in the 1960s the steepest slope was graded down and the whole area cleared and turned over to arable. Undoubtedly in 1645 a large part of these slopes must have been under furze with quite dense and impenetrable clumps of gorse bushes.[20]

Rupert, like any skilled commander, was fully prepared. He had with him several local people, presumably enlisted in Harborough the previous evening, who could guide him to a better place. According to Slingsby, it was not only

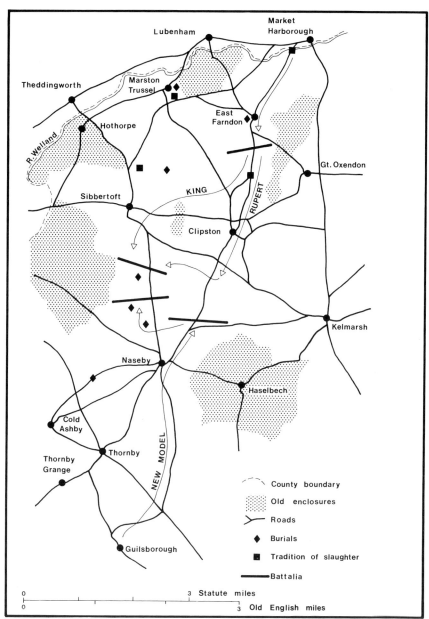

Fig.53. The pre-battle manoeuvres on the 14th June.

because of these unsuitable conditions that they wheeled about and marched to the west, Rupert also found the New Model horse were already 'marching up on ye side of ye Hill to ye place where after they imbattl'd their whole army'. Sprigge on the other hand claims that it was because Fairfax saw the Royalist army marching westwards, to gain the wind of the New Model, that he drew his army to the west. Burne has argued that Rupert probably made the first move and it certainly seems true that Rupert was taking the initiative throughout these early stages, as was his normal practice. However this must surely be the point at which, with the army already half drawn up, Cromwell had argued for a redeployment:

> 'Cromwell, who as though he had received direction from God himselfe, where to pitch the Battell; did advise, that the Batalia might stand upon such a ground, although it was being drawn up in another place, saying, "Let us I beseech you draw back to yonder hill, which will encourage the enemy to charge us, which they cannot doe in that place, without their absolute ruine." This he spake with so much cheerfull resolution and confidence, as though he had forseen the victory, and was therfore condiscended unto, and within an houre and halfe after, the effect fell out accordingly.'[21]

The scarp across the Clipston road would certainly have been a place where it would have been folly for the Royalist army to have attacked.

If it is uncertain who initiated the move, what is not in doubt is that such a flank march took place. Slingsby recorded that by 'our guides [we] were brought upon a fair peice of ground, partly corn and partly heath, under Naseby, about Half a mile distant from ye place.'[22] While the route across the open fields of Clipston and Sibbertoft will have been relatively easy for Rupert, the land between the Clipston and the Sibbertoft roads in Naseby is the most heavily dissected in the whole area. This is truly a 'place of little hills and vales', as one newspaper described the landscape.[23] It would have been very difficult for the New Model to have marched directly across this land, with its furze covered slopes and wet valley bottoms. Instead they must have marched westward along the ridge of high ground which extends through Gibbs Hill to Mill Hill. Several musket balls have been found on Gibbs Hill which may perhaps have been losses during the redeployment, because it seems unlikely, though not impossible, that this land saw any significant action later during the battle.[24] From Mill Hill the New Model could easily have marched north to the edge of Broadmoor, as indeed Slingsby implies they did. He says that as Rupert deployed his horse 'in sight of ye enemy', presumably on Dust Hill, the New Model were 'now come to ye top of ye Hill, and begin to draw down their Regiments upon ye side of ye hill: where they took their ground to imbattle their forces...'[25] In one of those minor local traditions which have the ring of truth, because they are so mundane and yet so well in tune with our knowledge of the place at that time, it is said that the Naseby cows, which would have been out grazing on this fallow field tended by the village cowherds, had to be driven out of the way of the contending armies as they drew up in battalia.[26] It was probably only now, seeing Fairfax was intent on fighting, that Rupert sent back instructions for the whole army to march up rapidly to join him and it has been claimed that this haste was caused by the belief that the New Model was retreating.[27] Was this perhaps the result of Fairfax marching south westwards onto Mill Hill when he followed Rupert's flank march or was it a result of his next decision, to pull back a hundred paces behind the cover of the hill to arrange his army in battalia?

If the decision on Friday night to turn and fight had been against Rupert's better judgement, there can be no doubt the events that morning which brought the two armies together on Naseby field were Rupert's responsibility. The decision to bring the Royalist army forward from the strong position at Farndon, where they were already deployed, to a poorer situation at Naseby has been presented as a disastrous mistake in several Royalist accounts and by most later authors who have written on the battle. One wonders whether Rupert, having been continually overruled by the King on the advice of courtiers like Digby and Ashburnham, was in one of his black moods. Frustrated at having to do something which he judged to be wholly unwise did he perhaps make the engagement happen whatever the cost? Almost certainly not, for it was in Rupert's character to carry out the King's instructions to the best of his ability, even if he disapproved of them.[28] It seems more likely, judging by Rupert's actions in previous engagements, that he was following a pre-determined strategy which demanded that he took the initiative. His friend Will Legge, defending Rupert from Digby's lies following Naseby, makes it quite clear the way in which Rupert worked: 'I am well acquainted with the Prince's ways that I am confident all his general officers and commanders knew beforehand how or in what manner he intended to fight.'[29]

If, as most commentators argue, the Royalist army was outnumbered in horse, why did Rupert not follow the most basic of principles laid down in the military manuals of the time: 'If your enemy surmount you in Horse, then endeavour to gain the Inclosures; if you exceed him therein, then make Choice of the Champane....'?[30] In Farndon field he could have deployed musketeers in the closes on his left wing, but instead he advanced to a position in Naseby field where the enemy could make exactly that sort of deployment against him. Walker also argued that, as a result of the disadvantage of the ground and the fact that their army marched up in battalia, Fairfax could see their deployment and thus had time to deploy his own troops to the best advantage.[31] Rupert, it would seem, had other priorities. In so many of his earlier engagements, such as Newark or Chalgrove, it was the speed and unexpectedness of his actions which had caught out his opponents allowing him to take advantage of their confusion. At Marston Moor, where he had been more cautious and had taken a defensive position behind the dyke, he had lost. Moreover, at Naseby there was no point in him taking a defensive stance because his cavalry, even though they probably did not outnumber those of the New Model, were still his greatest strength. If he was to have any chance of success he would have to use them to the greatest possible advantage and to do this he needed to take the initiative and carry the fight to the enemy.

The Royalist army at Farndon was already deployed in battalia. If they were to advance in haste there was no time to reorganise into line of march, nor would it have been sensible given the proximity of the enemy. So, over the next hour, the infantry and remaining horse marched forward 'in full

Campania' to join Rupert, the King marching at the head of the army. By the time they had marched about a mile and a half they could already see parties of the New Model horse on the high ground near Naseby.[32] Although this was essentially an open landscape, the Royalist advance was not easy. They must have marched to the north west of Clipston, to avoid the closes around the village, and then they had to negotiate the hedgerows of the old enclosed land of the deserted village of Nobold. They probably marched to the north of Nobold closes, but there was only limited room for manoeuvre because further north they were constrained by the deep coombs dropping steeply down to the Welland valley. If they had moved forward by brigade rather than in full battalia there would however have been sufficient room. The army must have destroyed a vast swathe of corn and other crops in the open fields of Farndon, Clipston and Sibbertoft as they advanced. Somewhere across that landscape, though not apparently in Sibbertoft, one of the great fields through which they marched was obviously laid down to beans that year, for many of the Royalists on the battlefield had put beanstalks in their hats as a field sign to tell friend from foe. It took about an hour for the troops to cover the two and a half miles from Farndon to Dust Hill, but at last the Parliamentarians saw the whole of the King's army as they 'marched in a very stately way in a whole Body towards us .... which was as much joy to us (who sought that above all)..'[133]

In order to understand the events which followed it is essential to establish how and where the two armies were deployed across the landscape as it was in 1645. Though there were variations in detail, most authors during the 19th and 20th centuries were in broad agreement over this deployment until Colonel H.C.B.Rogers published his account in 1968. He, by his own admission, was out of step with other historians, for he claimed that 'many Civil War historians make frontages much too short' and therefore he recalculated the width of the battalia at Naseby, placing the right wing as far east as the Clipston road and the left wing by Sulby Hedge. As a result, Rogers' interpretation has confused the understanding of the battle of Naseby ever since.[34] Local people have however always known exactly where the battlefield lay. The county historian, John Bridges, who visited Naseby in 1719, just within living memory of the events, was quite clear that the battle was fought in a 'Field of very large Extent' to the north west of Naseby, with the 'Field of Battle upon a plain, that plain on an Eminence'.[35] Sprigge provides even more specific evidence, saying the New Model was drawn up in 'a large fallow field on the Northwest side of Naseby, flanked on the left hand with a hedge...' and, repeating the comment from a newspaper, that 'the Field was a mile broad where the battail was fought, and from the outmost Flank of the right, to the left Wing, took up the whole ground.' This fallow field is clearly Turmore, one of the three great fields of Naseby, which lay to the north west of the village. An eye witness to the battle also reported that the troops drew up in battalia in 'Nasby fields, a place of little hills and vales, in a direct line equal to both parts, the ground some ploughed some Champion', which describes perfectly the landscape of the northern part of Turmore field.[36]

Streeter's engraving of the battle is the most important single source for the deployments.[37] It shows Butler's regiment of horse, which was on the far left of the New Model's battalia, just north of the corner of Sulby hedges. Though one must not take the exact positioning on Streeter's plan as though it was an accurately surveyed map, it does show that Ireton's cavalry must have been on Sulby Hill, from which the ground slopes to the south. It has been argued, not least by Carlyle, that the Parliamentarian army formed up on Mill Hill.[38] It is highly improbable that an army would have been formed up in battalia on Mill Hill and still have had its left wing against Sulby hedges, for a small but distinct valley intervenes. Moreover, Streeter's plan clearly shows the Parliamentarian army positioned to the north of Rutputt Hill, Fenny Hill and Mill Hill. The ground immediately east of Sulby Hill continues almost level as a ridge widening into a small, fairly level 'plateau' called Closter. This would accord very well with Bridges' 'plain on an Eminence'. Thereafter the ground narrows and rises gently to terminate as Sheddon or Lodge Hill, from which it falls away into the wet valley bottoms which divide Naseby and Clipston parishes. This conforms well with Sprigge's comment that 'we took the best advantage we could of the ground, possessing the ledge of a hill, running east to west...'. Lined along its whole length by New Model troops, the long scarp on the north side of the hill would have been a distinct and daunting feature facing the Royalists as they advanced onto Broadmoor. De Gomme clearly represents this scarp running eastward from Sulby hedges, with the Parliamentarian forlorn hope[39] on the northern slope, and he defines the ground between the two armies as 'the Descend of the Hill' with no other hills intervening between the forces. The hill we have described, running from Sulby Hedge to Lodge Hill does indeed encompass the whole width of Turmore Field from east to west as Sprigge describes and the distance, over 6300ft, is reasonably close to the estimate of one mile in the newspaper.

Another newspaper states that the army drew up in battalia near Naseby Warren.[40] This is confirmed by Sprigge who says that on the right wing the Parliamentarian horse, except for the left two divisions commanded by Whalley, 'advanced with great difficulty, also by reason of the unevenness of the ground, and a Coney-warren over which they were to march....'[41] A warren would have presented a problem both from the animal burrows and also perhaps from its boundary, for some warrens were enclosed by a wall. The extent of the rabbit warren has been identified and so this enables a remarkably accurate reconstruction of the deployment of the divisions of Cromwell's cavalry. Whalley's regiment must have been positioned just outside the warren to the west, while all the divisions to his right were within the warren.[42] There can be no doubt therefore that it was on the scarp overlooking Broadmoor that the New Model was drawn up in battalia. Fairfax

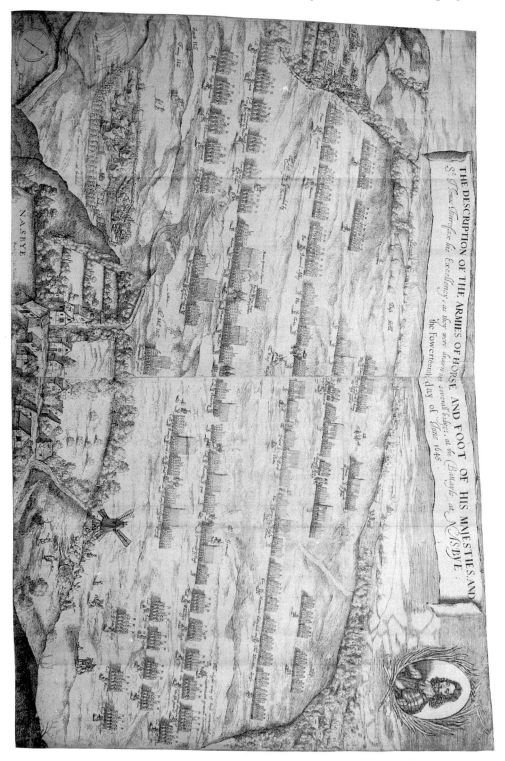

Fig. 54. An engraving of the battle by Streeter, published in 1647 in Sprigge's Anglia Rediviva. (Northamptonshire Libraries and Information Service)

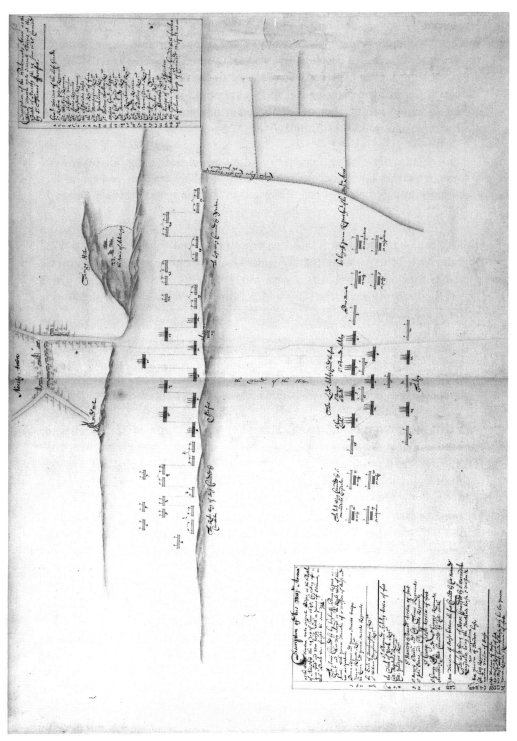

Fig.55. A plan of the battle by Bernard de Gomme. (By permission of The British Library, Add.16370)

had chosen a commanding position, protected from outflanking moves on the left by Sulby hedges and on the right by the furze and the small wet valleys in Clipston field. To gain the best advantage of his situation he had ordered the army to retreat 100 paces, about 480ft, from the top of the scarp.[43] In this way he could deploy his troops out of view of the enemy, for to the south of the scarp the hill top rises gently then levels out into the little plateau. The Royalists could see neither the deployment nor any confusion amongst the Parliamentarian ranks. As Slingsby says:

> 'they could easily observe in wt body we drew up our men, and ye utmost yt we were, wn as they lay wthout our sight, having ye Hill to cover ym, and appear'd no more to us yn wt they had drawn out in Battalio upon ye side of Nasby Hill.'[44]

It has been suggested that it was this withdrawal that caused Rupert to think that the New Model was retreating and so causing him to attack prematurely. Whether this withdrawal was a wise move or not can be questioned, for it seems likely that this was the issue which Lord Orrery discussed with Skippon some years after the battle:

> 'after my Lord Fairfax his army was drawn up in view of his Majesties, it having been judged that the ground a little behind them was better than that they stood upon, they removed thither [but Skippon] averred he was against it; but he obeyed the Orders for doing it only because he could not get them altered.'[45]

From the bottom of the gentle slope below the Parliamentarian lines the ground is almost flat across Broadmoor, rising again to the slightly lower Dust Hill. Streeter shows the Royalist army deployed with Dust Hill at their back and constrained on their right wing by the hedged enclosures of Sulby parish and on their left wing by furze. This would accord well with Bridges' statement that the Royalists formed up partly in Naseby and partly in Sibbertoft and that they had been 'much embarrassed by the bushes in Clipston and Naseby fields' in marching and countermarching. The road shown by Streeter running between the horse and foot on the Royalist left wing has caused much dispute in the past.[46] It has been claimed that this is the Clipston road because the Sibbertoft road was only created following the enclosure of Naseby in 1828. As we have demonstrated, there was in fact already a road crossing Turmore Field and running north through Sibbertoft field in 1645, and the position of the feature on Streeter's engraving would agree well with this road as it ran down off Dust Hill onto Broadmoor. Just as with the warren on the Parliamentarian right wing, this road would appear to enable accurate positioning of the horse of the Royalist left wing. However, as was noted earlier, Streeter's depiction of the battle should not be accepted without question. He has dramatically foreshortened the view to concentrate on the deployment of the armies, resulting in the appearance that the armies are far closer to Naseby village than they really were. This has resulted in the right wing of the Parliamentarian army appearing to extend eastward of the windmill and the Clipston road. Remove the foreshortening and the landscape features depicted by Streeter fall neatly into place. Even the hill on the Royalist left wing can be equated with Cawne Hill, just across the Clipston boundary. With regard to de Gomme's plan, one must also discount Rowley's attempt to overlay this directly on to a modern map. It was one of a series of plans compiled in almost identical fashion showing a number of contemporary battles, and drawn by an observer of the battle without the aid of a detailed survey of the parish. Indeed all of de Gomme's topographical information is derived directly from Streeter and so his plan cannot be taken as independent evidence as to positioning of the forces within the landscape.[47] Indeed, one account says Rupert first deployed in Sibbertoft field and another apparently reliable and detailed source claims that the Royalists took a hill and that the New Model took another hill half a mile to the south of them. This would indicate that the Royalists actually formed their battalia well back on Dust Hill, where they would have had the advantage of the slope. The deployment shown by Streeter may simply be a matter of artistic licence, for if the army had been shown on Dust Hill it would not have been clearly visible in the engraving. This is perhaps supported by Sprigge who says the Royalist army 'marched upon a plain ground towards us' and viewed from Closter and Sheddon Hill the whole Royalist battle formation advancing across Broadmoor would have been clearly seen by Fairfax. Symonds also says that they marched through, not from, a bottom full of furze bushes to approach the enemy.[48]

With certain specific exceptions, the plans by de Gomme and Streeter can however be taken as accurate representations of the arrangement of regiments relative to each other in each army. This is because both were apparently drawn up with access to reliable sources and with advice or information from senior commanders who participated in the battle. According to Warburton, de Gomme's plan was drawn up on Rupert's orders and was found in his papers.[49] The depiction by Streeter, or at least the copy of it by Sturt, was accurate according to Rushworth who says that he had to hand authentic plans of the deployments of both armies, the plan of:

> 'the King's Army being drawn up soon after by the Lord Ashley, who in an Engagement near Stow in the Wold was taken Prisoner; and whose Papers of Naseby Battel under his own hand I have by me, and that of the Parliament's Army given in approved by several of the Commanders in Chief therein concerned.'[50]

The deployments are also in reasonable accord with the newspaper accounts.[51] There is just one reservation. Sprigge specifically talks of Skippon and Fairfax putting 'the severall Brigades of Foot into order' and we have already seen that while at Northampton the New Model had been divided into brigades for

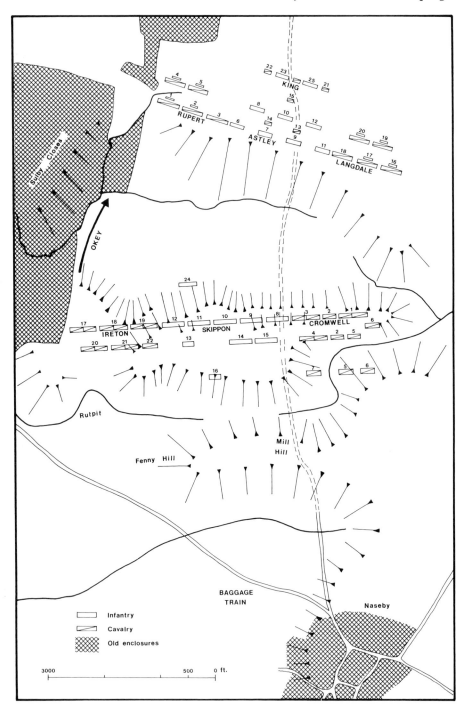

Fig.56. The deployment of regiments and brigades on the battlefield. Because of the difficulties of fully reconciling the calculation of frontages from troop numbers with that indicated by the topographical and archaeological evidence, the frontage of each regiment and brigade has been corrected according to the latter. (For the relative frontages as calculated from the estimated troop numbers see figure 60).

THE PARLIAMENTARIAN ARMY
(from Streeter)

THE ROYALIST ARMY
(from de Gomme)

The right wing of horse commanded
By Lieutenant general Cromwell

[1]The generall division of the life guard
[2]Sir Robert Pyes
[3]Col Whalleys Regt

[4]Coll.Sheffields division
[5]Coll.Fines
[6]Coll.Rosester
[7]the Associated horse *(Suffolk horse under Col.Gourdon)*

[8]The Generalls Regt
[9]Coll.Mountagues
[10]Coll.Pickering
[11]Sir Hardres Waller's
[12]Maior Generalls *(Skippon's)*

[13]Lieutenant Coll. Pride a Reserve *(described as Col.Bartlets)[52]*
[14]Coll.Hammond a Reserve
[15]Coll.Rainsborough Reserve

[16]Lt.Coll.Pride a Rear gard

The Left Wing Commanded by Commissary General Ireton

[17]Coll.Butler's Regiment
[18]Coll.Vermuyden's Regiment Commanded by Maior Huntinton
[19]Commis Generall Irctons

[20]Coll.Riches Regiment
[21]Coll.Fleetwood Regiment
[22]The troops of the Assosiation *(Suffolk horse under Col. Gourdon)[53]*

[23]The traine guarded with firelockes

[24]Forlorne hope of Musquetiers

5 divisions of Horse and 200 musketeers:
[1]Prince Rupert's & Prince Maurice's troops
[2]Prince Rupert's Regiment
[3]The Queen's and Prince Maurice's Regiments
[4]Earl of Northampton's Regiment
[5]Sir William Vaughan's Regiment

Sir Bernard Astley's tersia of foot
[6]The Duck of York Regiment
[7]Coll.Hopton's Regiment
[8]Coll. Paedges Regiment

Sir Hanery Baerd's tersia of foot
[9]Sir Hanery Baerd, and Coll.Thomas Regiments
[10]Sir John Owen's and Coll. Gerrat's Regiments

Sir George Lisle's tersia of foot
[11]Sir George Lisle's and St.Georges Regiments
[12]sherosbury foot commanded by Coll.Smith

[13,14,15]tree Division of Horse between the foot commanded by Coll. Hawerd *(2 divisions only shown by Streeter and with a different placing)*

The left wing of horse Commanded by Sir Marmaduke Langdale being the Noorthren horse 5 divisions & 200 musquetiers
[16,17,18] three divisions of Noordren horse
[19]Coll.Cary Regiment
[20]noordren division of horse

[21,22] two Divisions of Horse
[23]His Majesties Regiment of foot
[24]His Majesties Life Guarde of Horse
[25]Prince Rupert's Regiment of foote

the better organisation of the army.[54] That the regiments were brigaded is clear, because one newspaper says 'our armie being divided into several Brigades, diverse parties were drawn out.'[55] This is not to suggest that Streeter's representation of the deployment is incorrect, because the layout of the Parliamentarian regiments is compatible with a brigade structure as it is similar to the layout shown for the Royalist 'tercios', but Streeter seems to have simply named each New Model regiment rather than each brigade. One can suggest from the layout on the battlefield that Skippon's, Hardress Waller's and Pride's probably made up one brigade, Pickering's, Montague's and Hammond's another, while Fairfax's and Rainsborough's comprised the third. The actual commander of each brigade is not given by any source but Montague probably led the central brigade because he was the senior commander of the three and had brigade command later in the year. These brigades were not however fixed units, the composition was changed as the situation required. So, for example, later in the year Pickering's and Montague's found themselves brigaded with Hardress Waller's and Fairfax's at the siege of Bristol, while in the attack on Devizes and Laicock House Hammond's replaced Fairfax's in the brigade.[56] Contrary to the comments of some modern historians, Civil War armies normally employed a brigade structure in order to ease the difficulties in managing forces on the battlefield, the orders for the infantry at Naseby only having to be given to three brigade commanders rather than eight separate regimental commanders.[57]

Whereas the Parliamentarian army was organised essentially in two lines, the Royalists were deployed differently, in three lines with some cavalry between the infantry brigades and with musketeers interlining the cavalry. The interlining of the horse with musketeers was a practice which Rupert had followed in various battles, and indeed we find him deploying small numbers of musketeers with his cavalry in other situations, at the beginning of the campaign when he marched to Oxford in early May and then earlier on the 14th June when he marched forward from East Farndon to find the New Model. Were they the same commanded musketeers, who had perhaps been specially selected and trained to work with Rupert's cavalry? The creation of a second reserve, despite the limitations in numbers of troops available to Rupert, was presumably intended to give the flexibility to enable extra troops to be committed to exploit an advantage or, as at Marston Moor, to attempt to restore the balance if any part of the battle line began to buckle, but perhaps most importantly for the events which followed at Naseby it was also intended to secure a fighting retreat. A similar deployment had been employed by Rupert at the relief of Donnington Castle in the previous autumn. Roberts has argued that this form of deployment was intended to gain a tactical advantage and is simply the latest stage in the evolution of Rupert's ideas on deployment, which can be traced from the sequence of battle plans produced by de Gomme. However, it may also have been a response to the shortage of infantry because the Royalists were already suffering such problems, at least as much as the Parliamentarians, by the autumn of 1644 and especially during the Naseby campaign. This particular formation was to receive its first test at Naseby because the Donnington Castle episode had not led to a battle.[58]

It is possible to check the accuracy of our reconstruction of the deployments based upon topographical and documentary evidence by the independent calculation of the frontages of the two armies. The laying out of troops in battalia was a matter of detailed discussion amongst military authors of the period and followed strict rules, and so it is possible to calculate the ideal frontage and depth of each regiment and of the armies as a whole for the estimated troop numbers. Although the commanders would to some degree have compressed or widened the frontage to take account of the topography, the general extent would have been determined by the number of troops and the particular rules of deployment followed. What has not been attempted here is to accurately represent the exact size of each regiment for, although they undoubtedly varied, there is at present insufficient information as to exact regimental strengths. Instead, the overall estimates of the numbers of troops in the infantry and cavalry on each side have been evenly distributed between each regiment in this reconstruction.[59]

Formed up at 'order' the infantry would have a front of 3ft to each file, with half this at 'close order', with measurements in all cases being taken from the centre of each man and not between the men.[60] With the tactics employed at this stage of the war by both armies the infantry would be six deep at order. If one accepts the figure of about 7500 as the absolute maximum for the Parliamentarian infantry and assumes that this includes the officers, then deducting 550 for the troops defending the train and 300 for the forlorn hope one has at most 6600 in the main battalia. We have seen that Pride's regiment was supported by troops from Ingoldsby's and that it had to provide two separate units, one in the reserves and another as the rearguard. Streeter's stylised representation shows the rearguard with only one colour as opposed to three and with half the number of files compared to the other regiments. It would therefore seem valid to allocate about 400 men to the rearguard and an average of 800 to each of the other regiments. The majority of officers will have been within the main body, while the sergeants and some of the more senior officers who were controlling the action will have been positioned in the gaps between the blocks of pike and musket. Each regiment would then have a frontage of approximately 132 files, with 44 being pike and then the two flanking bodies of musket each with 44 files. For the pike this gives a 132ft frontage. The musketeers were divided into divisions to allow ranks to wheel off and march to the rear when firing by ranks, with Hexham indicating divisions comprising four files with a gap of 6ft between each division.[61] With five files per division this would give a frontage of 198ft for each body of musketeers. Therefore a regiment of 800 men would have a frontage of about 528ft. Streeter depicts a front line of five infantry regiments which gives a maximum frontage of 2640ft, but to this one must add gaps between the regiments.

It is here that we face the argument that Rogers first presented with regard
to the deployment of Civil War armies, that modern authors do not leave
sufficient space between regiments in each line. He states that the principles
of organisation defined in the military manuals required the spaces between
the regiments in the front line to be equal to that of the width of the regiments
in the second line and so forth, the regiments in each line covering the gaps
between the regiments in the line in front.[62] This argument is elaborated by
Roberts, who points out that such an arrangement results from the origin of
the battle formations in the 'chess board' type layout of the Republican Roman
Triplex Acies. This deployment enabled the regiments in the front, if broken,
to retreat behind their reserves to reform without disordering those reserves
and also to enable the reserves to be moved forward to support the front line.
De Gomme's plan of Naseby does indeed show such gaps between the bodies
of infantry and horse and if we apply the principal of equal gaps to the New
Model then the calculations do give a frontage much closer to the length
argued for by Rogers, almost 4800ft. However, as we have seen, the
topographical and documentary analysis for Naseby indicates quite clearly this
is wrong. Moreover, de Gomme's depiction of the deployment is in direct
conflict with Streeter's representation, which shows only small spaces
between the bodies of infantry and, as we have demonstrated, de Gomme's
information is only likely to be accurate and independent for the Royalist
deployment. Given his apparent attention to detail with regard to the
positioning and size of units, it seems strange that Streeter would have
compromised on this point. Roberts argues that, although unique in England,
the Streeter engraving is in the tradition of continental prospects of battles,
which also do not show the large gaps between regiments, but that the
'headquarters plans' from which such representations were compiled did show
such gaps and that this would explain the discrepancy between de Gomme and
Streeter. The independent evidence from Naseby would in fact strongly
support the accuracy of Streeter's representation in this regard, at least for the
New Model battalia. It is important to note therefore Roberts' comment that
there was dispute at the time as to the best practice in this matter of
deployment and that some manuals set distances between regiments which
were smaller than that of the regiments to their rear.[63]

There is another factor at Naseby which must be taken into account. This
is the depiction by Streeter of two artillery pieces between each of the
regiments of the Parliamentarian front line. That this is an accurate
representation by Streeter is confirmed by the fact that earlier in the campaign
it had been stated that two pieces of artillery marched between each infantry
regiment and the next. It was essential, if the army was to deploy rapidly into
battalia, that the artillery be already in place between the regiments while on
the march if that was where they were intended to end up in the battalia, given
the way in which the manuals show the battalia was formed. Whether such

placing of artillery in any way affects the rules as to how spacings were set between regiments, it is clear that it provides a minimum requirement, for which we may suggest 50ft. If we reduce the spacings between regiments at Naseby to this then for the spacing between the five regiments in the front line there must be 200ft, giving in all for the infantry, using the figures calculated above, a total of about 2850ft.

With regard to the spacing of the cavalry there was not, according to Cruso, a single 17th century view, though at close order some authorities give a spacing of either 2 paces or 3 ft between the horses excluding the horse itself.[64] In our reconstruction the calculation provided by Ward has been followed, for he states that each horse takes up 5ft for his station just as each man in the infantry takes up 3ft for his station.[65] If we accept the Parliamentarian cavalry strength at about 6600 men this averages out at about 550 for each of the 12 regiments, including the Association Horse as if it were a single regiment. Each was split into two divisions and, if formed up three deep as was normal by this time, each division would have a front of 91 horse giving 455ft per division.[66] Again we are faced by the problem of spacing between divisions, manuals often showing spacing equal to the width of the divisions themselves. This would give 5000ft for the six divisions on the left and 4100ft for the five divisions on the right wing. Again this can't be correct given the topographical evidence. If we were to allow just 20ft between each division of horse this still gives about 2830 ft for the six divisions on the left and about 2350 ft for the five divisions on the right, as indicated by Streeter.

Even using the lesser spacings this gives a total New Model frontage of about 8000ft, still substantially in excess of the width indicated by our topographical analysis. That there was a problem of space at Naseby is clear from Streeter who shows Cromwell's right wing of horse in three lines not two, while several accounts refer to Cromwell being constrained on the right by furze. A battalia would normally be laid out from the right, that being the most honourable position, but at Naseby it must have been deployed from the left. This will have been the result of the army being moved while already partially deployed, the left wing leading the march because they had to march to the left, whereas it would normally be expected to bring up the rear, and hence, exceptionally, the right wing was the last to reach its place. This meant that by the time Cromwell arrived, even before he had to deal with Rossiter's last minute appearance, he had insufficient space and so had to deploy in three lines. However, the commanders must surely have known before they laid out the army in its final position that there was insufficient room, so why were Ireton's wing of cavalry not similarly reorganised into three lines if they really had intended to allow substantial spaces between regiments and divisions? Unless there is a fundamental misunderstanding as to the method of deployment being used by Fairfax, the only other explanation can be that there has been a substantial overestimate of the Parliamentarian strength, even though in calculating the deployment we have taken the lower figure of 15000 rather than 17000.

Now there is the question of the spacing of the front and reserve lines, for which Hexham indicates 300ft for the infantry, while for the cavalry Vernon says each troop must be at least 100 paces (ie about 160 yards) behind the next, 'for the better avoiding of disorder....'.[67] There were three infantry regiments in the second line and then, at the very rear of the army, there was also Pride's rearguard. Fairfax had been forced to divide Pride's regiment in order to complete the battalia because he only had eight rather than the nine regiments he needed to cover the gaps between the regiments in the front line. The rearguard should theoretically have been placed double the distance behind the reserves in order to provide space for the first line to reform behind the reserves if it was forced to retreat in disorder. The appearance from Streeter that the rearguard was on Mill Hill is probably due to the foreshortening in the engraving. Such a positioning would have been very unlikely because a small but quite distinct valley would thus have divided it from the rest of the army, making it vulnerable and of little tactical value. It has been shown in our reconstruction 600ft behind the reserves. It would seem to be deployed to ensure that the other gap between the front regiments, which is not guarded by the reserves, is covered. This deployment in a third rather than in the second line will have left enough room for any front line regiment which broke to move between the regiments of the second line without disrupting them, even though the regiments were otherwise closely spaced. Perhaps this was in part a response to the tight situation within which the army had to be deployed at Naseby, but it seems more likely that this was an intentional arrangement arrived at by Fairfax earlier in the campaign, when he had to send Weldon's brigade to Taunton, so changing the number of regiments available to him, especially in view of the fact that he detached troops from one of Weldon's regiments at that time to march with Pride's regiment, an issue discussed below. The deployment of troops in battalia was after all a matter planned at an early stage of a campaign and the detaching of any troops will have demanded a redrawing of the battle plans, the numbers of regiments and companies to be detached being determined by the rules of deployment to be used. A commander could not leave himself with a number of regiments which could not be organised into a sensible battalia.

There is a further difficulty here because Sprigge comments that the train was 'well defended with firelocks, and a Rearguard left for that purpose'.[68] This is the only mention of a rearguard in his text and Pride's is the only rearguard identified on Streeter's engraving, published in Sprigge's book. In this comment Sprigge was probably following the newspaper account which states that it was 'Collonel Bartlets regiment and the Firelocks that guarded the Train'.[69] As we have seen, Bartlet's can be identified as Pride's regiment and therefore it might be suggested that Pride's rearguard should be placed with the baggage train and not in the Parliamentarian battalia. However, no other source refers to Bartlet's being with the train and, given the apparent care that Streeter took in accurately representing the Parliamentarian battalia, it would be reasonable to assume that there was indeed a rearguard on the battlefield and that perhaps the newspaper report was in error. The last deployment in the battalia was the placing of a forlorn hope of 300 commanded musketeers forward of the front line, to the bottom of the scarp and about carbine shot from the main battle line. They are shown by Streeter as a single body in front of Skippon's and Hardress Waller's regiments.

The completely independent archaeological evidence provides an excellent check upon the accuracy of the reconstruction based on topographical evidence and on the calculation of frontages. The distribution of musket balls on the hill top where the New Model infantry formed up undoubtedly reflects the location of the main infantry action. The concentration is very discrete in an east-west direction with a width of almost exactly 2000ft, compared to our calculation of the infantry frontage from the troop numbers of 2850ft. To accommodate the troops with the deployment suggested from the manuals it would require a reduction in the number of infantry by 1700, to give less than 5500 men, which seems highly improbable given there were over 7000 at the previous muster. The only other way in which the spacing could have been reduced was to reduce or remove the 6ft spacing between each division of musketeers, but this would mean they could not easily fire by ranks, as at least the reserves certainly did. A combination of the two alternatives seems the only solution, but there is an important issue here which places even greater demands for a clarification of the Parliamentarian troop numbers by detailed study of the Exchequer papers.

The gaps on either side of the musket ball distribution where almost no shot has been found must relate to the positioning of the cavalry. One might not perhaps expect a complete absence of large shot from the areas of cavalry action, for there were musketeers deployed between the lines of Royalist cavalry and there were also some dragoons deployed with the Parliamentarian cavalry. However, the horse will also have fired very few times compared to the infantry and so, although the carbines carried by some cavalry and the muskets carried by the dragoons will have left shot similar to that fired by the musketeers, the number of bullets deposited will have been very few in number compared to those left by the infantry. The almost total absence of pistol balls is primarily a result of the difficulty of recovery of such small shot during the survey. The gap in the distribution on the left side up to Sulby hedges is slightly over 2000ft, whereas our calculations of the frontage from estimated troop numbers requires 5000ft for the ideal deployment and 2830ft with a minimal spacing of 20ft between divisions. Therefore, to conform with the archaeological and topographical evidence, the numbers would have to be reduced by over 500 to give less than 2500 rather than 3000 troopers in Ireton's wing. On the right wing the ideal deployment would require over 4000ft but with the narrow spacing of 20ft there is about the right distance from the scatter to the eastern edge of the warren for all the right wing of horse. This still leaves just 700ft between the scatter and the warren boundary, whereas the two divisions of Whalley's horse which were outside the warren would require more than 900ft.

Though there may have been some slight lateral movement of the forces as the battle developed, the distribution of musket balls conforms reasonably well to the Parliamentarian deployment indicated by the topographical evidence, but both of these analyses suggests that the calculation of the frontages from troop numbers is overestimating the width of the units. This indicates that either the reduced spacings we have used are still too large, that a different method of deployment was used, or that the parliamentarian army strength has been significantly overestimated.

Similar calculations can be made for the Royalist army frontage. From the 4500 infantry 400 musketeers are allocated into eight bodies interlining the horse and, in the absence of adequate detailed information, the remaining 4100 are equally divided between the nine units to give 455 per body. With the infantry at six deep this gives a frontage of 76 files and hence 312ft at order. In contrast to the New Model, there is more than enough space for the deployment of the Royalist infantry in exactly the deployment shown by de Gomme, with gaps between each of the front line regiments equal to the width of the regiments in the second line. The 5200 horse have been shown deployed in 36 divisions, based upon the combined evidence of Streeter and de Gomme, giving approximately 144 per division and at three deep a frontage of 48 files, or 240ft per division.[70]

The topographical and archaeological evidence from Naseby is in close agreement and so clear cut that it is difficult to dispute. In contrast, the calculations of frontages using the wide spacings is in extreme conflict with this evidence for the New Model, and even with the severely reduced spacings we have applied there is still a significant discrepancy. One must therefore ask the question as to whether such ideal models applied from the manuals by Rogers and Roberts were actually ignored in practice in many situations on the battlefields of the English Civil War. Alternatively, was the situation at Naseby unique and one in which Fairfax and Cromwell had to compromise as a result of the particular restrictions of the ground? The compromise involved seems enormous but perhaps the advantages that Naseby field gave to Fairfax, enabling him to anchor both of his flanks securely, with Sulby hedges on the left and the furze on the right, was sufficient to justify such changes. Further detailed topographical and archaeological studies of other Civil War battlefields are essential if we are to answer this question, for only when we understand exactly how the military commanders actually deployed their troops on the battlefield can we hope to develop an effective understanding of how the battles were fought.

Finally it is necessary to identify the location of the baggage trains which accompanied the armies, both of which had a role in the battle. There is apparently no evidence as to the exact size of the Parliamentarian train, because although 33 new waggons had been ordered for the army in April they must have used many other waggons, and we certainly know that they had with them additional waggons from local villages to transport provisions.[71] Given the fact that the New Model was larger than the Royalist army one might expect its train to have been of at least a similar size, so the 175 waggons suggested above on the basis of the number of horses may be a reasonably accurate estimate. There were also a number of siege pieces with the train, none of which would have been deployed on the battlefield. The train must therefore have occupied a substantial area, perhaps something of the order of ten acres. In the past all authors have followed Streeter and placed the train close to Naseby village on the west side. For example, Hensman, writing early this century and following Gardiner, had little doubt that the train was on the south west of Naseby with the river Avon on its north side. Others, such as Smurthwaite, have placed it somewhat to the north west of Naseby.[72] If Streeter's engraving is accurate then the train was in fact immediately to the west of Naseby, on a small hill just outside the old enclosures of the village. Streeter shows it on the northern part of Leane Leys Hill, which he depicts as a furlong of open field strips between the Welford Road and Carvell's Lane, with the old enclosures of Naseby providing some protection from cavalry attack from the east. The firelocks guarding the train are shown deployed all around the waggons, the figures on the far side beginning to disappear beyond the brow of the hill. Leane Leys Hill still remains today with part of the area under ridge and furrow. However, there is one difficulty. Metal detecting in the area has so far failed to find any significant trace of military action, even though there was apparently a fierce engagement in which the defenders fired upon and drove off Rupert's cavalry. It is of course possible that the absence of finds is simply due to the fact that most of the land is under permanent pasture, although nothing was found either during the metal detecting survey which preceded the construction of the A14 road, which passes very close to the site, or during the watching brief on the construction.[73] It is possible, as with several other details, that Streeter was using a degree of artistic licence in his positioning of the train, but his specific reference to Leane Leys Hill implies that he had good local information on which to base his drawing. As we have seen, the train was guarded by the firelocks and possibly also by a rearguard composed of troops from Bartlet's regiment, which has been identified as Pride's. The regiment was already divided into two units on the battlefield and if it did really have another unit attached to the train it will have been severely overstretched, even with the additional companies from Ingoldsby's regiment, unless it was the local garrison troops that provided the bulk of the rearguard defending the train.

The Royalist baggage train is shown by Streeter just behind Dust Hill, but there is far more room here for artistic licence as it is a very distant view. It has even been argued that the Royalist train did not have time to move up to

Sibbertoft from Farndon and that it had no significant role in the later action but, although it is true that the waggons may have taken some time to catch up with the army, the little evidence which does exist would suggest that many did reach Sibbertoft as Streeter indicates.[74] With about 200 waggons the train will have extended for something like 2.5 miles in line of march, meaning that the first waggons would have arrived at East Farndon before the last had left Harborough, a distance of 2 miles. The army started marching at 6.00am and did not move from East Farndon until about 8.30am and so the waggons will have had plenty of time to reach Farndon at a speed of about 2 miles per hour.[75] From Farndon to Sibbertoft is 2.5 miles and so the first waggon would be arriving as the last waggon left. The army took an hour to march there, but at two miles an hour the first waggons would only have been arriving as the battle started and it seems unlikely that all the waggons would have reached Sibbertoft by the time the Royalists were retreating back towards the train. Streeter certainly shows the waggons still arriving as the battle began. It therefore seems reasonable to conclude that many, though probably not all the waggons did reach Sibbertoft before they were forced to flee. Slingsby makes it quite clear that the waggons had been left 'at a good distance' from the battle, which means they must have been well back from Dust Hill but, despite this, he says that in the pursuit the enemy gained the baggage. In this he is supported by a Parliamentarian account which says that Cromwell 'beat back the enemy from their Traine'.[76] As will become clear from the later discussion, this might indicate that the train was to the east of Sibbertoft village and adjacent to the Sibbertoft to Clipston road. This is a similar distance behind the Royalist lines as the Parliamentarian baggage was behind their lines and may be supported by the discovery in 1991 of a hoard of silver coins. If we are correct in our location of the Royalist baggage train then, like their Parliamentarian counterparts, the Royalists chose a site close to hedged enclosures which would give some protection from cavalry attack. This was also the first area of flat open ground which the waggon master would have reached once he ascended the hill from Clipston. With about 200 waggons and carriages, as well as six siege pieces drawn by up to 100 horses which will not have been deployed in the battle, the Royalist train must also have covered about ten acres, approximately the area surrounding the coin hoard site which is almost devoid of musket balls. Perhaps this blank area in the distribution has resulted from the fighting skirting around the cluster of waggons. It is to be hoped that further systematic survey work on both sites will yield more artefacts that confirm the location of the baggage trains.

As the officers of each regiment were busy deploying their men, the word for the day was passed down from the high command to each regiment via their major and then by the corporals to each of the company commanders.[77] For the New Model it was 'God is our strength', while on the Royalist side they had chosen 'Queen Mary'.[78] To further distinguish their soldiers many of the Royalists had beanstalks in their hats, while a few Parliamentarians had white linen or a piece of paper as their field sign.[79] The cavalry of course needed no such marks because, according to Vernon, every horseman should have had 'a skarfe of his Generall Colours.... as a good and visible mark in time of battell to know one another by...'[80] Once in place, the troopers probably made use of the brief lull in the action to prepare themselves. Pistols needed to be charged with powder and ball, if they had not been made ready earlier in the morning, and it is now they will have cocked or 'spand' their pistols with the spanner for, as Vernon advised, 'never span before you have just need, because many times the firelock pistols will not goe off if they have stood long spand.'[81] One can imagine Fairfax himself riding back and forth in front of the battle line, viewing his troops, the ensigns and cornets saluting with their colours as he passed. At such a time of great fear the ritual of flourishing of the colours, to display the honour of the regiment, might help a little in preparing for the coming danger, but for many it was however to more spiritual thoughts that their minds must have turned. As the troops stood in battalia Hugh Peters, the famous Independent chaplain, preached to the troops and, according to one report, even during the battle he 'rode from rank to rank with a Bible in one hand and a pistol in the other exhorting the men to do their duty'.[82] There must have been many there who prayed to God as the two armies prepared for battle, especially amongst the so called praying and preaching regiments of the New Model, who would undoubtedly soon be heard singing psalms as they marched forward, just as they had in previous engagements.[83] Cromwell later wrote:

> 'when I saw the enemy drawn up and march in gallant order towards us, and we a company of poor ignorant men to seek how to order our battle, the General having commanded me to order all the horse, I could not - riding alone about my business - but smile out to God in praises in assurance of victory....'[84]

Like Gustavus Adolphus before him, Cromwell had used the power of religion to weld his cavalry into an irresistible force. The belief that they were doing God's work was after all fundamental to many of the troops, as it had been in the Eastern Association, and this was already for many of its members a godly army with a destiny to fulfil.[85] The Royalists on the other hand, scornful of the religious extremism of the Independents, paraded 'a wooden Image, in the shape of a man, and in such a form, as they blasphemously called it the God of the Roundheads.'[86]

As he viewed the battlefield from Sulby Hill, while he oversaw the deployment of the left wing of cavalry, Cromwell must have recognised the importance of controlling the hedged enclosures on the left wing of the army, to stop any outflanking move by Rupert and to enable his own men to fire on the advancing enemy horse before they engaged Ireton's cavalry. It was for exactly such a task that the dragoons were designed and so Cromwell himself rode back behind the Parliamentarian lines to pass on the orders to the dragoon commander. Colonel Okey was issuing his men with ammunition about half a mile back in a 'meadow', probably the area of ley grass near to where the train was positioned. Cromwell instructed Okey to mount up and deploy his men as quickly as possible in a small close on the left wing. As the dragoons rode rapidly across the field, ten abreast, the Royalists will have perceived the threat as soon as Okey came over the brow of the hill. As they came to the little close, nine out of every ten of the dragoons will have alighted 'casting the bridle over Hthe next sideman's horse necke, and soe one in ten serves to keepe their horses, the rest performe the service.'[87] In Streeter's engraving the little groups of horses can be seen, set a little back from the action, being held by the tenth rider from each rank while the other dragoons line the hedge, firing on the Royalist horse. Rupert must have acted immediately to counter the move, because by the time the dragoons had delivered up their horses in the little close, the enemy was already advancing. Rushing forward Okey's men took cover behind the hedgerow facing towards the enemy, their muskets loaded and ready to meet the inevitable attack. The Royalists encompassed the dragoons' position on both sides, trying to drive them out of the close but, as Okey recounts:

> 'my men perceiving [this], they with shooting and rejoycing received them, although they were incompassed on the one side with the Kings Horse and on the other side with the Foot and Horse to get the Close; but it pleased God that wee beat off both the Horse and the Foot on the left, and the right Wing, and cleared the Field, and kept our ground.'[88]

This fighting may have taken place before the main battle started, because the Royalists could not afford to be outflanked, but it seems more likely, from Okey's brief description, that it occurred as the two armies closed. Indeed it may have been as a result of the last minute deployment of the dragoons that Rupert engaged his army sooner than he might have wished. Events earlier in the day would however suggest that Rupert already intended to attack first, once more taking the initiative by carrying the fight to the enemy, while Fairfax had no intention of attacking but rather wished to draw the enemy on to him. What is clear is that with this deployment of the dragoons the New Model had achieved an important advantage that had a significant impact on the events that followed. Not only would they protect the Parliamentarian left wing from being outflanked and cause serious damage amongst the right wing of Royalist horse as they charged, the dragoons would also probably keep some of the Royalist reserves out of the main action at a crucial later stage of the battle.

Streeter is the only source which gives a specific location for Okey, showing 'Lantford Hedge lined with Dragoones'. Lantford hedge was almost certainly that part of the hedge on the parish boundary with Sulby in the bottom of Broadmoor next to Lankyford furlong. Okey is quite specific in his account that they took a small close and were then encompassed by Royalists on both sides. Most of the closes in Sulby were massive sheep pastures, such as Coate Greene Pasture at 246 acres, and the only small closes were generally meadows near to the stream.[89] In 1645 one small triangular close did lie next to Lankyford furlong and this would match very well the location given by Streeter, but it is not very far forward of Ireton's front line, encompassing all the slope down to the stream in Broadmoor. Ireton's cavalry are said to have drawn down the brow of the hill to meet the Royalists while Slingsby is very clear that Okey had already fired on Rupert's men before they could fire on or charge Ireton. This small close seems too near to the Parliamentarian lines for such action. Most importantly, it seems highly improbable that the Royalists could have separately attacked Okey, and on both flanks, if he was so close to Ireton's cavalry, for they would have put themselves in great danger of being caught in the flank by an attack from Ireton. The only other close which would match Okey's description is that just in Sibbertoft parish called Archwrong Close, which can be seen as one of the two small closes behind the Royalist right wing on Streeter's engraving. In addition we have already suggested that Streeter has shown the Royalist army much too far forward.[90]

The archaeological evidence which lies within and around Archwrong and the adjacent close, the only significant concentration of finds that has been made on the western edge of the battlefield, suggests very strongly that this is the close occupied by Okey. In all more than 80 musket balls and eight pewter tops from powder 'boxes', from bandoliers of musketeers or dragoons, have been found here.[91] In contrast the 16 musket balls found along Sulby Hedges were the result of a very intensive search for evidence of the dragoons where Streeter placed them. The latter would perhaps have been from incoming fire hitting the hedge, while all the musket balls which were fired from the hedge and which missed their mark will have travelled three or four hundred yards before falling to earth. The evidence of intensive fire out from the hedge is almost completely absent here, with just three balls having been found, whereas the scatter further north might be consistent with the firing by dragoons from the cover of the hedgerow upon advancing Royalist cavalry. The pewter tops probably indicate the position of musketeers or dragoons who were firing, and more of these tops have been found around these closes than on the whole of the rest of the battlefield put together. It is possible that further survey will reveal a more extensive or different pattern, but the detectorists who conducted the survey have not suggested that there was any significant bias in recovery which might explain the discrete nature of the main concentration. Wogan, who was with Okey, says that they fired on the Royalists as they advanced and Slingsby makes it clear that the dragoons fired on the Royalists before they could charge Ireton, indicating that they were probably a considerable distance forward of the Parliamentarian lines.

It is with some concern that one suggests that such a specific statement by Streeter is in error. The artefact scatter around Archwrong may prove to be related to other action during the battle, but on balance it would seem likely that this archaeological evidence relates to the engagement with Okey's dragoons and that they were in Archwrong Close. If this interpretation is correct then it was a very bold, aggressive move by Cromwell, thrusting forward towards the enemy and threatening their right flank. Was it perhaps, like Skippon's deployment of the forlorn hope, in part a response to a clear build up of troops on the right side of the Royalist battalia, Cromwell seeing that Ireton's left wing of horse were going to be hard pressed? Certainly both Okey and Rushworth say that Rupert's wing of horse were more numerous than Ireton's.

Fig. 57. Musket and pistol balls together with lead caps to powder 'boxes' from musketeers' or dragoons' bandoliers, all from Naseby. (Northants CC).

Just before the armies engaged Cromwell had to deal with another last minute deployment, because Colonel Rossiter arrived on the field with 500 horse from Lincolnshire.[92] It was presumably too late for him to be sent to Ireton to reinforce the left wing and there was too little room on the right wing, which Cromwell had already deployed in three lines rather than two, and so Rossiter was squeezed in on the right in two divisions between the existing lines. This gave Cromwell a clear advantage in numbers over the Royalists that faced him, but it may also explain how it was that the New Model were somewhat in disorder, trying to rearrange the battalia, as the Royalists advanced.[93]

It was between about ten and eleven o'clock when finally the trumpets began to sound and the drums to beat. With colours to the fore, advanced and flying in the strong wind, the two armies began to march.[94] Fairfax was drawing his troops forward to the brow of the hill ready to meet the Royalist

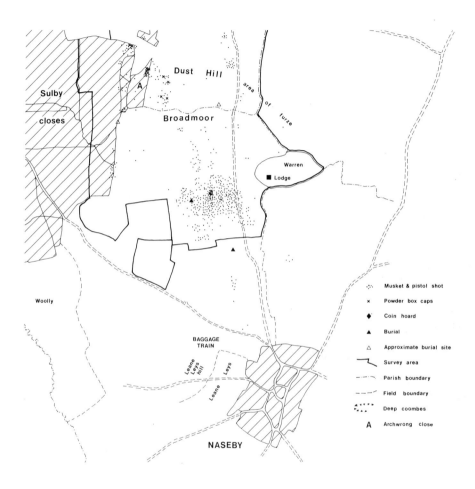

Fig.58. The distribution of finds from the southern part of the battlefield.

attack but he would not quit the advantage of the ground, and as they saw each other the soldiers from both sides 'with mighty shoutes exprest a hearty desire of fighting...'[195] According to one Royalist account their attack was premature, 'the Heat of Prince Rupert, and his Opinion they durst not stand him, engaged us before we had either turned our Cannon or chosen fit Ground to fight on.'[196] Though Rupert was renowned for his rashness, one cannot take at face value all the criticisms of his actions in the Royalist accounts written at a later date, for Rupert was to become a scapegoat for the defeat. In fact the early attack may have been intended to take advantage of the apparent incompleteness of the Parliamentarian battalia, but it is equally possible that it was the deployment of Okey's dragoons which prompted the Royalist right wing to advance first, for Rushworth reported that 'our Dragoones begun the Battaile Flanking the right wing of the Enemies Horse as they charged our left wing of Horse...'[197] However, according to other accounts it was the wish to gain the advantage of the wind, which was blowing from the north west, that brought the Parliament left and Royalist right into action first.[98] As the manuals make clear, whoever gained the advantage of the wind 'hath much the odds of the other.... because the Smoke that is made by both Sides, will annoy them much, who have not the benefit of the Wind.'[99] The other obvious reason for the Royalist right wing to move first was that at its west end Dust Hill is considerably further away from the Parliamentarian position than it is at its east end. Whatever the reason for the early attack, the resulting failure to employ the Royalist artillery at the beginning of the battle was not a significant factor in the defeat because the Royalist advance was such that even the Parliamentarian ordnance did little execution before the two armies joined.[100] Indeed, artillery seems rarely to have played a key role on Civil War battlefields and seldom broke or scattered infantry regiments.[101] Symonds claims that the Royalist shot just one piece and the Parliamentarians two before the armies met, all with little effect, while another account says five Parliamentarian cannon fired on the advancing Royalists.[102] It is interesting to note that although many cannon balls have been recovered from the battlefield over the centuries, in the mid 19th century the information collected by Fitzgerald suggested that the vast majority of them came from the southern part of Sibbertoft parish, confirming that the Royalist artillery did not play any significant role in the battle, but also that the Parliamentarian artillery must have fired far more than five rounds. Perhaps they continued to fire over the main infantry engagement at the Royalist reserves or perhaps later in the battle on the retreating enemy troops.

Several other accounts say that both armies deployed a forlorn hope and it was they that engaged first, seeking to gain the advantage of the wind and of the hill, although Streeter only depicts one. The Parliament forlorn was set in front of Skippon's and Waller's regiments one or two hundred yards forward of the main battalia, at the bottom of the hill, with orders to fall back when they were hard pressed. Skippon it would seem had no intention of quitting the advantage of the hill before the two bodies were fully engaged.[103] On this area of the battlefield, and this area only, there is a danger of confusing the archaeological evidence of the action at the beginning of the battle with that which took place later, because this was apparently the only part of the field where the two bodies of infantry were engaged when the Royalists were advancing and then later as they retreated. The scatter of nearly 40 musket balls on the slope and part way across Broadmoor might relate to the exchange of fire between the forlorn hope and the Royalist infantry as the battle began. As their forlorn hope fell back the musketeers in the front line regiments of the New Model had probably doubled their ranks to three deep, ready to fire a single volley as the two armies closed.

On the right wing Rupert led the Royalist horse. His tactics were to spearhead the first fierce cavalry attack himself, with superior forces in experience and determination if not also in numbers. Certainly Ireton lacked the experience that Rupert brought to the battle, for it was actually on the field that day that Colonel Ireton had been made up to Commissary General, filling the position which Vermuyden had wanted.[104] Rushworth claimed that Rupert's cavalry outnumbered Ireton's horse, saying 'Rupert and Maurice (having at least two thousand Horse more then ours that charged)'. There seems no obvious reason why he should have exaggerated this aspect of the Royalist army, because later he and others praised the Royalist infantry for their gallant fight when outnumbered, unless of course his informants wanted to excuse their defeat on the left wing.[105] Rupert's objective was to meet the enemy at a 'full career', breaking them with the sheer force of the impact, and some accounts imply that Ireton's cavalry were indeed routed at the first charge, Rupert 'driving them off their ground in some disorder'.[106] The action was in fact more protracted and less decisive. As the armies closed, Ireton drew his cavalry down the hill to meet the attack, but Rupert's charge was suddenly halted 'as if they had not expected us in so ready a posture', and Ireton also stopped briefly, because his formation had been disrupted by the 'disadvantage of the ground.'[107] The very brief accounts that we have of the action do not say so, but perhaps Rupert halted to enable the musketeers who interlined the cavalry to move up and fire on the Parliamentarians before the final cavalry charge, although these musketeers may already have been deployed against Okey's dragoons. According to Slingsby:

> 'they had possess'd an Hedge upon our right wing wch they had lin'd wth Musqueteers to Gall our horse, (as indeed they did) before we could come up to charge theirs. It fell upon Rupert to charge at yt disadvantage, and many of ye Regiment [were] wound'd by shot from ye hedge before we could joyne wth theirs on yt wing...'[108]

His reserves, the Earl of Northampton's regiment, also suffered in the same way as they seconded Rupert.[109] They must have kept as far from the hedge as possible to avoid the fire from Okey's dragoons and this may have put them at a disadvantage, in danger of being outflanked. After a brief pause, possibly resulting from being disordered through crossing the boggy ground along the parish boundary stream, to recover from the effects of Okey's firing or to widen their frontage now that the ground had widened out south of Archwrong Close, the Royalists resumed their charge and Ireton ordered the trumpets to sound a charge to meet them as, in his usual fashion, Rupert attacked 'with a full career up towards our men'. His famous cavalry charge had been first seen in a major Civil War battle at Edgehill, where Sir Richard Bulstrode described his tactics as 'Sword in Hand, to receive the Enemy's shot, without firing either Carbin or Pistol, till we broke in amongst the Enemy and then to make use of our Fire-Arms as need should require....'[110] It seems likely that Ireton's men fired their pistols before making the final charge but both sides depended upon shock action rather than firepower to break the opposition.[111]

The bodies of cavalry on either side will have advanced towards each other in 'closest order', as tightly packed as possible, with 'every left man's right knee .... close locked under his right hand man's left ham', three ranks deep with just three feet between each rank.[112] Each trooper will have had his sword in his hand, fastened to his wrist with a cord so not to lose it if they missed their blow, and with the pommel resting on his thigh. There in the middle of the front rank of each division the three cornets carried their standards proudly, each presumably leading their own troop, while at their side in the first rank rode 'the best and ablest men to receive the charge of the enemy.'[113] Ireton's men advanced down the slope, possibly even meeting the enemy in the bottom of Broadmoor. Approaching each other first at a 'good round trot', over the last few yards they broke into a 'full career', the two bodies crashing into each other at sword point. It must have been a terrifying sight, these armoured riders charging forward in a tight body, sword in hand. In sheer panic at Edgehill the inexperienced Parliamentarian cavalry had fled simply at the sight of Rupert's men charging towards them, but a great deal had changed since 1642. Here, as at Marston Moor, Rupert faced troopers who were often as experienced and as well disciplined as his own. Ireton's cavalry matched Rupert's charge and, unlike many of those who had faced him in previous engagements, withstood the attack. Keeping at close order to stop the enemy breaking through they fought fiercely for a time with sword and pistol, Rupert being 'handsomely' received and his attack repulsed.[114]

Only five of Ireton's front line divisions charged the enemy, Ireton's own division probably not taking part in this first charge. His was on the right wing of the cavalry's front line, the most honourable position, for careful inspection of Streeter's engraving shows that this division has four not three standards, while that to its left has only two. This is no coincidence because if one looks to the right wing of horse it will be seen that the right hand division of Cromwell's own regiment (nominally Fairfax's regiment) also has four standards, presumably showing the position of Fairfax's lifeguard, while his left division still has three standards. This is why Streeter depicts six files in each of the right wing divisions except Cromwell's, which has seven. In contrast, on the left wing five divisions have five files and only five divisions have six. In Ireton's regiment the left division has only four files, again perhaps representing the transfer of a troop to Ireton's own division. Though these files are only stylised representations the variations are not random and cannot be dismissed as simply artistic licence. It is even possible, given the other detail which is represented in the deployment, that the smaller number of files does indeed reflect an overall weakness amongst the regiments of the left wing of horse compared to the right. If this analysis is correct then it would make great sense for it to have been Ireton's own division that did not engage at the first charge. The events which followed certainly suggest that he had remained out of the action, standing back to judge the situation until he saw it appropriate to commit his reserves.

In this first charge the left two of Ireton's five front line divisions, commanded by Colonel Butler, were slower in their advance and failed to charge home because they had been disordered by the presence of water filled pits and ditches that they had not expected. As a result it was the Royalists that advanced upon them and so Butler's troops were 'overborn' by Rupert.[115] Given the importance of maintaining a solid body of horse, all at close order, and of meeting the charge with a charge, this was the worst possible thing for a division of cavalry, for once disordered they were very vulnerable. Scattered across Turmore field, in Sulby closes and across Dust Hill there are many small pits. Most have been ploughed over and are now visible only as slight depressions, but some are still quite deep and a few contain standing water. Several water filled pits still exist on Sulby Hill and it was features like these, but perhaps further north on the slope, that must have disrupted Butler's advance.[116] Once disordered and thrown back by the first charge, his regiment would have been very vulnerable to a charge from the Royalist reserves. However, as those reserves under the Earl of Northampton passed close by, the dragoons fired on them before they could discharge their pistols at Butler's men.[117] 'Had not wee by Gods providence been there', says Okey, 'there had been but few of Colonel Butlers Regiment left....', and yet even with his intervention Colonel Butler himself took a brace of bullets in the thigh and was put out of the action.[118]

The three right hand divisions of Ireton's cavalry, that is Vermuyden's former regiment and the left division of Ireton's regiment, had been the first to meet the enemy and fared much better. Although Vermuyden's right hand division did not charge home, the other two did and routed the enemy divisions. In their flight the two defeated Royalist divisions caused the division between them, which had not been charged, also to be carried away in the chaos. Indeed one of the Parliamentarian divisions, probably Ireton's, charged on and also routed the Royalist reserves that faced them. The success of this attack by Ireton's and Vermuyden's regiments may in part explain how the commanders of both Rupert's and Maurice's regiments and various of

their officers came to be killed or seriously wounded in the battle. Such was
this initial success that Ireton was able to turn his own division of horse to
attack the Royalist infantry to his right, which were already putting Skippon's
regiment under severe pressure. However, while charging amongst the
musketeers, Ireton was unlucky enough to suffer 'his horse being shot under
him, and himself run through the thigh with a Pike, and into the face with an
Halbert, [and he] was taken prisoner by the enemy......'[119] Indeed, one report
suggests that he would have 'had his braines knockt out, but for one of the
Kings Soldiers, who after in the turn became his Prisoner...' once the fortunes
of the infantry engagement were reversed, at which time, with the Royalists
in 'great distraction', he had the opportunity to offer his keeper his liberty if
he carried him off to safety.[120]

Whether Ireton's attack on the infantry was in any way significant in
turning the infantry battle there is no way of knowing, but what it did do was
to rob the left wing of horse of their commander at a critical moment. They
were facing the best of the Royalist cavalry led by one of Europe's most
famous cavalry commanders whose task was to break Ireton's wing. Rupert
knew that Cromwell was with the army and presumably that he was now
Lieutenant General and hence that he would lead the right wing of cavalry.
Rupert will have realised that the Royalist cavalry had little chance of
breaking through on that side and would simply have to depend upon Langdale
to hold the Ironsides. Instead the whole Royalist battle plan seems to have
focused upon the rapid destruction of the Parliamentarian left wing, for it was
here that Rupert had concentrated his best regiments of horse, and in this
objective Rupert could not afford to be deflected.

Despite their initial success and after a 'most terrible dispute; at length the
fury of the Enemy caused two Regiments of Horse to give ground a little'.[121]
Lacking their commander and at least one of their Colonels, under the force
of another Royalist charge which was well seconded, both the front line and
the reserves broke.[122] It was the coming on of the reserves, who would only
attack once the first troops had given their charge and were reformed behind
them ready for a second charge, that seems to have decided the engagement.[123]
Rupert believed that he should encourage his men by his own bravery and it
was such action that had given him the trust and respect of his men, and this
is why he led from the front. It is said that Rupert:

> 'charging with incredible Valour and fury, broke in upon and routed the three
> rightmost Divisions of that Left Wing...' and 'so behav'd himself in ye charge,
> yt he beat ym up upon yt wing beyond ye Hills, and had our success been ye
> like upon our left wing, in probability we might have had ye day.'[124]

However, contrary to some accounts, Rupert's cavalry did not 'bore all down
before them'.[125] Only two regiments of Ireton's wing seem to have been
routed, probably Vermuyden's and Fleetwood's judging by the casualty rates.
That it was the central regiment and its reserves that broke and fled is not

perhaps surprising, for they were after all facing Prince Rupert's own regiment, apparently the strongest of the Royalist regiments on that wing. They had done well to hold the first charge. As the Royalists broke through the divisions of Parliamentarian troopers 'above a thousand ran along with them...' and, as Kitson has commented from personal experience of horsemanship, it was probably the case that even if the riders wanted to stay to do battle, most would have been unable to stop their horses turning and joining the Royalists as they thundered through.[126] *The Weekly Account* admits that 'Rupert put our left to shamefull retreat', though that author did find several weak excuses for the failure, claiming that 'our men were new raised in the Associated Counties and better armed than hearted', which may have been true of some of the reserves, especially the single division of 200 Association troops from Suffolk, but not of the majority of the cavalry which had come from experienced regiments in Essex's and the Eastern Association armies.[127] But the majority of the Parliamentarian troops, although disordered and pushed back, did not apparently flee.[128] So, this intense engagement on the left wing, which had lasted rather less than half an hour, was not an immediate or by any means a total rout for Ireton.[129] It is also unclear how many of the Royalist horse that had been driven back by Ireton's first charge had rallied and rejoined the attack and so accompanied Rupert in the pursuit. Vaughan's regiment, which was the reserve to Rupert's regiment of horse, certainly followed the Prince because Digby reported that Sir William Vaughan had 'charged quite through those bodies' of Parliamentarian troops.[130] However, some of the reserves under the Earl of Northampton may have remained on the battlefield and have supported the infantry action, for at least one account refers to Skippon's infantry being attacked by Royalist horse as well as foot, though these could equally have been Howard's horse which had been deployed between the infantry units. Okey's account also suggests that the majority of Ireton's cavalry had already been driven back before Northampton charged Butler's regiment.

Few had ever managed to withstand Rupert's charge but what his enemies had been able to exploit was the ensuing chaos and this was to be the case at Naseby because, once he had broken the Parliamentarian regiments, his men thundered on across Turmore field. Having driven them off their ground in disorder, Rupert pursued the fleeing Parliamentarian troopers almost as far as Naseby village, indeed some of the troopers appear to have fled to the very gates of Northampton, bringing news of the defeat of Fairfax's army.[131] The cavalry pursuit was probably a chaotic affair, for the remains of at least one trooper are said to have been found early this century during the construction of the reservoir, over a mile to the west of Naseby village. The problem in resolving exactly where the cavalry pursuit led is the fact that the recovery of pistol shot has proved so difficult and that so few shots will have been fired, although it is just possible that the small quantity of musket balls found on Mill Hill and further south relate to dragoons, or to royalist cavalry carrying carbines, firing during the pursuit.[132] Despite his success, Rupert had not however achieved his objective. He had broken through and disordered Ireton's cavalry but he had not destroyed them or even driven the majority off the battlefield, perhaps as many as 1500 troopers remaining on the field.

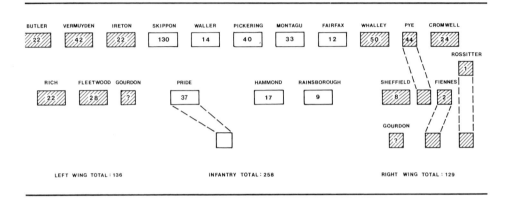

Fig.59. The distribution of wounded between the various regiments of the Parliamentarian army. Not displayed on the plan are the numbers for Fairfax's lifeguard (3) who were probably with Cromwell, Okey's dragoons (2), the artillery (2) and the baggage train (7), while a handful of those listed cannot at present be allocated to a regiment. A more detailed summary is in appendix 3.

A total of 535 Parliamentarians are named as being seriously wounded in the battle, most with a record of their company and regiment, of which 45 eventually died of their wounds. It would appear to be a fairly complete record of the casualties, except those killed outright, although interpretation is hampered by the lack of detailed information as to the exact strength of each regiment from which they came.[133] If this limitation is kept in mind, one finds that the casualty rates do accord well with the positions of regiments on the field and the degree to which they are known to have been hard pressed.[134] In total there were 136 seriously wounded Parliamentarian troopers from the left wing of cavalry, only 7 more than in the right wing, but they were not evenly distributed amongst the regiments. In the centre, where Rupert appears to have broken through, Vermuyden's old regiment, now commanded by Major Huntington, had 42 wounded and lost at least one captain and one corporal killed, as well as a lieutenant, two cornets and one corporal wounded. His reserve, Fleetwood's regiment, which incorporated two companies from Cromwell's original Ironsides, had 28 wounded and also lost a captain killed. In contrast all the other three regiments had 22 casualties each, except for the Association Horse for which no figures seem to exist. In addition, Ireton's own regiment lost Captain Hoskins killed and Ireton himself and a corporal wounded, while in Butler's regiment the colonel himself, a major and a lieutenant were wounded and in Rich's regiment a lieutenant and a reformado[135] were wounded. There were apparently few if any comparable losses of officers in the right wing of horse. That Ireton's reserves suffered almost equally to the front line regiments is surely a reflection of the fact that most of the front line were broken, and that all the reserves were heavily engaged in their attempt to hold Rupert's second charge. Though one might expect the highest casualty rates to occur where regiments broke and fled, the disordered troops being far more vulnerable, this is not borne out when we examine the casualty rates suffered by the right wing of cavalry. This might suggest that, for the cavalry at least, casualty rates are a direct reflection of the intensity of the engagement itself. In analysing all these casualty figures it must also of course be remembered that most of the regiments will have had significant fighting ahead of them in the later stages of the battle, but the scale and distribution of losses here on the left wing between the various regiments, as in the rest of the battalia, would seem to correlate well with the events of the first period of the battle when the fighting was fiercest and was 'very doubtful' for the New Model.

In the infantry action the Parliamentarians had also suffered badly in the first half hour. As the two armies came together the New Model artillery had only discharged at most five pieces and these overshot the enemy. Then, as the forlorn hope retired back to the main body, the New Model infantry marched forward to the brow of the hill. The musketeers are most likely to have doubled their ranks to three deep to fire a single salvo before the two armies closed and, according to one Royalist account, this volley overshot because the two bodies hardly saw each other until they were within carbine range.[136] Having fired, the infantry continued to close but 'the Foot charged not each other till they were within twelve paces one of another, and could not charge above twice, but were at push of Pike.'[137] In each regiment the block of two or three hundred pikemen, in the centre of the line in ranks six deep, will all have been at close order and packed tight. With the pikes of the front ranks lowered at charge to create a solid, impenetrable wall they must have advanced in perfect step with the beating drums so as to maintain their order. Already the ensigns will have withdrawn for protection to the half files of the pike, that is in the centre of the body, and will have furled their colours and brought them down to the charge. As the smoke of the first volley blew back into the faces of the Parliamentarian soldiers the musketeers, in blocks of two or three hundred and again probably six deep on either flank of each body of pike, will not have had time to reload before the two bodies met. This was probably just at the break of slope, approximately where the 1930s monument now stands, although it is possible that it was further back towards the top of the hill, depending how one takes Sprigge's comment that the New Model regained the ledge of the hill before the two armies met. At first as the two bodies of infantry crashed together the wall of pikes remained intact, while on their flanks Rupert's musketeers are likely to have fallen on immediately with the butt end of muskets. The most reliable Parliamentarian accounts suggest that the initial stages did not go too badly for Skippon's men because at first some of the Royalist foot 'gave a little backe', but so too did some of the New Model infantry.[138] This first charge must have taken some minutes as the front line regiments struggled for the advantage but, although it would have been a fearsome experience, so long as the ranks of pikemen and musketeers remained intact then there was relatively limited damage that could be inflicted. It seems that overall the New Model might have had the better of the first charge and have pushed the Royalists back. Astley's men now prepared for a second charge. As the huge blocks of infantry lumbered towards each other once more it is said that the Royalists were now being driven on by the divisions of Howard's horse, with which Rupert had interlined his infantry, just as they had been at the storming of Leicester. Whether forcing the infantry forward or simply supporting their attack, the use of cavalry within the infantry battle was an aggressive tactic popular amongst German commanders and it seems this caused problems for the Parliamentarian infantry. Again, just as on his right wing of cavalry, Rupert needed to break through quickly and decisively, for in a long gruelling battle of attrition he knew his outnumbered infantry were almost bound to lose.

This time the intensity of the action was such that in the second charge the pikemen came to 'push of pike', although Rushworth's exact meaning here is unclear. Firth argues that by this period there was little use of sword by infantry, but Walker's description of the early infantry action at Naseby, quoted below, would seem to imply that the pikemen did draw their swords. Certainly in one good late 16th century description of pike action we see hand to hand fighting in which the pikes were dropped and the pikemen fell on with sword.[139] On either side the musketeers also closed to the enemy. Very few of them will have drawn their swords, most preferring in the confined space to turn their muskets around and use them as fearsome clubs, swinging them above their heads to crash down on the enemy. So long as the block remained intact then the soldiers were relatively safe, and if one man was to fall then the man behind him would push forward into his place. Only if the enemy were able to break into the ranks or outflank the body did the situation become desperate, and it would appear that this is exactly what soon happened. Walker says that the Royalist troops, 'falling in with Sword and butt end of Musquet did notable Execution; so much as I saw their Colours fall, and their Foot in great Disorder.'[140]

Although it has been long understood that the Royalist infantry were heavily outnumbered, there has not been a detailed consideration of the actual implications of this on the battlefield, especially in view of the fact that those infantry were deployed in three line compared to what was effectively two lines in the Parliamentarian battalia. Only if the Royalist infantry were deployed according to the manuals and exactly as de Gomme shows, with a gap between the front line regiments equal to the width of the corresponding regiment in the second line, would Astley have been able to engage more than half of Skippon's front line. Moreover, even when deployed in this way, he would still not have been able to effectively engage the regiment on Skippon's right wing, explaining why Fairfax's were not hard pressed. Perhaps of even greater importance is the fact that each of the bodies of infantry in Astley's front line will have been outnumbered by almost two to one. Perhaps this is why in the first charge the Royalists were thrown back. When they advanced again they must have brought up the reserves of the second line into the gaps in the first line to support the attack, for surely only then will they have had sufficient strength to push back the New Model. They would then have been roughly equal in numbers to the Skippon's front line, excluding Fairfax's. This must explain how they were able, because they were more experienced and hardened troops, to break the New Model front line, especially when supported by Royalist horse. But Astley's left wing will have been dangerously exposed to an attack from Fairfax's regiment now that all his second line had been committed to the attack, especially as they were, as we shall see, quite safe from any cavalry attack from Langdale. To stop Fairfax's regiment from wheeling around on Lisle's left flank, Prince Rupert's regiment of foot from the reserves in the third line must surely have been brought forward to cover Lisle's left flank, though certainly not to engage Fairfax's regiment. These two moves, the commitment of the second line and the moving up of Rupert's bluecoats, if the interpretation is correct, would help to explain several of the key events of the next stage of the battle which are discussed below.

The collapse of the New Model's front line must have happened very rapidly, within the first half hour, because Skippon's regiment was in trouble well before Ireton's wing of horse had been defeated. But it was not just the two infantry regiments on the left which were pushed back, for according to Baillie the Royalist attack saw 'the Independent Colonels Pickering and Montacue flee like men', although a Parliamentarian newspaper, which seemingly reported Fiennes' account of the battle to the House of Commons, stated that only one regiment of foot had been routed.[141] It is usually assumed that all Rupert's cavalry charged away from the battlefield in pursuit of Ireton's men, but at least one Parliamentarian source suggests that some of Rupert's cavalry did turn on the New Model infantry. In Colonel Pickering's obituary, written in the following November, it is said that 'at the battell of Naseby when his men retreated our Wing being routed, which gave the Enemies horse leave to fall upon them yet did he keep to the body, choosing rather to die, than to leave the field.'[142] It is of course possible that the author of the obituary was wrongly informed and that the cavalry involved were just Howard's divisions which had supported Astley's foot from the beginning, but this description is supported by Bishop's letter which says that once Ireton's cavalry were routed the retreat was upon Skippon's and Hardress Waller's regiments.[143] Indeed, Okey's description suggests that the Earl of Northampton's regiment at least were still on the field once Rupert's brigade had broken through. Already hard pressed by Astley's more experienced infantry and apparently now attacked by Howard's if not other horse, Pickering's and Montague's, and perhaps also Waller's, were driven off in disorder behind the reserves. Skippon's regiment were now probably left completely exposed.

The total number of wounded in the New Model infantry was almost identical to that for the whole of the cavalry, being 258 compared to 265, and if the maximum strengths for the army are taken then the ratios overall are about 1 in 34 for the infantry and 1 in 25 for the cavalry. Until we have accurate figures as to the numbers of men in each regiment there cannot be a definitive analysis of this important data, but already it will be seen that the distribution of the casualties between regiments reinforces the evidence of the accounts of the battle in a remarkably detailed way.

Skippon's regiment was the most severely affected with 130 wounded, which represents just over half the total of infantry casualties! His regiment had not only been hard pressed by Astley's tercio, once Ireton's wing had been routed Skippon's regiment almost certainly had to deal with cavalry attack upon their exposed left flank. Skippon's suffered a casualty rate, excluding those killed, of 1 in 9 if the regiment was at full strength and more like 1 in 6 if our estimates of average strengths are correct. Moreover, the losses were not simply of common soldiers, they included senior officers, with Skippon himself wounded and the effective regimental commander, Lieutenant Colonel Francis, his lieutenant and his ensign all wounded and later dying of their injuries, as well as two other Ensigns, one sergeant and one corporal all wounded. This was a regiment which had been severely mauled. Interestingly the casualties are concentrated mainly in two companies, the colonel's and lieutenant colonel's, and even if one assumes that all the companies were at full strength then the differences in the size of each company still does not explain the discrepancy. The lieutenant colonel's own company suffered more casualties than the whole of Montague's regiment put together, with a ratio of about 1 in 4 and in the colonel's company a ratio of about 1 in 5. In each regiment within the body of pike and the two flanking bodies of musketeers the men are likely to have been organised according to the dignity of the companies, as the manuals indicate by the positioning of colours, the men of the colonel's company being in the files on the right flank and the men of the lieutenant colonel's company in the files on the left flank of the body.[144] The losses would therefore suggest that the regiment suffered attack on both flanks, with the companies whose troops were towards the centre of the body being far less heavily affected. The attack on their left flank was probably by Northampton's brigade of cavalry, while the attack on their right flank would be understandable if all three centre regiments of the front line had broken and left Skippon's regiment exposed. This is only a suggestion and a more detailed analysis taking account of the total numbers of men in each company, if adequate records survive in the Exchequer papers, and analyzed in relation to the evidence of other drill manuals may disprove the hypothesis. The one thing that is clear is that it cannot be mere chance that the casualties were so heavily concentrated in a few companies.

COMPANY	NUMBERS		CASUALTIES	RATIO	
	ideal	(estimated)	actual		
Colonel's	200	(167)	33	1 in 6	(1 in 5)
L.Colonel's	160	(133)	34	1 in 5	(1 in 4)
Major's	140	(116)	11	1 in 12	(1 in 10)
1st Captain	100	(83)	7	1 in 14	(1 in 12)
2nd Captain	100	(83)	4	1 in 25	(1 in 21)
3rd Captain	100	(83)	6	1 in 16	(1 in 14)
4th Captain	100	(83)	9	1 in 11	(1 in 9)
5th Captain	100	(83)	14	1 in 7	(1 in 6)
6th Captain	100	(83)	4	1 in 25	(1 in 21)
7th Captain	100	(83)	7	1 in 14	(1 in 12)

Table 1. Casualty rates, excluding those killed outright, in each company of Skippon's regiment.

The two regiments which were named as breaking in the fight, Pickering's and Montague's, also had high casualty rates, 40 and 33 respectively, giving ratios of about 1 in 25 and 1 in 33. The highest company casualty rate was 9 for the lieutenant colonel's company of both Pickering's and Montague's, but this was only a ratio of 1 in 18, compared to 1 in 4 for Lieutenant Colonel Francis' company in Skippon's regiment, and showing overall a far more even distribution between the companies. This would suggest that although these two regiments broke and fell back in disorder behind the reserves, they did not suffer anything like the same pressure as Skippon's. The confusing figure is the casualty rate for Sir Hardress Waller's regiment, which had just 14 wounded even though it was in the front line between Skippon's and Pickering's and had suffered, like Skippon's, as a result of Ireton's defeat. This is a casualty rate of 1 in 100, similar to that for Fairfax's regiment which is specifically said not to have been hard pressed. If the adjacent regiments suffered such high casualties, why did Hardress Waller's not suffer in the same way? The explanation may be that, as we have already suggested, his regiment was seriously under strength, perhaps with certain companies simply not present. This can be supported by the fact that there were nine casualties in the lieutenant colonel's company, identical to that for Pickering's and

Montague's, yet there are losses listed under only three other companies. If there were really 800 recruits waiting to join the regiment then at just 400 strong Hardress Waller's would have had a similar casualty ratio, at 1 in 28, to that seen in Pickering's and Montague's regiments.

When the centre regiments of the front line broke and fell back in disorder behind the reserves, how fierce was the fighting and how hard pressed were the reserves? Modern accounts of the battle suggest that they were under severe pressure and only Cromwell's cavalry saved the infantry. However, if one judges by the casualty figures they may not have been hard pressed at all. Hammond's had 17 casualties, a ratio of 1 in 57, Rainsborough's only 9, a ratio of 1 in 111. These figures appear similar to Fairfax's regiment, at 12 wounded, which presumably also played a key role in this second phase of the infantry battle. Pride's on the other hand had just 3 wounded, a ratio of 1 in 333. It is true that in the case of Pride's the situation is further complicated by the fact that part of the regiment had been detached as a rearguard, but the very low numbers of wounded in the regiment has its only comparison in the reserves of the right wing of cavalry, which did not apparently become engaged at all with Langdale's forces, suggesting that Pride's may not even have been committed at this stage of the battle.

The relative lack of musket balls on the slope down into Broadmoor might be consistent with the firing of just one volley as the two bodies closed and then, because the troops rapidly became engaged in hand to hand fighting, they will not have produced a dense distribution of musket balls. We cannot therefore expect the archaeological evidence to tell us how far the infantry units pushed first one way then the other. Whatever the exact detail of this first half hour of fighting, the Parliamentarian foot were soon driven back and driven so far that the Royalists captured six pieces of artillery.[145] The gunners themselves did not give up without a fight for Miles White, a gentleman of the Ordnance was killed, another died of his wounds and a third lost his hand.[146] How far back on the hill top the cannon were placed is unclear, though to have fired on the Royalist troops as they advanced onto Broadmoor the Parliamentarians must have been on or forward of the crest and so they could not have been any further back than the burial pit on Closter. If Streeter is correct in showing two artillery pieces deployed between each of the infantry regiments then the fact that six not twelve pieces were taken may assist in understanding how far back Skippon's infantry were pushed. Fairfax's regiment was not hard pressed and, according to Sprigge, they stood their ground while the cavalry on their right were certainly never forced to retreat, but 'almost all of the rest of the main Battail being overpressed, gave ground and went off in some disorder, falling behind the Reserves...'[147] We must therefore conclude that the whole battle line pivoted on Fairfax's regiment with Skippon's falling back the furthest, though not breaking, and the artillery pieces taken presumably being those between the four front line regiments on the left of the infantry.

It is unclear how far the broken regiments went in their flight from the main battle, but it seems very unlikely that the minor scatter of musket balls on the southern slope of Mill Hill and the presence of at least one burial pit on Mill Hill itself relates to infantry action. The space between the reserves and the rearguard was intended for broken regiments of the front line to reform, so that they could be brought back into the action as a new reserve. It is not impossible that further survey work there will eventually reveal that Skippon's men were pushed back as far as Mill Hill, but these bullets are perhaps more likely to relate to cavalry action during Rupert's pursuit of Ireton's men or even the attack on the baggage train if Smurthwaite's positioning of the train proves correct. There is however some difficulty with the archaeological evidence here due to the presence of a number of fields under permanent pasture and the relative lack of survey work on Fenny Hill. What is clear is that the distribution of musket balls falls off quite rapidly southward before this area of pasture and unsurveyed land is reached, probably indicating that the intense infantry fighting was restricted to the hill top called Closter.[148] This is exactly where local tradition, recorded from the early 18th century onwards, has always placed the most intense part of the action, John Bridges' 'plain on an eminence'. It is also here, on the left wing of the Parliamentarian infantry, that Fitzgerald excavated a burial pit in the mid 19th century, in the area in which one would expect the dead from the fiercest engagement, that involving Skippon's regiment, to be buried.

The dense distribution of musket balls on this hill top provides the clearest evidence for the next stage of infantry action and would appear to show how far back the Royalists pushed the New Model foot.[149] The distribution trends at an angle to the original battalia and is consistent with the battle line pivoting on Fairfax's regiment with Skippon's being pushed back the furthest. However Skippon was not apparently pushed off the hill top, for it must be remembered that the majority of the musket balls represent overshots. These are likely to be at most 1200ft from the point from which they were fired, while the enemy at which they were being fired would have been at well under 600ft, the maximum effective killing range of the musket, and probably well below 300ft, the effective killing range giving reasonable accuracy.[150] The implication of this archaeological evidence is that the two bodies stood back for a period of time facing and firing at each other, because in all nearly 400 musket balls have been recovered from the plateau during the survey. What percentage this represents of the total fired cannot even be guessed at, because of the numerous biases in the data which we have already considered, but it must be remembered that a single volley of all the musketeers in the front lines on both sides would produce something like 5000 bullets!

Once the centre regiments of the Parliamentarian front line infantry had broken and fallen back in disorder, Skippon led forward the reserves to hold the Royalist advance. It was essential for the reserves to be brought in immediately because the Royalist front line will themselves probably have been somewhat disordered as a result of breaking the New Model regiments and so were at their most vulnerable.

It was apparently at this point, as he brought up the second line of foot, that Skippon was wounded. A musket ball, said to have been fired accidentally by one of his own men while wheeling off, pierced right through his body despite his armour, because, as they assumed at the time, the shot was fired from such close range.[151] As a result Skippon 'was in a great measure disabled to perform the Duty of his Place that day, tho extreamly desirous to do it.'[152] But it was not the wounding of Skippon that had placed the Parliamentarian infantry in such a predicament, the problems had already developed, indeed it was from this point onwards that Parliamentarian fortunes began to revive. Fairfax wrote after the battle that Skippon:

> 'was shot through the side but notwithstanding he continued in the field with great resolution; And when I desired him to goe off the field He answered, he would not goe so long as a man would stand, still doing his Offices as a valiant and wise Commander.'[153]

Though Pickering and various other officers had apparently fallen in with the reserves to support them at this most dangerous moment, some of the officers must have fallen back with their broken regiments and eventually managed to rally them. Not surprisingly, given the great difficulty of reforming a broken regiment, it would be some time before those troops could be brought back into the action, but the important thing to note is that they had both the time and the freedom to rally their men, for nowhere is there any indication that the reserves were thrown back or retreated before they halted the Royalist advance.[154]

It was probably at this point, as the reserves were brought forward, that the majority of the firing took place. Though the musketeers during the war would often fire by 'salvee' - the massive volley fire used to such great effect by Gustavus Adolphus in the Thirty Years War, and which both armies had apparently used as they had clashed at the beginning of the battle - they would also in appropriate situations fire by ranks. Judging from the comment made about the soldier who wounded Skippon having accidentally fired as he 'wheeled off', the infantry reserves advanced using some form of firing by ranks. Barriffe says in his manual that:

> 'Advancing of two ranks to fire, ten paces before the Front, is most commonly used, when one or both Battells march against each other; the Musquettiers being led forth by two ranks together ten or twenty paces, before the front of the body; that so they may come neare enough to do certaine execution. A Serjeant from each flanke, leading up the two fore-most ranks, (according as they shall have order) the first ranke of each flanke is to present, and give fire, wheeling either all off to the right, or to the right and left....'.

That rank then rejoined the back of the regiment and the next rank marched on and fired as soon as the front rank was clear:

> 'and so successively, the rest of the ranks advancing, firing, and wheeling off ... This way they may give fire, once or oftner over, as the enemy doth advance... All this while ... if there be no fear of the enemies horse, then the Pikes may move shouldered and close forward to their Order; by that means saving their Pikes from being shattered and broken by the bullets that flie at randome.'

Once the bodies come close together then the pikes are lowered to the charge, pointing straight forward at the enemy, the men standing shoulder to shoulder, and 'so at length come to push of pike.' The musketeers would then advance no closer than the half files of the pikes, that is with their front rank level with the fourth rank of the pikes, and from there they could continue to fire in the same way as before and so 'may do execution with their shot and be out of danger of the Pikes.'[155] The number of musket balls concentrated on the hill top would suggest that the charge continued in this or a similar fashion for some considerable time. This was THE decisive moment of the English Civil War, because the New Model had been 'so overborn, one wing in a manner broken, and many of the Foot routed, and all in danger to be lost...' that if Skippon's reserves were broken then the battle would be lost.[156]

Once the Royalist cavalry attack had swept away Ireton's left wing of horse and the Royalist foot and horse had pushed Skippon's infantry back across the top of the hill, Okey says 'we gave ourselves up for lost men, but wee resolved every man to stand to the last....'[157] They will have been completely isolated down in the valley bottom, but they still posed a significant threat to the Royalists. It seems likely that the King had to commit some of his reserves to deal with the dragoons, otherwise Okey would have been free to mount up and charge into the rear or flank of the Royalist army, as he did with such good effect later in the day. Such a diversion of Royalist troops, perhaps the King's own regiment of foot, at this critical point in the battle may have had a significant effect on the King's ability to support Astley as the tables began to turn. Whatever exactly happened around the small close, Okey maintained his position without losing a single man and at the end of the day had in all only 3 wounded in his whole regiment.[158]

As the two armies had closed at the beginning of the battle Cromwell, who was in command of the right wing of cavalry, the usual place for the Lieutenant General of Horse, found himself facing Langdale's Northern horse with the Newark horse as their reserve.[159] Langdale was to suffer a great deal of the blame for the destruction of the Royalist army, but much of this criticism may be unwarranted and it would appear that his men, like Rupert, were to a degree made scapegoats for the defeat. For example, one Royalist account says that their left wing of horse were the last to engage, 'and had our left Wing but at this time done half so well as either the Foot or right Wing, we had got in few Minutes a glorious Victory.'[160] According to the author of the *Iter Carolinum* the army was 'utterly defeated through the cowardice of the horse, which fled to the walls of Leicester, 16 miles; never faced nor rallied till there.'[161] These criticisms are repeated by Whitelocke who says 'Langdale's men having been in some discontent before, did not in this Fight behave themselves as they used to doe in others, as their own party gave it out of them....'[162] Sir Philip Warwick was even more specific, explaining that in Langdale's brigade 'there were some trivial but pernicious, disputes, betwixt him and the Commander of the Newark - horse' which caused them to be routed so soon. The criticism does not however derive solely from Royalist accounts, for Rushworth, who had no reason to lie, added to his report of the battle written on the 15th June that 'Langdels Brigade ran away basely, and lost the King the day.'[163]

Symonds recorded in his diary that 'they kept their grownd on the top of the hill, and wee marched up to them through a bottome full off furse bushes....', but Cromwell did not receive the charge where he stood, his cavalry moved forward to meet the Royalists on the slope above Broadmoor.[164] Whalley, commanding the left two divisions of the cavalry, was the first to charge against two divisions of Langdale's horse. Despite later criticism, Langdale's horse are said to have 'made a very gallant resistance, and firing at a very close charge, they came to sword'.[165] We hear nothing of the role played by the 200 musketeers that de Gomme records as supporting Langdale's cavalry, but if they were indeed deployed in this way then they must have provided a damaging fire as Cromwell's men advanced. This type of deployment had been developed by Gustavus Adolphus as an effective method of checking an enemy charge of horse, because the musket was far more effective than the pistol against armour. That Langdale's men did indeed put up stiff resistance is confirmed by the casualty rates amongst the Parliamentarian horse. Whalley's regiment suffered more casualties than any other Parliamentarian cavalry regiment on the field, with 50 seriously wounded and yielding a casualty rate of 1 in 12. Given the number that were wounded in his regiment, and hence the sharpness of the fight, it is not surprising to hear that, though unharmed, Colonel Whalley 'had his coat cut in many peeces'.[166] In contrast, Colonel Sheffield's regiment, who were Whalley's reserve and were committed by Cromwell to support Whalley in this action, did not apparently have a particularly stiff fight, suffering only 8 casualties, a ratio of just 1 in 75.

Whalley routed the two divisions he faced, driving them back behind Rupert's bluecoats in the Royalist infantry reserve, where they fled for shelter and then rallied.[167] By this time those reserves must have marched across Broadmoor in support of the first two lines of Royalist infantry and so Langdale's men did not have to fall back very far. Whalley's divisions may have followed up the attack for Symonds claimed that the Parliamentarian forces had certain intelligence of the King's position because they left all others and charged up to his body of horse.[168] The rest of the front line of Cromwell's horse had their order disrupted as they advanced because they had to march over the rabbit warren before they could charge the Northern horse, while on the far right their freedom for action was also restricted by the presence of a dense area of furze. Despite these limitations they came up to and routed the remaining divisions of Langdale's horse, but again the casualty rates indicate a very severe engagement. Pye's regiment had 44 wounded, giving a casualty rate of 1 in 14 and yet only one of his divisions was in the front line. If the second division suffered as little as those of Sheffield's regiment, which seconded Whalley, then the losses suffered by Pye's first division may have been as high as 1 in 8. Cromwell's regiment suffered even lower casualties, half that of Whalley's, with just 24 seriously injured and a ratio of 1 in 25, but here again the issue may be more complicated. Like Ireton on the left wing, Cromwell undoubtedly held back with his own division in order to be able to oversee the action and to decide when and where to commit his reserves as the fight developed. If this was the case then a much higher proportion of the casualties may have been borne by his left hand division, but only if all the regiment's losses were in that division would they have matched the 1 in 12 suffered by Whalley. What is clear is that Cromwell's regiment were heavily committed and took substantial casualties whereas their reserves, even more so than those which supported Whalley, suffered hardly at all. Rossiter had only one and Fiennes only two casualties, ratios of 1 in 500 and 1 in 250. Indeed, it seems quite likely that it was only the reserves to Whalley's and Pye's that Cromwell actually needed to commit at this time. Fiennes, Rossiter and presumably Gourdon were to be given their opportunity later.

A newspaper report claimed that at the first shock Cromwell's cavalry gave such a thorough charge that the enemy on that side were never able to rally again, and 'that which made our Horse so terrible to them, was the thicknes of our reserves and their orderly and timely comming on, not one failing to come on in time.'[169] The Ironsides were 'like a torrent driving all before them...' and both Langdale's front line and his reserves were broken.[170] They put the Royalists 'into great confusion, not one body of the enemies horse which they charged, but they routed, and forced to flie beyond all their Foot, except some that were for a time sheltered by the Brigade of Foot before mentioned.'[171] That Cromwell himself was involved in the thick of the fighting at various times during the day is certain, though one may question the story, recounted in Banks' *Life of Cromwell*, that a cavalier commander fought with him, knocking his helmet from his head, Cromwell only being saved by his own men riding to his rescue.[172]

It is hardly surprising to find that Langdale was defeated. Not only was he outnumbered, with five Royalist bodies of horse against Cromwell's 'seven great Bodies', he was also fighting up slope and, most importantly, he was facing what was surely the most formidable force that ever took to a Civil

War battlefield. The front line of the right wing were almost wholly Cromwell's Ironsides. In the Eastern Association it had been a double regiment of 14 troops but now most of them were in the regiments of Whalley and of Fairfax, the latter though nominally the Lord General's regiment still remaining under Cromwell's personal command, with just one other division in the centre of the front line, a division of Pye's which was a regiment from Essex's army. The Ironsides were the most feared of all Parliamentarian cavalry, the crack troops of the New Model Army, well equipped, well trained and most importantly well disciplined and strongly committed. They were a force to be feared and in practically every battle they had fought had driven the enemy before them. It is not surprising that Cromwell should have chosen to commit these two regiments first. It was therefore the Ironsides that smashed the Northern horse, with Cromwell carrying 'all the Field before him; just as they did at Marston-Moore.' Langdale was simply outclassed, outnumbered and overwhelmed.[173] Slingsby, who was on the receiving end of this assault, recorded in his diary that Langdale's men were:

> 'out front'd and overpour'd by their assailants, after they were close joyn'd, they stood a pritty while, and neither seem'd to yeild, till more came up to their flanks and put ym to rout, and wheeling to our right took ym in disorder, and so presently made our whole horse run...'[174]

Another Royalist defended Langdale's attempt to hold Cromwell's attack, saying 'Yet I must needs say ours did as well as the Place and their Numbers would admit; but being outflanked and pressed back, they gave Ground and fled'[175] The losses suffered by Langdale's cavalry are also a good reflection of the fight that they put up, with one account of the capture of horses with saddles reporting that the losses fell 'most on Langdales men, who were most forward in the charge', while Sir Philip Monckton who rode with them is said to have had three horses killed under him that day.[176]

The first phase of the Royalist strategy had worked. Rupert had defeated the Parliamentarian left wing of horse and Astley's infantry had driven off much of the Parliamentarian front line infantry in disorder. There were now two key questions. Did the King have sufficient reserves and the necessary discipline to capitalise upon this initial success? Alternatively, could Skippon's infantry hold off the Royalist attack for long enough to enable Cromwell to defeat Langdale and then turn his reserves on the Royalist foot. It would not matter how strong Cromwell's cavalry were, they would be unable to continue the fight if they had no infantry support.

It was now that major problems began to arise for the Royalists, some very much of their own making. Rupert had broken Ireton's cavalry, but what he or the commander of his reserves failed to do was to ensure that all Ireton's men were driven from the field and then to deploy cavalry units to ensure that they could not be brought back into the fight. About a thousand of Ireton's men, mainly from two regiments, were chased from the field and Rupert did pursue these and presumably ensured that they could not return to the battlefield. But, in doing so he travelled far from the main battle at a crucial time and so when his cavalry were most needed, to exploit the success and then to stop a Parliamentarian recovery, they were nowhere to be seen. It is easy to criticise a cavalry commander from the comfort of one's study having never experienced the chaos of a real battle or the sheer momentum of a cavalry charge. Other commanders on the field that day had been in very similar situations to that in which Rupert now found himself. Fairfax, for example, had led the right wing cavalry charge at Marston Moor where he too had broken through, charging on in pursuit of the enemy only to discover when he returned to the field that the rest of his wing of horse had been defeated. At Naseby the problem was not simply Rupert's lack of self discipline and his recklessness, nor was it just that he had led from the front rather than holding back so that he could direct the action. A decisive factor may have been that Rupert had to commit all of his reserves of horse to defeat Ireton, but there was also the discipline of the New Model cavalry who, apart from the 1000 that had fled, remained on the field and were soon reformed and brought back into the action. Similarly, Astley had probably already used the reserves of foot in his second line and Howard's cavalry to break Skippon's front line regiments. In contrast, on the right wing Cromwell was able to keep several regiments in reserve which he did not have to commit in the attack on Langdale. Either now, or possibly later in the battle, he also did what Rupert should have done, he deployed four divisions, presumably Whalley's and Pye's regiments, to follow Langdale's retreating cavalry in good order, to face them and stop them being brought back into the fight.[177]

Whereas there is general agreement and relative clarity amongst most of the sources for the events up to this time, when it comes to the next stage of the battle they are much more confused. In a single brief statement Sprigge deals with the recovery of the Parliamentarian infantry: 'The Reserves advancing .... repelled the Enemy, forcing them to a disorderly retreat'.[178] Slingsby also devotes just a few words to the rest of the infantry battle, saying that with the flight of their left wing of horse the Royalist 'foot thus left nak'd were fourc'd to lay down their arms.'[179] In these brief phrases lie the key to the battle, for this was the turning point, but how was a battle 'very doubtful' transformed into such a dramatic victory? In developing the following interpretation it has been necessary to give greater weight to Rushworth's letter, which seems to be the official account provided to Parliament by Fairfax, in place of Sprigge's account as on several key points the two seem to conflict. It may be that some of the detail in the following pages, particularly the sequence of the events, could be reconstructed in a different way, but there can be little doubt that a fundamental reinterpretation similar to that presented here is essential, given the archaeological evidence that is now available.

After the battle Royalist prisoners are supposed to have said that but for Cromwell's horse the Parliamentarians would have lost the day.[180] Of this there can be no doubt. However, if it was the Royalist strategy to throw their greatest strength into the attack on their right, both horse and foot, then Cromwell was simply responding to that strategy once he had dealt with the Royalist threat on his side of the field. Rupert had probably asked far too much of Langdale while giving him too few resources. After all, with nearly 2400 men, Whalley's, Pye's, Cromwell's and Sheffield's regiments together were as strong as Langdale's whole wing. Once Langdale was thrown back, Cromwell's reserves could wheel to the left against the Royalist infantry.[181]

The various accounts conflict as to the exact role played by Fairfax at this time, some placing him with Skippon in command of the foot while others suggest he was with the right wing of cavalry, but these accounts cannot always be trusted, one for example saying that Cromwell commanded the left wing and Fairfax the right! Perhaps far closer to the truth is the following description:

> 'The general as all the army observe was raised to a pitch as much above us as his place was he never stood still but in the midst between the two armies before and whilst they were charging, moving from body to body giving orders in the midst of dangers.'[182]

What is not in doubt is his involvement at the heart of the fighting, indeed he is said to have lost his headpiece while fighting on the right wing.[183] It would not therefore be unreasonable to assume that it was Fairfax who, having recognised the problem on the left and in the centre, rode across to the right wing to get Cromwell to dispatch his reserves against the infantry. Cromwell after all will not have been able to see how the battle had progressed on the left simply because it is impossible to see that part of the field from either Lodge Hill or from down on Broadmoor. These reserves, which were in the second and third line and so had not yet been engaged with the enemy, included Fiennes' regiment and Rossiter's, who it is said 'charged where the Generall was'.[184] Fairfax's lifeguard under Captain D'Oyley also moved against the Royalist foot.[185] Just as at Marston Moor, the battle was being turned around by Cromwell's cavalry, while at the same time those of Ireton's cavalry who remained in the field were rallied by their officers.[186]

> 'Then the right wing of our Horse (wherein the Generall was in person) charged in the Flanke of the blew regiment of the Enemies Foot, who stood to it, till the last man, abundance of them slaine, and all the rest surrounded, wounded, and taken..'[187]

The attack seems to have been on the third rather than second line of reserves. This may be because Astley had already committed all his second line to the main attack, moving Rupert's foot across to cover Fairfax's regiment. In this situation the destruction of Rupert's bluecoats would threaten the whole Royalist infantry because it would leave them without a reserve. This episode however highlights the problem of conflicting evidence, for another source, if it refers to Rupert's regiment, suggests they were destroyed by infantry:

> 'The Blue regiment of the Kings stood to it very stoutly, and stir'd not, like a wall of brasse, though encompassed by our Forces, so that our men were forced to knock them down with the But end of their Musquets: It is conceived that a great part of them were Irish, and chose rather to die in the field than be hanged.'[188]

Elton's manual shows how an infantry regiment might hope to withstand such a ferocious attack on all sides, the troops being deployed in a ring for 'it is one of the most serviceable Figures that can be made, to secure the Souldier from danger against the furious charge of horse in Campania, the accomplishing or making of it up, being easily and suddainly performed....'[189] The pikes will not however have been charged to foot, the typical posture shown in most of the manuals, because Elton, who is probably our best guide to actual practice during the English Civil War, says this was 'of little use in a desperate charge' and that he 'never met with any souldier that hath been abroad upon any service that ever saw the charging of pikes at the foot.' Instead he advises the pikemen to close to their closest order, porting their pikes and 'locking themselves one within another' to create an impenetrable wall of pike points. One can imagine the bluecoats in their ring, the pikes at closest order to receive the attacking horse. Protected from the cavalry onslaught the musketeers beneath the shafts of the pikes could fire volley after volley into the attackers, while in the centre of the ring were the colours, each held up defiantly by the ensigns. The ensign's was without doubt the most dangerous duty, as Fairfax by his own hand would soon demonstrate, for the colours were both a sign of strength for the defenders, who were to protect them with their life, and for the attackers a great prize to be gained. According to Vernon:

> 'it will be very neccessary for the Cavalry to have some pretty stratageme, in the charging of the Foote: or else it will be very difficult routing of the foot.... you are to divide your Troop or parties into three squadrons, ... who are to charge in ful career all at one instant upon the Front Reer and Flank of the Foot.'[190]

It was possibly at this point that Fairfax again took a major hand in the thick of the fighting, once more following the instructions of the manuals to the letter, in an episode recounted by Whitelocke.[191]

> 'The general had his helmet beat off, and riding in the field bareheaded up and down from one part of his army to another, to see how they stood, and what advantage might be gained, and coming up to his own lifeguard commanded by Colonel Charles D'Oyley, he was told by him that he exposed himself to too

much danger, and the whole army there by, riding bareheaded in the fields, and so many bullets flying about him, and D'Oyley offered his general his helmet, but he refused it, saying, "It is well enough, Charles;" and seeing a body of the King's foot stand, and not at all broken, he asked D'Oyley if he had charged that body, who answered, that he had twice charged them, but could not break them. With that, Fairfax bid him to charge them once again in the front, and that he would take a commanded party, and charge them in the rear at the same time, and they might meet together in the middle; and bade him, when Fairfax gave the sign, to begin the charge. D'Oyley pursued his general's orders; and both together charging that body put them into a confusion, and broke them; and Fairfax and D'Oyley met again in the middle of them, where Fairfax killed the ensign, and one of D'Oyley's troopers took the colours, bragging of the service he had done in killing the ensign and taking the chief colours. D'Oyley chid the trooper for his boasting and lying, telling him how many witnesses there were who saw the general do it with his own hand; but the general himself bade D'Oyley to let the trooper alone, and said to him, 'I have honour enough, let him take that to himself.'[192]

This was not propaganda. Fairfax's lifeguard were certainly in the thick of the action, for they had at least three men seriously wounded, of which one died, a significant number for a single troop of horse. Moreover, knowing Fairfax's previous experience in the war, this was the sort of action that one would have expected of him for, as so many times before in Yorkshire and elsewhere, 'Our Generall was in some danger, hazarding his own person, but blessed to God came off well.'[193] Indeed, at Naseby he had so far shown great restraint in order that he could properly fulfil his role as commander of the army, a role which on the Royalist side Rupert was unwilling or, more likely, not allowed to fulfil. Under this sustained attack and without the support of Rupert's or Langdale's cavalry, the Royalist's last reserve of infantry could not hope to maintain the fight. It may also have been now, rather than later, that Fiennes attacked the King's regiment of foot. The 'stout old souldiers ....stood like a wall of brasse to receive his charge' but eventually he broke the regiment, taking the King's own and 14 other colours.[194]

Less than an hour before, the New Model had been staring defeat in the face, as comrades fell or fled and as the Royalists threw everything into the attack. Rupert had applied a well thought out strategy, playing upon his greatest strengths. On other battlefields during the war he had been used to meeting forces superior in number and defeating them through the audacity of his tactics, the fierceness of his attack or by sheer courage and determination, but at Naseby, just as at Marston Moor nearly a year before, Rupert had met his match. Yet as the Royalist army slid from the brink of apparent victory towards the depths of defeat Rupert was not with the army. The King himself had the task of recovering the situation as best he could, in the hope that Rupert's cavalry would return to their aid before all was lost. The Parliamentarian accounts from the battlefield give the Royalist infantry their due, saying they 'did as gallantly, as ever men on earth could doe', surprising their opponents who admitted that before the battle it was the Royalist infantry that they least valued.[195] 'The Kings main battle fought bravely, maintaining their ground for a considerable time; but were at last overpowered with numbers, and forced to retreat....'[196] Having committed his second line reserves in order to break Skippon's front line and with the loss of their third line reserve, Astley had nothing left to throw into the fight to hold Skippon's counter attack. This was the turning point of the battle and of the war, for on the hill top called Closter, in Naseby field, the Royalist tide was halted and thrown back. What happened to the King's army over the next hour would be repeated for his whole cause over the following year.

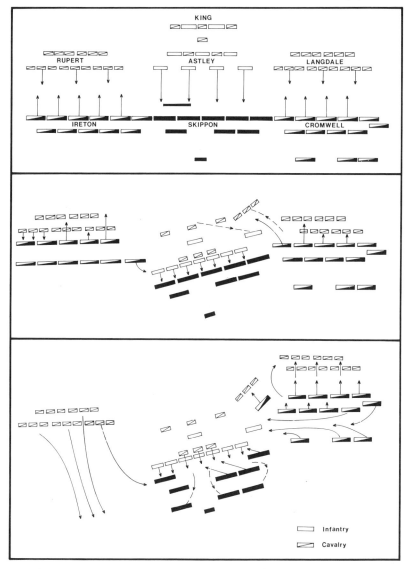

Fig.60. The early phases of the battle. Frontages here are as calculated from estimated troop numbers.

The early and crucial phases of the battle can now be summarised, suggesting the Royalist tactics, how they may have been countered and why they probably failed. They had committed the greatest strength of their horse, at least in experience and possibly also in numbers, to the right wing under Rupert, exploiting his ability to rapidly destroy the enemy with his devastating cavalry charge, which had succeeded in various battles from Edgehill onwards. The Royalist tactics may have been clear to Fairfax even before the battle began. Why else would he have deployed the forlorn hope on the far left of the infantry frontage unless it was to break up the advance of the strongest of the Royalist infantry? The New Model commanders could after all, as every witness agrees, see exactly how the Royalist army was being deployed. What did they see as Rupert and Astley formed their battalia on Dust Hill? Astley's tercio was far stronger than all the others, for not only did it comprise three bodies, Astley had brought the largest number of infantry to the army in May, some 3300 foot. This is not to suggest that they were all in his tercio but it might indicate that his was the strongest wing. One must also ask whether Rupert packed his right wing with extra bodies of horse. Rushworth was certain in his letter that Rupert had a considerable advantage in numbers of cavalry.[197] Another factor may have been that Fairfax saw the Royalists were bringing in their right wing to attack first and that the momentum of this attack had to be countered. The Parliamentarian strategy was clearly quite the opposite to Rupert's, as can be seen from Cromwell's earlier proposal that the army withdraw to 'yonder hill' in order to draw the Royalist army on to attack them. As the stronger army, they did not want to deter the weaker Royalist army from fighting.

The Parliamentarian infantry was so strong, and hence had so wide a frontage, that Astley had to commit his second line reserves to ensure the success of the second charge, driven on or supported by Howard's horse. The King's reserves of foot may perhaps have been committed to deal with Okey, while Rupert's bluecoats from the same third line reserves may have been moved forward and to the left to cover Lisle's brigade from flank attack by Fairfax's regiment of foot, who were not facing any infantry regiment. With the majority of their infantry committed to the attack Astley began to push back Skippon's front line on its left wing, the right being anchored by Fairfax's regiment. Ireton had had initial success against Rupert, saw the deteriorating situation on his right and tried to support Skippon's infantry by attacking the flank of the Duke of York's regiment on Astley's right wing. The situation may well have been already critical. But Ireton's right hand regiments now broke under Rupert's second attack leaving just Butler's and his reserve on the field to face part of the Earl of Northampton's brigade which were Rupert's reserve. Skippon's regiment now probably came under flank attack by Northampton's cavalry and fell back even further, while the centre regiments, Pickering's and Montague's, probably under attack from Howard's horse as well as the foot, broke and ran. Skippon's regiment were now a key to the infantry battle, for they were attacked on both flanks but apparently held. Fairfax's regiment now presumably moved in to hold Lisle's while Skippon's held the Duke of York's regiment. With both ends of the Parliamentarian front line still anchored, the Royalists could not afford to push through in the centre in pursuit of the broken regiments otherwise they would totally disorder their own line. This gave Skippon the chance to bring on the reserves, marching forward firing by ranks with Hammond's and Rainsborough's, to fill the gap where the front line had broken. Pride's were retained as a reserve, and this must explain their very low casualty rate. Behind this new front line the broken regiments had the opportunity to regroup in safety. Meanwhile, although Rupert had driven off about a thousand of Ireton's wing of horse the rest were now presumably brought back into the action to counter any of Northampton's remaining troops, while on the right, Fairfax himself led in Cromwell's third line reserves of horse to destroy Rupert's bluecoats, perhaps the only remaining Royalist reserve of foot. Once this reserve was gone and now facing a complete battle line of mainly fresh Parliamentarian infantry, the Royalist army began to fall back in a disorderly retreat.

It is now that the archaeological evidence comes dramatically to the fore, demanding a comprehensive review of all the historical sources for the events of the final hour of the battle. This analysis, which combines historical with archaeological and topographical evidence, has led to a complete reinterpretation of the last stages of the battle and a redefinition of the battlefield. According to Rushworth, once the Royalists had lost their best infantry their remaining forces retreated. The various accounts differ as to whether this decisive action took half an hour or even longer, for according to one account the whole of Fairfax's army having been rallied 'with one hot charge did attack then for almost an hour driving the King's men from their ordnance.' Several apparently reliable Parliamentarian accounts, written on the day itself or soon after, agree that they 'charged the Enemy both Horse and Foot through and through; and beat them quite out of the Field before them.'[198] Another account says the Royalist 'Horse and Foot gave backe, wee advanced on after them in order, our Horse flanking our Foot...'[199] The New Model was now an army which had recovered its composure and confidence and would fulfil the greatest expectations of its creators. The Royalists had despised and taunted them, but now in response a Parliamentarian regiment 'tooke one Colours of Horse, with a paire of horns, Come Cuckolds, was the Motto; as soon as our men had it in possession, they held the Hornes and Motto towards the Enemy, and so charged them.'[200] That the majority of the foot were thus driven out of the field is crucial to the understanding of the events that followed for, as we shall see, when the sources say 'field' they probably do mean the open field of Naseby.

This was a disorderly retreat, though not a total rout. The scatter of musket balls, in small groups of between ten and thirty, both on the northern slope of

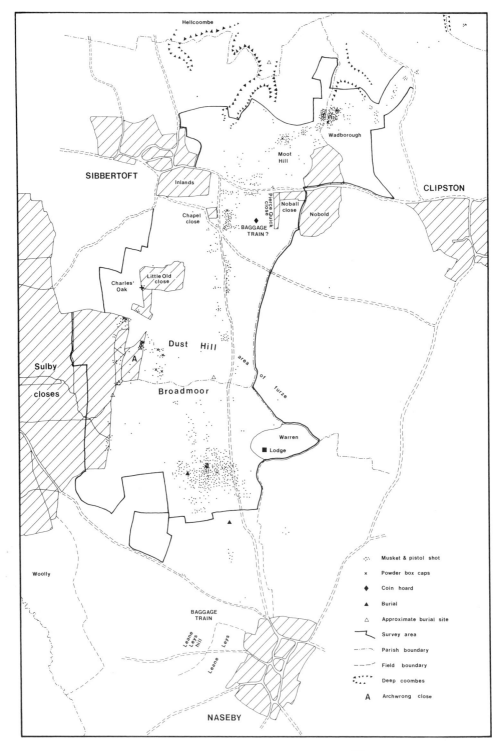

Fig.61. The distribution of finds from the whole battlefield.[201]

Closter and in Broadmoor (if these were not the result of the original action of the forlorn hope) and then across Sibbertoft field on either side of the road, might suggest a fighting retreat.[202] To move rapidly back across the standing corn, or what was left of it, in Sibbertoft Field, the troops seem to have followed close by the road, perhaps taking what cover they could from the furze in the common on the east side of the road. Perhaps the gaps in the distribution of musket balls to east and west of the road reflect the presence of cavalry with the retreating infantry because several of the accounts do say that both horse and foot retreated. The clusters of musket balls might indicate that bodies of infantry which still retained their order stood and fired at the advancing New Model troops, then falling back behind another body which itself provided covering fire and so forth. This cannot have been a retreat covered by the third line Royalist reserves, if Rushworth is correct, because at least the bluecoats had been destroyed before the retreat took place. It might have been the King's regiment that supported the retreat, if Fiennes destruction of them did not occur until later. This may however be reading too much into the distribution of artefact. Though the exact method of retreat is not clear, the Royalist infantry and what cavalry still remained with them fell back more than a mile across the Sibbertoft plateau behind Dust Hill. Okey, who for more than an hour had been isolated down on Broadmoor holding off the Royalist attempts to dislodge him, saw the New Model's right wing of horse and the foot push back the enemy. With the Royalists in retreat he was now able to leave the cover of the small close and at last his dragoons could rejoin the main battle. As Okey himself reports, having seen Cromwell drive the enemy before him, he ordered his men to mount up and to charge the enemy foot. [203]

Most of the accounts now dispose of the Royalist foot in a single sentence, as the New Model drove the enemy from their artillery and their train and finally destroyed Astley's infantry.[204] To judge from the archaeological evidence, these few words encompass another fierce fight, for about 130 musket balls have been recovered from the area between Sibbertoft village and Nobold closes. As the infantry retreated north they must have approached the site occupied by the baggage train and, as they fell back, the train probably began to flee. Its position may be signified by the gap in the distribution of musket balls adjacent to Pierce's Quick Close, for it is here that a hoard of silver coins was found in 1991. Another hoard, including some gold coins of James I & Charles I, was also found at some time before 1866 in an unidentified field in Sibbertoft parish.[205] There are also a few coins scattered to the north and north east of this location which might be indicative of other losses during the battle, either by soldiers or from the fleeing waggons, but it is difficult to confirm this. As one Royalist account reports:

'ye enemy in pursuit of us gain'd bag and baggage all we had, wch they found to be a very rich pillage: and tho' our Waggons were left at a good distance yet could not be carry'd off, but some were taken, and some overthrown and monys shaken out, wch made our soulgiers to venture their lives once more, wch was but to stay and take it up.'[206]

Perhaps the questions will be resolved by more systematic survey to see how genuine this loose concentration of coins really is, and whether there are other artefacts associated with them which might indicate the destruction of the train.

Fig.62. A hoard of 44 silver coins found at Sibbertoft in 1991. The coins range in date from Elizabeth I to Charles I, with several minted around May 1644 and the latest coin minted between May 1644 and May 1645, these latest coins showing no signs of wear. It may have been buried by someone with the baggage train, but if the field was under corn as the account from Sibbertoft would suggest, then it would not be surprising if a purse was lost in the chaos of the flight of Royalist troops, or perhaps during the plundering of the baggage train which may have been sited here. The face value of the hoard is £2/3/6d, that is the equivalent of 65 days pay for a foot soldier. As Rushworth reported, 'one great incouragement to the common souldiers to fall on, was the rich Plunder the enemy had (their purses also being fully of Money, the Plunder of poore Leicestershire, God turned to be one meanes of their ruine, and indeed our souldiers got plenty...'[207]

If the gap in the distribution of musket balls does not mark the position of the baggage train then it may be the initial position to which Langdale's horse retreated alongside their foot. Whichever is the case, the Royalists may briefly have attempted to hold a line between the Chapel Close and Pierce's Quick

Close, because there is a much denser concentration of musket balls in this area, including a small group of bullets of an unusually large bore.[208] Could this perhaps represent action by a particular unit defending the train? Though seriously wounded, Skippon still led up the Parliamentarian infantry to the second charge and, in Rushworth's words, the New Model 'after one charge more, became Masters of all their Infantry, and took about three thousand prisoners', but as we have seen from the earlier action, a single 'charge' could last for half an hour or more.[209] That this final infantry action is described as a charge would suggest similar action to that in which Skippon had earlier used his reserves to halt the original Royalist advance in Naseby field. The position near Chapel Close was not held, for the musket ball distribution continues on northward. So far the retreat had been funnelled northward by the old enclosures on the east and west, but any further north beyond the Sibbertoft-Clipston road and the land falls away steeply down towards one of the many coombs which provide a dramatic edge to the Sibbertoft plateau. Their retreat therefore now swung north eastward, between Nobold enclosures and the scarp, but here some of the troops, perhaps both horse and foot, seem to have broken and run. There is a slight scatter of musket balls running down the slopes at the north end of Sibbertoft parish, towards the deep coombs by Castle Yard. These may represent firing upon fleeing men, for it is said that some were 'slaine in the fields running away'.[210] A few may have escaped this way, but there is a tradition that in their flight some Royalists were 'overtaken in a deep ravine near Sibbertoft, called Hellcoombe, and there sold their lives dearly.'[211] Hellcoombe is one of those remarkable deep valleys north of Sibbertoft village and in an odd position in relation to the rest of the action to have been chosen for a spurious local tradition.[212] It was also reported in the 19th century that graves had been found close to Castle Yard, in what was by then known as Marston Woods, though in 1645 this was probably open ground.[213] It may have been some of these men, pursued by parties of New Model troops, that finally made their way out into the Welland valley to Marston Trussell.

The majority of the troops probably remained with the main body as the retreat continued, because the scatter runs across Moot Hill, exactly where the tradition recorded in 1719 says the King's standard was raised.[214] This story makes very little sense in terms of the early stages of the battle, for all that action took place nearly two miles to the south, but the tradition could well relate to this final stage of the battle. Did the King attempt once more to rally his troops here? If so, he failed and they were pushed back yet again towards their last stand, the location of which seems to be pinpointed very clearly by the archaeological evidence. On a small hill, called Wadborough, on the north west side of Clipston parish is a concentration of musket balls as intense, though nowhere near as extensive, as that seen on Closter in Naseby where the decisive stages of the infantry action had been fought. Over 130 musket balls have been recovered on Wadborough, in addition to the scatter of more than 50 on the adjacent Moot Hill. The intense concentration of musket balls on Wadborough itself must surely represent the last stand of the old infantry. As the horse and foot stood there, the last point before the land began to fall down into yet another valley, perhaps several thousand foot and some of Langdale's and Northampton's remaining horse tried to hold the Parliamentarian advance. As throughout the battle, the King had probably fallen back with the final reserve of horse, his lifeguard, behind the main battle and now he must have been some distance back from the main action.

Was it at this very moment, as the infantry most needed cavalry support, that the famous episode involving Lord Carnwath occurred? The King knew that if they were left unprotected by cavalry then Astley's remaining regiments would be destroyed, yet Langdale's horse were once more being driven back chased by four divisions of Cromwell's horse, while the rest charged the Royalist foot. Clarendon records that:

'The King's reserves of horse - which was his own guards, with himself in the head of them - were even ready to charge the enemy horse who followed those of the left wing, when on a sudden, such a panic fear seized upon them that they all ran near a quarter of a mile without stopping. This happened upon an extraordinary accident, which hath seldom fallen out, and might well disturb and disorder very resolute troops, as these were the best horse in the army. The King....was even upon the point of charging the enemy, in the head of his guards, when the Earl of Carnwath, who rode next to him - a man never suspected for infidelity, nor one from whom the King would have received counsel in such a case - on a sudden laid his hand on the bridle of the King's horse, and swearing two or three full mouthed Scots' oaths (for of that nation he was) said, "Will you go upon your death in an instant?" and, before his majesty understood what he would have, turned his horse round. Upon this a word ran through the troops that they should march to the right hand; which was away both from charging the enemy, or assisting their own men. Upon this they all turned their horses and rode upon the spur, as if they were every man to shift for himself. It is very true that, upon the more soldierly word Stand, which was sent to run after them, many of them returned to the King; though the former unlucky word carried more from him.'[215]

This event seems to be encompassed in Rushworth's typically economical statement that, as the Royalist foot were being finished off, 'the Enemies Horse ran a pace.'[216] However, those horse that came back to the King did make a charge 'wherein some of them fell' and several accounts do suggest that the King himself led the attack, but the attempt failed and the King seems to have been driven back once more.[217]

It was now that Rupert's cavalry finally returned to the battle, but where had he been over the last crucial hour? When he had broken through the Parliamentarian left wing Rupert had ridden on in pursuit of about a thousand of Ireton's cavalry who fled the field. That Rupert had to maintain the pursuit was obvious. He had to be sure that, once broken, the Parliamentarians did not regroup and re-enter the battle. He achieved this but at what cost? Where Cromwell dispatched just four divisions to a similar task and brought the rest of his troops back into the action, Rupert seems to have taken a large part of his wing of cavalry to follow the broken regiments. Rupert eventually turned back from the pursuit when he reached Naseby village, but this will have taken him at least a mile and a half from the battlefield. Then, instead of returning immediately, he turned aside to summon the Parliamentarian train. If the Royalist army was really as seriously outnumbered as all modern accounts would have us believe, then why did Rupert waste vital time in action which could in no way influence the outcome of the battle? When he had left the field the New Model infantry had been reeling from the combined assault of Astley's infantry and various bodies of horse, while most of Ireton's remaining cavalry were in total disorder. Did Rupert believe that his strategy had succeeded? Did he attack the train with the intention of stopping Fairfax's army from rapid pursuit over the following days, as he had done to the Earl of Essex the day before Edgehill, or was this simply a lack of self discipline? Rushworth, who was with the train, must have seen the event at first hand for he records the initial encounter in some detail:

> 'A party of theirs that broke through the left wing of Horse, came quite behind the rear to our traine, the Leader of them being a person somewhat in habit like the Generall, in a red Mountero, as the generall had, he came as a friend; our Commander of the gaurd of the traine went with his hat in his hande, and asked him how the day went, thinking it had been the Generall; the Cavalier whom we since heard was Rupert, asked him and the rest, if they would have quarter, they cryed no, Gave fire and instantly beat them off.'[218]

This may not however have been such a brief and relatively innocuous encounter as Rushworth makes it appear. We have seen how elsewhere in the battle he has dismissed quite significant action in a few words and there is various evidence that would suggest this was in fact quite a fierce engagement. It is not simply the loss of the Great Houghton cart and team at Naseby fight, there were at least nine seriously wounded men who were probably with the baggage train during the battle. Of these it might be argued that the two Commissaries, Captain Potter, who was 'sore wounded in diverse places' and Captain Cooke, both of whom later died of their wounds, may have been on the field, rather than with the train.[219] There can be no such doubt about some of the others who were seriously wounded:

> 'William Wells belonging to the traine.... John Skidmore provost marshall to ye traine.... Isiah Clothey master of ye Mynors..... Thomas Benton carpenter to the carriages... Jesper Williams sevant to Lt.Norman.... Jeremiah Williams wagginman... Thomas Britton belonging to ye Carriages...'[220]

Sprigge also lists Master Robert Wolsey, Assistant to Quartermaster General of Foot, as being wounded at Naseby. To have inflicted such casualties, Rupert's cavalry must surely have made a sustained attack and perhaps even have broken in amongst some of the waggons, but the rearguard and the Firelocks that guarded the train 'fired with admirable courage on the Princes horse'.[221] It must be asked how it was that the relatively small number of troops defending the train, no more than 130 firelocks and perhaps just three or four hundred commanded musketeers, could have driven off nearly 2000 enemy horse, while Rushworth's description certainly does not give the impression that a vast body of cavalry were with Rupert, describing them as just 'a party of theirs'. This is further evidence that Rupert did not have all the cavalry of his right wing with him.

Fig.63. The Parliamentarian baggage train as depicted by Streeter.

It must have taken Rupert some time to rally his cavalry before he attacked the train, then to regroup them again after that engagement and so it is not perhaps surprising that as much as an hour had passed before Rupert finally returned to the main action. As Whitelocke says, Rupert's 'long stay so far from the Main Body was no small prejudice to the King's Army.'[222] Contrary to the impression given by various accounts, including Sprigge, what Rupert cannot have known is how badly the Royalist cause had deteriorated. From the valley to the south of Mill Hill, where the Parliamentarian baggage train was located, it is impossible to see the hill top of Closter, let alone Dust Hill or beyond. Also contrary to most later commentaries on the battle, Rupert did manage to rally and reform his cavalry. As he finally rode back across Mill Hill and then through the position where the Parliamentarian army had formed up in battalia earlier in the day he will have found the battle had moved on a long way into the distance. To his left there must have been a scatter of bodies where the decisive action had been fought and there may even have been some of Skippon's infantry shepherding Royalist prisoners, if they had not all moved forward with the action. But Rupert was not free to act. Fairfax and Cromwell were well aware that there was a large body of cavalry away to the south which could at any moment reappear to charge the army from the rear, and so they had deployed some of their own cavalry to meet this threat. Certainly when Rupert reached the Royalist infantry 'with a good Body of Horse from the right Wing...', even though he found the infantry 'in such a general distresse...' he could do nothing for them. His horse were not in order and they were being pursued by detachments of cavalry from Ireton's, Rich's, Fleetwood's, Vermuyden's and Butler's horse, the very regiments Rupert had defeated at the beginning of the battle.[223] According to Belasyse, Rupert 'could not retreat in order to our other bodies, being broken in the retreat, and after charged by the same body of their horse which had before beaten our left wing...'[224] So, passing by the infantry and 'instead of attempting anything in the rescue of them ...... he made up further, untill he came to the ground where the King was rallying the broken horse of his Left wing, and there joined with them, and made a stand.'[225]

Cromwell's right wing, having beaten Langdale beyond the foot 'about a quarter of a mile beyond the place where the battail was fought', had not pursued the advantage and had simply sent a body of horse to stop them returning to the aid of the foot.[226] According to Slingsby:

'Ye enemy did not pursue, wch gave time to us to stop, and really our men, ye prince on ye one hand, and Sr. Marmaduke Langdale on ye other, (ye King yet being upon ye place) having got together as many as they could, made an offer of a [second] charge....'[227]

The Royalists had put themselves in good order again, as best they could given the shortness of time and the fact that Fairfax was pressing close upon them.[228] Apart from the detachments which had been sent forward to stop the Royalist horse from re-engaging, the rest of the army was busy dealing with the remaining Royalist infantry and it was only when the infantry action was assured that Fairfax then brought up the rest of the Parliamentarian horse to face the King. For a short space of time the two sides stood within Carbine shot, no more than 200 yards apart, and faced each other in silence.[229] This was not simply out of exhaustion at the previous hours of battle, for Rushworth makes clear, 'our Horse, though one would have beaten ten, (such a feare was the Enemy possessed with all) would not pursue in heate but take the Foot to flancke them...'[230] The New Model infantry were at least a quarter of a mile behind the horse, probably around Wadborough hill dealing with Astley's infantry which had now all surrendered, and so Fairfax called up those regiments of the Parliamentarian foot that had been disordered in the first part of the battle but which had now been rallied and presumably had followed up as the new reserve in Skippon's advance. They marched rapidly forward and took up their position between the cavalry, who were already drawn up in two wings. In this way Fairfax was able to create a completely new battalia at the end of the battle to face the remaining Royalist horse. According to a witness at Charles' trial, the King was there in back, breast and helmet, with sword drawn trying to rally his troops.[231] Surrounded by his courtiers, the Duke of Richmond, Lord Lichfield, Earl of Lindsay, George Digby, Lord Belasyse, the Earl of Carnwath and others, Charles called upon his cavalry to make one final charge, as though that could somehow recover the day.[232]

Wogan implies that the place in which the King made his last stand was 'the top of the hill towards Harborough'. There is another hill further east of Wadborough called Mill Hill, along which the modern road runs towards Marston Trussell and it might be here, in quite a commanding position that the King stood for the last time with his horse. This area is however the least well surveyed of any part of the battlefield, and it is uncertain whether the scatter of musket balls and the small but significant number of pistol shot seen in the valley below is a representative distribution or if there are other concentrations to be found. We must await the results of further survey work before answering this question. What seems clear is that a retreat continued towards East Farndon, still following what seems to have been the line of the army's approach to the field several hours before. It may be that the cavalry fled even further north east, up to the position in East Farndon field where the Royalist army had first formed their battalia early that morning, which would certainly be in accord with Wogan's statement about the hill towards Harborough. Given the increasing proportion of pistol shot amongst the finds from Moot Hill onwards it would certainly appear that the Royalist troopers had followed Vernon's advice to:

> 'alwaies reserve one of thy Pistols readie charged, primed, spand and cocked in thy houlster, so that if thou shouldst be forced to retreat, and thine Enemie pursue thee, though maist be able to reward him with that Messenger in thy Houlster...'[233]

It may not prove possible to identify with any certainty the hill on which the cavalry made their last stand, because the action was brief and apparently just involved dragoon firing, so the number of artefacts may be minimal. Okey's dragoons began the attack before the Royalists could attempt another charge and neither the King's efforts 'nor the endeavours of those that waited on him could ever prevail with those shattered and frightened troops either to give or stand one charge more.'[234] In the last throws of Naseby fight the King was trying to do the impossible. He should have recognised that all was lost and that his and Rupert's duty was to organise a rearguard action to cover their retreat to enable as many as possible of his cavalry to escape but, as was later the case with the war as a whole, Charles could not accept the inevitable and asked more than he should of his supporters even though they faced certain defeat. So, as Slingsby says, the Royalist horse 'could not abide it; they being horse and foot in good order, and we but a few horse only, and those mightily discourag'd; yt so we were immediately made to run...'[235] Both the front regiments and their reserves turned and fled, running clear away from the battlefield. This was now a total rout, 'and happy was he that was best mounted...'[236]

In all the battle had taken about three hours but in the last half hour 'it was sharpe and fell very heavy upon the enemy'.[237] The accounts suggest it was about noon or slightly later by the time the battle was over and:

> 'by one of the clocke in the afternoone there was not a Horse or man of the Kings Army to be seene in Northamptonshire but the prisoners, the Horse being in haste gone towards Leicester, and our Foot were gathering the pillage while our Horse followed the flying Enemy.' [238]

If it was just the archaeological evidence that suggested the action extended right across Sibbertoft field and into Clipston, then there might be considerable doubt about the interpretation presented here. It might for example be argued that a major concentration of musket balls could represent simply the overturning of a supply waggon during the flight, for we know that many Royalist waggons suffered this fate, though this cannot of course explain the vast majority of the finds. It could also be asked why there have apparently been no burials found in the area to the east of Sibbertoft if so much action took place there. Graves have been reported just to the north in Marston Woods while other finds have been reported from Clipston parish, including at least one sword.[239] Many questions still remain and further work will undoubtedly require the revision of the story presented here, for there are still contradictory elements in the various contemporary accounts, some supporting and some casting doubts on the present interpretation. However, the broad sweep of this interpretation is supported by further crucial documentary evidence, the significance of which has in the past been overlooked. We have already seen that the Royalists, both horse and foot, were driven back beyond both their artillery and their train, which means they must have been pushed back beyond Dust Hill. Far more significant are the accounts of distribution of the dead. One, written by 'a gentleman from Northampton', who was present and who viewed the battlefield once the action was over, reported that 'the bodies lay slaine about foure miles in length, the most thick on the hill the Kings men stood on..'[240] A second report, published some days after the battle, which appears to be accurate in many details and claims to have been compiled by someone who, 'being upon the place, made more strict enquirie than first I could do...' He claimed to have viewed the field and reported that:

> 'In 2 miles space on their ground lay slaine about three hundred, and on our ground about an hundred. In the pursuit (beyond the two miles) I conceive, is

an hundred more slaine for ten miles space in Leicestershire, as comparing the maps will shew you....'[241]

From Broadmoor to Wadborough in Clipston, following the scatter of musket balls, is two miles and surely represents 'their ground'. 'Our ground' must be interpreted as Closter hill where the New Model army had formed up on the morning of the 14th, where the early action had been fought and where the New Model undoubtedly suffered most of its casualties. The two miles, containing 300 bodies, will have been that over which the Royalist were forced into a disorderly retreat, while the four miles of the other account might accord with the full length across the landscape almost to East Farndon, over which the scatters of musket and pistol shot have been found. 'The hill the King's men stood on' where the greatest number of bodies were to be seen is most likely to be Wadborough where the infantry probably made their last stand.[242]

In three hours the New Model army had achieved 'after a doubtful battle a most glorious victory, greater than that of York.'[243] But the battle of Marston Moor, near York, had not begun until sometime between five and seven in the evening and so there was no time for a destructive pursuit of the defeated Royalist forces. At Naseby not only was the victory itself far more complete than at Marston Moor, the battle was over so early that there was no limit to the pursuit. So it was that the Royalist army 'fled and we after at the breech of them, killing as fast as we could all we found in Armes.[244] However, the majority of the infantry did not have the opportunity to run, for 'The Generall hath so broken the Enemies Foot, that hee could not heare or see that they brought off a hundred'.[245] The New Model drove them out of the field:

> 'and with such speed and earnest prosecution, that no man can say yet, there was one of the Kings Foot got away, and but few of his Horse in any order, though it be thought neere foure thousand of them got out of the Field, but were pursued by our Horse.'[246]

That evening, as the first accounts of the battle were being written, the Parliamentarian cavalry were still 'upon the chase knocking them down, and taking them Prisoners, for at least five miles in the way towards Leicester.'[247]

With their will finally broken the cavalry had fled in various directions.[248] It was almost a case of every man for himself and so we find that Slingsby, with Lieutenant Colonel Atkinson from the Northern horse and three others, passed around the east side of Harborough whereas all the other Royalists rode to the west or even through the town. Not surprisingly, those that were not caught or killed, arrived at Leicester long before Slingsby.[249] While the battle itself took between two and three hours, the flight continued for six hours over some thirteen miles of Northamptonshire and Leicestershire, 'the longest pursuite that was since this unhappy war began.'[250] Cromwell had dispatched detachments of horse to chase the fleeing Royalists and, unlike Rupert's ill conceived attack on the Parliamentarian train, Fairfax had not made a similar mistake.[251] For some time now the royalist waggons must have been streaming down along the Clipston road, some simply having turned and fled without ever reaching Sibbertoft. According to Wogan, a captain with Okey's dragoons:

> 'Presently a noise was spread among our horse, that no man must light to plunder on pain of death, and forthwith to follow the King's horse; which accordingly we did, but very leisurely being much discontented to leave all the plunder of the field to our foot.'[252]

Cromwell's cavalry continued to within sight of Leicester, just two miles from the defences of the town, with Rossiter's and Rich's regiments, together with Major Harrison of Fleetwood's regiment, having the vanguard in the pursuit.[253] The Northampton and Rockingham horse, who had not fought in the battle, and the Hertfordshire Horse who had also arrived too late to fight, also joined in the chase and did good service.[254] As one correspondent reported, 'we pursued them with full bodies ..... the enemy never making face against us, but once at a bridge, from which we soon beat them.'[255] The flight was a chaotic affair and inevitably in the hours following the battle there were conflicting reports, with various rumours, some true and others wildly in error, circulating within the army.[256] Some, such as that telling of the capture of Prince Rupert, turned out later to be wrong whereas others may well be true, such as the claim that 'Sir Jacob Ashley was neere taking, we got the Cap of his head...'[257]

Uncovering the details of the flight using archaeological evidence will prove far more difficult than exploring the battle itself. If the various accounts are to be believed then the paths will have divided and to follow such scatters across many square miles of Northamptonshire will not be a simple task! Once past Farndon we must, for the moment at least, depend upon documentary sources, local tradition and chance discoveries. It would appear that a substantial number headed on to Harborough along the main road, for the point at which the Farndon road crosses the Welland from Northamptonshire into Leicestershire is called Bloodyman's ford, where it is said that some of the Royalists were caught and killed.[258] The accounts of the King's flight from the battlefield tell how at one point the Parliamentarian horse were actually ahead of him and that he was almost taken, though the rumour that he had been wounded in the arm proved to be wrong.[259] It is said that the King's own pistols 'that he did charge himself' were taken, but that Charles himself escaped across a ford or small brook on the county boundary. But it was not a simple escape, for:

> 'the King himself in person being necessitated, with his own troop only, to charge through the body for his escape' and it is said that his flight was aided

by 'a gentleman of the Bedchamber, that stood next the King, and cryed, hold your hands the King will yield his person, which while they did, hee got away, and so escaped.'[260]

It is surely here at Bloodyman's ford, across which the King had undoubtedly ridden out from Harborough that morning, that the Civil War was almost ended by the capture or death of the King. Any further east there is only the stone bridge into Harborough, while Slingsby says that no others travelled east of Harborough, and further west the flight will have been deterred by the hedged fields of the old enclosed township of Thorpe Lubenham. As we follow the King north from Harborough, heading towards Leicester, other traditions take him via Tur Langton, where since at least the early 19th century a spring by the village has been known as Charles's Well, because supposedly Charles stopped there to water his horse during the flight, while a more dubious tradition suggest he changed horses at Wistow Hall.[261]

Others from the baggage train also seem to have followed this route of escape via East Farndon, but apart from the regular sighting of a ghostly carriage supposedly seen speeding across the Clipston to Marston road near Twantry Farm, there is no real evidence that any of those from the train set out across the fields. They may have followed the road to Clipston and then north to Farndon because of the difficulty of moving waggons and carriages quickly over ploughland. According to tradition it was along the Clipston to Farndon road that the massacre of women from the baggage train took place. These were some of the 500 'common rabble' or 'common vermin' taken on foot, many of them 'Irish women, of cruel countenance some of them were cut by our soldiers when they took them...'[262] In the 19th century and even early this century local people would still point out to visitors the place where the Royalist women were killed or slashed during the flight.[263] Unlike many traditions, this one has a fairly secure basis as it was first recorded within living memory of the battle:

> 'In the south part of Farndon-field, within the gate-place in the road between Naseby and Farndon, the Parliament horse galloping along, as Mr Morton (the author of the Natural History of Northamptonshire) was informed by an eye witness, cut and slashed the women, with this sarcasm at every stroke, "Remember Cornwall, you whores!" Sir Ralph Hopton, as they said, having used their women in Cornwall in the like manner.'[264]

That a massacre did take place is confirmed by a contemporary report that:

> 'The Irish women Prince Rupert brought on the field (wives of the bloody Rebels in Ireland, his Majesties dearly beloved subjects) our soldiers would grant no quarter too, about 100 slain of them, and most of the rest of the whores that attended that wicked Army are marked in the face or nose, with a slash or cut.'[265]

It is reported that a mass grave of about 30 bodies was found in East Farndon churchyard some years before 1842 and this has been suggested as being of men or women killed in the pursuit, though there is no proof.[266]

It is perhaps not surprising to see that at Naseby, as elsewhere, the Irish troops and their civilian camp followers were badly treated and even killed. There had been a flood of refugees from Ireland during the war and many stories, whether propaganda or not, which told of massacres of good protestants by evil catholics. There was also the news of a treaty between the King and the rebels which would enable more Irish to be brought over to swell the King's forces. Though not condoning the killing, one can begin to understand why it occurred. That the Irish should be treated very differently from the rest of the Royalists was not just the wild action of the common soldiers, it was endorsed by a Parliamentary ordinance of October 1644 which said no quarter was to be given to any Irish. Fairfax wrote that 'Some Irish are among the prisoners as I am informed, I have not time to make inquiry into it; I desire they may be preceded against above, according to ordinance of Parliament.'[267] Parliamentarian attitude to the Irish is after all mirrored in the Royalist attitude to the Scots and so when considering the killing of the Irish at Naseby we must remember Symonds' words about the sack of Leicester: 'There were many Scotts in this towne, and no quarter was given to any in the heat.'[268] That attention in later times concentrated on the Parliamentarian atrocity at Naseby is perhaps a reflection of who finally won the peace not the war.

While these 'common rabble' were on foot, other of the women were in waggons and carriages. There were 'wagons carrying the middle sort of Ammunition Whores, who were full of money and rich apparell', in all some 1500 of them, while the genteel sort were in coaches, at least seven of which managed to reach Harborough before they were taken. Some waggons from the train travelled even further east, presumably through Oxendon and thus towards Harborough on the Northampton road, because one report speaks of a waggon:

> 'drawn by twenty six Horses, carrying a twenty foure pound bullet; they carried off the ground over Harborough bridge (as I was told in Harborough, by one that stood to watch) but six Carts or Waggons, one whereof was taken in the Towne by our Horse, and the other about a mile off the Towne, as I was told...'

Many of the waggons are said to have contained rich plunder while in others there were about 50 load of muskets, pike and powder match and bullet, and an abundance of trunks which the soldiers soon emptied.[269]

Other fleeing cavalry, as we have already seen, may have taken a more direct route into Leicestershire well before the King's last stand, fleeing down the coombs and heading north towards Marston Trussell. Some quite elaborate traditions have built up around the events which apparently occurred that afternoon. In the 19th century the village used to be known as pudding-poke

Fig.64. Marston Trussell village viewed from the south. The road running eastward from the village was constructed in the 19th century and prior to this the High Street was a dead end road running to the church. Immediately to the right of the church is a field called Slaughterford, which contains the earthwork remains of a moated medieval manor house. This is the traditional site of a skirmish as Royalist troops fleeing from the battlefield were caught and killed. The tradition says they were trapped in the dead end street. A mass grave was found in the churchyard in the 19th century and at least one cannon ball is said to have been recovered from the village. In the surrounding landscape can be seen the ridge and furrow remains of the open field system.[270] (reproduced by permission of Northamptonshire County Council)

Marston because the High Street was a dead end road which ran up to the church, and it is said that some Royalist troops were caught outside the churchyard gate and slaughtered.[271] This story is rather fanciful, but what does seem to be genuine is the fact that the field by the church, where a track crossed the stream, was known from at least the early 19th century as Slaughterford, and that the tradition that 'several' royalists were killed there was recorded in 1792, well before the discovery in the later 19th century of a mass grave at the east end of the churchyard, by the chancel wall, known ever since as the 'Cavaliers' Grave'.[272] From Marston the fleeing Royalists were supposedly caught once more in Foxton field, just a mile or two to the north.[273] It would seem likely that most of the fleeing Royalists were making their way towards the main Leicester road to the north of Harborough, as the most direct and quickest route back to the relative safety of Leicester. That some did take this course is clear, for Slingsby reports that 'The horse were pursued by a body of the enemys horse and loose scowters, to Great Glyn, and there the Earle of Lichfield charged their loose men with halfe a score horse and beate them back.'[274] But this was just one minor event of many, with the Royalist cavalry being caught in minor engagements across miles of the Leicestershire countryside in a long afternoon and evening of skirmishing that continued almost to the gates of Leicester and in which some 300 Royalists are said to have been killed.[275] Many more were captured, including some late that night when the pursuers fought with the rearguard, including the Duke of York's lifeguard, which lost most of its troopers and all its colours. Sir John Norwich, in command of the Rockingham horse, was apparently involved in this last action of the day, for he himself took Colonel Neville and, not surprisingly, conveyed the prisoners to Rockingham Castle.[276] From a force of perhaps near 12000 there were less than 4000 Royalists that reached safety, and some of those severely wounded. In almost twelve hours of fighting on Saturday the 14th June 1645 the King's main field army had literally been destroyed by Parliament's New Model Army.

NOTES

1. *A Relation of the Victory. Moderate Intelligencer*, 15th June. Symonds, p.193.

2. Vernon, 1644, p.78.

3. Nichols, vol 2, p.505-6, is followed by Gardiner, 1893, vol.2, p.242, and most other writers on the battle, though the exact details of deployment vary between authors, if they hazard a detailed interpretation. Holme, 1891, claims that the left wing was on the summit of Farndon Hills, that is immediately south of East Farndon village, while the right flank was on the ancient fortress at Sibbertoft, the medieval Castle Yard. This is quite impossible given the broken topography and the distance.

4. Slingsby, p.150. *The Kingdomes Weekly Intelligencer*, 10th-17th June, says that the battalia was on 'Clipston Hill', but this is an unreliable source.

5. It is just possible that Slingsby was referring to the chapel which once stood in the deserted village of Little Oxendon, just north of the ridge, but it had probably been demolished by this time. It is unlikely, but further documentary research might show that Little Oxendon chapel, last recorded in 1525, still stood in 1645. Northamptonshire Sites and Monuments Record, site number 7384001.

6. Bridges, 1791, vol.2, p.9. Little Bowden Inclosure Award, 1840, NRO ZA4181.

7. Markham is one of the few writers on the battle to have studied the local topography and local traditions. However, perhaps as a result of Bridges' mention of Moot Hill, he places the first Royalist battalia at Sibbertoft and the Parliament army on Mill Hill. Markham, 1870, p.209-226.

8. Walker, 1705.

9. An alternative conclusion must be that Walker is unreliable in his details about Naseby, perhaps he was even influenced by Digby's lies. If so then some of the events which follow may have been misrepresented, particularly where they reflect on Rupert's actions.

10. Digby to Legge, quoted by Morrah, 1976, p.188.

11. Slingsby, p.150. Walker, 1705. Cruso, 1632, p.60.

12. Sprigge says 3:00 am but 6:00 am is given by Leighton & Herbert.

13. Sprigge, 1647, p.33.

14. Leighton and Herbert.

15. Recorded in 1865 by J.N.Simpkinson, quoted by Stead, 1891, p.69.

16. *Northampton Daily Reporter*, 25th August 1891, reporting a tradition recorded by Mr Stead.

17. Fitzgerald to Carlyle, Terhune & Terhune, 1980, vol.1, p.358.

18. Sprigge, 1647, p.34.

19. Slingsby, p.151.

20. This description is based on detailed field inspection and discussion with the landowner, Mike Westaway.

21. *A Just Apology.* This may be the withdrawal, discussed below, with which Skippon disagreed but that has in the present interpretation been taken to be a separate event later in the morning. It is conceivable that Cromwell's proposal also relates to the later event.

22. Slingsby, p.151. Sprigge, 1647, p.34. Various authors have debated this flank march. Burne, 1950, p.254-5, concludes that Rupert turned first on the basis that a defending force would not quit a good position across a road unless his opponent moved first. Woolrych, 1961, p.122, dismisses this mile long westward flank march by the New Model. This seems to be based upon his error in placing Fairfax's original position along the Sibbertoft road. Fairfax would never have marched in this direction, to the west of Harborough, knowing that the King was at Harborough and might in fact be marching away to the north east.

23. *A More Particular and Exact Relation.*

24. The landowners, the Chapmans, kindly showed me the finds they have from the fields. There are 2 musket balls and 2 pistol balls of lead, and an iron stirrup which may or may not be contemporary with the battle. These were found by their father at some time around the 1930s when ploughing with horses. Only three fields were ploughed at that time, those on the eastern part of Mill Hill. There has also been the more recent discovery of several other musket balls from the hill top.

25. Slingsby, p.151. Okey says the Royalists came into the field and were ready to advance before the New Model was in battalia. However, Okey was by his own admission not on the field at this time. *A more particular and exact relation.*

26. *Northampton Daily Reporter*, 25th August 1891, reporting a tradition recorded by Stead, 1891, p.72.

27. Walker, 1705. Clarendon, vol.2, p.507. Slingsby, p.151.

28. Kitson, 1994, p.47.

29. Warburton, vol.3, p.129.

30. J.B., 1661, p.37.

31. Walker, 1705.

32. Rushworth letter. Walker, 1705. Symonds, p.193. Witnesses at trial of Charles I, Rushworth, 1722, vol.7, p.1410-1.

33. Leighton and Herbert. Okey. *A True Relation of a Victory.*

34. Rogers, 1968, p.45. His interpretation is repeated in various publications including Baker, 1986, p.92-95; Denton, 1988 and Rowley, 1989. Many modern published accounts of the battle, too numerous to list, broadly follow Gardiner's interpretation. See for example Woolrych, 1961, p.112-138; Kinross, 1979, p.84; Asquith, 1981. The 19th century accounts include, in addition to Gardiner, Mursell, 1861, p.34; Holme, 1891, p.76; Warburton, vol.3, p. 102 n.3 & p.106; Rimmer, 1892, p.83; Whellan, 1849, p.378.

35. Bridges, 1791, p.575. Also the record of Bridges' visit to Naseby and Sibbertoft during September 1719, in Bridges' notes.

36. Sprigge, 1647, p.34. *A more exact and perfect Relation.*

37. The foreground of Streeter's engraving was undoubtedly drawn from the church tower, as a visit will confirm. This must after all be why the church is not shown on the engraving, something that has puzzled many students of the battle. The middle ground contains no topographical detail at all, only the Parliament battalia. The distant parts of the view are in quite a different proportion and could not have been drawn from the tower. These were undoubtedly

the result of separate drawings made in the open field, probably from Sulby Hill and Lodge Hill.

38. Carlyle, 1858, p.174.

39. A forlorn hope was a body of commanded musketeers drawn out from various regiments who were sent forward of the main body to fire upon and thus disrupt the initial enemy advance.

40. *A True Relation of a Victory.*

41. Sprigge, 1647, p.36.

42. Mastin recognised that this enabled Cromwell's cavalry to be accurately located. The annotation on the copy of Streeter's engraving produced for Mastin's book quite inexplicably places the 'Rabbit Burrows' within the Royalist lines in complete contradiction to Mastin's text. Mastin, 1792, p.135.

43. Sprigge, 1647, p.34. It is assumed that the normal double pace is meant; see chapter 1 n.13.

44. Slingsby, p.151.

45. Sprigge, 1647, p.34. Orrery, 1677, p.153. There is a problem here in that both Cromwell and Skippon refer to withdrawal and may both be referring to the same incident, but it is difficult to reconcile the two accounts. It is conceivable that this slight withdrawal was the redeploying to 'yonder hill' argued for by Cromwell, not the move from the Clipston road scarp, but it seems less likely as a move of only 100 paces was required, not a major transfer of the army to another hill. If it was this move then the reason for the move was not to be able to deploy out of sight but rather to encourage the Royalist attack.

46. See for example Rowley, 1989, p.11.

47. The disposition of Parliamentarian forces and the topography behind their lines on de Gomme's plan is clearly based upon Streeter's engraving. The features shown in Naseby village, the windmill and its associated hills are identical to Streeter; 'Taming Hill' behind the Parliament baggage appears to be a misreading of 'Fainny Hill' on Streeter's engraving; even the description of the Parliament forces is identical to Streeter's down to the finest detail, as for example with the 'Assosiated horse' on the right wing and 'The troops of the Assosiation' on the left wing. Only with regard to the disposition of the Royalist forces do the two disagree, suggesting that it was only here that de Gomme had independent and more accurate information.

48. *A More Exact and Perfect Relation.* Leighton and Herbert. Slingsby, p.151. *The Weekly Account*, 11th-18th June.

49. Warburton, vol.3, p.102-4.

50. Rushworth, vol.6, p.42. Roberts argues that Astley's plan will have been a fair copy of a 'headquarters plan' produced by Rupert for the campaign, probably modified a short time before the battle to take account of the particular troops available and then made available to the brigade commanders. The difference between Astley's (as reproduced by Streeter) and de Gomme's plans may therefore have been a result of the different recollections of the two men. Roberts, pers.comm..

51. *A more particular and exact Relation.*

52. *A More Particular and Exact Relation.*

53. *A More Particular and Exact Relation.*

54. Sprigge, 1647, p.35.

55. *A Glorious Victory.*

56. Foard, 1994, p.95.

57. Young, 1985, for example, specifically says that there was no brigade system used by the New Model Army at Naseby. This is clearly wrong.

58. Keith Roberts, pers.comm.. See also Roberts, 1995.

59. Rogers, 1968, also attempted to analyze the frontages by making calculations from information published in Elton's manual. Unfortunately he made a number of important errors and, in failing to consult a wider range of contemporary manuals, was unaware of the ways in which different authors elaborate upon, and occasionally contradict, the statements of others.

60. Hexham, 1642, part 2, 19-20, states that at open order 'outstretched hands may meet', confirming that the 6ft is meant to include the man as well as the space between him and the next man. He also gives a frontage of 75ft for 25 files at order. Hexham is supported by a manual of 1643, representing the official requirements, Anon, 1643. Cruso, 1632, p.45, is even more specific:'...here we must observe a difference between the manner of taking distance.... for in the foot, the distance is taken from the center of the souldiers bodie...'.

61. Hexham, 1642, part 2, p.20.

62. Rogers, 1968, especially p.234-5. Puysegur, 1659 quoted by Lloyd, 1908.

63. In the absence of a comprehensive study of the evidence of all the available manuals it is dangerous to take information from just one or two cases, because there are so many other variables in the nature of the deployments that could lead to errors in interpretation. For example the plans at the end of Hexham, 1642, give spacings of various sizes between units but they relate to a variety of brigade and other systems, many of which may not be relevant to the English Civil War.

64. Cruso, 1632, p.45.

65. Ward, 1639, defines measurements in a table at end of the work.

66. For the cavalry Hexham gives a 200ft frontage for a division of 300 horse, presumably in 5 ranks.

67. As elsewhere in the text it has ben assumed that the normal contemporary measurement of double paces is meant. Vernon, 1644, p.86.

68. Sprigge, 1647, p.38.

69. *The Weekly Account*, 11th-18th June.

70. Young states that each of the divisions of the Royalist horse was divided into two squadrons. There is no explanation given for this, though it appears to derive from de Gomme's depiction of two standards with each division of horse. Streeter clearly depicts three squadrons to each. However, de Gomme also shows two standards with each of the divisions of the New Model regiments even though they were not sub divided. Thus the depiction may not represent two squadrons in the Royalist horse.

71. Mungeam, 1968.

72. Typescript lecture by Hensman, given at Loughborough, 25th February 1908. This is the interpretation followed by Baker, 1986, p.92, and others. Smurthwaite, 1984, p.167.

73. Pers.comm., G.Cadman, Northamptonshire Heritage.

74. Smurthwaite, 1994.

75. In the 17th century the stage-waggons, precursors of the stage-coach, are said to have averaged about two miles per hour and 20 miles per day. Burke, 1942, p.34.

76. Slingsby, p.152-3. Leighton & Herbert.

77. Vernon, 1644, p.37. Leighton and Herbert.

78. Rushworth letter. *The Parliament Post*, 10th-17th June 1645. *The Weekly Account*, 11th-18th June. According to *Mercurius Civicus*, 12th-18th June and *The Kingdomes Weekly Intelligencer*, 10th-17th June, the word was *'God and Queen Mary'*. *'God and King Charles'* according to *The Parliament Post*, 10th-17th June 1645.

79. Rushworth letter. *Mercurius Civicus*, 12th-18th June.

80. Vernon, 1644, p.41.

81. Vernon, 1644, p.45.

82. Stearns, 1954.

83. According to Luke the 'chiefest' preaching and praying regiments were Skippon's, Pickering's, Montague's, Rainsborough's, Hammond's, Fairfax's and Fleetwood's. Tibbutt, 1963, p.324.

84. *Good News out of the West*.

85. *A More Particular and Exact Relation*.

86. Sprigge, 1647, p.45.

87. Vernon, 1644, p.42-3.

88. *A More Particular and Exact Relation.*

89. Survey of the Manor of Sulby, 1582, NRO FH272, and information from A.E.Brown.

90. The reconstruction of the old enclosures of Sibbertoft has proven very difficult in certain places and it is just possible that the Archwrong Close is not exactly as reconstructed here.

91. Later orders for the New Model refer to bandoleers with boxes of wood and others with boxes of double plate. Another (April 1646) requires boxes of wood 'the Heade to bee of wood', implying that some orders at least in the past had wooden boxes with metal heads. An order of January 1646 required boxes of strong plate, the heads the same. Mungeam, 1968.

92. Sprigge, 1647, p.36.

93. Sprigge, 1647, p.43.

94. *A True Relation of a Victory.* Leighton & Herbert. *A Glorious Victory.* Clarendon, 1702, vol.2, p.507. *A more particular and exact relation. Moderate Intelligencer*, 15th June. Only one source says at 9.00 am., *A more exact and perfect relation.* Symonds says about 12:00, as does Baillie, 1775, vol.2, p.116-7.

95. Leighton and Herbert.

96. Walker, 1705.

97. Rushworth letter.

98. *A Relation of the Victory. A More Particular and Exact Relation.*

99. J.B., 1661, p.37.

100. *A more exact and perfect Relation.* Rushworth letter. *A True Relation of a Victory. A Relation of the Victory.*

101. Carlton, 1994, p.140.

102. Symonds, p.193. *A more exact and perfect Relation.*

103. Leighton and Herbert. Rushworth,vol.6, p.42.

104. *The Parliament Post*, 10th-17th June.

105. *Rupert's Life.* Rushworth letter.

106. *A more exact and perfect Relation.*

107. Sprigge, 1647, p.37.

108. Slingsby, p.151-2.

109. Okey. He mistakenly claims that the King was in the second line of the Royalist right wing of horse.

110. Quoted by Tincey, 1993, p.20.

111. Okey says that when the reserves attacked they did fire their pistols before they charged.

112. Vernon, 1644, p.71, 43 & 45. Vernon states that the troop giving the first charge is 'to be at their Close Order, every left hand man's right knee must be close locked under his right hand man's left ham...' as they advance at an easy pace, and then they are to charge '...keeping still in their Close Order...'. Later in the century Lord Orrery, quoted by Firth, 1962, p.142, supports this practice: 'When the squadrons advance to charge the trooper's horses and their own knees are as close as they can well endure.'

113. Vernon, 1644, p.46.

114. Rushworth, vol.6, p.42. *The Weekly Account*, 11th-18th June. According to Sir Philip Warwick, Ireton 'made a soldierly and notable defense'. Warwick, 1701, p.287.

115. Sprigge, 1647, p.38.

116. As Mastin's references to gravel digging in the 18th show, many of these probably post date the battle, a few may relate to the burial of those killed in 1645, but some were in existence at the time of the battle.

117. Okey incorrectly identifies the reserves as the King's regiment.

118. *Three Letters. A more exact and perfect relation.* Okey.

119. Sprigge, 1647, p.37.

120. *The Moderate Intelligencer*, 12th-19th June.

121. *A More Particular and Exact Relation.*

122. Rushworth, vol.6, p.42. Walker, 1705.

123. Vernon, 1644, p.86.

124. *Rupert's Life*, p.18. Slingsby, p.151-2.

125. Walker, 1705.

126. Leighton and Herbert.

127. *The Weekly Account*, 11th-18th June.

128. *A More Particular and Exact Relation*.

129. *A True Relation of a Victory*.

130. Warburton, 1849, vol.3, p.127.

131. *A more exact and perfect Relation. Rupert's Life*, p.18. Wogan.

132. In the absence of information on the distribution of shot of different bore across the battlefield it is impossible to define where the smaller balls fired from carbines have been found.

133. Throughout the text when casualty rates are referred to they denote those wounded sufficiently to warrant hospital treatment, including those that died of their wounds, but not those killed outright on the battlefield.

134. A listing by regiment naming each soldier wounded at Naseby who was brought to Northampton on 14th June and thereafter. *Accompt of Maior and Mr Rushworth of Northampton, June 1645 concerning the £700...*', PRO SP28/173 unfol.. The total of 535 corresponds reasonably well with the estimate of 600 wounded given on the 15th June, *Moderate Intelligencer*, 12th-19th June. The list of course does not take account of those who died on the field or did not survive long enough to warrant any payments for their support. The listing is not absolutely complete as will be seen from the occasional references to others known to have been injured at Naseby, but these seem mainly to be officers.

135. A reformado was an officer brought into a regiment from another but without being given command of troops.

136. Walker, 1705.

137. Rushworth letter.

138. Rushworth letter.

139. *A more exact and perfect Relation*. Firth, 1962, p.74. Sir John Smythe's late 16th century description of pike action quoted by Lloyd, 1908, p.89.

140. Walker, 1705.

141. 17th June, Baillie, 1775, vol.2, p.116-7. *The Kingdomes Weekly Intelligencer*, 17th-24th June.

142. *The Moderate Intelligencer*, 27th November to 4th December.

143. *A More Particular and Exact Relation*.

144. Elton, 1650, p.141 and Barriffe, 1661, p.6 et.seq.

145. Walker, 1705. *A True Relation of a Victory*.

146. Northampton wounded account, PRO SP28/173 unfol..

147. Sprigge, 1647, p.36.

148. Though our interpretation may well be correct, until detailed survey work has been possible in the rest of the area on Fenny Hill and Mill Hill we cannot be certain, especially as there may be problems of mineralisation of the soil and of wetness in the slade bottom which is causing the fall off on in the distribution southward.

149. One report suggests that the greatest concentration of artefacts was in fact to be found 'on the Sibbertoft side, and as most of the bullets have been found there it supports the theory that the fight was the hottest at that spot.' Holloway, 1912. This is in conflict not only with modern survey evidence but also with the study by Fitzgerald in the 19th century and most other reports which all agree that the main concentration was on Closter.

150. Newman, 1981, p.75, quoting Ross, 1887, p.129.

151. The author of *A more exact and perfect Relation* states that 'this wound he tooke in bringing up the Foote, where they were first disordered, and yet led them up after he was wounded'. He was a significant observer on this matter for he spoke with Skippon on his sickbed. However George Bishop claims it was in the first charge that Skippon was wounded. *The Kingdomes Weekly Intelligencer*, 24th June-1st July.

152. Ludlow, 1698, vol.1, p.151-3.

153. *Three Letters* - Fairfax.

154. *A more exact and perfect Relation*.

155. Barriffe, 1661, p.82-4.

156. *A Sacred Record*.

157. *A More Particular and Exact Relation*.

158. Okey himself says three although the record of wounded lists only two.

159. Slingsby, p.152.

160. Walker, 1705.

161. *Iter Carolinum*.

162. Whitelocke, p.145.

163. Rushworth letter.

164. Symonds, p.193. Sprigge, 1647, p.35.

165. Sprigge, 1647, p.35.

166. *The True Informer*, 21st June.

167. Sprigge, 1647, p.35.

168. Symonds, p.193.

169. *The Parliament Post*, 10th-17th June. Rushworth letter.

170. *A More Particular and Exact Relation*.

171. Sprigge, 1647, p.36.

172. Banks, 1739, p.22-3.

173. *A Relation of the Victory*. Walker, 1705.

174. Slingsby, p.152.

175. Walker, 1705.

176. *A more exact and perfect Relation*. Young, 1985, p.273.

177. Sprigge, 1647, p.38. Walker, 1705. It must be admitted that some of the casualties suffered by the two regiments might be accounted for by them having to face and hold off all the defeated Northern and Newark horse. However, not one of the accounts suggest that Langdale charged these two regiments during this phase of the battle.

178. Sprigge, 1647, p.36.

179. Slingsby, p.152.

180. *Moderate Intelligencer*, 15th June.

181. *The Parliament Post*, 10th-17th June.

182. *A True Relation of a Victory. Moderate Intelligencer*, 15th June. *The Weekly Account*, 11th-18th June. *The Parliament Post*, 10th-17th June. *A Glorious Victory. The Kingdomes Weekly Intelligencer*, 10th-17th June. *A More Particular and Exact Relation*.

183. *A More Particular and Exact Relation*.

184. Rushworth letter.

185. Walker, 1705.

186. *A True Relation of a Victory. The Parliament Post*, 10th-17th June. Ludlow, 1698, vol.1, p.151-3.

187. Rushworth letter. *A More Exact and Perfect Relation*.

188. *The Kingdomes Weekly Intelligencer*, 10th-17th June.

189. Elton, 1650, p.160.

190. Vernon, 1644, p.87.

191. This is the part of the action where Rushworth and Sprigge are in conflict. Rushworth is clear that the Blue Regiment were broken and then the Royalist horse and foot retreated, after which the foot was destroyed in a final charge. Sprigge has Fairfax breaking this last tercio at the end of the infantry battle. As Rushworth's letter was written immediately after the battle and apparently with information from the high command his account has been given precedence here over Sprigge's.

192. Whitelocke, p.145.

193. *A Glorious Victory*.

194. *The Kingdomes Weekly Intelligencer*, 17th-24th June.

195. Rushworth letter.

196. *Rupert's Life*, p.18.

197. The evidence from Symonds on regimental and related strengths when plotted does not provide a clear picture, indeed it suggests weaknesses where strengths would have been expected, particularly with regard to Rupert's right wing of horse.

198. *A Relation of the Victory. A more exact and perfect Relation. The Kingdomes Weekly Intelligencer*, 10th - 17th June, refers only to foot.

199. Rushworth letter.

200. Rushworth letter.

201. This cannot be taken as a highly accurate distribution plan as most of the evidence was plotted by eye at 1:10,000 scale, much of it a significant time after many of the discoveries were made. Although for these reasons every single musket ball cannot be claimed to be accurately plotted, a problem which has been compounded by the difficulties of presentation of so much detail on such a small plan, the overall pattern at the scale presented is a very good representation of the actual distribution of artefacts. No attempt has been made to distinguish the small number of pistol shot on this plan. The small number of artefacts identified outside the survey area are from minor survey activity which did not cover a significant area.

202. The archaeological evidence in the south west corner of Sibbertoft parish, if it does not relate to Okey as we have suggested it does, must represent the destruction of one of the Royalist regiments of foot during the retreat. The caps to powder boxes might then be concentrated here for the very reason that the men fought to the last in a severe action. The scatter of artefacts in the adjacent closes might perhaps reflect the flight of small groups of musketeers from the main body as it was shattered, taking refuge behind the hedges and firing upon the cavalry which were mopping up the last survivors.

203. Okey.

204. Leighton and Herbert.

205. Curteis, 1992. *Proceedings of the Society of Antiquaries*, 1866, vol.2, p.346. Besly, 1987, p.107. Just to the north of the silver coin hoard, close to Lowe Farm, a possible 17th century horse harness fitting has also been found, though unlike the hoard it is impossible to say if it relates in any way to the battle.

206. Slingsby, p.152-3.

207. Rushworth letter.

208. The balls are of 20mm as opposed to the more normal 17mm or below seen elsewhere on the battlefield.

209. *Moderate Intelligencer*, 15th June. Rushworth letter.

210. Rushworth letter.

211. Anon, 1881, p.137. Hensman, who collected material in the early 20th century for a history of the Civil War in Northamptonshire, transcribed information from a document by someone called Trusloe supposedly recording an account of a local man in the battle: 'Now another party of their men did we trap down a valley nigh to the battlefield, sparing none as were our orders, and so left them, lying as they had fought, back against back. Others of their rout, as I have heard say turn to harbour until our men hasten up with fire destroy their refuge, and so bear all before our hand.' This is one of the earliest references to the Hellcoombe

slaughter tradition.

212. Hellcombe is recorded in the 19th century as being the coomb at the bottom of Jacob's Ladder, *JNNHS&FC*, vol.12, p.49. Local information, via Mr Kendal of Starr's Lodge, places Jacob's Ladder at the head of 'The Coombes'. This is confirmed by the Marston field name map (NRO) which gives 'Elcombs' at SP687839. Thanks to A.E.Brown for this reference. It appears to be incorrectly located by Markham, 1870, plan opposite p.213.

213. Fitzgerald to Carlyle, 30th September 1842, Terhune & Terhune, 1980, vol.1, p.366.

214. Bridges' notes.

215. Clarendon, p.508.

216. Rushworth letter.

217. Walker, 1705. *A True Relation*.

218. Rushworth letter.

219. *A More Exact and Perfect Relation*.

220. Northampton wounded account, PRO SP28/173, unfol..

221. *The Weekly Account*, 11th-18th June. Repeated by Sprigge, 1647, p.38.

222. Whitelocke, p.145.

223. Walker, 1705. Sprigge, 1647, p.38.

224. Belasyse.

225. Sprigge, 1647, p.38.

226. Sprigge, 1647, p.36.

227. Slingsby, p.152-3.

228. Sprigge, 1647, p.39.

229. *A More Particular and Exact Relation*.

230. Rushworth letter.

231. Rushworth, 1722, vol.7, p.1411.

232. Rushworth letter. Symonds, p.193.

233. Vernon, 1644, p.35.

234. Okey. Belasyse.

235. Slingsby, p.152-3.

236. Rushworth letter.

237. Leighton & Herbert. *The Weekly Account*, 11th-18th June, suggests just one and a half hours.

238. Leighton and Herbert. *A more exact and perfect Relation*.

239. NRO Placenames index, Clipston. The sword was presented to Miss Wake in the 1950s but the object is not now in the Record Office and so the card has been removed from the index. There is no record of the present location of the sword.

240. *A more exact and perfect Relation*.

241. *The True Informer*, 16th-21st June.

242. 'Tradition affirms the carnage to have been most deadly on the site of Mr Smeeton's farmhouse, and here I believe, most of the relics of the battle have been found.' J.Smeeton had Broadmoor Farm in 1849. Whellan, 1849.

243. Rushworth to Luke, 14th June, Tibbutt, 1963, p.576.

244. *A True Relation of a Victory*.

245. *A Relation of the Victory*. Whetham to Luke, 14th June, Tibbutt, 1963, p.576. Okey.

246. *A more exact and perfect Relation*.

247. *A Relation of the Victory*.

248. *Moderate Intelligencer*, 15th June.

249. Slingsby, p.153.

250. *A True Relation of a Victory*. *The True Informer*, 21st June. *The Kingdomes Weekly Intelligencer*, 10th-17th June.

251. Rushworth letter.

252. Wogan, reprinted in Young, 1985.

253. *Moderate Intelligencer*, 15th June.

254. *Moderate Intelligencer*, 15th June. *A True Relation of a Victory*.

255. *The True Informer*, 21st June.

256. *A Glorious Victory*.

257. Rushworth letter. *A Glorious Victory*.

258. Bland, 1924, p.60. Today the road crosses by a small bridge.

259. Okey.

260. *The Moderate Intelligencer*, 12th-19th June. *Iter Carolinum. A more exact and perfect Relation*.

261. Nichols, vol.2, p.506, quoting William Hanbury, rector of Langton. Tennant's suggestion that some fleeing troops passed through and plundered Rugby in the flight is even less plausible because Rugby is in completely the wrong place. This event may have been incorrectly associated with the 14th June and in fact related to the preceding week. Tennant, 1992, p.262.

262. *A more exact and perfect relation*.

263. Philips, 1828. Typescript by Strongman on the battle, c.1935, LRO DE 2132/54, p.36.

264. Nichols, vol.2, p.506, quoting Morton. Ryves, 1685. Bridges 1791, vol.1, p.574-5.

265. Rushworth letter. *Mercurius Civicus*, 12th-18th June. *The Kingdomes Weekly Intelligencer*, 10th-17th June. According to one report between 300-400 '*whores*' were killed. *A True Relation of a Victory*. Nichols vol.3, p.531.

266. Fitzgerald to Carlyle, 7th October 1842, Terhune & Terhune, 1980, vol.1, p.374.

267. *Three Letters* - Fairfax.

268. Symonds, p.180.

269. *A more exact and perfect Relation*.

270. Northampton Museum accession register, D.52/1927.

271. F.Cooke, circa 1926, Notes of Parish of Marston Trussell., p.5, refers to receipt bill for repairs to churchyard gate which had been broken down by the Cavaliers and Roundheads. Then p.13 refers to the east end of the church saying 'The cross on here was knocked off in the battle, and two cannon balls were dug up in the churchyard between the south door and the ditch.' Elsewhere in a loose paper in book of lecture notes say 'most likely knocked off...' It refers to a receipt/bill for repairs to churchyard gate which had been broken down by the Cavaliers and Roundheads. NRO Marston Trussell Parish Records \37. All Law's interpretations of the documents in so far as they relate to the battle are very dubious.

272. Mastin, 1792, p.146. Murray, 1901, p.101. In 1881 it was reported that human bones, buttons and a knife were 'not long since found buried in the clay' at Marston Trussell. Anon, 1881, p.137. James, 1864. James was the vicar of Sibbertoft. At some time before the Second World War 'Mr John Burdett of Lubenham and William Cheney went to drain a field at Marston and said 'On laying the first drain, they dug through a mass of human bones. Evidently all had been buried in one deep trench. During the day Squire Bennett visited the field to inspect the work and was horrified at the sight of it. The Squire sternly rated the farm foreman for allowing, as he said, the awful desecration of human remains; he had the drain carefully filled in and the pipes drawn away and never attempted to drain it again. John Burdett was a man who would fairly give the facts. The name of the field was (I think) Slaughterford or Slaughterfield or some similar name!' Market Harborough Advertiser, quoted by James McCloghry, undated (post 1979), *Our Marston*, typescript in NRL. The discoveries of bodies in the field are perhaps most likely to be the result of a shrinkage in the size of the churchyard, for the burials were, according to recent accounts in the village, found adjacent to the churchyard boundary. A photograph of the site of the 'Cavalier Grave' is given in Bond, 1927, figure 12.

273. News cuttings on the history of Foxton, 1944, LRO DE 3389/214 item 2.

274. Symonds, p.193.

275. Rushworth letter.

276. Rushworth to Luke, 15th June, Tibbutt, 1992, p.577. Leighton & Herbert.

CHAPTER 9

THE AFTERMATH

'There being now through the great goodness of God
so happy an opportunity offered of finishing these unhappy troubles
by giving us this early and unexpected victory, we would leave
no means unattempted that might contribute thereto.'
Committee of Both Kingdoms

Following the battle the greater part of the New Model infantry together with the train 'soberly marched towards Leicester', staying that night at Market Harborough, and so it was that in the space of a few hours the Royalist headquarters became those of the Parliamentarian army and a great number of the troops that had marched out with thoughts of victory that morning returned in the evening as prisoners.[1] Though the majority travelled north, Fairfax must have detached part of his forces to deal, amongst other things, with the wounded on both sides. Large numbers of troops certainly remained at Naseby, for later the village recorded that 'the night after the fight wer had verie many quarterd in every howse besides of maymed souldiers on both sides a good while after.'[2] Some of the horse may have been stationed much closer to Leicester, but others who had been in the pursuit were, it would seem, recalled towards Market Harborough. Certainly Rossiter's regiment, which had been in the vanguard of the chase, was in the small village of Marston Trussell on the night of the 14th, just two miles north of the battlefield. There they were quartered on all the houses in the village, with as many as 50 or 60 men allocated to some households, while the adjacent hamlet of Hothorpe, which lay within Marston parish, was also required to provide provisions for Rossiter's men.[3] Other troops may have been quartered at Rockingham, returning perhaps together with Sir John Norwich's men with their prisoners after a successful pursuit.[4]

At Harborough that night, as the army regrouped, Fairfax assessed the situation and planned his next move. He also made sure that a detailed account of the battle was conveyed immediately to Parliament, while both he and Cromwell sent their own brief reports to the Speaker.[5] In his letter Fairfax requested 'that the honour of this great never to be forgotten mercy, may be given to God in an extraordinary day of thanksgiving...'[6] In response Parliament would declare Thursday 26th June a day of thanksgiving in all the churches and chapels in London and the following day in the rest of the country, with the London celebration being accompanied by a collection for those people of Leicester who had fled to the capital.[7] For many however the next day, Sunday the 15th June, was a day to celebrate the great success, as at Newport Pagnell where the governor had himself ordered a public thanksgiving in the church.[8] The messengers who brought Parliament the news from the army were handsomely rewarded, as presumably was Fairfax's own chaplain who had been dispatched to give the House a first hand account of the battle. Parliament would also vote £700 for an enamel and diamond locket which was to be made for Fairfax in recognition of his great service in the victory at Naseby.[9]

This had been a victory so complete and so cheaply won that the New Model remained in a good condition to continue the campaign with vigour. By the night of the 14th the army was of course 'wearied out and tyred' and the horses 'worne off their legs', but reserves had already arrived to restore the situation.[10] It was reported at the time that 'our Army [is] not at all weakened hereby, but by the accesse of Colonel Rossiters Horse and Dragoones, the Northampton Troopes and some Foot, with other supplies from the Associated Counties, is made more numerous.'[11] Sir John Gell, who had also been too late to participate in the battle, reached the army with his fresh forces soon after and, it was said:

> 'will be very useful for the prosecution of that happy victory, and give a few days' rest to the horse of the General wearied and harrassed with duty in the late service, and so enable them to complete the victory by the utter dissipation of the remainder of those beaten forces.'[12]

On the 15th the army was 'in a verie good posture, and willing on their way, as ever I saw any, being much refreshed, and supplyed with money, apparell, and other accomodations, out of the Kings store.'[13] There were also exceptional financial rewards for individual soldiers because, as Rushworth reported on the night after the battle, 'the Souldiers have already brought in to the Generall above 40 Standards and Colours, he gives each man a reward.'[14] But for most of the troops the greatest profit came in plunder they had taken from the captured Royalists and their baggage train:

> 'The soldiers that were slaine and taken were verie full of money, scarce any poor rogue but had in his pocket fortie or fiftie shillings, some five pounds, some ten pounds, some twentie pounds, besides plate and rings and all which they had plundered in Leicester and the counties in their march...'[15]

Indeed, this was to prove one of Fairfax's main problems. The army had already suffered from desertion, but now many of the common soldiers had more money than they had ever had before and for some this was more than they could cope with. A week or so later Fairfax would write to Parliament complaining that:

> 'My Horse are much weakened; many Men who git rich Booty being gone to bestow it in Places of Safety, and many Men lie wounded in the Garrisons. It is so with my Foot, of whom I believe I have not Half the Number according to the Establishment....'[16]

Though he might be expected to have exaggerated the impact in order to encourage Parliament to deal more swiftly with his needs, the New Model was clearly suffering just as the Eastern Association army had in the weeks after Marston Moor.[17]

Meanwhile, though no longer fleeing for their lives, the King and his supporters did not stay at Leicester to await the inevitable siege. As Rupert had done after the defeat at Marston Moor, when he fled York leaving it to the Parliamentarians, so the King abandoned Leicester. Without an effective field army the defence of such a garrison against the New Model was impossible and so, as a newspaper reported, 'diverse thousands of his Majesties men are run severall wayes.'[18] 'We heare some of the Kings Forces are taken towards Litchfield, but it is thought the greatest part of those that are left, are flying towards Newark, whither its said the King himselfe is going.'[19] It was in fact the Northern horse who marched to Newark, closely missing Gell's 2000 cavalry who were marching south to join Fairfax.[20] For many of the Royalists there was little they could now do but fall back on their home garrisons and wait, as with the Earl of Northampton's horse, some 500 of whom would return to Banbury on the 20th June.[21]

On the evening following the battle the King made sure that arrangements were in hand to treat the wounded at Leicester and then, towards night 'this dismall Saturday', having been rejoined by the two princes and some of his cavalry, Charles marched to Ashby castle where they arrived at daybreak.[22] Just two regiments of horse, the Queen's and Colonel Cary's, were left at Leicester to support Lord Loughborough's garrison.[23] On the 16th Fairfax reported that most of the King's horse were around Ashby and some at Newark, but in fact Charles had not stopped at Ashby.[24] On the afternoon of the 15th he had marched with all the horse to Lichfield, where they left Colonel Bagot who was fatally wounded, and then the next day on to Wolverhampton, then to Bewdley, where he stayed for two nights, then on again to Bromyard, reaching Hereford on the Thursday.[25] Rupert wished to see the surviving remnants of the cavalry united with Goring's Western army, because he recognised that this was the last chance to build a force capable of withstanding the New Model, but yet again he was ignored. Instead the King marched on to Raglan Castle and there he was entertained for some weeks by the Earl of Worcester, during which time Goring's army was defeated.[26] Rupert could see, in a way that Charles would not, that all was lost. The King's supporters were now deserting him daily and Rupert made it clear to Charles that the idea of troops from Ireland restoring his fortunes was an illusion. But the King would not take notice of Rupert, indeed already by late June the blame for the defeat at Naseby had begun to be placed at Rupert's door. It was even being said that it was he, against the advice of Lord Astley, who had argued they should fight the New Model. Not surprisingly it was Digby who was behind these lies, causing Will Legge to reply in defence of Rupert that:

'where your Lordship would excuse him of the particular and general
aspersions, yet you come with such objections against the conduct of that
business, as would, to men ignorant of the Prince, make him incapable of
common sense in his profession...'[27]

Given the animosity that already existed within the Royalist cause it is not
surprising that the conflict between the various factions intensified, for the
impact of Naseby on the Royalist army had been devastating. All the accounts
agree that the whole of the Royalist infantry were either killed or taken
prisoner. Rumours amongst the New Model on the afternoon of the 14th had

Fig. 65. St. Dionysius, a chapel of ease to Great Bowden church, lay in the market place at Market Harborough. It was the largest and most easily secured building in the town and so was used on the night of the 14th June as a prison for many of the captured Royalists.

suggested that there were as few as two thousand Royalists taken or killed, but
more informed sources soon confirmed that between four and five thousand
prisoners had been taken on the field and in the flight to Market Harborough.
That evening the Provost Marshal claimed to have in his charge some four
thousand prisoners of which over 400 were officers, including four colonels
and 12 lieutenants and ensigns, while other prisoners were taken as the
Royalist cavalry fled towards Leicester.[28] The latter, many of which were
apparently taken to Rockingham castle, may not have been brought together
with the other prisoners until at least the Sunday, and this may explain the
discrepancy between the numbers of prisoners reported on the 14th and the
figures quoted in later accounts. Of these 4000-5000 prisoners there were

probably between one and two thousand horse, although other sources claim that in foot alone there were 4000 taken.[29] Some of these prisoners may have been quartered on the night of the 14th in Naseby village, but the majority were marched up with the army to Market Harborough.[30] There, presumably joined by some of the prisoners taken during the flight, they were held overnight in St.Dionysius Chapel in the centre of the town. The use of churches to temporarily house prisoners was a common practice during the Civil War, simply because they were the only buildings of sufficient size in which prisoners could be locked up in relative security, and as we follow the prisoners on their way to London we find them being held in a number of churches en route. The first stage of this journey began the following day when 4508 were marched south to Northampton. As they entered the Parliamentarian garrison the defeated soldiers are supposed to have said that their commanders had told them that on Sunday night 'we should enter this Towne and so wee do, though those that told us so are run away from us.'[31] That night they were held in the various medieval churches in the town, though there is a tradition at the nearby village of Ecton which claims that prisoners were held there as well. However this and the record of provisions sent to Ecton from nearby villages may relate to the care of the wounded discussed below.

Fig.66. St.Sepulchre's Church in Northampton, which had been built on the model of the circular Holy Sepulchre in Jerusalem on the return from the Crusades, was one of the places where Royalist prisoners were held on the night of Sunday 15th June, while various of the wounded would later be buried in its churchyard.

Colonel John Fiennes, assisted by Colonel Gourdon's Suffolk horse and other troops out of the local garrisons, was given the task of escorting the prisoners to the capital.[32] As none of them were New Model troops, and so would not be marching with the army, they could be spared for these duties. The two regiments may also have been somewhat more fresh than the other troops, for they had been in the reserves of Horse and so were generally not hard pressed during the battle and had suffered very few casualties. This is not to suggest that Fiennes' men had seen no action, for they had apparently lost many horses during the battle and Fiennes himself was said to have 'fought with courage, and did notably in the action.'[33] The convoy however proved too weak for the job, not least because some of Fiennes' regiment had initially been left behind with the army, and so he requested that Luke provide additional troops from Newport Pagnell to join him on the 17th at Olney. He also requested Luke to send out scouts towards Banbury and Boarstall House to gain intelligence, for his prisoners had expressed an expectation of being set free. He did not want the great victory to be in any way undone by a Royalist attack on his convoy which would release the prisoners and allow the King to rebuild his army.[34] Luke refused to send out any troops to assist, claiming that he needed authorization from the Committee of Both Kingdoms. The dead hand of bureaucracy, which had so weakened the war effort in previous years, still lay heavy on all but the New Model, providing any commander with an excuse not to give essential support. However, at least supplies and surgeons were dispatched from Newport Pagnell, revealing that some of the wounded were made to march with the other prisoners.[35]

Although the convoy had left for London on the 16th June there were still more prisoners being brought in Northampton over the following few days, most of whom may have been officers for one account refers to 'Knights and Colonels fresh brought in'.[36] These new prisoners may perhaps explain why it was that on 30th September 1645 the Northampton accounts record that William Garrett was reimbursed for the allowance of 1d per day for each of the cavaliers 'taken prisoner at Naseby fight and other places and sent into his custody', though whether any of the prisoners stayed long in the town is not known.[37] On Monday night the convoy had reached Olney and this must be when Cogenhoe, and presumably other villages in Northamptonshire, had to provide provisions to Olney for the prisoners.[38] From there they marched via Bedford, reaching Dunstable and Luton on Tuesday.[39] It was at Luton that some of the prisoners tried to set fire to a barn in which they were locked up for the night and then on Thursday, when at St.Albans, they apparently broke up the pews and caused other damage in the church in which they were held. The prisoners had been ordered to remain at St.Albans temporarily while it was decided where they could be held in London and at the same time the Hertfordshire Committee were also required to provide additional guards.[40] By Friday the convoy had moved on to Barnet.[41] Not surprisingly the Royalists propaganda tried to put the best possible face on the disastrous situation:

> 'The rebels at London are very insolent upon their late victory, and extremely averse to peace, as I hear. I have advertisement that at Barnet, within ten miles of London, the King's soldiers (prisoners) fell out with their convoy; and fighting with them, many of them got away, insomuch, as it is believed, there were not carried into London above six or seven hundred prisoners, though they emptied all their garrisons of Northampton, Newport Pagnell, and of the prisoners which they had long detained to increase the show....'[42]

Given the trouble on previous nights it is not surprising that there were some losses, though the numbers involved were obviously grossly exaggerated in the Royalist sources. The following day the convoy set off again with Fiennes' and Gourdon's regiments and the Hertfordshire Trained Bands as the guard, divided into various divisions, but as a precaution against further trouble they were further reinforced at Islington with several companies of the Green, White and Yellow regiments of the London Trained Bands.[43]

On Saturday 21st June, exactly a week after the battle, about 3000 prisoners were escorted through London to Westminster and the 55 captured colours and standards carried with the prisoners through the streets. From Islington they marched by Mount Hill at Aldersgate to St. Martin's Lane near Charing Cross, leaving the chief officers at Peterhouse while the rest were held in the Mews at Charing Cross under the guard of the Trained Bands. In case there was any disorder amongst the prisoners a gibbet was set up nearby. A French observer who saw the prisoners paraded through the capital was amazed at how well they looked, saying that this was not an army whose hearts had been in their cause or who had fought to the last.[44] Here was more support for Belasyse's claim that the battle was poorly contested by the King's men. The parade of prisoners was not the only spectacle, for at least one of the carriages captured after the battle, with its feather bed, rich clothes and other plunder, was also brought through the streets, driven by the trooper who had taken it.[45]

Colonel Fiennes and other gentlemen who came to London with the prisoners and carried the colours and the letters from the General were 'called into the House, and made a particular Narration of the fight.' As was common practice, these messengers were well rewarded, one being given £100 and another £40, as were the men who carried the captured colours.[46] On the 26th it was ordered that these colours and cornets taken at Naseby be brought to the Herald's Office, registered and then hung up in Westminster Hall.[47] A record was indeed made, for 33 of these Royalist colours are depicted by Turmile, including the King's own standard with the lion and crown with the motto 'Dieu et mon droit', all the colours of the King's regiment of foot and of his lifeguard, all those of the Queen's regiment and of Prince Rupert's together with the Duke of York's Standard. In all some 80 colours had been taken but the rest did not come up to London until later.[48] The captured senior officers, the knights and colonels, had also not yet been brought up to the capital but at least their names and ranks could be published, as were various letters from the army that gave first hand accounts of the battle.[49] Naseby was to be turned into as great a propaganda victory as it had been a military victory and the underlying message they wished to convey was that the King's cause was now hopeless.

The prisoners were held during the following days in the Artillery Ground near Tuttle Fields while a committee was appointed by Parliament to consider how they should be disposed of.[50] The Irish prisoners, who originally were to have been executed, were now simply to be imprisoned. As for the others, it was eventually decided to send home those 'that would give Security for their living peaceably for the future; but such as did not, which was much the greater Number, were shipped off to serve in Foreign Parts upon Conditions.'[51] In all about 800 'volunteered' for Ireland, others went to Europe to fight for the Spanish and the French, but most of the rest spent the next year or more in prison.[52] In this, as in all other things about the campaign, the Parliamentarian action was designed to end the war as rapidly as possible by denying the King the ability or time to rebuild his forces. At Cropredy bridge Charles had not destroyed Waller's army, even though he had the opportunity, and at Lostwithiel he had failed to turn Essex's humiliating defeat into the destruction of his army, for he allowed Skippon to march away with his troops. Those men were then able to fight again at the second battle of Newbury a short time later. It may be true that these Parliamentarian forces suffered badly from desertion and that Waller's army effectively disintegrated, but the officers and seasoned troops of both armies had remained available to be incorporated into the New Model. In contrast, after Naseby the Royalist soldiers and officers taken prisoner were removed from the war once and for all. In this way they did not give the King the opportunity to rebuild his army, just as in the flight they were pursued mercilessly almost to the gates of Leicester. The objective was to destroy the Royalist military machine. This was the action of men that intended to win the war as quickly and completely as possible.

The prisoners of quality, the Royalist officers, were held separately from the common soldiers.[53] Though the accounts vary in detail there seem to have been about 340 inferior officers and 120 senior officers taken on the 14th June.[54] Of the 187 officers of the rank of ensign and above listed as prisoners on the night after the battle, 159 were from the infantry and only 28 from the cavalry. Though these did not represent all the cavalry officers taken in the pursuit, some of which were held at Rockingham, the figures do indicate how heavily the number of prisoners was weighted towards the infantry. It is therefore reasonable to assume that most of the 460 officers listed were also from the infantry. These officers had not been brought into Northampton on the Sunday, indeed some were still being taken to London by waggon as late as the 25th June and, whereas the common soldiers were put in the military grounds, the officers were held separately under guard in London House.[55]

Fig. 67. The wounded brought back into Naseby after the battle would have found a village very different to that which we see today.[56] At that time, although it was one of the larger of the county's villages, there were only about 65 houses and a population of around 400.[57] The houses in which the wounded were quartered for many days after the battle were mainly built of cob, that is of mud and straw, or were timber framed. Seen here in 1855 are some of those houses before their demolition later in the century. Ironically the bells in the village church, which were perhaps the first to have rung out to mark the great victory, bear the image of Charles I and the inscription 'GOD SAVE THE KING'![58]

If one takes into account all the sources which relate the numbers captured, it would appear likely that the most accurate figure for the common soldiers was that recorded when they marched into Northampton on the 15th June, a total of 4508. Not only does this have the appearance of an official and accurate total, it was provided at a time when they had almost all been collected together and when information should have been readily available, whereas most of the other figures seem to be those which had been estimated on the day of the battle itself. To this of course must be added at least 460 officers who, as we have seen, were dealt with separately. This gives almost 5000, but these figures do not apparently include the seriously wounded, some of whom could not be moved immediately, who numbered at least 500. In all then there were about 5500 prisoners captured on the 14th June. Of these perhaps 1000 were cavalry, for around 1000 horses were taken.[59] In addition, about 200 wounded Royalists managed to escape to Leicester after the battle, including the four Lords who 'came mortally wounded to Harborough but durst not stay.[60] While the other prisoners were apparently marched to Market Harborough, the wounded were not moved and so the night following the battle found 'many lying in the adjacent villages, besides the prisoners taken.'[61] It is not surprising therefore to find the constable of Naseby recording that on the night of the 14th and for a good while after, many of the wounded soldiers were quartered in every house in Naseby village.[62] These clearly included some quite high ranking officers, for at least one lieutenant colonel, Sir Edward Littledon, was said to 'lyeth wounded at Navesby'.[63]

On the evening of the 14th or soon after at least fifty other wounded soldiers were brought to the small garrison town of Rockingham to be treated, for one villager, Mr Thomas Harrison, later tried to claim payment 'For 50 Menes dyett being wounded at Nasebey fight yt Came to my wife for Cure £5.'[64] Whether they were Parliamentarian or Royalist troops is not stated, but they may well have been those wounded in the pursuit during the afternoon and evening following the battle, for we know that some of the prisoners taken during the pursuit were brought back to Rockingham. The majority of the wounded were however taken into Northampton in the days following the battle.[65] These are said to have included all the Parliamentarians and at least 500 Royalist wounded who had been taken in the fight but who were not brought up to London because they were so ill.[66] These men were quartered in many of the houses in Northampton and in surrounding settlements up to ten miles away, for in August payments were made for the quartering of wounded Parliamentarian soldiers in Wellingborough, Overstone and other places.[67] The dispersal of wounded men into the villages around Northampton was probably not an uncommon practice, for in May a trooper from the Northampton garrison, under Captain Clerke, lay 'under surgeons hand at Wilby'.[68] There is a tradition that the pub called the World's End at Ecton, between Wellingborough and Northampton, gained its name from the fact that wounded Royalist soldiers were held there after the battle. It is said that many of the wounded died there, and thus for them it became the world's end.[69] Although aspects of the tradition may be wrong, there is some supporting evidence, because the nearby village of Cogenhoe had to supply provisions to the value of £2 to Ecton after Naseby fight.[70]

The estimates given in the various sources immediately after the battle as to the numbers of wounded vary considerably. For Parliamentarian wounded the estimates are between 200 and 600.[71] The lower estimate of 200 is accompanied by a figure of 1000 Royalists, whereas other sources say the numbers were about equal, one specifying around 600 on each side.[72] Perhaps the most accurate figure for Royalist wounded taken prisoner was the 500 specified as being 'in the Villages and the Townes about Northampton, which in regard of the desperatenesse of their wounds were not brought up with the rest', but it is clear that these men were only the most severe cases because when Fiennes marched south with the convoy of prisoners he had required the services of surgeons, while there were also the two hundred or so wounded who escaped to Leicester. Perhaps a figure of 1000 is not too wild as an overall estimate for the Royalist wounded. For the Parliamentarian side we have far more accurate statistics.[73] Because of the great significance of the victory they had won, Parliament granted a substantial sum of money to meet the costs of the maintenance and care of their own troops wounded in the fight. On 20th June they assigned £500 to the mayor and aldermen of Northampton 'for the maintenance of our maimed men in Northampton; which Town and County ... very kind and loving to all ours there, yet are they not able to support so many.'[74] Later there was a further £200, again from the Committee of the Army, for the 'releife, mayntenance and care of ye souldiers wounded att Navesby battell under ye command of ye Honourable Sir Thomas Fairfax.' It is as a result of the careful accounting for this money, by the officials at Northampton, that we have a full record, by name and regiment, of every man in the Parliamentarian army that fought at Naseby and who was wounded severely enough to need treatment over the following weeks, as well as the way in which they were cared for and the costs of that care. The account lists 535 wounded soldiers. It might be argued that this record did not cover all the seriously wounded but it is likely to have been fairly comprehensive because a report in the *True Informer* states that 'Our wounded and sick men are all brought to Northampton'.[75] There may have been some discrepancies, for Okey states that he had 3 men wounded and none killed yet the Northampton account records payments for only two of Okey's men, while several other individuals, mainly senior officers, mentioned by Sprigge as wounded are not on the Northampton list.[76] Possibly such discrepancies occur because some men were not so seriously injured and were able to remain with the army.

The enormous number of seriously wounded men, both Parliamentarian and Royalist, completely overwhelmed the limited medical resources available in Northamptonshire and it was reported as late as the 24th June that surgeons were still very much wanted in Northampton and that 'many are likely to perish if they come not.'[77] At least 40 of the most seriously wounded were cared for in the 'hospital barne' in Northampton. There were two hospitals in the town in 1645, both in Bridge Street. St.Thomas's, which was by far the smaller, lay immediately outside the south gate, while St.John's lay just inside the gate. The medieval Hospital of St.John had been maintained after the dissolution as a hospital for the town and it was managed during the war by Francis Rushworth and Joseph Sergeant.[78] It is these two aldermen whose names are appended to the account of the payments for the Naseby wounded, indicating that it was at St.John's that the seriously wounded men were cared for. There were not even enough beds in the hospital to take the most serious cases and so we find payments for the construction of beds and the purchase of bedding, and then later the purchase of wood and nails to make a further 20 beds. There are various payments for beer, straw and suchlike, as well as the purchase of 184 shirts for the casualties. It was probably because of the

Fig.68. St.John's Hospital at the bottom of Bridge Street in Northampton, where the most severely wounded from the battle were cared for, as it was in the early 19th century. The medieval infirmary, known in the 17th century as the 'domicile' because it was the almshouse in which the poor lived, is the main building in this view. It still survives today together with the adjoining hospital chapel, set back and to the left, which was rebuilt in the 19th century. The hospital had seen the burial of soldiers from the Battle of Northampton in 1460 and in the 19th century it still had a burial ground at the rear. The Master's House, made out of the medieval refectory, lay to the left of the chapel but was pulled down in 1871. There is no evidence to show exactly where the hospital barn lay, in which the Naseby wounded were cared for, but John Speed's map of the town does show several other buildings within the hospital precinct in 1610 (fig.41).[79]

great strain placed on the town to care for these men, and particularly the lack of surgeons, that 19 very seriously wounded men were fairly soon transported up to hospitals in London in specially hired coaches, at the cost of £5/3/0d, and then later in July a further 18 men and thereafter yet more.[80] A short time after the battle, perhaps just a few days later, we find evidence of other wounded soldiers being transported out of Northampton, presumably returning to their homes. The constable of Great Houghton, a village which stood close by the Northampton to Bedford road, records a number of payments in connection with the transport of wounded soldiers. They may have been troops from the former Eastern Association regiments on their way back home to East Anglia or they may simply have been travelling via Olney or Bedford to London:

'payd for A miamed shoger and horse on night 8d...., payd to John Denton for on horse to Bedford two days to Carrie the maymed shogers 2/-, payd for another horse for my selfe two days to goe with the maymed shogers suche shom againe 2/-, spent shum two days of my selfe 1/4'.

Only at one other time do we find Houghton visited by wounded soldiers, when troops from Waller's army were quartered there and in other villages about Northampton following his defeat at Cropredy bridge.[81] Undoubtedly the payments made by the constable at Great Houghton are only the tip of the iceberg, for if the parish records for other villages survived, especially those on the main roads and adjacent to the main garrisons, both Royalist and Parliamentarian, we would have a far more detailed picture of the dispersal of the wounded from the battle.

In all there were at least nine surgeons employed by the Northamptonshire Committee to care for the wounded. Mr Humfry Cole, a surgeon to the garrison, was paid the sum of £7 'for his paines and materrialls in dressing wounded soldiers' for the period 18th June to 17th July, while Richard Ewin, surgeon to the infantry of the garrison, was paid £8 for the period 2nd to 31st July.[82] Undoubtedly both men were involved for some of this time in the treatment of Naseby casualties, however the surgeons to the garrison were in continual service during the war and seven or eight pounds was a typical monthly remuneration.[83] Those specifically paid for treating the Naseby wounded included Colonel Rich's surgeon and Mr Clarke, a surgeon at Wellingborough, who were supported by at least six surgeon's mates, in addition to at least four nurses who attended the sick. These surgeons were paid between one and ten pounds at various times for their attendance on the soldiers. Some had been specially brought into Northampton to deal with the great influx of wounded and so they also needed to be provided with quarters. Hence we find that a Mr Francis Gray was paid £2 for quartering the surgeon Mr.Fothergill, his mate, two servants and their horses for three weeks. Medical supplies were also naturally in great demand. Fothergill for example was paid a total of £13/01/05d to meet his bills in connection with the Naseby wounded. Whereas the most seriously wounded were treated in the hospital barn, the majority of the men were simply quartered on inns and private households, who apparently provided the nursing themselves and were reimbursed by the Committee. So for example Nicholas Harman was paid 30/- on the 23rd June for the billeting and carriage of soldiers wounded at Naseby field.[84] Some of these payments were for periods of three or four weeks, but other soldiers required longer term care and so some payments for quarter were for up to eight and ten weeks and even then, in late August, some soldiers were still said to lie sick. The actual sums made available for the support of individual men vary quite considerably and a few who were particularly ill were given second payments. Generally however the sum paid out for the common infantryman was about 6/-, that for the cavalryman most commonly 15/-, while for officers the sums tended to be commensurate with their rank. So whereas for one corporal the sum was £1 and for a provost marshal £1/10/0d, that for one ensign was £2 and a lieutenant £2/5/0d. There were of course variations from this pattern which undoubtedly related to the severity of the man's injuries and the time during which he was laid up.

Despite the care they were given, inevitably not all the men recovered. Some of those recorded as lying 'veary sick' or 'sorely wounded', and those for whom a second sum had to be paid because they continued to lay 'very weak', seem to have pulled through. Others however did not, for there are payments to the sexton for digging graves and the purchase of 76 shrouds for the dead. In all 42 wounded Parliament soldiers are listed as having died of their wounds, so perhaps the other shrouds were used for Royalists. Whereas the Parliamentarian soldiers were treated in the hospital and at inns and private houses, at least some of the wounded Royalists were held in the prison in Northampton castle, for on 23rd July payments were made to Philip Cave regarding their custody in the castle, for shrouds for the dead prisoners and for the cost of their burial from 28th June to 21st July.[85]

The one group of Parliamentarian wounded who are not consistently covered by the Northampton account are the senior officers. In particular, Skippon, Ireton, Colonel Butler, Major Huntington, Major Horton and Captain Blevin are not mentioned. Only four senior officers are listed in the account, Captains Potter, Cooke and Bush and Lieutenant Colonel Francis, all of whom died of their wounds within a few days of the battle. As with the prisoners, so with the wounded, the senior officers were inevitably treated very differently to the common soldiers. For some of course the wounds were of little consequence and they remained in command. Cromwell for example supposedly had a 'knock above his eye', but nothing serious enough to keep him from the action.[86] Others did not fare so well. Ireton, who had been injured in the thigh by a pike and in the face by a halberd, and Captain Butler, who had taken a brace of bullets in the thigh, were both sorely wounded and it was feared that they would die. Both did survive and in Ireton's case it was not many weeks before he was back on active service. Without doubt the greatest concern was for Major General Skippon and we have a good deal of information as to how he was treated in the weeks following the battle, which shows the very different care given to senior officers as compared to the common soldier. Skippon was taken to 'Master Stanlies house' at Brixworth and about 500 men with two pieces of ordnance were left there to guard him until he could be moved.[87] George Bishop, who was with the army and was the author of one of the accounts of the battle, actually took Skippon to the house in Brixworth and saw his wound dressed: 'I said to him, Sir, your wound hath caused a little cloud on this glorious day; hee answered, by no means let mine Eclipse its Glory, for it is my honour that I received a wound, and it was my God that strengthened mee.'[88] All the accounts agree that Skippon had acted very courageously on the field and therefore on the 20th June the Commons wrote a letter of thanks to Skippon and sent a 'physician', Dr Clarke, to visit him.[89] The provision of a guard for the commander was essential because later in the month the Earl of Northampton threatened to fetch him away, despite his wounds.[90] It was for this reason that on the 28th June the Major General was moved by horse litter from Brixworth to

Northampton, even though he was not really fit enough to travel. On the 30th a letter from Skippon arrived in Parliament informing of his progress and in response the House ordered £200 to be sent to him and a further £200 to pay his doctor's, surgeon's, apothecary's and other costs.[91] Doctors were again sent to attend on Skippon and still they found him seriously ill:

> 'At the comming down of Doctor Meverell, and Doctor Dunne they found him very weake and much spent, his wounde being on the right side of his brest, not far from the mouth of his stomack, the bullet coming out within three or four inches of the back bone, the danger was the greater for that he having his Armour on, which weighed 58lb weight, and the mouth of the piece being so neere shot (as is conceived) by one of his own souldiers in wheeling off, besides his taking extraordinary paines for four houres in the field after he received his wound, the blood much running down his body, and the loss of blood and spirits very great.'[92]

He was to require various surgery because of a piece of armour that had lodged in his wound. However, by the 15th July he had recovered sufficiently to be brought to London and so the Northampton Committee hired a horse litter to carry him there.[93] Inevitably, for such a hero, as he approached the capital 'divers Gentlemen and Citizens of worth rode forth to meet him.' It would however be almost a year before he was able to rejoin the army.[94]

Some other wounded officers did not fare so well. Captain Bush had died of his wounds and been buried at All Saints church in Northampton on the 16th June, as was 'a cornett from Abram Mainard'. Of Captain Potter, acting as one of Parliament's Commissioners to the Army, it was said he was 'dangerously wounded, but hopes of his recovery, so is Captaine Cooke.' They appear to have been moved to Northampton but they also died and were buried at All Saints church, Potter on the 28th and Cooke on the 29th June.[95] Unlike those killed outright on the battlefield, all those who died later of their wounds, whether senior officers or common soldiers, were properly interred in a churchyard. We find in Northampton that during June at least 30 common soldiers were buried at All Saints church, while in July there were Cornet Davis 'a soldier from the Swan', 'a clarke of the Band' and 'a solder from Will.Lanes'. Most if not all of these were presumably Naseby casualties.[96] Some of the Parliamentarian dead may have been buried in the hospital cemetery, for the most seriously injured were treated in the hospital and the sexton was paid for digging graves.[97] It must have been a similar story in all the churches in the town and in the other villages where the wounded had been dispersed, though very few burial registers survive to detail the men who died. In the Church of the Holy Sepulchre we find 'Robert Harris, souldier under Major Huntington' was buried on 15th June, then from mid July there was Captain Brampton Ferne and 13 more soldiers, several of unknown name. These undoubtedly included Royalists as well as Parliamentarians, but it is only with the senior officers that we can usually distinguish. On the 16th June for example the ardent Royalist Sir Edward Littledon, one of three members of the same family in Lisle's regiment of foot captured at Naseby, was buried at Holy Sepulchre, while Sir Thomas Dallison, 2nd Baronet Laughton of Lincolnshire, who was in Prince Rupert's Brigade at Naseby, died on the 20th June and was buried at St.Giles' church.[98] As we have seen, there were still wounded lying sick in the town during August and a few may still have been dying then or even later.[99]

About 200 wounded Royalist cavalry and officers had managed to reach Leicester following the battle. After Leicester had been retaken by Fairfax it would appear that some of the wounded moved on to the Belvoir Castle garrison in late June, when the constable's accounts for Branston, a village just three miles south of Belvoir, record for the very first time payments to wounded people, both soldiers and civilians. For the period the 20th June to 5th July the constable recorded:

'Item given to a Cart load of Maigmed people which were brought to ye towne from Walthid 6d, Item spent with Capt: Maisons soliers 1/4d, Item given to 2 soldiers who were Maigmed 4d....', Aug 7: 'Item given to 2 Maighmed soldiers 7d'.

That these wounded were indeed from the Naseby campaign seems likely because, although there were various soldiers from Belvoir quartered in the village again in August and September, there is only one more reference to wounded soldiers, after the 20th October, when the constable 'payd for Ale for 2 Maigmed soldiers 6d'.[100] Other wounded Royalists may have marched with the King to their home garrisons, like Colonel Bagot, governor of Lichfield, who returned to the city only to die some days later.[101]

There were some wild Parliamentarian reports which suggested that there were only about 100 Parliamentarian dead whereas between one and two thousand Royalists died in the battle.[102] Others claim the Royalist dead numbered about 600 and the Parliamentarians about 100, but the lowest estimate, of 50 common soldiers on the Parliamentarian side, was qualified with the comment 'as far as can be guessed until they come to bury the dead.'[103] The higher estimates of 100-150 come from the Parliament commissioners and Rushworth who were probably better informed and are the ones most commonly repeated by the newspapers.[104] Indeed, perhaps the most reliable source is Rushworth's letter which estimates a total of 1000 dead: 'we had slaine on our part none above a Captaine I yet hear of, and in all not 150 to my best judgement and I viewed the ground where the bodies lay.' Later he continues:

'I viewed the dead bodies, from the Battell to Harborough truly I estimate them not to be above 700, together with those slaine in the fields running away, but in pursuit between Harborough and Leicester, and by townes, conceived about 300 more slaine...'[105]

Another contemporary account broadly agrees, going on to say the number killed was 'as great in the pursuite, as upon the place..'[106] The estimates of the various eye witnesses generally indicate that at least 400 Royalists were killed on the battlefield, together with some 300 horses, while another 300 or so men were killed in the flight. According to Clarendon there were 900 Royalists killed of whom 150 were officers and gentlemen.[107] Whereas the Royalists lost many of their officers of high rank and birth, from the Parliamentarian army two captains were the most senior officers killed, though several higher ranking men would die of their wounds within a few days of the battle.[108] If we accept the figure of 700 - 1000 Royalists killed outright on the day then to this must be added those who survived only to die later of their wounds. Of the 535 on the Parliamentarian side who were seriously wounded 44 subsequently died. If the numbers on either side were in any way proportional in this respect then one must expect between about 100 and 300 Royalists to have died later of their wounds. That there was a far greater impact on the Royalist army is borne out by the relative numbers of officers killed, though of course care must be taken in drawing such conclusions as the Royalist army was supplied with a far greater number of officers than the New Model. So the total killed seem to have numbered in all between 1000 and 1500. However one looks at the figures, they would seem to support Belasyse's claim that the losses at Naseby were relatively light for such a major battle, something closer to 10% rather than the 20% which has been previously suggested.[109] They were considerably less than at Marston Moor where the dead have been estimated at 4000, a difference which cannot be wholly accounted for by the greater number of men involved in that engagement. If one adds the number of Royalists captured, at about 5000, to the number very seriously wounded, between 700 and 1000, and to the number killed, about 1000, then we can see that with a total of around 7000 the Royalist army had quite literally been destroyed.

The clearance of the battlefield must have been a dismal task, because there were bodies strewn for miles across the landscape. Undoubtedly a few of those who had at first been taken for dead were discovered still to be alive, as tradition records was the case with a Mr Mansell who was found to be alive by a young woman who then nursed him back to health.[110] The bodies of the dead were probably buried close to where they fell, for graves have been found in various parts of Naseby and Sibbertoft field. According to Mastin an old man in the village in the late 18th century still told the story which his grandfather had told him, who had been the boy tending the cattle in the field on the day of the battle and who had been present when the dead were buried. According to him it was done by the country people who came in from all the surrounding villages, who stripped some of the dead but buried others in their clothes, generally in mass graves so shallow that within a short time they 'became very offensive, that matter issued from the graves and ran several yards upon the ground, which, having subsided the cattle ate those spots, for several years, remarkably bare.'[111] The arms and equipment were, as far as possible, collected from the battlefield, though not all by representatives of the army or of the County Committee. As Rushworth reported, 'Wee tooke 5000 Armes on the field, but the Soldiers were so greedy of Plunder and pursuing the enemy, that the Countrey got some of them.'[112] Certain items must have remained in the cottages and houses in Naseby and nearby until a hundred or two hundred years later when antiquaries visited Naseby and purchased or were given these relics of the battle. Though some may have been dug up, many of those which survive in museum collections today can be seen, from the survival of leather fittings and the lack of rust, never to have lain in the ground. Due to the enterprise of these country folk, warrants had to be sent out to relevant parts of the county 'about gathering up arms after Navesby fight...'[113] This must have been a very substantial task because a number of different people were paid to complete the work. On 1st July 1645 a man was paid by the County Committee for himself and five others 'collecting up Armes after the fight in Nasebie feild and likewise for expenses upon Cartes in conveying the same to this Garrison £20.'[114] Later a certain Mr Palmer was paid six shillings for six days work fetching arms and carts from Naseby field and then on the 5th July 1645 Henry Divers was paid for his expenses 'finding and bringing arms to and carts to this garrison after ye late fight in Naseby field £3/0/2d.'[115]

The estimates of the numbers of arms actually captured in the battle range from 5000 to 10000, but not all will have been taken directly from soldiers for the Royalist train included waggons carrying 50 loads of muskets, pikes, powder, match and bullets.[116] Also taken were many horses with saddles and pistols as well as all the Royalist ordnance.[117] The latter comprised twelve of the fourteen pieces which had been drawn out of the artillery park at Magdalen College in early May, being two great demi-cannon, two demi-culverin and eight sakers as well as one mortar.[118] All the supplies for the ordnance were also captured with the train, consisting of twelve waggons and including 40 barrels of powder and proportionate match as well the ammunition, both shot and ball.[119] One of these waggons carrying a load of twenty four pound cannon balls was drawn by twenty six horses, while twelve other waggons carried the boats with their cables and anchors, which were for the transport of the artillery across rivers.[120] In all there were probably about two hundred waggons and carriages taken with the train, though one account says there were as many as 300. Some of these waggons contained 'great store of Bisket and Cheese (a seasonable refreshment for our souldieers that had marched so hard, and the night before had not a bit of Bread to a Regiment for their refreshment)...'[121]

The senior commanders may have escaped but their possessions were all captured, including Prince Rupert's sumpter horse and Sir Jacob Astley's coach, which were carrying 'great store of Plunder' and also some letters of 'Nicholas the lyer' where he says the Parliament has ordered the King to be killed.[122] In all the plunder that day was said to have been worth as much as a hundred thousand pounds in gold, silver and jewels.[123] Even the King's own waggon was taken with all 'the King's stuff' and some of his servants, and it was in this that the most important of all the items captured was found, 'the King's cabinet' containing his personal correspondence.[124] On the 23rd June the letters were brought before Parliament and referred to a Committee to be deciphered.[125] They were to have dramatic propaganda value, soon being published as *The King's Cabinet Opened*. They were a damning indictment of Charles, revealing both his untrustworthy character and the treaties he had tried to negotiate with Irish catholics and other foreign powers to bring troops into England.[126] Lady Hutchinson says 'This summer there was a much greater progress made in the war than had been before' and the King was beaten:

> 'in that memorable battle at Naseby, where his coach and cabinet of letters were taken; which letters being carried to London were printed, and manifested his falsehood, how that, contrary to his professions, he had endeavoured to bring in Danes and Lorrainers, and Irish rebels, to subdue the good people here, and had given himself up to be governed by the queen in all affairs both of state and religion.'[127]

These were undoubtedly destructive revelations that must have encouraged the desertion of many of the King's already wavering supporters.

When the train was taken the Parliamentarians also recovered large numbers of cattle that had been plundered from the country people, to whom it is said they were now returned.[128] If true, this will have been some comfort for the local people, but many had suffered greatly not just from the plundering but also from the battle itself. The open field landscape of Northamptonshire may have been ideal for the conduct of large set piece battles and have made it possible for the Royalist army to march some three miles in battle formation from Farndon to Naseby, however the impact of such a march and the action of the battle itself was dramatic for the local villagers. Though the field to the north west of Naseby, where the main action was fought, was fallow in 1645 this was not the case with the fields to the south and east of Sibbertoft, and probably not of Farndon and Clipston through which the action also passed. We know that many of the Royalist troops had bean stalks in their hats as field signs to distinguish their comrades from the enemy and the local people knew only too well where the bean stalks had come from! A large part of the crops in Sibbertoft seem to have been destroyed as a result of the movements of the armies, for the village estimated that 'The losse which was sustained in the fields of Sibbertoft att Navesbye fight in wheatte Rye barlye peasse oates and grasse was att the least to the value of £300.'[129] Also, given the sheer scale of the plundering and taxation by the Royalist army, which is clearly documented, we can believe it was not just propaganda when a Parliamentarian newspaper reports that 'the Country, though much plundered, are much satisfied, to see their revenge wrought so suddenly on their enemies; and the very Malignants rejoyce to see them led prisoners, that did so lately abuse them as well as others.'[130]

This victory was not to be frittered away as that at Marston Moor had been nearly twelve months before. The New Model had achieved their first and greatest objective, the destruction of the main Royalist field army. There was now an immediate and easy opportunity to restore the balance of power in the region by retaking Leicester. Not only had Naseby cast fear in all the Royalists, but the King had left the town very poorly garrisoned as the Rockingham governor had reported over a week before.[131] Fairfax wrote from Harborough on Sunday the 15th June, 'we intend to move to Leicester, as soon as we have taken Order with our prisoners, and wounded men...'[132] Later that day, when the prisoners had been dispatched to Northampton and with the wounded already being cared for, the army marched north along the main road towards Leicester.[133] That night the headquarters were at Great Glen, where Rupert had established his headquarters on the march south less than a fortnight before, and already the guards and sentinels were close to Leicester itself, which 'so alarm'd the Nobles and Gentry that had fled thither for security, that they departed thence in much haste, leaving the Lord Hastings to defend that Place.'[134]

Despite the provisions taken with the Royalist baggage train, there was still the need to maintain the supply of the Parliamentarian army, so we find on the following day that supplies were being sent in from the villages in north Northamptonshire. Welford, a large village on the Leicestershire border, reported 'we sent the second day after Navsby fight to Sr Thomas Fairfax hed quarters as much provisions as was valued by Mr Comesarie General at £3', while at Harrington, to the south east of Naseby a villager reported: 'these was taken from Mee by the gennerall Fairfax his army presently after naseby feeild one gray stond horse worth £10'.[135] Other supplies came in from places such as Sibbertoft, which had already been hard hit by the Royalists, and also from villages in north east Warwickshire, such as Long Lawford which several days later sent beer to Leicester for Fairfax's men.[136] Undoubtedly the Hundreds of south Leicestershire had also been sent warrants to supply the army, but the parish accounts for the county apparently do not survive.

Though the majority of the King's cavalry had already fled the region there were still Royalist troops who were easy game for the jubilant Parliamentarians. On the 16th the Derbyshire horse under Gell encountered a party of the Royalist cavalry capturing 200, while another party fell on some of the Newark horse and took 42.[137] Fairfax's first objective was to recapture Leicester and so on the 16th they marched on to Knighton, a village immediately south of the town, to prepare the siege. At about noon the whole army stood before Leicester and Fairfax sent a summons to Lord Loughborough. The response suggested that the Royalists would defend the town to the last, so a Council of War was convened and it was decided to storm the defences. Fairfax did not have the time for a long siege, he had other more pressing priorities, and so warrants went out to all the surrounding Hundreds to bring in materials and equipment, including hay, straw, ladders and carts, needed for the attack. The next day a battery was prepared in the same place the Royalists had used just over a fortnight before, and the same artillery pieces were set up to bombard the Newark wall. Rumour still abounded at this time for, while they were preparing to storm the town, Fairfax received intelligence that the King was advancing with 4000 horse towards them.[138] As Lord Loughborough knew only too well, there was in fact no chance of relief and so he sent out a trumpeter to request a parley. Two commissioners, Colonels Pickering and Rainsborough, were appointed to discuss the surrender. Early the next morning, before the surrender agreement could be properly implemented, in a spontaneous move the Royalists began laying down their arms, the gates were opened and Lord Loughborough and his officers quit the town leaving it in a state of chaos. Such was the King's attitude, now that his cause was so desperate, that Lord Loughborough was briefly imprisoned by Charles for delivering Leicester up to Fairfax without a fight, even though it would have resulted in a pointless loss of life.[139] Several months later Prince Rupert himself would be treated equally badly after the fall of Bristol. When Fairfax finally marched into Leicester later that morning he found that various commanders who had been wounded at Naseby, including Sergeant Major General Eyres, Colonel Lisle and others, were still in the town. He also took fourteen pieces of ordnance, thirty colours, 2000 arms, 500 horse and 50 barrels of powder with ammunition and match. As Sprigge records:

'The poor Inhabitants were overjoyed at their deliverance, though in a sad Condition, being so plundered by the Enemy at first taking the towne, that many had nothing left but the bare walls, who before had their shops and houses well furnished....'[140]

That same day the money for the army finally arrived, having been brought by convoy via Newport Pagnell, and so Fairfax mustered his troops and issued their pay. After a brief rest, on the 20th the army set out on its rapid march into the South West. The Scottish army was also now marching south and already the Royalist garrisons had begun to tumble, first Carlisle, then Scarborough and soon many others would follow. In contrast to the situation in late May, the Royalists no longer posed any great threat in the Midlands or East Anglia. Though later in the summer the King would regroup some of his forces at Newark and briefly break into the Association, taking the very lightly defended town of Huntingdon, it was not a significant threat because the Association had sufficient men in arms to meet the challenge. The local garrisons were generally more than a match for the remaining Royalists although, as before, the Newark forces in particular were still capable of destructive sallies across into Lincolnshire and so convoys were still needed to guard traffic moving north along Ermine Street, and it would not be until the siege of Newark was successfully concluded in 1646 that the problems would finally cease.[141] The Royalist garrisons in the Midlands were very heavily fortified and capable of withstanding prolonged siege, as the events of late 1645 and 1646 were to prove, but they did not provide a significant threat to the Parliamentarian cause now that the King's field army had been destroyed. Neither did they control enough territory to support or raise a new army, they were hard enough pressed simply to maintain themselves, and so the local Parliamentarian commanders could safely be left to deal with them.

It was the South West and to a lesser extent Wales and the Welsh Marches that still had the potential to supply a new army and contained the ports which could enable Irish forces and supplies from the continent to reach the King. Though Charles remained in South Wales trying to raise a new army, it was in the South West, where Goring still had a substantial Royalist force, that his greatest opportunity lay. Already in early 1645 it had been recognised, following the fall of Shrewsbury which was the key to North Wales, just as Gloucester was the key to South Wales, that the King:

> 'must now rely only upon Somerset, Devonshire, and Cornwall, for men and contribution; for I make account he is so straightened and wasted in his head-quarter about Oxford, that there are neither men, moneys, horses, nor victuals to be had there.'[142]

The ports such as Exeter and Fowey were the main route for the import of supplies from the continent and the transfer of the Prince of Wales, with key advisors such as Hyde, into the South West in early 1645, to reorganise and improve the war effort, had been a recognition that this region was the most important remaining base for the maintenance and supply of the Royalist war effort. After Naseby there was a desperate need for arms and equipment if a new field army was to be rebuilt, and Goring's army was the core around which Rupert saw it must be created. Fairfax was well aware of this and also knew only too well the immediate threat to Taunton, for in late May Lord Goring, Hopton and Grenville had joined forces and defeated Weldon's brigade.[143] On the 12th June letters had arrived from Taunton saying speedy relief was essential and Fairfax had also intercepted letters from Goring to the King which showed he was confident of reducing Taunton within a few days, which would greatly strengthen the Royalist grip on the region.[144] It was inevitable therefore that Fairfax should march as rapidly as possible into the South West. He had no intention of allowing the Royalists the opportunity to rebuild their forces. Moreover, he knew how urgent it was to complete the tasks quickly, for in the weeks after the battle the New Model would see a major loss of men through desertion, just as the Eastern Association army had during the previous summer. An army was always a wasting asset and so it was a resource that should be used as quickly and effectively as possible. This is exactly what Fairfax would do over the coming months.[145]

Having recaptured Leicester on the 18th June 1645, Fairfax had restored the balance of power in the region and reopened vital communications. He then put the garrison in the capable hands of Colonel John Needham who immediately, on the 20th June, laid siege to Ashby de la Zouch castle, where Lord Loughborough had retreated. Though it would be late February 1646 before Ashby surrendered it was no longer a significant threat and one by one the other Royalist fortresses in the region would come under siege, mainly by local troops, in a concerted effort to destroy the last pockets of resistance. In a sense therefore the beginning of the siege of Ashby castle marked the end of the Naseby campaign, because the King's army had been destroyed, the victorious New Model was marching rapidly south westward to a new challenge, while the fate of the region had returned once more into the hands of the local Parliamentarian commanders.[146]

Fig. 69. The ruins of the castle at Ashby de la Zouch, Leicestershire, as they existed in the 18th century. The castle was slighted in 1648, after the Second Civil War.

NOTES

1. *A True Relation of a Victory*. Rushworth letter. Rushworth to Luke, 14th June 1645, Tibbutt, 1963, p.577. Nichols, vol.2, p.505.
2. PRO SP28/171, f.199.
3. '... June the [ ] 1645 After Naisbey fight men and horses under the Comand of Colonell Rocester': 20 men, £1/00/0d; 24 men & some horses, £1/16/0d; 46 men & 52 horses, £4/00/0d; 45 men & as much grasse, £8/00/0d; 30 men, £1/10/0d; 36 men & 36 horses, £2/00/0d; 10 men, £0/10/0d; 50 men & almost as many horses, £5/00/0d; 50 men & 30 horses, £3/05/0d; 60 men and horses, £2/10/0d; 60 horses, £1/00/0d; 9 men, £0/04/6d; 24 men, £0/12/0d; 4 men, £0/02/0d; men and horses, £0/10/0d; 12 men & horses, £0/12/0d; 6 men, £0/03/0d; 6 men, £0/03/0d; 5 men, £0/02/6d; 6 men, £0/03/0d; grass eaten to value of £1/00/0d; 9 men & horses, £0/09/0d; 6 men & 1 horse, £0/03/6d; men & horses, £1/05/0d. Marston Trussell account, PRO SP28/173 unfol.. The Marston account refers to Thomas Sprigge. This may be a relation of Joshua Sprigge, whose family came originally from the Harborough district, though

Joshua himself was from Banbury. Hothorpe account, PRO SP28/238, f.23-4. Dated June 1644 but clearly relating to June 1645.

4. Though undated, the constable's claim is between a reference to the fall of Leicester and one to the wounded troops from Naseby fight. There are references to infantry taking free quarter to the value of 9/6d. The constable also records a cost of 8/- spent on Fairfax's soldiers 'goeing northwards staying with us' as well as five acres of meadow grass, worth £5/10/0d, eaten by some of the horses in Cromwell's regiment at their rendezvous there. *A Particular of the Lord Rockingham's Account*, PRO SP28/171 unfol..

5. *The True Informer*, 21st June.

6. *Three Letters* - Fairfax.

7. *Lords Journals*, 16th June. Whitelocke, p.146, says 19th June.

8. Rushworth, vol.6, p.48. Whitelocke, p.146.

9. *Lords Journals*, 16th June 1645.

10. Rushworth letter.

11. *A more exact and perfect Relation.*

12. Committee of Both Kingdoms to Gell, 18th June 1645, *CSPD*, p.600.

13. *The True Informer*, 21st June.

14. Rushworth letter.

15. *The Kingdomes Weekly Intelligencer*, 10th-17th June. *Scottish Dove*, 13th-20th June.

16. *Lords Journals*, 27th June.

17. Foard, 1994, p.68.

18. *The Moderate Intelligencer*, 12th-19th June.

19. *A Glorious Victory*.

20. Rushworth, vol.6, p.42.

21. Tibbutt, 1963, p.328.

22. Symonds, p.194. *Iter Carolinum.*

23. Symonds, p.194.

24. *Lords Journals*, 18th June.

25. Slingsby, p.153. Symonds, p.194-5.

26. Wedgwood, 1974, p.459.

27. Warburton, vol.3, p.129.

28. Rushworth letter.

29. *A Glorious Victory. Three Letters* - Fairfax. *A True Relation of a Victory.* Leighton and Herbert. *A more exact and perfect relation. Moderate Intelligencer*, 15th June. *The Weekly Account*, 11th-18th June. *The Kingdomes Weekly Intelligencer*, 10th-17th June.

30. The Naseby account implies this is the case, PRO SP28/171, f.199.

31. *The True Informer*, 21st June.

32. Fiennes to Luke, 16th June, Tibbutt, 1963, p.579. *The Exchange Intelligencer*, 18th-24th June.

33. *A True Relation of a Victory. CSPD*, 1645, p.6.

34. Fiennes to Luke, 16th June, Tibbutt, 1963, p.579 & 581.

35. Luke to Fiennes, 16th June, and Fiennes to Luke, 17th June, Tibbutt, 1963, p.325 & 581.

36. *The True Informer*, 21st June. Sheriff of Northampton, 18th June, *A more particular and exact relation.*

37. The date is when he was paid, not when he held the prisoners, but it does imply that he held them for some days. PRO SP28/35, f.460.

38. 'provision carried to Olney for the prisoners after Nazby fight £1/10/0d', PRO SP28/171, f.610-1.

39. Tibbutt, 1963, p.581. *The True Informer*, 21st June.

40. *Lords Journals*, 18th June.

41. *Kingdomes Weekly Intelligencer*, 17th-24th June.

42. Nicholas to Rupert, 23rd June, Warburton, vol.3, p.120.

43. *The Exchange Intelligencer*, 18th-24th June. *The Manner how*.

44. Wedgwood, 1974, p.457. *The Manner how*.

45. *Mercurius Verdicus*, 14th-21st June.

46. *Kingdomes Weekly Intelligencer*, 17th-24th June. Whitelocke, p.146-7.

47. Whitelocke, p.147.

48. Dr Williams' Library, MS Modern f.7. Rushworth letter. *The Kingdomes Weekly Intelligencer*, 10th-17th June. *Mercurius Civicus*, 12th-18th June. There is a full list and description of the colours in *The Manner how*.

49. *Three Letters*.

50. The Military Yard in St.Martin's Field according to *Lords Journals*, 21st June.

51. Ludlow, 1698, vol.1, p.156-7. The prisoners were held in the Military Yard, *Mercurius Civicus*, 18th-25th June. Whitelocke, p.146.

52. Kenyon, 1988. Wedgwood, 1974, p.457. Gardiner, 1893, vol.2, p.257.

53. *A more exact and perfect Relation*.

54. *Mercurius Civicus*, 12th-18th June.

55. *The True Informer*, 21st June. Whitelocke, p.147. *A Diary or an Exact Journal*, 19th-26th June.

56. It is incorrectly stated by the editor of *CSPD*, p.594, that Naseby was a market town. Goodfellow, P., 1987, 'Medieval Markets of Northamptonshire', *NP&P*, vol.5, p.305-324.

57. Naseby Map of 1630 depicts 65 houses. Compton Census 1676 gives the population of the village as 400, comprising 70 families. This accords well with the 74 houses with 95 hearths recorded in the Hearth Tax of 1674.

58. *Architectural Notices of the Churches of the Archdeaconry of Northampton*, p.239. Some of the bells were recast in 1936.

59. *A more exact and perfect relation*.

60. Rushworth letter.

61. *The True Informer*, 21st June.

62. PRO SP28/171, f.199.

63. *Mercurius Civicus*, 12th-18th June. *Three letters*.

64. PRO SP28/171, f.391.

65. *The True Informer*, 21st June.

66. *Mercurius Civicus*, 18th-25th June.

67. Northampton wounded account, PRO SP28/173, f.18.

68. PRO SP28/238, f.244.

69. Pipe, 1990, p.105-6. It is also claimed that the pub was built in the 18th century and was originally called the Globe, and was renamed when William Hogarth, the 18th century artists who often stayed at Ecton, painted a new inn sign and took the name the World's End from the adjoining paddock. Cole, 1825, p.46. This is clearly wrong because the pub already had the name in 1675 and 1679. Ogilby, 1675, plate 61. VCH, 1937, vol.4, p.122.

70. PRO SP28/171, f.610-1.

71. *The Moderate Intelligencer*, 12th-19th June.

72. *The True Informer*, 21st June. *Moderate Intelligencer*, 15th June.

73. *Mercurius Civicus*, 18th-25th June.

74. *The Moderate Intelligencer*, 19th-26th June.

75. *The True Informer*, 21st June.

76. Okey.

77. *The Moderate Intelligence*r, 19th-26th June.

78. VCH, 1930, vol.3, p.59-61. Serjeantson, 1911-1914. Dryden, 1875.

79. Serjeantson, 1911-14. A detailed description of the buildings before demolition of the Master's House is given in Dryden 1873.

80. Northampton wounded account, PRO SP28/173, f.18-19.

81. Though not dated, the items for 1645 appear to be in chronological order. The references to maimed soldiers appear immediately after the providing of supplies to the army at Kislingbury and the loss of the team at Naseby and so must relate to the period of days and weeks after the battle. These payments to maimed soldiers are quite different to the standard payment to Northampton towards the costs of maintaining the gaol and for supporting maimed soldiers, which was an annual payment made by all parishes. Great Houghton parish records, NRO 175P/38.

82. 17th July 1645, PRO SP28/35 f.344. PRO SP28/35, f.463.

83. 23rd January 1645-6, Richard Ewyn surgeon, PRO SP28/35, f.417.

84. 23rd June 1646, PRO SP28/238, f.316.

85. PRO SP28/239 unfol.. There are also various payments to the surgeon which may relate to the care of these prisoners.

86. *The True Informer*, 21st June.

87. *Mercurius Civicus*, 18th-25th June.

88. *A More Particular and Exact Relation*.

89. *A Relation of the Victory*. Whitelocke, p.146.

90. *The Kingdomes Weekly Intelligencer*, 24th June-1st July.

91. Whitelocke, p.147.

92. *The Kingdomes Weekly Intelligencer*, 24th June-1st July.

93. 'paid to paull grene for a horse that carryed up Major general Scippon £1/10/0d', PRO SP28/173, Northampton wounded account, f.20.

94. *Mercurius Civicus*, 10th-17th July. Sprigge, 1647, p.248.

95. Rushworth letter. Serjeantson, 1901, p.152-3.

96. Serjeantson, 1911, p.204-5.

97. St.John's was in the parish of All Saints, so it is possible that the 30 listed as being buried in the church may be the same men. No attempt has been made to compare the names in the list of wounded with that in the registers, though this could be done to get a more complete list of the Parliamentarian dead.

98. Cox & Serjeantson, 1897, p.195-7. Serjeantson, 1911, p.204-5.

99. A soldier who died at Mr Blake's in Harborough was buried on the 29th August 1645 but it seems highly unlikely that he was a Naseby casualty. 'Samuell Garner a souldier that was wounded and died at Mr Blakes and was buried August 29th.' Market Harborough parish register. Equally unlikely is the entry from All Saints register in Northampton for 6th February 1646 to the burial of 'a souldier under Corronell Prids regiment.'

100. In 1646 and 1647 there are just two references to maimed soldiers and this seems to be the general payment made by all parishes rather for soldiers actually in the village. Constable's accounts, Branston, LRO DE 720-30. .

101. *Kingdomes Weekly Intelligencer*, 8th-15th July.

102. *Scottish Dove*, 13th-20th June.

103. *A more exact and perfect Relation*.

104. *Mercurius Civicus*, 12th-18th June. *The Weekly Account*, 11th-18th June.

105. Rushworth letter.

106. *A True Relation of a Victory*.

107. Clarendon, bk.9, p.42.

108. 600 Royalist killed and not above 100 Parliamentarians, Leighton and Herbert. About 400 dead and about 300 horses on the field. 50 of ours killed, *A more particular and exact Relation*.

109. Carlton, 1994, p.202.

110. Ireland, 1794. *NN&Q*, 1886-7, vol.2, item 284.

111. Mastin, 1792, p.117-8.

112. Rushworth letter.

113. On 25th November 1645 Walter Oldham was paid for two several journeys of 5 days delivering warrants in the county. PRO SP28/239 unfol..

114. PRO SP28/35, f.476.

115. PRO SP28/239 unfol.. A further payment is recorded in January 1646 for the transport of arms and equipment to the garrison, but it is unclear whether this was simply a late payment or whether there were still arms being collected from the surrounding villages seven months after the battle. 11th-26th January 1645-6, Philip Cave's Second Account, PRO SP28/172 unfol..

116. *The Kingdomes Weekly Intelligencer* 10th-17th June. *The Weekly Account* 11th-18th June. *Mercurius Civicus* 12th-18th June. Leighton and Herbert. *A True Relation of a Victory. A more exact and perfect relation.*

117. *A more exact and perfect Relation.*

118. Leighton and Herbert. *An Ordinance* - Cromwell and Fairfax letters. *A Relation of the Victory.* Rushworth letter. *Mercurius Civicus,* 12th-18th June. *The Weekly Account,* 11th-18th June. *The Kingdomes Weekly Intelligencer,* 10th-17th June.

119. *Mercurius Civicus,* 12th-18th June. *The Kingdomes Weekly Intelligencer,* 10th-17th June.

120. *Mercurius Civicus,* 12th-18th June. *The Kingdomes Weekly Intelligencer,* 10th-17th June. *Parliament's Post,* 10th-17th June.

121. Rushworth letter.

122. *A True Relation of a Victory.* Rushworth letter.

123. Wedgwood, 1974, p.455, quoting Hull letters.

124. *Three Letters* - Cromwell. Leighton & Herbert. *Iter Carolinum.* Possibly two carriages escaped. *The Kingdomes Weekly Intelligencer,* 10th-17th June. *Mercurius Civicus,* 12th-18th June. All the coaches etc except the King's and Digby's, *A more particular and exact Relation.* Also taken according to Whitelocke, p.153, was a book 'wherein were the names of divers members of the House, with summs of money supposed to have been contributed by them to the King, and his Majestie's hand in many places of it.'.

125. Whitelocke, p.147.

126. *The King's Cabinet Opened,* 1645. Maddison, 1966.

127. Hutchinson, 1908, p.224.

128. *The True Informer,* 21st June. *A more exact and perfect relation.*

129. PRO SP28/171, f.124.

130. *The True Informer,* 21st June.

131. Sprigge, 1647, p.48.

132. *Three Letters* - Fairfax.

133. Rushworth letter.

134. Rushworth,vol.6, p.48.

135. PRO SP28/173 unfol.. PRO SP28/172 unfol..

136. Tennant, 1992, p.262.

137. Whitelocke, p.146-7.

138. Whitelocke, p.146.

139. Hensman, 1911.

140. Sprigge, 1647, p.50.

141. Davies, 1964, p.36. *The City Scout. The Moderate Intelligencer,* 21st-28th August. *The True Informer,* 30th August.

142. Letter from Chaloner to Lord Fairfax, 24th February, Bell, 1849, vol.1, p.164.

143. Sprigge, 1647, p.23.

144. Whitelocke, p.144. Rushworth, vol.6, p.48. Sprigge, 1647, p.47.

145. The records of quartering and supply suggest that the New Model took the road through Lutterworth and Rugby, where they picked up one parish team to carry supplies to the next headquarters at Lillington near Warwick, where they joined the Warwick to Stratford road. Naturally Fairfax sent units of cavalry forward in advance of the army, to prepare the way and

to cover the advance. So, while the headquarters were at Lutterworth, Rich's regiment was already at Kineton, presumably to deter any attack from Banbury, and they remained there for three days as the army marched south. In contrast to such cavalry units, the infantry appear to have been kept close together at or immediately adjacent to the headquarters. So for example when the headquarters were at Lillington, near Warwick, regiments of foot were also in the adjacent villages of Milverton, Offchurch and Leamington. Tennant, 1992.

146. Nichols, vol.3, p.611.

CHAPTER 10

AN ASSESSMENT

'This is no other but the hand of God,
to him alone be the glory,
wherein none are to share with him.'
Oliver Cromwell

The starting point for any assessment of the Naseby campaign must be the question as to whether the Royalists had already lost the ability to win the war. It seems clear that by the beginning of 1645 Rupert and various other of the King's advisors had reached this conclusion, because they argued that Charles should use the substantial military resources that were still under his control to achieve the best negotiated peace he could. From the beginning of the war Parliament had the advantage in resources through its control of the wealthiest areas of England. The King's best chance of winning was in the early stages, in 1642-3, when he had important advantages, such as the quality of his cavalry compared to that of his enemy. There seems little doubt that, as the war progressed, but for the incompetence and lack of commitment of its senior commanders, Essex and Manchester, Parliament's command of resources should have enabled it to win the war far sooner. By 1645 their ability to wage war had improved even further relative to the King as a result of military successes both regionally and nationally. At a regional level, as we have seen in the south east Midlands, the territories under Royalist control were contracting under Parliamentarian pressure and as the territories shrank so the ability of the Royalist forces to maintain their military machine at a local level was reduced. This created a downward spiral which, unless broken, would inevitably lead to defeat. The same was true at a national scale.

Some have argued that it was in fact the battle of Marston Moor that was the turning point of the war because it resulted in the King losing almost the whole of the north of England. This was certainly a severe blow to his ability to wage war, for the North was a large recruiting ground from which the Earl of Newcastle had been able to build and maintain a substantial army. As the area under Royalist control reduced so that territory which the King retained was placed under increasing pressure in order to maintain an army capable of challenging Parliament's main field army. The result was a massive strain on the resources of those territories and by the spring of 1645 this caused the local populations to rise up against their oppressors in a way which was not seen in the main areas of Parliamentarian control. This is why Hutton has argued that, although battles decisively affected the course of events, 'in the last analysis it was the local community, not Parliament, which defeated Charles I, not from hatred of his cause but from hatred of the war itself.'[1] In reality the two are intimately interlinked because the problems with the local communities were to a large degree the result of the deteriorating military situation. The inexorable slide towards total defeat could only be reversed by decisive military victory by a large force but, particularly by 1645, the mobilisation of such an army required the stripping of troops from local garrisons, and the almost immediate result in May 1645 in the Midlands was the fall of Evesham. Without a rapid, major victory over Parliament's main field army, which would release the King's forces to recapture large parts of England, there was no chance of the downward spiral being broken.

The Royalist forces had always been divided into a number of separate armies. Now that they were under such pressure it was even more important that those forces be combined into a single army which could be efficiently managed according to a single strategy. Although Rupert had made some attempt at reorganisation, the Royalists never matched the bold decision by Parliament to completely remodel its forces in order to win the war. Indeed the King's actions in promoting Goring to an independent command had exactly the opposite effect. Had the Royalists attempted a fundamental reorganisation then there were probably still sufficient military resources available, particularly in Wales, the Marches and the South West to create a formidable army that might have been capable of defeating the New Model. Very belatedly an initiative of this kind was proposed, after the battle of Naseby, when it was suggested that most of the Royalist garrisons be abandoned in order to marshal sufficient troops to create a new field army, but this was a desperate measure when it was far too late to be effective. However, through his untiring work during the spring of 1645 and against all the odds, Rupert had rebuilt an army capable of fighting a major campaign.

It was not the Royalists but the Parliamentarians that had learnt the lessons of three years of war and achieved the reconstruction of their forces to create a single major army. This is why Everitt has seen the battle of Naseby as 'the triumph of the state over the county community as much as of Parliament over the King'.[2] There was the creation of a national army in spite of the county based military organisation which had dominated Parliament's military operation throughout most of the war. The County Committee system, with the associated local military command structure, was however better than any administrative system that the Royalists imposed in the territories they held. It was an important building block enabling the efficient raising of both taxes and recruits and so there was no attempt to replace it. Instead these local interests were made subservient to the national interest and they became very much more a local government tool acting for a national government, at least in military terms. Though it had taken a long time and a great deal of effort from a small but determined group of MPs, led by the Independents, to get a fundamental shift in Parliament's military policy, once the decision was made it was not easily undone. The King on the other hand could and did change his mind frequently, resulting in a complete lack of continuity and of sound management. Overawed by those around him, unable to fully accept his lack of ability, yet unwilling to relinquish control to anyone capable of implementing a coherent strategy, he was always there to dabble and to undermine. In this the Royalist cause suffered from the old problems of the monarchical system, with a single person in overall control as a result of birth not of ability. His advisors might win the argument a hundred times, but Charles was still their King and could change his mind as and when he wished, and often did. In contrast in Parliament it was possible for leaders to be overturned and replaced, providing the possibility for new leaders to implement new policies. As a result Parliament achieved a major development in national and local administration of the war effort just as it had developed the Committee system as the forerunner of cabinet government. In a sense the Parliamentarian response to the war can be seen as innovative, presaging future developments in English government while the Royalist approach was reactionary, based on individual personal authority.

The Royalist army should have been able to muster a larger number of troops at Naseby than it did, in particular those of Goring, who had been instructed to rendezvous with the King well before the 14th June. It was Charles who had sent Goring back into the South West in early May and it was Charles who had given him the independent command which he would exploit in order to achieve his own objectives. Sir Philip Warwick was quite clear that this was a major reason for the defeat, saying that:

'if the state of affairs had bin duly and fully weighed, a necessity lay on his Majestie to have kept all his forces close together, or to have bin in such a nearnes for conjunction, as might have made one day the decider of the whole controversy, but wee still wanted some daring resolution....'[3]

This was comparable to the failures of Parliamentarian commanders in previous campaigns, dividing their forces and unable to establish a single overall command structure. Charles never gave Rupert, or any other commander, the authority they needed to manage the war effort effectively and this resulted in regional and personal interests being put before national interests. In effect, Goring put the capture of Taunton above the defeat of the New Model Army, indeed Bulstrode, who actually wrote Goring's reply to his instructions to rendezvous with the King in early June, hints at more sinister intentions. Goring's personal ambition was also perhaps coming before that of the Royalist cause.[4]

It has been argued that events might have turned out very differently had Goring and Gerard joined the King's army before the battle was fought. In any such assessment what must be taken into account is the large number of Parliamentarian troops which might also have been available to Fairfax. Firstly, Goring's troops were in the South West to counter the action of a brigade of New Model troops under Weldon that had been sent to relieve Taunton. Weldon's brigade could equally have been called up to join the New Model and indeed, one might argue that they should never have been detached from the New Model in the first place, whatever the condition of Taunton. Second, there were large numbers of troops close to joining Fairfax or which could have been brought up to the army within a few days, and the timing of the battle was after all of Fairfax's choosing. There were the Hertfordshire horse that arrived in time to join in the pursuit on the 14th June, the 2000 horse under Gell who arrived the next day, 3400 troops in the Association almost ready to march but which Cromwell had left behind in order to join the army swiftly, while Kingston has estimated that East Anglia had in all some 15000 men in arms in June 1645.[5] Only if the New Model had been drawn into battle in the South West could the table of advantage have been turned, for only in the South West did the Royalists have the necessary resource base to raise substantial forces, Goring having some 11000 men in arms in the region by June. It could be argued that this was the fundamental mistake, not focusing the campaign in or near the South West, where the King's army would have been closest and the Parliamentarians furthest from the areas where they could muster their largest number of troops.

However, Rupert and the King knew only too well that they would be unable to carry the Northern horse with them if they did not march into the North, and that would deprive them of substantial experienced cavalry forces. The alternative, which Rupert favoured, was to centre the campaign of 1645 in the North. There the King did have potential advantages, with a large tract of territory which could be returned into Royalist hands where there were many who would rally to the King's standard, and enabling a reconstruction of the Royalist resource base for a continuation of the war. This was after all where most Parliamentarians believed the King would march, right up until the fall of Leicester, and it was also where Rupert continually argued the army should be. Where the campaign certainly should not have been fought from the Royalist point of view was in the south east Midlands, exactly where the King chose to bring his army. This was a war torn region which did not hold the key to the Civil War but it was where the Parliamentarians were on home territory, closest to where they could muster the greatest number of additional troops and where the Royalists were furthest from were they could assemble such support.

In the early stages of the campaign the command of the New Model was maintained at a distance by the Committee of Both Kingdoms and this placed the army in a situation as dangerous as did the King's incompetent management of the Royalist campaign. Through the bureaucratic hand of the Committee of Both Kingdoms, Essex and Manchester retained a control over the action of the New Model, and this was why the new army began the campaign following an ineffective and destructive strategy similar to that seen in previous years. There was the division of the New Model into several separate brigades which were sent to opposite ends of the country in order to pursue several different objectives at once, destroying one of the most fundamental advantages that the new army had over its Royalist opponents.

This was the point at which the New Model was at its most vulnerable and might have been destroyed by the sort of swift Royalist action that Goring was arguing for, but bold action was the last thing that Charles was capable of and he was unwilling to delegate the authority to someone who was. If he had acted decisively and followed one of the several courses of action proposed by his advisors in May then he would have had a far greater chance of success. As always however, he avoided making a choice and ended up with no effective strategy at all. The creators of the New Model had realised that the way to win the war was to repeat the success they had achieved at Marston Moor, by destroying the King's field armies, because this would enable all other objectives to be achieved. As soon as the last phase of the remodelling process was complete, with the transfer of control of the army from the Committee of Both Kingdoms to the Lord General and his Council of War, this original strategy, which must have been arrived at by Cromwell and Fairfax long before, was applied immediately. Once this had been put in train then the Royalists' fate was sealed. If they were to have met this challenge then Charles needed to have acted in the preceding winter by giving Rupert the authority to completely reorganise the Royalist army, and for the Prince to implement his own strategy for the conduct of the campaign in 1645. Rupert was as capable as Cromwell and Fairfax of seeing that the first objective, once sufficient forces had been assembled, should be the destruction of the enemy's field army.

Arguments have been made about the decision taken at Market Harborough on the night of the 13th June. Despite later lies, the blame for this decision can be placed with Digby, for his advice to the King, and with Charles for taking the advice of courtiers on such crucial military matters against the judgement of his senior military commanders. In reality however it was probably already too late even by the 12th June for the Royalist army to avoid a battle, and because the convoy had been sent to Oxford there was no way that the army could have marched any earlier. If they had not fought at Naseby then they are likely to have been caught at some point hardly less disadvantageous as they retreated northward, and as they marched they would be moving yet further from the reinforcements that Goring and Gerard were supposed to bring up to the army. In contrast Fairfax could look to the support of the Parliamentarian forces in the North and to the Scottish army. The Royalists would only have been delaying the inevitable. Rupert's strategy in the North would only have worked if they had marched there much earlier, when they were free to act without the attentions of the New Model. In that respect the crucial decisions were those made by the King at Market Drayton, Burton on Trent and Leicester between the 20th May and the 3rd June, when he decided to stay in the Midlands because of worries about Oxford.

For Hutton and Gentles the battle of Naseby was simply a case of suicide whereas for Morrah it was a 'near-run thing' that up to almost the end might have gone the other way. The truth seems to lie somewhere between the two extremes.[6] No one can dispute that the New Model had the advantage in numbers, though the degree of their superiority would seem to have been overestimated by some commentators and so, although this was a significant advantage, it was not the single overwhelming factor that various authors would suggest. Indeed, many at the time saw the New Model's success as a remarkable and unexpected victory. According to Ludlow for example 'This Success was astonishing, being obtained by Men of little Experience in Affairs of this nature, and upon the account despised by their Enemies...'[7] The victory was described in the Sermon given in Parliament on the 19th as 'this late great, and unexpected Victory' with the comment that 'They were an Army despised by our Enemies, and little lesse then despaired of by our Friends, as men from whom little was to bee looked for...'[8]

In reality the situation was very different, and the senior Parliamentarian commanders knew this only too well. The troops that fought under Fairfax at Naseby were a single professional army, even if only newly created. There were no militia forces within it and only a small percentage of the troops were drawn from local garrisons. It was well organised and its commanders generally had the trust of their men. Many of the infantry officers had fought in several of the major battles of the war while the cavalry were even more experienced. As a newspaper reported after the battle, our officers 'performed all poynts of souldery as well, though Envy hath frequently bespattered them, as not able to command, and therefore deserted by so many out of feare...'[9] The Royalists certainly had a much larger number of officers and they had a far greater experience of warfare, which may in part have contributed to the early success of the Royalists on their right wing and in the centre. However, the King's army must have suffered from all the tensions arising from the combination of many smaller bodies of troops, and despite some limited attempt at reorganisation they had never overcome this fundamental weakness. Moreover, the Northern horse had almost mutinied just before Naseby and it was argued by several commentators at the time that it was the failure of the Northern horse to fight with conviction that was a major factor in the defeat. For Belasyse however it was a much wider lack of commitment amongst the Royalist forces which contributed to the destruction of the King's army. The New Model infantry had of course suffered from desertion, but this was an inevitable problem with any Civil War army, and they may also have had problems due to the number of new recruits and the tensions between Presbyterian and Independent, especially in the two centre regiments which broke at Naseby. It was even considered by some Parliamentarian commanders that the common infantryman in the Royalist army was generally better than his equivalent in the Parliamentarian army, but what was most important at Naseby was the degree of commitment, discipline and experience of the majority of the New Model cavalry and of the infantry officers.

Whatever the differences in number and quality of the two armies or the quality of their equipment, the ability of the senior commanders on the field and the effectiveness of their tactics could be decisive. Smaller armies, during the Civil War in England and elsewhere, sometimes defeated far larger forces as both Rupert and Montrose had demonstrated. However, unlike their predecessors, the senior commanders of the New Model had a genuine commitment to winning the battle and the war. They were more than just competent commanders and they were willing to lead by example. An eye witness had reported after the battle of Naseby that 'Sir Thomas Fairfax hath merited exceedingly, shewing such courage and resolution as hath rarely been seen, which did so animate the souldiers, as is hardly to be exprest.' There were similar reports as to the courage of Cromwell, Skippon and Ireton which cannot be dismissed as simply propaganda.[10] There was, perhaps for the first time in the war, a Parliamentarian army which had a wholly united and effective command structure. Fairfax had full authority to command, the ability and experience to exercise that authority and the right team to implement his orders, with all three senior commanders each playing a vital role in controlling the battle. Although they did not have the benefit of long experience in continental wars, Fairfax and Cromwell had learned their trade well during the three years of Civil War, in defeat as well as in victory. Only in the later stages at Naseby, at key points in the action, did they become fully involved in the fighting. They worked together effectively and with clear purpose and thought, stamping their authority on the battle. On the right wing Cromwell was in full control of the situation throughout. In the centre Skippon was determined and decisive in the face of great adversity, bringing on the reserves and ensuring that the collapse of the front regiments did not lead to the collapse of the whole centre. Fairfax fulfilled the duties of a commander in chief with great energy and effectiveness, ensuring that all the forces at his disposal were used when and where they were most needed.

Cromwell had sufficient forces to maintain an uncommitted reserve. He was able to flank Langdale through superior numbers and by driving off several of Langdale's divisions using the strength of the Ironsides. He had the discipline to control the forces at his disposal and he had also managed to rally many of the broken regiments of the left wing to cover the rear. Moreover, though forced to commit his infantry reserve to hold the Royalist advance, Fairfax managed to rebuild a reserve from the regiments which had broken and in the later stages of the battle he was able to commit these reserves again to complete the destruction of the Royalist army. Who rallied and led up these troops we are not told, perhaps it was one of the brigade commanders, but as Sprigge says, it was an unusual thing for broken regiments to be rallied so quickly and be returned into the action. Once disordered it was very difficult to bring troops back into order, yet that is what the New Model achieved in both its left wing of horse and its front line of infantry. This above anything else proves that the criticisms about the competence of the New Model's officers were unfounded. The New Model took everything that Rupert threw at it, there were considerable doubts for a time but it managed to absorb the punishment and then exert its dominance. When success was assured there was a steady, controlled but overwhelming exploitation of the advantage. Nothing was left to chance and nothing was allowed to get in the way of the central objective of completely destroying the Royalist army. So, in contrast to Rupert's ill-conceived attack on the Parliamentarian baggage train, Fairfax strictly forbade the cavalry from plundering the Royalist baggage because they had to follow up in the pursuit. There had been no elaborate manoeuvres, no complex strategies, just the steady and effective use of the resources which were available.

The decisive force on the battlefield was without doubt Cromwell's cavalry, as the Royalist prisoners admitted, while an eye witness reported that Cromwell 'behaved himself to the utmost routed the Adversary as on Marston Moore and then relieved our Army on the other Party, which was like to be undone....'[11] It had been Cromwell's careful and deliberate preparation over several years, particular with the Eastern Association cavalry, that underpinned the success at Naseby. Rupert may have been an innovative tactician and have experimented with different battle formations, but unlike Cromwell he did not perhaps pay sufficient attention to the creation of the units he would employ on the field. Although one must remember Clarendon's antipathy towards Rupert, his assessment of the key difference between the Royalist and Parliamentarian cavalry has a fundamental truth:

> 'That difference was observed all along, in the discipline of the King's troops and of those which marched under the command of Fairfax and Cromwell, that though the King's troops prevailed in their charge, and routed those they charged, they seldom rallied themselves again in good order, nor could be brought to make a second charge again the same day. Whereas the other troops, if they prevailed, or though they were beaten and routed, presently rallied again and stood in good order till they received their new orders.'[12]

Clarendon was wrong in that Rupert did rally his men after their pursuit as far as Naseby village but they were disordered again as they returned to the main action and Rupert even worked to reform them a third time when he had rejoined the King. However, the general truth of Clarendon's observation cannot be denied, for although Ireton's wing of horse were broken, only 1000 fled, the rest remaining on the field, soon being reformed and thrown back into the battle.

Whereas Fairfax could afford to approach the battle in a more defensive and deliberate way, because of his advantage in numbers, Rupert needed all his famed audacity and inventiveness if he was to have any chance of success. From the events of the battle one can perhaps begin to suggest his battle plan, of which his senior commanders will have been well aware. It was in Rupert's character to act decisively and with great courage, particularly when under pressure. Whether in a skirmish like Chalgrove or a more major action such as Newark, he would always try to throw the enemy off guard by rapid movement and unexpected initiatives. At Naseby he did not wait for Fairfax to come on to Farndon, he moved quickly forward, choosing the ground and possibly even making Fairfax move from his much stronger position across the Naseby-Clipston road. Once the rest of his army had marched up, Rupert attacked quickly, before the Parliamentarian forces were completely ready. Whatever he lost as a result, with the lack of artillery support and the disadvantage of the ground, he probably more than gained by taking the initiative and carrying the fight to the enemy. His strategy seems to have been to strike fast and hard on the right wing, leading the cavalry attack himself, and to support this with a strong push on the right wing of the infantry, where he presumably committed his first line of reserves at an early stage, in an attempt to roll up the New Model's left wing and break not only Ireton's cavalry but also shatter Skippon's infantry. The idea must have been to press so hard that the New Model simply did not have time to recover. This may explain why it was Rupert's right wing that engaged first and it was perhaps why the Parliamentarian forlorn hope was placed in front of the left of the infantry line, because Fairfax and Skippon could perhaps see the build up on the Royalist right. No one would have criticised Rupert's impetuosity if the strategy had succeeded, and at first it looked as though it had been successful because, as Cromwell was to report, the battle was in the early stages 'very doubtfull'. Rupert's confidence and daring had once more provided a chance of success and indeed his strategy might have succeeded against the sort of armies that Essex and Waller had commanded. But now the Royalists were facing commanders, officers and cavalry that were at least their equals.

The Royalists may already have committed most if not all their reserves of foot and most of their horse to achieve this early success and they may simply have had nothing left to meet the counter-attack when it came. Once they had broken the Parliamentarian front line the Royalists' own front line will also inevitably have been in disorder and hence vulnerable to Skippon's counter-attack. In this context it is significant that it was the King's and Rupert's own regiments of foot, which were the pride of the infantry and had been in the King's reserve in the third line, that the New Model cavalry had destroyed and that it was only then that the Royalist army retreated. What we are not told is whether they had been instrumental in breaking the front line of the New Model or, more likely, were being brought forward to engage and break Skippon's reserves when they were tackled by Cromwell's cavalry.

The Royalist defeat cannot however be attributed simply to the lack of numbers. Whereas the New Model commanders controlled the battle throughout, Rupert has been criticised by many for having committed himself with his troops on the right wing, which took him out of the action at a critical moment in the battle. It is argued that he should have stayed with the main body, like Fairfax, and have commanded the whole battle to be able to ensure the reserves were committed as and where necessary. Rupert may not have had anyone of Cromwell's abilities to fill the post of commander of horse but there were other commanders, like Maurice and Northampton, who had the experience and courage to lead the right wing of horse. Kitson has argued that Rupert was simply doing what the other great commanders of the period did, leading from the front, and he makes a direct comparison with Fairfax, but this argument does not stand up. Fairfax had been an equally dashing and courageous, if not at times foolhardy, cavalry commander. However, once he had command of a major army he delegated the responsibilities to lead the cavalry and, whatever his personal inclination, at Naseby Fairfax held back sufficiently to maintain control of the battle, though he did of course lead in the reserves of horse against the infantry. A more significant factor in Rupert's decision may simply have been that he believed his strategy had far more chance of success if he personally commanded the crucial cavalry charge, for without rapid success on the right wing there could be no possibility of victory, because if it became a matter of sustained attrition then Fairfax's advantage in numbers would be decisive. It has also been suggested that Rupert fought with the right wing simply because he could not face being overruled by the King in the crucial battlefield decisions. The real answer must however surely be that the King was, as Captain General, the overall commander and he probably considered he should exercise that authority, especially after his successes at Cropredy and Lostwithiel and Rupert's defeat at Marston Moor. In this situation it would have been pointless for Rupert to have remained in the centre simply to be overruled yet again by the King. After all, at Marston Moor, where he was in overall command, he did remain with the reserve and only committed himself to the action when he had to lead the reserve to try to halt the collapse of his right wing of horse.

The most telling criticisms of Rupert's action at Naseby are those that relate to his absence from the field during the critical middle hour. Kitson attempts to excuse Rupert, saying he was not in fact away from the battle for very long but this is simply not true. Rupert had not only spent precious time in the pursuit but also in the totally pointless attack on the Parliamentarian baggage train. There are several important examples, such as the battle of Vlotho, where Rupert had through his courageous, devastating cavalry charges provided the opportunity for victory only to then carry his charge too far so leading to defeat.[13] In this respect Naseby was perhaps just another example of his recklessness, but whether his return to the battlefield half an hour or so earlier would have turned the tables once more seems unlikely, though we shall never know for certain. Rupert has also been criticised for the chaos of the final flight, but this like many other criticisms of his actions seems quite unreasonable. It had taken a great effort to rally the horse for the final stand and when the Royalist cavalry finally turned and fled they were a totally broken force which no one could make stand.

In the Royalist post mortem on the battle it was upon Rupert that many sought to place the blame, which is exactly what Rupert himself had anticipated: 'Pray let me know what is said among you concerning our last defeat. Doubtless the fault of it will be put upon [me].' Lord Digby was blaming the whole disaster on Rupert and in later years various authors would feed upon Digby's misinformation and lies, further distorting the truth, blaming Rupert for each of the disastrous decisions which were in fact all taken by the King himself and against Rupert's advice.[14] Thus Whitelocke for example wrote that at Harborough 'it was resolved (and chiefly by P.Rupert's eagerness, old Commanders being much against it) to give Battel: and because Fairfax had been so forward, they would no longer stay for him, but seek him out.'[15] Despite more recent revision of Rupert's role, in the end it may be that Digby has still succeeded in his distortion of the truth for the closer one looks at the one major Royalist account of the battle and the campaign, that by Walker, the more one wonders how faithfully it reports what actually happened from the Royalist perspective and how much this may have distorted our view of Rupert's actions before and during the battle.[16]

Not surprisingly, what the Royalist accounts do not do is place the blame for the Naseby defeat where it really belongs, with the King himself and with his courtier advisors, particularly Digby. The decisions which led to the battle were all taken by Charles, who was there in person throughout and took overall command of the army. One would have thought it impossible for Charles to escape the blame for the dramatic miscalculation and incompetence of the Royalist actions of the battle and the weeks preceding it, yet somehow, from the moment the battle was lost, the real reasons for this devastating defeat were being distorted, so much so that within a very short space of time, and exactly as Rupert predicted, they all came to be placed at Rupert's door. It is remarkable how history could so often have failed to treat Charles with the contempt that he deserves, but rather to have seen him as a martyr who was let down by his closest supporters. An incompetent leader in any sphere of human activity will encourage, through his weakness, conflict amongst those he leads. With Charles it seems that he actually maintained control of situations by dividing the authority of his best commanders, which further encouraged dissention and conflict. The result in the Naseby campaign was that Goring's troops never arrived and the advice of Rupert and the other military commanders was ignored. Charles had done exactly the same before Edgehill, giving Rupert command of the cavalry independent of Lord Lindsay, his senior commander. Rupert had been willing to exploit the King's mismanagement when it was to his advantage, but in the Naseby campaign this rebounded upon him with a vengeance. Charles was a man who had respect and loyalty because of his birth, in spite of his incompetence. Fairfax, Cromwell and Rupert had that respect and loyalty because of their ability.

Markham would have us believe that 'it was Fairfax whose genius won the fight at Naseby...' and that Cromwell was no more than 'his very efficient general of horse.'[17] Many commentators have presented the story in such a way, both at Marston Moor and at Naseby, so as to undermine the role of Cromwell. For both Morrah and Kitson the two great commanders of the first

Civil War were Rupert and Fairfax. Cromwell's time they say had yet to come.[18] That Fairfax commanded at Naseby and that Cromwell followed his orders cannot be denied. Fairfax contributed much to the battle itself and on the evidence of Waller, speaking after his experience in March 1645, we know that Cromwell was a loyal and effective officer who would efficiently carry out the orders of his commander. Fairfax was certainly not Cromwell's puppet, as some contemporary, Presbyterian critics claimed and Cromwell did not run the New Model Army in the way that he had run the Eastern Association army under Manchester. Fairfax was a courageous and skilled general, but that was all he was. The underlying basis for the success at Naseby was that Parliament was able to marshal the largest, best organised and best equipped army with the best trained cavalry. For this Cromwell must take the greatest credit. He had provided the crucial military understanding which ensured that the political battles during the winter of 1644-5 achieved exactly what was needed in military terms. In many respects the New Model Army was already Cromwell's army even though Fairfax was the undisputed commander. It is true that Fairfax, with Skippon's assistance, played a major role in turning the new army into an effective fighting force, but the strength of the New Model, especially at Naseby, was first and foremost in the core of committed and well trained troops that it had inherited from the Eastern Association army which Cromwell had shaped. By 1645 his enemies, both Royalist and Parliamentarian, had no doubt as to who was the real driving force and their remaining assessment and predictions certainly proved correct over the following decade.

Baillie wrote of the battle on the 17th June: 'This accident is like to change much of the affairs here. We hope the back of the malignant party is broken...'[19] Marston Moor had resulted in the fall of the North to Parliament, but this had only weakened the Royalist cause. Naseby was in contrast the decisive battle, for although it did not end the war it provided the opportunity for complete victory, an opportunity which Fairfax immediately capitalised upon. At Naseby the main Royalist field army had been almost completely destroyed. They had lost up to 10000 arms together with 40 barrels of powder and twelve pieces of ordnance and 200 carriages. The loss was damaging but not disastrous. There were artillery pieces in Oxford, including some 26 brass pieces and although difficult it would perhaps not have been impossible for the Oxford and Bristol armouries to replace the other equipment lost at Naseby, while there were still substantial military supplies coming into England from the continent via the ports of the South West.[20] What the King could not replace was the officer corps which he lost on the 14th June, extending from senior officers right down to corporals and even the experienced infantrymen. For the first and only time in the war in a major battle one side had lost the whole of their infantry at a stroke. The King had also lost a good number of officers from the cavalry, not to mention all the gunners and support staff of the artillery train. They could not be replaced, for Parliament ensured that the prisoners were kept out of the rest of the war. If he had acted swiftly the King might have rebuilt a substantial if less experienced army from the remaining troops around the country, using Goring's army of the South West as the core. However, Charles did not act on the advice he was given. Instead it was Fairfax who moved rapidly and with clear purpose, his strategy being to destroy Goring's army before it could be built into a major force. This he achieved at Langport within less than four weeks of Naseby. With the destruction of Goring's army the last hope of the Royalists was gone. Naseby saw not only the destruction of his army, but also the destruction of his supporters' trust in him, for with the publication of Charles' letters, captured at Naseby, many saw that he did not recognise the Parliament at Westminster, even though he had agreed to this in the negotiations of the Treaty of Uxbridge, that he was trying to organise an Irish army to support him, whatever the cost to the protestant faith, and was even seeking the support of a foreign army. No one could now be in any doubt as to his duplicity.

For the Independents the victory at Naseby was both the fulfilment of their primary military objective and the seal upon their political success. Their military arguments were vindicated and their control of the military machine was assured, because the Commons motion to restore the authority of the Committee of Both Kingdoms over Fairfax and his Council of War was easily defeated. Cromwell had developed a power base within the Eastern Association army, by bringing in people as regimental commanders who were his close supporters and who shared his religious beliefs and attitudes, men like Pickering and Montague. This power base had now been transferred successfully to the New Model Army and the winning of the political battle over the army officer list had led other of his opponents to refuse to serve in the army allowing Cromwell to move his people into places of rank and influence, with his close ally Ireton being appointed Commissary General of Horse. Cromwell's military reputation and his personal position in the army, and that of his allies, was secured by the victory at Naseby. In the flush of success, Parliament ordered that Cromwell 'continue Lieutenant General of the Horse under Sir Thomas Fairfax during the pleasure of the Houses, notwithstanding the Self-denying Ordinance....' Though the Lords restricted this to a period of three months, his position was assured, creating the potential for him to take over the army and ultimately the government. Naseby was thus the culmination of one process and the starting point for another and so in a sense one may say that at Naseby Parliament won the war but lost the peace.

Whatever the details of the assessment of the actions of the commanders and the men on both sides on the day, the underlying and most significant of all factors was political. If the victory at Naseby had been made possible by the success of the arguments of the most able soldier in Parliament, so it was lost as a result of the failure of the King to accept the arguments of the most capable soldier in the Royalist Council of War.

NOTES

1. Hutton, 1982, p.203.
2. Everitt, 1969, p.9.
3. Warwick, 1701, p.285.
4. Bray, 1827, vol.5, p.129n.
5. Kingston, 1897, p.208.
6. Hutton, 1982, Gentles, 1992. Morrah, 1976.
7. Ludlow, 1698, vol.1, p.156-7.
8. *A Sacred Record.*
9. *A True Relation of a Victory.*
10. *A True Relation of a Victory.*
11. *A More Particular and Exact Relation.*
12. Clarendon, 1702.
13. Kitson, 1994, p.59.
14. Warburton, vol.3, p.129. Rupert to Legge, 18th June, Warburton, vol.3, p.119.
15. Whitelocke, p.144.
16. Walker, 1705.
17. Markham, 1870, p.iv.
18. Morrah, 1976. Kitson, 1994.
19. 17th June, Baillie, 1775, vol.2, p.116-7.
20. For example, Hyde reported in late May the arrival at Dartmouth and Falmouth of two ships with over 500 barrels of powder and great quantities of match. Clarendon to Rupert, May 1645, Warburton, vol.3, p.95-6. Roy, 1964, p.57.

ANTIQUARIES AND TOURISTS, PREACHERS AND POLITICIANS

'this is Naseby Field; them's Sulby Hedges.
That's the way the King come;
and that's the way Bounaparte come!'
Naseby labourer, 1865

Naseby has always held a special place in the popular mind as THE event of the English Civil War. When celebrations were to be held for the tercentenary of Cromwell's birth it was to Naseby, not to Marston Moor, Dunbar or any other of his victories that the main attention was given. It was at Naseby that tradition, though spurious, ascribes Cromwell's burial. In the 19th century it was to Naseby that nonconformists and radical politicians looked as the cradle of their tradition. There is in fact a whole history of later study of and interest in the battle, a fascinating social history which brings us into contact with not just historians but with antiquaries, tourists, poets, politicians and nonconformist ministers.

Attitudes towards the battle have altered quite dramatically as society has evolved and changed over the last 350 years. First there were the perspectives at the time of and immediately following the battle, from both sides in the conflict, that we have used to explore the events of the Naseby campaign. Then there were the views, under the Commonwealth and Protectorate, of Naseby as a great victory over tyranny. Following the Restoration there was a revision of history in which the Revolution came to be seen, for nearly two centuries, as a disruption of the natural order. Only with the revival of the power struggle of the masses against the landed and commercial classes during the 19th century, allied with the ascendancy of the nonconformist religious sects, was there a revival of a positive attitude towards Naseby. Finally, in the present century we have been able to step back from the deep felt commitments of one side or the other as our modern society moves so much further away from the beliefs and values of the mid 17th century. Yet we have not escaped completely from involvement in the politics of the war, even if it is only expressed today in the side one chooses in joining a Civil War re-enactment society! There are still political and religious undercurrents in the way we view the battle of Naseby 350 years after the event.

It was in the homes of people at the two opposite ends of the social spectrum that awareness of the event was mainly kept alive during the 18th and earlier 19th centuries. On the one hand there were the farmers and poor labourers of Naseby who found the artefacts and bones on the battlefield as they ploughed the land. They kept them in their homes or sold them to their 'betters', who were increasingly visiting the village as antiquaries or tourists.

The second group were the gentry of the neighbourhood with their antiquarian interests - families like the Hanburys of Kelmarsh and the Cockaynes of Rushton. It was on the views of such families of substance that the history of the war and of the battle were to be mainly based from the time of the Restoration until the mid 19th century. They were the ones with the resources who could afford to make collections of artefacts from the battle or to carry out or sponsor the antiquarian and historical studies.

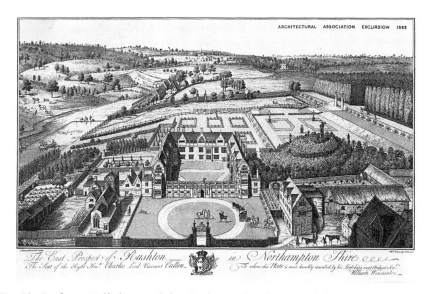

Fig. 70. Rushton Hall, home of the Cockayne family, one of the Northamptonshire gentry who maintained the interest in the battle of Naseby during the 18th century. In the Hall they collected relics of the battle and in the grounds they built a 'temple', where they placed a tablet with a poem on the battle and in which one could sit and muse upon the distant view of Naseby.

There was continued interest in Naseby throughout the 17th century, as witnessed for example by the painting of the battle, now in Daventry Museum, which was produced in the late 17th century. However the great flowering of historical and antiquarian interest was during the 18th century. The first antiquary to write about Naseby was probably Gibson, in his revision of Camden's *Britannia* published in 1695:

> 'Naseby, eminent in late years for the bloody battel fought there in the year 1645, between his Majesty King Charles the first, and the Parliament-Army. There are now no signs of the fight remaining, except some few holes, which were the burying-places of the dead men and horses.'[1]

Morden's map of Northamptonshire, published in Gibson's volume, recorded the site of the battle with a single sword placed between Naseby and Sibbertoft. The first antiquary to visit the battlefield with serious intent was

John Bridges, Northamptonshire's county historian, who came on one of his antiquarian perambulations of the county in September 1719. His brief observations, which included information from local informants as to exactly where the battle was fought, survive in his notebooks. Then in August 1721 he sent his artist, the dutchman Peter Tillemans, to draw a view of the battlefield, but sadly Tillemans' drawing was never published and the original does not survive.[2] At about the same time John Morton, another local antiquary, also took note of the battle, recording the tradition in East Farndon of the slaughter of the Royalist women from the baggage train. For both Bridges and Morton however Naseby held only a passing interest.

It was not until later in the century that antiquaries began to pay more sustained attention. In the 1770s Rowland Rouse, from Market Harborough, who assisted Nichols with his county history of Leicestershire:

'went over to Naseby, and secured by purchase from cottagers and others what relics he could of the battle. These comprised a buff doublet, a flint lock musket, and four officers' swords, and an instrument of brass used by some Officers of the Ordnance.'

The latter was 'engraved all over with calculations, the names of the different pieces of ordnance, and the weight of powder and ball each carried.' Samuel Ireland also visited Naseby, in 1794, to collect material for his book on the river Avon and was 'fortunate enough to form a considerable assemblage of curious articles which had been dug up in the field of battle, viz. large Jack Boots, similar to those worn by the drivers of the Diligences in France, musket balls, gloves, etc;'[3] While some Naseby 'relics' like these were undoubtedly collected years or centuries later from the battlefield, many of the objects must surely have been in the hands of local families ever since 1645, presumably collected by them from the battlefield in the hours or days after the fight. Rouse's collection was inherited by Matthew Holbeche Bloxham who, in 1874, still retained the buff coat, musket and two swords. The other two swords and the instrument he gave to his friend Sir Samuel Rush Meyrick, who illustrated the swords in his book on ancient armour.[4] Another important collection of Naseby artefacts was made by the Cockayne family of Rushton Hall, 10 miles north east of Naseby. The Cockaynes were Royalists during the Civil War, Charles Lord Cockayne, Viscount Cullen, raising a troop of horse for the King.[5] In about 1824 the chamber next to the 'Gothic Hall' at Rushton was 'occupied by the furniture found in the tent of Charles the First, on the fatal field of Naseby.' There were various other things of antiquarian interest at Rushton, for it was reported that 'in another part of the building was a wainscoted chamber, in which the Duke of Monmouth was for some time concealed after the battle of Sedgemoor' together with other 'strange specimens of the furnishing of olden time....'[6] The Naseby objects comprised:

346 <a

'a curiously carved oblong table and two small round ones, a pair of candlesticks, a large covered punch-bowl, and four small drinking cups, taken from the camp at Naseby after the battle, in which Charles Cokayne, the first Viscount Cullen, had a command in the King's forces. All the articles are of black oak, or teak, and with the exception of the cups, are richly chased and inlaid with ivory. The table was known as King Charles' Wassail Table.'[7]

The table was illustrated by Meyrick in his book on ancient furniture, but in August 1855 the furniture, pictures and other items at Rushton were sold by auction and dispersed.[8]

According to Sir Charles Isham, 'The best collection of relics was at Kelmarsh Hall, collected immediately after the battle.'[9] Kelmarsh, just three miles from the battlefield, was the seat of William Hanbury FSA(1748-1807), the most prolific collector of artefacts from Naseby.[10] He was also interested in the details of the battle itself, because in about 1771 Hanbury wrote to a friend in Clipston, who was also an author and antiquary, enclosing a copy of Sprigge's *Anglia Rediviva* which he says contains 'a very curious chart of Naseby Field, and the Position of the Armies...'[11] Hanbury's collection was moved out of the county in about 1860 when Lord Bateman sold Kelmarsh Hall and moved to Shobden in Herefordshire.[12] The title is now extinct and there is no record of the whereabouts of the Naseby objects, except for those which were given by Bateman to Sir Charles Isham, which comprised '1. Cavalier Helmet with vizor 2. A Roundhead ditto. 3. A back piece with straps and Buckles. 4. Three Cannon Balls. 5. A pistol Holster.'[13] These items are now in Northampton Museum, some of the few Naseby artefacts which can now be easily traced. The Isham family themselves already had at least one object said to have been associated with the battle of Naseby. This was the blood stained buff coat which, according to tradition, was from one of Prince Rupert's troopers, who had been hidden in an apple loft at the Hall after the battle, 'a pretty romance that there is no means of disproving'.[14]

The largest collection of artefacts in Naseby itself was built up by the Ashby family, who were also patrons to the local historian John Mastin. They had originally kept their collection in the Shuckburgh manor house, opposite the church, but the objects were moved out of the village to Naseby Woolleys when they acquired that house later in the 19th century.[15] Captain Ashby Ashby was bankrupted in 1887, which led to an auction in which his collection was sold.[16] According to the sale catalogue of 1888 the auction included 'well authenticated relics of the Battle of Naseby' and the newspaper report remarked upon 'the careful manner in which all were labelled with their known history; and were undoubtedly as genuine as they were reported to be. Captain Ashby Ashby kept a record of the place whence each was derived.'[17] Sadly the artefacts have been dispersed and the records of their provenance apparently lost.[18] The Naseby lots comprised:

Helmet, 2 horseshoes : £2

old spur, 2 horseshoes, part of antique sword pomel : 8/-
3 horse shoes and cannon ball : 14/-
3 horseshoes, bones, spearhead : 11/-
curious oval marble vase, an antique mortar, a quantity of bullets : £1/4/0d
rapier from Naseby Field : £2/15/0d
part of a stirrup, horseshoe, bones etc : 10/-
bowl, of antique British enamelled pottery, said to be hidden in a well from
soldiers at the Battle of Naseby, and glass bottle : £2/15/0d
rapier, antique sword and scabbard : £3
oak table : £6

The country houses in the area still continued to act as the main repository for Naseby relics well into the 20th century and a few remain there even today. For example, Mr Albert Pell of Haselbech reported in the early 20th century the finding some time before 'of certain relics, consisting of soldiers' accoutrements, that were discovered when the Naseby Reservoir was constructed'. By 1904 these had found a home in Stanford Hall, the home of Lord Braye who is said to have collected various objects from Naseby and nearby, including 'some jewellery worn by Royalist officers'.[19] Perhaps the most impressive items held in any local collection are the two saddles preserved in Wistow Hall. They were described earlier this century:

'Charles' saddle is of Italian make, in crimson velvet, quilted with gold braid, and Rupert's is a more workman-like affair of leather with some embroidery on it. It is a good deal worn. Charles's stirrups are beautifully finished, of brass gilt over, and having down the sides an ornament of grapes; .... Rupert's are of steel, a nice piece of forging; the latter still attached to the stirrup leathers. The bits are very heavy. There is a pair of pistols which may have belonged to Rupert, who was an expert in their use. Another pair might possibly have belonged to the King.... The King's sword, which was probably attached to the saddle, was left by him, but this was given by Sir Henry the physician to George IV, whom he attended....'[20]

Other artefacts which have survived and retained their provenance are those which were at some time in the past deposited in local parish churches for safe keeping and display. At Lubenham church there is the chair said to have been used by the King on the night of the 13th June.[21] At Ravensthorpe until the 1960s there were seven pieces of armour hung on the east wall of the north chapel which, according to local tradition, came from Naseby battlefield, just seven miles away. Naseby church also has its relics, which were all deposited there in the 20th century. There were two swords, said to be from Naseby field, mounted on the north wall of the north aisle, together with a single iron stirrup. Sadly one of the swords was stolen in 1992.[22] The association of these artefacts and others such as those in Foxton church should not however be accepted without question. In the 17th century there was a requirement upon all parishes to maintain 'town armour' for the men it had to supply for the militia and hence one finds in various parish churches even today there are pieces of 17th century armour. Examples still exist at Raunds church, where there are two incomplete sets of pikeman's armour, while earlier this century other examples existed in Higham Ferrers church.[23]

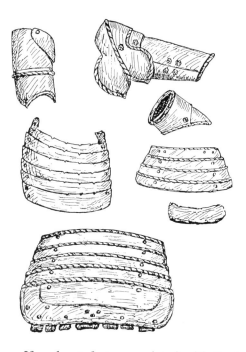

Fig. 71. Markham's drawing of the pieces of armour, said to have come from Naseby battlefield, which used to be displayed in Ravensthorpe church but are now preserved in Northampton Museum. This was apparently part of an officer's armour, similar to though of lesser quality than that being worn by Charles I in figure 18.

If such artefacts associated with the battle go astray, or even if they lose their provenance, then something of the history of the battle is irretrievably lost. The story of just one object will give an idea of the vagaries of fortune which enable an artefact to survive through to the present but equally shows how so many have come to be lost. Before 1773 there was a large oak table in Shuckburgh House in Naseby which an antiquary was told by the then tenants of the Hall that 'a party of the King's life guards were surprised by Ireton, as they were sitting down to supper at this very table, the evening before the battle.'[24] When Henson visited Naseby in the early 19th century his attention was directed to 'an antique Oak Table, placed in a gloomy apartment of a house, erected on the site of a venerable old Mansion, the seat of the Shuckbrughs.'[25] This great oak table, 9ft long and 3ft wide, was shown in 1828 to Philips but by then it was said to be 'the table at which the council of the Parliament officers deliberated before the battle.'[26] Ashby, owner of the house, transferred the table to Naseby Woolleys after he purchased the house from the Fitzgerald family and this seems to be why Rimmer was later to wrongly identify the Woolleys as the place where the Royalist troopers had been caught 'carousing'.[27] By 1888 the story had changed yet again. The report of the sale, presumably drawing upon Ashby's detailed records of the provenance of the items in his collection, says the table formerly belonged to the Everard family:

> 'members of which were conspicuous actors in the Cromwellian army. One,
> Robert Everard, was a captain in the army; and he was associated with the
> Baptist Chapels in Northampton, East Haddon, and Ravensthorpe. It is said that
> it was at this table that Oliver Cromwell dined before the battle of Naseby.'[28]

*Fig. 72. An early 20th century postcard showing the Cromwell Table in the Reading
Room in Naseby village.*

Page, working from Mastin's *History*, returned to the tradition about the table
which associated it with the Royalist troopers, but then we find that Holloway
elaborates the story yet again, saying that after they had captured or killed
their foes, the Parliamentarian troopers sat down at the table to the meal
prepared for their enemies.[29] This story may have originated because the table
was for a long time in the Shuckburgh's manor house which lay opposite the
church, next to the vicarage. The house itself has also over the years been an
object of interest to antiquaries. In the late 19th century Page visited Naseby
and the manor house was one stop on his itinerary:

> 'There is nothing very attractive in the outside of this latter structure, but we
> shall have missed an important part of our duty if we pass on without entering
> its doors. In the back part of the house, the original walls of which still exist,
> we can stand in an old room (now used as a scullery) which tradition points out
> as the spot where Ireton surprised and slaughtered that picket of revelling
> Royalists on the eve of the battle. Not long since, the table around which some

of them were seated at the time of their surprise, was seen here.'[30] In 1891 another visitor reported: 'The spacious fireplace, from which you can look up into the sky, is still in use - the rafters of the roof are as rough and rude as they were two centuries since; but alas! the place that knows them now will soon know them no more. The present tenant, who asked distainfully, "What use was it?" has determined to improve it out of existence. In a few months the last relic of the skirmish that brought on Naseby fight will have given place to a brand-new building...'[31]

At the auction in 1888 the Cromwell table had it seems been purchased by Lord Clifden and was later placed in safe keeping by Lord Annaly at Holdenby House.[32] It had presumably been bought for the village but if so it was not until 1904 that it returned to Naseby, when it was temporarily kept in the house of Mr Austin Butlin.[33] By 1912 the table had found a more permanent home in the village Reading Room but here it apparently had to be 'surrounded by high iron railings to prevent it being chipped by relic hunters.' By 1932, after the closure of the Reading Room, the table was transferred to the parish church, where it remains to this day.[34]

Most collections of Naseby artefacts have proved vulnerable. For example, in the 19th century there were various relics from Naseby in the art museum at Rugby School, but recent enquiries have completely failed to locate them.[35] A sword found at Clipston was deposited with the Northamptonshire Record Office in February 1947 and again there is now no trace of it, though the Record Office do have a pair of stirrups said to be from Naseby but they have never been authenticated and their provenance is unknown.[36] There are many similar examples. What, one wonders, has become of the sword, two horse-shoes and three bullets from the battlefield that in 1912 were with Mr G.W.Brunner, headmaster of Guilsborough School?[37] Some items can be traced for a while, from newspaper and other reports, but then they disappear from view. Such is the case with the 'gold medal (the only one known) giving a representation of Fairfax's head' on one side and on the reverse 'Post hoc meliora meruisti, 1645', which was found on Naseby field in 1850. It was later in the possession of the Rev.T.James, vicar of Sibbertoft and Theddingworth, and by 1894 it was owned by his nephew Mr Sutherland of Theddingworth, who also owned a bullet, a stirrup much eaten by rust and a two-edged sword.[38] Then in the early 20th century there was the collection of artefacts at Broadmoor Farm made by Mr Kimbell, which has again apparently disappeared without trace.[39] Other items were scattered around various private collections far and wide, such as the 'pair of leather stirrups from Naseby' which were in the ownership of Peterborough Natural History Society in 1892.[40] The fate of the private collections of artefacts made by the various antiquaries depended very much upon the vagaries of family fortune. When Captain Ashby's collection at Naseby Woolleys was sold the 'curiosities' fetched more than was expected because they were so well provenanced, but this did little for us, for most of those at the sale were dealers. The destination of several of the Naseby artefacts can be traced, the Cromwell Table which, as we have seen, was purchased for £6 by Lord Clifden, and the spurs, two horse-shoes and part of an antique old sword pommel which were purchased for eight shillings for Northampton Museum by the curator Mr George.[41] Over the years various Naseby artefacts from other collections were also given to the museum. So, for example, in 1894 Mr J.Robinson of Ravensthorpe presented a two edged sword, which was in excellent condition and said to be from Naseby field, which had been in the family's ownership for some 150 years.[42] Other Naseby artefacts were given to Market Harborough museum by Guy Paget of Sulby Hall.

One might have thought that deposition in a local museum would have been the safest way in which such items could have been secured for the future. Sadly this has not proved to be the case. For example, in 1927 an antiquarian collection from Marston Trussell was presented to Northampton Museum which included a bronze object 'probably from Baggage Waggon', a cannon ball, a small cannon ball, four bullets, a battle axe, and a small spoon, all from Naseby, together with various other prehistoric and later antiquities, geological specimens, fossils and several ethnographic items.[43] Like various other objects deposited with the museum over the last century or so, they have all either been lost, misplaced or have lost their provenance. Only the items loaned to the museum by the Isham family can be securely identified, because when they were given they already had the information written on them in white paint!

Unfortunately, not only have most of the archaeological finds from the battlefield been lost, most of them were never properly recorded by anyone, even though this would have told us a great deal about the nature and location of the action. But to criticise antiquaries of the 18th or 19th century for such failings would be wrong, especially as we have often equally failed in the 20th century. Equipment, bullets and bones have been discovered on the battlefield almost continuously since the enclosure of Sibbertoft in 1650, when the labourers digging the ditches and banks for the hedgerows came across the mouldering remains of horses and men in a mass grave, and the reported discoveries must be only a small proportion of the many finds which have been made over the centuries. Of the 18th century discoveries we know almost nothing. There is just Mastin's report of having seen burials revealed in a gravel pit on Mill Hill in the 1790s and the reference to the 'dragoon boot' found in a mire near Sulby hedge. The majority of reported finds were made in the 19th century, it being stated in 1849 that 'In cultivating the soil bullets, cannon-balls, and fragments of arms, are frequently turned up', however such discoveries were already becoming increasingly rare.[44] In 1842 Fitzgerald reported to Carlyle that 'Bullets of all kinds used to be very common: bits of armour: my blacksmith says the children rolled about the cannon balls for playthings.'[45] The more substantial objects still continued to be discovered occasionally throughout the 19th century, as for example by the

Ordnance Survey team working at Naseby at some time before 1892 who discovered a pair of spurs said to be of mid 17th century date.[46] By far the most common find from the battlefield was not surprisingly the lead bullet, which is still the case today, but as early as 1828 Phillips reported 'I collected one bullet found on the field, but I was told, that tourists and antiquaries had made every relic scarce.'[47] The increasing rarity of such items is not surprising given the fact that later in the century Captain Ashby bought up all the bullets he could at 3d each, while Sir Charles Isham paid double that when he happened to call at a shepherd's house near Naseby in 1893, 'close to a turnip field where most of (the bullets) had been turned up; his wife had one for me for which I gave her 6d.'[48] Even Carlyle had picked up a bullet when he visited in 1841.[49] As a result, by 1891 when Stead visited Naseby he found that whereas:

> 'fifty years ago bullets were common, today they are seldom found. A ploughboy occasionally turns one up in the furrow, so white with chalk deposit that it might be mistaken for a marble; but there are probably not more than a score to be found in that parish. The ploughboy's tariff for the bullets is 9d each - the price paid by the village publican, who sells them to collectors for as much as he can get. The publican has two treasures which he will not sell - a fragment of chain shot, a lump of lead with iron imbedded in the centre; and a silver groat of Philip and Mary. At Clipstone, Mr Haddon, whose father once farmed part of Naseby Field, has the rusted remains of a two-edged sword; the tenant of Millhill ploughed up a gold ring, which he incontinently sold for a sovereign to a Harborough jeweller; but of other relics there is but small trace.'[50]

Even so, the antiquaries and historians, just like the tourists, continued to buy up the bullets. Because they were willing to buy so the labourers were willing to collect them, something that will have been fairly easy for them to do as they walked along behind the plough with their eye to the furrow. At the end of the century John Page, the local historian of the Civil War in the county, could still himself collect one or two such mementos and early in the 20th century the Wilford family, who lived at the farm cottage on Lodge Hill, still used to glean the musket balls and sell them at 6d each.[51] In 1912 there was even an advert placed in the Northampton Independent by a 'Collector' for any relics of Naseby battlefield! The labourers still collected musket balls well into the present century, men like William Haynes who had a box of musket balls which he had collected when he led the team of horses when ploughing, but with the passing of the horse drawn plough so the collection stopped.[52] The antiquaries who bought these relics can be excused, for they were not aware of the potential that these objects, if left in the ground for future systematic collection, could offer in terms of information about the battle. The same cannot be said today, when battlefield sites are being stripped of their archaeological remains far more intensively and with an equal lack of recording or concern.

There have never been any archaeological features on the battlefield related to the action other than the burial pits. These have been well known ever since the battle but, as Fitzgerald found out in the 1840s, the local knowledge as to exactly which pits were burial pits and which simply quarry pits was by the 19th century wholly unreliable. By that time almost any of the dozens, if not hundreds of pits across the battlefield would be said to be a burial pit. According to Holme, 'They are chiefly sunk in hollows that except in extremely dry weather they constitute ponds, and being left waste round their borders, have become fringed with brambles and wild flowers.' It was claimed by Whellan in 1849 that the graves were never ploughed over, but this is contradicted by Fitzgerald who was investigating the pits at exactly this time. Some may have remained undisturbed, but by 1890 Isham reported further destruction and today almost every one has been ploughed flat. [53]

After the brief visit by John Bridges in 1719 and apart from their collection of artefacts which had come from the battlefield, few of the antiquaries produced any significant information about or insight into the battle. The next and possibly the best known local historian associated with the study of the battle was the Reverend John Mastin (1748-1829). He was curate of Naseby from 1778-1783 and then vicar until his death in 1829.[54] Mastin seems a formidable figure, 'largely formed, but not corpulently covered. His dress was of the old School, black coat and waistcoat and knee breeches with black stockings.'[55] There were, as we shall see, others who later did far more to reveal the story of the battle than he, but it was mainly because of the publication of his book on the history of Naseby that he is remembered. He was visited by various antiquaries over the years who came to see the battlefield. They included Ireland, Henson and Phillips, who each made a pilgrimage to Naseby.[56] Henson visited the village before enclosure of the parish and became a good friend of Mastin, frequently riding across to the village during the four or five years he was in Northamptonshire to meet the rector and to discuss the battle and other matters.[57] There was also a steady trickle of writing on Naseby through the 19th century with Henry Lockinge, Mastin's successor as curate, contributing another small volume on the history of the village and battle in 1830. The following decades saw a major revival of interest in the study of the Civil War, exemplified by the work of Carlyle and then Gardiner. The 200th (1845) and especially the 250th (1895) anniversary of the war and then the 300th (1899) anniversary of Cromwell's birth led to an upsurge of interest in the Civil War and there are innumerable newspaper articles in the latter part of the 19th century, both locally and occasionally nationally. The period also saw the appearance of a number of local antiquaries and historians with a detailed interest in the battle of Naseby, and in the Civil War in the county as a whole. Perhaps the most prolific of these was J.T.Page of West Haddon.[58] In 1893 he published what is still the most comprehensive account of Northamptonshire in the Civil War and was a frequent contributor to local newspapers on the subject of the Civil War and particularly Naseby. J.C.Cox, rector of Holdenby, was another noted local historian who developed an interest in the war and hence in the battle.

There were numerous historians and antiquaries that took an interest in Naseby over the centuries, most of them clerics like Mursell, Simpkinson, Mastin and Lockinge simply because of the nature of antiquarian study in the 18th and 19th centuries. However, despite the large number of such people involved in one way or another with Naseby over the years, it is remarkable to note that the first and until recently the only significant analysis of the battlefield to take account of its archaeological potential was undertaken by a mid 19th century poet and translator! In the 1840s Thomas Carlyle, who was preparing Cromwell's letters and speeches for publication, had the unique opportunity of befriending Edward Fitzgerald, whose family owned a large part of Naseby battlefield. Fitzgerald, well known later as the translator of the *Rubayat of Omakyam*, proved to be not only very interested in the battle but also a willing and extremely capable investigator. He had already examined and become fascinated in the battlefield in 1830 and, following a meeting organised by a friend, Fitzgerald agreed to collect information from Naseby for Carlyle, who had completely misinterpreted the location of the battlefield on his visit with the historian Dr Arnold earlier in 1842.[59]

Unfortunately, not only was Fitzgerald's excellent work largely ignored or misused by Carlyle, who never visited the battlefield with Fitzgerald despite numerous invitations, it has been ignored or misinterpreted ever since.[60] In the absence of photography, Fitzgerald even produced watercolour views of the battlefield and surrounding countryside for Carlyle.[61] He also collected information from local people, and on the 17th-century landscape from documents including the 1630 map, and was thus able to accurately locate Leane Leys, Fenny Hill, Rutpit Hill, Mill Hill, Lantford hedges, the warren and the windmill.[62] He also questioned local informants about previous discoveries of human remains and military artefacts and was told that it was from Cloisterwell that most bullets had been found, a conclusion that is supported by modern survey. Apparently most cannon balls came from the other side of Broadmoor, confirming that it was only the Parliamentarian artillery who were able to lay down a significant barrage during the battle, the Royalist artillery having initially been left behind in the hasty advance from East Farndon.[63] There was also a sword reported from Broadmoor but most objects, such as the 'curious powder-horn found on Naseby Field', were not accurately provenanced.[64] When Fitzgerald studied the battlefield in 1842 much of the land was pasture and many more pits were visible at the surface than can be seen today. He reported that 'most of the graves are to be traced in and about Cloisterwell and down by Langfordy.'[65] He had local reports of burials in both places, and had himself seen part of a skull and iron heel of a boot, found in 1823, said to have come from a rider found buried together with his horse in a marsh near Langford.[66]

In September 1842 Fitzgerald, assisted by two local farmers, began a brief

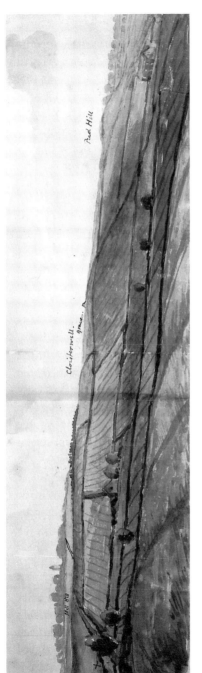

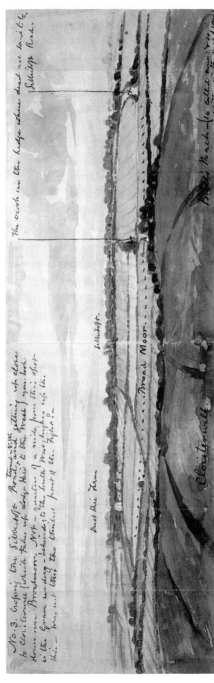

Fig. 73. Fitzgerald's watercolours of the battlefield. Above: View from Dust Hill showing the spoil heap of his successful excavation. Below: Dust Hill from Cloisterwell with the traditional burial site in Broadmoor. (Cambridge University Library)

campaign of excavation. He dug into one pit at Langford and one across Broadmoor 'on Charles's side' but found nothing, the ground being undisturbed below 2ft deep.[67] The latter was the traditional place where burials had been found at the enclosure of Sibbertoft field, Bridges having already reported in 1719 that the 'Extent of the place of battle further appears by Mens Bones dug up in making the fences of the further south part of Sibbertoft enclosure', but he had not identified the location.[68] The pit that Fitzgerald examined can be accurately located from his watercolour view of Broadmoor and Dust Hill taken from Cloisterwell. Fitzgerald also conducted excavations on Cloisterwell on 'several hollows, overgrown with rank vegetation, which tradition had always pointed to as the Graves of the Slain', which may have been the 'two hollows...where the Dead buryd' recorded by Bridges.[69] One of these was found to contain skeletons closely packed.[70] Fitzgerald reported of this burial pit that 'a soil of animal matter mixed with crumbling jaw-bones, arm bones, skulls etcc, is found about four feet under the surface.'[71] They only opened a trench 7ft long by 3.5 ft wide in the grave and discovered seven or eight skeletons, laying alternately east and west tightly packed with one 'jammed in' across them, but the bones were generally in poor condition except for the teeth. He estimated from the overall size of the pit that it might have contained above 100 men. People had frequently dug into the other pits on the field and found nothing, and this was the result when Fitzgerald opened up three other 'little valleys about that Closterwell ground.' His conclusion is an important lesson for any future campaign of archaeological excavation on the battlefield: 'The truth is that little marle-pits etcc, have become confounded with the graves: so it is only by chance (now the ground has been so ploughed over) that you get upon a grave.'[72] The excavated burial pit, previously incorrectly located by the Ordnance Survey, can be positioned from Fitzgerald's previously unpublished watercolour view of the battlefield taken from Dust Hill, which shows the spoil heap of the excavation on the skyline.[73] It is near the crest of the hill in the area of Closter furlong, in a field later known as West Cloister Hill or Bills Bitch West.[74] A large pit is still visible in the field as a slight depression, though now ploughed over, and this is probably where Fitzgerald dug.

In 1906 local tradition also indicated that depressions in Doctor's Close were burial pits but modern fieldwork has enabled a large number of pits across Naseby, Sibbertoft, Sulby and Clipston fields to be accurately located and, given Fitzgerald's evidence, we must treat with care any statements which suggest they are graves.[75] Another problem is that many of the burials at Naseby may have been disturbed by later cultivation, for there are various local reports of the discovery of human bones in cultivation. This is not surprising if local tradition, reported in the late 18th century, about the shallowness of the graves is to be believed. The only other reasonably well located discovery of burials are those said to have been found during gravel digging on Mill Hill in 1792 and 1794.[76] These may have come from the large pits which are still visible immediately north of Mill Hill farm but no accurate information is available. The burials which Fitzgerald found would certainly appear to lie at the focus of the early infantry action, whereas it may be that the other stray discoveries mainly relate to fleeing cavalry, because they have been found scattered far and wide. For example, between Cold Ashby and Guilsborough in a marshy place two skeletons, with helmets on their heads, were found together in a gravel pit in 1817.[77]

Although the results of Fitzgerald's detailed study was never made available, in the later 19th and early 20th century there was little confusion as to the general location of the battlefield. Interpretations did vary in detail, some placing the battle in the valley of Broadmoor and one even misplacing Broadmoor as the whole area between Dust Hill and Mill Hill.[78] The clearest description is that by Mursell in 1860:

'Pausing here a moment, let us turn aside to indicate the locality of this memorable fight. The traveller along the road from Naseby to Clipston and Sibbertoft, about a mile from the first-named village, passes over a low, undulating ridge, which local courtsey has dignified by the name of Mill Hill. To his left are three similar elevations, known as Fenny, Learnlease and Rutput hills. Advancing along the road he crosses another wider ridge, which bears the names in different parts of its extent, of Lodge-hill, Billsbitch hill and Red hill. Descending this he crosses broadmoor, leaving Naseby Rabbit Warren on his right. The road he ascends and passes over two or three lower elevations, opposite to these we have mentioned, the land of which is known as Dust hill.The space over which we thus go, between Mill hill and Fenny hill on the one hand, and Dust hill on the other was the field of the battle.....'[79]

Hamson, writing in 1906, correctly dismisses the analysis which place the Parliament forces on Mill Hill and Fenny Hill.[80] It can be seen therefore that our analysis of the battlefield is not so different from that which has been current for much of the past 350 years. Only in its extension of the events northwards in Sibbertoft does it differ from previous analysis, and even there it is preceded by the comments made by John Bridges about Moot Hill.

Interest in the battle found its first expression in monumental form in 1771 when George Ashby placed a rustic altar in a grove in the grounds of his Hall at Haselbech. This modest little monument carried the following inscription:

'Sacred to Monarchy, Freedom, and Peace. This small monument was placed in sight of Naseby Church, 30th January, 1771, by G.Ashby. May the best of Kings be afraid of nothing so much as encroaching upon the rights of the people. May the subject, however fond of liberty, be quiet, be thankful, so long as he has no grievances to be redressed.'[81]

Ashby was or soon became lord of one of the Naseby manors and, as we have seen, began a collection of artefacts from the battlefield.[82] A few years later another wealthy landowner built a small temple or 'alcove' situated on a low

Fig. 74. The Naseby obelisk, erected on the windmill mound in 1823, seen here in the early 20th century on one of the many postcards published by the village photographer and postmaster Mr Halford. The inscription on the monument reads: 'TO COMMEMORATE THAT GREAT AND DECISIVE BATTLE FOUGHT IN THIS FIELD ON THE XIV DAY OF JUNE MDCXLV BETWEEN THE ROYALIST ARMY COMMANDED BY HIS MAJESTY KING CHARLES THE FIRST, AND THE PARLIAMENT FORCES HEADED BY THE GENERALS FAIRFAX AND CROMWELL, WHICH TERMINATED FATALLY FOR THE ROYAL CAUSE, LED TO THE SUBVERSION OF THE THRONE, THE ALTAR, AND THE CONSTITUTION, AND FOR YEARS PLUNGED THIS NATION INTO THE HORRORS OF ANARCHY AND CIVIL WAR: LEAVING A USEFUL LESSON TO BRITISH KINGS NEVER TO EXCEED THE BOUNDS OF THEIR JUST PREROGATIVE, AND TO BRITISH SUBJECTS NEVER TO SWERVE FROM THE ALLEGIANCE DUE TO THEIR LEGITIMATE MONARCH. THIS PILLAR WAS ERECTED BY JOHN AND MARY FRANCES FITZGERALD, LORD AND LADY OF THE MANOR OF NASEBY: A.D. MDCCCXXIII. '

mound in the gardens at Rushton Hall which commanded an admirable view of Naseby field, some ten miles to the south west. Several walks radiated from the alcove and the hedges to the walks were carefully clipped so that the view towards the battlefield was not obscured. Though now in a sorry state, due to the decline of the Hall and its grounds, the temple does still exist.[83] In about 1820 John Purcell Fitzgerald, a Lancashire landowner and coal mine proprietor, and father of Edward Fitzgerald, inherited one of the Naseby manors. His influence on Naseby seems to have been quite dramatic because enclosure of the parish followed almost immediately, he renovated the church, gave land for the building of a Methodist chapel, replaced the market cross with a large Celtic style cross and built Naseby Woolleys on the newly enclosed land in the west of the parish. Then, in 1823, he erected a monument to the battle.[84] It was an obelisk placed on the highest ground in Naseby parish, on the old windmill mound where, if Streeter's engraving is to be taken literally, the villagers had watched from a safe distance as the battle began to unfold. This obelisk was meant to be seen from a distance as a landscape feature and was very much in the romantic tradition of the earlier monuments at Haselbech and Rushton. It was not important whether it sat on the exact site of the battle, it lay at least in Naseby field. It was a reminder of the battle and local people knew very well that the actual battlefield lay more than a mile to the north west.[85] In later years Carlyle, like many visitors, was confused by the presence of the obelisk, but others were well aware that, by chance, the monument 'though a mile or two away from the actual battlefield, ... serves to mark the spot where the forces of the Parliament mustered on the morning of the day....'[86]

All these monuments, and indeed the whole 18th and early 19th century interest in the battle, was one of reinforcing the status quo - the privilege and power of the few. It was perhaps an omen for the future that the mason who carved the inscribed tablets for the obelisk monument had at least one failure. The place in which the stone finally came to rest was one from which a new and very different interest in the battle would soon be resurrected, because in 1880 a mural tablet dated 1831 was removed from the King Street Independent Chapel in Northampton and on its reverse was found part of the Naseby obelisk inscription. As the reporter noted, 'it is a curious irony of fate that a tablet which inculcates the duty of non-resistance should come to be affixed to the wall of a Dissenting meeting house....'[87] It was these nonconformists, in the mould of the Civil War Independents, or so they often saw themselves, who would inherit the Naseby mantle - not as romantic Royalists but rather as modern warriors in Cromwell's footsteps.

The general revival of interest in the Civil War in the second half of the 19th century was very different in many respects from that in previous generations. At this time the political changes which England was undergoing was bringing to fruition some of the key objectives of the more radical Parliamentarians of the Civil War. In a pre-Marxist era, and certainly before

Fig. 75. A romantic Victorian view of the battle of Naseby, inspired by the great wave of interest in the battle and in the Civil War in general which developed in the 19th century.

the creation of any sort of modern socialist revolution, the campaigns of the English Civil War provided a valuable heritage for the new campaigners for democracy and equality. Indeed Vincent has suggested, in his study of the origins of the Liberal party, that political attitudes of the 1860s 'had nothing to do with the industrial revolution, much to do with the Civil War.'[88] These beliefs underpinned the work of various of the historians who studied the war at that time, with Markham for example writing in 1870 that 'the Independents were simply what every English politician in these days is, or pretends to be, advocates of civil and religious liberty!'[89] For the agricultural trade unionists in particular, Naseby became the focus of their interest as the place where the Civil War was won. In 1873 the Naseby branch of Joseph Arch's Agricultural Labourer's Union was founded. Arch had a close alliance with the Liberal party, later becoming a member of Parliament, and was active in the moves to widen the franchise. He claimed that his ancestors had fought in the Civil War against tyranny and oppression and for the liberty of the people and in his speeches he frequently harked back to that time, an interest that is most clearly seen in his encouragement of the Naseby demonstrations. The workers of Naseby were particularly proud of their connection with this revolutionary past and so 1874 saw the Union's first demonstration at Naseby. 220 people were given tea in a booth set up outside the Fitzgerald Arms, for the landlord was a friend of the Union. Thomas Halford, who we shall also meet in another connection as a local photographer of the battlefield, was also a Union member. The demonstration in the following year drew a crowd of 2000, marching with a band and then listening to an address by Joseph Arch himself. Arch saw the great propaganda value of holding meetings on the site of the battle which overturned oppressive authority in the 17th century, just as they in their own way were struggling with oppression in their own century. Further demonstrations were held between 1876 and 1880 which specifically celebrated the outcome of the battle, all of which Arch attended, being introduced in 1876 as 'Our Cromwell'. The demonstration itself saw the organisation of petitions for the extension of the franchise, while in June 1877 Arch also spoke at a great Liberal rally at Naseby.[90]

There was at this time a close link, just as there had been in the mid 17th century, between radical politics and nonconformist religion. In the intense and very partisan revival of interest in the battle of Naseby these political and religious beliefs were firmly intertwined. Stead in 1891 expressed the feelings well:

> 'from the point of view of church order and political history, Baptists and Congregationalists are Independents..... Independency is not anarchy, but it is liberty - it is so devoted to liberty that, if need arises, it does not shrink from consenting to submit to the severest discipline. The Independents, like their immortal leader, are at once the most idealist and the most opportunist of men......The Independents owe to Cromwell their imperial ideas, their conception of England's responsibility for the exercise of power, and their belief in the grandeur of her destinies.... Again and again in recent years the inspiration that springs perennial from the life of the Lord Protector has perceptibly deflected the course of English politics at home and abroad.'[91]

We find the Naseby vicar reporting to his bishop at this time that three quarters of the population of Naseby were dissenters and that their dissent was more political than religious, the new chapel having become the focus of opposition to the vicar and the squire. The Union and Liberal demonstrations were soon followed by nonconformist meetings, which were not only important in a religious context but were an important force in Northamptonshire Liberalism in the 1880s and 1890s. Whereas the victory gained in the battle of Naseby had been largely reversed with the Restoration, the struggle of the 19th century did bear lasting fruit. In 1885 rural labourers were finally given the vote and in 1894 they had the opportunity to exercise that vote locally with the creation of the first representative parish councils. In the first parish council election the old order in Naseby was swept from power, although they would not give up without a fight, literally, and so came about what was reported at the time as the second battle of Naseby.[92] Unwilling to simply accept the results of the wider democracy, these men actually came to blows at a meeting in the church with those who, with true popular support, now controlled the new parish council.

Near the turn of the century, on the 250th anniversary, there were various events which generated popular interest in the Civil War. For example, 1892 saw an important exhibition of artefacts from the Stuart period in the Hall of the Worshipful Company of Saddlers in Cheapside, London. Here various items associated with Naseby field were displayed, including the Wistow saddles of Prince Rupert and King Charles.[93] Perhaps of the greatest significance however was the 300th anniversary of Cromwell's birth, in 1899, which saw a 'wave of appreciation of Cromwell's merits... passing over the nation at large'. The 'Free Churches' established a Cromwell Memorial Fund as well as a range of celebrations in London, at Huntingdon and more locally at places such as Market Harborough and Wellingborough.[94] The political nature of these events is clearly seen from the Wellingborough celebration in April.[95] As the *Northampton Herald* reported, 'both addresses had an unmistakable tinge of Radicalism about them, and the object in view was as much the promotion of party interest as the honouring of the memory of Cromwell.'[96] Inevitably Naseby also figured in the celebrations. Advertisements appeared in the local papers encouraging people to attend Naseby on the 27th April, for the celebration of the birth of 'the greatest Englishman'. Tea was to be served in the schoolroom at 6d per head, followed by a public meeting at 7.00pm.[97]

For the anniversary of the battle of Naseby in that year there were plans for the greatest of all the celebrations. The 'demonstration' proposed by the Free Church Council was to have brought together ten or twelve thousand people. It fell through simply because of the logistical problem of transporting so many people to rural Northamptonshire so far from a railway.[98] Instead a far more modest meeting rather similar to earlier celebrations was organised by the Northampton and Naseby nonconformists which, thanks to promotion in the local papers, was 'very largely attended by the people from all the surrounding district.'[99] 'The day was delightfully fine and the demonstration proved a complete success from every point of view. The villagers had very heartily entered into the spirit of the affair and flags floated from almost every house.' Music was provided by the Long Buckby Silver Band and about 450 sat down for tea. Later some inspected the obelisk, others the site of the thickest fighting, while some took in the magnificent view from the church tower and by six thirty that evening, when the public meeting began on the recreation ground, there were nearly a thousand people. They had come in brakes, on bicycles and all sorts of other vehicles. As the newspapers reported, this gathering 'showed that the spirit of Oliver Cromwell was not dead. They had met to show their adhesion to the principles for which Cromwell contended.'[100] There was a service with hymns, prayers and speeches and it was said to have been 'one of the best representations of sturdy and militant Nonconformity that has been held in the neighbourhood for some time past.'[101]

There had in fact been two separate Naseby meetings to mark Cromwell's tercentenary, due to the differences in view between the nonconformists and

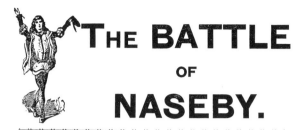

THE BATTLE
OF
NASEBY.

ANNIVERSARY ~
~ CELEBRATIONS
On the Battle Field,
Thursday, June 15, 1899.

Committee :—Rev. JABEZ BELL (President), Mr. J. LINNETT (Vice-President),
Mr. W. RUSSELL (Treasurer), Mr. C. HALFORD (Secretary), Rev. J. J COOPER,
Mr. Councillor E. LEWIS, Mr. T. D. LEWIS, Mr A ABRAMS (Northampton),
Mr. R. CHAPMAN, Mr. J. H. SMEETON, Mr. G. WILFORD,
Mr. D. W. WRIGHTON, Mr. J. MARTIN, and Mr. E. BURDETT (Naseby).

PUBLIC TEA at 4.30. Tickets 6d.

Grand Demonstration
On the RECREATION GROUND,
At SIX p.m.
SPEAKERS AND SUPPORTERS:

Rev. J. HIRST HOLLOWELL

Rev. W. L. LEE, Rev. HARRY COLLINGS, Rev. T. ROWSON,
Rev. W. E. SCAMELL, Rev. W. G. HOOPER,
WALTER HADDON, Esq., W. FITCHETT, Esq., (London),
F. BARLOW, Esq., J.P., JOHN SMEETON, Esq., C.A.,
HENRY COOPER, Esq., J. JUDGE, Esq.

MUSIC AND SONGS OF FREEDOM.

LONG BUCKBY TOWN SILVER PRIZE BAND
Will play Selections during the day.
Collection to Defray Expenses.   Surplus given to the Cromwell Library Scheme.

 Wagonette Return Fare 1s. 9d.   Northampton Friends can secure Tickets
from Mr. A. Abrams, 7, Horsemarket, not later than Monday, June 12.

" Evening Telegraph " Offices, Guildhall Road, Northampton.

Fig. 76. Advertisement for the Naseby celebration in 1899. There was even a hymn specially composed for the event.[102]

others. This alternative celebration on the 26th April 1899 was addressed by the well known local historian the Rev.J.C.Cox.[103] As his speech makes clear, the nonconformists did not have a monopoly of interest in the Cromwell anniversary or in the battlefield at Naseby:

'It seems to me somewhat petty and pitiable for a small and extreme section of the Protestant party of today to try, in their ignorance, to identify the memory of Oliver Cromwell with the Kensit's and the Walsh's who happen just now, in their campaign of slander, to be feebly strutting across one obscure corner of the stage of English public affairs. Many of us churchfolk, at all events, are glad to be permitted to have some share in the wave of appreciation of Cromwell's merits that is now happily passing over the nation at large.'[104]

For Cox the battle of Naseby did not represent radical politics, it was a triumph of morality and liberty over license and despotism. Different groups clearly brought very different meaning to the same events. This split in the protestant churches is a strange reminder of the Independent/Presbyterian split of Cromwell's time. There was even an opposing camp, for the exploitation of the battle by radical political and religious leaders had also drawn criticism from local Tories. One of these corresponded with the *Northampton Chronicle* in December 1898, presumably in response to the plans for the Cromwell tercentenary celebrations in the coming year. He reported a supposed conversation with a labourer near Clipston on matters of land, labour and similar topics, clearly harking back to the Agricultural Workers' actions at Naseby, and later hinting at the nonconformist rallies. The report claimed that a labourer near Clipston reported seeing 'a spectral horseman mounted on a white charger, riding like mad o'er the fields not far from the village of Naseby', and after close questioning on matters of appearance and dress the correspondent recording the story concluded that:

'the uneasy spirit of the uncrowned King has returned to the scene of one of his greatest battles and successes. The reason why I come to this conclusion is because I hear on pretty good authority that during the last few months prayers have been offered up in many Chapels to Almighty God for the spirit of Oliver Cromwell to arise, or rather return, from the spirit world, and regenerate the land; and I find, in consulting American papers, that the same strange phenomenon has been observed in some of the States. What can this possibly portend? Do we want another Oliver Cromwell? Can it be that some of our enterprising friends are anxious to re-fight the Battle of Naseby over again? God forbid that anyone should harbour such thoughts without cause. Will all true patriots help to lay this restless spirit? It does seem queer to me that he should disturb us after close on three centuries of silence. My advice to all is - Watch. Watch the East, the West, the North, the South; for when Cromwell's spirit is abroad there's mischief brewing.'[105]

With such tensions it is perhaps not so surprising that the scheme to erect a statue to Cromwell at Huntingdon collapsed in August 1899 although, after some political controversy, a statue was unveiled at Westminster on 14th November 1899.[106]

To leave a permanent reminder at Naseby of the anniversary celebrations and the public awareness of the importance of the battle and of Cromwell's part in it, Cox and the other speakers at the Naseby tercentenary commemoration in April 1899 formed a committee to create a library. It was to deal with the life and times of the great man or any aspect of the Civil War, from all points of view, to permanently mark the anniversary of Cromwell's birth. It would, according to Cox, be useful for the village and district and prove an attraction to visitors. Both J.C.Cox and J.T.Page took an active role, while Dr Gardiner, the most important of living authors on the Civil War, was said to have taken a 'kindly interest in the scheme'.[107] The list of subscribers included Smeeton, a Baptist farmer, and the Baptist minister of Long Buckby, a prominent Liberal.[108] It was hoped that the collection could be presented to Naseby on the 14th June and be housed in the existing Naseby Reading Room which had been established in 1884, part of the process of late 19th century educational development.[109] After some considerable delays, the Cromwell Library was finally opened there on the 27th June 1901.

Within a few years we find that the initial impetus had gone and the care of the collection left a great deal to be desired. As Holloway wrote in 1912, the small library was locked up in a corner cupboard which the visitor must inspect under the eye of the caretaker, but at least the books had 'escaped the mice better than the modern magazines, especially poor Mr Stead's splendid articles on the battle, which have been reduced almost to ribbons by the rodents.'[110] This was a reflection of a general decline in interest in the English Revolution. The nonconformist religious links of the Liberal and socialist movement gradually declined and, most significantly perhaps, modern revolutionary champions appeared in the 20th century to give a new focus on which to concentrate. The political demands of the 19th century had been largely achieved, fulfilling the promise of a redistribution of power that victory at Naseby had led some to believe might be realized in the mid 17th century. With the achievement of these aims the agenda moved on in ways for which the 17th century revolution no longer provided the central model and so interest in the Civil War, and therefore also in Naseby, as a political and religious focus declined. It seems sad that the Cromwell Library, the one lasting monument to the great flowering of interest in the battle of Naseby in the late 19th century has now lost its identity and is hidden away in the County Record Office in Northampton with almost no one aware of its existence.[111]

These great anniversary events had a significant effect in promoting the importance of Naseby, but they were not the origin of popular interest in the battlefield. People were already coming to Naseby, not only as antiquaries and historians to study the battle but also a modest number of tourists. There has

Fig. 77. The Cromwell Library, established to mark the 300th anniversary of Oliver Cromwell's birth. It is seen here, on one of Halford's postcards, when it was housed in the Reading Room at Naseby. The collection of books is now buried away from public view in the Northamptonshire Record Office store room. However, although the bookcase is lost, the Record Office still has the signing in book recording all those who used Library in its early years and bundles of tickets, issued at 1d a time to the readers. There is even one book with a hole eaten right through the middle by mice!

been an almost continual interest in the battle both locally and nationally throughout the last 350 years, though the nature of that interest has changed dramatically with the political and religious context of century or class. Though she did not turn aside from her route to visit Naseby, Celia Fiennes when passing Bosworth Field recorded 'This is a great flatt full of good enclosures; near this is Narsby where was the great battle fought between King Charles I and the Parliament of England....'[112] In 1724 Daniel Defoe, who wrote the *Memoirs of a Cavalier*, reported of Naseby:

> 'A little way off of Northampton is Naseby, where the bloody and fatal Battle was fought between the Royalists and Parliamentarians, upon a fine Plain, where at present stands a Wind-mill; and on it, are the Marks of several great Holes, where the Slain were buried.'[113]

In 1763 Martin wrote:

> 'Naseby, said to be the very Center of England, and the highest Ground; that therefore, it's right Name is Navelsby. It was the Field of that fatal Battle between the Forces of the King and Parliament, June 14, 1645. There are no Traces of it remaining, but a few Holes which were the Burying places of the dead Men and Horses.'[114]

There was it seems an increased interest in the battlefield during the early 19th century, unless of course it is simply that we become more aware of that interest. The erection of the monument in 1823 was therefore perhaps not simply the whim of a landowner, but rather a reflection of a wider growth of interest in the battle. This gradually led to the development of a genuine if very modest tourist trade. In the *New British Traveller* of 1819 Naseby was described as having 'considerable claims to notice .... from its connection with a great historical fact', and in 1825 it was 'a small village, but on many accounts interesting to the traveller, and will ever be conspicuous on the face of history.'[115] While the antiquaries of the late 18th and early 19th century would beat a path to Mastin's door, the ordinary visitor could look to the local inns as a source of historical information. In 1815, according to Cole:

> 'in one of the rooms of an inn near the spot, used to be a series of pictures, representing the manoeuvres of both armies on that perilous day. They served to impress the mind of the travellers with the particulars of this memorable battle.'[116]

In the late 19th century when Page visited the battlefield he found that the landlady of the Royal Oak had a copy of Mastin's history of the village to hand. There he could find 'rare and interesting information respecting the place itself and also many details of its famous battle, as well as the relative positions of the rival armies when they took the field.'[117] Carlyle had said of Mastin's and Lockinge's books that 'there are two modern books about Naseby and its battle, both of them are without value....'. In writing this he did not give a thought to their usefulness for the ordinary visitor to the battlefield, which was considerable because Mastin provided a verbatim account of the battle from Sprigge and from three contemporary dispatches.[118] Such information was otherwise quite inaccessible, and generally remains so even today. Any tourist who wanted more basic information only had to ask the locals. There are various stories like that of the Rev. John Simpkinson, rector of Brington, who rode over to Naseby in the summer of 1865 to examine the battlefield. There he fell in with an old labourer of over 80 who showed him 'various spots where the battle had been hottest, as was evident by bullets and fragments of weapons, which are still turned up occasionally by the plough.'[119] However one visitor would seem to have been rather less fortunate than most:

> 'In 1865 I was driving through Naseby. Wanting some information my brother alighted, and made some enquiries of a passing labourer, whose reply was amusing, but hardly instructive, "this is Naseby Field; them's Sulby Hedges. That's the way the King come; and that's the way Bounaparte come!"'

One cannot help but think that it was in fact the local who had the last laugh, but what must have annoyed the people of Naseby most of all was to have outsiders telling them the truth of the matter, as has happened again in recent years, when they knew very well where the battle was fought and its importance. One can therefore only guess what the villagers thought when they read the article in the County Magazine in 1932:

> 'It is not so bad now, but still very few seem to have any idea of the importance of the fight or the issues at stake. The populace, however, generally know the ground on which the battle was fought, thanks to compulsory education in elementary schools and a general increase in historical knowledge.'[120]

By the mid 19th century a change was beginning in the way in which the battle was viewed. This new concern with accuracy and fact rather than romantic feelings, was reflected in the wish of Fitzgerald and Carlyle that a small inscribed monument of Portland stone be erected on the battlefield itself, to make up for the 'blockhead of a monument' that Fitzgerald's father had put up on the old windmill site. It was to have marked the site of the mass grave which Fitzgerald had excavated, but his family had sold the Naseby estate in 1855 and the trustees of the new owners would not allow a monument to be placed on their land.[121] Had Fitzgerald succeeded in erecting this marker and had Carlyle published Fitzgerald's results properly, then in more recent years there need have been no confusion over the location of the decisive action of the battle. The inscription was to have read:

> 'Here and for .... yards to the rearward, lies the Dust of men slain in the Battle of Naseby, 14 June 1645. Hereabouts appears to have been the crisis of the struggle, hereabouts the final charge of Oliver Cromwell and his Ironsides, that day. This Ground was opened, not irreverently or with reluctance, Saturday 23

September 1842, to ascertain the fact, and render the contemporary records legible. Peace henceforth to these old Dead.
Edward Fitzgerald (date)'[122]

The various late Victorian anniversaries not surprisingly led to a wave of tourist interest in Naseby, with various visits being made to the village, as for example in July 1891 when the National Cyclists came to Naseby.[123] There must have been many such organised trips, though more often than not they will have been more local events, such as when Serjeantson and Poynton led an anniversary visit by the Northamptonshire Natural History Society and Field Club, on Thursday 16th June 1904. Fifty two members from Northampton were joined by others at Naseby making a party of some eighty or more, who took tea at the Fitzgerald Arms. Poynton described the battlefield, which they viewed from the Parliament side, looking across Broadmoor. Mr George, curator of Northampton Museum, reported later that:

'we could follow Mr Poynton's relation as to the disposition of the various troops, and realise that nothing could bring to our minds more vividly this momentous encounter like a personally conducted visit to the actual place of conflict under well informed leaders.'

They had walked down across Broadmoor to view relics from the battlefield in Broadmoor Farm and then to view 'the field where the slain were buried, the spots being still visible.' Finally they returned to the village to see the Cromwell Table.[124]

By the early 20th century Hamson could write that 'during the summer there are numerous visitors to Naseby...' and it was this growing interest in the battlefield that led him in 1906 to publish what must be one of the earliest of battlefield guides. The popularity of the place as a genuine if modest tourist destination is borne out by the advertisements for the local pub and the guest

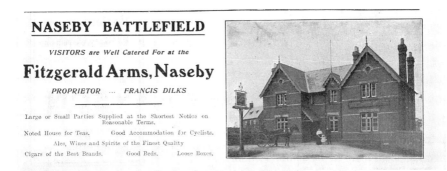

Fig. 78. An early 20th century advertisement for accommodation at the Fitzgerald Arms, opposite the church in Naseby. This reflects the very modest tourist trade in the late 19th and early 20th century related to the battle.

house. There were also the numerous postcards on battle subjects produced by Halford, the local photographer who ran the post office, which were offered for sale in the village at this time. By the 1920s Halford even had an advertisement for the post office displayed next to the obelisk monument! The local labourers were also able to make a little extra money from the visitors, by collecting musket balls from the battlefield and selling them to the tourists.[125]

Another response to this great interest in the battle was the installation of some of the very first battlefield interpretation panels, two 'memorial boards' erected in 1908 by the parish council. The one on the north side, on Dust Hill, read:

'Battle of Naseby, June 14th, 1645. Left Wing of Royalist Army and position of Sir Marmaduke Langdale's Cavalry. Westward along the crest were the positions of Astley's Infantry in the centre, with King Charles in the rear and Prince Rupert's Horse on the right wing.'

Fig. 79. The unveiling of the Naseby battlefield monument on 26th May 1936. This 'round headed' monument was designed by the Northamptonshire architect J.A. Gotch for Mr C.E. Reich, who gave it into the care of the County Council. He had been so concerned that there was no monument on the actual battlefield that he paid for one himself and gave it to the people of Northamptonshire in the hope, as he himself said at the unveiling, that 'you and your children, and your children's children will remember that here at Naseby occurred one of the most important events in the history of your county.'[126]

On the opposite side, on Lodge Hill, the board read:

> 'Battle of Naseby, June 14th, 1645. Right Wing of Parliamentarian Army, and
> position of Cromwell's Horse. Westward on the crest were the positions of
> Skippon's Infantry in the centre and Ireton's Horse on the left wing.'[127]

Simple, but effective, this was the best interpretation the battlefield was to see
until the late 1980s. In the intervening period there was however still an
interest in the battlefield, for in 1936 a battlefield monument was finally
erected overlooking Broadmoor. We have seen that Carlyle and Fitzgerald
wanted to place a new monument to mark the centre of the main action, but
that their plans had been thwarted. The new monument was about 500 metres
north east of the burial pit excavated by Fitzgerald but still well placed to
mark the principal action of the battle, which took place on the hill top
immediately to the south, although it is a little too far west for the inscription
it carries, which claims that it stands close to the location from which
Cromwell made his first charge.

In tracing the Naseby campaign we have seen that folk memories can have
a relevance, if only minor, to the understanding of the actual events. Perhaps
more significant is the insight they give into local interest in the battle over the
centuries. No other single event in the whole history of Northamptonshire
seems to have generated more local traditions. Strongman, an amateur
archaeologist and local historian who studied the traditions of the Market
Harborough area, was in no doubt as to the all pervading effect of the battle
of Naseby on the historical consciousness of the people in the area:

> 'The Old Hall [at Lubenham] has been spoken of as the house where King
> Charles was hidden after his disastrous encounter at Naseby. This ancient gossip
> concerning King Charles and his supposed Naseby flight movements recall other
> stories equally misleading. A stranger wandering around the Harborough district
> in search of historical data, could be excused if he came to the conclusion that
> locally, history commenced and finished on Naseby Field. During the many
> years spent in pursuing these interesting inquiries, it has been a constant
> experience to hit up against either King Charles or Oliver Cromwell as the
> persons responsible for the erection or destruction of this, that, or the other
> object about which a keen interest has been aroused. Charles, local gossip says,'
> threw up those earthworks on East Farndon Hill, even Harrod, in his history of
> Harborough claims that "In the Hall Close adjoining the Old Hall at Lubenham,
> the Kings Army threw up four entrenchments N.S.E.W. and in which they
> lay."'

Whereas in earlier centuries the traditions developed as stories which were
handed down by word of mouth, in the 20th century one may be excused for
thinking it is perhaps the newspaper reporter above all other who is
responsible for the evolution of spurious stories. This was certainly the way
Strongman felt, for his excavation at Lubenham was later reported, to his

great disgust, as a hunt for King Charles' Treasure, buried during the flight from Naseby battlefield![128]

Traditions have been recorded throughout the last 300 years, starting with the time when Morton was able to speak to people within living memory of the battle. The earlier the tradition is first recorded and the more mundane the subject, the more likely it is that it has a core of truth. Most of the traditions were however recorded during the 19th century by local historians from stories they were told by elderly village residents. James, who was writing in 1855, dismissed 'these memorials and corresponding traditions', saying that they 'have sprung up in compliance with the renewed interest latterly taken in the spot.'[129] There are indeed many stories which would seem to fit James' assessment. One of the most improbable is the supposed account of John Trusloe, related in about 1815-1825 when he was an old man, of the events which befell his grandfather during the flight from Naseby. It was said to have been recorded by a Mr Green who lived as a child in Market Harborough in about the 1820s, where he picked up various traditions from the old men of the town. These stories were said to have been recorded in a manuscript from which a certain Mr Clarke made a copy for the local historian Hensman early this century. The provenance is tortuous, the story quite unbelievable and yet it is still fascinating.[130] The man was supposedly a Parliamentarian soldier from the 'Buckingham troops' and had moved up from Daventry where they changed horses. Then at Naseby:

> 'we were out before daylight and put in a hollow way, sort of blind lane, hedges as high as our heads. Here we had to dismount and lie as still as poachers. The fight began on the farthest side but we heard shouts soon enough and the thud of hard ridden horses came near ... every firelock had been cleaned, loaded and charged ... we fired through the hedges. Horses and riders tumbled fast so then we were soon upon our horses and after the flying rout. That trick of ours won the day as I well know. On the far side they had been worsted....'

The story would appear to be a distorted combination of the information from Sprigge and a knowledge of Sulby hedges as they were in the later 19th century. The account continues:

> 'Naseby fight was on the afternoon before and we had followed the King's crowd right up to dark cutting down all we caught up with as were our orders. It was in the pudding-bag, Marston, the crowd was the thickest and they stuck there like huddled sheep. Most had thrown away their arms, but a few set their backs against the church and fought desperately. The crowd was soon gone, and those who were killed were stacked up against the church door leading to the chancel. Then we laid ourselves down to sleep.'

Later that night a woman and child came around, asking after Prince Rupert - was he killed? The lady supposedly was Rupert's wife and the baby his also and, so the story goes, they both died that night and were buried there at Marston! Was it perhaps the discovery of the mass grave in the churchyard at Marston Trussell, near to the Chancel wall, in the second half of the 19th century which provided the basis for this part of the story? Indeed one begins to ask whether any of the traditions associated with Marston are actually genuine, because there is no contemporary account of a skirmish at Marston by name. It is just possible that it is all a fabrication based in some form around the archaeological discoveries, some of which may in fact prove to be just ordinary churchyard burials but which now lie outside the churchyard because the boundary has contracted over the centuries. Even the mass grave in the churchyard has not been demonstrated as being of Civil War date. However, the traditions and the discoveries, together with the field name of Slaughterford, do all together suggest it is likely a skirmish took place there. This is at least one of the few places where the issue could undoubtedly be resolved by a properly recorded metal detecting survey.

There are many traditions which are related in some way or other to objects or buildings. Another skirmish during the Royalist flight from the battlefield is said to have happened at Foxton, a couple of miles north east of Marston. Fighting is said to have occurred as the fleeing Royalists were nearing Foxton village. It is claimed that the dead were given Christian burial in the churchyard and their arms and armour were collected and deposited in a large oak chest in the church. This equipment was still there in 1860 and is said to have included about 20 heavy pistols, with barrels a foot long, the same number of swords and helmets, and several cuirasses. In about 1870 the vicar of Laughton and Foxton sold these ancient weapons, causing a great stir in the village. Was this all a genuine folk memory, or was it simply that Foxton had somehow retained its village armour and weapons from the 17th century and an elaborate story was woven about the objects to explain their presence in the church?[131] Other stories, which are even more likely to be spurious are centred around archaeological sites or ruined buildings. Such is the case of Knaptoft, where we can actually begin to see how the tradition evolved. A report in 1944 was very clear as to the reasons for the ruined condition of the church there:

> 'After the battle of Naseby a party of Royalists, hotly pursued by Cromwell's cavalry, took refuge in Knaptoft Church and refused to surrender. Cromwell's men brought some gunpowder, and blew in the church door. But it is said they used too much gunpowder, and not only did they blow the church down, but many of Cromwell's soldiers who stood near were killed. This story had been handed down in the Glover family from Commonwealth days. At the time they were large farmers in Lubenham.'[132]

One can trace the tradition back to the second half of the 19th century where an explanation appears for part of the elaborate 20th century story:

'About 1850 a large part of the tower of the north side fell; the tenant of the
farm cleared all the fallen parts away and found charred beams... this seems to
show that the church was destroyed by fire after the Battle of Naseby, which is
the tradition.'[133]

The source of the tradition can be traced back to Nichols in the early 19th
century who wrote: 'The church was standing in 1630; but was probably
dilapidated during the ravages of the civil war.'[134] This appears to have been
mere conjecture on Nichols' part, but in the following hundred years or more
a very elaborate and apparently completely spurious tradition built up around
the church based on his comment. In fact the ruins of the building lie amongst
the earthwork remains of the deserted medieval village of Knaptoft, the
process of decline began long before the Civil War and the reasons for the
loss of the church are undoubtedly related to the desertion of the village not
to Parliamentarian cavalry pursuing Royalists from Naseby field.[135] Another
deserted village has also become linked to the battle, because in 1870 a Mr
North exhibited some artefacts found on the site of Little Oxendon. They were
said to be:

'a few antiquities connected with the Battle of Naseby......Tradition says that
when the victorious Parliamentary troops, routing the Royalists, pursued them
towards Market Harborough, they came across the little village of Little
Oxendon, and finding its inhabitants favourable to the cause of their King,
almost totally destroyed the place....'[136]

Like Knaptoft, Little Oxendon had no association with the battle. It was a
medieval village which had been deserted at least a century before the Civil
War.

Various other archaeological discoveries have over the years been
explained by reference to the battle. At Stanford on Avon for example we find
a record in 1883 that 'some few years ago a number of skeletons, found in
"the gravel holes", and supposed to be fugitives from Naseby, were removed
to the north-west of the churchyard.'[137] Then again, in about 1936 'in a close
at Hothorpe, called Deadman's Close, in making a drain, a human skeleton
was discovered, which might have been one of these stragglers from the great
battle....'[138] But the linking of these discoveries with the battle has not,
apparently, led to the development of a tradition in these places. Perhaps by
the late 19th century it was simply too late for completely new traditions to
begin to form, although existing traditions have certainly continued to evolve
over the last hundred years.

The Wistow tradition is one where it is possible to see very well the way
in which a tradition can become elaborated progressively with the telling. In
this case the development can be traced because the story has been recorded
a number of times over the last 200 years.[139] We know from the *Iter
Carolinum* that Charles I was indeed at Wistow on the 4th June 1645, but the

tradition has become focused in particular around the two elaborate saddles which are preserved in the Hall, which were probably left at that time by the King as a gift for the owner of Wistow. From Charles having stayed there ten days before the battle it became in the 19th century a story that Charles had slept there the night before Naseby.[140] This seems to be a common change in traditions, probably resulting from the description 'before Naseby', meaning some days before, being misunderstood later as meaning the night before. According to John Halford in the late 19th century the saddles were 'left by the unfortunate monarch, perhaps on the occasion of his visit on June 4th; more probably, I think, in his hasty flight towards Leicester immediately after his disastrous defeat.'[141] By the 1930s it had become a fact that they had been left there when Charles and Rupert fled from the battlefield, changing horses at the Hall.[142] Not satisfied with this, another author tried to 'reconstruct' Charles' flight from Naseby using local tradition and the account he gives of Wistow is woven elaborately around the claim that bullet holes had been found in the door of the drawing room, which was supposedly once the original entrance to the Hall. The brief halt of the King at the Hall in earlier stories now becomes a fighting retreat with Parliamentarian forces firing on the King as he flees, bullets smashing into the fabric of the Hall. We step from history into tradition and eventually find ourselves in complete fiction.[143]

Some stories can be completely dismissed through careful research. For example, there is the case of the large, plain Celtic style cross in the churchyard at Naseby. Barrett in 1896 claimed, on no particular authority, that it had been erected in memory of those who had been killed on Naseby field and buried in the churchyard. By 1914 Treen reported that the cross marked the site where many Royalists were buried. In fact it is well documented that the cross was erected in about 1825 by the lord of the manor to replace the old and dilapidated market cross which stood nearby in the street. There was no connection at all to the battle![144] It seems quite likely that the 1881 report of Civil War burials is also wrong: 'parliamentarian officers who fell were, it is said, buried under the tower of Naseby church, where some bones have been found.'[145] Another spurious idea was disproved by research in the 18th century. The church tower used to have 'little more than half a pyramidal spire covered with lead, and a notion did prevail that it was decollated at the time of the battle; but, upon examination, dates were discovered upon the lead prior to 1645; a proof that this was not the case.'[146] Other stories can be dismissed simply because the places involved are not in a sensible location relative to the battlefield, such as the claim that 'After the battle, Cromwell visited Aylesbury and Dinton Hall, and left behind him his sword as a property, not to any particular family, but to the mansion of Dinton for ever.' The owner of Dinton Hall, Simon Mayne was a regicide and a friend of Cromwell and he may well have visited the Hall and have presented the owner with his sword but it is certain that he did not visit Dinton immediately after the battle.[147] Yet another tradition places Cromwell at

Woollaton, Lord Middleton's house, the night after Naseby while another story claims that Charles I visited Belton in Rutland, where he is said to have rested on the plain stone which today forms the base of the war memorial.[148]

But for every tradition that can be shown to be wrong there is another which may well have a genuine basis, as we have seen for example with Cromwell's associations with Thornby Grange and Hazelrigg House. Another story which may also be genuine is that relating to Tur Langton, half way from Naseby to Leicester. Not far from the busy modern road in a pasture field is a very undistinguished spring. Nichols, writing in the late 18th century, recorded the local tradition that as he fled from the battlefield Charles watered his horse in this spring in Langton field 'which, from that incident, was called, and still retains the name of, King Charles' Well'.[149] This is fairly close to the course that anyone fleeing to Leicester would have taken and the event is mundane enough to be true. Nearby at Great Glen, on the road many of the fleeing Royalists undoubtedly used, there is another story which was reported fairly early, at the end of the 18th century (though one might suggest reasons for the person concerned to have fabricated the story). Throsby recorded that:

> 'I have been told that Mr Hobson, who resided at or near this village.... was raised to opulence by the following circumstance: Immediately after the battle at Naseby, a servant, going into the field, saw a stranger on horse-back, riding hastily, throw a portmanteau over a hedge into a ditch; which the boy, after the stranger was gone, picked up, and brought to his master, who found it to contain mostly money, which master told him were only hob-nails. Mr Hobson after keeping the property for some time, and finding that no enquiry was made after it, turned the good fortune to his own account, after rewarding the boy who found the portmanteau. Mr Hobson frequently told the story at the decline of his life; from whose account of the transaction it was then generally believed that a thief had taken advantage of the confusion attendant on an army after the defeat, and, being pursued, threw it into a ditch, with an intent to return for it again, or to prevent being detected.'[150]

However, simply because a story was recorded at a very early date does not always mean it is true. The least likely of all stories associated with Naseby was first written down in the 17th century, the idea that Cromwell himself was buried on Naseby field, the place of one of his greatest triumphs.[151]

Though many of the stories can be dismissed, each must be treated with care for some of the more unlikely ones in the end prove to have a significant core of truth. This is best exemplified by the claim that Shawell rectory, in south west Leicestershire, was burnt down after Naseby fight because of the strong Royalist sympathies of the rector.[152] This might have been very quickly dismissed as fanciful, but recently quite independent contemporary information has been discovered in the Exchequer papers revealing that Rupert burnt the village at a cost to the villagers of £235. This presumably took place in the week or so preceding the battle when the whole region was being plundered and when threats of this kind were being made. So, the tradition had a genuine basis but the perpetrator and the timing of the destruction had been completely changed![153] Indeed, where destruction has been involved, whether spurious or genuine, it seems to be the Parliamentarians who are usually if not always said by tradition to have been responsible. According to Everitt:

'after 1660 the Great Rebellion became a sensitive and embarrassing subject in most local communities.... Everywhere Cavalier legends were spawning themselves, like mushrooms in the dark, even in such unlikely counties as Suffolk and Northamptonshire.'[154]

The Shawell case reveals how the new environment of the post Restoration period must have demanded genuine traditions be completely changed, so that they were favourable to the King and his cause.

In the end however some of the stories simply leave one confused and wondering what on earth they mean and where and how they originated. Such is the tradition of King Charles' Oak in Sibbertoft, for which the earliest record I have found is in the 1930s in Strongman's notes.[155] The tree itself was destroyed a few years ago but its site was pointed out to me by Peter Burton. The remarkable thing is that of all the hedgerows such a tree could have been in, this oak was at the south west corner of Little Old Close. This is one of the very few places in Sibbertoft field where any tree could have existed at the time of the battle! The tradition must surely be a very early one, for within five years of the battle there were hundreds of trees planted in new hedgerows across the whole of Sibbertoft parish. But what could the tradition possibly mean? It is such cases that make one treat more carefully the other local stories. Should we perhaps take more seriously the story that Peter was told by his father, that the place where the King's army camped before the battle was to the south west of Lowe Farm? Is this a folk memory of the site occupied by the Royalist baggage train during the battle, or is it a much more recent fabrication that just happens to fit with recent discoveries?

Such is the popular awareness of the battle that, ever since the 17th century, it has also been surrounded not only by traditions but also by tales of ghostly apparitions. There were many such stories from various parts of Northamptonshire in the early 18th century for Morton recorded 'Reports we have had of strange Appearances of Military Skirmishes in the Air, or of Armies of Aerial Warriours disputing in Battel-Array for Victory.' But Morton was not taken in by these stories:

'....peradventure [they] saw a great many small Clouds of uncouth Shapes, from which there flash'd out Lightening, and now and then they heard a Thunder-Crack. This 'tis likely was the whole of the Matter, and all the rest the Product of thir own Superstitious Imaginations.'[156]

Though we have seen at least one ghost story from Naseby was in fact a political statement there are those who have reported ghostly apparitions in good faith, believing the truth of their experiences. In the mid 19th century one visitor wrote:

> 'I paid a visit to Naseby, which from my earliest acquaintance with history had been surrounded with a glamour of fascinating interest.... It was the summer season and the gorse was in bloom, making the wide and silent plain gay with its golden sheen.'

There he met a local labourer who recounted how he had often heard the legend of the great battle being fought again at midnight every year on the anniversary of the battle.[157] The tales even led one of the more poetically minded visitors to write *The Spectral Battle*.[158] The Naseby ghost stories are continually being added to even to this day. On the evening of the 14th June 1949 a couple cycling in the area stopped near Naseby where they saw across the road what they described as an old drovers road and there they were amazed to see men wearing leather jerkins labouring down the old road with wooden carts.[159] Though such stories improve with the telling and can hold an audience, the reality is often rather mundane when one can actually get at the truth. At least one of the apparent ghost stories is no such thing. The story as heard by Mastin in the mid 18th century was that:

> 'some years ago, on a Shrove-Tuesday two women of the village had a violent dispute in the church-yard; from words they proceeded to blows, and fought most furiously; when a man, who was shot in the battle of Naseby, came out of a grave and parted them. The fact was, one Humphrey Thompson, a parishioner of Naseby, a quarter-master, valiantly fighting for his Royal master in this field, was wounded, but not mortally: he, after quitting the army, was made parish-clerk and sexton, and was digging a grave when the above-mentioned quarrel happened.'[160]

Today the stories of ghosts associated with the battle are still recounted, and new sightings are still reported, like the carriage said to be seen crossing the back road from Clipston to Marston near Twantry Farm, which just so happens to be on what we now know to be the main line of Royalist flight from the battlefield.[161] Whatever the truth of the various traditions and ghost stories, they help us to reassess Greenall's comment that 'the battle faded in importance in the Naseby consciousness until its memory was revived for propaganda as well as antiquarian purposes in Victorian times.'[162] What the many folk memories tell us, above all else, is that the battle of Naseby has remained a significant event in the collective consciousness of the whole region throughout the last 350 years.

While many of us give little credence to such ghost stories we cannot usually claim that the people are reporting anything other than what they genuinely believe they have seen. However such honesty is not associated with everything surrounding Naseby. The enormous rise in interest in the Civil War in the 19th century inevitably led to the perpetration of forgeries for profit or simply out of mischief. Most notable is the map of the battle supposed to have been drawn by Cromwell.[163] Said to have been found in 1876 in a mid 17th century book, it was validated by 'several eminent literary men' as being in Cromwell's hand.[164] There was also the 'lance head from Naseby Field' which was given to Norwich Museum in 1839 by Squire, who is now known as a major forger of both documents and of artefacts of the Civil War and other periods. Carlyle himself, who was briefly taken in by some of Squire's forgeries, wrote of him 'there was no mischief but what he was capable of and you could not tell what he was up to.'[165] The malaise was in fact quite widespread. At Daventry one finds that the Plough and Bell Inn tried to wrest from the Wheatsheaf the honour of having accommodated the King while the Royalist army was in the town in June 1645, presumably because they thought it might attract a few more customers. Even Naseby itself was not immune. In the late 19th century, farm labourers in the village took the opportunity to make a little extra money in a rather underhand way from the growing interest in the battle. Rather than collect the bullets from the battlefield, which were now becoming rather scarce, they simply made or acquired bullets and passed them off as genuine battlefield relics, selling them to gullible tourists at a few pence a time. [166]

Fig. 80. The plan of the battle of Naseby signed by Cromwell which was in fact a 19th century forgery.

To end on such a depressing note would however be quite wrong, for thankfully it represents a very minor element of the Naseby story. Over the centuries the battle has held a great fascination and has drawn many to the clayland of Northamptonshire on the watershed between the Welland, Nene and Avon. Most were simply tourists, some were antiquaries intent on serious historical and archaeological study, others came for political or religious reasons but, whatever their reasons for visiting, many were taken by the romance of the event and of the place. This had led Cockayne, Ashby and Fitzgerald to erect their monuments to the battle, but others created more ephemeral monuments. These are the poems which, though not perhaps outstanding works of art, reflect as clearly as anything the very distinct feelings of the different classes and centuries for the events of the 14th June 1645. The *Scottish Dove* published a Parliamentarian poem within days of the battle:[167]

> 'The Dove from Naseby-field doth Triumph bring,
> And of redundant benefit doth sing:
> The sues, that God for mercies may have praise
> Who turnes our mournings into Halceon dayes:
> Brave Rossiter did Newark Noddies cheat,
> And Venables hath Birons Buzzards beat;
> Shrewsbury by Mackworths worth did make
> A Royall partie fall, some crouch some quake:
> Noble Fairfax Leicester hath regained,
> Though men despise, Gods hand is not restrain'd.'

By the 18th century, not surprisingly, the message is very different. On a wooden tablet dated August 1783 within the 'temple' in the grounds of Rushton Hall, a garden which had been frequented by great authors like Dryden, was the poem by Dr Bennel, Bishop of Cork.[168] From this summer house one could sit and look out across to Naseby, ten miles away in the distance and muse:

> 'Where yon blue field scarce meets our streaming eyes,
> A fatal name for England, NASEBY lies.
> There hapless CHARLES beheld his fortune cross'd,
> His forces vanquish'd, and his Kingdom lost.
> There gallant Lisle, a mark for thousands stood,
> And Dormer seal'd his loyalty in blood;
> Whilst down yon hill's steep side with headlong force,
> Victorious Cromwell chac'd the northern horse.
> Hence Anarchy our church and state profan'd,
> And tyrants in the mask of Freedom reign'd.
> In times like these, when Party bears command,
> And Faction scatters Discord thro' the land;
> Let these sad scenes an useful lesson yield,
> Lest future NASEBYS rise in every field.'[169]

Following the enclosure of Naseby in 1823 Joseph Tyler, rector of Gt Addington, wrote a Latin poem in which Naseby figures prominently. Here it is presented in Gould's recent translation:

'If it pleases thee to recall the hardships and gloomy reign of the Stuarts and to remember the Britons exhausted with Civil War, Naseby will yield evidence. Naseby, now by a new law dividing her acres in many parts, she indeed once witnessed the unmerited sorrows of Charles, turning his back in flight and exiled from the throne of his fathers; saw brothers perish wounded by brothers; saw the Aufona red with blood from its very source; saw troops celebrate a mad triumph and rebel standards scattered over the wide fields. So a stranger wandering most sadly among these very fields calls to mind the wantonness of a cruel fate, the glory of a fragile reign and its fallen sceptr. And as he turns the sod, once drenched with English blood, stands amazed at the tokens of a bygone war, broken swords, javelins eaten away with the decay of age, and helmets riddled with bullet-marks, or removes black cakes of mud from iron bullets. Often too the terrified farmer hears the snap of bones as he turns his harrow, and he grasps his handle more carefully in his trembling hands, fearing to violate the hidden graves.'[170]

Later in the 19th century even the famous historian Macaulay, who completed his *History of England* in 1861, set pen to paper. The result was the rather long and overbearing poem *The Battle of Naseby. By Sergeant Obadiah-Bind-their-Kings-in-Chains, and-their-Nobles-in-Links-of-Iron, Sergeant in Ireton's Regiment*. Just a few of the fifteen stanzas will give a flavour of the work:

'It was about the noon of a glorious day of June
We saw their banners dance and their cuirasses shine,
And the Man of Blood was there with his long essenced hair,
And Astley, and Sir Marmaduke, and Rupert of the Rhine.

Like a Servant of the Lord with his Bible and his sword
The General rode along us to form us to the fight,
When a murmuring sound broke out, and swelled into a shout
Among the godless horsemen upon the Tyrant's right.

And hark! like the roar of the billows on the shore,
The cry of battle rises along their charging line;
'For God! for the Cause! for the Church! for the Laws!
For Charles King of England, and Rupert of the Rhine!'

In the 19th century such was the interest in the battle that a number of works of, not particularly good, fiction were also composed around the events.[171] For example, in 1898 the Northampton Mercury serialised the Reverend A.J.Foster's 'fascinating romance' called *The Broken Tester*.[172] In the present century Harrison, a minor poet of the Northamptonshire landscape, has left us his view of Naseby. Following as it does the 19th century restoration of Cromwell and of the English Revolution to respectability, it lacks the factional political message seen in the 18th century poem, though the author's perspective is not wholly impartial:[173]

'Upon this Summer's morn I rest awhile,
Beneath a hedge that hides a broken stile;
The shadow of the obelisk is thrown
Across the swaying grass by breezes blown,
And thus a touch of gold, a glint of green
Just ebbs and flows with shadows blue between.
I hear the piping of a joyous bird,
The song that Cromwell's Roundheads might have heard,
On that fair day when through this stricken field
The morning sunlight gleam'd on sword and shield.

Beyond the field the peaceful village stands,
Surrounded by deep woods and fertile lands;
The homesteads nestle down moss-grown with age,
Like pictures culled from life's historic page;
One room remains with table and with chairs,
Where Cromwell sat to shape the morn's affairs;
Near four cross roads still stands the whipping stone,
An ancient relic of days sad and lone,
A grim reminder of the bitter creed
That knew no solace for another's need.

The Welland and the Avon, crystal clear,
From bubbling springs commence their journeys here;
One flows through flow'ring fields its eastward way,
By lofty elms and drooping willows grey;
The other, turning westward from its source,
Meanders softly on its level course,
By Stratford, where the 'Bard of Avon' sleeps,
To meet the Severn; there fair Malvern sweeps
Her rolling hills across the tranquil skies,
And Bredon's breezy uplands gently rise.

And as I linger, thoughts just come and go
Like waves across the grass that ebb and flow.
I seem to see the battle through the field,
And Rupert's henchmen to stern Cromwell yield.
Of little streams that flow, and flow to bless
Far distant meads with beauty's soft caress;
To grow more full and winding, fresh and free,
Through English meadows to the open sea.
Still I can hear that piping joyous bird,
The song that Cromwell's Roundheads might have heard.'

NOTES

1. Camden, 1722, vol.1, p.520.

2. Bridges, 1791, vol.1, p.575. Bridges notes. Brown & Foard, 1994, p.183, 185 & 200.

3. Henson, 1893, p.59. It was Rouse who drew the picture reproduced in fig.65.

4. Matthew Holbeche Bloxham, 'Naseby', 3rd December 1874, unprovenanced newspaper cutting in NRL.

5. Cockayne, 1869, p.9.

6. 'Rushton Hall and its Owners', *NN&Q*, vol.6, item 846.

7. Gotch et al, 1896. The table is shown in Neale's view of the interior of the Hall in 1825 and is engraved in Rush Meyrick's *Ancient Furniture*.

8. 'Rushton Hall and Its Owners', *NN&Q*, 1894-5, vol.4, p.10 and item 824. *Sale Catalogue of Furniture etc of Hon.Mrs.Cockayne Medlycott of Rushton Hall*, Weds 27th September 1826, NRL. The table is now apparently in the Victoria and Albert Museum.

9. Letters from Sir Charles Isham to J.T.Page, reported in *Northampton Herald*, 6th January 1894.

10. Wall, 1927, p.22. Some of Hanbury's correspondence is preserved in the British Library but is not relevant to Naseby. Henson, 1893, p.59.

11. NRO H(K)203.

12. *Northampton Herald*, 6th January 1894.

13. Letter from Lord Bateman, 17th April 1865 to Sir Charles Isham, quoted by Isham, 1969.

14. According to Sir Charles Isham writing in the 19th century the coat, which had always been in the family, had no history. A front and back view of it were published by Scott, where it was wrongly said to have belonged to Fairfax. *British Battles on Land & Sea*, part 18, p.234. The coat is of thick hide, weighing 16 lbs and yet the blood has soaked right through. The buttons are silver wired. *Northampton Herald*, 6th January 1894. Scott, 1868, p.446, plates 54 & 55. Isham, 1955, p.xli. The buff coat is now in the Victoria and Albert Museum.

15. Page, 1886.

16. He changed his name from Capt.George Ashby Maddock and later again to George Ashby Ashby. *Northampton Mercury*, 18th June 1887. 'Relics of Naseby Fight', *NN&Q*, vol.III, 1888-9, item 414.

17. *Northampton Mercury*, 11th February 1888.

18. *Sale Catalogue of Naseby Woolleys*, February 1888, NRL. *NN&Q*, New Series, 1921-3, vol.5, item 283; Old Series, 1889, vol.3, p.48 & 66-8.

19. T.J.George, *JNNHS&FC*, Vol.12, no.98, p.193. Holme, 1891, p.46n. Holloway, 1912. The pieces of armour have since been said to date from the time of Henry VIII. Information from Lady Braye.

20. Information from Lord Cottesloe of Wistow in c.1935. LRO DE 2102, 2, *The Wistow Hall Tradition*, c.1935, typescript by Frank P.Strongman. *NN&Q*, 1888-9, vol.3, item 522.

21. Anon, 1881, p.135. Nichols vol.3, p.539 & plate LXX. fig.30.

22. One of the swords, was given to the village in the 1930s and has a provenance via Major Renton of Naseby Hall, Mr Fox of Northampton, having been found on the battlefield in the 19th century. *Northampton Independent*, 5th June 1936, p.3.

23. Markham, 1921. An example of the maintenance of this armour is seen in the account of the constable of Irchester in 1634, referring to receipts of £1/0/5d for the town arms. NRO, Irchester Parish Records, 177P/IrBi.

24. Mastin, 1792, p.74-5.

25. Henson, 1893. Page worked out that this History must have been written in about 1847, *Northampton Herald*, 21st April 1894. Of course the visits to Naseby were much earlier.

26. Phillips, 1828.

27. Greenall, 1974, p.10. Page, 1886. Rimmer, 1892, p.85-6.

28. 'Relics of Naseby Fight', *NN&Q*, vol.3, item 433. *Sale Catalogue of Naseby Woolleys*, February 1888, NRL. *Northampton Mercury*, 11th February 1888.

29. Holloway, 1912.

30. Page, 1886.

31. Stead, 1891, p.69.

32. Page, 1894.

33. George, *JNNHS&FC*, vol.12, no.98, p.195.

34. Anon, 1932, p.3.

35. Holme, 1891, p.46n.

36. The sword was indexed as Map 1131, the card saying 'with Miss Wake'. The index card has now been removed.

37. 'The sword, which is in a splendid state of preservation as regards the elaborate metal work of the hilt, was discovered broken by a former parish constable of Naseby, who sharpened the severed blade to a point and hung it at the head of his bed as a useful protection.... It has three edges, but is not made like a bayonet, being formed of a flat blade out of which a central ridge is worked, with a corresponding groove in the other side.' It was given by the constable's granddaughter to Mr Brunner. Holloway, 1912.

38. Holme, 1891, p.46n. Correspondence from Mr Stewart Sutherland to J.T.Page, *Northampton Herald*, 3rd February 1894. This was Canon Thomas James, 1809-1863. Longden, 1940, vol.7, p.259. Engraved on the sword blade was 'Gloria virtutem sequitur Vivit post funera virtus 1618' on one side and on the other 'Stalzius Reviler me fecit Soling. Constantes fortuna juvat.'

39. George, *JNNHS&FC*, 1904, vol.12, no.98, p.194.

40. *Northampton Daily Chronicle*, 18th June 1892.

41. *Northampton Mercury*, 11th February 1888.

42. The sword was given to Mr Whitney who then passed it to the museum. *Northampton Daily Reporter*, 10th, 11th, 12th July 1894; *Northampton Daily Chronicle*, 11th July 1894.

43. NRO, Marston Trussell parish records /42.

44. Whellan, 1849, p.382. *Northampton Herald*, 6th January 1894. One of the more improbable was that supposedly made by labourers digging out a bog on the north side of Naseby in 1823. They claimed to have found a portrait of Charles I, probably a 'modern' one, painted on velum, wrapped in lead, put in a bottle and again wrapped in lead. Unnamed newspaper cutting, possibly from the *Northampton Mercury*, 1823, in NRL. A Fairfax gold medal, again post dating the battle, was also found in about 1855.

45. Fitzgerald to Carlyle, 23rd September 1842, Terhune & Terhune, 1980, p.354.

46. They were displayed at the exhibition in 1892, lent by Captain Woollett.

47. Phillips, 1828.

48. *Northampton Herald*, 6th January 1894.

49. Carlyle's letter, 10th May 1842, *NN&Q*, vol.1, 1884-5, item 111. John Alt Porter, *NN&Q*, 1884-5, item 183.

50. Stead, 1891, p.69.

51. *Northampton Herald*, 9th December 1893. Pers. comm. Mike Westaway.

52. *Northampton Independent*, 22nd June 1912, p.10. Pers.comm Mike Westaway.

53. Cole, 1815, p.126-7. Holme, 1891, p.46. Carlyle to Mrs Aitkin, 10th May 1842, *NN&Q*, old series, 1886, vol.1, p.138.. Whellan, 1849, p.382. *Northampton Herald*, 3rd February 1894. The most improbable claim is that the bones from the battlefield were collected up at some time after the battle and deposited in the crypt at Rothwell church.

54. Longden, 1940, vol.9, p.171.

55. Henson, 1893, p.60.

56. Phillips, 1828.

57. Henson, 1893, p.53-61.

58. *Northampton Reporter*, 1st May 1899.

59. Fitzgerald wrote in November 1830: 'This is a very curious place with bones and bullets of the fight at Naseby'. Terhune & Terhune, 1980, vol.1, p.93. Fitzgerald to Pollock, 16th September 1842, & notes by Fitzgerald. Terhune and Terhune, 1980, vol.1, p.339-342. Carlyle to Mrs Aitkin, 10th May 1842, *NN&Q*, old series, 1886, vol.1, p.138.

60. Fitzgerald's letters to Carlyle, accompanied by eight annotated sketches and watercolours of the battlefield, Cambridge University Library, Dept. of Manuscripts & University Archives, Add.7062. This manuscript volume also contains a plan and views of Winceby battlefield. The letters are transcribed and one sketch and two watercolours are reproduced in Terhune & Terhune, 1980, vol.1, p.27-8, 339-49, 351-401 & plates 4 & 5. The grave pit excavated by Fitzgerald is incorrectly placed at grid reference SP66978013 on the Ordnance Survey Archaeological Record Card SP68SE5, and repeated by RCHM, 1981, p.186. For Carlyle's failure see: T.Carlyle, 1858, vol.1 p.173-5 & vol.3, p.393-5. Fitzgerald to Bernard Barton, 14th May 1845, Terhune & Terhune,1980, vol.1, p.489. Carlyle, 1850, p.231-2. The corrections Fitzgerald made to Carlyle's proofs also show that Fitzgerald was working without the benefit of his original letters and watercolours, Add.7062. Carlyle wrote to Fitzgerald in 1845: 'I dare not open the big packet, fruit of our joint investigations long ago', instead he wrote from memory never amending the text despite Fitzgerald correcting the drafts! Fitzgerald wrote 'Carlyle gets on with his book...He has entirely misstated all about Naseby, after all my trouble...', Terhune & Terhune, 1980, p.488-9.

61. Cambridge University Library, Add. MS.7062.

62. Fitzgerald to Carlyle, 23rd September 1842. Terhune & Terhune,1980, vol.1, p.352. Later finds similarly lack accurate provenances, as with the gold medal of 1645 from the battlefield. *Proceedings of the Society of Antiquaries*, 1873, vol.5, p.443.

63. 'Of cannon balls Charles had enough of them on the other side of Broadmoor'. Fitzgerald to Carlyle, 23rd September 1842. Terhune & Terhune, 1980, vol.1, p.357. As a result of enclosure the former areas of Closterwell and Closter furlong had become confused by the mid 19th century.

64. 27th September & 9th October 1842, Terhune & Terhune, 1980, vol.1, p.378.

65. Fitzgerald to Carlyle, 23rd Sept 1842, Terhune & Terhune, 1980, vol.1, p.354.

66. Fitzgerald to Carlyle, 27th September 1842. Terhune & Terhune, 1980, vol.1, p.357.

67. Fitzgerald to Carlyle, 28th September 1842 & 2nd October 1842. Terhune & Terhune, 1980, vol.1, p.369.

68. 'A little way up Dust Hill from the Broadmoor runs a hedge, with a slight turn in it; which turn was made (it is recorded) when that field was enclosed the second year after the battle, in order to avoid a great buried heap of men and horses'. Fitzgerald to Carlyle, 23rd Sept 1842, Terhune & Terhune, 1980, vol.1, p.354. Bridges, 1791.

69. Bridges notes.

70. Fitzgerald to Samuel Lawrence, 28th September 1842, Terhune & Terhune, 1980, vol.1, p.342 & 360.

71. Fitzgerald to Carlyle, 23rd September 1842, Terhune & Terhune, 1980, vol.1, p.354.

72. Fitzgerald to Carlyle, 28th Sept.1842, Terhune & Terhune, 1980, vol.1, p.357.

73. Fitzgerald roughly plotted the grave and other pits on a sketch plan, printed in Terhune & Terhune, 1980, vol.1, p.353. They were said to lie behind the viewpoint on the watercolour plate 3, and were nearer the crown of the hill 'on the Parliament slope' not at the bottom and certainly not in Broadmoor. Fitzgerald to Carlyle, January 1846. Terhune & Terhune, 1980, vol.1, p.517.

74. Hamson, 1906. 1932 Field Name Map at NRO.

75. Hamson, 1906, p.14. Lockinge's engraving of the battle is very inaccurate in many respects and his location of the 'graves of the slain' cannot be accepted as accurate. Lockinge, 1830.

76. Mastin, 1792, p.113.

77. Fitzgerald to Carlyle, 30th September 1842, Terhune & Terhune, 1980, vol.1, p.365.

78. Mursell, 1861, p.34. Holme, 1891, p.76. Warburton, vol.3, p.102 n.3 & p.106. Rimmer, 1892, p.83. Whellan, 1849, p.378.

79. Mursell, 1861, p.32.

80. Hamson, 1906, p.5.

81. 'Pleasant Places : Naseby', *Northampton Daily Times*, 19th June 1895, newspaper cutting in NRL.

82. Mastin, 1792, dedication. Nichols, vol.3, p.295.

83. *The Beauties of England and Wales : Northamptonshire*, vol.11, December 1809, p.162. Holme, 1891, p.51. Gotch et al, 1896.

84. Greenall, 1974, p.27.

85. James, 1864, p.28. Whellan, 1849, p.382.

86. Evans, 1924, p.243.

87. *Northamptonshire Guardian*, 1880, quoted in *Evening Telegraph*, 26th April 1899.

88. Vincent, 1966, p.xxix.

89. Markham, 1870, p.192.

90. Greenall, 1974, p.41-2. Horn, 1968-9. Horn, 1971, p.122-128.

91. Stead, 1891, p.74.

92. Greenall, 1974, p.41-2.

93. *Northampton Daily Chronicle*, 18th June 1892.

94. Cox, 1899. *Kettering Leader*, 31st March 1899.

95. *Christian World*, 27th April 1899.

96. *Northampton Herald*, 29th April 1899.

97. *Northampton Mercury*, 21st April 1899.

98. *Evening Telegraph*, 16th June 1899.

99. *Wellingborough News,* 16th June 1899. *Kettering Leader*, 9th June 1899. *Northampton Daily Reporter*, 14th June 1899.

100. *Evening Telegraph*, 16th June 1899.

101. *Kettering Leader*, 12th May 1899. *Northampton Mercury*, 16th June 1899.

102. *Christian World*, 22nd June 1899.

103. *Peterborough Standard*, 29th April 1899. *Northampton Herald*, 29th April 1899. Cox, 1899. *Northampton Daily Chronicle*, 28th April 1899.

104. Cox, 1899, p.4.

105. Correspondent under the name of 'Vigilant' to the *Northampton Chronicle*, 19th December 1898.

106. *Evening Telegraph*, 4th August 1899. *Daily Telegraph*, 15th November 1899.

107. *Northampton Mercury*, 19th May 1899. *Northampton Daily Reporter*, 27th May 1899. A list of books given or purchased for the library was given in *Northampton Daily Reporter*, 1st June 1899.

108. Greenall, 1974, p.41-2.

109. *Northampton Mercury*, 5th May 1899.

110. Holloway, 1912.

111. A catalogue of the books is in NRO ZA5284.

112. Morris, 1959, p.164.

113. Defoe, 1724, p.364-5.

114. Martin, 1763, p.124-5.

115. *The New British Traveller*, 1819, vol.3, p.664. Cooke, 1825, p.152-4.

116. Cole, 1815, p.126-7.

117. Page, 1886.

118. Carlyle, 1858, vol.1, p.174.

119. Longden, 1941, vol.12, p.179. Simpkinson was author of *The Washingtons, a Tale of the Seventeenth Century. Northampton Daily Reporter*, 21st July 1891.

120. Anon, 1932, p.7.

121. Terhune & Terhune, 1980, vol.1, p.178; vol.3, p.313, 351-4, 373, 417, 428, 431, 440-1.

122. Terhune & Terhune, 1980, vol.2, p.180.

123. *Northampton Daily Reporter*, 29th July 1891.

124. T.J.George, 1904, *JNNHS&FC*, vol.12, no.98, p.192-6.

125. J.Hamson, 1906, p.3. A collection of Halford's postcards are in the NRL postcard collection. 1929 card of Obelisk, NRL post card collection.

126. *Northampton Independent*, 5th June 1936. B.Giggins, 1993, *The Naseby Battlefield Monument*, unpublished report in Northamptonshire Sites and Monuments Record.

127. Anon, 1932, p.8.

128. Articles and papers by Strongman, LRO DE 2101/131/6, p.2.

129. James, 1864, p.27-8.

130. Letter from Clarke to Hensman, 9th Sept 1915. His widow of Werrington Green, Lansdowne House, Stoneygate had the manuscript. NRO, Hensman Civil War Notes.

131. Newspaper cuttings on the history of Foxton, 1944, LRO DE 3389/214 item 2.

132. Newspaper cuttings, 1944, LRO DE 3389/214 item 3.

133. Green, 1893, p.88.

134. Nichols, vol.4, p.221.

135. Pevsner, 1984, p.195.

136. *Transactions of the Leicestershire Architectural and Archaeological Society*, vol.2, 1870, p.258-260. Stead, 1891, p.74.

137. Sandon, 1883, p.129.

138. Typescript of lecture by Strongman on Naseby Battle, c.1935, DE 2132/54, p.33

139. Page, 1893.

140. *Strand Magazine*, November 1893.

141. *Northampton Herald*, 9th December 1893.

142. Information from Lord Cottesloe of Wistow in c.1935, *The Wistow Hall Tradition*, c.1935, typescript by Frank P. Strongman, LRO DE 2102, 2.

143. R.C.Timms, 1929, *Great Glen and Gt Stretton*, typescript, LRO L914.2GRE, p.2. F.P. Strongman, c.1935, *The Wistow Hall Tradition*, typescript, LRO DE 2102, 2.

144. Barrett, 1896, p.381; repeated in A.E.Treen, *Souvenir of the Drive to Naseby*, 20th June 1914. *Northampton Herald*, 6th & 11th April 1901.

145. Anon, 1881, p.139.

146. Letters from Mr Prattent, *NN&Q*, vol.III, item 462, referring to *Gentleman's Magazine*, February and November 1793.

147. *Peterborough Standard*, 29th April 1899. Mastin, 1792, p.182.

148. Stead, 1891, p.72. Mee, 1967, p.196.

149. Nichols, vol 2, p.506, quoting William Hanbury, rector of Langton. *Leicestershire and Rutland Notes and Queries*, vol.11, p.300. Ordnance Survey 1:2500 1st edition map. According to Hill, 1867, p.85, it is 'Carles' Trough'. Harrod, 1808, p.82. From early 20th century, a photo of a rectangular, brick lined water filled well in middle of field, titled as being at Naseby, but must be at Tur Langton, F.Lumbers, Leicester, NRO P/3275.

150. Throsby, 1791, vol.2, p.319-20.

151. *Harleian Miscellany*, vol.2, p.286. Harrod, 1880, p.81. Tole, 1888-9. *Northampton Herald*, 19th August 1899. Mastin, 1792, p.202-3, quoting Banks, 1739.

152. Firth, 1926, p.185.

153. Tennant, 1992, p.257.

154. Everitt, 1969, p.3.

155. *The Wistow Hall Tradition*, c.1935, typescript by Frank P. Strongman, LRO DE 2102, 2. The tradition was repeated to Burne in the 1940s. Burne, 1950, p.256.

156. Morton, 1712, p.351.

157. 'Legends and Stories of Northamptonshire', *Northampton Mercury* , pre 1880, newspaper cutting NRL.

158. Taken from Story, 1883.

159. Slater, 1992, p.21-24.

160. Page, 1886. Henson, 1893, p.60.

161. Information from Stuart Kendal of Sibbertoft.

162. Greenall, 1974, p.16.

163. *NN&Q*, 1886-7, vol.2, item 261.

164. *Wellingborough News*, 16th June 1899.

165. Rye, 1925, p.76-7.

166. Edgar, 1923, p.60. 'On Naseby battlefield relics are often ploughed up, and when the visitors make unusual demand for such, the bullets "made in Birmingham" are said to be offered as real Naseby shot of the 17th century.' *Peterborough Standard*, 29th April 1899.

167. *Scottish Dove*, 13th to 20th June 1645.

168. Campion, 1878.

169. *Beauties of England and Wales : Northamptonshire*, vol.11, Dec.1809, p.162.

170. Rev.J.Tyley, 1823, *Inclosure of Open Field*, NRO, Gt Addington parish records. Gould, 1991, p.57-8.

171. *King Charles at Naseby or Royalty in Northamptonshire and what came of it* was published in the Northampton Daily Reporter on the 13th March 1882. Then in July 1886 there was a short fictional tale woven around the events of the battle. *Chambers' Journal*, 17th July 1886.

172. *Northampton Mercury*, February 1898.

173. Harrison, 1928.

CHAPTER 12

A FUTURE FOR THE PAST

'....nothing could bring to our minds more vividly this momentous encounter
like a personally conducted visit to the actual place of conflict...'
T.J.George, Northampton Museum curator, 1904

The transformation of the landscape of the battlefield from that which
existed in 1645 to that which we see today took place progressively over the
centuries. The first enclosure was of Sibbertoft, within just five years of the
battle, other parishes followed in the second half of the 18th century, while
the very last place in the area to see enclosure was Naseby itself. Henson
visited the parish some years before enclosure and described it in glowing
terms as a 'scene of beauty, sublimity and rusticity'. But to others in the early
19th century, like William Pitt, it was a backward area which could not
escape the Agricultural Revolution for much longer and surprisingly it was
John Mastin, the best known of the local historians of the battle and parish,
that was the strongest promoter of enclosure at Naseby. Mastin argued long
and hard for the improvement of the parish and finally this came in 1820.
When Phillips visited in 1828 he still saw a landscape very similar to that of
1645, but he said 'The lordship has recently been divided and enclosed, so
that in the next generation, hedges and trees will disguise the scite of the
lately-open field where the battle was fought.'[1] Following enclosure, in the
1820s and 1830s, there were also a number of new farms built away from the
village where none had existed before. By 1890 visitors to the battlefield
found a very different landscape to that over which the battle had been fought:

'Gone are the thickets of gorse and the trecherous rabbit-holes that hampered
on that memorable day the movements of the cavalry. The labourer's spade has
drained and filled the pits of water and other peeces of ditches that checked the
Parliamentary charge....'[2]

By 1912 Holloway could write that 'had the people of Naseby purposely set
about abolishing all their associations with the great battle they could hardly
have been more successful....'[3]

Sadly I find myself, when taking a party to Naseby, recounting similar
feelings about the continuing loss. When I first visited the village in search of
the story of the battle I ventured down Carvell's Lane to see the site of the
Parliamentarian baggage train, down a narrow, deeply hollowed medieval
road lined with trees and with a rough surface of earth and stone. One could
step back in time just for a moment to the summer of 1645 and imagine the
waggons and carriages rumbling down the old lane. Now it has been given
modern metalling and a house is being built at the bottom of the hill.

Approaching the battlefield along the narrow country roads from the village one came across Fenny Slade, the shallow valley which Rupert must have ridden across when he attacked the baggage train. It was a quiet scene of cattle in fields of ridge and furrow, but today the peace is shattered and the prospect dominated by traffic thundering along a dual carriageway. How soon will it be before the last of the remaining ridge and furrow also disappears? In a fashion reminiscent of Mastin's promotion of enclosure, the founder of the tiny battle and farm museum, Eric Westaway, told me on one of my visits to Naseby that he remembered ploughing up many fields of ridge and furrow after the Second World War. It had been with great pride that he had levelled the furrows very neatly in just a year or so of ploughing, by the clever trick of ploughing down the centre of the ridge, exactly opposite to the way they had been formed. Then again it was Mike Westaway, who has spent so much time and effort in the study of the battlefield, who told me, as we explored the land where Fairfax had formed up his army for the first time on the morning of the battle, how in the 1960s he had cleared away from the slopes here, with great efficiency, one of the last fragments of furze in Naseby. Indeed it has been over the last 50 years that the extensive remains of the 17th century landscape, both living and fossilised as archaeological features, have been almost totally obliterated from the battlefield. All the furze is gone and there is nothing to stop the last small areas of ridge and furrow from also being lost.

Fig. 81. Traffic now thunders past Naseby on the new A14. It has cut a swathe through what was a peaceful and very pleasant landscape of hedged fields containing ridge and furrow near to where the Parliamentarian baggage train stood. Thankfully this is almost a mile from the site of the main battlefield action, lying well beyond Mill Hill Farm which can be seen on the skyline.

The sweeping away of the links with the past to make way for the more efficient management of the land to meet the needs of the present is a constant and inevitable trend. Yet the value of such links cannot be over emphasised. At Naseby we are not dealing with just any piece of the landscape, this was the stage for one of the most dramatic and influential events in English history. In researching for this book I returned once more to walk over the whole of the battlefield with Mike Westaway, revisiting the places we had viewed together on my first visit less than ten years before. We returned to Sulby Hill, where the so called 'graves of the slain' are recorded. I can remember the magic of the moment when I had walked over the brow of the hill the first time, with the accounts of the battle clearly in my mind, and saw Sulby hedge and there on the hill top found the water pits, still with their rushes and standing water, just as Ireton's troopers had encountered them on the 14th June. But this time we found that they are being filled in as the land is 'improved' yet further. How long will it be before they grub up Sulby hedge or the hedge which still marks the perimeter of the rabbit warren across which Cromwell had to advance?

In the village itself a similar process has taken place. In 1842 Naseby was still 'a venerable hamlet..... all built of mud, but trim with high peaked roofs, and two feet thick of smooth thatch on them, and plenty of trees scattered round and among.'[4] The cob buildings of the village were lost to an improving landlord in the 1870s and the local authority housing committee in the inter war period so that today just two of the old cob buildings with their thatched roofs remain. The modern character of Naseby was established in the 1870s and 1880s when Viscount Clifden spent large sums of money building new labourers' cottages 'of a much better type' in red brick.[5] Even the old stump of the market cross was moved. Sadly the process of change in the village has continued in more recent years so that today even the 'gem of all the old buildings' in Naseby, the timber framed Tithe Barn, which Holloway could say in 1912 'makes one step back in fancy to the days of Cromwell', is now gone![6] Even the more recent 'history of the history' is being lost. The Cromwell Library, for example, has left Naseby and is now hidden away in the County Record Office, unknown to anyone whereas it was intended as a lasting and accessible monument to Cromwell and to the greatest battle of the English Civil War.

Although the battlefield was systematically scoured for arms and equipment immediately after the battle, despite the cultivation in intervening centuries and the removal of many objects from the battlefield to serve the demand for relics, and even the occasional antiquarian excavation, much evidence still lays buried in the ground at Naseby. Ever since 1645 pistol, musket and cannon shot, pieces of armour, swords and other items have been collected in quantity from the field, but over the last 150 years antiquaries have reported the decline of such finds as the battlefield was stripped. Even where material was collected for its historical value the exact find spots were rarely if ever recorded and most of the material is now lost or dispersed. Yet, as this book has hopefully demonstrated, the distribution of artefacts across the landscape, when combined with the documentary and topographical evidence, can add a dramatic new dimension to a battlefield analysis. The number of Civil War and later battlefields on the draft English Heritage Register is just 26, but a significant number of these sites will not be amenable to systematic study because they have been affected by development, mineral extraction or other land use which has destroyed much of the evidence. By comparison with other archaeological sites in England, battlefields are therefore a rare 'monument class', while the evidence they contain is very vulnerable. The invention of the metal detector has made both the study and the destruction of the evidence possible but sadly the latter seems to be the norm. If the artefact distributions which exist on our battlefields are of high importance to the understanding of the battles, as the evidence presented here for the battle of Naseby would suggest they are, then it is essential that this archaeological evidence is protected, or at the very least is subjected to properly funded, detailed systematic study before it is further damaged or completely destroyed.

The lesson that is clear from Naseby is that if we do not actively conserve then our contact with and potential to understand the past will be continually eroded. We can see how earlier visitors to the place, even visitors just twenty or fifty years ago, had a far better link with the events of 1645 than we do today. It is inevitable that there is change in the landscape, but for at least a few of the major events in our country's history there is the need to retain something of the context within which they took place, so that later generations have more than just words to link them to these momentous events. The value of conserving our man made heritage has been recognised for generations. The Ancient Monument Protection Act of 1882 provided protection for some archaeological sites and has been revised and updated on a number of occasions, most recently in the Ancient Monuments and Archaeological Areas Act 1979. The Town and Country Planning Act 1947 provided protection for historic buildings and in 1967 the Civic Amenities Act provided for Conservation Areas to conserve the wider built environment, legislation that was updated and consolidated in the Planning (Listed Buildings and Conservation Areas) Act 1990. However, until very recently our battlefields have been sadly neglected.

One might argue that it was at Naseby that the case for the conservation of battlefields as important historic sites was officially recognised in England for the first time, as a result of the battle over the construction of the new A14 road. However, that struggle is the exact opposite of the model of how to achieve conservation. In 1974 plans were unveiled for a new road to link the Midlands to the east coast ports, by connecting the M1 to the A1. The exact course of this new road, now known as the A14, was not yet fixed. Indeed even the need for a major new road was challenged by many, especially as a similar road was to be constructed along the Nene valley. Others questioned

Fig. 82. The A14 road under construction in 1992, looking north from Naseby village.

the course to be taken, arguing for it to run through south Leicestershire and by Market Harborough and only then through Northamptonshire, well to the east of Naseby. In the village of Naseby itself there was universal opposition, almost every adult in the village signing a petition which was presented to the local MP in May 1975. The potential impact on the Civil War battlefield meant that important national figures, academics and politicians, were drawn into the conflict. Naturally too the Civil War re-enactment societies rose to the challenge, and in February 1975 some 300 members of the Sealed Knot and of the Roundhead Association, in uniform, staged a protest in the village, one of a number of such appearances. Four months later The Society for the Preservation of the Field of the Battle of Naseby was formed, under the patronage of Sir John Betjeman and with the involvement of leading historians such as Sir Arthur Bryant and Mr Burn-Callander.[7] But, once it became clear that the road was unlikely to be stopped and it was simply a choice of routes, north or south of Naseby, both of which had significant environmental impact, the matter became far more complicated. The events which followed over almost twenty years justifiably warrant the name of the 'Second Battle of Naseby'. Like a civil war it set cousin against cousin, neighbour against neighbour and disrupted the whole community and the lives of the main protagonists. Like a civil war, none were wholly in the wrong - apart perhaps from the Department of Transport!

Though the public enquiry decided upon the northern route, running through what can be viewed as the far southern edge of the battlefield, the conflict rumbled on until construction finally began in 1991. The misinformation, of which both sides were guilty, and in the later years the increasingly bizarre antics of some protestors, soured relations and set back the cause of battlefield conservation and interpretation at Naseby by decades. Today the repercussions are still being felt. The road should never have been built where it was, but it did not destroy the battlefield as protestors claimed it would. Now that the road is completed the storm has begun to abate, just a little, and although it will be a long time before the memory and the deeply held feelings fade, we can at least begin to talk once more of the facts without raising a hornet's nest of protest from one side or the other because those facts do not fit with their particular cause.

At least, if nothing else, the conflict over Naseby did lead to a heightened awareness of the value of battlefields and was instrumental in the formation of the Battlefields Trust. Coming at a time of increasing concern for the heritage, as part of the wider movement for environmental conservation, the 'Second Battle of Naseby' was perhaps the catalyst that led to the establishment of the Register of Historic Battlefields. The placing of a responsibility with English Heritage in 1990 for the creation and maintenance of the Register marked an important turning point in England's attitude towards its battlefields, with a recognition that they were nationally important heritage sites.[8] Planning Policy Guidance Notes published by the Department of the Environment have recently strengthened the hand of conservation within the planning process, recognising the importance of battlefields and making clear that such sites are a material consideration in the planning process. With the publication of the Battlefields Register in June 1995 the first step along the path of battlefield conservation on a national scale will have been taken. The guidance published by English Heritage to accompany the Register recognises the archaeological potential of battlefields as well as the need for conservation of their character and the development of their interpretation, but the objectives set in the guidelines are far too modest and the powers available to local planning authorities, upon whom the responsibility for conserving the sites has been placed, are far too weak.[9] The proper understanding of our major battles is being jeopardised by the destruction of the archaeology of the battlefields, mainly through the uncontrolled removal of artefacts, yet there are no powers to halt such destruction. We have also seen how the last man made features in the landscape around Naseby which survive from the 17th century are under threat of destruction, yet there are no powers provided to conserve those features. Indeed, if the recent planning appeal decision at Tewkesbury is a guide to the future, even those powers which are said to be available under the Town and Country Planning Act 1990 may count for nothing![10] Our battlefields are nationally important historic and archaeological sites and they should be treated as such. The Register must be seen as just a first step. If it is to have a real impact, and if the Government are to be persuaded of the need to extend statutory protection to these sites, then archaeologists and landscape historians must work together with military historians to provide detailed studies of other battlefields, to demonstrate both the potential and the threat. The absence of any proposals for action from English Heritage in connection with the Battlefields Register reflects the almost complete failure of the archaeological profession to take the study of battlefields seriously. The investigation of these historically important sites has been left to non archaeologists who, as at Naseby, have in several cases produced very valuable evidence, but in recognition of the pioneering work they have done it is essential that a proper methodology of battlefield archaeology is developed and that effective conservation of the evidence is instituted before it is too late.

At Naseby at some time in the future it will be appropriate to initiate a carefully thought out programme of archaeological survey and excavation, further exploring the artefact distributions and the burial pits. This will undoubtedly yield important new evidence for the battle, although a comprehensive study will not be quick or easy. Although there has been some study of the archaeology of other battlefields in England, most notably Marston Moor, we cannot at present draw upon this as the work has yet to be adequately published. Direct comparison with the methodology and problems of fieldwalking study is relevant here, because the issues are very similar. One needs the recovery of artefacts in as consistent a fashion as is possible to provide a representative picture of the distribution of artefacts in the ploughsoil. When this evidence is available then the pattern can be analyzed and an attempt made to correct for variations in land use, both past and present, for previous removal of objects and for other factors such as the background effects of geology.[11] Random data collection, such as that used at Naseby, is not wholly adequate because it builds in its own biases, with typically far more artefacts being recovered from areas of higher density because survey time is inevitably concentrated on those areas producing the most finds. Other biases also need to be explored, such as the differential recovery of musket as to pistol shot, which is currently a reflection of the size and hence ease of recovery, not of their actual density and distribution. Other artefacts may be far more rare, but they may prove of great significance in pinpointing particular actions, such as the distribution of the pewter tops from the powder 'boxes' on the bandoliers of the musketeers or dragoons. It may be that other geophysical survey techniques might also be usefully applied to the battlefield. The use of ground radar has for example been considered in order to locate burial pits and other features of the contemporary landscape on the battlefield at Culloden.[12] However, given the sheer size of Naseby battlefield and the vast number of pits of various dates that are scattered across that landscape, as Fitzgerald discovered, this would not perhaps be appropriate at Naseby.

With all the work that has already been done at Naseby, can we now define the extent of the battlefield and the requirements for its long term conservation? Should the battlefield be seen as the whole area over which bodies and artefacts have been found and across which events are recorded? This would mean that the battlefield extended as far afield as Marston Trussell and Cold Ashby. Should it include the areas where the two armies first formed up and marched across the landscape to their final positions before the battle? This would still encompass an impossibly large area of some 20 square kilometres from East Farndon to Naseby. Should it cover the area extending from the Parliamentarian baggage train site by Naseby village across to Wadborough hill in Clipston where we believe the Royalist infantry made their last stand? This would encompass an area of up to 10 square kilometres. The answer must surely be that no simple boundary could or should be drawn, but rather that the responses should be tailored to the needs. The control of metal detecting should probably be across the whole area where the artefacts are known or expected to exist. The individual burial pits, if they can be identified, should be given their own specific protection from both further cultivation damage and from non archaeological investigation. Such sites may include detached locations like Marston Trussell and Hellcoombe, if the sites can be confirmed by archaeological survey, as well as the main area of fighting. These and other places, such as Bloodyman's ford between East Farndon and Market Harborough which is now within an urban area, should be identified as potentially important archaeological sites that should be conserved or investigated like any other such sites, through the planning process, if they come under threat from any form of development. The management of the landscape itself should encompass the conservation and enhancement of all the significant features which were present at the time of the battle and especially those which influenced the events of the battle. These included the hedgerows of Sulby closes and Archwrong Close, but they should also include the ridge and furrow in Naseby and Clipston which preserves, for all to see, the pattern of the landscape as it was in 1645. What should not be done is simply to define where the first and most significant part of the battle took place and restrict any conservation to that area. As in all matters of historic landscape management, a balance must of course be drawn between what might be desirable and what it is practically possible and reasonable to implement, but that balance has certainly not been adequately defined at present.

Only if we collectively take a stake in this important landscape and create a plan for its long term management will the battlefield be secured. There must be money which will enable the landowners to benefit while still conserving, whether it be through schemes like the Countryside Commission's Countryside Stewardship or by management grants from English Heritage. We should look to conserve and enhance those features which remain from the 17th century and even consider, in the longer term, returning this landscape to something like the character it had in 1645. It would be possible to restore the hedgerows which existed, gapping up the Sulby hedge where it is decayed, to remove those hedges which did not exist at the time of the battle, perhaps even to re-establish the furze. Though elsewhere conservationists would throw up their hands in horror at the idea of grubbing up hedgerows, perhaps here at Naseby is one of the few places where we should contemplate this as an enhancement of the landscape's historic value. One cannot put back the open field system or recreate the warren, but one could create a feeling of the openness of the landscape as it was in 1645 and so enable the visitor to gain an impression of the sheer scale of the battle. There should also be the opportunity in the future for the visitor to walk out across this landscape and to see where the great events took place. If we cannot as a nation achieve this at Naseby, one of our two or three most important battlefields, then what can be achieved anywhere? These may be very long term goals, but what we must achieve now is the effective conservation of that which still exists so that it is there for any future management schemes which may become possible.

Commemoration of those that died was the focus of some of the anniversary events which have taken place over the last 150 years at Naseby, but strong political and religious beliefs underlay the 18th and early 19th century interest of the gentry in the battle of Naseby, while the great popular upsurge of interest in the battle in later 19th century was certainly underpinned by the radical political and nonconformist religious struggle of the Victorian era. Today we are much more of a secular society and the political issues have moved a long way from the 19th century situation for which the Civil War had direct relevance. Though time heals wounds, memories fade and relevance is lost, strangely the Civil War can still raise political and religious feeling even today, but the main focus of interest is now the more objective understanding of the battle and its significance in English history.

Interpretation of Naseby battlefield has seen some minor advances. Popular local interest in the battle has since 1975 been maintained primarily by Eric Westaway with his Battle and Farm Museum. Holloway would have appreciated Eric's efforts, for he wrote in 1912: 'If only the village could secure ... a suitable repository for their relics they might recover more of their lost posessions.'[13] A few have indeed returned, thanks to the generosity of Leicestershire Museum Service who have loaned a few items to Eric, but the need for a professional and adequately funded approach to the whole matter cannot be put off much longer. We have seen what has and continues to happen to the many artefacts associated with the battle. There are also many visitors to Naseby who must go away very disappointed at the lack of interpretation facilities which do full justice to the importance of the site. The County Council have long been responsible for the two monuments at Naseby, but even here the steps have been faltering and small. In 1924 Evans wrote the Naseby obelisk 'were it not almost entirely planted out by trees would serve as an historic landmark for the county around [instead it is] rendered as insignificant and unmeaning as possible, by planting it out... with trees.'[14] We ought to follow Evans' guidance and recapture the original romantic image of an eye catching feature seen from a distance. In this small matter as in so much else to do with the battlefield there is the need for a vision that matches the scale of the event itself. In the late 1980s when I was given responsibility to oversee the management of the County Council's 'Properties in Care' we installed new interpretation panels at both monuments. This was a very modest attempt by the Council to meet a real need while trying to mend relationships with the village, which had been soured after the disastrous attempt some years earlier to take the first steps in the establishment of a battlefield interpretation centre. In the shadow of the tension, mistrust and anger which surrounded the Second Battle of Naseby any such major initiative was doomed to failure, but this particular initiative, to judge by the comments of some of the locals, set back the cause of battlefield interpretation by many years. Only now, since the road has been finished, and because there has been a major turnover in the population of the village, have the tensions begun to subside. But for some the memories will linger on. It may be many years before we see an interpretation centre on the battlefield at Naseby, but eventually it must surely come. This is one of the best documented of all our battles, where events and topography can be intimately linked on what is still one of the least spoilt of English battlefields. Naseby could provide THE Civil War interpretation centre around which the story of the English Revolution should be told. However, it can and must only come with the consent and encouragement of the villagers and landowners of Naseby and Sibbertoft.

A century or more ago Naseby led the way. It saw perhaps the first genuine campaign of battlefield archaeology, the construction of one of the first battlefield monuments, the erection of some of the earliest battlefield interpretation panels and publication of one of the first battlefield guides. It was the venue for great working class and nonconformist demonstrations and great commemoration events which drew thousands of visitors. It even had its own Cromwell Library! The 350th anniversary should be the starting point for a new approach to Naseby, one that is more long lasting and more far reaching than those of the Victorian era. The foolish lack of imagination of many in the 20th century, with such acts of vandalism as the demolition of the Tithe Barn and its replacement with undistinguished modern houses, should not be repeated. In that little piece of destruction we have lost the opportunity which Holloway saw: 'The barn in its picturesque surroundings adjoining the church and with its old-world appearance, would make an ideal museum for Naseby relics...'[15] The need still exists because so many genuine objects associated with the battle are scattered the length and breadth of the country, increasingly over the years in danger of losing their provenance and hence their significance. The famous 'King's Cabinet' - is it still at Sudeley Castle? The collection of Naseby arms and armour that was at Kelmarsh Hall - where did it go when the last Lord Bateman died? What will happen to all the metal detecting finds from the battlefield? We should set ourselves the objective of bringing together as many as possible of these objects at Naseby for all to see.

What of the interpretation of and access to the battlefield itself? There is a

Fig. 83. A very modest step in the development of interpretation of the battle was the installation of panels at each of the monuments at Naseby in 1989. As the 350th anniversary commemoration programme for 1995 reveals, there is a great popular interest in the battle and an enormous educational potential which is just waiting to be realised.(reproduced by permission of Northamptonshire County Council)[16]

great story to be told that takes us through one of the most momentous events of our history and across a small corner of one of the most pleasant yet undiscovered landscapes of Midland England. The countryside between East Farndon, Naseby and Marston Trussell may have been transformed by enclosure since 1645, yet it has not been spoilt by modern development. Even the A14 does not intrude too badly into the scene. The Sulby closes are still there, the land still down to pasture; nearby are a few of the 'water pits' encountered by Ireton's cavalry; in Broadmoor the Archwrong Close still remains as does the mound and pond at the site of one of the traditional burial pits of men and horses. Further north, though now shrouded in trees, there is the great but unexpected chasm of Hellcoombe, and down in the Welland valley the quiet pasture field of Slaughterford at Marston. Even a few small fragments of ridge and furrow survive on the battlefield, while away in Clipston great swathes of it still remain, the landscape across which the King's army marched that morning.

How should we interpret Naseby? Our 19th century forbears, who also fought for the rights we take for granted today, would have had no doubts. They would have presented Naseby as a Parliamentarian victory of dramatic proportions over a King who wanted absolute authority and who, through incompetence and obstinacy, had dragged his country into a bloody civil war. Though we should not be so strident in our presentation, that is still essentially the story to be told. We have seen how 'political correctness' following the Restoration distorted the facts in folk memory - we should not allow the same to happen now. Today we live with the benefits of Parliamentary democracy and freedom of religion for which men fought and died on Naseby field. While we should respect the military abilities and honour the courage of the King's army, as in 1646 Colonel Butler came to respect Prince Rupert, the enemy he had faced in the battle, we should not excuse the cause for which they fought.

Here on the 14th of June 1645 some of the greatest characters of our history, known to almost every Englishman from that day to this, played for the highest stakes. Here our first truly professional army won its most important battle and it is to Naseby that many look as the place where Parliamentary democracy was secured. Here in just three hours our Great Civil War was decided, a king and kingdom was lost and a republic made possible. We have failed dismally in the present century to conserve and to present Naseby battlefield, even though it is one of our greatest historic sites. We must ensure that it fares better in the new millennium.

NOTES

1. Phillips, 1828.
2. *Leicestershire Mercury*, 31st May 1890.
3. Holloway, 1912.
4. Carlyle to Mrs Atkin describing visit with Dr Arnold of Rugby in 1842 to Naseby, *NN&Q*, old series, 1886, vol.1, p.138.
5. Greenall, 1974, p.22 & 44. P.Horn, 1968-9, p.172 n.25.
6. The Tithe Barn was reportedly identified by Markham as dating from 1651, six years after the battle, but elsewhere it is said to have been dated '1601 E.S.', supposedly built by Edward Shuckburgh, one of the two lords of the manor. C.A.Markham, *NN&Q*, New Series, vol.3, p.37. *Northampton County Magazine*, vol.3, 1930, p.154. *Northampton Mercury*, 18th September 1908. Page, 1886.
7. Anon, 1975, *Naseby Past and Present*, privately published booklet in NRL.
8. DOE, 1990, p.128.
9. DOE, 1990a & 1994. English Heritage, 1994a.
10. *British Archaeological News*, December 1994, p.1.
11. Just such a systematic metal detecting study is currently under way by the Midland Archaeological Research Society on the Grafton Regis siege site of 1643 in Northamptonshire.
12. *The Times*, 14th December 1994.
13. Holloway, 1912.
14. Evans, 1924, p.243-4. George, *JNNHS&FC*, vol.12, no.98, p.196.
15. Holloway, 1912.
16. Leicestershire County Council, 1995, *The Decisive Campaign, Official Souvenir Brochure*. Northamptonshire Chamber of Commerce & Leicestershire County Council, 1995, *Naseby Trail* leaflet. Northamptonshire County Council, 1995, *The Battle of Naseby*, leaflet.

APPENDICES

APPENDIX 1 : THE KING'S MARCHES

The King's marches as described in *Iter Carolinum*.

May 1645
Wednesday 7th - Oxford to Woodstock, 1 night, 6ml
8th - to Stow, Mr Jones's, 1, 13ml
9th, to Evesham, Aldeman Martin's, 1, 12ml
10th, Inkberrow, the vicarage, 1, 6
11th, Droitwich, Mr Barrett's, 3, 9
14th, Coftonhall, Mrs Skinner's; Hawksley House taken by Prince Maurice in our march, a garrison, 1, 10
15th, Hemley nr Wolverhampton, Mr War's, 1, 12
16th, Bishberry nr Stourbridge, Mr Grosvenor's, 1,6
17th, Chetwin, nr Newport, Mr Pigot's, 3, 12
20th, Beaton, nr Drayton, Mr Church's, 2, 8
22nd, Park-hall, nr Stone, Mr Crompton's, 2,10
24th, Eaton in the Clay, Sir Thomas Millware's, 1, 10
26th, Tutbury, dinner, Lord Loughborow's, 2, 6
27th, Ashby, E of Huntingdon's, 1,9
28th, Coat's, nr Loughborough, Sir H.Skipwith's, 1, 9
Thurs 29th, remarched to Elstone nr Leicester 'which we faced with soldiers, the R. defaced with fire', 2, 10
Sat the last, 'to Leicester, which was taken by his majesty at two; many soldiers rewarded with the plunder; the slain equal on both sides; the Countess of Devonshire's we demolished with fire', 4, 3

June 1645
Weds 4th, Wistow, Sir Richard Halford's, 1,5
5th, Lubenham, Mr Collin's, 2, 7
7th, Daventry, the Wheatsheaf 'from whence Oxford was relieved from a siege, and victualled', 6, 14
13th 'remarched again to Lubenham, Mr Collin's', 1, 14
'Saturday the 14th, an alarm affrighted the king and army from Lubenham at two o'clock in the morning, to Harborow, the general's quarter; thence, about seven, towards Naseby, where the parliament's army quartered; rashly fought with them; were utterly defeated, through the cowardice of the horse, which fled to the walls of Leicester, 16 miles; never faced nor rallied till there, whereby many of the horse, all the foot, were either slain or taken prisoners, with some of his majesty's servants; all the ordnance, ammunition, the king's stuff, household carriages, and all the baggage of the army, were totally lost; the parliament having the clearest victory given them from the beginning; the king himself in person being necessitated, with his own troop only, to charge through their body for his escape. From Leicester we marched to Ashby de la Zouch in the night, and came thither about break of day, and halted there', 1, 28
15th, Litchfield, the governor's in the close, 1 ,12
16th Wolverhampton, Mrs Barnford's, a widow, 1, 12
17th Bewdley, the Angel, 2,13
19th Bramyard, dinner; to Harriford, supper, 12, 24
Thence Abergavenny, 3, 15; Ragland, 12,7; Cardiff, Tredegar, 18th Ragland ...'The Scots approach, and our own causeless apprehension of fear, made us both demur and doubt; on the first what to resolve, and in the latter, how to steer our resolutions, which involved us in a most disasterous condition...'
Then in August through Bridgenorth, Welbeck, Newark, Belvoir, Stanford, 24th Huntingdon, 26th Woburn, Ascot, Oxford 28th.

APPENDIX 2 : THE SOURCES FOR THE BATTLE

A BRIEF ASSESSMENT OF THE MAIN SOURCES

A Glorious Victory:
Anonymous Parliamentarian letter of 14th June 1645, initialled JW. Appears to have wild errors but several specific details appear significant.

A More Exact and Perfect Relation:
Parliamentarian letter of 15th June from a Gentleman in Northampton who was an eye witness. A general account with apparently good independent information and one of the clearest descriptions of the sequence of events.

A Relation of the Victory:
Summary from an anonymous Parliamentarian letter of 14th June 1645 which appears to be that in *A True Relation*.

A True Relation:
Anonymous Parliamentarian letter of 14th June 1645. Some significant information but very brief and probably not involved in the action.

Belasyse:
Royalist account from Lord Belasyse who was with the King's lifeguard at Naseby. Written some years after the battle but appears to be a genuine eye witness account rather than a compilation from other sources. Significant details.

Bishop (*A More Particular and Exact Relation*):
Parliamentarian letter by George Bishop written on 16th June 1645. He was an eye witness with detailed information.

Clarendon, 1702:
Royalist account written within two years of the battle but as a secondary work based on Walker's account. Places Rupert's actions in a bad light.

Cromwell (*Three Letters*):
Brief letter of 14th June 1645 by the Parliamentarian Lieutenant General, containing little useful detail.

Fairfax (*Three Letters*):
Brief letter of 15th June 1645 by the Parliamentarian commander. Important list of prisoners attached to these letters.

Leighton & Herbert (*Three Letters*):
Parliamentarian letter of 14th June 1645 from the two Parliamentarian Commissioners with the army but not eye witnesses to the battle itself. Brief but some significant detail.

Mercurius Civicus, 12th-18th June:
Secondary Parliamentarian account of no particular significance.

Okey:
Parliamentarian letter by Colonel Okey himself written on 15th or 16th June 1645. Possibly unreliable on the preliminary stages because he was not present when the deployments were being made, but a key source for the main action especially on the Parliamentarian left wing.

Parliament Post, 10th-17th June 1645:
Secondary Parliamentarian account, muddled and of no real significance.

Rushworth Letter:
Apparently the official account for Parliament written by Rushworth, Fairfax's Secretary, on 15th June, referred to in Fairfax's own letter and authenticated by Thomason as being by Rushworth. One of the most important sources which apparently gives an overall, balanced and well informed account including information from senior officers such as the Provost Marshal. One of the most reliable Parliamentarian sources for an overview of the sequence of events.

Rushworth, 1722:
Parliamentarian account but a secondary historical work compiled from other sources, particularly from Sprigge.

Slingsby:
Royalist diary eyewitness account by a senior figure fighting alongside Langdale's horse. Likely to be reliable because a personal diary. Major source for the action of the Royalist horse.
Sprigge, 1647:
Parliamentarian account by Fairfax's chaplain who may not have been present at Naseby.
An historical work partly compiled from newspapers and other accounts but with much additional detail not present in other sources, suggesting some information may have been derived directly from those involved in the battle. Appears that he may occasionally have misinterpreted or mixed up the events referred to in the original sources. A key source.
Symonds:
Royalist diary eyewitness account by a member of the King's lifeguard. Likely to be reliable and relatively unbiased because it was a personal record. A major source.
The Kingdomes Weekly Intelligencer, 10th-17th June:
Secondary Parliamentarian account, confused in places but drawing upon other published letters.
The Moderate Intelligencer, 12th-19th June 1645:
Secondary Parliamentarian account of no great significance for the battle itself, as opposed to the preceding and succeeding events.
The Scottish Dove, 13th-20th June 1645:
Secondary account of no particular significance.
The True Informer, 16th-21st June 1645:
Parliamentarian letter written several days after the battle by an eyewitness who claims to have revisited the field several days after the battle. Only a few words on the main action but appears to have genuine, unique information of significance collected thereafter.
The Weekly Account, 11th-18th June 1645:
Anonymous Parliamentarian letter. Very generalised but appearing to give a few pieces of significant information.
Walker, 1705:
Royalist account by Sir Edward Walker, Secretary of War, who was with the King's lifeguard at Naseby. Prepared for Clarendon's use. The 'official' Royalist account, it may place Rupert's actions in a bad light but not as clearly as Clarendon. A key source.
Wogan:
Parliamentarian account written some years after the battle by a captain who was with Okey's dragoons at Naseby. A somewhat conflated account but with significant unique information.

A TRANSCRIPT OF KEY LETTERS

A number of the sources are reprinted in Young 1985, but three of the most important were omitted by Young and so they are reprinted here from Baker's transcription.

Rushworth's Letter:

Annotated, in Thomason's own hand according to Carlyle, saying 'Mr Rushworth's letter being ye Secretary to his Excellence'

'The Copie of a letter sent from a Gentleman of publicke employment in the late service neere Knaseby
Both Armies were drawne in Battalia in a great field neere Knavesby by ten in the morning, each wing of both sides charged the other, with that eagernesse that they had not patience to shoot one peece of Ordnance, our Dragoones begun the Battaile Flanking the right wing of the Enemies Horse as they charged our left wing of Horse, the Foot charged not each other till they were within twelve paces one of another, and could not charge above twice, but were at push of Pike, the Enemies Foot gave a little backe, and so did some few of ours, and then the right wing of our

Horse (wherein the Generall was in person) charged in the Flanke of the blew regiment of the Enemies Foot, who stood to it, till the last man, abundance of them slaine, and all the rest surrounded, wounded, and taken these (the hope of their Infantry) being lost Horse and Foot gave backe, wee advanced after them in order, our Horse flanking our Foot, and after one charge more, became Masters of all their Infantry, and tooke about three thousand prisoners, the Enemies Horse ran a pace, but still our Horse, though one would have beaten ten, (such a feare was the Enemy possessed with all) would not pursue in heate but take the Foot to flanke them, the King cryed out, face about once and give one charge and recover the day, our Men Horse and Foot came on with that courage, that before ever wee gave fire they faced about and ran cleere away, and happy was he that was best mounted, and Lieutenant Generall Cromwell, pursued with the Horse after them on a Carreire about twelve or thirteen miles, within two or three miles of Leicester, and having taken eight pieces of Ordnance in the Field, whereof two were Demi cannon, one whole Culverine, tooke all the rest of their Ordnance and their Carriages, Bag and Baggage abundance of Coaches, and rich Plunder, Carts with Boates and great store of Bisket and Cheese (a seasonable refreshment for our souldiers that had marched so hard, and the night before had not a bit of Bread to a Regiment for their refreshment,) the Foot and the Traine Marched this night to Harborough (foure miles) where our head quarter is. Time will not give me leave to enlarge my self on particulars otherwise it were worth your knowledge and fit to be had in memory. I shall not attribute more to one Commander than to another, for indeed they did as gallantly, as ever men on earth could doe, and so did the Enemies foote, which before the battaile wee least valued, Rupert and Maurice (having at least two thousand Horse more then ours that charged were so well received by our men though our left wing gave backe a little as their hearts were broake at the first, that which made our Horse so terrible to them, was the thickness of our reserves and their orderly and timely comming on, not one failing to come on in time; About the beginning the day was doubtfull, but blessed be the name of our God, in one halfe houre the field was won and the Enemy gone, to God alone be the praise, it becomes not me to say any thing of my Generalls, Major Generalls, or Lieutenant Generall Crumwells carriage in this Battaile, I leave it to all men on the place to relate it, who cannot but admire their valour, and thus hath the Lord gone along with this new moulded Army, so much contemned by many and left as sheepe to the slaughter by others, but from the beginning I was confident, a blessing from heaven did attend this Army, there were in it so many pious men, men of integrity, hating vice, fighting not out of ambitiousnesse or by ends, but ayming at Gods glory and the preservation of Religion and Liberty, and the destruction of the Enemy which was never in so faire a way as now is, if peoples hearts would yet be moved to redeeme themselves from slavery and all joyne as one man. If this advantage be improved (as what a wearied out and tyred Army is able to doe, will be done) with the blessing of God, and an addition of some fresh horse, ours being worne off their legs, the Enemy in all probability will not this Summer get head againe, and I hope in the Lord never more considerable in the field, some observations I had in the time of the Battell in the carriage of things that one great incouragement to the common souldiers to fall on, was the rich Plunder the enemy had (their purses also being full of Money, the Plunder of poore Leicestershire, God turned to be one meanes of their ruine, and indeed our souldiers got plenty, the Irish women Prince Rupert brought on the field (wives of the bloody Rebels in Ireland his Majesties dearly beloved subjects) our souldiers would grant no quarter too, about 100 slain of them, and most of the rest of the whores that attended that wicked Army are marked in the face or nose, with a slash or cut. I viewed the dead bodies, from the Battell to Harborough truly I estimate them not to be above 700, together with those slaine in the fields running away, but in pursuit between Harborough and Leicester, and by townes, conceived about 300 more slaine, abundance wounded, persons of great note fell, one with a starre and a red crosse on his coat, conceived to be the Duke of Lenox four Lords came mortally wounded to Harborough, but durst not stay, we tooke all the foot Colours in the field, the Kings owne Colours, with the Lyon and Crowne, with this Motto *Dieu et mon droit*; The Queenes Colours, and the Princes Colours, and the Duke of Yorkes Standard; We got the Plunder of the Kings Coach, his Cabinet etc. The enemies word was, *Queen Mary*, ours *God is our strength*, and so he was indeed. They had beane stalkes in

their hats, we nothing; some of ours of their owne accord had white linnen, or paper in their hats. A party of theirs that broke through the left wing of Horse, came quite behind the rear to our traine, the leader of them being a person somewhat in habit like the Generall, in a red Mountero, as the Generall had, he came as a friend; our Commander of the gaurd of the Traine went with his hat in his hande, and asked him how the day went, thinking it had been the Generall; The Cavalier whom we since heard was Rupert, asked him and the rest, if they would have quarter, they cryed no, Gave fire and instantly beat them off; It was a happy deliverance we had slaine on our part none above a Captaine I yet hear of, and in all not 150. to my best judgement, and I viewed the ground where the bodies lay, the honest and valiant Major generall wounded, Collonell Butler, Colonell Francis, Major Horton, Captaine Potter, one of the Commons of Parliament, Colonell Ireton, and some other Officers of note wounded; The Provost Marshall saith, he hath in all about foure thousand Prisoners, whereof above 400 are Officers four Collonels, 12 Lieutenants and Ensignes. The souldiers have already brought into the Generall above 40. Standards and Colours, he gives each man a reward. Sir Jacob Ashley's Coach was taken with great store of Plunder, also some Letter, of Nicholas the lyer wherein he hath this expression in his Letter to the King. That the Parliament had given particular Direction to the Generall to kill the King, and to give him no quarter, the rest of his stories are like this; Wee tooke 5000 Armes on the field, but the souldiers were so greedy of Plunder and pursuing the enemy, that the Countrey got some of them. Sir Jacob Ashley was neere taking, we got the Cap of his head; The Army is marching towards Leicester, and will not give the Enemy time to rally; our Horse are close in the reare of them, Collonel Rossiter came seasonable to the engagement, and charged where the Generall was, and is still in pursuit of the enemy, I could say more had I time to sleepe, I rest Yours etc
Harborough June 15
two in the morning

We tooke one Colours of Horse, with a pair of hornes, *Come Cuckolds*, was the Motto; as soon as our men had it in possession, they held the Hornes and Motto towards the Enemy, and so charged them.
Langdels Brigade ran away basely, and lost the King the day.'

Letter from a Gentleman in Northampton:

'A more exact and perfect Relation of the great victory... Being a letter from a Gentleman in Northampton...'

After a brief account of the days leading up to the battle:
'The Kings men perceiving our neere approach, and that they could not march away so fast as we pursued, having neere 300 Carriages of one kind or another, they resolved to take the advantage of ground on a large hill in Navesby Field, about nine miles from Northampton, and three from Harborough; and were ready before wee could get to them; who found another Hill about halfe a mile on the South of them, equally commodious with theirs, about nine of the clock on Saturday morning, June 14. we joyned battell with them with much resolution on both sides; the Kings left wing first charging our left, and driving them off their ground in some disorder, our right wing doing as much for their left wing, the body in the meane while being strongly ingaged, our Foot at first charge gained ground of the enemy, with some losse on the Enemies part, but they being driven on by their horse, at the second charge drove ours to some disorder, but by the care of the Field-Officers was soon drawne into a body againe, and by this time our left wing had rallied againe, and the whole Army with one hot charge in all the parts of it did so bestirre them for almost an houre, that they drove all Kings men from their Ordnance (which before had not time to doe much execution on either side) and the right wing following their advantage they had first got, put the Kings Army to a general Rout, so that our Army drove them

quite out of the Field Horse and Foot, and that with such speed and earnest prosecution, that no man can say yet, there was one of the Kings Foot got away, and but few of his Horse in any order, though it be thought neere foure thousand of them got out of the Field, but were pursued by our Horse. By one of the clocke in the afternoone there was not a Horse or man of the Kings Army to be seene in Northamptonshire but the prisoners, the Horse being in Haste gone towards Leicester, and our Foot were gathering the pillage while our Horse followed the flying Enemy. I saw the field so bestrewed with Carcases of Horse and Men, as was most sad to behold, because subjects under one Government, but most happy in this, because they were most of them professed enemies of God, and the government of his Son: The Field was about a mile broad where the Battell was fought, and from the outmost Flanke of the right, to the left wing, tooke up the whole ground; The bodies lay slaine about four miles in length, the most thick on the hill the Kings men stood on; I cannot think there was few lesse then four hundred men slaine, and truly I think not many more, and neere 300. Horses: Wee tooke at least four thousand Prisoners on the ground between Navesby and Harborough, neere three hundred Carriages, whereof twelve of them were Ordnance, one drawne by twenty six Horses, carrying a twenty foure pound bullet; they carried off the ground over Harborough bridge (as I was told in Harborough, by one that stood to watch) but sixe Carts or Waggons, one whereof was taken in the towne by our Horse, and the other about a mile off the Towne, as I was told; there was many of the Wagons laden with rich plunder, and others with Arms and Ammunition, about 50 loads of Muskets, Pikes, Powder, Match, and Bullets, abundance of Trunks, which the Souldiers soone emptied, as they did the Waggons that carried the middle sort of Ammunition Whoores, whoe were full of money and rich apparell, there being at least 1500 of that tribe, the gentiler sorts in Coaches, whereof I only saw 7 Coaches with Horses taken stuffed with that commodity, and the common rabble of common vermin of foot, 500. of them at least being taken and kept without gaurd, untill order was taken to dispose of them and their mates, many of these Irish women, of cruel countenances, some of them were cut by our Souldiers when they tooke them; there was taken above 1000. live Horses, and many Cows; they had robbed the Country of besides many Horses with Saddles and Pistols, it falling most on Langdales men, who were most forward in the charge. Amongst the prisoners there is about 100 Field Officers, I was told, five that were sometimes Parliament men, now were Colonels, and knowne Gentlemen, they are secured by themselves, with others that are knowne to be men of quality, one Gentleman of the Bedchamber, that stood next the King, and cryed, hold your hands the King will yield his person, which while they did, hee got away, and so escaped for this time by getting over a Forde or small Brooke that parts two Counties of Leicester and Northamptonshire. I shall not take upon me to set forth the deportment of the Generall, Lieutenant Generall, and our Major Generall, which in their severall places behaved themselves to admiration, not sing to the praise of this or that Colonell, Captaine, or Souldier, though I acknowledge many deserve as much as any pen can expresse, but shall now tell you impartially our losse on the place, so near as I can: The truly religious Major General Skippon hath received a wound on the right side with a Musket bullet, piercing his Armour and body quite through, but as I hear the Chyrurgion say, it had not entred into the hollow part of his body, it is about five or six inches between the hole it made going in and comming out, this wound he tooke in bringing up the Foote, where they were first disordered, and yet led them up after he was wounded; there is great hopes of his recovery, and though for present he manifests much christian patience, saying, That though he might groane, he would not grudge under it; and taking my leave of him for that night he called on me to beg God a sanctified use of that affliction for him; which I pray God we may heartily do, both for him and ourselves. Colonel Ireton is also wounded, and so is Colonel Butler with a brace od bullets in the thigh, who gallantly charged both the Princes before he came off; Captain Potter, one of the Commissioners of the Army is also sore wounded in diverse places; one Foot Captaine of Colonell Pickerings Regiment slaine, a Welch man; And the Cornet to Colonell Whaleys owne Troope, a stout and godly man, as all that knew him affirme about 50 Common Souldiers, as neer as can be at present guessed untill they come to bury the dead. Our Horse it is said are within a few miles of Leicester, and the Foote this Saturday night quarter in Leicesteshire, our head quarters being Harborough this night, which was the Kings last; our Army not at all weakened hereby, but by the accesse of Colonel Rossiters Horse and Dragoones, the Northampton Troopes and soome Foot, with other supplies from the Associated Counties, is made more numerous. The Generall lost his Headpiece in the midst of the fight, yet had no hurt. The whole Army is very desirous to prosecute the Victory to the utmost advantage with all faithfulnesse, that if it may be, an end may be put to these sad times....

15 June 1645'

The letter of George Bishop, a Gentleman in the Army

'A More Particular and Exact Relation .... Being two letters, the one written by G.B. a Gentleman in the Army, unto Lieutenant Colonell Roe, Scoutmaster Generall for the City of London....'

'You have heard at large I beleeve of the good successe God hath given unto us how hee hath raised us out of our graves and caused our dead hopes to live again, by that fearfull overthrow he hath given the Adversary; the particulars of which Battail I could give you, but suppose you have heard it already, therefore I forbear, onely in short thus; About 11 of the clock wee were drawn both Armies into Battalia in Naseby fields, a place of little hills and vales, in a direct line equall to both parts, the ground some ploughed some Champion. Our Battaile was thus ordered; Lieutenant Generall Cromwell commanded all the Horse, Major Generall Skippon the Foot; the Generall not in one place, but every where as occasion required. In our right Wing of Horse were the Generalls, (sometimes Lieutenant Generall Cromwells,) Colonell Whaleys, Col.Pyes, Col.Rossiters, Col.Fines, and Col.Sheffields Regiments. In the left wing were Colonell Iretons, (who was made Commissary Generall of the Horse in the field) Colonell Fleetwoods, Col.Rich, Col.Butler, Col.Vermuydens, and the Suffolke Regiments, Dragoons equally divided on both parts. The Infantry thus ordered; in the right wing, the Generalls, Colonell Mountagues, Col.Pickerings, Col.Sir Herdus Wallers Regiment. In the left, Major Generall Skippon's, Colonell Bartlets, Col.Rainsboroughs, Col.Hammons Regiments. The wind was North west, and before we joyned battail, blew stiffe, equall on both parts; onely the Enemy had it somewhat more advantagious for them: in regard the wind was that way; both parties sought to get the winde, which occasioned our left wing of Horse, and of Foot, and their right, first to engage; where was most terrible dispute; at length the fury of the Enemy caused two Regiments of Horse to give ground a little, the rest stood, the retreat was upon Major Generall Skippons Regiment, being the utmost of that Wing, and the Regiment next to him; the Enemy pursued, and came neere the Train: In the mean time Lieutenant Geneerall Cromwell routed the Kings left Wing, drove them cleare away from that side, having made not the least retreat; but was like a torrent driving all before them; In which the Generall charged valiantly, and lost his Head-piece, who seeing the left scattered, he with Lieutenant Generall Cromwell faced about to that Wing, with some Divisions of Horse, charged bareheaded within push of Pike, routed the Enemy; after this both parts rallyed, and stood very neere each other, having silence for a short space, but ours advancing to charge, the Enemy fled, ours pursued them for the space of 14 miles, within two miles of Leicester, cutting them off as they went; all their foot were cut off and taken, wee have about 4 or 5000 Prisoners, of Horse at least 2000. All the traine and Coaches, except the Kings and Digbies Coaches. All their Armes,, Provisions,, Ordinance, etc Bag and Baggage. Abundance of rich plunder for the souldiers, about 400 slaine in the place, besides the chase; about 50 of ours conceived to be slaine: one slaine that had a Plush Coat, with a Starre in Silver on it, conceived the Duke of Lenox, Sir Marmaduke Langdale, the Lord Grandenson, and many others of note, as we conceive, and are informed besides abundance wounded on the place and 200 carryed that night wounded into Leicester; many Women slaine that in their Army, and many taken, which are every one wounded. By a Waggoner of the Kings taken, we understand that the King was wounded in the Arm, and that he saw it bleed, and that at one time our horse were beyond him.

On our part slaine, Captain Tomkins, Lieutenant Generall Cromwells Cornet, Colonell Whaleys Cornet, and a few others; but many wounded: viz. Major Generall Skippon shot through the right side, Colonell Ireton wounded in foure places, but not mortall, Colonell Butler, Captain Blevin, and many others wounded. Our men came on with brave valour and agility, as could be expected from men, the best demonstration of the Officers valour is their wounds. I do not heare of one but discharged his Duty: and cannot praise one above another, least I should detract from any: Onely, concerning the Generalls.

Sir Thomas Fairfax never appeared with that alacrity of Spirit, and that pleasant countenance, as then; greatly encouraging his Souldiers, and promised by his countenance Victory: before the fight, his former lookes were like to a dead man, to what he had when he went to ingage: and the truth is, his very countenance discovered an Embleme of true valour, as ever we saw; and had a spirit heightened above the ordinary spirit of man, hee was to and againe in the front, carrying Orders, bringing on Divisions in the midst of Dangers, with gallant bravery, and received not the least wound; though hee ingaged bare headed, and routed the Enemy.

That Noble Lieutenant Generall Cromwell behaved himself to the utmost routed the Adversary as on Marston Moore and then releieved our Army on the other Party which was like to bee undone; whom God mightily honoured. And now hath given Prince Rupert his other Iron-side. And as for Major Generall Skippon, worthy to bee continually in the best thoughts of truest English: behaved himselfe with that valour and Gallantry, as possibly a man could doe; I heard the Generall speak wonderfully to him in his praise; with great expressions.

In the first charge he received his wound, shot through the right side under the ribbes, through Armour, and Coat, but not mortall, yet notwithstanding hee kept his Horse, and discharged his place, and would by no means bee drawn off till the Field was wonne; for the space of two houres and a half.

Truely Sir, you would scarce beleeve that undauntednesse that was in him I helped him to a House, and carryed him to his Chamber, stript him, and saw his wound drest; and never beheld such gallant spirit in my life to bear such a wound. And when I said to him, Sir, your wound hath caused a little cloud on this glorious day; hee answered, hy no means let mine Eclipse its Glory, for it is my honour that I received a wound, and it was my God that strengthened mee.

Sir these three Generalls I suppose have not their fellows in the world, all things considered.... I had thought to have been short, yet I have made somewhat a long narration; you will pardon the prolixity of my lines, which cannot be so digested in regard of our hasty march: I hope shortly to give you a good account of Leicester. This is all at present.

June 16. 1645   Your humble servant
Great Glinne   George Bishop'

APPENDIX 3 : PARLIAMENTARIAN WOUNDED

In late June or early July 1645 £500 and in August £200 was received by the Northamptonshire County Committee from the Committee of the Army. This document, 'The Accompt of the Maior and Mr Rushworth of Northampton June 14th 1645', records the disbursement of that money, listing the payments to sick and wounded men under Fairfax that came to Northampton after the 14th June 1645. From the newspaper accounts it would appear that every wounded soldier that needed proper care was brought up to the town, although some of them were apparently dispersed in villages and towns nearby. The document names each soldier but in the following summary only the total number of men for each company is normally provided. There is potential for further detailed analysis, particularly if detailed records of each regiment are also recovered from within the Exchequer papers. It should be noted, from the variation in the payments made, that ranks may not have been listed in every case.

'The Accompt of Joseph Sargeant and Francis Rushworth Aldermen of Northampton Concerning seaven hundred pounds advanced from the Treasurers att Warr for the Releife, Mayntenance and care of ye souldiers wounded att Navesby battell under ye command of ye Honourable Sir Thomas Fairfax' (PRO SP28/173 unfol..)

Capt. Potter Commisary - died	£0
Capt. Cooke Commissary - died	£0
Lt Col.Francis - died	£0
Lt.Norman to Col Francis - died	£2/5/0d
Ensign Green to Col Francis - died	£2/0/0d
Ensign Sinick	£1/0/0d
Wm Wels belonging to the traine	£0/12/0d
John Skidmore provost marshall to ye traine	£1/10/0d
Isaiah Clothey master of ye Mynors	£0/15/0d
Richard Symons of ye life guard - died	£1/0/0d
Ric Roberts corp. of a troup to ye General	£1/0/0d
Ric Crawford same troup	£1/0/0d
Robert Guilbert matross who lost his hand	£1/0/0d
Cornelius Morgan under Major Finxher	£0/10/0d
Kill French a deminer (gunner?) - died	£0/10/0d
Tho Beneton carpenter to ye carriages	£0/8/0d
Jesper Williams servant to Lt Norman	£0/8/0d
Jeremiah Williams wagginman	£0/8/0d
7 men under Cap.parker troupe	5 x £0/16/0d; £0/11/0d; £0/6/0d
John Gullen ye Generals owne command	£0/8/0d
John Feild - Capt While	£0/6/0d
2 men under Cap Muskett	£0/6/0d each
2 men under Capt Gaudey	£0/6/0d each
2 men under Capt Mainester	£0/6/0d each
4 men under Lt.Col.Jackson	£0/6/0d each
1 man under Major Cooke	£0/6/0d
Tho Briton belonging to ye Carriages	£0/8/0d
total :39	

Soldiers wounded under Maj Gen Skippon:

30 men under Lt Col. Francis	£0/6/0d each - of which 2 died
Walter Joanes gentleman of ye pike	£0/12/0d
17 men under Capt. Lt Symonds	£0/6/0d each
total 49	
16 men under Capt.Lt.Symonds	£0/6/0d each of which 1 died
Wm Sitchill ensign under Major Ashfield	£0/10/0d
Mathew Thowrogood corp. under Maj.Ashfield	£0/8/0d
9 men under the same	£0/6/0d each except onc at £1/0/0d
5 men under Capt. John Harrison	£0/6/0d each of which 1 died
Tobias Morgan serjeant (under Harrison?)	£1/0/0d
14 men under Capt. Boein	£0/6/0d each of which 1 died
4 men under Cap Gybbins	£0/6/0d each
total 51	
8 men under Capt Winkfeild	£0/6/0d each
4 men under Capt. Streeter	£0/6/0d each
7 men under Capt Coppits	£0/6/0d each
17 men under Capt. Park	£0/6/0d each of which 1 died
1 man under Cap Winkfeild	£0/6/0d
more to Wm Price under Lt Col Francis	£0/3/0d

more to John Spinke lying veary sick	£0/10/0d (listed above under Capt. Gybbins)
Ric Wilkin under Lt Col. Francis	£0/10/0d
total 40	

Soldiers under Col.Pickering:

5 men under Maj Junnes	£0/6/0d each
7 men under Lt Col.Hewson	£0/6/0d each except 1 that died who was paid 8/-
4 men under Capt. gale	£0/6/0d each
4 men under Capt Tomkins	£0/6/0d each except 1 man
1 man under Capt Axtell	£0/6/0d
2 men under Capt. Margerum	£6/0/0d each
4 men under Capt Silverwood	£0/6/0d each of which 1 died
2 men under Capt Davie	£0/6/0d each
3 men under Capt Carter	£0/6/0d of which 2 died paid £0/8/0d & £0/10/0d
Corp David Barrett under Carter	£0/10/0d
4 men under Capt Husbands	£0/6/0d each
2 men under Lt Col. Hewson	£0/12/0d each
total 48	
1 Man under Capt. Price	£0/6/0d

Soldiers under Col Muntague:

9 men under Lt Col.	£0/6/0d each
4 men under Maj Kelsie	£0/6/0d each
7 men under Cap Disnee	£0/6/0d each of which 1 died paid £0/8/0d
3 men under Capt Newin	£0/6/0d each
4 men under Capt Wikes	£0/6/0d each
5 men under Capt Blenkin	£0/6/0d each
2 men under Cap Saunders	£0/6/0d each
2 men under Quartermaster branch	£0/6/0d each of which 1 died
1 under Capt Blenkin	£0/6/0d
1 under Capt Bisco	£0/6/0d
total 39	

Under Col Hammond:

9 men under Lt Col Heward	£0/6/0d each, 1 sorely wounded £1/10/0d & 1 died £0/8/0d
1 under Capt Boys	£0/6/0d
1 drummer under Capt Puckle	£0/8/0d died
1 under Capt Smith	£0/6/0d
1 under Capt Disye	£0/6/0d
1 under Capt Eaton	£0/6/0d
1 under Capt Noehear	£0/6/0d
1 under Capt Skelton	£0/6/0d
1 under Lt Col	£0/6/0d

Under Col Rainsboro:

Robert Dearye lieut	£1/0/0d
John Nicoles serj to his own Company	£0/10/0d
2 under Capt Horsley	£0/10/0d each
2 under Capt Sanford	£0/6/0d each
2 under Capt Cross	£0/6/0d each
1 under Capt Creamor	£0/6/0d
more to John Joanes under Capt Horsley	£0/15/0d died
total 27	

Under Col Waler:
9 under Lt Col. Scotchford   £0/6/0d each
1 under Capt Hill   £0/6/0d
2 under Capt Wade   £0/6/0d each
2 under Capt Holdin   £0/6/0d each
Under Col Bartlitt:
3 men under Col Bartlitt   £0/6/0d each
total 17
Under Col Pye:
14 under Major Tomlinson   £0/15/0d each of which 1 died
10 under Capt Lt.Hamden   4 x £0/17/6d, 2 x £1, 1 x £0/18/0d, 1 x
                                              £0/15/0d, 1 x £0/10/0d
7 under Capt Knight   £0/15/0d each except 1 x £0/10/0d
4 under Capt Margery   2 x £1, 2 x £0/15/0d
3 under Capt Rawlins   1 x £1 died, 2 x £0/17/6d
5 under Capt Barrey   £1, 2 x £0/17/6d, 2 x £0/15/0d
1 under Capt Barrows   £0/10/0d
more to JohnPalmer lying very weak   £0/10/0d
total 44
Under Vermuden:
Capt Bush - died   £1/5/0d
1 under him   £0/16/0d
4 under capt Bush   £0/17/0d, £0/19/0d, 2 x £0/10/0d
John Hanks corp under Maj Huntington   1/10/00d
8 under Maj Huntington   £0/17/0d, 4 x £0/15/0d, 1 x £0/10/0d, 1 x
                                              £1/10/0d died
9 under Capt.Lt Curson   2 x £1, 6 x £0/15/0d, 1 x £0/10/0d
Lt Edw Sharpe to Capt Middleton   £2/0/0d
Wm Standley cornet to same   £1/15/0d
2 under Capt Middleton   £0/15/0d & £0/17/6d
6 under Capt Reynolds   £0/15/0d died, £1/10/0d, £1/0/0d, £0/17/6d,
                                              2 x £1
5 under Capt Jenkins   3 x £1, £0/15/0d, £0/17/6d
John Chapman cornet to same   £1/8/0d
Robert Farey corp to same - died   £1/5/0d
1 under Capt Hoskins   £0/15/0d
total 42
under Col Fleetwood:
11 under Capt John Selby   5 x £1 of which 2 died 5 x £0/15/0d of which
                                              1 died, 1 x £0/10/0d
6 under Maj Harrison   2 x £0/15/0d, 3 x £0/10/0d, 1 x £0/5/0d
8 under Capt Lt Blissit   3 x £1, 2 x £0/15/0d of which 1 died, 2 x
                                              £0/10/0d, 1 x £0/5/0d
2 under Capt Lehunt   1 x £1 died, 1 x £0/15/0d
1 under Capt Coleman   £0/15/0d died
total 38
Under Col. Ireton:
Henry Pocock corp under Major Sedascue   £1/2/0d
2 under same   £1/0/0d, £0/15/0d
6 under Capt Guilliam   3 x £1 of which 1 died, £1/2/6d, £0/16/0d,
                                              £0/10/0d
5 under Capt Gybbons   3 x £1 of which 1 died, £0/17/6d, £0/15/0d
4 under Colonel's own troupe   £0/18/0d, £0/15/0d, 2 x £0/10/0d

4 under Capt Hoskins	3 x £1, £0/10/0d
total 22	
Under Col Butler:	
8 under Capt Perry	4 x £1 of which 1 died, £0/17/6d, 2 x £0/15/0d, £0/10/0d
Thos Sparling Lt to Capt Pennyfather	£1/5/0d died
7 under Capt Pennyfather	2 x £0/17/6d, £0/18/0d, 2 x £0/15/0d, £0/10/0d, £0/16/0d
3 under Capt Foeley	£0/15/0d each
1 from Col's own troup	£1
2 under Capt Gardner	£0/10/0d each
total 22	
Under Col. Rich:	
Tale Howley a reformado	£1
2 under Maj Alford	£1, £0/15/0d
5 under Col's own troup	3 x £1 (one a lieutenant) of which 1 died, 2 x £0/15/0d, £0/15/0d
7 under Capt Dandie	4 x £1, 3 x £0/15/0d
6 under Capt. Nevell	3 x £0/15/0d, £0/12/0d, 2 x £0/10/0d
1 under Capt Ireton	£1/5/0d
total 23	
Under Lt Gen Cromwell:	
4 in Cromwell's own troup	£0/8/0d each
5 under Capt Lawrence	£0/8/0d each
1 under capt Desborow	£0/8/0d
The Quartermasters man	£0/8/0d
1 under capt Grove	£0/12/0d
6 under Capt Berrye	5 x £0/8/0d, £0/12/0d
total 18	
Under Col Sheffield:	
2 under Col's troup	£0/6/0d died, £1/7/0d sorely wounded
1 under Major Fincher	£0/15/0d
2 under Capt Rainsborow	£0/15/0d, £0/5/0d
1 under Capt Martin	£0/15/0d
1 under Capt Robotham	£0/15/0d
Under Col Oakeley:	
2 under Capt.Mercers	£0/12/0d, £0/10/0d
Under Col. Fines:	
2 under Capt Temple	£0/15/0d, £0/10/0d
1 under Col Rossetar:	£0/8/0d
total 12	
Under Col Whaley:	
4 under Maj Bethel	2 x £0/15/0d, £0/12/0d, £0/8/0d
7 under Colonel's troupe	2 x £0/15/0d, 4 x £0/12/0d, £0/8/0d
19 under Capt Camion	2 x £1, 3 x £0/15/0d of which 1 died, 8 x £0/12/0d, 4 x £0/8/0d, 2 x £0/12/0d
1 under Cpt Portar	£1
7 under Capt Grove	£0/15/0d, £0/8/0d, £0/12/0d, 4 x £0/8/0d
total 38	
12 under Capt Swallow	£0/17/6d, 5 x £0/15/0d of which 2 died, 2 x £0/12/0d, 4 x £0/8/0d
total 12	

f.18 dorse: purchases of 184 shirts, 76 shrouds; costs of 40 much wounded in the hospital barne for a fortnight, making of beds in the hospital, bedding, and continued attendance at hospital to 26 July 1645, beer, 'paid for Carriage of 19 of them very much wounded in Coaches up to London £5/3/0d', paid Mr Clarke surgeon of Wboro £1, Col.Rich his surgeon £2, 6 surgeons mates £3.

f.19-20 : summary of main payments to 30 July 1645: carriage of 18 wounded men to London to ye hospital, paid 4 nurses that attended the wounded men £1/16/0d, straw, the Sexton for digging graves, payment for quarter, for supplies, for men in the 'hospitall barne', various payments to people for nursing wounded men, payments for wood, nails etc for making 20 beds in the hospital barne, payment to the surgeon of Wboro.

f.20 'paid paull grene for a horse that carryed up Major general Scippon £1/10/0d', carriage of others to London.

p.21: 18 Aug 1645 - paid for wounded soldiers quartered at Wboro, Overstone and other places, soldiers quartered on various people in the places for periods of 3 or 4 weeks in some cases up to 8 and 10 weeks some soldiers said to still lie sick.

f. 22: 'pd Mr Francis Gray for quartering Mr Fothergill Surgeon his mate and 2 servants with their horses 3 weeks £2', the 9 surgeons paid for their paines sums between £10 and £1, and finally 'ye Appothicary as by his bills will appeare £13/1/5d'

APPENDIX 4 : NEW MODEL ARMY SUPPLY CONTRACTS

Summary of orders placed before June 1645 (from Mungeam, 1968).

TRAIN:
11 open waggons, 14 close waggons; 6 close waggons for Sir Thomas Fairfax, 2 close waggons for the Major General, 300 harnesses, 100 harnesses - every fifth harness for a Thill horse (1 April). 400 pick axes (8 April), 800 shovels and spades (4 April), 200 tents for the train (3 April)

ARMS & ORDNANCE etc:
300 grenado shells for the great morter (24th May), 600 round shot for demi culverin & 2000 for saker, 1000 hand grenades saker bore; brass morter (7th April), barrels of powder, 8 ton match (1 April). 5000 matchlock muskets (1 April), 600 matchlock muskets (10 April)
50 snaphaunce muskets (10 April), 1000 snaphaunce muskets - English full bore (3 April)
6000 bandeleers (1 April), 5 tons musket bullets (3 April), 1000 cartrages (9th April)
600 pikes (1 April), 100 pikes (15th May), 1000 long pikes (9 April) (elsewhere long pikes purchased were 16ft) 200 long pikes (15th May), 400 long pikes (10th April), 100 long pikes (30th May). 9000 swords & belts (1 April)

INFANTRY CLOTHES & EQUIPMENT
3000 shirts (1 April), 1000 shirts (10th April), 5000 pairs shoes, 2000 pair Irish stockings - (1 April), 1500 pair Irish stockings (8 April), 2000 snapsacks (8 April), 200 leather snapsacks, 4000 coats & breeches the tape white, blue, green, yellow, 100 coats & breeches the tape orange (1 April). 60 drums (1 April)

CAVALRY EQUIPMENT
100 dragoon saddles (30th May), 500 dragoon saddles (4 April), 500 saddles (250 to be padsaddles) (3 April), 100 Padsaddles (10th April), 1400 saddles (1 April). 1100 back, breast and pot (where they are ordered later it is with horse equipment)(elsewhere 200 pots with 3 bars English) (1 April). 1400 pistols & holsters (1 April), 300 pistols & holsters (1st May), 550 pair pistols & holsters (3 April), 200 horseman swords (1 April). 250 horse harness (8 April), 50 horse harness (9th April), 50 horse harness (1 May), 50 horse harnesses (23 May).

ABBREVIATIONS

A Glorious Victory :*A Glorious Victory obtained by Sir Thomas Fairfax ..... A True Relation of a Great Victory,* including a letter from IW. (BL TT E288/21)

A Just Apology : *A Just Apology for an Abused Army, 1647* (BL TT E372/22)

A more exact and perfect Relation : *A more exact and perfect Relation of the great Victory* - letter from a Gentleman in Northampton (BL TT E288/28)

A More Exact Relation : *A More Exact Relation of the Siege laid to the Town of Leicester* (BL TT E287/6)

A more perfect and exact relation : *A Narration of the Siege of the Town of Leicester... , with a more perfect and exact relation of the taking...* reprinted by Nichols,vol.3, appendix 4

A Perfect Relation : *A Perfect Relation of the Taking of Leicester with the several Marches of the King's Army....*(BL TT E287/6) reprinted in Nichols, vol.3, appendix 4

A More Particular and Exact Relation : *A More Particular and Exact Relation of The Victory obtained* - letters by Okey, George Bishop and the Sheriff of Northampton (BL TT E288/38)

A Relation of the Victory : *A Relation of the Victory obtained by Sir Thomas Fairfax* - summary of a letter from the army brought by the City Scout (BL TT E288/25)

A Sacred Record : *A Sacred Record to be made of Gods Mercies to Zion: A Thanksgiving Sermon Preached to the two Houses of Parliament, 19th June* (BL TT E288/36)

A True Relation of a Victory : *A True Relation of a Victory obtained over the Kings Forces* -a letter from an unnamed source (reprinted in Young, 1985, p.371-374) (BL TT E288/22)

AASR : *Association of Architectural Societies Reports*

Belasyse : *A Briefe Relation of the Life and Memoires of John Lord Belasyse* (extract reprinted in Young, 1985, p.320-322)

BL : British Library

Bod.Lib. : Bodleian Library, Oxford

Bridges' notes : Bodleian Library MS Top. Northants e.2 p.119-120 and f.1 p.149-151

CSPD : *Calendar of State Papers Domestic 1644-5*

DOE : Department of the Environment

Eayre map : *The County of Northampton as surveyed and planned by Thomas Eyre revised by Thomas Jefferys*, second edition 1791 (reprinted 1975 by Northamptonshire Libraries)

Good News out of the West : *Good News out of the West, 23 July 1645* (BL TT E293/18)

HMC : Historic Manuscripts Commission, 1891, *Portland Manuscripts*, vol.1

Iter Carolinum : Manley, T., 1660, *Iter Carolinum, being a succinct Relation of the necessitated Marches, Retreats... of Charles I*

JNNHS&FC : *Journal of the Northamptonshire Natural History Society and Field Club*

Leighton & Herbert : *Three Letters* (BL TT E288/27)

LRO : Leicestershire Record Office

Narration of the siege : *Narration of the siege and taking of the town of Leicester*, reprinted in Nichols, vol.3, appendix 4, p.46-49.

NN&Q : *Northamptonshire Notes and Queries*

NP&P : *Northamptonshire Past and Present*

NRO : Northamptonshire Record Office

Okey : *A More Particular and Exact Relation* - a letter from Colonel John Okey (reprinted in Young 1985, p.338-340) (BL TT E288/38)

PRO : Public Records Office

RCHM : Royal Commission of Historical Monuments

Rupert's Life : Anon, 1683, *Historical Memoires of the Life and Death of that wise and valliant Prince Rupert*

Rushworth letter : *An Ordinance of the Lords and Commons ....with two exact Relations of the said Victory* - the second letter said by Carlyle (1858, vol.1, p.175) to be annotated in Thomason's own hand as being Rushworth (BL TT E288/26)

<u>Short Memorials</u> : *Short Memorials of Thomas Lord Fairfax, written by himself, 1699*, reprinted in Scott, 1811.

<u>Slingsby</u> : Parsons, D., (ed.), 1836, *The Diary of Sir Henry Slingsby*

<u>Speed maps</u> : John Speed, 1616, *Theatrum Imperii Magnae Britanniae* (reprinted in N.Nicolson, & A.Hawkyard, 1988, *The Counties of Britain : A Tudor Atlas by John Speed*)

<u>Symonds</u> : Long, C.E., (Ed.), 1859, *Richard Symonds' Diary*

The manner how: The manner how the prisoners are to be brought into London (BL TT E288/48)

<u>Three Letters</u> : *Three Letters from the Right Honourable Sir Thomas Fairfax* - letters from Fairfax, Cromwell and Leighton & Herbert (reprinted in Young, 1985, p.335-337) (BL TT E288/27)

<u>TT</u> : Thomason Tracts

<u>VCH</u> : Victoria County History

BIBLIOGRAPHY

Adams, I.H., 1976, *Agrarian Landscape Terms*

Adamson, J.H. & Folland, H.F., 1973, *Sir Harry Vane, His Life and Times 1613-1662*

Anon, 1643, *Instructions for Muster and Armes and the use thereof*, National Army Museum 7506-22

Anon, 1881, *Our Own Country*

Anon, 1932, 'Our County villages : Naseby', *Northampton County Magazine*, vol.5

Anon, 1824, *History of Ashby Castle*

Anon, 1683, *Historical Memoires of the Life and Death of that wise and valliant Prince Rupert*

Ashley, M., 1992, *The Battle of Naseby and the Fall of King Charles I*

Asquith, S.A., 1981, *The New Model Army*

Atkin, M., and Laughlin, W., 1992, *Gloucester and the Civil War*

Baillie, R., 1775, *Letters and Journals*

Baker, G., 1822-1830, *History and Antiquities of the County of Northampton*

Baker, A., 1986, *A Battlefield Atlas of the English Civil War*

Banks, J., 1739, *Life of Oliver Cromwell*

Barrett, C.R.B., 1896, *Battles and Battlefields in England*

Barriffe, W., 1661, *Militarie Discipline or the Young Artillery-Man* (reprinted 1988 with an introduction by K.Roberts)

Beesley, A., 1841, *The History of Banbury*

Bell, R., (ed.) 1849, *Memorials of the Civil War Comprising Correspondence of the Fairfax Family*

Bennett, M., 1980, 'Henry Hastings and the Flying Army of Ashby de la Zouch', *Transactions of the Leicestershire Archaeological Society*, vol.56, p.62-70

Beresford, M.W., 1974, *History on the Ground*

Besly, E., 1987, *English Civil War Coin Hoards,* British Museum Occasional Paper 51

Blackmore, D., 1990, *Arms and Armour of the English Civil Wars*

Bland, J., 1924, *Bygone Days in Market Harborough*

Bond, W.G., 1927, *The Wanderings of Charles I and his Army in the Midlands in the Years 1442-1645*

Bray, W., (ed.), 1827, *Memoirs of John Evelyn*

Bridges, J., 1791, *The History and Antiquities of Northamptonshire*

Brown, A.E., 1991, *Early Daventry*

Brown, A.E., & Foard, G., 1994, *The Making of A County History : John Bridges' Northamptonshire*

Bull, F.W., 1900, *A History of Newport Pagnell*

Burke, T., 1942, *Travel in England*

Burne, A.H., 1950, *The Battlefields of England*

Butcher, R., 1646, *The Survey and Antiquity of the town of Stamford*

Camden, W., 1722, *Britannia*, revised by Edmund Gibson, Second Edition

Campion, S.S., 1878, *Rushton, Historical, Biographical, Archaeological*

Carlton, C., 1994, *Going to the Wars*

Carlyle, T., 1858, *Cromwell's Letters and Speeches*

Carte, T., 1759, *A Collection of Original Letters and Papers concerning the affairs of England from the year 1641 to 1660 found among the Duke of Ormonde's Papers*

Clarendon, Earl of, 1702, *The History of the Great Rebellion*

Cockayne, A.E., 1869, *Cockayne Memoranda*

Cole, J., 1815, *The History of Northampton and its Vicinity*

Cole, J., 1825, *The History and Antiquities of Ecton*

Cooke, G.A., 1825, *A Topographical and Statistical Description of the County of Northampton*

Courtney, P. & Y., 1992, 'A Siege examined: the Civil War archaeology of Leicester', *Post*

Medieval Archaeology, vol.26, p.47-90

Cox, J.C., & Serjeantson, R.M., 1897, *History of Church of Holy Sepulchre, Northampton*

Cox, J.C., 1898, *The Borough Records of Northampton*

Cox, J.C., 1899, *Cromwell and the Great Civil War*

Cox, T., 1738, *Magna Britannia*

Cruso, J., 1632, *Militarie Instructions for the Cavallrie*, reprinted 1972, edited by P.Young

Curteis, M., 1992, 'The Sibbertoft Civil War Coin Hoard', *Northamptonshire Archaeology*, vol.24, p.109-111

Darby, H.C., 1976, *A New Historical Geography of England before 1600*

Dare, M.P., 1926, 'Old-time Lawkeepers', *AASR*, vol.38, p.106-165

Davies, C., 1992, *Stamford and the Civil War*

Davies, J.C., 1964, *Bowden to Harborough*

Davies, J.C., & Brown, M.C., 1984, *The Book of Market Harborough*

Defoe, D., 1724, *Tour through Great Britain*

Defoe, D., 1854, *Memoirs of a Cavalier*

Denton, B., 1988, *Naseby Fight*

DOE, 1990, *This Common Inheritance, Britain's Environmental Strategy*

DOE, 1990a, *Planning Policy Guidance Note 16 : Planning and Archaeology*

DOE, 1994, *Planning Policy Guidance Note 15 : Planning and the Historic Environment*

Dore, R., 1984, *Letter Books of Sir William Brereton*, Lancashire and Cheshire Record Society

Dore, R.N., 1957, 'Sir William Brereton's Siege of Chester and the Naseby Campaign', *Transactions of the Lancashire and Cheshire Antiquarian Society*, vol.67

Dryden, A., (ed.), 1911, *Memorials of Old Leicestershire*

Dryden, H.E.L., 1875, 'Hospital Dedicated to St.John the Baptist at Northampton', *AASR*, vol.12, p.211-234

Dyson, A.H., 1913, *Lutterworth*

Edgar, W., 1923, *Borough Hill and Its History*

Elton, R., 1650, *The Compleat Body of the Art Military*

English Heritage, 1994, *Battlefields : The proposed Register of historic battlefields*

Evans, H.A., 1924, *Highways and Byways in Northamptonshire and Rutland*

Evans, H.A., 1938, *Highways and Byways in Oxford and the Cotswolds*

Everitt, A.M., 1969, *The Local Community and the Great Rebellion*

Finch, P., 1901, *History of Burley on the Hill, Rutland*

Firth, C.H., 1890, 'Chronological Survey of Oxon, Berks and Bucks 1642-6' in *Proceedings of the Oxford Architectural and Historical Society* (New Series), vol.5 p.280-292

Firth, C.H., 1898, 'The Journal of Prince Rupert's Marches', *English Historical Review*, vol.13

Firth, C.H., 1947, *Oliver Cromwell*

Firth, C.H., 1962, *Cromwell's Army*

Firth C.H. & Davies, G., 1940 *The Regimental History of Cromwell's Army*

Firth, J.B., 1926, *Highways and Byways in Leicestershire*

Fleming, D., 1981-2, 'Faction and Civil War in Leicestershire', *Transactions of the Leicestershire Archaeological Society*, vol.57

Foard, G., 1978, 'Systematic fieldwalking and the investigation of Saxon settlement in Northamptonshire', *World Archaeology*, vol.9, p.357-374

Foard, G., 1992, *An Analysis of the Civil War Battlefield at Naseby*, unpublished report

Foard, G., 1994, *Colonel John Pickering's Regiment of Foot 1644-1645*

Foard, G., 1994a, 'The Civil War defences of Northampton', *NP&P*, vol.9, no.1, p.4-44

Gardiner, S.R., 1893, *History of the Great Civil War*

Gentles, I., 1992, *The New Model Army*

Gibbs, R., 1885, *History of Aylesbury*, p.154-173

Goring, J. & Wake, J., 1975, *Northamptonshire Lieutenancy Papers 1580-1614*

Gotch, J.A., et al, 1896, 'Rushton Hall & its Owners', reprinted from *NN&Q*, vol.6

Gould, J., 1991, *Gothick Northamptonshire*

Green, J.H., 1893, *Notes on Mowsley and Knaptoft*

Greenhall, R., 1974, *Naseby : A Parish History*

Gresley, J.M., (ed.), 1856, *Some Account of Crowland Abbey*

Halford, H., 1813, *An Account of what appeared on opening the coffin of Charles the First in the vault of King Henry the Eighth in St.George's Chapel at Windsor*

Hall, S., 1989, *Boarstall Tower*, National Trust guide

Hall, D.N., 1977, 'Naseby Parish Survey 1976', *CBA Group 9 Newsletter*, vol.7, p.48-57

Hall, D.N., & Harding, R., 1979, 'Clipston Parish Survey 1976', *CBA Group 9 Newsletter*, vol.9, p.21-31

Hamson, J., 1906, *Topographical Guide to Naseby Battlefield*

Harrington, P., 1992, *Archaeology of the English Civil War*

Harrison, G., 1928, *Poems and Sketches*

Harrison, G., 1948, *A Wanderer in Northamptonshire*

Harrod, W., 1808, *History of Market Harborough and its vicinity*

Haythornthwaite, P., 1983, *The English Civil War 1642-1651*

Hensman, E.W., 1911, 'Henry Hastings, Lord Loughborough, and the Great Civil War', in Dryden, 1911.

Henson, 1893, *A Concise History of the County of Northampton*

Herrick, R., 1648, *Hesperides, or, the Works, both Humane and Divine*

Hexham, H., 1639, *The Principles of the Art Militarie*

Hill, J.H., 1875, *The History of Market Harborough and the Gartree Hundred*

Historic Manuscripts Commission, 1891, *Portland Manuscripts*, vol.1

Hobson, P., 1647, *A Garden Inclosed* and *Wisdom justified only of her children*

Holles, D., 1699, *Memoirs*

Hollings, 1840, *Leicestershire during the Civil War*

Holloway, W.H., 1912, 'A Visit to Naseby', *Northampton Independent*, 15th-29th June, rewritten and republished as W.H.Holloway, *The Story of Naseby*

Holme, C., 1891, *A History of the Midland Counties*

Holmes, C., 1974, *The Eastern Association*

Horn, P., 1971, *Joseph Arch*

Horn, P., 1968-9, 'Nineteenth Century Naseby Farm Workers', *Northamptonshire Past and Present*, IV, p.167-173

Hoskins, W.G., 1955, *The Making of the English Landscape*

Hutchinson, L., 1908, *Memoirs of the Life of Colonel Hutchinson*

Hutton, R., 1982, *The Royalist war effort 1642-1646*

Hutton, R., 1987, *Charles II*

Ireland, S., 1794, *Warwickshire Avon*

Isham, G. (ed.), 1955, *The Correspondence of Bishop Brian Duppa and Sir Justinian Isham 1650-166*

Isham, G. (ed.), 1955, *The Duppa-Isham Correspondence 1650-1660*, Northamptonshire Record Society, vol.17

Isham, G., 1969, 'The Kelmarsh "Naseby Relics"', *The Northamptonshire Antiquarian Society*, vol.LXVI, p.16-17

Isham, G., 1962, 'Naseby: A Note on the Preliminaries of the Battle', *NP&P*, vol.2, p.10

J.B., 1661, *Some Brief Instructions for the Exercising of the Cavalry*, published in Barriffe, 1661

James, T., 1864, *The History and Antiquities of Northamptonshire*, reprinted from the *Quarterly Review*, 1850

Johnson, A.M., undated, *Buckinghamshire 1640-1660*, Thesis at University of Wales

Jones, 1829, *Views*

Kenyon, J., 1988, *The Civil Wars of England*

Kingston, A., 1897, *East Anglia and the Great Civil War*

Kinross, J., 1979, *The Battlefields of Britain*

Kishlansky, M., 1979, *The Rise of the New Model Army*

Kitson, F., 1994, *Prince Rupert, Portrait of a Soldier*

Klingelhofer, E., 1983-4, 'Rockingham Castle in 1250', *Northamptonshire Past and Present*, vol.7, p.11-25

Laing, (ed.), 1841, *Baillie's Letters and Journals*

Lilly, W., 1715, *History of his Life and Times*

Lloyd, E., 1908, *A review of the History of Infantry*

Lockinge, H., 1830, *Historical Gleanings on the Memorable Field of Naseby*

Long, C.E., (ed.), 1859, *Richard Symonds' Diary*

Longden, H.I., 1940, *Northamptonshire and Rutland Clergy*

Ludlow, E., 1698, *Memoirs*

Maddison, R.E., 1966, 'The King's Cabinet Opened : a case study in pamphlet history', *Notes and Queries*, 2142, p.2-9

Manley, T., 1660, Iter Carolinum, reprinted in Scott, 1811,vol.5, p.263

Markham, C.A., 1870, *A Life of the Great Lord Fairfax*

Markham, C.A., 1921, 'Arms and Armour in Churches', *AASR*, vol.36, p.87-94

Martin, B., 1763, *The Natural History of England*

Mastin, J., 1792, *The History and Antiquities of Naseby*

Mee, A., 1945, *The King's England : Northamptonshire*

Mee, A., 1967, *The Kings England : Leicestershire*

Morrah, P., 1976, *Prince Rupert of the Rhine*

Morris, C. 1959, *The Journeys of Celia Fiennes*

Morton, J., 1712, *The Natural History of Northamptonshire*

Mungeam, G.I., 1968, 'Contracts for the Supply of Equipment to the New Model Army in 1645', *Journal of the Arms and Armour Society*, vol.VI, No.3, p.53-115

Murray, 1901, *Handbook for Northants and Rutland*

Mursell, J., 1861, *The Principal Historical Associations of Northamptonshire*

Newman, P., 1981, *Marston Moor*

Nichols, J., 1795-1811, *The History and Antiquities of the County of Leicester*

Nicolson, N., & Hawkyard, A., 1988, *The Counties of Britain : A Tudor Atlas by John Speed*

O'Neil, B.H.St.John, 1960, *Castles and Cannon*

Ogilby, J., 1675, *Britannia,* reprinted 1939

Orrery, Earl of, 1677, *A Treatise of the Art of War*

Page, J.T., 1886, 'A Visit to Naseby', *Rugby Advertiser*, 30th September

Page, J.T., 1889, 'Things Old and New : Reminiscences of Naseby Field', *Northampton Mercury*, 14th September

Page, J.T., 1894, 'Relics of Naseby Fight', *Northampton Herald*, 6th January

Page, J.T., 1893a, 'The Night before Naseby', *Northampton Herald*, 25th November

Page, J.T., 1893, 'The Great Civil War in Northamptonshire', *East London Magazine*, Vol.1, no.30-32, p.285-320

Palmer, J. & M., 1972, *A History of Wellingborough*

Parsons, D., (ed.), 1836, *The Diary of Sir Henry Slingsby*

Petrie, C., (ed.), 1968, *The Letters of King Charles I*

Pettit, P.A.J., 1968, *The Royal Forests of Northamptonshire*, Northamptonshire Record Society, vol.23

Pevsner, N., 1973, *The Buildings of England: Buckinghamshire*

Pevsner, N., 1973a, *The Buildings of England : Northamptonshire*

Pevsner, N., 1984, *The Buildings of England : Leicestershire and Rutland*

Philips, R., 1828, *A Personal Tour through the United Kingdom*

Pipe, M., 1990, *Tales of Old Northamptonshire*

Pitt, W., 1809, *General View of the Agriculture of the County of Northampton*

Puysegur, 1659, *Instructions Militaires*

Ramsey, R.W., 1949, *Henry Ireton*

Rastall, W.D., 1787, *History of Southwell*

Ravenhill, W., (ed.), 1992, *Christopher Saxton's 16th Century Maps : The Counties of England and Wales*

RCHM, 1913, *An Inventory of the Historical Monuments in Buckinghamshire*

RCHM, 1926, *An Inventory of the Historical Monuments in Huntingdonshire*

RCHM, 1964, *Newark Upon Trent : Civil War Siegeworks*

RCHM, 1981, *An Inventory of the Archaeological Sites in North West Northamptonshire*

Richards, J., 1988, 'The Greys of Bradgate', *Transactions of the Leicestershire Archaeological Society*, vol.62

Rimmer, A., 1892, *Rambles round Rugby*

Roberts, K., 1989, *Soldiers of the English Civil War (1) : Infantry*

Roberts, K., 1995, 'English Civil War Battle Plans', *English Civil War Times*, no.51

Rogers, H.C.B., 1968, *Battles and Generals of the Civil Wars 1642-1651*

Ross, W.G., 1887, 'Military Engineering During the Civil War', *Professional Papers of the Corps of Royal Engineers*, vol.13

Ross, W.G., 1888, The Battle of Naseby, English Historical Review, vol.3, p.668-679

Rowley, C., 1989, *The Battle of Naseby*

Roy, I., 1964, *The Royalist Ordnance Papers 1642-1646*, parts 1 & 2, Oxfordshire Record Society, vol.43 & vol.49

Roy, I., 1962, 'The Royalist Council of War 1642-1646', *Bulletin of the Institute of Historical Research*, no.35

Rushworth, J., 1722, *Historical Collections*, vol.6

Rye, W., 1925, *Two Cromwellian Myths*

Ryves, B., 1685, *Mercurius Rusticus: or, the countries complaint*

Sandon, W.H., 1883, 'Stanford Church and its Registers', *ASSR*, vol.17, p.121-153

Savage, *1671, Coritani Lacrymantes*, printed in Rastall, 1787, p.430-432

Scott, S., 1868, *The British Army*

Scott, W. (ed.), 1811, *Somers Tracts: A Collection of Scarce and Valuable Tracts*, 2nd edn, vol.5

Serjeantson, R.M., 1901, *History of the Church of All Saints, Northampton*

Serjeantson, R.M., 1911, *History of the Church of St.Giles, Northampton*

Serjeantson, R.M., 1911-1914, 'The Hospital of St.John, Northampton', *JNNHS&FC*, vol.16, p.221-237 & 265-291; vol.17, p.1-24 & 49-78

Shehan, J.J., 1862, *History and Topography of Buckinghamshire*

Sherwood, R.E., 1974, *Civil Strife in the Midlands 1642-1651*

Sherwood & Pevsner, 1974, *The Buildings of England : Oxfordshire*

Slater, A.R., 1992, *Ghostly Tales and Hauntings of South Leicestershire*

Smurthwaite, D., 1984, *The Complete Guide to the Battlefields of Britain*

Smurthwaite, D., 1994, *Naseby 1645*, English Heritage Proposed Battlefields Register

Smyth, W.H., 1864, *Addenda to the Aedes Hartwellianae*

Sprigge, J., 1647, *Anglia Rediviva*

Staines, J., 1842, *A History of Newport Pagnell*

Stainwright, T.L. 1991, *Windmills of Northamptonshire*

Stead, 1891, 'Cromwell and His Independents', *The Review of Reviews*

Steane, J.M., 1974, *The Northamptonshire Landscape*

Stearns, R.P., 1954, *The Strenuous Puritan : Hugh Peter 1598-1660*

Stocks, H., (ed.), 1923, *Records of the Borough of Leicester 1603-1688*

Story, A., 1883, *Historical Legends of Northamptonshire*

Stukeley's Diaries and Letters, vol.2, 1883, Surtees Society

Temple, 1986, 'The Original Officer List of the New Model Army', *Historical Institute Journal*, vol.59

Tennant, P., 1992, *Edgehill and Beyond*

Terhune, A., & Terhune, A.B., (eds), 1980, *The Letters of Edward Fitzgerald*

Throsby, J., 1791, *The History and Antiquities of the Ancient Town of Leicester*

Tibbutt, H.G., 1955, *Colonel John Okey, 1606-1662*, Befordshire Historical Record Society, vol.35

Tibbutt, H.G. 1963, *The Letter Books of Sir Samuel Luke*

Tincey, J., (ed.), 1993, *Vernon's The Young Horseman*

Tole, F.A., 1888-9, 'Cromwell in Northamptonshire', *NN&Q*, vol.3, item 398

Toynbee, M., (ed.), 1961, *The Papers of Captain Henry Stevens*, Oxfordshire Record Society, vol.42

Varley, F.J., 1932, *The Siege of Oxford*

Vernon, J., 1644, *The Young Horseman*, reprinted as J.Tincey (ed.), 1993

VCH, 1930-7, *A History of the County of Northampton*

VCH, 1959, *A History of the County of Oxford*, vol.6

Vicars, J., 1646, *England's Parliamentarie Chronicle*

Vincent, J., 1966, *Formation of the Liberal Party 1857-68*

Walker, E., 1707, *Historical Collections*, p.112-132, (reprinted in Young, 1985, p.312-320)

Wall, J.C., 1927, *Kelmarsh*

Walpoole, G.A., 1784, *The New British Traveller*

Warburton, E., 1849, *Memoirs of Prince Rupert and the Cavaliers*

Ward, R., 1639, *Animadversions of Warre*

Warwick, P., 1701, *Memoires of the Reign of King Charles I*

Wedgewood, C.V., 1974, *The King's War*

Wharton, G., 1645, *An Astrological Judgement* (BL TT E.286/31)

Whellan, W., 1849, *History Gazetteer and Directory of Northamptonshire*

Whetham, C.D., and Whetham, W.C.D., 1907, *A History of the Life of Colonel Nathaniel Whetham : A Forgotten Soldier of the Civil Wars*

Whitelocke, B., 1682, *Memorials from the English Affairs*

Wilson, J., 1985, *Fairfax*

Wogan, E., *The Proceedings of the New Moulded Army from ...1645, till .... 1647*, in Carte, 1759, reprinted in Young, 1985, p.367-371

Woolrych, A., 1961, *Battles of the English Civil War*

Young, P., 1954, 'The Northern Horse at Naseby', *Journal of the Society for Army Historical Research*

Young, P. (ed.), 1972, *Militarie Instructions for the Cavallrie*

Young, P., 1985, *Naseby 1645 : The Campaign and the Battle*

Young. P., & Holmes, R., 1974, *The English Civil War*

INDEX